CENSUS OF INDIA 1911

Census of India 1871-1951, 9 Sets In 384 Bindings (9788121258876) Rs. 700000

Census of India 1911, 23 Vols. In 41 Bindings (9788121271271) Rs. 69000

1. India - Report (9788121275071) Rs. 2475 (Vol. I, Pt. 1)
2. India - Tables (9788121275057) Rs. 2225 (Vol. I, Pt. 2)
3. Andaman and Nicobar Islands - Report & Tables (9788121275033) Rs. 900 (Vol. II, Pt. 1 & 2)
4. Assam - Report (9788121275019) Rs. 1000 (Vol. III, Pt. 1)
5. Assam - Tables (9788121274999) Rs. 1300 (Vol. III, Pt. 2)
6. Baluchistan - Report & Tables (9788121274975) Rs. 950 (Vol. IV, Pt. 1 & 2)
7. Bengal, Bihar And Orissa And Sikkim - Report (9788121274951) Rs. 3100 (Vol. V, Pt. 1)
8. Bengal - Tables (9788121274937) Rs. 2250 (Vol. V, Pt. 2)
9. Bihar And Orissa - Tables and Bengal And Sikkim - Chapter I of Administrative Volume (9788121274913) Rs. 1800 (Vol. V, Pt. 3 & 4)
10. City of Calcutta - Report and Tables and Administrative (9788121274876) Rs. 1300 (Vol. VI, Pt. 1 & 2 & 3)
11. Bombay - Report (9788121274814) Rs. 1950 (Vol. VII, Pt. 1)
12. Bombay - Imperial Tables and Administrative Report (9788121274791) Rs. 3300 (Vol. VII, Pt. 2 & 3)
13. Bombay (Town And Island) - Report And Tables (9788121274753) Rs. 1250 (Vol. VIII, Pt. 1 & 2)
14. Burma - Report (9788121274739) Rs. 2250 (Vol. IX, Pt. 1)
15. Burma - Tables (9788121274715) Rs. 1480 (Vol. IX, Pt. 2)
16. Central Provinces And Berar - Report (9788121274692) Rs. 1475 (Vol. X, Pt. 1)
17. Central Provinces And Berar - Tables (9788121274678) Rs. 1900 (Vol. X, Pt. 2)
18. Coorg - Report And Tables Madras - Report (9788121274630) Rs. 1740 (Vol. XI & Vol. XII, Pt. 1)
19. Madras - Imperial And Provincial Tables (9788121274616) Rs. 1500 (Vol. XII, Pt. 2)
20. Madras - Administrative Report and city of Madras (9788121274593) Rs. 630 (Vol. XII, Pt. 3 & 4)
21. North - West Frontier Province - Report & Tables (9788121274579) Rs. 2150 (Vol. XIII, Pt. 1 & 2)
22. Punjab - Report (9788121274555) Rs. 3000 (Vol. XIV, Pt. 1)
23. Punjab - Tables (9788121274531) Rs. 2200 (Vol. XIV, Pt. 2)
24. Punjab - Appendices To The - Imperial Tables (9788121274517) Rs. 950 (Vol. XIV, Pt. 3)
25. United Provinces of Agra And Oudh - Report (9788121274494) Rs. 2225 (Vol. XV, Pt. 1)
26. United Provinces of Agra And Oudh - Tables (9788121274470) Rs. 4000 (Vol. XV, Pt. 2)
27. United Provinces of Agra And Oudh - Provincial Tables And Appendices (9788121274456) Rs. 570 (Vol. XV, Pt. 3)
28. Baroda - Report (9788121274432) Rs. 2000 (Vol. XVI, Pt. 1)
29. Baroda State - The Imperial Tables (9788121274418) Rs. 850 (Vol. XVI, Pt. 2)
30. Central India Agency - Report And Tables (9788121274395) Rs. 1470 (Vol. XVII)
31. Cochin - Report And Imperial Tables (9788121274371) Rs. 1150 (Vol. XVIII, Pt. 1 & 2)
32. Hyderabad State - Report (9788121274357) Rs. 890 (Vol. XIX, Pt. 1)
33. Hyderabad State - Imperial And Provincial Tables (9788121274333) Rs. 1750 (Vol. XIX, Pt. 2)
34. Kashmir - Report (9788121274319) Rs. 950 (Vol. XX, Pt. 1)
35. Kashmir - Tables (9788121274296) Rs. 1170 (Vol. XX, Pt. 2)
36. Mysore - Report (9788121274272) Rs. 1200 (Vol. XXI, Pt. 1)
37. Mysore - Tables (9788121274258) Rs. 1500 (Vol. XXI, Pt. 2)
38. Rajputana And Ajmer-Merwara - Report (9788121274234) Rs. 1470 (Vol. XXII, Pt. 1)
39. Rajputana And Ajmer-Merwara - Tables (9788121274210) Rs. 1700 (Vol. XXII, Pt. 2)
40. Travancore - Report (9788121274197) Rs. 1870 (Vol. XXIII, Pt. 1)
41. Travancore - Imperial Tables (9788121274173) Rs. 870 (Vol. XXIII, Pt. 2)

Owing to the antiquity and rarity of this book, certain pages are regrettably absent, and readability is compromised due to the blurring of the original text. If you possess any insights regarding the availability of these missing sections, kindly inform us. Your assistance is crucial in ensuring the completion of this significant work for the benefit of future generations.

CENSUS OF INDIA, 1911

VOLUME - XIV

PUNJAB

PART III - APPENDICES TO THE - IMPERIAL TABLES

PANDIT HARIKISHAN KAUL

GYAN

Published by

Gyan Publishing House
5, Ansari Road
Daryaganj, New Delhi-110002
Phone: 011-47034999, 9811692060
E-mail: books@gyanbooks.com

Distribution Network
gyanbooks.com
India, USA, Canada, UK, Australia

ISBN: 978-81-212-7127-1 (Set) 23 Vols. In 41 Bindings

ISBN: 978-81-212-7451-7 (PB) Vol. XIV, Pt. III

First Published, 1912

2nd Impression 2024

Printed at: Gyan Press, Delhi.

CENSUS OF INDIA 1911

CENSUS OF INDIA, 1911.

VOLUME XIV.

PUNJAB.

PART III.

APPENDICES

TO THE

IMPERIAL TABLES

BY

PANDIT HARIKISHAN KAUL, R.B., C.I.E.

SUPERINTENDENT OF CENSUS OPERATIONS,

PUNJAB.

Lahore:

PRINTED AT THE "CIVIL AND MILITARY GAZETTE" PRESS,

1912.

Agents for the sale of Punjab Government Publications

In London.

Constable & Co., 10, Orange Street, Leicester Square, W. C.

Grindlay & Co., 54, Parliament Street, S. W.

Henry S. King & Co., 65, Cornhill, E. C.

P. S. King & Son, 2 and 4, Great Smith Street, Westminster, S. W.

Kegan Paul, Trench, Trübner & Co., 43, Gerrard Street, Soho, W.

B. Quaritch, 11, Grafton Street, New Bond Street, W.

T. Fisher Unwin, 1, Adelphi Terrace, W. C.

W. Thacker & Co., 2, Creed Lane, London, E. C.

Luzac & Co., 46, Great Russell Street, London, W. C.

On the Continent.

Friedlander & Sohn, 11, Carlstrasse, Berlin.

Otto Harrassowitz, Leipzig.

Karl W. Hiersemann, Leipzig.

Ernest Leroux, 28, Rue Bonaparte, Paris.

Martinus Nijhoff, The Hague.

In India.

Thacker, Spink & Co., Calcutta & Simla.

Newman & Co., Calcutta.

R. Cambray & Co., Calcutta.

Thacker & Co., Bombay.

Higginbotham & Co., Madras.

T. Fisher Unwin, Calcutta.

V. Kalyanaram Iyer & Co., 189, Esplanade Row, Madras.

G. A. Natesan & Co., Madras.

Superintendent, American Baptist Mission Press, Rangoon.

A. Chand & Co., Imperial Book Depôt Office, Delhi.

Gulab Singh & Sons, Mufid-i-'Am Press, Lahore.

Manager, Punjab Law Book Depôt, Anárkali Bazar, Lahore.

S. Mumtaz Ali & Son, Rafah-i-'Am Press, Lahore [for Vernacular Publications only].

Manager, "The Aryan Printing, Publishing and General Trading Co., Limited, Lahore."

N. B. Mathur, Superintendent and Proproprietor, Nazair Kanun Hind Press Allahabad.

D. B. Taraporevala Sons & Co., Bombay.

TABLE OF CONTENTS.

TABLE VIII (APPENDIX).

LITERACY IN THE VERNACULARS.

The figures for general literacy and literacy in English have been given in the prescribed form in Imperial Table VIII. The figures in this table show literacy in the Vernaculars and the arrangement of having sub-divisions of each Vernacular is peculiar to this Province. The sub-divisions under each Vernacular show the script employed by literates in that Vernacular. All the dialects used in the Province have been grouped into 3 main Vernaculars, namely Urdu, Hindi and Punjabi. The column 'Others' under Urdu and Hindi shows persons using some script other than that specified in the table. These scripts are given below :—

	Urdu.			Hindi.	
	Males.	Females.		Males.	Females.
Nagri	1,824	180	Gurmukhi	658	53
Laude	5,669	235	Gujrati	117	11
Gurmukhi	480	49	Bengali	181	3
Gujrati	96	...	Tankri	100	48
Bengali	47	...	Persian	140	8
Tankri	2	18	Roman	...	1
Roman	221	54			
Total ...	7,839	536	Total ...	1,196	124

The column 'Others' at the end of the Vernaculars shows figures for literates in Vernaculars of other Provinces and Countries. The details of these are noted below :—

	Others.			Others.	
	Males.	Females.		Males.	Females.
			Brought forward ...	3,210	406
Gojrati	325	137	Garhwali	5	...
Bengali	743	113	Telugu	2	...
Sindhi	17	...	Burmese	1	...
Marhathi	42	11	Chinese	1	...
Arabic	119	75	Portuguese	6	...
Pashto	26	1	Greek	...	1
Tamil	7	5	Canary	3	...
Nepali	1,304	50	Tibetan	194	20
Bhoti	627	14	Unspecified	18	38
Total ...	3,210	406	Total ...	3,440	465

APPENDIX TO IMPERIAL TABLE VIII.—

PART A.—PROVINCIAL SUMMARY.

PUNJAB.

Serial No.	Religion and Age.	Literate in Vernacular.														
		Total.			Urdu.							Hindi.				
					Total.			*Persian.*		*Others.*		*Total.*			*Nagri.*	
		Persons.	Males.	Females.	Persons.	Males.	Females.	Males.	Females.	Males.	Females.	Persons.	Males.	Females.	Males.	Females.
		1	2	3	4	5	6	7	8	9	10	11	12	13	14	15
1	**ALL RELIGIONS** ...	**867,224**	**812,388**	**54,836**	**402,728**	**385,091**	**17,637**	**377,252**	**17,101**	**7,839**	**536**	**149,336**	**137,985**	**11,351**	**65,538**	**9,937**
2	0—10 ...	11,942	8,876	3,066	6,501	5,616	885	5,562	865	54	20	2,148	1,303	845	707	735
3	10—15 ...	74,329	65,255	9,074	48,134	45,080	3,054	44,704	2,961	376	93	9,218	7,182	2,036	3,598	1,844
4	15—20 ...	104,909	94,746	10,163	59,329	55,772	3,557	54,913	3,463	859	94	16,170	13,870	2,300	6,701	2,046
5	20 and over ...	676,044	643,511	32,533	288,764	278,623	10,141	272,073	9,812	6,550	329	131,800	115,630	6,170	54,532	5,312
6	**HINDU** ...	**484,668**	**457,758**	**26,910**	**166,540**	**162,153**	**4,387**	**155,365**	**4,020**	**6,788**	**367**	**137,73 9**	**126,994**	**10,745**	**61,565**	**9,484**
7	0—10 ...	6,151	4,599	1,552	2,814	2,555	259	2,507	248	46	11	2,015	1,203	812	667	709
8	10—15 ...	39,535	34,651	4,884	22,465	21,420	1,045	21,077	981	343	64	8,521	6,549	1,972	3,414	1,787
9	15—20 ...	59,488	53,763	5,725	27,611	26,242	1,369	25,507	1,305	735	64	14,957	12,760	2,197	6,818	1,963
10	20 and over ...	379,494	364,745	14,749	113,650	111,936	1,714	106,274	1,486	5,662	228	112,246	106,482	5,764	51,158	5,025
11	**SIKH** ...	**169 363**	**155,155**	**14,208**	**40,525**	**39,944**	**581**	**39,533**	**532**	**411**	**49**	**4,160**	**3,995**	**165**	**1,826**	**104**
12	0—10 ...	2,622	1,740	882	687	645	42	644	39	1	3	32	23	9	16	5
13	10—15 ...	14,468	12,327	2,141	6,251	6,178	73	6,161	60	17	13	219	199	20	63	18
14	15—20 ...	18,848	16,675	2,170	6,768	6,675	93	6,654	87	21	6	395	367	28	175	20
15	20 and over ...	133,425	124,410	9,015	26,819	26,446	373	26,074	340	372	27	3,514	3,406	108	1,572	58
16	**JAIN** ...	**12,239**	**11,717**	**522**	**3,907**	**3,813**	**94**	**3,335**	**60**	**478**	**34**	**5,748**	**5,415**	**333**	**1,429**	**272**
17	0—10 ...	145	115	30	67	61	6	58	4	3	2	66	46	20	26	17
18	10—15 ...	985	916	69	465	450	15	443	14	7	8	380	339	41	108	37
19	15—20 ...	1,488	1,400	88	601	585	16	509	9	76	7	643	586	57	184	50
20	20 and over ...	9,621	9,286	335	2,774	2,717	57	2,325	37	392	20	4,659	4,444	215	1,117	168
21	**BUDDHIST** ...	**609**	**584**	**25**	**11**	**11**	...	**11**	...	...	...	**12**	**12**	...	**12**	...
22	0—10 ...	1	1	...	...	...	...	...	...	...	...	...	...	..	...	...
23	10—15 ...	19	19	...	...	...	...	...	...	...	...	1	1	...	1	...
24	15—20 ...	51	51	...	2	2	...	2	...	...	...	...	...	...	...	...
25	20 and over ...	538	513	25	9	9	...	9	...	...	...	11	11	...	11	...
26	**ZOROASTRIAN** ...	**403**	**259**	**144**	**84**	**56**	**28**	**54**	**28**	**2**	...	**16**	**15**	**1**	**10**	...
27	0—10 ...	24	15	9	5	2	3	2	3	...	...	...	...	...	...	...
28	10—15 ...	33	13	20	7	1	6	1	6	...	...	3	3	...	1	...
29	15—20 ...	32	14	18	3	2	1	2	1	...	.	...	...	...	...	...
30	20 and over ...	314	217	97	69	51	18	49	18	2	...	13	12	1	9	...
31	**MUHAMMADAN** ...	**193,540**	**183,010**	**10,520**	**185,920**	**175,675**	**10,245**	**175,585**	**10,226**	**90**	**19**	**1,418**	**1,388**	**30**	**562**	**17**
32	0—10 ...	2,743	2,253	490	2,692	2,213	479	2,211	478	2	1	26	26	...	1	....
33	10—15 ...	18,212	16,768	1,444	17,892	16,488	1,404	16,481	1,401	7	3	91	89	2	11	1
34	15—20 ...	23,830	22,202	1,628	23,249	21,665	1,584	21,854	1,581	11	3	146	143	3	19	2
35	20 and over ...	148,755	141,787	6,968	142,087	135,309	6,778	135,239	6,766	70	12	1,155	1,130	25	531	14
36	**CHRISTIAN** ...	**6,393**	**3,900**	**2,493**	**5,737**	**3,436**	**2,301**	**3,368**	**2,235**	**68**	**66**	**212**	**136**	**76**	**134**	**59**
37	0—10 ...	256	153	103	236	140	96	140	93	...	3	9	5	4	3	1
38	10—15 ...	1,077	561	516	1,054	543	511	541	503	2	8	8	2	1	...	1
39	15—20 ...	1,171	638	533	1,095	601	494	585	460	16	14	29	14	15	7	11
40	20 and over ...	3,889	2,548	1,341	3,352	2,152	1,200	2,102	1,159	50	41	201	145	56	124	46
41	**JEW** ...	**9**	**5**	**4**	**4**	**3**	**1**	**1**	...	**2**	**1**	**1**	...	**1**	...	**1**
42	0—10 ...	...	...	...	...	...	...	...	...	...	...	...	...	...	...	...
43	10—15 ...	...	...	...	...	...	...	...	...	...	...	...	...	...	...	...
44	15—20 ...	1	...	1	...	...	...	...	...	...	...	...	...	...	...	...
45	20 and over ...	8	5	3	4	3	1	1	...	2	1	1	...	1	...	1

EDUCATION (BY RELIGION AND AGE).

PART A.—PROVINCIAL SUMMARY.

PUNJAB.

LITERATE IN VERNACULAR.																				
HINDI,				PUNJABI.													OTHERS.			
Lande or Mahajani.		Others.		Total.			Gurmukhi.		Lande or Mahajani.		Nagri.		Tankri.		Persian.					
Males.	Females.	Males.	Females.	Persons.	Males.	Females.	Males.	Females.	Males.	Females.	Males.	Females.	Males.	Females.	Males.	Females.	Persons.	Males.	Females.	Serial No.
16	17	18	19	20	21	22	23	24	25	26	27	28	29	30	31	32	33	34	35	
71,251	1,290	1,196	124	311,255	285,872	25,383	121,066	20,734	120,720	1,326	24,281	2,910	17,136	327	2,669	86	3,905	3,440	435	1
585	105	11	5	3,238	1,925	1,313	1,226	1,107	487	68	143	125	51	9	18	4	55	32	23	2
3,516	179	68	13	16,814	12,880	3,934	6,564	3,212	4,516	151	1,035	589	420	28	356	4	163	113	50	3
7,082	241	87	13	28,982	24,749	4,233	10,550	3,397	10,036	210	2,059	641	1,107	47	398	32	428	355	73	4
60,068	765	1,030	84	262,221	246,318	15,903	102,726	13,018	105,081	891	21,055	1,705	15,558	243	1,898	46	3,259	2,940	319	5
64,683	1,178	746	83	177,888	166,326	11,562	29,759	7,402	95,276	1,057	23,376	2,754	16,816	321	1,069	28	2,501	2,285	216	6
528	99	8	4	1,300	826	474	235	294	390	58	136	115	51	9	14	3	22	15	7	7
3,087	172	48	13	8,450	6,603	1,847	1,412	1,179	3,611	124	977	516	409	28	194	...	99	79	20	8
6,371	228	78	6	16,629	14,507	2,122	2,617	1,365	8,609	174	1,915	515	1,081	47	205	21	291	251	37	9
54,697	679	617	60	151,509	144,390	7,119	25,495	4,564	82,666	706	20,268	1,609	15,305	237	656	4	2,089	1,937	152	10
1,922	33	247	28	124,560	111,101	13,459	89,503	13,143	20,281	209	608	92	82	2	527	10	118	115	3	11
7	1	...	...	1,903	1,072	831	980	808	84	15	6	8	...	...	2	...	...	...	...	12
181	2	5	...	7,997	5,949	2,048	5,092	2,016	743	18	27	14	1	...	86	...	1	1	...	13
192	4	...	4	11,678	9,630	2,048	7,820	1,996	1,870	31	35	20	19	...	86	1	7	6	1	14
1,592	26	242	24	102,982	94,450	8,532	75,611	8,326	17,884	145	540	50	62	2	353	9	110	108	2	15
3,881	61	125	...	2,557	2,464	93	60	19	2,149	21	166	50	81	1	8	2	27	25	2	16
26	3	...	...	12	8	4	1	2	6	...	1	2	...	...	...	...	...	...	...	17
222	4	9	...	140	127	13	4	8	102	2	16	8	2	...	3	...	...	...	...	18
394	7	8	...	240	226	14	3	5	197	4	23	5	2	...	1	...	4	3	1	19
3,219	47	108	...	2,165	2,103	62	52	9	1,844	15	126	35	77	1	4	2	23	22	1	20
...	...	...	...	2	2	...	...	...	...	...	...	...	2	...	...	...	584	559	25	21
...	...	...	...	...	...	...	...	...	...	...	...	...	...	...	...	...	1	1	...	22
...	...	...	...	...	...	...	...	...	...	...	...	...	...	...	...	...	18	18	...	23
...	...	...	...	...	...	...	...	...	...	...	...	...	...	...	...	...	49	49	...	24
...	...	...	...	2	2	...	...	...	...	...	...	...	2	...	...	...	516	491	25	25
1	...	4	1	4	4	...	4	...	...	...	...	...	...	...	...	...	299	184	115	26
...	...	...	...	...	...	...	...	...	...	...	...	...	...	...	...	...	19	13	6	27
...	...	2	...	...	...	...	...	...	...	...	...	...	...	...	...	...	23	9	14	28
...	...	...	...	...	...	...	...	...	...	...	...	...	...	...	...	...	29	12	17	29
1	...	2	1	4	4	...	4	...	...	...	...	...	...	...	...	...	228	150	78	30
771	13	55	...	5,932	5,752	180	1,537	105	2,913	34	123	7	124	3	1,055	31	270	195	75	31
24	...	1	...	17	13	4	4	3	7	...	...	...	...	...	2	1	8	1	7	32
76	1	2	...	208	185	23	41	11	60	7	5	1	8	...	71	4	21	6	15	33
128	1	1	...	401	375	26	100	12	160	6	5	1	5	...	105	7	34	19	15	34
548	11	51	...	5,306	5,179	127	1,392	79	2,686	21	112	5	111	3	877	19	207	169	38	35
13	5	19	12	312	223	89	203	62	1	5	8	7	1	...	10	15	102	75	27	36
...	2	2	1	6	6	...	6	...	...	...	...	...	...	...	...	...	5	2	3	37
...	...	2	...	19	16	3	15	3	...	...	...	...	...	...	1	...	1	...	1	38
2	1	5	3	34	11	23	10	19	...	1	...	...	...	...	1	3	13	12	1	39
11	2	10	8	253	190	63	172	40	1	4	8	7	1	...	6	12	83	61	22	40
...	...	...	...	...	...	...	...	...	...	...	...	...	...	...	...	...	4	2	2	41
...	...	...	...	...	...	...	...	...	...	...	...	...	...	...	...	...	...	...	...	42
...	...	...	...	...	...	...	...	...	...	...	...	...	...	...	...	...	...	...	...	43
...	...	...	...	...	...	...	...	...	...	...	...	...	...	...	...	...	1	...	1	44
...	...	...	...	...	...	...	...	...	...	...	...	...	...	...	...	...	3	2	1	45

APPENDIX TO IMPERIAL TABLE VIII.—

PART A.—PROVINCIAL SUMMARY.

BRITISH TERRITORY.

Serial No.	Religion and Age.	Literate in Vernacular.														
		Total.			Urdu.							Hindi.				
					Total.			Persian.		Others.		Total.			Nagri.	
		Persons.	Males.	Females.	Persons.	Males.	Females.	Males.	Females.	Males.	Females.	Persons.	Males.	Females.	Males.	Females.
		1	2	3	4	5	6	7	8	9	10	11	12	13	14	15
1	**ALL RELIGIONS** ...	**743,631**	**693,750**	**49,881**	**364,307**	**347,782**	**16,525**	**340,486**	**16,030**	**7,296**	**495**	**121,443**	**111,331**	**10,112**	**51,872**	**8,897**
2	0—10 ...	10,916	8,052	2,864	6,055	5,217	838	5,167	820	50	18	1,896	1,110	786	650	693
3	10—15 ...	67,468	58,890	8,578	44,766	41,816	2,950	41,469	2,860	347	40	7,969	6,069	1,900	3,064	1,722
4	15—20 ...	92,029	82,645	9,384	54,077	50,705	3,372	49,878	3,285	827	87	13,644	11,548	2,096	6,601	1,863
5	20 and over ...	573,218	544,163	29,055	259,409	250,044	9,365	243,972	9,065	6,072	300	97,934	92,604	5,330	42,557	4,619
6	**HINDU** ...	**404,201**	**379,929**	**24,272**	**148,061**	**143,952**	**4,109**	**137,661**	**3,772**	**6,291**	**337**	**111,128**	**101,563**	**9,565**	**48,244**	**8,473**
7	0—10 ...	5,563	4,111	1,452	2,600	2,349	251	2,305	240	44	11	1,791	1,034	757	814	669
8	10—15 ...	35,179	30,600	4,579	20,685	19,671	1,014	19,352	953	319	61	7,377	5,536	1,841	2,893	1,670
9	15—20 ...	50,987	45,697	5,290	24,856	23,535	1,321	22,831	1,263	704	58	12,641	10,641	2,000	5,258	1,784
10	20 and over ...	312,472	299,521	12,951	99,920	98,397	1,523	93,173	1,316	5,224	207	89,319	84,352	4,967	39,484	4,350
11	**SIKH** ...	**145,172**	**132,350**	**12,822**	**36,534**	**36,001**	**533**	**35,621**	**485**	**380**	**48**	**3,795**	**3,659**	**136**	**1,720**	**96**
12	0—10 ...	2,394	1,572	822	632	592	40	591	37	1	3	31	23	8	16	7
13	10—15 ...	13,237	11,203	2,034	5,775	5,707	68	5,691	55	16	13	207	188	19	60	17
14	15—20 ...	16,627	14,657	1,970	6,080	5,993	87	5,972	81	21	6	349	323	26	163	20
15	20 and over ...	112,914	104,918	7,996	24,047	23,709	338	23,367	312	342	26	3,208	3,125	83	1,481	52
16	**JAIN** ...	**10,522**	**10,058**	**464**	**3,584**	**3,494**	**90**	**3,018**	**57**	**476**	**33**	**5,194**	**4,886**	**308**	**1,275**	**252**
17	0—10 ...	136	107	29	61	55	6	52	4	3	2	63	44	19	19	16
18	10—15 ...	878	817	61	414	400	14	393	9	7	5	352	315	37	100	33
19	15—20 ...	1,284	1,204	80	551	536	15	460	8	76	7	582	530	52	165	46
20	20 and over ...	8,224	7,930	294	2,558	2,503	55	2,113	36	390	19	4,197	3,997	200	991	157
21	**BUDDHIST** ...	**503**	**491**	**12**	**11**	**11**	...	**11**	...	...	...	**1**	**1**	...	**1**	...
22	0—10 ...	1	1	...	...	...	...	...	...	...	...	...	...	...	...	...
23	10—15 ...	19	19	...	...	...	...	...	...	...	...	1	1	...	1	...
24	15—20 ...	49	49	...	2	2	...	2	...	...	...	...	...	...	...	...
25	20 and over ...	484	422	12	9	9	...	9	...	...	...	...	...	...	...	...
26	**ZOROASTRIAN** ...	**385**	**245**	**140**	**76**	**48**	**28**	**48**	**28**	...	...	**16**	**15**	**1**	**10**	...
27	0—10 ...	24	15	9	5	2	3	2	3	...	...	...	...	...	...	...
28	10—15 ...	33	13	20	7	1	6	1	6	...	...	3	3	...	1	...
29	15—20 ...	30	12	18	1	...	1	...	1	...	...	...	...	...	...	...
30	20 and over ...	298	205	93	63	45	18	45	18	...	...	13	12	1	9	...
31	**MUHAMMADAN** ...	**176,681**	**166,917**	**9,764**	**170,497**	**160,955**	**9,542**	**160,873**	**9,525**	**82**	**17**	**1,081**	**1,052**	**29**	**498**	**16**
32	0—10 ...	2,558	2,103	455	2,530	2,085	445	2,083	444	2	1	7	7	...	1	...
33	10—15 ...	17,056	15,684	1,372	16,842	15,501	1,341	15,496	1,338	5	3	26	24	2	9	1
34	15—20 ...	21,913	20,407	1,506	21,522	20,054	1,468	20,044	1,465	10	3	44	41	3	14	2
35	20 and over ...	135,154	128,723	6,431	129,603	123,315	6,288	123,250	6,278	65	10	1,004	980	24	474	13
36	**CHRISTIAN** ...	**6,158**	**3,755**	**2,403**	**5,540**	**3,318**	**2,222**	**3,253**	**2,163**	**65**	**59**	**227**	**155**	**72**	**124**	**59**
37	0—10 ...	240	143	97	227	134	93	134	92	...	1	4	2	2	...	1
38	10—15 ...	1,066	554	512	1,043	536	507	536	499	...	8	3	2	1	...	1
39	15—20 ...	1,138	619	519	1,065	585	480	569	467	16	13	28	13	15	6	11
40	20 and over ...	3,714	2,439	1,275	3,205	2,063	1,142	2,014	1,105	49	37	192	138	54	118	46
41	**JEW** ...	**9**	**5**	**4**	**4**	**3**	**1**	**1**	...	**2**	**1**	**1**	...	**1**	...	**1**
42	0—10 ...	...	...	...	...	...	...	...	...	...	...	...	...	...	...	...
43	10—15 ...	...	...	...	...	...	...	...	...	...	...	...	...	...	...	...
44	15—20 ...	1	...	1	...	...	...	...	...	...	...	...	...	...	...	...
45	20 and over ...	8	5	3	4	3	1	1	...	2	1	1	...	1	...	1

EDUCATION (BY RELIGION AND AGE)—*continued.*

PART A.—PROVINCIAL SUMMARY.

BRITISH TERRITORY.

LITERATE IN VERNACULAR.																				
HINDI.				PUNJABI.													OTHERS.			
Lande or Mahajani.		*Others.*		*Total.*			*Gurmukhi.*		*Lande or Mahajani.*		*Nagri.*		*Tankri.*		*Persian.*					
Males.	Females.	Males.	Females.	Persons.	Males.	Females.	Males.	Females.	Males.	Females.	Males.	Females.	Males.	Females.	Males.	Females.	Persons.	Males.	Females.	Serial No.
16	17	18	19	20	21	22	23	24	25	26	27	28	29	30	31	32	33	34	35	
58,513	1,114	946	101	254,256	231,451	22,805	99,153	19,039	98,765	1,118	19,203	2,391	12,297	189	2,033	68	3,625	3,186	439	1
450	88	10	5	2,915	1,697	1,218	1,092	1,038	425	60	120	113	44	9	16	3	50	28	22	2
2,950	165	56	13	14,575	10,897	3,678	5,812	3,060	3,704	128	819	476	265	13	297	1	158	108	50	3
5,876	222	71	11	23,901	20,055	3,846	8,940	3,148	8,436	192	1,599	446	783	29	297	31	407	337	70	4
49,237	639	810	72	212,865	198,802	14,063	83,309	11,798	86,200	738	16,665	1,356	11,205	138	1,423	33	3,010	2,713	297	5
52,720	1,012	599	80	142,647	132,259	10,388	25,229	7,032	75,637	866	18,464	2,278	12,086	187	843	25	2,365	2,155	210	6
413	84	7	4	1,153	716	437	215	275	330	47	113	108	44	9	14	8	19	12	7	7
2,606	158	37	13	7,023	5,319	1,704	1,262	1,132	2,857	102	775	457	260	13	165	...	94	74	20	8
5,330	210	58	6	13,215	11,280	1,935	9,220	1,310	6,591	153	1,543	422	760	29	166	21	275	241	34	9
44,371	560	497	57	121,256	114,944	6,312	21,532	4,315	65,859	564	16,033	1,296	11,022	136	498	1	1,977	1,828	149	10
1,762	32	177	8	104,727	92,577	12,150	72,571	11,869	19,094	195	491	77	64	1	357	8	116	113	3	11
7	1	...	...	1,731	957	774	867	759	82	13	6	6	...	...	2	...	...	...	...	12
128	2	5	...	7,254	5,307	1,947	4,501	1,917	712	17	23	13	1	...	70	...	1	1	...	13
160	4	...	2	10,191	8,335	1,856	6,642	1,808	1,591	29	30	19	18	...	54	...	7	6	1	14
1,472	25	172	6	85,551	77,978	7,573	60,561	7,391	16,709	136	432	37	45	1	231	8	108	106	2	15
3,486	56	125	...	1,724	1,660	64	53	14	1,392	20	152	27	69	1	4	2	20	18	2	16
25	3	...	...	12	8	4	1	2	6	...	1	2	...	...	...	...	...	...	...	17
208	4	9	...	112	102	10	3	3	80	2	16	5	1	...	2	...	...	...	...	18
357	6	8	...	148	136	12	2	5	112	3	21	4	1	...	...	...	3	2	1	19
2,898	43	108	...	1,452	1,414	38	47	4	1,184	15	114	16	67	1	2	2	17	16	1	20
...	...	...	...	...	...	...	...	...	...	...	...	...	...	...	...	...	491	479	12	21
...	...	...	...	...	...	...	...	...	...	...	...	...	...	...	...	...	1	1	...	22
...	...	...	...	...	...	...	...	...	...	...	...	...	...	...	...	...	18	18	...	23
...	...	...	...	...	...	...	...	...	...	...	...	...	...	...	...	...	47	47	...	24
...	...	...	...	...	...	...	...	...	...	...	...	...	...	...	...	...	425	413	12	25
1	...	4	1	4	4	...	4	...	...	...	...	...	...	...	...	...	289	178	111	26
...	...	...	...	...	...	...	...	...	...	...	...	...	...	...	...	...	19	13	6	27
...	...	2	...	...	...	...	...	...	...	...	...	...	...	...	...	...	23	9	14	28
...	...	...	...	...	...	...	...	...	...	...	...	...	...	...	...	...	29	12	17	29
1	...	2	1	4	4	...	4	...	...	...	...	...	...	...	...	...	218	144	74	30
532	13	22	...	4,855	4,737	118	1,099	61	2,651	32	90	4	77	...	820	18	248	173	75	31
5	...	1	...	13	10	3	3	8	7	...	...	...	...	...	...	...	8	1	7	32
15	1	...	...	167	158	14	31	5	55	7	5	1	3	...	59	1	21	6	15	33
27	1	...	...	314	294	20	68	6	142	6	5	1	4	...	77	7	33	18	15	34
485	11	21	...	4,861	4,280	81	999	50	2,447	19	80	2	70	...	684	10	186	148	38	35
12	1	19	12	299	214	85	197	60	1	5	6	5	1	...	9	15	92	68	24	36
...	...	2	1	6	6	...	6	...	...	...	...	...	...	...	...	...	8	1	2	37
...	...	2	...	19	16	3	15	3	...	...	...	...	...	...	1	...	1	...	1	38
2	1	5	3	83	10	23	10	19	...	1	...	...	...	...	...	3	12	11	1	39
10	...	10	8	241	182	59	166	38	1	4	6	5	1	...	8	12	76	56	20	40
...	...	...	...	...	...	...	...	...	...	...	...	...	...	...	...	...	4	2	2	41
...	...	...	...	...	...	...	...	...	...	...	...	...	...	...	...	...	...	...	...	42
...	...	...	...	...	...	...	...	...	...	...	...	...	...	...	...	...	...	...	...	43
...	...	...	...	...	...	...	...	...	...	...	...	...	...	...	...	...	1	...	1	44
...	...	...	...	...	...	...	...	...	...	...	...	...	...	...	...	...	3	2	1	45

APPENDIX TO IMPERIAL TABLE VIII.—

PART A.—PROVINCIAL SUMMARY.

NATIVE STATES.

Serial No.	Religion and Age.	Literate in Vernacular. Total. Persons.	Total. Males.	Total. Females.	Urdu. Total. Persons.	Urdu. Total. Males.	Urdu. Total. Females.	Urdu. Persian. Males.	Urdu. Persian. Females.	Urdu. Others. Males.	Urdu. Others. Females.	Hindi. Total. Persons.	Hindi. Total. Males.	Hindi. Total. Females.	Hindi. Nagri. Males.	Hindi. Nagri. Females.
	1	2	3	4	5	6	7	8	9	10	11	12	13	14	15	16
1	ALL RELIGIONS ...	123,593	118,638	4,955	38,421	37,309	1,112	36,766	1,071	543	41	27,893	26,654	1,239	13,666	1,04
2	0—10 ...	1,026	824	202	446	399	47	395	45	4	2	252	193	59	57	4
3	10—15 ...	6,861	6,365	496	3,368	3,264	104	3,235	101	29	3	1,249	1,113	136	534	12
4	15—20 ...	12,880	12,101	779	5,252	5,067	185	5,035	178	32	7	2,526	2,322	204	1,100	18
5	20 and over ...	102,826	99,348	3,478	29,355	28,579	776	28,101	747	478	29	23,866	23,026	840	11,975	69
6	HINDU ...	80,467	77,829	2,638	18,479	18,201	278	17,704	248	497	30	26,611	25,431	1,180	13,321	1,01
7	0—10 ...	588	488	100	214	206	8	202	8	4	...	224	169	55	53	4
8	10—15 ...	4,356	4,051	305	1,780	1,749	31	1,725	26	24	3	1,144	1,013	131	521	11
9	15—20 ...	8,501	8,066	435	2,755	2,707	48	2,676	42	31	6	2,310	2,119	197	1,063	17
10	20 and over ...	67,022	65,224	1,798	13,730	13,538	191	13,101	170	438	21	22,227	22,130	797	11,684	67
11	SIKH ...	24,191	22,805	1,386	3,991	3,943	48	3,912	47	31	1	365	336	29	106	1
12	0—10 ...	228	168	60	55	53	2	53	2	...	...	1	...	1	...	...
13	10—15 ...	1,231	1,124	107	476	471	5	470	5	1	...	12	11	1	3	...
14	15—20 ...	2,221	2,021	200	688	682	6	682	6	...	...	46	44	2	12	...
15	20 and over ...	20,511	19,492	1,019	2,772	2,737	35	2,707	34	30	1	306	281	25	91	1
16	JAIN ...	1,717	1,659	58	323	319	4	317	3	2	1	554	529	25	154	20
17	0—10 ...	9	8	1	6	6	...	6	...	...	...	3	2	1	1	1
18	10—15 ...	107	99	8	51	50	1	50	1	...	...	28	24	4	8	4
19	15—20 ...	204	196	8	50	49	1	49	1	...	...	61	56	5	19	4
20	20 and over ...	1,397	1,356	41	216	214	2	212	1	2	1	462	447	15	126	11
21	BUDDHIST ...	106	93	13	...	...	...	...	...	...	...	11	11	...	11	...
22	0—10 ...	...	...	...	...	...	...	...	...	...	...	...	...	...	...	...
23	10—15 ...	...	...	...	...	...	...	...	...	...	...	...	...	...	...	...
24	15—20 ...	2	2	...	...	...	...	...	...	...	...	...	...	...	...	...
25	20 and over ...	104	91	13	...	...	...	...	...	...	...	11	11	...	11	...
26	ZOROASTRIAN ...	18	14	4	8	8	...	6	...	2	...	...	...	...	...	...
27	0—10 ...	...	...	...	...	...	...	...	...	...	...	...	...	...	...	...
28	10—15 ...	...	...	...	...	...	...	...	...	...	...	...	...	...	...	...
29	15—20 ...	2	2	...	2	2	...	2	...	...	...	...	...	...	...	...
30	20 and over ...	16	12	4	6	6	...	4	...	2	...	...	...	...	...	...
31	MUHAMMADAN ...	16,859	16,093	766	15,423	14,720	703	14,712	701	8	2	337	336	1	64	1
32	0—10 ...	185	150	35	162	128	34	128	34	...	...	19	19	...	...	...
33	10—15 ...	1,156	1,084	72	1,050	987	63	985	63	2	...	65	65	...	2	...
34	15—20 ...	1,917	1,795	122	1,727	1,611	116	1,610	116	1	...	102	102	...	5	...
35	20 and over ...	13,601	13,064	537	12,484	11,994	490	11,989	486	5	2	151	150	1	57	1
36	CHRISTIAN ...	235	145	90	197	118	79	115	72	3	7	15	11	4	10	...
37	0—10 ...	16	10	6	9	6	3	6	1	...	2	5	3	2	3	...
38	10—15 ...	11	7	4	11	7	4	5	4	2	...	...	...	...	...	...
39	15—20 ...	33	19	14	30	16	14	16	13	...	1	1	1	...	1	...
40	20 and over ...	175	109	66	147	89	58	86	54	1	4	9	7	2	6	...
41	JEW ...	...	...	...	...	...	...	...	...	...	...	...	...	...	...	...
42	0—10 ...	...	...	...	...	...	...	...	...	...	...	...	...	...	...	...
43	10—15 ...	...	...	...	...	...	...	...	...	...	...	...	...	...	...	...
44	15—20 ...	...	...	...	...	...	...	...	...	...	...	...	...	...	...	...
45	20 and over ...	...	...	...	...	...	...	...	...	...	...	...	...	...	...	...

EDUCATION (BY RELIGION AND AGE)—*continued.*

PART A.—PROVINCIAL SUMMARY.

NATIVE STATES.

LITERATE IN VERNACULAR.																				
HINDI.				PUNJABI.													OTHERS.			
Lande or Mahajani.		*Others.*		*Total.*			*Gurmukhi.*		*Lande or Mahajani.*		*Nagri.*		*Tankri.*		*Persian.*					
Males.	Females.	Males.	Females.	Persons.	Males.	Females.	Males.	Females.	Males.	Females.	Males.	Females.	Males.	Females.	Males.	Females.	Persons.	Males.	Females.	Serial No.
17	18	19	20	21	22	23	24	25	26	27	28	29	30	31	32	33	34	35	36	
12,738	176	250	23	56,999	54,421	2,578	21,913	1,695	21,955	208	5,078	519	4,839	138	636	18	280	254	26	1
135	17	1	...	323	228	95	134	74	62	8	23	12	7	...	2	1	5	4	1	2
566	14	13	...	2,239	1,983	256	752	152	812	23	206	63	155	15	58	3	5	5	...	3
1,206	19	16	2	5,081	4,694	387	1,610	249	2,200	24	459	95	324	18	101	1	21	18	3	4
10,831	126	220	21	49,356	47,516	1,840	19,417	1,220	18,881	153	4,390	349	4,353	105	475	13	249	227	22	5
11,963	166	147	3	35,241	34,067	1,174	4,530	370	19,639	191	4,912	476	4,760	134	226	3	136	130	6	6
115	15	1	...	147	110	37	20	19	60	6	23	12	7	...	...	...	3	3	...	7
481	14	11	...	1,427	1,284	143	150	47	754	22	202	59	149	15	29	...	5	5	...	8
1,041	18	15	...	3,414	3,227	187	397	55	2,018	21	452	93	321	18	39	...	16	13	3	9
10,326	119	120	3	30,253	29,446	807	3,963	249	16,807	142	4,235	312	4,283	101	158	3	112	109	3	10
160	1	70	20	19,833	18,524	1,309	16,932	1,277	1,287	14	117	15	18	1	170	2	2	2	...	11
...	...	...	...	172	115	57	113	55	2	2	...	...	...	...	...	...	...	...	...	12
8	...	...	...	743	642	101	591	99	31	1	4	1	...	...	16	...	...	...	...	13
32	...	...	2	1,487	1,295	192	1,178	188	79	2	5	1	1	...	32	1	...	...	...	14
120	1	70	18	17,431	16,472	959	15,050	935	1,175	9	108	13	17	1	122	1	2	2	...	15
375	5	...	...	833	804	29	7	5	767	1	14	23	12	...	4	...	7	7	...	16
1	...	...	...	...	...	...	...	...	...	...	...	...	...	...	...	...	...	...	...	17
16	...	...	...	28	25	3	1	...	22	...	...	3	1	...	1	...	...	...	...	18
37	1	...	...	92	90	2	1	...	85	1	2	1	1	...	1	...	1	1	...	19
321	4	...	...	713	689	24	5	5	600	...	12	19	10	...	2	...	6	6	...	20
...	...	...	...	2	2	...	...	...	...	...	...	...	2	...	...	...	93	80	13	21
...	...	...	...	...	...	...	...	...	...	...	...	...	...	...	...	...	...	...	...	22
...	...	...	...	...	...	...	...	...	...	...	...	...	...	...	...	...	...	...	...	23
...	...	...	...	...	...	...	...	...	...	...	...	...	...	...	...	...	2	2	...	24
...	...	...	...	2	2	...	...	...	...	...	...	...	2	...	...	...	91	78	13	25
...	...	...	...	...	...	...	...	...	...	...	...	...	...	...	...	...	10	6	4	26
...	...	...	...	...	...	...	...	...	...	...	...	...	...	...	...	...	...	...	...	27
...	...	...	...	...	...	...	...	...	...	...	...	...	...	...	...	...	...	...	...	28
...	...	...	...	...	...	...	...	...	...	...	...	...	...	...	...	...	...	...	...	29
...	...	...	...	...	...	...	...	...	...	...	...	...	...	...	...	...	10	6	4	30
239	...	33	...	1,077	1,015	62	438	41	262	2	33	3	47	3	235	13	22	22	...	31
19	...	...	...	4	3	1	1	...	...	...	...	...	...	...	2	1	...	...	...	32
61	...	2	...	41	32	9	10	6	5	...	...	...	5	...	12	3	...	...	...	33
96	...	1	...	87	81	6	34	6	18	...	...	...	1	...	28	...	1	1	...	34
63	...	30	...	945	899	46	393	29	239	2	33	3	41	3	193	9	21	21	...	35
1	4	...	...	13	9	4	6	2	...	...	2	2	...	...	1	...	10	7	3	36
...	2	...	...	...	...	...	...	...	...	...	...	...	...	...	...	...	2	1	1	37
...	...	...	...	...	...	...	...	...	...	...	...	...	...	...	...	...	...	...	...	38
...	...	...	...	1	1	...	...	...	...	...	...	...	...	...	1	...	1	1	...	39
1	2	...	...	12	8	4	6	2	...	...	2	2	...	...	...	...	7	5	2	40
...	...	...	...	...	...	...	...	...	...	...	...	...	...	...	...	...	...	...	...	41
...	...	...	...	...	...	...	...	...	...	...	...	...	...	...	...	...	...	...	...	42
...	...	...	...	...	...	...	...	...	...	...	...	...	...	...	...	...	...	...	...	43
...	...	...	...	...	...	...	...	...	...	...	...	...	...	...	...	...	...	...	...	44
...	...	...	...	...	...	...	...	...	...	...	...	...	...	...	...	...	...	...	...	45

APPENDIX TO IMPERIAL TABLE VIII.—

PART B.—DETAILS FOR

Serial No.	District or State.	Religion and age.	Literate in Vernacular.														
			Total.			Urdu.							Hindi.				
						Total.			Persian.		Others.		Total.			Nagri.	
			Persons.	Males.	Females.	Persons.	Males.	Females.	Males.	Females.	Males.	Females.	Persons.	Males.	Females.	Males.	Females.
	1	2	3	4	5	6	7	8	9	10	11	12	13	14	15	16	17
1	HISSAR.	ALL RELIGIONS ...	20,567	20,024	543	5,072	4,925	147	4,898	132	27	15	14,344	14,001	343	3,996	241
2		0—10 ...	174	144	30	51	50	1	50	1	...	...	116	90	26	27	20
3		10—15 ...	1,350	1,274	76	554	539	15	537	14	2	1	743	693	50	269	40
4		15—20 ...	2,592	2,499	93	778	756	22	752	17	4	5	1,718	1,653	65	456	41
5		20 and over ...	16,451	16,107	344	3,689	3,580	109	3,559	100	21	9	11,767	11,565	202	3,244	140
6		HINDU ...	16,285	15,894	391	2,617	2,577	40	2,558	31	19	9	13,122	12,791	331	3,905	236
7		0—10 ...	142	116	26	32	32	...	32	...	...	...	109	83	26	27	20
8		10—15 ...	1,044	986	58	345	340	5	339	5	1	...	675	626	49	260	40
9		15—20 ...	2,058	1,984	74	438	431	7	428	4	3	3	1,575	1,511	64	448	40
10		20 and over ...	13,041	12,808	233	1,802	1,774	28	1,759	22	15	6	10,763	10,571	192	3,170	136
11		SIKH ...	920	884	36	130	130	...	130	...	...	...	289	284	5	28	2
12		0—10 ...	7	4	3	2	2	...	2	...	...	...	...	...	...	...	...
13		10—15 ...	52	45	7	15	15	...	15	...	...	...	14	14	...	4	...
14		15—20 ...	91	89	2	20	20	...	20	...	...	...	40	40	...	6	...
15		20 and over ...	770	746	24	93	93	...	93	...	...	...	235	230	5	18	2
16		JAIN ...	1,172	1,172	...	293	293	...	293	...	...	...	826	826	...	22	...
17		0—10 ...	9	9	...	1	1	...	1	...	...	...	7	7	...	...	...
18		10—15 ...	94	94	...	37	37	...	37	...	...	...	53	53	...	5	...
19		15—20 ...	158	158	...	54	54	...	54	...	...	...	92	92	...	...	...
20		20 and over ...	911	911	...	201	201	...	201	...	...	...	674	674	...	17	...
21		MUHAMMADAN ...	2,139	2,047	92	1,995	1,907	88	1,901	88	6	...	103	99	4	40	1
22		0—10 ...	13	13	...	13	13	...	13	...	...	...	...	...	...	...	...
23		10—15 ...	157	147	10	154	145	9	144	9	1	...	1	...	1	...	...
24		15—20 ...	276	266	10	260	250	10	249	10	1	...	10	10	...	2	...
25		20 and over ...	1,693	1,621	72	1,568	1,499	69	1,495	69	4	...	92	89	3	38	1
26	ROHTAK.	ALL RELIGIONS ...	14,602	14,187	415	9,954	9,653	301	5,338	165	4,315	136	4,613	4,508	105	1,179	70
27		0—10 ...	101	92	9	79	71	8	39	5	32	3	21	20	1	1	1
28		10—15 ...	1,366	1,292	74	1,075	1,020	55	792	24	228	31	285	267	18	38	16
29		15—20 ...	2,133	2,062	71	1,597	1,542	55	1,034	37	508	18	532	517	15	137	12
30		20 and over ...	11,002	10,741	261	7,203	7,020	183	3,473	99	3,547	84	3,775	3,704	71	1,003	41
31		HINDU ...	11,511	11,251	260	7,278	7,117	161	3,138	52	3,979	109	4,221	4,125	96	1,101	67
32		0—10 ...	73	69	4	54	51	3	20	2	31	1	19	18	1	1	1
33		10—15 ...	1,093	1,030	63	821	776	45	548	19	228	26	271	254	17	38	16
34		15—20 ...	1,680	1,640	40	1,206	1,180	26	724	14	456	12	472	458	14	97	11
35		20 and over ...	8,665	8,512	153	5,197	5,110	87	1,846	17	3,264	70	3,459	3,395	64	965	39
36		JAIN ...	1,113	1,076	37	734	704	30	391	3	313	27	379	372	7	74	2
37		0—10 ...	12	10	2	10	8	2	7	...	1	2	2	2	...	...	...
38		10—15 ...	79	74	5	66	61	5	61	...	...	5	13	13	...	...	...
39		15—20 ...	172	166	6	113	107	6	57	...	50	6	59	59	...	40	...
40		20 and over ...	850	826	24	545	528	17	266	3	262	14	305	298	7	34	2
41		MUHAMMADAN ...	1,877	1,782	95	1,872	1,777	95	1,757	95	20	...	5	5	...	1	...
42		0—10 ...	10	9	1	10	9	1	9	1	...	...	...	...	...	...	...
43		10—15 ...	182	178	4	182	178	4	178	4	...	...	...	...	...	...	...
44		15—20 ...	275	252	23	275	252	23	250	23	2	...	...	...	...	...	...
45		20 and over ...	1,410	1,343	67	1,405	1,338	67	1,320	67	18	...	5	5	...	1	...
46	GURGAON.	ALL RELIGIONS ...	14,931	14,418	513	6,012	5,823	189	5,779	185	44	4	8,895	8,579	316	5,099	288
47		0—10 ...	135	106	29	67	57	10	56	10	1	...	67	49	18	30	17
48		10—15 ...	1,456	1,361	95	804	771	33	768	32	3	1	652	590	62	413	59
49		15—20 ...	2,103	2,004	99	1,122	1,074	48	1,068	47	6	1	978	927	51	582	47
50		20 and over ...	11,237	10,947	290	4,019	3,921	98	3,887	96	34	2	7,198	7,013	185	4,074	165
51		HINDU ...	11,284	10,984	300	3,194	3,177	17	3,141	17	36	...	8,065	7,784	281	4,868	256
52		0—10 ...	101	83	18	40	38	2	37	2	1	...	61	45	16	29	15
53		10—15 ...	1,091	1,031	60	494	493	1	490	1	3	...	597	538	59	398	56
54		15—20 ...	1,531	1,485	46	630	625	5	619	5	6	...	900	859	41	588	38
55		20 and over ...	8,541	8,365	176	2,030	2,021	9	1,995	9	26	...	6,507	6,342	165	3,868	147
56		JAIN ...	840	820	20	178	177	1	177	1	...	...	662	643	19	116	19
57		0—10 ...	9	7	2	3	3	...	3	...	...	...	6	4	2	1	2
58		10—15 ...	64	60	4	13	12	1	12	1	...	...	51	48	3	13	3
59		15—20 ...	97	94	3	31	31	...	31	...	...	...	66	63	3	10	3
60		20 and over ...	670	659	11	131	131	...	131	...	...	...	539	528	11	92	11
61		MUHAMMADAN ...	2,606	2,515	91	2,467	2,382	85	2,374	81	8	4	139	133	6	105	4
62		0—10 ...	19	16	3	19	16	3	16	3	...	...	...	...	...	...	...
63		10—15 ...	258	249	9	254	245	9	245	8	...	1	4	4	...	2	...
64		15—20 ...	425	405	20	419	401	18	401	17	...	1	6	4	2	4	2
65		20 and over ...	1,904	1,845	59	1,775	1,720	55	1,712	53	8	2	129	125	4	99	2

EDUCATION (BY RELIGION AND AGE).
DISTRICTS AND STATES.

LITERATE IN VERNACULAR.																				
HINDI.				PUNJABI.													OTHERS.			
Lande or Mahajani.		Others.		Total.			Gurmukhi.		Lande or Mahajani.		Nagri.		Tankri.		Persian.					
Males.	Females.	Males.	Females.	Persons.	Males.	Females.	Males.	Females.	Males.	Females.	Males.	Females.	Males.	Females.	Males.	Females.	Persons.	Males.	Females.	Serial No.
18	19	20	21	22	23	24	25	26	27	28	29	30	31	32	33	34	35	36	37	
9,947	98	58	4	1,135	1,086	49	583	38	435	4	25	7	...	...	43	...	16	12	4	1
60	5	3	1	7	4	3	1	3	3	...	...	...	...	...	...	...	...	...	...	2
415	10	9	...	53	42	11	15	9	18	1	4	1	...	...	5	...	...	...	...	3
1,187	24	10	...	94	89	5	32	2	47	1	2	2	...	...	8	...	2	1	1	4
8,285	59	36	3	981	951	30	535	24	367	2	19	4	...	...	30	...	14	11	3	5
8,833	92	58	3	540	522	18	168	7	330	4	24	7	...	...	5	...	6	4	2	6
53	5	3	1	1	1	...	...	...	1	...	...	...	...	...	...	...	...	...	...	7
357	9	9	...	24	20	4	4	2	10	1	4	1	...	...	2	...	...	...	...	8
1,053	24	10	...	45	42	3	11	...	29	1	2	2	...	...	...	...	...	...	...	9
7,370	54	31	2	470	459	11	148	5	290	2	18	4	...	...	3	...	6	4	2	10
254	3	2	...	501	470	31	410	31	50	...	...	...	...	...	10	...	...	...	...	11
...	...	...	...	5	2	3	1	3	1	...	...	...	...	...	...	...	...	...	...	12
10	...	...	...	23	16	7	11	7	4	...	...	...	...	...	1	...	...	...	...	13
34	...	...	...	31	29	2	20	2	5	...	...	...	...	...	4	...	...	...	...	14
210	3	2	...	442	423	19	378	19	40	...	...	...	...	...	5	...	...	...	...	15
804	...	...	...	53	53	...	...	...	53	...	...	...	...	...	...	...	...	...	...	16
7	...	...	...	1	1	...	...	...	1	...	...	...	...	...	...	...	...	...	...	17
48	...	...	...	4	4	...	...	...	4	...	...	...	...	...	...	...	...	...	...	18
92	...	...	...	12	12	...	...	...	12	...	...	...	...	...	...	...	...	...	...	19
657	...	...	...	36	36	...	...	...	36	...	...	...	...	...	...	...	...	...	...	20
56	3	3	...	41	41	...	10	...	2	...	1	...	...	...	28	...	...	...	...	21
...	...	...	...	...	...	...	...	...	...	...	...	...	...	...	...	...	...	...	...	22
...	1	...	...	2	2	...	...	...	...	...	...	...	...	...	2	...	...	...	...	23
8	...	...	...	6	6	...	1	...	1	...	...	...	...	...	4	...	...	...	...	24
48	2	3	...	33	33	...	9	...	1	...	1	...	...	...	22	...	...	...	...	25
3,303	35	26	...	35	26	9	23	9	1	...	...	...	...	...	2	...	...	...	...	26
19	...	...	...	1	1	...	1	...	...	...	...	...	...	...	...	...	...	...	...	27
227	2	2	...	6	5	1	5	1	...	...	...	...	...	...	...	...	...	...	...	28
375	3	5	...	4	3	1	3	1	...	...	...	...	...	...	...	...	...	...	...	29
2,682	30	19	...	24	17	7	14	7	1	...	...	...	...	...	2	...	...	...	...	30
2,998	29	26	...	12	9	3	6	3	1	...	...	...	...	...	2	...	...	...	...	31
17	...	...	...	...	...	...	...	...	...	...	...	...	...	...	...	...	...	...	...	32
214	1	2	...	1	...	1	...	1	...	...	...	...	...	...	...	...	...	...	...	33
356	3	5	...	2	2	...	2	...	...	...	...	...	...	...	...	...	...	...	...	34
2,411	25	19	...	9	7	2	4	2	1	...	...	...	...	...	2	...	...	...	...	35
298	5	...	...	...	...	...	...	...	...	...	...	...	...	...	...	...	...	...	...	36
2	...	...	...	...	...	...	...	...	...	...	...	...	...	...	...	...	...	...	...	37
13	...	...	...	...	...	...	...	...	...	...	...	...	...	...	...	...	...	...	...	38
19	...	...	...	...	...	...	...	...	...	...	...	...	...	...	...	...	...	...	...	39
264	5	...	...	...	...	...	...	...	...	...	...	...	...	...	...	...	...	...	...	40
4	...	...	...	...	...	...	...	...	...	...	...	...	...	...	...	...	...	...	...	41
...	...	...	...	...	...	...	...	...	...	...	...	...	...	...	...	...	...	...	...	42
...	...	...	...	...	...	...	...	...	...	...	...	...	...	...	...	...	...	...	...	43
...	...	...	...	...	...	...	...	...	...	...	...	...	...	...	...	...	...	...	...	44
4	...	...	...	...	...	...	...	...	...	...	...	...	...	...	...	...	...	...	...	45
3,480	27	...	1	14	8	6	7	6	...	...	...	...	...	...	1	...	10	8	2	46
19	1	...	...	1	...	1	...	1	...	...	...	...	...	...	...	...	...	...	...	47
177	3	...	...	...	...	...	...	...	...	...	...	...	...	...	...	...	...	...	...	48
345	4	...	...	2	2	...	2	...	...	...	...	...	...	...	...	...	1	1	...	49
2,939	19	...	1	11	6	5	5	5	...	...	...	...	...	...	1	...	9	7	2	50
2,921	24	...	1	1	...	1	...	1	...	...	...	...	...	...	...	...	4	3	1	51
16	1	...	...	...	...	...	...	...	...	...	...	...	...	...	...	...	...	...	...	52
140	3	...	...	...	...	...	...	...	...	...	...	...	...	...	...	...	...	...	...	53
291	3	...	...	...	...	...	...	...	...	...	...	...	...	...	...	...	1	1	...	54
2,474	17	...	1	1	...	1	...	1	...	...	...	...	...	...	...	...	3	2	1	55
527	...	...	...	...	...	...	...	...	...	...	...	...	...	...	...	...	...	...	...	56
3	...	...	...	...	...	...	...	...	...	...	...	...	...	...	...	...	...	...	...	57
35	...	...	...	...	...	...	...	...	...	...	...	...	...	...	...	...	...	...	...	58
53	...	...	...	...	...	...	...	...	...	...	...	...	...	...	...	...	...	...	...	59
436	...	...	...	...	...	...	...	...	...	...	...	...	...	...	...	...	...	...	...	60
28	2	...	...	...	...	...	...	...	...	...	...	...	...	...	...	...	...	...	...	61
...	...	...	...	...	...	...	...	...	...	...	...	...	...	...	...	...	...	...	...	62
2	...	...	...	...	...	...	...	...	...	...	...	...	...	...	...	...	...	...	...	63
...	...	...	...	...	...	...	...	...	...	...	...	...	...	...	...	...	...	...	...	64
26	2	...	...	...	...	...	...	...	...	...	...	...	...	...	...	...	...	...	...	65

APPENDIX TO IMPERIAL TABLE VIII.—

PART B.—DETAILS FOR

Serial No.	District or State.	Religion and Age.	LITERATE IN VERNACULAR. Total. Persons.	Total. Males.	Total. Females.	Urdu. Total. Persons.	Urdu. Total. Males.	Urdu. Total. Females.	Urdu. Persian. Males.	Urdu. Persian. Females.	Urdu. Others. Males.	Urdu. Others. Females.	Hindi. Total. Persons.	Hindi. Total. Males.	Hindi. Total. Females.	Hindi. Nagri. Males.	Hindi. Nagri. Females.
	1	2	3	4	5	6	7	8	9	10	11	12	13	14	15	16	17
1	GURGAON.	CHRISTIAN ...	178	83	95	152	66	86	66	86	...	...	26	17	9	13	8
2		0—10 ...	5	...	5	5	...	5	...	5	...	...	...	...	...	...	...
3		10—15 ...	41	19	22	41	19	22	19	22	...	...	...	...	...	...	...
4		15—20 ...	45	16	29	40	15	25	15	25	...	...	5	1	4	...	3
5		20 and over ...	87	48	39	66	32	34	32	34	...	..	21	16	5	13	5
6	DELHI.	ALL RELIGIONS ...	35,782	32,423	3,359	19,653	18,105	1,548	17,874	1,460	231	88	14,499	12,838	1,661	8,176	1,485
7		0—10 ...	601	395	206	343	268	75	265	72	3	3	244	122	122	95	110
8		10—15 ...	3,267	2,777	490	2,258	2,012	246	1,996	236	16	10	957	728	229	481	206
9		15—20 ...	4,635	4,063	572	2,847	2,568	279	2,537	258	31	21	1,644	1,368	276	868	246
10		20 and over ...	27,279	25,188	2,091	14,205	13,257	948	13,076	894	181	54	11,654	10,620	1,034	6,732	923
11		HINDU ...	22,282	20,387	1,895	9,056	8,744	312	8,572	235	172	77	12,660	11,186	1,474	7,433	1,336
12		0—10 ...	359	229	130	135	122	13	119	11	3	2	213	103	110	82	100
13		10—15 ...	2,002	1,742	260	1,130	1,091	39	1,076	29	15	10	824	616	208	427	188
14		15—20 ...	2,939	2,620	319	1,426	1,367	59	1,348	43	19	16	1,450	1,203	247	797	223
15		20 and over ...	16,982	15,796	1,186	6,365	6,164	201	6,029	152	135	49	10,173	9,264	909	6,127	825
16		SIKH ...	1,130	1,093	37	191	169	22	164	22	5	...	31	29	2	23	2
17		0—10 ...	2	1	1	2	1	1	1	1	...	...	...	...	...	...	...
18		10—15 ...	10	7	3	8	5	3	5	3	...	...	...	...	...	...	...
19		15—20 ...	85	81	4	24	21	3	21	3	...	...	3	3	...	3	...
20		20 and over ...	1,033	1,004	29	157	142	15	137	15	5	...	28	26	2	20	2
21		JAIN ...	2,175	1,996	179	565	550	15	550	15	...	...	1,597	1,435	162	599	133
22		0—10 ...	34	21	13	7	5	2	5	2	...	...	27	16	11	13	10
23		10—15 ...	191	168	23	63	61	2	61	2	...	...	128	107	21	53	18
24		15—20 ...	253	224	29	74	71	3	71	3	...	...	176	151	25	66	22
25		20 and over ...	1,697	1,583	114	421	413	8	413	8	...	...	1,266	1,161	105	467	83
26		MUHAMMADAN ...	9,379	8,486	893	9,171	8,280	891	8,262	885	18	6	140	138	2	92	2
27		0—10 ...	148	121	27	147	120	27	120	26	...	1	1	1	...	...	...
28		10—15 ...	901	782	119	899	780	119	779	119	1	...	2	2	...	...	...
29		15—20 ...	1,195	1,057	138	1,183	1,045	138	1,045	136	...	2	4	4	...	...	...
30		20 and over ...	7,135	6,526	609	6,942	6,335	607	6,318	604	17	3	133	131	2	92	2
31		CHRISTIAN ...	764	428	336	658	355	303	319	298	36	5	66	45	21	24	12
32		0—10 ...	56	22	34	52	20	32	20	32	...	...	3	2	1	...	...
33		10—15 ...	161	77	84	158	75	83	75	83	...	...	2	2	...	...	...
34		15—20 ...	160	80	80	140	64	76	52	73	12	3	11	7	4	2	1
35		20 and over ...	387	249	138	308	196	112	172	110	24	2	50	84	16	22	11
36	KARNAL.	ALL RELIGIONS ...	18,258	17,727	531	7,671	7,418	253	7,208	233	210	20	10,439	10,194	245	2,687	203
37		0—10 ...	131	116	15	61	58	3	57	2	1	1	68	58	10	18	7
38		10—15 ...	1,160	1,096	64	673	642	31	635	28	7	3	483	453	30	181	29
39		15—20 ...	2,301	2,208	93	1,100	1,048	52	1,016	47	32	5	1,190	1,155	35	310	30
40		20 and over ...	14,666	14,307	359	5,837	5,670	167	5,500	156	170	11	8,698	8,528	170	2,228	137
41		HINDU ...	13,414	13,158	256	3,686	3,657	29	3,608	25	49	4	9,678	9,455	223	2,542	190
42		0—10 ...	95	85	10	32	31	1	30	1	1	...	63	54	9	16	7
43		10—15 ...	852	817	35	415	410	5	408	3	2	2	436	406	30	117	29
44		15—20 ...	1,689	1,652	37	561	557	4	549	3	8	1	1,126	1,095	31	296	27
45		20 and over ...	10,778	10,604	174	2,678	2,659	19	2,621	18	38	1	8,053	7,900	153	2,113	127
46		SIKH ...	354	331	23	261	259	2	136	2	123	...	28	27	1	6	1
47		0—10 ...	1	1	...	1	1	...	1	...	...	...	...	...	...	...	...
48		10—15 ...	17	15	2	15	15	...	11	...	4	...	...	...	...	...	...
49		15—20 ...	27	24	3	21	21	...	7	...	14	...	...	...	...	...	...
50		20 and over ...	309	291	18	224	222	2	117	2	105	...	28	27	1	6	1
51		JAIN ...	831	813	18	173	171	2	138	...	33	2	658	642	16	124	8
52		0—10 ...	8	7	1	3	3	...	3	...	...	...	5	4	1	2	...
53		10—15 ...	70	70	...	25	25	...	24	...	1	...	45	45	...	14	...
54		15—20 ...	85	81	4	26	25	1	16	...	9	1	59	56	3	12	2
55		20 and over ...	668	655	13	119	118	1	95	...	23	1	549	537	12	96	6
56		MUHAMMADAN ...	3,523	3,350	173	3,427	3,264	163	3,264	163	...	...	65	64	1	9	...
57		0—10 ...	24	21	3	22	21	1	21	1	...	...	...	...	...	...	...
58		10—15 ...	208	190	18	205	188	17	188	17	...	...	2	2	...	...	...
59		15—20 ...	482	445	37	475	439	36	439	36	...	...	4	4	...	2	...
60		20 and over ...	2,809	2,694	115	2,725	2,616	109	2,616	109	...	...	59	58	1	7	...
61		CHRISTIAN ...	136	75	61	124	67	57	62	43	5	14	10	6	4	6	4
62		0—10 ...	3	2	1	3	2	1	2	...	...	1	...	...	...	...	...
63		10—15 ...	13	4	9	13	4	9	4	8	...	1	...	...	...	...	...
64		15—20 ...	18	6	12	17	6	11	5	8	1	3	1	...	1	...	1
65		20 and over ..	102	63	39	91	55	36	51	27	4	9	9	6	3	6	3

EDUCATION (BY RELIGION AND AGE).

DISTRICTS AND STATES—*continued.*

LITERATE IN VERNACULAR.																				
HINDI.				PUNJABI.													OTHERS.			
Lande or Mahajani.		*Others.*		*Total.*			*Gurmukhi.*		*Lande or Mahajani.*		*Nagri.*		*Tankri.*		*Persian.*					
Males.	Females.	Males.	Females.	Persons.	Males.	Females.	Males.	Females.	Males.	Females.	Males.	Females.	Males.	Females.	Males.	Females.	Persons.	Males.	Females.	Serial No.
18	19	20	21	22	23	24	25	26	27	28	29	30	31	32	33	34	35	36	37	
4	1	...	...	...	...	...	...	...	...	...	...	...	...	...	...	...	...	...	...	1
...	...	...	...	...	...	...	...	...	...	...	...	...	...	...	...	...	...	...	...	2
...	...	...	...	...	...	...	...	...	...	...	...	...	...	...	...	...	...	...	...	3
1	1	...	...	...	...	...	...	...	...	...	...	...	...	...	...	...	...	...	...	4
3	...	...	...	...	...	...	...	...	...	...	...	...	...	...	...	...	...	...	...	5
4,248	122	414	54	864	830	34	819	16	5	1	4	17	...	...	2	...	766	650	116	6
21	8	6	4	1	1	...	1	...	...	...	...	...	...	...	...	...	13	4	9	7
227	15	20	8	2	2	...	2	...	...	...	...	...	...	...	...	...	50	35	15	8
474	23	26	7	55	52	3	52	3	...	...	...	...	...	...	...	...	89	75	14	9
3,526	76	362	35	806	775	31	764	13	5	1	4	17	...	...	2	...	614	536	78	10
3,443	93	310	45	54	33	21	29	3	...	1	4	17	...	...	...	...	512	424	88	11
18	7	3	3	1	1	...	1	...	...	...	...	...	...	...	...	...	10	3	7	12
177	12	12	8	1	1	...	1	...	...	...	...	...	...	...	...	...	47	34	13	13
889	20	17	4	3	1	2	1	2	...	...	...	...	...	...	...	...	60	49	11	14
2,859	54	278	30	49	30	19	26	1	...	1	4	17	...	...	...	...	395	338	57	15
1	...	5	...	810	797	13	790	13	5	...	...	...	...	...	2	...	98	98	...	16
...	...	...	...	...	...	...	...	...	...	...	...	...	...	...	...	...	...	...	...	17
...	...	...	...	1	1	...	1	...	...	...	...	...	...	...	...	...	1	1	...	18
...	...	...	...	52	51	1	51	1	...	...	...	...	...	...	...	...	6	6	...	19
1	...	5	...	757	745	12	738	12	5	...	...	...	...	...	2	...	91	91	...	20
771	29	65	...	...	...	...	...	...	...	...	...	...	...	...	...	...	13	11	2	21
3	1	...	...	...	...	...	...	...	...	...	...	...	...	...	...	...	...	...	...	22
48	3	6	...	...	...	...	...	...	...	...	...	...	...	...	...	...	...	...	...	23
81	3	4	...	...	...	...	...	...	...	...	...	...	...	...	...	...	3	2	1	24
639	22	55	...	...	...	...	...	...	...	...	...	...	...	...	...	...	10	9	1	25
31	...	15	...	...	...	...	...	...	...	...	...	...	...	...	...	...	68	68	...	26
...	...	1	...	...	...	...	...	...	...	...	...	...	...	...	...	...	...	...	...	27
2	...	...	...	...	...	...	...	...	...	...	...	...	...	...	...	...	...	...	...	28
4	...	...	...	...	...	...	...	...	...	...	...	...	...	...	...	...	8	8	...	29
25	...	14	...	...	...	...	...	...	...	...	...	...	...	...	...	...	60	60	...	30
2	...	19	9	...	...	...	...	...	...	...	...	...	...	...	...	...	40	28	12	31
...	...	2	1	...	...	...	...	...	...	...	...	...	...	...	...	...	1	...	1	32
...	...	2	...	...	...	...	...	...	...	...	...	...	...	...	...	...	1	...	1	33
...	...	5	3	...	...	...	...	...	...	...	...	...	...	...	...	...	9	9	...	34
2	...	10	5	...	...	...	...	...	...	...	...	...	...	...	...	...	29	19	10	35
7,431	40	76	2	121	97	24	87	23	...	...	10	1	...	...	...	...	27	18	9	36
40	3	...	...	...	...	...	...	...	...	...	...	...	...	...	...	...	2	...	2	37
315	1	7	...	3	1	2	1	2	...	...	...	...	...	...	...	...	1	...	1	38
842	5	3	...	8	3	5	3	5	...	...	...	...	...	...	...	...	3	2	1	39
6,234	31	66	2	110	93	17	83	16	...	...	10	1	...	...	...	...	21	16	5	40
5,853	31	60	2	49	45	4	36	3	...	...	9	1	...	...	...	...	1	1	...	41
38	2	...	...	...	...	...	...	...	...	...	...	...	...	...	...	...	...	...	...	42
282	1	7	...	1	1	...	1	...	...	...	...	...	...	...	...	...	...	...	...	43
796	4	3	...	2	...	2	...	2	...	...	...	...	...	...	...	...	...	...	...	44
5,737	24	50	2	46	44	2	35	1	...	...	9	1	...	...	...	...	1	1	...	45
5	...	16	...	65	45	20	44	20	...	...	1	...	...	...	...	...	...	...	...	46
...	...	...	...	...	...	...	...	...	...	...	...	...	...	...	...	...	...	...	...	47
...	...	...	...	2	...	2	...	2	...	...	...	...	...	...	...	...	...	...	...	48
...	...	...	...	6	3	3	3	3	...	...	...	...	...	...	...	...	...	...	...	49
5	...	16	...	57	42	15	41	15	...	...	1	...	...	...	...	...	...	...	...	50
518	8	...	...	...	...	...	...	...	...	...	...	...	...	...	...	...	...	...	...	51
2	1	...	...	...	...	...	...	...	...	...	...	...	...	...	...	...	...	...	...	52
31	...	...	...	...	...	...	...	...	...	...	...	...	...	...	...	...	...	...	...	53
44	1	...	...	...	...	...	...	...	...	...	...	...	...	...	...	...	...	...	...	54
441	6	...	...	...	...	...	...	...	...	...	...	...	...	...	...	...	...	...	...	55
55	1	...	...	5	5	...	5	...	...	...	...	...	...	...	...	...	26	17	9	56
...	...	...	...	...	...	...	...	...	...	...	...	...	...	...	...	...	2	...	2	57
2	...	...	...	...	...	...	...	...	...	...	...	...	...	...	...	...	1	...	1	58
2	...	...	...	...	...	...	...	...	...	...	...	...	...	...	...	...	3	2	1	59
51	1	...	...	5	5	...	5	...	...	...	...	...	...	...	...	...	20	15	5	60
...	...	...	...	2	2	...	2	...	...	...	...	...	...	...	...	...	...	...	...	61
...	...	...	...	...	...	...	...	...	...	...	...	...	...	...	...	...	...	...	...	62
...	...	...	...	...	...	...	...	...	...	...	...	...	...	...	...	...	...	...	...	63
...	...	...	...	...	...	...	...	...	...	...	...	...	...	...	...	...	...	...	...	64
...	...	...	...	2	2	...	2	...	...	...	...	...	...	...	...	...	...	...	...	65

APPENDIX TO IMPERIAL TABLE VIII.—
PART B.—DETAILS FOR

Serial No.	District or State.	Religion and Age.	Literate in Vernacular.														
			Total.			Urdu.							Hindi.				
						Total.			Persian.		Others.		Total.			Nagri.	
			Persons.	Males.	Females.	Persons.	Males.	Females.	Males.	Females.	Males.	Females.	Persons.	Males.	Females.	Males.	Females.
	1	2	3	4	5	6	7	8	9	10	11	12	13	14	15	16	17
1	AMBALA.	ALL RELIGIONS ...	29,249	27,880	1,369	16,236	15,512	724	13,641	558	1,871	166	5,454	5,127	327	1,694	230
2		0—10 ...	212	164	48	162	128	34	119	23	9	11	30	21	9	6	7
3		10—15 ...	1,902	1,720	182	1,479	1,375	104	1,305	74	70	30	203	149	54	33	40
4		15—20 ...	3,414	3,168	246	2,333	2,209	124	2,053	97	156	27	448	382	66	95	55
5		20 and over ...	23,721	22,828	893	12,262	11,800	462	10,164	364	1,636	98	4,773	4,575	198	1,560	128
6		HINDU ...	17,395	16,747	648	8,786	8,546	240	6,989	125	1,557	115	5,045	4,733	312	1,682	225
7		0—10 ...	121	101	20	86	76	10	70	2	6	8	27	18	9	6	7
8		10—15 ...	1,115	1,021	94	831	800	31	742	13	58	18	184	132	52	33	38
9		15—20 ...	2,024	1,901	123	1,346	1,302	44	1,163	25	139	19	422	358	64	95	54
10		20 and over ...	14,135	13,724	411	6,523	6,368	155	5,014	85	1,354	70	4,412	4,225	187	1,548	126
11		SIKH ...	5,227	4,969	258	1,365	1,319	46	1,144	6	175	40	165	159	6	2	...
12		0—10 ...	21	14	7	9	6	3	5	...	1	3	...	...	...	...	...
13		10—15 ...	291	266	25	172	160	12	154	1	6	11	5	5	...	...	...
14		15—20 ...	579	534	45	223	216	7	216	1	...	6	3	2	1	...	...
15		20 and over ...	4,336	4,155	181	961	937	24	769	4	168	20	157	152	5	2	...
16		JAIN ...	740	713	27	440	425	15	296	11	129	4	202	193	9	...	5
17		0—10 ...	8	8	...	5	5	...	3	...	2	...	3	3	...	...	...
18		10—15 ...	52	49	3	35	34	1	28	1	6	...	14	12	2	...	2
19		15—20 ...	89	87	2	62	61	1	45	1	16	...	22	21	1	...	1
20		20 and over ...	591	569	22	338	325	13	220	9	105	4	163	157	6	...	2
21		MUHAMMADAN ...	5,583	5,241	342	5,395	5,055	340	5,054	340	1	...	34	34	...	7	...
22		0—10 ...	61	40	21	61	40	21	40	21	...	...	...	...	...	...	...
23		10—15 ...	420	372	48	417	369	48	369	48	...	...	...	...	...	...	...
24		15—20 ...	672	619	53	659	606	53	606	53	...	...	...	...	...	...	...
25		20 and over ...	4,430	4,210	220	4,258	4,040	218	4,039	218	1	...	34	34	...	7	...
26		CHRISTIAN ...	298	205	93	246	163	83	154	76	9	7	8	8	...	3	...
27		0—10 ...	1	1	...	1	1	...	1	...	...	...	...	...	...	...	...
28		10—15 ...	24	12	12	24	12	12	12	11	...	1	...	...	...	...	...
29		15—20 ...	49	27	22	43	24	19	23	17	1	2	1	1	...	...	...
30		20 and over ...	224	165	59	178	126	52	116	48	8	4	7	7	...	3	...
31	SIMLA.	ALL RELIGIONS ...	4,881	4,534	347	2,528	2,422	106	2,411	104	11	2	1,635	1,442	193	1,425	192
32		0—10 ...	91	70	21	62	54	8	54	8	...	...	14	6	8	6	8
33		10—15 ...	421	379	42	308	289	14	288	13	1	1	71	45	26	45	26
34		15—20 ...	559	501	58	296	286	10	285	10	1	...	152	116	36	115	36
35		20 and over ...	3,810	3,584	226	1,867	1,793	74	1,784	73	9	1	1,398	1,275	123	1,259	122
36		HINDU ...	3,463	3,225	238	1,373	1,348	25	1,348	25	...	...	1,556	1,376	180	1,372	180
37		0—10 ...	66	51	15	40	37	3	37	3	...	...	14	6	8	6	8
38		10—15 ...	334	304	30	221	219	2	219	2	...	...	71	45	26	45	26
39		15—20 ...	422	378	44	186	183	3	183	3	...	...	147	112	35	112	35
40		20 and over ...	2,641	2,492	149	926	909	17	909	17	...	...	1,324	1,213	111	1,209	111
41		SIKH ...	233	220	13	69	68	1	61	...	7	1	17	16	1	10	1
42		0—10 ...	2	2	...	...	...	...	...	...	...	...	...	...	...	...	...
43		10—15 ...	11	10	1	8	7	1	6	...	1	1	...	...	...	...	...
44		15—20 ...	29	25	4	11	11	...	11	...	...	...	...	...	...	...	...
45		20 and over ...	191	183	8	50	50	...	44	...	6	...	17	16	1	10	1
46		MUHAMMADAN ...	1,012	951	61	981	922	59	922	59	...	...	20	19	1	18	1
47		0—10 ...	20	17	3	20	17	3	17	3	...	...	...	...	...	...	...
48		10—15 ...	71	63	8	69	61	8	61	8	...	...	...	...	...	...	...
49		15—20 ...	90	83	7	89	83	6	83	6	...	...	...	...	...	...	...
50		20 and over ...	831	788	43	803	761	42	761	42	...	...	20	19	1	18	1
51		CHRISTIAN ...	117	93	24	80	66	14	62	13	4	1	27	19	8	19	7
52		0—10 ...	1	...	1	...	...	...	...	...	...	...	...	...	...	...	...
53		10—15 ...	4	2	2	4	2	2	2	2	...	...	...	...	...	...	...
54		15—20 ...	11	10	1	10	9	1	8	1	1	...	1	1	...	1	...
55		20 and over ...	101	81	20	66	55	11	52	10	3	1	26	18	8	18	7
56	KANGRA.	ALL RELIGIONS ...	30,514	29,430	1,084	7,416	7,327	89	7,321	89	6	...	3,077	2,756	321	2,682	313
57		0—10 ...	316	277	39	162	159	3	159	3	...	...	47	29	18	29	18
58		10—15 ...	2,137	1,999	136	1,358	1,351	7	1,350	7	1	...	167	120	47	118	47
59		15—20 ...	2,967	2,804	163	1,271	1,253	18	1,250	18	3	...	277	225	52	213	51
60		20 and over ...	25,094	24,350	744	4,625	4,564	61	4,562	61	2	...	2,586	2,382	204	2,322	197
61		HINDU ...	28,700	27,728	972	6,435	6,400	35	6,395	35	5	...	3,039	2,726	313	2,655	309
62		0—10 ...	291	255	36	143	142	1	142	1	...	...	45	28	17	28	17
63		10—15 ...	2,007	1,878	129	1,256	1,253	3	1,253	3	...	...	166	119	47	117	47
64		15—20 ...	2,804	2,659	145	1,175	1,167	8	1,164	8	3	...	275	224	51	212	50
65		20 and over ...	23,598	22,936	662	3,861	3,838	23	3,836	23	2	...	2,553	2,355	198	2,298	195

MEANS OF LIVELIHOOD.

DISTRICTS AND STATES—*continued.*

OF MATERIAL SUBSTANCES—*continued.*

—*continued.*

—*concluded.*

31.—Other insufficiently described textile industries.						7.—Hides, skins, and hard materials from the animal kingdom. Total Order.						32.—Tanners, curriers, leather dressers, etc.						33.—Makers of leather articles such as trunks, bags, etc.						
Total workers and dependents.	Actual workers. Total.		Partially agriculturist.		Dependents.	Total workers and dependents.	Actual workers. Total.		Partially agriculturist.		Dependents.	Total workers and dependents.	Actual workers. Total.		Partially agriculturist.		Dependents.	Total workers and dependents.	Actual workers. Total.		Partially agriculturist.		Dependents.	Serial No.
	Males.	Females.	Males.	Females.			Males.	Females.	Males.	Females.			Males.	Females	Males.	Females.			Males.	Females.	Males.	Females.		
206	207	208	209	210	211	212	213	214	115	216	217	218	219	220	221	222	223	224	225	226	227	228	229	
23,575	4,669	3,729	2	3	15,177	89,577	28,516	2,322	1,546	15	58,739	77,199	24,951	2,138	1,190	14	50,115	12,094	3,503	184	354	1	8,407	
22,843	4,508	3,418	2	3	14,917	78,373	24,375	2,113	1,285	15	51,885	66,398	20,962	1,936	952	14	43,500	11,725	3,363	172	331	1	8,190	
19,294	3,517	2,353	...	...	13,424	22,303	7,077	672	492	2	14,554	11,209	3,862	517	168	1	6,830	10,966	3,195	150	324	1	7,621	
19	...	1	...	...	18	3,311	1,174	65	65	...	2,072	3,298	1,169	65	64	...	2,064	13	5	...	1	...	6	1
188	...	163	...	...	25	5,438	1,246	131	382	1	4,061	1,192	393	28	59	...	776	4,246	853	108	323	1	3,285	2
17	8	10	...	...	4	3,385	1,135	147	17	...	2,103	1,137	361	126	17	...	650	2,246	773	21	...	...	1,452	3
18,886	3,419	2,177	...	...	13,290	4,670	1,512	69	1	...	3,089	774	139	57	1	...	578	3,870	1,359	12	...	...	2,499	4
...	...	...	...	...	...	1,420	405	154	9	...	861	1,166	388	149	9	...	629	154	12	...	...	...	142	5
184	95	2	...	...	87	3,805	1,391	106	18	1	2,308	3,366	1,198	97	18	1	2,073	437	193	9	...	...	235	6
...	...	...	...	...	...	274	214	...	...	...	60	274	214	...	...	...	60	...	...	...	...	...	...	7
1,215	391	396	2	1	428	44,572	13,159	1,131	570	18	30,282	44,460	13,139	1,116	569	13	30,205	111	19	15	...	...	77	
3	2	...	...	...	1	88	18	15	...	...	55	88	18	15	...	...	55	...	...	...	...	...	...	8
150	8	128	...	...	14	23,708	7,791	962	369	13	14,955	23,684	7,791	957	369	12	14,936	24	...	5	...	...	19	9
1,039	364	266	2	1	407	17,945	4,516	113	194	...	13,316	17,920	4,513	103	194	...	13,304	25	3	10	...	...	12	10
23	17	...	...	...	6	1,187	328	28	8	...	831	1,124	311	28	2	...	785	62	16	...	...	...	46	11
...	...	...	...	...	...	1,644	506	13	4	...	1,125	1,644	506	13	4	...	1,125	...	...	...	...	...	...	12
2,125	548	571	...	2	1,006	8,493	3,226	262	202	...	5,005	8,300	3,189	261	202	...	4,850	174	25	1	...	...	148	
131	76	12	...	2	43	1,242	411	7	14	...	824	1,101	398	6	14	...	697	136	11	1	...	...	124	13
1,769	464	444	...	...	861	1,490	733	11	19	...	746	1,462	719	11	19	...	732	24	11	...	...	...	13	14
1	...	...	...	...	1	1,529	498	8	8	...	1,028	1,516	489	8	8	...	1,024	7	3	...	...	...	4	15
216	5	115	...	...	96	3,034	1,114	154	156	...	1,766	3,024	1,113	154	156	...	1,757	6	...	...	...	...	6	16
8	3	...	...	...	5	1,198	470	87	5	...	641	1,197	470	87	5	...	640	1	...	...	...	...	1	17
190	51	93	...	...	46	1,704	473	20	14	...	1,211	1,360	889	18	8	...	953	320	81	2	6	...	237	
...	...	...	...	...	...	694	190	4	7	...	500	473	122	2	1	...	349	216	67	2	6	...	147	18
57	3	49	...	...	5	34	22	1	...	...	11	18	11	1	...	...	6	12	9	...	...	...	3	19
74	47	...	...	...	27	279	88	10	1	...	181	194	87	10	1	...	97	84	1	...	...	...	83	20
1	...	...	...	...	1	638	150	4	4	...	484	624	150	4	4	...	470	...	...	...	...	...	...	21
29	1	20	...	...	8	58	22	1	2	...	35	51	19	1	2	...	31	7	3	...	...	...	4	22
29	...	24	...	...	5	1	1	...	...	...	...	...	...	...	...	...	...	1	1	...	...	...	...	23
19	1	5	...	...	13	1,301	440	28	7	...	833	1,069	883	24	5	...	682	154	43	4	1	...	107	
...	...	...	...	...	...	46	7	...	...	...	39	10	3	...	...	...	7	8	1	...	...	...	7	24
...	...	...	...	...	...	737	255	2	...	...	460	694	246	2	...	...	446	7	2	...	...	...	5	25
10	...	5	...	...	5	68	17	...	1	...	51	1	1	...	...	...	...	67	16	...	1	...	51	26
...	...	...	...	...	...	246	58	26	...	...	162	220	52	22	...	...	146	24	5	4	...	...	15	27
6	...	...	...	...	6	62	24	...	1	...	36	2	2	...	...	...	...	48	19	...	...	...	29	28
3	1	...	...	...	2	142	79	...	5	...	63	142	79	...	5	...	63	...	...	...	...	...	...	29
732	161	311	...	...	260	11,204	4,141	209	261	...	6,854	10,801	3,989	197	238	...	6,615	369	140	12	23	...	217	
...	...	...	...	...	...	21	16	1	9	...	4	21	16	1	9	...	4	...	...	...	...	...	...	30
...	...	...	...	...	...	38	14	...	...	...	24	38	14	...	...	...	24	...	...	...	...	...	...	31
...	...	...	...	...	...	27	9	...	...	...	18	27	9	...	...	...	18	...	...	...	...	...	...	32
1	...	1	...	...	...	543	177	...	...	...	366	543	177	...	...	...	366	...	...	...	...	...	...	33
1	...	...	...	...	1	...	...	...	...	...	...	...	...	...	...	...	...	...	...	...	...	...	...	34
8	*3*	*2*	...	...	*3*	*226*	*118*	*10*	*23*	...	*98*	*59*	*25*	...	...	...	*34*	*167*	*93*	*10*	*23*	...	*64*	
...	...	...	...	...	...	3	...	...	...	...	3	3	...	...	...	...	3	...	...	...	...	...	...	35
...	...	...	...	...	...	14	...	...	...	...	14	14	...	...	...	...	14	...	...	...	...	...	...	36
...	...	...	...	...	...	...	...	...	...	...	...	...	...	...	...	...	...	...	...	...	...	...	...	37
...	...	...	...	...	...	...	...	...	...	...	...	...	...	...	...	...	...	...	...	...	...	...	...	38
...	...	...	...	...	...	...	...	...	...	...	...	...	...	...	...	...	...	...	...	...	...	...	...	39
...	...	...	...	...	...	42	25	...	...	...	17	42	25	...	...	...	17	...	...	...	...	...	...	40
6	3	2	...	...	3	167	93	10	23	...	64	...	...	...	...	...	...	167	93	10	23	...	64	41
1	1	...	...	...	...	...	...	...	...	...	...	...	...	...	...	...	...	...	...	...	...	...	...	42
...	...	...	...	...	...	...	...	...	...	...	...	...	...	...	...	...	...	...	...	...	...	...	...	43
124	24	49	...	...	51	5,321	1,612	90	101	...	3,619	5,314	1,608	90	101	...	3,616	...	...	...	...	...	...	44
13	4	...	...	...	9	275	109	11	...	...	155	222	90	11	...	...	121	26	11	...	...	...	15	45
...	...	...	...	...	...	172	65	...	1	...	107	172	65	...	1	...	107	...	...	...	...	...	...	46
1	...	...	...	...	1	2	...	1	...	...	1	...	...	...	...	...	...	2	...	1	...	...	1	47
498	116	232	...	...	150	4,044	1,835	89	116	...	2,120	3,932	1,833	88	116	...	2,011	112	2	1	...	...	109	48
6	...	...	...	...	6	224	62	...	9	...	162	214	55	...	9	...	159	10	7	...	...	...	3	49
79	13	27	...	...	39	240	91	1	2	...	148	220	80	1	2	...	139	20	11	...	...	...	9	50
...	...	...	...	...	...	71	83	6	...	...	32	39	17	6	...	...	16	32	16	...	...	...	16	51
18,382	3,403	1,839	...	...	13,140	2,019	645	30	...	...	1,844	409	24	18	...	...	367	1,584	607	12	...	...	965	52
119	76	4	...	...	39	420	199	...	4	...	221	397	189	...	4	...	208	18	8	...	...	...	10	53
1,395	463	84	...	...	848	738	412	9	...	...	317	712	398	9	...	...	305	22	11	...	...	...	11	54

TABLE XV A.—OCCUPATION OR

DETAILS FOR

Serial No.	CLASS … / SUB-CLASS … / ORDER … / GROUP … / DISTRICT OR STATE.	B.—PREPARATION AND SUPPLY — III.—INDUSTRY — 7.—Hides, skins, and hard materials from the animal kingdom. — 34.—Furriers. Total workers and dependents.	Actual workers. Total. Males.	Actual workers. Total. Females.	Partially agriculturist. Males.	Partially agriculturist. Females.	Dependents.	35.—Bone, ivory, horn, &c., workers. Total workers and dependents.	Actual workers. Total. Males.	Actual workers. Total. Females.	Partially agriculturist. Males.	Partially agriculturist. Females.	Dependents.	Total Order. Total workers and dependents.	Actual workers. Total. Males.	Actual workers. Total. Females.	Partially agriculturist. Males.	Partially agriculturist. Females.	Dependents.
		230	231	232	233	234	235	236	237	238	239	240	241	242	243	244	245	246	247
	PUNJAB …	93	7	1	…	…	85	191	55	4	2	…	132	482,740	168,148	10,227	19,380	703	304,365
	BRITISH TERRITORY	93	7	1	…	…	85	157	43	4	2	…	110	423,692	146,834	9,071	16,879	677	267,787
	DELHI DIVISION …	85	…	1	…	…	84	43	20	4	…	…	19	64,618	24,931	931	2,817	98	38,756
1	Hissar … …	…	…	…	…	…	…	…	…	…	…	…	…	7,266	3,110	74	630	1	4,082
2	Rohtak … …	…	…	…	…	…	…	…	…	…	…	…	…	9,828	3,319	81	712	4	6,478
3	Gurgaon … …	…	…	…	…	…	…	2	1	…	…	…	1	9,046	3,185	85	347	6	5,778
4	Delhi … …	…	…	…	…	…	…	26	14	…	…	…	12	9,187	3,797	238	167	…	5,152
5	Karnal … …	85	…	1	…	…	84	15	5	4	…	…	6	13,945	5,197	292	617	81	8,456
6	Ambala … …	…	…	…	…	…	…	…	…	…	…	…	…	14,469	5,737	186	327	6	8,546
7	Simla … …	…	…	…	…	…	…	…	…	…	…	…	…	875	586	26	17	…	264
	JULLUNDUR DIVISION …	…	…	…	…	…	…	1	1	…	1	…	…	82,746	30,239	3,108	4,041	165	49,399
8	Kangra … …	…	…	…	…	…	…	…	…	…	…	…	…	14,515	5 384	1,871	1,525	140	7,260
9	Hoshiarpur … …	…	…	…	…	…	…	…	…	…	…	…	…	20,665	6,990	734	969	23	12,941
10	Jullundur … …	…	…	…	…	…	…	…	…	…	…	…	…	18,818	6,817	169	479	…	11,832
11	Ludhiana … …	…	…	…	…	…	…	1	1	…	1	…	…	11,945	4,672	160	337	1	7,104
12	Ferozepore … …	…	…	…	…	…	…	…	…	…	…	…	…	16,803	6,376	165	731	1	10,262
	LAHORE DIVISION …	6	6	…	…	…	…	13	8	…	…	…	7	116,083	38,436	912	5,574	23	76,735
13	Lahore … …	…	…	…	…	…	…	5	2	…	…	…	3	24,833	8,983	268	1,557	7	15,582
14	Amritsar … …	…	…	…	…	…	…	4	3	…	…	…	1	22,777	7,740	204	865	1	14,838
15	Gurdaspur … …	6	6	…	…	…	…	…	…	…	…	…	…	17,135	6,073	140	651	4	10,922
16	Sialkot … …	…	…	…	…	…	…	4	1	…	…	…	3	28,654	8,348	145	1,266	5	20,161
17	Gujranwala … …	…	…	…	…	…	…	…	…	…	…	…	…	22,684	7,292	155	1,235	6	15,287
	RAWALPINDI DIVISION …	…	…	…	…	…	…	24	3	…	…	…	21	70,868	24,304	1,202	2,506	4	44,862
18	Gujrat … …	…	…	…	…	…	…	5	1	…	…	…	4	17,395	6,435	98	632	2	10,862
19	Shahpur … …	…	…	…	…	…	…	4	2	…	…	…	2	14,339	4,694	179	692	…	9,466
20	Jhelum … …	…	…	…	…	…	…	1	…	…	…	…	1	13,957	4,515	207	354	…	9,235
21	Rawalpindi … …	…	…	…	…	…	…	14	…	…	…	…	14	8,863	3,485	93	295	…	5,285
22	Attock … …	…	…	…	…	…	…	…	…	…	…	…	…	9,992	3,137	544	258	2	6,311
23	Mianwali … …	…	…	…	…	…	…	…	…	…	…	…	…	5,822	2,038	81	275	…	3,703
	MULTAN DIVISION …	2	1	…	…	…	1	76	13	…	1	…	63	89,877	28,924	2,918	1,941	387	58,035
24	Montgomery … …	…	…	…	…	…	…	28	3	…	…	…	25	14,268	4,730	504	193	326	9,034
25	Lyallpur … …	…	…	…	…	…	…	36	7	…	…	…	29	14,962	5,207	66	446	…	9,689
26	Jhang … …	…	…	…	…	…	…	…	…	…	…	…	…	16,264	5,195	147	299	…	10,922
27	Multan … …	2	1	…	…	…	1	…	…	…	…	…	…	22,665	7,432	620	340	57	14,613
28	Muzaffargarh … …	…	…	…	…	…	…	12	3	…	1	…	9	11,238	3,570	336	386	2	7,332
29	Dera Ghazi Khan …	…	…	…	…	…	…	…	…	…	…	…	…	10,480	2,790	1,245	277	2	6,445
	NATIVE STATES …	…	…	…	…	…	…	34	12	…	…	…	22	59,048	21,314	1,156	2,501	26	36,578
30	Loharu … …	…	…	…	…	…	…	…	…	…	…	…	…	67	26	13	…	2	28
31	Dujana … …	…	…	…	…	…	…	…	…	…	…	…	…	358	156	1	…	…	201
32	Pataudi … …	…	…	…	…	…	…	…	…	…	…	…	…	318	94	2	2	…	222
33	Kalsia … …	…	…	…	…	…	…	…	…	…	…	…	…	801	258	…	30	…	543
34	Nahan … …	…	…	…	…	…	…	…	…	…	…	…	…	1,610	804	52	49	6	754
	SIMLA HILL STATES …	…	…	…	…	…	…	…	…	…	…	…	…	2,574	1,090	123	76	…	1,361
35	*Simla Hill States.* Jubbal …	…	…	…	…	…	…	…	…	…	…	…	…	349	204	8	8	…	187
36	Bashahr …	…	…	…	…	…	…	…	…	…	…	…	…	114	74	…	…	…	40
37	Keonthal …	…	…	…	…	…	…	…	…	…	…	…	…	99	63	9	…	…	27
38	Baghal …	…	…	…	…	…	…	…	…	…	…	…	…	53	7	21	…	…	25
39	Bilaspur …	…	…	…	…	…	…	…	…	…	…	…	…	750	222	49	3	…	479
40	Nalagarh …	…	…	…	…	…	…	…	…	…	…	…	…	777	336	6	48	…	435
41	Minor Hill States …	…	…	…	…	…	…	…	…	…	…	…	…	432	184	30	17	…	218
42	Mandi … …	…	…	…	…	…	…	…	…	…	…	…	…	1,149	483	279	7	1	407
43	Suket … …	…	…	…	…	…	…	…	…	…	…	…	…	121	50	8	4	…	63
44	Kapurthala … …	…	…	…	…	…	…	7	4	…	…	…	3	6,134	1,946	55	204	…	4,133
45	Malerkotla … …	…	…	…	…	…	…	27	8	…	…	…	19	1,243	404	3	14	…	836
46	Faridkot … …	…	…	…	…	…	…	…	…	…	…	…	…	1,331	470	20	81	…	841
47	Chamba … …	…	…	…	…	…	…	…	…	…	…	…	…	502	209	66	26	3	227
48	*Phulkian States* Patiala …	…	…	…	…	…	…	…	…	…	…	…	…	21,515	8,237	802	1,176	7	12,976
49	Jind …	…	…	…	…	…	…	…	…	…	…	…	…	3,617	1,244	14	248	…	2,359
50	Nabha …	…	…	…	…	…	…	…	…	…	…	…	…	5,889	1,668	16	150	…	3,705
51	Bahawalpur … …	…	…	…	…	…	…	…	…	…	…	…	…	12,319	4,195	202	334	7	7,922
52	*Cities* Delhi … …	…	…	…	…	…	…	26	14	…	…	…	12	3,782	1.994	178	…	…	1,615
53	Lahore… …	…	…	…	…	…	…	5	2	…	…	…	3	5,679	2,442	28	109	…	3,209
54	Amritsar …	…	…	…	…	…	…	4	3	…	…	…	1	4.336	1,925	12	8	…	2,899

MEANS OF LIVELIHOOD.

DISTRICTS AND STATES—*continued.*

OF MATERIAL SUBSTANCES—*continued.*

—*continued.*

8.—Wood.												9.—Metals.						
36.—Sawyers, carpenters, turners, &c.						37.—Basket makers and other industries of woody materials.						Total Order.						
Total workers and dependents.	Actual workers.				Dependents.	Total workers and dependents.	Actual workers.				Dependents.	Total workers and dependents.	Actual workers.				Dependents.	Serial No.
	Total.		Partially agriculturist.				Total.		Partially agriculturist.				Total.		Partially agriculturist.			
	Males.	Females.	Males.	Females.			Males.	Females.	Males.	Females.			Males.	Females.	Males.	Females.		
248	249	250	251	252	253	254	255	256	257	258	259	260	261	262	263	264	265	
380,629	134,873	1,494	17,225	292	244,262	102,111	33,275	8,733	2,155	411	60,103	241,331	80,979	1,748	10,225	48	158,604	
332,258	117,317	1,310	14,902	289	213,631	91,434	28,517	7,761	1,977	385	54,156	210,183	69,917	1,007	8,814	24	139,259	
53,611	20,440	137	2,429	85	33,084	11,007	4,491	794	388	13	5,722	51,245	18,577	253	1,783	4	32,415	
5,927	2,564	8	570	1	3,355	1,339	546	66	60	...	727	5,932	2,779	27	246	1	3,126	1
8,272	2,678	23	625	3	5,571	1,556	641	8	87	1	907	6,545	2,221	26	399	2	4,298	2
8,291	2,874	7	323	6	5,410	757	311	78	24	...	368	5,460	1,998	50	248	1	3,412	3
6,350	2,733	6	142	...	3,611	2,837	1,064	232	25	...	1,541	13,579	4,076	30	294	...	9,473	4
11,406	4,156	89	426	75	7,161	2,539	1,041	203	191	6	1,295	9,252	3,164	86	413	...	6,002	5
12,553	4,874	3	328	...	7,676	1,916	863	183	1	6	870	10,074	4,103	22	183	...	5,949	6
812	561	1	17	...	250	63	25	24	...	...	14	403	236	12	...	...	155	7
64,976	24,110	400	3,334	31	40,466	17,770	6,129	2,708	707	134	8,933	33,006	10,920	260	1,832	8	21,826	
6,253	2,522	129	1,011	18	3,602	8,262	2,862	1,742	514	122	3,658	6,493	2,201	30	933	5	4,262	8
17,211	5,862	103	858	11	11,246	3,454	1,128	631	111	12	1,695	6,787	2,520	62	391	2	4,205	9
16,934	6,171	51	473	..	10,712	1,884	646	118	6	...	1,120	8,259	3,009	19	202	...	5,231	10
11,008	4,273	104	330	1	6,631	937	399	65	7	...	473	5,696	1,437	116	98	1	4,143	11
13,570	5,282	13	662	1	8,275	3,233	1,094	152	69	...	1,987	5,771	1,753	33	208	...	3,985	12
105,435	35,518	382	5,324	18	69,535	10,648	2,918	530	250	5	7,200	63,640	20,460	324	3,029	7	42,856	
22,620	8,295	63	1,438	5	14,262	2,213	688	205	119	2	1,320	12,215	3,932	31	581	2	8,252	13
21,454	7,243	102	859	...	14,109	1,323	497	102	6	1	724	14,831	5,161	66	472	1	9,604	14
13,163	5,304	73	611	4	7,786	3,972	769	67	40	...	2,136	11,038	3,403	97	351	4	7,538	15
26,973	7,742	46	1,214	3	19,183	1,681	606	97	52	2	978	12,831	3,997	13	743	..	8,821	16
21,225	6,934	96	1,202	6	14,195	1,459	358	59	33	...	1,042	12,725	3,967	117	682	...	8,641	17
46,665	16,916	128	2,334	4	29,621	23,703	7,388	1,074	172	...	15,241	33,632	10,503	109	1,674	2	23,020	
13,984	5,174	58	605	2	8,752	3,411	1,261	40	27	...	2,110	8,202	2,372	25	373	2	5,805	18
11,695	3,938	21	662	...	7,736	2,644	756	158	80	...	1,730	6,664	2,146	18	325	...	4,500	19
6,478	2,245	13	303	...	4,220	7,479	2,270	194	51	...	5,015	4,551	1,459	25	292	...	3,067	20
5,241	2,402	11	261	...	2,828	3,622	1,083	82	34	...	2,457	3,899	1,392	2	141	...	2,505	21
5,058	1,669	18	241	2	3,371	4,934	1,468	526	17	...	2,940	7,303	2,264	34	390	...	5,005	22
4,209	1,488	7	262	...	2,714	1,613	550	74	13	...	989	3,013	870	5	153	...	2,138	23
61,571	20,333	263	1,481	151	40,975	28,306	8,591	2,655	460	236	17,060	28,660	9,457	61	496	3	19,142	
9,782	3,345	154	145	151	6,283	4,486	1,385	350	48	175	2,751	3,958	1,310	6	41	2	2,642	24
12,578	4,473	25	300	...	8,080	2,384	734	41	146	...	1,609	8,520	2,798	14	198	1	5,708	25
11,312	3,461	45	151	...	7,806	4,952	1,734	102	148	...	3,116	4,619	1,429	13	51	...	3,177	26
13,100	4,367	19	234	...	8,714	9,565	3,065	601	106	57	5,899	6,936	2,314	17	81	...	4,605	27
8,010	2,596	11	383	...	5,403	3,228	974	325	3	2	1,929	2,325	775	6	69	...	1,544	28
6,789	2,091	9	268	...	4,689	3,691	699	1,236	9	2	1,756	2,302	831	5	56	...	1,466	29
48,871	17,556	184	2,323	3	30,631	10,677	3,758	972	178	23	5,947	31,148	11,062	741	1,411	19	19,345	
36	17	1	...	...	18	31	9	12	...	2	10	23	14	...	3	...	9	30
347	156	...	...	...	191	11	...	1	...	...	10	352	26	...	...	...	326	31
307	90	...	2	...	217	11	4	2	...	...	5	54	15	...	...	...	39	32
758	235	...	29	...	523	43	23	...	1	...	20	636	213	...	1	...	423	33
1,035	573	...	34	...	462	575	231	52	15	6	282	1,478	580	...	118	...	898	34
1,321	652	34	56	...	635	1,253	438	89	20	...	726	3,073	1,194	125	188	1	1,754	
322	201	8	8	...	113	27	3	...	...	...	24	68	24	...	...	...	44	35
87	54	...	...	...	38	27	20	...	...	...	7	45	9	...	...	...	38	36
33	...	9	...	...	24	66	63	...	...	...	3	218	105	28	1	...	85	37
...	...	...	...	...	...	53	7	21	...	...	25	277	128	...	39	...	149	38
207	67	17	...	...	123	543	155	32	3	...	356	1,248	462	91	62	...	695	39
398	207	...	38	...	191	379	129	6	10	...	244	659	246	3	53	1	410	40
274	123	...	10	...	151	158	61	30	7	...	67	558	220	3	33	...	335	41
291	149	39	3	...	108	858	314	240	4	1	304	1,722	645	407	21	3	670	42
39	13	...	...	...	26	82	37	8	4	...	37	375	132	8	9	...	235	43
5,402	1,874	11	201	...	3,717	732	272	44	3	...	416	2,879	940	11	131	...	1,928	44
1,194	380	3	14	...	811	49	24	...	...	...	25	1,125	413	1	14	...	711	45
1,080	408	1	77	...	671	251	62	19	4	...	170	816	269	1	3	...	546	46
237	113	11	12	...	113	265	96	55	14	3	114	249	106	6	29	...	137	47
19,141	7,319	68	1,122	3	11,754	2,374	918	234	54	4	1,222	10,067	3,656	129	630	18	6,282	48
3,034	1,044	1	299	...	1,989	583	200	13	49	...	370	2,623	863	1	188	1	1,759	49
5,125	1,571	13	150	...	3,541	264	97	3	...	...	164	1,926	740	42	22	1	1,144	50
9,024	3,162	2	324	...	5,860	3,295	1,033	200	10	7	2,062	3,750	1,256	10	54	...	2,484	51
2,549	1,507	2	...	...	1,040	1,233	487	171	...	...	575	7,680	2,335	...	...	...	5,345	52
5.378	2,375	23	109	...	2,980	301	67	5	...	...	229	4,532	1,533	22	30	1	2,977	53
4,040	1,803	5	3	...	2,282	296	122	7	...	...	167	3,608	1,531	8	3	...	2,069	54

TABLE XV A.—OCCUPATION OR

DETAILS FOR DISTRICTS,

Serial No.	CLASS ... / SUB-CLASS ... / ORDER ... / GROUP ...	B.—PREPARATION AND SUPPLY / III.—INDUSTRY / 9.—METALS: 38.—Forging and rolling of iron and other metals.						39.—Plough and agricultural implement makers.						40.—Makers of arms, guns, etc.					
	District or States.	Total workers and dependents.	Actual workers. Total. Males.	Actual workers. Total. Females.	Actual workers. Partially agriculturist. Males.	Actual workers. Partially agriculturist. Females.	Dependents.	Total workers and dependents.	Actual workers. Total. Males.	Actual workers. Total. Females.	Actual workers. Partially agriculturist. Males.	Actual workers. Partially agriculturist. Females.	Dependents.	Total workers and dependents.	Actual workers. Total. Males.	Actual workers. Total. Females.	Actual workers. Partially agriculturist. Males.	Actual workers. Partially agriculturist. Females.	Dependents.
		266	267	268	269	270	271	272	273	274	275	276	277	278	279	280	281	282	283
	PUNJAB ...	1,560	243	55	36	...	1,282	22,187	7,548	146	1,082	13	14,493	115	44	...	10	...	71
	BRITISH TERRITORY	1,302	137	55	34	...	1,110	12,493	4,139	25	503	...	8,329	72	25	...	...	...	47
	DELHI DIVISION ...	486	110	5	29	...	371	4,434	1,802	4	276	...	2,628	...	...	...	...	...	...
1	Hissar	...	...	...	...	...	...	10,77	627	4	52	...	446	...	...	...	...	...	...
2	Rohtak	220	37	4	29	...	179	71	54	...	2	...	17	...	...	...	...	...	...
3	Gurgaon	223	52	1	...	...	170	32	10	...	2	...	22	...	...	...	...	...	...
4	Delhi	29	10	...	...	...	19	3,047	986	...	205	...	2,061	...	...	...	...	...	...
5	Karnal	10	7	...	...	...	3	178	125	...	15	...	53	...	...	...	...	...	...
6	Ambala	4	4	...	...	...	...	29	...	...	...	...	29	...	...	...	...	...	...
7	Simla	...	...	...	...	...	...	...	...	...	...	...	...	...	...	...	...	...	...
	JULLUNDUR DIVISION ...	...	...	...	...	...	...	3,312	758	7	88	...	2,547	18	6	...	...	...	12
8	Kangra	...	...	...	...	...	...	489	121	...	19	...	368	4	2	...	...	...	2
9	Hoshiarpur	...	...	...	...	...	...	...	...	...	...	...	...	...	...	...	...	...	...
10	Jullundur	...	...	...	...	...	...	1,697	623	3	69	...	1,071	...	...	...	...	...	...
11	Ludhiana	...	...	...	...	...	...	1,120	14	4	...	...	1,102	1	...	...	...	...	1
12	Ferozepore	...	...	...	...	...	...	6	...	...	...	...	6	13	4	...	...	...	9
	LAHORE DIVISION ...	781	4	50	...	...	727	1,401	573	...	56	...	828	20	8	...	...	...	12
13	Lahore	8	4	...	...	...	4	1	1	...	...	...	...	1	1	...	...	...	...
14	Amritsar	...	...	...	...	...	...	...	...	...	...	...	...	6	3	...	...	...	3
15	Gurdaspur	771	...	50	...	...	721	1,114	563	...	56	...	551	...	...	...	...	...	...
16	Sialkot	2	...	...	...	...	2	286	9	...	...	...	277	2	1	...	...	...	1
17	Gujranwala	...	...	...	...	...	...	...	...	...	...	...	...	11	3	...	...	...	8
	RAWALPINDI DIVISION ...	4	1	...	...	...	3	890	281	9	26	...	600	16	8	...	...	...	13
18	Gujrat	...	...	...	...	...	...	8	...	...	...	...	8	3	...	...	...	...	8
19	Shahpur	...	...	...	...	...	...	13	...	...	...	...	13	...	...	...	...	...	...
20	Jhelum	1	1	...	...	...	...	...	...	...	...	...	...	...	...	...	...	...	...
21	Rawalpindi	3	...	...	...	...	3	90	33	...	8	...	57	13	8	...	...	...	10
22	Attock	...	...	...	...	...	...	702	233	9	14	...	460	...	...	...	...	...	...
23	Mianwali	...	...	...	...	...	...	77	15	...	4	...	62	...	...	...	...	...	...
	MULTAN DIVISION ...	31	22	...	5	...	9	2,456	725	5	57	...	1,726	18	8	...	...	...	10
24	Montgomery	...	...	...	...	...	...	140	3	1	...	...	136	...	...	...	...	...	...
25	Lyallpur	31	22	...	5	...	9	443	161	...	23	...	282	...	...	...	...	...	...
26	Jhang	...	...	...	...	...	...	54	...	...	...	...	54	5	4	...	...	...	1
27	Multan	...	...	...	...	...	...	1,784	546	4	34	...	1,234	...	...	...	...	...	...
28	Muzaffargarh	...	...	...	...	...	...	21	8	...	...	...	13	...	...	...	...	...	...
29	Dera Ghazi Khan ...	...	...	...	...	...	...	14	7	...	...	...	7	13	4	...	...	...	9
	NATIVE STATES ...	278	106	...	2	...	172	9,694	3,409	121	579	13	6,164	43	19	...	10	...	24
30	Loharu	...	...	...	...	...	...	...	...	...	...	...	...	...	...	...	...	...	...
31	Dujana	...	...	...	...	...	...	242	...	...	...	...	242	...	...	...	...	...	...
32	Pataudi	...	...	...	...	...	...	...	...	...	...	...	...	...	...	...	...	...	...
33	Kalsia	...	...	...	...	...	...	...	...	...	...	...	...	...	...	...	...	...	...
34	Nahan	61	60	...	2	...	1	...	...	...	...	...	...	7	1	...	...	...	6
	SIMLA HILL STATES ...	184	22	...	...	...	162	...	...	...	...	...	...	10	5	...	...	...	5
35	*Simla Hill States.* Jubbal ...	59	22	...	...	...	37	...	...	...	...	...	...	...	...	...	...	...	...
36	Bashahr ...	...	...	...	...	...	...	...	...	...	...	...	...	...	...	...	...	...	...
37	Keonthal ...	...	...	...	...	...	...	...	...	...	...	...	...	...	...	...	...	...	...
38	Baghal ...	...	...	...	...	...	...	...	...	...	...	...	...	4	...	...	...	...	4
39	Bilaspur ...	125	...	...	...	...	125	...	...	...	...	...	...	4	4	...	...	...	...
40	Nalagarh ...	...	...	...	...	...	...	...	...	...	...	...	...	2	1	...	...	...	1
41	Minor Hill States	...	...	...	...	...	...	...	...	...	...	...	...	...	...	...	...	...	...
42	Mandi	31	23	...	...	...	8	...	...	...	...	...	...	...	...	...	...	...	...
43	Suket	2	1	...	...	...	1	...	...	...	...	...	...	...	...	...	...	...	...
44	Kapurthala	...	...	...	...	...	...	...	...	...	...	...	...	...	...	...	...	...	...
45	Malerkotla	...	...	...	...	...	...	65	31	...	...	...	34	...	...	...	...	...	...
46	Faridkot	...	...	...	...	...	...	...	...	...	...	...	...	...	...	...	...	...	...
47	Chamba	...	...	...	...	...	...	...	...	...	...	...	...	...	...	...	...	...	...
48	*Phulkian States.* Patiala ...	...	...	...	...	...	...	9,385	3,278	121	579	13	5,886	...	...	...	...	...	...
49	Jind ...	...	...	...	...	...	...	2	...	...	...	...	2	...	...	...	...	...	...
50	Nabha ...	...	...	...	...	...	...	...	...	...	...	...	...	...	...	...	...	...	...
51	Bahawalpur	...	...	...	...	...	...	...	...	...	...	...	...	26	13	...	10	...	13
52	*Cities* Delhi ...	8	...	...	...	...	6	...	...	...	...	...	...	...	...	...	...	...	...
53	Lahore ...	...	...	...	...	...	...	1	1	...	...	...	...	1	1	...	...	...	...
54	Amritsar ...	...	...	...	...	...	...	...	...	...	...	...	...	4	1	...	...	...	3

EDUCATION (BY RELIGION AND AGE).
DISTRICTS AND STATES—*continued.*

LITERATE IN VERNACULAR.																				
HINDI.				PUNJABI.													OTHERS.			
Lande or Mahajani.		*Others.*		*Total.*			*Gurmukhi.*		*Lande or Mahajani.*		*Nagri.*		*Tankri.*		*Persian.*					
Males.	Females.	Males.	Females.	Persons.	Males.	Females.	Males.	Females.	Males.	Females.	Males.	Females.	Males.	Females.	Males.	Females.	Persons.	Males.	Females.	Serial No.
18	19	20	21	22	23	24	25	26	27	28	29	30	31	32	33	34	35	36	37	
...	...	...	...	19	16	3	15	3	...	...	1	...	...	...	...	...	1	1	...	1
...	...	...	...	...	...	...	...	...	...	...	...	...	...	...	...	...	...	...	...	2
...	...	...	...	...	...	...	...	...	...	...	...	...	...	...	...	...	...	...	...	3
...	...	...	...	1	...	1	...	1	...	...	...	...	...	...	...	...	...	...	..	4
...	...	...	...	18	16	2	15	2	...	...	1	...	...	...	...	...	1	1	...	5
856	12	31	4	12,744	11,776	968	8,532	827	2,266	51	786	88	2	..	190	2	33	9	24	6
9	...	...	...	186	128	58	109	48	13	5	5	4	...	...	1	1	2	...	2	7
55	1	1	...	795	641	154	479	132	106	1	26	21	...	...	30	...	4	1	3	8
91	2	1	1	1,340	1,196	144	863	126	214	2	75	16	2	...	42	...	9	2	7	9
701	9	29	3	10,423	9,811	612	7,081	521	1,933	43	680	47	...	...	117	1	18	6	12	10
762	10	27	4	4,669	4,382	287	1,603	166	1,915	42	715	78	2	...	147	1	...	...	...	11
9	...	...	...	51	35	16	18	8	11	5	5	2	...	...	1	1	...	...	...	12
50	1	1	...	259	216	43	72	23	95	1	22	19	...	...	27	...	...	...	...	13
82	2	1	1	525	487	38	194	22	192	2	62	14	2	...	37	...	...	...	...	14
621	7	25	3	3,834	3,644	190	1,319	113	1,617	34	626	48	...	...	82	...	...	...	...	15
26	1	4	...	7,587	6,947	640	6,742	631	156	1	44	8	...	...	5	...	...	...	...	16
...	...	...	...	129	88	41	86	40	2	...	...	1	...	...	...	...	...	...	...	17
1	..	...	...	506	396	110	389	109	3	...	4	1	...	...	...	...	...	...	...	18
...	...	...	...	767	669	98	652	96	9	...	8	2	...	...	...	...	...	...	...	19
25	1	4	...	6,185	5,794	391	5,615	386	142	1	32	4	...	...	5	...	...	...	...	20
62	...	...	...	180	173	7	12	...	149	5	12	2	...	...	...	...	...	...	..	21
4	...	...	...	1	...	1	...	...	...	...	...	1	...	...	...	...	...	...	...	22
	...	...	...	9	8	1	...	...	8	...	...	1	...	...	...	...	...	...	...	23
9	...	...	...	16	16	...	2	...	13	...	1	...	...	...	...	...	...	...	...	24
49	...	...	...	154	149	5	10	...	128	5	11	...	...	...	...	...	...	...	...	25
6	1	...	...	266	243	23	144	19	46	3	15	...	...	...	38	1	33	9	24	26
...	...	...	...	...	...	...	...	...	...	...	...	...	...	...	...	...	2	...	2	27
...	...	...	...	8	8	...	5	...	...	...	...	...	...	...	3	...	4	1	3	28
...	...	...	...	20	19	1	10	1	...	...	4	...	...	...	5	...	9	2	7	29
6	1	...	...	238	216	22	129	18	46	3	11	...	...	...	30	1	18	6	12	30
...	...	...	...	42	31	11	31	11	...	...	...	...	...	...	...	...	..	...	...	31
...	...	...	...	5	5	...	5	...	...	...	...	...	...	...	...	...	...	...	...	32
...	...	...	...	13	13	...	13	...	...	...	...	...	...	...	...	...	...	...	...	33
...	...	...	...	12	5	7	5	7	...	...	...	...	...	...	...	...	...	...	...	34
...	...	...	...	12	8	4	8	4	...	...	...	...	..	...	...	...	...	...	...	35
3,257	48	2	...	15,007	14,076	931	8,310	816	4,603	54	683	54	8	1	472	6	21	17	4	36
48	6	...	...	194	81	113	61	105	17	6	2	2	...	...	1	...	...	...	...	37
227	4	...	...	854	681	173	367	165	199	4	47	3	...	1	68	...	...	...	...	38
364	5	...	...	1,551	1,406	145	658	124	587	12	80	8	2	...	79	1	3	...	3	39
2,618	33	2	...	12,408	11,908	500	7,224	422	3,800	32	554	41	6	...	324	5	18	17	1	40
2,930	38	...	...	6,727	6,469	258	1,699	174	3,974	35	632	47	7	1	157	1	6	4	2	41
45	5	...	...	47	34	18	18	10	14	2	2	1	...	...	...	...	...	...	...	42
205	4	...	...	361	341	20	108	14	170	2	42	3	...	1	26	...	...	...	...	43
324	4	...	...	811	770	41	148	24	518	10	78	6	1	...	27	1	2	...	2	44
2,356	25	...	...	5,508	5,324	184	1,430	126	3,274	21	510	37	6	...	104	...	4	4	...	45
181	4	...	..	7,787	7,131	656	6,463	629	486	18	33	5	...	.	149	4	...	...	...	46
2	...	...	...	144	45	99	41	95	3	4	...	...	...	...	1	...	...	...	...	47
16	...	...	...	466	313	153	258	151	20	2	3	...	...	...	32	...	...	...	...	48
25	...	...	...	698	598	100	507	97	63	1	...	2	...	...	28	...	...	...	...	49
138	4	...	...	6,479	6,175	304	5,657	286	400	11	30	3	...	...	88	4	...	...	...	50
100	5	...	...	122	120	2	1	...	108	1	9	1	...	...	2	...	...	...	...	51
1	1	...	...	1	...	1	...	...	...	...	...	1	...	...	...	...	...	...	...	52
5	...	...	...	13	13	...	...	...	9	...	2	...	...	...	2	...	...	...	...	53
13	1	...	...	7	6	1	...	...	4	1	2	...	...	...	...	...	...	...	...	54
81	3	...	...	101	101	...	1	...	95	...	5	...	...	...	...	...	...	...	...	55
45	1	...	...	318	316	2	108	1	35	...	8	...	1	...	164	1	2	2	...	56
...	...	...	...	1	1	...	1	...	...	...	...	...	...	...	...	...	...	...	...	57
1	...	...	...	12	12	...	4	...	...	...	...	...	...	...	8	...	...	...	...	58
2	...	...	...	31	31	...	2	...	4	...	...	...	1	...	24	...	...	...	...	59
42	1	...	...	274	272	2	101	1	31	...	8	...	...	...	132	1	2	2	...	60
...	...	...	...	58	40	13	39	12	...	...	1	1	...	...	...	...	...	...		61
...	...	...	...	1	1	...	1	...	...	...	...	...	...	...	...	...	...	...	...	62
...	...	...	...	2	2	...	2	...	...	...	...	...	...	...	...	...	...	...	...	63
...	...	...	...	4	1	3	1	3	...	...	...	...	...	...	...	...	...	...	...	64
...	...	...	...	46	36	10	35	9	...	...	1	1	...	...	...	...	...	...	...	65

APPENDIX TO IMPERIAL TABLE VIII.—
PART B.—DETAILS FOR

Serial No.	District or State.	Religion and Age.	Literate in Vernacular. Total. Persons.	Total. Males.	Total. Females.	Urdu. Total. Persons.	Urdu. Total. Males.	Urdu. Total. Females.	Urdu. Persian. Males.	Urdu. Persian. Females.	Urdu. Others. Males.	Urdu. Others. Females.	Hindi. Total. Persons.	Hindi. Total. Males.	Hindi. Total. Females.	Hindi. Nagri. Males.	Hindi. Nagri. Females.
	1	2	3	4	5	6	7	8	9	10	11	12	13	14	15	16	17
1	LAHORE.	ALL RELIGIONS ...	61,908	52,885	9,023	40,192	35,262	4,930	35,105	4,907	157	23	8,365	5,689	2,676	3,973	2,313
2		0—10 ...	1,597	983	614	1,053	712	341	710	341	2	...	421	197	224	145	170
3		10—15 ...	6,423	4,487	1,936	4,437	3,253	1,184	3,250	1,179	3	5	1,202	637	565	496	495
4		15—20 ...	9,983	7,415	2,568	6,691	5,271	1,420	5,232	1,416	39	4	1,663	868	795	742	689
5		20 and over ...	43,905	40,000	3,905	28,011	26,026	1,985	25,913	1,971	113	14	5,079	3,987	1,092	2,590	959
6		HINDU ...	30,815	24,992	5,823	16,237	14,138	2,099	14,004	2,093	134	6	8,128	5,474	2,654	3,829	2,291
7		0—10 ...	856	448	408	352	205	147	205	147	...	...	418	196	222	144	168
8		10—15 ...	3,678	2,215	1,463	2,129	1,380	749	1,379	746	1	3	1,154	591	563	493	493
9		15—20 ...	6,024	3,973	2,051	3,451	2,479	972	2,446	969	33	3	1,641	850	791	727	685
10		20 and over ...	20,257	18,356	1,901	10,305	10,074	231	9,974	231	100	...	4,915	3,837	1,078	2,465	945
11		SIKH ...	9,147	8,752	395	3,107	2,973	134	2,971	129	2	5	64	63	1	20	1
12		0—10 ...	50	27	23	29	14	15	14	15	...	...	...	...	...	...	...
13		10—15 ...	700	667	33	306	297	9	297	9	...	...	40	40	...	...	...
14		15—20 ...	956	874	82	350	316	34	316	34	...	...	2	2	...	2	...
15		20 and over ...	7,441	7,184	257	2,422	2,346	76	2,344	71	2	5	22	21	1	18	1
16		JAIN ...	352	334	18	148	143	5	143	5	...	...	74	61	13	48	13
17		0—10 ...	10	7	3	8	7	1	7	1	...	...	2	...	2	...	2
18		10—15 ...	26	23	3	18	16	2	16	2	...	...	2	1	1	1	1
19		15—20 ...	62	57	5	31	30	1	30	1	...	...	16	12	4	11	4
20		20 and over ...	254	247	7	91	90	1	90	1	...	...	54	48	6	36	6
21		MUHAMMADAN ...	20,637	18,249	2,388	19,924	17,563	2,361	17,544	2,354	19	7	64	63	1	50	1
22		0—10 ...	626	462	164	622	458	164	456	164	2	...	1	1	...	1	...
23		10—15 ...	1,863	1,506	357	1,843	1,492	351	1,490	349	2	2	2	2	...	1	...
24		15—20 ...	2,714	2,395	319	2,658	2,342	316	2,336	316	6	...	3	3	...	1	...
25		20 and over ...	15,434	13,886	1,548	14,801	13,271	1,530	13,262	1,525	9	5	58	57	1	47	1
26		CHRISTIAN ...	830	477	353	758	430	328	428	323	2	5	27	20	7	20	7
27		0—10 ...	42	28	14	42	28	14	28	14	...	...	...	...	...	...	...
28		10—15 ...	141	68	73	138	68	70	68	70	...	...	1	...	1	...	1
29		15—20 ...	209	106	103	201	104	97	104	96	...	1	1	1	...	1	...
30		20 and over ...	438	275	163	377	230	147	228	143	2	4	25	19	6	19	6
31	AMRITSAR.	ALL RELIGIONS ...	38,548	35,584	2,964	18,776	17,894	882	17,888	867	6	15	4,623	4,269	354	4,105	354
32		0—10 ...	758	590	168	389	367	22	367	22	...	...	78	49	29	47	29
33		10—15 ...	3,694	3,253	441	2,341	2,191	150	2,191	145	...	5	288	227	61	215	61
34		15—20 ...	4,781	4,353	428	2,750	2,583	167	2,581	165	2	2	417	357	60	344	60
35		20 and over ...	29,315	27,388	1,927	13,296	12,753	543	12,749	535	4	8	3,840	3,636	204	3,499	204
36		HINDU ...	15,858	14,929	929	6,522	6,390	132	6,390	132	...	...	3,981	3,650	331	3,570	331
37		0—10 ..	293	244	49	159	154	5	154	5	...	...	71	45	26	44	26
38		10—15 ...	1,278	1,147	131	762	746	16	746	16	...	...	250	193	57	190	57
39		15—20 ..	1,975	1,834	141	1,029	1,010	19	1,010	19	...	...	350	295	55	287	55
40		20 and over ...	12,312	11,704	608	4,572	4,480	92	4,480	92	...	...	3,310	3,117	193	3,049	193
41		SIKH ...	12,983	11,708	1,275	3,432	3,393	39	3,393	39	...	...	565	548	17	481	17
42		0—10 ...	316	216	100	87	86	1	86	1	...	...	7	4	3	3	3
43		10—15 ...	1,342	1,169	173	545	542	3	542	3	...	...	34	30	4	22	4
44		15—20 ...	1,587	1,448	139	565	554	11	554	11	...	...	62	60	2	56	2
45		20 and over ...	9,738	8,875	863	2,235	2,211	24	2,211	24	...	...	462	454	8	400	8
46		JAIN ...	364	343	21	103	100	3	100	3	...	...	33	30	3	29	3
47		0—10 ...	5	3	2	2	2	...	2	...	...	...	...	...	...	...	...
48		10—15 ...	37	34	3	20	20	...	20	...	...	...	2	2	...	1	...
49		15—20 ...	40	34	6	18	17	1	17	1	...	...	2	1	1	1	1
50		20 and over ...	282	272	10	63	61	2	61	2	...	...	29	27	2	27	2
51		MUHAMMADAN ...	8,928	8,414	514	8,365	7,859	506	7,856	506	3	...	38	38	...	22	...
52		0—10 ...	128	122	6	127	121	6	121	6	...	...	...	...	...	...	...
53		10—15 ...	973	889	84	953	869	84	869	84	...	...	2	2	...	2	...
54		15—20 ...	1,117	1,023	94	1,079	988	91	987	91	1	...	1	1	...	...	...
55		20 and over ...	6,710	6,380	330	6,206	5,881	325	5,879	325	2	...	35	35	...	20	...
56		CHRISTIAN ...	388	172	216	351	150	201	147	186	3	15	6	3	3	3	3
57		0—10 ...	14	4	10	14	4	10	4	10	...	...	...	...	...	...	...
58		10—15 ...	62	14	48	61	14	47	14	42	...	5	...	...	...	...	...
59		15—20 ...	62	14	48	59	14	45	13	43	1	2	2	...	2	...	2
60		20 and over ...	250	140	110	217	118	99	118	91	2	8	4	3	1	3	1
61	GURDASPUR.	ALL RELIGIONS ..	24,722	23,365	1,357	14,442	13,913	529	13,913	529	...	...	1,588	1,425	163	1,085	141
62		0—10 ...	414	[illegible]	50	308	285	23	285	23	...	...	20	12	8	9	8
63		10—15 ...	2,883	2,[illegible]45	233	2,106	2,021	85	2,021	85	...	...	99	58	41	51	38
64		15—20 ...	2,901	2,677	224	1,959	1,870	89	1,870	89	...	...	125	104	21	87	21
65		20 and over ...	18,724	17,874	850	10,069	9,737	332	9,737	332	...	...	1,344	1,251	93	938	74

EDUCATION (BY RELIGION AND AGE).

DISTRICTS AND STATES—*continued.*

LITERATE IN VERNACULAR.																				
HINDI.				PUNJABI.													OTHERS.			
Lande or Mahajani.		*Others.*		*Total.*			*Gurmukhi.*		*Lande or Mahajani.*		*Nagri.*		*Tankri.*		*Persian.*					
Males.	Females.	Males.	Females.	Persons.	Males.	Females.	Males.	Females.	Males.	Females.	Males.	Females.	Males.	Females.	Males.	Females.	Persons.	Males.	Females.	Serial No.
18	19	20	21	22	23	24	25	26	27	28	29	30	31	32	33	34	35	36	37	
1,714	363	2	...	13,246	11,872	1,374	6,493	927	4,859	155	430	264	3	8	77	26	105	62	43	1
52	54	...	...	110	63	47	21	25	39	1	3	21	...	...	...	...	13	11	2	2
139	70	2	...	775	592	183	880	94	167	33	45	56	...	...	...	...	9	5	4	3
126	106	...	...	1,611	1,266	345	710	232	502	37	52	48	1	8	1	20	18	10	8	4
1,397	133	...	...	10,750	9,951	799	5,382	576	4,161	84	330	139	2	....	76	...	65	36	29	5
1,645	363	...	...	6,450	5,380	1,070	1,263	641	3,650	137	405	264	3	8	59	20	...	...	...	6
52	54	...	..	86	47	39	9	17	35	1	3	21	...	...	...	...	...	...	...	7
98	70	...	...	395	244	151	71	67	129	28	44	56	...	...	...	...	...	...	...	8
123	106	...	...	932	644	288	192	177	399	35	52	48	1	8	...	20	...	...	...	9
1,372	133	...	...	5,037	4,445	592	991	380	3,087	73	306	139	2	...	59	...	...	...	...	10
43	...	...	...	5,976	5,716	260	5,099	256	604	4	13	...	...	...	...	...	...	...	...	11
...	...	...	...	21	13	8	12	8	1	...	...	...	...	...	...	...	...	...	...	12
40	...	...	...	354	330	24	307	24	23	...	...	...	...	...	...	...	...	...	...	13
...	...	...	...	604	556	48	511	48	45	...	...	...	...	...	...	...	...	...	...	14
3	...	...	...	4,997	4,817	180	4,269	176	535	4	13	...	...	...	...	...	...	...	...	15
13	...	...	...	123	123	...	7	...	116	...	...	...	...	...	...	...	7	7	...	16
...	...	...	...	...	...	...	...	...	...	...	...	...	...	...	...	...	...	...	...	17
...	...	...	...	6	6	...	2	...	4	...	...	...	...	...	...	...	...	...	...	18
1	..	...	...	15	15	...	...	...	15	...	...	...	...	...	...	...	...	...	...	19
12	...	...	...	102	102	...	5	...	97	...	...	...	...	...	...	...	7	7	...	20
13	...	...	...	649	623	26	94	15	499	11	12	...	...	...	18	...	...	...	...	21
...	...	...	...	3	3	...	...	...	3	...	...	...	...	...	...	...	...	...	...	22
1	...	...	...	18	12	6	...	1	11	5	1	...	...	...	...	...	...	...	...	23
2	...	...	...	53	50	3	6	1	43	2	...	...	...	...	1	...	...	...	..	24
10	...	...	...	575	558	17	88	13	442	4	11	...	...	...	17	...	...	...	...	25
...	...	...	...	44	26	18	26	15	...	3	...	...	...	...	...	...	1	1	...	26
...	...	...	...	...	...	...	...	...	...	...	...	...	...	...	...	...	...	...	...	27
...	...	...	...	2	...	2	...	2	...	...	...	...	...	...	...	...	...	...	...	28
...	...	...	...	7	1	6	1	6	...	...	...	...	...	...	...	...	...	...	...	29
...	...	...	...	85	25	10	25	7	...	3	...	...	...	...	...	...	1	1	...	30
161	...	3	...	15,119	13,401	1,718	9,358	1,588	3,549	86	426	38	1	...	67	6	30	20	10	31
2	...	...	...	289	173	116	128	111	42	4	3	1	...	...	...	...	2	1	1	32
12	...	...	...	1,063	835	228	653	212	161	12	11	4	...	...	10	...	2	..	2	33
13	...	...	...	1,614	1,413	201	972	173	414	18	26	8	...	...	1	2	...	...	...	34
134	...	3	...	12,153	10,980	1,173	7,605	1,092	2,932	52	386	25	1	...	56	4	26	19	7	35
77	...	3	...	5,354	4,889	465	1,808	373	2,715	60	363	32	...	...	3	...	1	...	1	36
1	...	...	...	63	45	18	16	15	29	2	...	1	...	...	...	...	...	...	...	37
3	...	...	...	266	208	58	84	47	117	7	7	4	...	...	...	...	...	...	...	38
8	...	...	...	596	529	67	165	48	341	11	23	8	...	...	...	...	...	...	...	39
65	...	3	...	4,429	4,107	322	1,543	263	2,228	40	333	19	...	...	3	...	1	...	1	40
67	...	...	...	8,986	7,767	1,219	7,379	1,197	318	21	37	1	1	...	32	...	...	...	...	41
1	...	...	...	222	126	96	111	94	13	2	2	...	...	...	...	...	...	...	...	42
8	..	...	...	763	597	166	565	161	29	5	1	..	...	...	2	...	...	...	...	43
4	...	...	...	960	834	126	797	121	35	5	2	...	...	...	...	...	...	...	...	44
54	...	...	...	7,041	6,210	831	5,906	821	241	9	32	1	1	...	30	...	...	...	...	45
1	...	...	...	228	213	15	23	9	171	2	19	4	...	...	...	...	...	...	...	46
...	...	...	...	3	1	2	...	2	...	...	1	...	...	...	...	...	...	...	...	47
1	...	...	...	15	12	3	...	3	11	...	1	...	...	...	...	...	...	...	...	48
...	...	...	...	20	16	4	...	3	15	1	1	...	...	...	...	...	...	...	...	49
...	...	...	...	190	184	6	23	1	145	1	16	4	...	...	...	...	...	...	.	50
16	...	...	...	522	514	8	131	2	345	3	6	...	...	...	32	3	3	3	...	51
...	...	...	...	1	1	...	1	...	...	...	...	...	...	...	...	...	...	...	...	52
...	..	...	...	18	18	...	4	...	4	...	2	...	...	...	8	...	...	...	...	53
1	...	...	...	37	34	3	10	...	23	1	...	...	...	...	1	2	...	...	...	54
15	...	...	...	466	461	5	116	2	318	2	4	...	...	...	23	1	3	3	...	55
...	...	...	...	29	18	11	17	7	...	...	1	1	...	...	...	3	2	1	1	56
...	...	...	...	...	...	...	...	...	...	...	...	...	...	..	...	..	...	...	...	57
...	...	...	...	1	...	1	...	1	...	...	...	...	...	...	...	...	...	...	...	58
...	...	...	...	1	...	1	...	1	...	...	...	...	...	...	...	...	..	...	...	59
...	...	...	...	27	18	9	17	5	...	...	1	1	...	...	...	8	2	1	1	60
340	10	...	12	7,334	6,719	615	3,092	414	1,710	20	1,048	170	339	6	530	5	1,358	1,308	50	61
3	...	...	...	77	58	19	17	14	10	3	18	2	...	...	13	...	9	9	...	62
7	2	...	1	444	339	105	114	67	54	5	64	82	4	1	103	...	34	32	2	63
17	...	...	...	635	538	97	191	55	99	3	143	36	24	1	81	2	182	165	17	64
313	8	...	11	6,178	5,784	394	2,770	278	1,547	9	823	100	311	4	333	3	1,133	1,102	31	65

APPENDIX TO IMPERIAL TABLE VIII.—

PART B.—DETAILS FOR

Serial No.	District or State.	Religion and Age.	Literate in Vernacular.															
			Total.			Urdu.							Hindi.					
						Total.			Persian.		Others.		Total.			Nagri.		
			Persons.	Males.	Females.	Persons.	Males.	Females.	Males.	Females.	Males.	Females.	Persons.	Males.	Females.	Males.	Females.
	1	2	3	4	5	6	7	8	9	10	11	12	13	14	15.	16	17
1	GURDASPUR.	HINDU ...	13,837	13,234	603	6,122	6,064	58	6,064	58	...	...	1,536	1,386	150	1,049	129
2		0—10 ...	188	172	16	112	110	2	110	2	...	...	19	12	7	9	7
3		10—15 ...	1,334	1,225	109	917	910	7	910	7	...	...	97	57	40	50	37
4		15—20 ...	1,493	1,387	106	744	735	9	735	9	...	...	124	104	20	87	20
5		20 and over ...	10,822	10,450	372	4,849	4,809	40	4,809	40	...	...	1,296	1,213	83	903	65
6		SIKH ...	3,740	3,446	294	1,631	1,611	20	1,611	20	...	...	39	29	10	26	9
7		0—10 ...	58	43	15	29	27	2	27	2	...	...	1	...	1	...	1
8		10—15 ...	356	309	47	229	227	2	227	2	...	...	1	1	...	1	...
9		15—20 ...	481	446	36	319	319	...	319	...	...	...	1	...	1	...	1
10		20 and over ...	2,845	2,649	196	1,054	1,038	16	1,038	16	...	...	36	28	8	25	7
11		MUHAMMADAN ...	6,692	6,365	327	6,274	5,949	325	5,949	325	...	...	7	7	...	7	...
12		0—10 ...	129	114	15	128	113	15	113	15	...	...	...	...	...	...	...
13		10—15 ...	887	840	47	855	808	47	808	47	...	...	...	...	...	...	...
14		15—20 ...	853	799	54	823	771	52	771	52	...	...	...	...	...	...	...
15		20 and over ...	4,823	4,612	211	4,468	4,257	211	4,257	211	...	...	7	7	...	7	...
16		CHRISTIAN ...	410	290	120	387	270	117	270	117	...	...	3	2	1	2	1
17		0—10 ...	36	33	3	36	33	3	33	3	...	...	...	...	...	...	...
18		10—15 ...	102	75	27	102	75	27	75	27	...	...	...	...	...	...	...
19		15—20 ...	73	46	27	72	45	27	45	27	...	...	...	...	...	...	...
20		20 and over ...	199	136	63	177	117	60	117	60	...	...	3	2	1	2	1
21	SIALKOT.	ALL RELIGIONS ...	28,911	26,983	1,928	19,231	18,332	899	18,307	897	25	2	2,109	1,904	205	1,312	190
22		0—10 ...	326	251	75	214	195	19	195	19	...	...	60	36	14	25	14
23		10—15 ...	3,068	2,634	434	2,611	2,362	249	2,360	248	2	1	139	91	48	78	45
24		15—20 ...	3,590	3,269	321	2,852	2,704	148	2,704	147	...	1	215	187	28	155	26
25		20 and over ...	21,927	20,829	1,098	13,554	13,071	483	13,048	483	23	...	1,705	1,590	115	1,054	105
26		HINDU ...	12,418	11,779	639	6,648	6,580	68	6,570	66	10	2	1,648	1,462	186	1,037	174
27		0—10 ...	148	121	27	82	80	2	80	2	...	...	45	31	14	21	14
28		10—15 ...	1,206	1,082	124	959	951	8	950	7	1	1	118	72	46	62	43
29		15—20 ...	1,501	1,400	101	1,085	1,076	9	1,076	8	...	1	157	134	23	113	22
30		20 and over ...	9,563	9,176	387	4,522	4,473	49	4,464	49	9	...	1,328	1,225	103	841	95
31		SIKH ...	5,268	4,813	455	1,874	1,859	15	1,847	15	12	...	297	287	10	267	9
32		0—10 ...	64	34	30	20	20	...	20	...	...	...	4	4	...	4	...
33		10—15 ...	456	386	70	270	267	3	266	3	1	...	18	16	2	16	2
34		15—20 ...	646	566	80	371	369	2	369	2	...	...	42	38	4	37	4
35		20 and over ...	4,102	3,827	275	1,213	1,203	10	1,192	10	11	...	233	229	4	210	3
36		JAIN ...	523	510	13	111	111	...	111	...	...	...	149	140	9	6	7
37		0—10 ...	5	5	...	4	4	...	4	...	...	...	1	1	...	...	..
38		10—15 ...	37	35	2	17	17	...	17	...	...	...	3	3	...	...	...
39		15—20 ...	77	75	2	35	35	...	35	...	...	...	15	14	1	5	...
40		20 and over ...	404	395	9	55	55	...	55	...	...	...	130	122	8	1	7
41		MUHAMMADAN ...	10,006	9,466	540	9,909	9,372	537	9,370	537	2	...	15	15	...	2	...
42		0—10 ...	104	89	15	103	89	14	89	14	...	...	...	...	...	...	...
43		10—15 ...	1,129	1,047	82	1,125	1,043	82	1,043	82	...	...	...	...	...	...	...
44		15—20 ...	1,232	1,141	91	1,227	1,137	90	1,137	90	...	...	1	1	...	...	...
45		20 and over ...	7,541	7,189	352	7,454	7,103	351	7,101	351	2	...	14	14	...	2	...
46		CHRISTIAN ...	689	410	279	689	410	279	409	279	1	...	...	...	...	...	...
47		0—10 ...	5	2	3	5	2	3	2	3	...	...	...	...	...	...	...
48		10—15 ...	240	84	156	240	84	156	84	156	...	...	...	...	...	...	...
49		15—20 ...	134	87	47	134	87	47	87	47	...	...	...	...	...	...	..
50		20 and over ...	310	237	73	310	237	73	236	73	1	...	...	...	...	...	...
51	GUJRANWALA.	ALL RELIGIONS ...	28,851	26,720	2,131	17,027	16,307	720	16,307	720	...	...	1,302	1,206	96	712	75
52		0—10 ...	458	327	131	294	256	38	256	38	...	...	12	7	5	7	5
53		10—15 ...	3,176	2,808	368	2,422	2,330	92	2,330	92	...	...	91	60	31	82	16
54		15—20 ...	3,680	3,321	359	2,527	2,406	121	2,406	121	...	...	155	143	12	100	12
55		20 and over ...	21,537	20,264	1,273	11,784	11,315	469	11,315	469	...	...	1,044	996	48	573	42
56		HINDU ...	12,624	11,791	833	6,199	6,104	95	6,104	95	...	...	1,060	967	93	658	74
57		0—10 ...	226	159	67	129	119	10	119	10	...	...	12	7	5	7	5
58		10—15 ...	1,403	1,228	175	1,000	991	9	991	9	...	...	74	44	30	31	15
59		15—20 ...	1,678	1,524	154	1,004	983	21	983	21	...	...	142	130	12	100	12
60		20 and over ...	9,317	8,880	437	4,066	4,011	55	4,011	55	...	...	832	786	46	520	42
61		SIKH ...	7,525	6,838	687	2,620	2,602	18	2,602	18	...	...	193	190	3	36	1
62		0—10 ...	97	59	38	32	30	2	30	2	...	..	...	...	...	...	...
63		10—15 ...	813	699	114	486	482	4	482	4	...	...	16	15	1	...	1
64		15—20 ...	924	819	105	462	461	1	461	1	...	...	13	13	...	...	...
65		20 and over ...	5,691	5,261	430	1,640	1,629	11	1,629	11	...	...	164	162	2	36	...

EDUCATION (BY RELIGION AND AGE).

DISTRICTS AND STATES—*continued*.

LITERATE IN VERNACULAR.																				
HINDI.				PUNJABI.													OTHERS.			
Lande or Mahajani.		*Others.*		*Total.*			*Gurmukhi.*		*Lande or Mahajani.*		*Nagri.*		*Tankri.*		*Persian.*					
Males.	Females.	Males.	Females.	Persons.	Males.	Females.	Males.	Females.	Males.	Females.	Males.	Females.	Males.	Females.	Males.	Females.	Persons.	Males.	Females.	Serial No.
18	19	20	21	22	23	24	25	26	27	28	29	30	31	32	33	34	35	36	37	
337	9	...	12	4,826	4,481	345	1,308	152	1,649	20	1,026	166	332	6	166	1	1,359	1,308	50	1
3	...	...	...	48	41	7	4	2	8	3	17	2	...	...	12	...	9	9	...	2
7	2	...	1	286	226	60	40	23	52	5	61	31	4	1	69	...	34	32	2	3
17	...	...	..	443	383	60	65	21	99	8	142	35	24	1	53	...	182	165	17	4
310	7	...	11	4,049	3,831	218	1,199	106	1,490	9	806	98	304	4	32	1	1,128	1,097	31	5
3	1	...	...	2,070	1,806	264	1,723	260	32	...	15	4	1	...	35	...	...	...	...	6
...	...	...	...	28	16	12	13	12	1	...	1	...	...	...	1	...	...	...	...	7
...	...	...	..	126	81	45	72	44	...	...	1	1	...	...	8	...	...	...	...	8
...	...	...	...	161	126	35	123	34	...	...	1	1	...	...	2	...	...	...	...	9
3	1	...	...	1,755	1,583	172	1,515	170	31	...	12	2	1	...	24	...	...	...	...	10
...	...	...	...	406	404	2	43	...	23	...	7	...	2	...	329	2	5	5	...	11
...	...	...	...	1	1	...	...	...	1	...	...	...	...	...	...	...	...	...	...	12
...	...	...	...	32	32	...	2	...	2	...	2	...	...	...	26	...	...	...	...	13
...	...	...	...	30	28	2	2	...	...	...	...	...	...	...	26	2	...	...	...	14
...	...	...	...	343	343	...	39	...	20	...	5	...	2	...	277	...	5	5	...	15
...	...	...	...	20	18	2	18	2	...	...	...	...	...	...	...	...	...	...	...	16
...	...	...	...	...	...	...	..	...	...	...	...	...	...	...	...	...	...	...	...	17
...	...	...	...	...	...	...	...	...	...	...	...	...	...	...	...	...	...	...	...	18
...	...	...	...	1	1	...	1	...	...	...	...	...	...	...	...	...	...	...	...	19
...	...	...	...	19	17	2	17	2	...	...	...	...	...	...	...	...	...	...	...	20
582	11	10	4	7,564	6,742	822	2,942	769	3,550	37	245	16	4	...	1	...	7	5	2	21
11	...	...	...	62	20	42	18	40	...	1	2	1	...	...	...	...	...	...	...	22
13	...	...	3	318	181	137	107	128	68	3	11	6	...	...	...	...	...	...	...	23
32	2	...	...	523	278	145	160	131	192	12	26	2	...	...	...	...	...	...	...	24
526	9	10	1	6,661	6,163	498	2,657	470	3,295	21	206	7	4	...	1	...	7	5	2	25
419	9	6	3	4,122	3,737	385	743	338	2,838	32	156	15	4	...	1	...	...	...	...	26
10	...	...	...	21	10	11	9	10	...	...	1	1	...	...	...	...	...	...	...	27
10	...	...	3	129	59	70	14	63	40	2	5	6	...	...	...	...	...	...	...	28
21	1	...	...	259	190	69	43	56	132	11	15	2	...	...	...	...	...	...	...	29
378	8	6	...	3,718	3,478	235	677	209	2,661	19	135	7	4	...	1	...	...	...	...	30
18	...	2	1	3,097	2,667	430	2,180	427	469	8	18	...	...	...	...	...	...	...	...	31
...	...	...	...	40	10	30	9	29	...	1	1	...	...	...	...	...	...	...	...	32
...	...	...	...	168	103	65	92	65	11	...	...	...	...	...	...	...	...	...	...	33
1	...	...	...	233	159	74	117	74	41	...	1	...	...	...	...	...	...	...	...	34
17	...	2	1	2,656	2,395	261	1,962	259	417	2	16	...	...	...	...	...	...	...	...	35
134	2	...	...	263	259	4	2	2	188	1	69	1	...	...	...	...	...	...	...	36
1	..	...	...	...	...	...	...	...	...	...	...	...	...	...	...	...	...	...	...	37
3	...	...	...	17	15	2	...	...	9	1	6	1	...	...	...	...	...	...	...	38
9	1	...	...	27	26	1	..	1	16	...	10	...	...	...	...	...	...	...	...	39
121	1	...	...	219	218	1	2	1	163	...	53	...	...	...	...	...	...	...	...	40
11	...	2	...	82	79	3	17	2	60	1	2	...	...	...	...	...	...	...	...	41
...	...	...	...	1	...	1	...	1	...	...	...	...	...	...	...	...	...	...	...	42
...	...	...	...	4	4	...	1	...	3	...	...	...	...	...	...	...	...	...	...	43
1	...	...	..	4	3	1	...	...	3	1	...	...	...	...	...	...	...	...	...	44
10	...	2	...	73	72	1	16	1	54	...	2	...	...	...	...	...	...	...	...	45
...	...	...	...	...	...	...	...	...	...	...	...	...	...	...	...	...	...	...	...	46
...	...	...	...	...	...	...	...	...	...	...	...	...	...	...	...	...	...	...	...	47
...	...	...	...	...	...	...	...	...	...	...	...	...	...	...	...	...	...	...	...	48
...	...	...	...	...	...	...	...	...	...	...	...	...	...	...	...	...	...	...	...	49
...	...	...	...	...	...	...	...	.	...	...	...	...	...	...	...	...	...	...	...	50
494	21	...	...	10,522	9,207	1,315	3,697	1,227	5,350	69	148	19	12	...	...	...	...	...	...	51
...	...	...	...	152	64	88	46	80	15	7	3	1	...	...	...	...	...	...	...	52
28	15	...	...	663	418	245	233	236	173	3	11	6	1	...	...	...	...	...	...	53
43	...	...	...	998	772	226	344	209	413	14	14	3	1	...	...	...	...	...	...	54
423	6	...	...	8,709	7,953	756	3,074	702	4,749	45	120	9	10	...	...	...	...	...	...	55
309	19	...	...	5,365	4,720	645	1,108	577	3,486	51	128	17	...	...	...	...	...	...	...	56
...	...	...	...	85	33	52	18	45	12	6	3	1	...	...	...	...	...	...	...	57
13	15	...	...	329	193	136	78	129	105	1	10	6	...	...	...	...	...	...	...	58
30	...	...	...	532	411	121	125	105	272	13	14	3	...	...	...	...	...	...	...	59
266	4	...	...	4,419	4,083	336	887	298	3,097	31	99	7	...	...	...	...	...	...	...	60
154	2	...	...	4,712	4,046	666	2,552	649	1,480	16	14	1	...	...	...	...	...	...	..	61
...	...	...	...	65	29	36	27	35	2	1	...	...	...	...	...	...	...	...	...	62
15	...	...	...	311	202	109	154	107	48	2	...	...	...	...	...	...	...	...	...	63
13	...	...	...	449	345	104	218	103	127	1	...	...	...	...	...	...	...	...	...	64
126	2	...	...	3,887	3,470	417	2,153	404	1,303	12	14	1	...	...	...	...	...	...	...	65

APPENDIX TO IMPERIAL TABLE VIII.

PART B.—DETAILS FOR

Serial No.	District or State.	Religion and Age.	LITERATE IN VERNACULAR.														
			Total.			Urdu.							Hindi.				
						Total.			Persian.		Others.		Total.			Nagri.	
			Persons.	Males.	Females.	Persons.	Males.	Females.	Males.	Females.	Males.	Females.	Persons.	Males.	Females.	Males.	Females.
	1	2	3	4	5	6	7	8	9	10	11	12	13	14	15	16	17
1	GUJRANWALA.	JAIN ...	273	271	2	87	86	1	86	1	...	...	12	12	...	12	...
2		0—10 ...	7	7		6	6	...	6	...	...	...			...		...
3		10—15 ...	34	34	...	19	19	...	19	...	...	...	...	...	...	...	...
4		15—20 ...	29	28	1	15	15	...	15	...	...	...	...	...	...	...	...
5		20 and over ...	203	202	1	47	46	1	46	1	...	...	12	12	...	12	...
6		MUHAMMADAN ...	8,063	7,544	519	7,761	7,244	517	7,244	517	...	...	37	37	...	6	...
7		0—10 ...	128	102	26	127	101	26	101	26	...	...			...		...
8		10—15 ...	866	796	70	857	787	70	787	70	...	...	...	...	...	...	...
9		15—20 ...	983	896	87	980	893	87	893	87	...	...	1	1	...	1	...
10		20 and over ...	6,086	5,750	336	5,797	5,463	334	5,463	334	...	...	36	36	...	5	...
11		CHRISTIAN ...	366	276	90	360	271	89	271	89	...	...	...	...	...	...	...
12		0—10 ...	...	...	...	...	...	...	...	...	...	...	...	...	...	...	...
13		10—15 ...	60	51	9	60	51	9	51	9	...	...	...	...	...	...	...
14		15—20 ...	66	54	12	66	54	12	54	12	...	...	...	...	...	...	...
15		20 and over ...	240	171	69	234	166	68	166	68	...	...	...	...	...	...	...
16	GUJRAT.	ALL RELIGIONS ...	23,182	21,728	1,454	14,150	13,669	481	13,669	481	...	...	546	501	45	313	25
17		0—10 ...	348	281	67	187	187	10	187	10	...	...	8	3	5	2	4
18		10—15 ...	2,539	2,298	241	1,956	1,876	80	1,876	80	...	...	26	18	8	4	6
19		15—20 ...	2,776	2,553	218	2,038	1,962	76	1,962	76	...	...	26	22	4	14	1
20		20 and over ...	17,519	16,591	928	9,959	9,644	315	9,644	315	...	...	486	458	28	293	14
21		HINDU ...	7,042	6,631	411	3,983	3,938	45	3,938	45	...	...	438	405	33	244	24
22		0—10 ...	91	73	18	62	60	2	60	2	...	...	6	2	4	2	4
23		10—15 ...	774	695	79	613	608	8	608	8	...	...	24	16	8	4	6
24		15—20 ...	858	779	79	645	633	12	633	12	...	...	21	19	2	14	1
25		20 and over ...	5,319	5,084	235	2,660	2,637	23	2,637	23	...	...	387	368	19	224	13
26		SIKH ...	7,626	7,005	621	1,714	1,696	18	1,696	18	...	...	94	83	11	65	...
27		0—10 ...	149	107	42	27	26	1	26	1	...	...	2	1	1	...	...
28		10—15 ...	749	655	94	326	321	5	321	5	...	...	2	2	...	...	...
29		15—20 ...	846	770	76	322	321	1	321	1	...	...	5	3	2	...	...
30		20 and over ...	5,882	5,473	409	1,039	1,028	11	1,028	11	...	...	85	77	8	65	...
31		MUHAMMADAN ...	8,381	8,009	372	8,327	7,956	371	7,956	371	...	...	9	9	...	...	...
32		0—10 ...	98	92	6	98	92	6	92	6	...	...	...	...	...	...	...
33		10—15 ...	1,004	940	64	1,002	939	63	939	63	...	...	...	...	...	...	...
34		15—20 ...	1,051	996	55	1,050	995	55	995	55	...	...	...	...	...	...	...
35		20 and over ...	6,228	5,981	247	6,177	5,930	247	5,930	247	...	...	9	9	...	...	...
36		CHRISTIAN ...	117	70	47	117	70	47	70	47	...	...	...	...	...	...	...
37		0—10 ...	9	8	1	9	8	1	8	1	...	...	...	...	...	...	...
38		10—15 ...	11	7	4	11	7	4	7	4	...	...	...	...	...	...	...
39		15—20 ...	21	13	8	21	13	8	13	8	...	...	...	...	...	...	...
40		20 and over ...	76	42	34	76	42	34	42	34	...	...	...	...	...	...	...
41	SHAHPUR.	ALL RELIGIONS ...	27,319	24,795	2,524	12,178	11,938	240	11,937	240	1	...	668	536	132	370	130
42		0—10 ...	403	290	113	195	185	10	185	10	...	...	22	6	16	4	16
43		10—15 ...	2,605	2,146	459	1,435	1,410	25	1,409	25	1	...	57	13	44	12	44
44		15—20 ...	3,316	2,854	462	1,649	1,615	34	1,615	34	...	...	79	52	27	42	25
45		20 and over ...	20,995	19,505	1,490	8,899	8,728	171	8,728	171	...	...	510	465	45	312	45
46		HINDU ...	13,715	12,572	1,143	4,516	4,486	30	4,485	30	1	...	615	485	130	356	128
47		0—10 ...	181	126	55	93	90	3	90	3	...	...	21	5	16	4	16
48		10—15 ...	1,292	1,045	247	678	676	2	675	2	1	...	54	11	43	11	43
49		15—20 ...	1,764	1,534	230	735	731	4	731	4	...	...	77	50	27	41	25
50		20 and over ...	10,478	9,867	611	3,010	2,989	21	2,989	21	...	...	463	419	44	300	44
51		SIKH ...	6,903	5,724	1,179	1,266	1,254	12	1,254	12	...	...	36	36	...	10	...
52		0—10 ...	141	90	51	22	22	...	22	...	...	...	...	...	...	...	...
53		10—15 ...	757	567	190	211	209	2	209	2	...	...	1	1	...	...	...
54		15—20 ...	831	629	202	203	203	...	203	...	...	...	1	1	...	1	...
55		20 and over ...	5,174	4,438	736	830	820	10	820	10	...	...	34	34	...	9	...
56		MUHAMMADAN ...	6,591	6,415	176	6,293	6,117	176	6,117	176	...	...	15	15	...	4	...
57		0—10 ...	79	72	7	78	71	7	71	7	...	...	1	1	...	...	...
58		10—15 ...	545	525	20	537	517	20	517	20	...	...	1	1	...	1	...
59		15—20 ...	704	677	27	694	667	27	667	27	...	...	1	1	...	...	...
60		20 and over ...	5,263	5,141	122	4,984	4,862	122	4,862	122	...	...	12	12	...	3	...
61		CHRISTIAN ...	106	82	24	101	79	22	79	22	...	...	...	...	...	...	...
62		0—10 ...	1	1	...	1	1	...	1	...	...	...	...	...	...	...	...
63		10—15 ...	10	9	1	9	8	1	8	1	...	...	...	...	...	...	...
64		15—20 ...	17	14	3	17	14	3	14	3	...	...	...	...	...	...	...
65		20 and over ...	78	58	20	74	56	18	56	18	...	...	...	...	...	...	...

EDUCATION (BY RELIGION AND AGE).

DISTRICTS AND STATES—*continued.*

LITERATE IN VERNACULAR.																				
HINDI.				PUNJABI.														OTHERS.		
Lande or Mahajani.		*Others.*		*Total.*			*Gurmukhi.*		*Lande or Mahajani.*		*Nagri.*		*Tankri.*		*Persian.*					
Males.	Females.	Males.	Females.	Persons.	Males.	Females.	Males.	Females.	Males.	Females.	Males.	Females.	Males.	Females.	Males.	Females.	Persons.	Males.	Females.	Serial No.
18	19	20	21	22	23	24	25	26	27	28	29	30	31	32	33	34	35	36	37	
...	...	...	...	174	173	1	6	1	153	...	2	...	12	...	...	...	...	...	...	1
...	...	...	...	1	1	...	1	...	...	...	...	...	...	...	...	...	...	...	...	2
...	...	...	...	15	15	...	1	...	12	...	1	...	1	...	...	...	...	...	...	3
...	...	...	...	14	13	1	...	1	12	...	...	...	1	...	...	...	...	...	...	4
...	...	...	...	144	144	...	4	...	129	...	1	...	10	...	...	...	...	...	...	5
31	...	...	...	265	263	2	26	...	231	1	6	1	...	...	...	...	...	...	...	6
...	...	...	...	1	1	...	...	...	1	...	...	...	...	...	...	...	...	...	...	7
...	...	...	...	8	8	...	...	...	8	...	...	...	...	...	...	...	...	...	...	8
...	...	...	...	3	3	...	1	...	2	...	...	...	...	...	...	...	...	...	...	9
31	...	...	...	253	251	2	25	...	220	1	6	1	...	...	...	...	...	...	...	10
...	...	...	...	6	5	1	5	...	...	1	...	...	...	...	...	...	...	...	...	11
...	...	...	...	...	...	...	...	...	...	...	...	...	...	...	...	...	...	...	...	12
...	...	...	...	...	...	...	...	...	...	...	...	...	...	...	...	...	...	...	...	13
...	...	...	...	...	...	...	...	...	...	...	...	...	...	...	...	...	...	...	...	14
...	...	...	...	6	5	1	5	...	...	1	...	...	...	...	...	...	...	...	...	15
188	20	...	...	8,486	7,558	928	5,134	813	2,285	71	51	44	33	...	55	...	...	...	...	16
1	1	...	...	143	91	52	82	46	8	1	...	5	1	...	...	...	...	...	...	17
14	2	...	...	557	404	153	351	126	47	15	1	12	3	...	2	...	...	...	...	18
8	3	...	...	712	574	138	454	111	118	14	...	13	1	...	1	...	...	...	...	19
165	14	...	...	7,074	6,489	585	4,247	530	2,112	41	50	14	28	...	52	...	...	...	...	20
161	9	...	...	2,621	2,288	333	750	224	1,433	68	45	41	33	...	27	...	...	...	...	21
...	...	...	...	23	11	12	5	6	5	1	...	5	1	...	...	...	...	...	...	22
12	2	...	...	134	71	63	37	37	30	14	1	12	3	...	...	...	...	...	...	23
5	1	...	...	192	127	65	50	38	76	14	...	13	1	...	...	...	...	...	...	24
144	6	...	...	2,272	2,079	193	658	143	1,322	38	41	11	28	...	27	...	...	...	...	25
18	11	...	...	5,818	5,226	592	4,378	587	842	3	5	2	...	...	1	...	...	...	...	26
1	1	...	...	120	80	40	77	40	3	...	...	...	...	...	...	...	...	...	...	27
2	...	...	...	421	332	89	314	88	17	1	...	...	...	...	1	...	...	...	...	28
3	2	...	...	519	446	73	404	73	42	...	...	...	...	...	...	...	...	...	...	29
12	8	...	...	4,758	4,368	390	3,583	386	780	2	5	2	...	...	...	...	...	...	...	30
9	...	...	...	45	44	1	6	1	10	...	1	...	...	...	27	...	...	...	...	31
...	...	...	...	...	...	...	...	...	...	...	...	...	...	...	...	...	...	...	...	32
...	...	...	...	2	1	1	...	1	...	...	...	...	...	...	1	...	...	...	...	33
...	...	...	...	1	1	...	...	...	...	...	...	...	...	...	1	...	...	...	...	34
9	...	...	...	42	42	...	6	...	10	...	1	...	...	...	25	...	...	...	...	35
...	...	...	...	...	...	...	...	...	...	...	...	...	...	...	...	...	...	...	...	36
...	...	...	...	...	...	...	...	...	...	...	...	...	...	...	...	...	...	...	...	37
...	...	...	...	...	...	...	...	...	...	...	...	...	...	...	...	...	...	...	...	38
...	...	...	...	...	...	...	...	...	...	...	...	...	...	...	...	...	...	...	...	39
...	...	...	...	...	...	...	...	...	...	...	...	...	...	...	...	...	...	...	...	40
166	2	...	...	14,472	12,321	2,151	3,990	2,034	7,054	65	279	37	831	14	167	1	1	...	1	41
2	...	...	...	186	99	87	70	79	26	6	1	2	2	...	...	...	...	...	...	42
1	...	...	...	1,113	723	390	348	373	306	8	14	9	26	...	29	...	...	...	...	43
10	2	...	...	1,588	1,187	401	422	386	631	7	22	6	95	2	17	...	...	...	...	44
153	...	...	...	11,585	10,512	1,273	3,150	1,196	6,091	44	242	20	708	12	121	1	1	...	1	45
129	2	...	...	8,584	7,601	983	1,165	894	5,315	42	268	34	783	13	70	...	...	...	...	46
1	...	...	...	67	31	36	15	31	13	4	1	1	2	...	...	...	...	...	...	47
...	...	...	...	560	358	202	69	188	233	6	14	8	25	...	17	...	...	...	...	48
9	2	...	...	952	753	199	144	189	499	2	22	6	76	2	12	...	...	...	...	49
119	...	...	...	7,005	6,459	546	937	486	4,570	30	231	19	680	11	41	...	...	...	...	50
26	...	...	...	5,601	4,434	1,167	2,801	1,140	1,568	28	9	3	17	1	39	...	...	...	...	51
...	...	...	...	119	68	51	55	48	13	2	...	1	...	...	...	...	...	...	...	52
1	...	...	...	545	357	188	277	185	72	2	...	1	1	...	7	...	...	...	...	53
...	...	...	...	627	425	202	277	197	127	5	...	...	16	...	5	...	...	...	...	54
25	...	...	...	4,310	3,584	726	2,192	710	1,356	14	9	1	...	1	27	...	...	...	...	55
11	...	...	...	283	283	...	22	...	171	...	2	...	31	...	57	...	...	...	...	56
1	...	...	...	...	...	...	...	...	...	...	...	...	...	...	...	...	...	...	...	57
...	...	...	...	7	7	...	3	...	1	...	...	...	...	...	4	...	...	...	...	58
1	...	...	...	9	9	...	1	...	5	...	...	...	3	...	...	...	...	...	...	59
9	...	...	...	267	267	...	19	...	165	...	2	...	28	...	58	...	...	...	...	60
...	...	...	...	4	3	1	2	...	...	...	...	...	...	...	1	1	1	...	1	61
...	...	...	...	...	...	...	...	...	...	...	...	...	...	...	...	...	...	...	...	62
...	...	...	...	1	1	...	...	...	...	...	...	...	...	...	1	...	...	...	...	63
...	...	...	...	...	...	...	...	...	...	...	...	...	...	...	...	...	...	...	...	64
...	...	...	...	3	2	1	2	...	...	...	...	...	...	...	...	1	1	...	1	65

APPENDIX TO IMPERIAL TABLE VIII.

PART B.—DETAILS FOR

Serial No.	District or State	Religion and age	Literate in Vernacular. Total. Persons.	Males.	Females.	Urdu. Total. Persons.	Males.	Females.	Urdu. Persian. Males.	Females.	Urdu. Others. Males.	Females.	Hindi. Total. Persons.	Males.	Females.	Hindi. Nagri. Males.	Females.
	1	2	3	4	5	6	7	8	9	10	11	12	13	14	15	16	17
1	JHELUM.	ALL RELIGIONS ...	22,519	21,050	1,469	13,363	13,082	281	13,054	280	28	1	1,241	1,198	43	1,153	37
2		0—10 ...	814	241	73	164	158	6	158	6	...	...	6	6	1	3	1
3		10—15 ...	2,051	1,799	252	1,508	1,469	39	1,469	39	...	..	28	17	11	13	9
4		15—20 ...	2,741	2,476	265	1,930	1,879	51	1,879	51	...	...	111	106	5	105	5
5		20 and over ...	17,413	16,534	879	9,761	9,576	185	9,548	184	28	1	1,096	1,070	26	1,032	22
6		HINDU ...	7,907	7,418	489	3,785	3,745	40	3,719	39	26	1	1,202	1,163	39	1,131	34
7		0—10 ...	107	89	18	69	68	1	68	1	...	...	5	4	1	3	1
8		10—15 ...	669	580	89	502	499	3	499	3	...	...	26	16	10	12	9
9		15—20 ...	973	890	83	632	625	7	625	7	...	...	108	104	4	103	4
10		20 and over ...	6,158	5,859	299	2,582	2,553	29	2,527	28	26	1	1,063	1,039	24	1,013	20
11		SIKH ...	6,415	5,668	747	1,585	1,570	15	1,570	15	...	...	27	23	4	19	3
12		0—10 ...	143	93	50	34	34	...	34	...	...	...	...	...	...	...	...
13		10—15 ...	609	480	129	241	239	2	239	2	...	...	2	1	1	1	...
14		15—20 ...	700	560	140	251	247	4	247	4	...	...	2	1	1	1	1
15		20 and over ...	4,963	4,535	428	1,059	1,050	9	1,050	9	...	...	23	21	2	17	2
16		MUHAMMADAN ...	8,077	7,872	205	7,907	7,706	201	7,704	201	2	...	11	11	...	2	...
17		0—10 ...	64	59	5	61	56	5	56	5	...	...	1	1	...	...	...
18		10—15 ...	762	730	32	755	723	32	723	32	...	...	...	...	...	...	...
19		15—20 ...	1,052	1,016	36	1,032	997	35	997	35	...	...	1	1	...	1	...
20		20 and over ...	6,199	6,067	132	6,059	5,930	129	5,928	129	2	...	9	9	...	1	...
21	RAWALPINDI.	ALL RELIGIONS ...	28,074	24,183	3,891	16,467	15,958	514	15,951	511	2	3	2,166	1,967	199	1,899	196
22		0—10 ...	749	462	287	360	324	36	324	36	...	...	29	7	22	7	22
23		10—15 ...	3,317	2,635	682	2,153	2,085	68	2,085	68	...	...	110	76	34	74	33
24		15—20 ...	3,811	3,182	629	2,516	2,439	77	2,439	77	...	...	185	154	31	146	31
25		20 and over ...	20,197	17,904	2,293	11,438	11,105	333	11,103	330	2	3	1,842	1,730	112	1,672	110
26		HINDU ...	9,020	7,837	1,183	4,143	4,065	78	4,065	78	...	...	1,914	1,738	176	1,693	173
27		0—10 ...	252	165	87	138	128	10	128	10	...	...	29	7	22	7	22
28		10—15 ...	990	807	183	650	642	8	642	8	...	...	98	66	32	64	31
29		15—20 ...	1,318	1,109	209	812	800	12	800	12	...	...	158	135	23	132	23
30		20 and over ...	6,460	5,756	704	2,543	2,495	48	2,495	48	...	...	1,629	1,530	99	1,490	97
31		SIKH ...	9,196	6,934	2,262	2,883	2,836	47	2,836	47	...	...	94	88	6	77	6
32		0—10 ...	355	174	181	81	73	8	73	8	...	...	...	...	...	...	...
33		10—15 ...	1,385	942	443	585	575	10	575	10	...	...	6	5	1	5	1
34		15—20 ...	1,223	875	348	474	469	5	469	5	...	...	10	8	2	8	2
35		20 and over ...	6,233	4,943	1,290	1,743	1,719	24	1,719	24	...	...	78	75	3	64	3
36		JAIN ...	340	323	17	86	86	..	86	...	...	...	88	81	7	70	7
37		0—10 ...	1	1	...	1	1	...	1	...	...	...	...	...	...	...	...
38		10—15 ...	37	34	3	17	17	.	17	...	...	...	6	5	1	5	1
39		15—20 ...	44	38	6	14	14	...	14	...	...	...	15	10	5	5	5
40		20 and over ...	258	250	8	54	54	...	54	...	...	...	67	66	1	60	1
41		MUHAMMADAN ...	9,189	8,864	325	9,115	8,805	310	8,805	310	...	...	44	41	3	40	3
42		0—10 ...	128	111	17	128	111	17	111	17	...	...	...	...	...	...	...
43		10—15 ...	880	835	45	879	834	45	834	45	...	...	...	...	...	...	...
44		15—20 ...	1,186	1,134	52	1,181	1,133	48	1,133	48	...	...	...	...	...	..	...
45		20 and over ...	6,995	6,784	211	6,927	6,727	200	6,727	200	...	...	44	41	3	40	3
46		CHRISTIAN ...	280	193	87	232	157	75	155	72	2	3	26	19	7	19	7
47		0—10 ...	12	11	1	12	11	1	11	1	...	...	...	...	..	...	...
48		10—15 ...	22	17	5	22	17	5	17	5	...	...	...	...	...	...	...
49		15—20 ...	40	26	14	35	23	12	23	12	...	...	2	1	1	1	1
50		20 and over ...	206	139	67	163	106	57	104	54	2	3	24	18	6	18	6
51	ATTOCK.	ALL RELIGIONS ...	15,472	14,248	1,224	7,369	7,282	87	7,280	85	2	2	601	575	26	176	18
52		0—10 ...	153	119	34	59	59	...	59	...	...	...	3	3	...	...	...
53		10—15 ...	1,497	1,290	207	929	915	14	915	14	...	...	16	12	4	3	3
54		15—20 ...	1,728	1,533	195	1,057	1,043	14	1,043	13	...	1	43	37	6	19	4
55		20 and over ...	12,094	11,306	788	5,324	5,265	59	5,263	58	2	1	589	623	16	154	11
56		HINDU ...	4,398	3,940	458	1,520	1,508	12	1,506	10	2	2	348	327	21	169	15
57		0—10 ...	28	22	6	16	16	...	16	...	...	...	3	3	...	...	...
58		10—15 ...	385	312	73	217	217	...	217	...	...	...	7	3	4	3	3
59		15—20 ...	474	407	67	248	244	4	244	3	...	1	21	18	3	18	3
60		20 and over ...	3,511	3,199	312	1,039	1,031	8	1,029	7	2	1	317	308	14	148	9
61		SIKH ...	6,294	5,604	690	1,220	1,219	1	1,219	1	...	...	228	235	3	4	1
62		0—10 ...	112	84	28	30	30	...	30	...	...	...	...	...	...	...	...
63		10—15 ...	629	509	120	236	236	...	236	...	...	...	8	8	...	...	...
64		15—20 ...	645	527	118	207	207	...	207	...	...	...	22	19	3	1	1
65		20 and over ...	4,908	4,484	424	747	746	1	746	1	...	...	208	208	...	3	...

EDUCATION (BY RELIGION AND AGE).

DISTRICTS AND STATES—*continued.*

LITERATE IN VERNACULAR.																				
HINDI.				PUNJABI.													OTHERS.			
Lande or Mahajani.		*Others.*		*Total.*			*Gurmukhi.*		*Lande or Mahajani.*		*Nagri.*		*Tankri.*		*Persian.*					
Males.	Females.	Males.	Females.	Persons.	Males.	Females.	Males.	Females.	Males.	Females.	Males.	Females.	Males.	Females.	Males.	Females.	Persons.	Males.	Females.	Serial No.
18	19	20	21	22	23	24	25	26	27	28	29	30	31	32	33	34	35	36	37	
45	6	...	...	7,909	6,765	1,144	3,894	1,046	2,401	35	436	60	21	1	13	2	6	5	1	1
2	...	...	...	144	78	66	60	59	13	4	5	3	...	...	...	...	...	...	...	2
4	2	...	...	515	313	202	238	183	63	4	9	14	1	1	2	...	...	...	...	3
1	...	...	...	700	491	209	319	194	144	6	24	9	...	...	4	...	...	...	...	4
88	4	...	...	6,550	5,883	667	3,277	610	2,181	21	398	34	20	...	7	2	6	5	1	5
32	5	...	...	2,920	2,510	410	466	339	1,714	15	320	55	7	1	3	...	..	...	...	6
1	...	...	...	33	17	16	4	11	9	3	4	2	...	...	...	...	...	...	...	7
4	1	...	...	141	65	76	13	60	41	2	8	13	1	1	2	...	...	...	...	8
1	...	...	...	233	161	72	35	62	109	2	16	8	...	..	1	...	...	...	..	9
26	4	...	.	2,513	2,267	246	414	206	1,555	8	292	32	6	...	...	...	...	...	..	10
4	1	...	...	4,803	4,075	728	3,419	706	546	18	109	4	...	...	1	...	...	...	...	11
...	...	...	...	109	59	50	56	48	2	1	1	1	...	...	...	...	...	...	...	12
...	1	...	...	366	240	126	225	123	14	2	1	1	...	...	...	...	...	...	...	13
...	...	...	...	447	312	135	283	132	21	3	8	...	...	...	...	...	...	...	...	14
4	...	...	...	3,881	3,464	417	2,855	403	509	12	99	2	...	...	1	...	...	...	..	15
9	...	...	...	159	155	4	8	1	131	1	7	1	...	...	9	1	...	...	..	16
1	...	...	...	2	2	...	...	...	2	...	...	...	...	...	...	...	...	...	...	17
...	...	...	...	7	7	...	...	...	7	...	...	...	...	...	...	...	...	...	...	18
...	...	...	...	19	18	1	1	...	14	...	...	1	...	...	3	...	...	...	...	19
8	...	...	...	131	128	3	7	1	108	1	7	...	...	...	6	1	...	...	...	20
68	3	...	...	9,300	6,163	3,137	5,196	3,093	710	12	157	27	98	1	2	4	141	100	41	21
...	...	...	...	359	131	228	122	225	5	1	3	2	1	...	...	...	1	...	1	22
2	1	...	...	1,043	470	573	425	586	34	1	11	6	...	...	...	...	11	4	7	23
8	...	...	...	1,098	581	517	488	507	77	4	9	4	6	...	1	2	12	8	4	24
58	2	...	..	6,600	4,981	1,819	4,161	1,795	594	6	134	15	91	1	1	2	117	88	29	25
45	3	...	..	2,866	1,964	902	1,875	878	422	5	107	19	60	...	...	...	97	70	27	26
...	...	...	...	85	30	55	21	52	5	1	3	2	1	...	...	...	...	...	...	27
2	1	...	...	234	95	139	67	134	22	...	6	5	...	...	...	...	8	4	4	28
3	...	...	...	337	167	170	110	166	51	2	1	2	5	...	...	...	11	7	4	29
40	2	...	...	2,210	1,672	538	1,177	526	344	2	97	10	54	...	...	...	78	59	19	30
11	...	...	...	6,219	4,010	2,209	3,798	2,204	173	4	25	1	14	...	...	...	...	...	...	31
...	...	...	...	274	101	178	101	173	...	...	...	...	...	...	...	...	...	...	...	32
...	...	...	...	794	362	432	357	432	5	...	...	...	..	...	...	...	...	...	...	33
...	...	...	...	739	398	341	377	338	18	2	2	1	1	...	...	...	...	...	...	34
11	...	...	...	4,412	3,149	1,263	2,963	1,261	150	2	23	...	13	...	...	...	...	...	...	35
11	..	...	...	166	156	10	...	...	109	3	23	6	24	1	...	...	...	...	...	36
...	...	...	...	..	...	..	...	...	...	...	...	...	...	...	...	...	...	..	...	37
...	...	...	.	14	12	2	...	...	7	1	5	1	...	...	...	...	...	...	...	38
5	...	...	...	15	14	1	...	...	8	...	6	1	...	...	...	...	...	...	...	39
6	...	...	...	137	130	7	...	...	94	2	12	4	24	1	...	...	..	...	...	40
1	...	...	...	30	18	12	10	7	6	...	...	1	...	...	2	4	...	...	...	41
...	...	...	...	...	...	..	..	..	...	...	...	...	...	...	...	...	...	...	...	42
...	...	...	...	1	1	...	1	...	...	...	...	...	...	...	...	...	...	...	...	43
...	...	...	...	5	1	4	...	2	...	...	...	...	...	...	1	2	...	...	...	44
1	...	...	...	24	16	8	9	5	6	...	...	1	...	...	1	2	...	...	...	45
...	...	...	...	19	15	4	13	4	...	...	2	...	...	...	...	..	3	2	1	46
...	..	...	...	...	...	...	..	...	...	...	...	...	...	...	...	...	...	...	...	47
...	...	...	...	...	...	...	...	...	...	...	...	...	...	...	...	...	...	...	...	48
...	...	...	...	2	1	1	1	1	...	...	...	...	...	...	...	...	1	1	...	49
...	...	...	..	17	14	3	12	3	...	...	2	...	...	...	...	...	2	1	1	50
398	2	1	6	7,498	6,387	1,111	3,423	1,094	2,963	15	1	2	...	...	...	...	4	4	...	51
3	...	...	...	91	57	34	55	34	2	...	...	...	...	...	...	...	...	...	...	52
9	...	...	1	551	362	189	280	189	82	...	...	...	...	...	...	...	1	1	..	53
18	...	...	2	628	453	175	287	172	166	2	...	1	...	...	...	...	...	...	..	54
368	2	1	3	6,228	5,515	713	2,801	699	2,713	13	1	1	...	...	...	...	3	3	...	55
157	2	1	4	2,530	2,105	425	816	418	1,288	5	1	2	...	...	...	...	...	...	...	56
3	...	...	...	9	3	6	3	6	...	...	...	...	...	...	...	...	..	...	...	57
...	...	...	1	161	92	69	60	69	32	...	...	...	...	...	...	...	...	...	...	58
...	...	...	...	205	145	60	66	57	79	2	...	1	...	...	...	...	...	...	...	59
154	2	1	3	2,155	1,865	290	687	286	1,177	3	1	1	...	...	...	...	...	...	...	60
231	...	...	2	4,836	4,150	686	2,601	676	1,549	10	...	...	...	...	...	...	...	...	...	61
...	...	...	...	82	54	28	52	28	2	...	...	...	...	...	...	...	...	...	...	62
8	...	...	...	386	265	120	220	120	45	...	...	...	...	...	...	...	...	...	...	63
18	...	...	2	416	301	115	220	115	81	...	...	...	...	...	...	...	...	...	...	64
205	..	...	...	3,953	3,530	423	2,109	413	1,421	10	..	...	...	...	...	...	...	...	...	65

APPENDIX TO IMPERIAL TABLE VIII.—

PART B.—DETAILS FOR

Serial No.	District or State.	Religion and age.	LITERATE IN VERNACULAR. Total. Persons.	Total. Males.	Total. Females.	Urdu. Total. Persons.	Urdu. Total. Males.	Urdu. Total. Females.	Urdu. Persian. Males.	Urdu. Persian. Females.	Urdu. Others. Males.	Urdu. Others. Females.	Hindi. Total. Persons.	Hindi. Total. Males.	Hindi. Total. Females.	Hindi. Nagri. Males.	Hindi. Nagri. Females.
	1	2	3	4	5	6	7	8	9	10	11	12	13	14	15	16	17
1	ATTOCK.	MUHAMMADAN ...	4,762	4,690	72	4,619	4,547	72	4,547	72	...	..	11	11	...	1	...
2		0—10 ...	13	13	...	13	13	...	13	...	...	...	...	...	...	...	...
3		10—15 ...	480	466	14	474	460	14	460	14	...	...	1	1	...	...	...
4		15—20 ...	609	599	10	602	592	10	592	10	...	...	...	...	...	...	...
5		20 and over ...	3,660	3,612	48	3,530	3,482	48	3,482	48	...	...	10	10	...	1	...
6		CHRISTIAN ...	9	5	4	5	3	2	3	2	...	...	4	2	2	2	2
7		0—10 ...	...	...	..	...	...	...	...	...	...	...	...	...	...	...	...
8		10—15 ...	...	...	...	...	...	...	...	...	...	...	...	...	...	...	...
9		15—20 ...	...	...	...	...	...	...	...	...	...	...	...	...	...	...	...
10		20 and over ...	9	5	4	5	3	2	3	2	...	...	4	2	2	2	2
11	MIANWALI.	ALL RELIGIONS ...	11,143	10,793	350	5,229	5,127	102	5,127	102	...	...	65	32	33	32	33
12		0—10 ...	149	123	26	105	98	7	98	7	...	...	7	1	6	1	6
13		10—15 ...	1,002	928	74	729	713	16	713	16	...	...	18	5	13	5	13
14		15—20 ...	1,421	1,369	52	916	899	17	899	17	..	...	7	4	3	4	3
15		20 and over ...	8,571	8,373	198	3,479	3,417	62	3,417	62	...	...	33	22	11	22	11
16		HINDU ...	7,353	7,180	173	2,324	2,313	11	2,313	11	-	...	61	29	32	29	32
17		0—10 ...	102	84	18	67	64	3	64	3	...	...	7	1	6	1	6
18		10—15 ...	666	621	45	432	431	1	431	1	...	...	18	5	13	5	13
19		15—20 ...	899	873	26	466	465	1	465	1	...	...	7	4	3	4	3
20		20 and over ...	5,686	5,602	84	1,359	1,353	6	1,353	6	...	...	29	19	10	19	10
21		SIKH ...	1,072	982	90	318	314	4	314	4	...	...	1	...	1	...	1
22		0—10 ...	13	9	4	4	4	...	4	...	...	...	...	...	...	...	...
23		10—15 ...	75	61	14	37	37	...	37	...	...	...	...	...	...	...	...
24		15—20 ...	123	112	11	55	54	1	54	1	...	...	...	...	...	...	...
25		20 and over ...	861	800	61	222	219	3	219	3	...	...	1	...	1	...	1
26		MUHAMMADAN ...	2,691	2,612	79	2,567	2,488	79	2,488	79	...	...	3	3	...	3	...
27		0—10 ...	32	30	2	32	30	2	30	2	...	...	...	...	...	...	...
28		10—15 ...	260	245	15	259	244	15	244	15	...	...	...	...	...	...	...
29		15—20 ...	396	382	14	392	378	14	378	14	...	..	...	...	...	...	...
30		20 and over ...	2,003	1,955	48	1,884	1,836	48	1,836	48	...	...	3	3	...	3	...
31	MONTGOMERY.	ALL RELIGIONS ...	17,803	16,726	1,077	6,725	6,384	341	6,384	341	...	...	436	401	35	160	33
32		0—10 ...	276	197	79	163	120	43	120	43	...	...	5	3	2	...	2
33		10—15 ...	1,445	1,248	197	691	641	50	641	50	...	...	11	8	3	5	3
34		15—20 ...	1,795	1,613	182	841	790	51	790	51	..	...	23	21	2	4	1
35		20 and over ...	14,287	13,668	619	5,030	4,833	197	4,833	197	...	...	397	369	28	151	27
36		HINDU ...	6,938	6,460	478	1,953	1,882	71	1,882	71	...	...	289	259	30	157	30
37		0—10 ...	92	62	30	49	39	10	39	10	...	...	4	2	2	...	2
38		10—15 ...	555	462	93	241	235	6	235	6	...	...	8	5	3	5	3
39		15—20 ...	540	446	94	229	206	23	206	23	...	...	12	11	1	4	1
40		20 and over ...	5,751	5,490	261	1,434	1,402	32	1,402	32	...	...	265	241	24	148	24
41		SIKH ...	6,969	6,637	332	1,055	1,044	11	1,044	11	...	...	137	137	...	1	...
42		0—10 ...	85	69	16	15	15	...	15	...	...	...	1	1	...	...	...
43		10—15 ...	596	537	59	158	158	...	158	...	...	...	8	8	...	...	...
44		15—20 ...	809	749	60	176	175	1	175	1	..	...	10	10	...	...	...
45		20 and over ...	5,479	5,282	197	706	696	10	696	10	...	...	123	123	...	1	...
46		MUHAMMADAN ...	3,834	3,588	246	3,664	3,422	242	3,422	242	...	...	8	5	3	2	1
47		0—10 ...	99	66	33	99	66	33	66	33	...	..	...	...	...	...	...
48		10—15 ...	290	247	43	289	246	43	246	43	...	...	...	...	...	...	...
49		15—20 ...	434	414	20	424	405	19	405	19	...	...	1	...	1	...	...
50		20 and over ...	3,011	2,861	150	2,852	2,705	147	2,705	147	...	...	7	5	2	2	1
51		CHRISTIAN ...	53	36	17	50	33	17	33	17	...	...	...	...	...	...	...
52		0—10 ...	...	...	...	...	...	...	...	...	...	...	...	...	...	...	...
53		10—15 ...	2	1	1	2	1	1	1	1	...	...	...	...	...	...	...
54		15—20 ...	12	4	8	12	4	8	4	8	...	..	...	...	...	...	...
55		20 and over ...	39	31	8	36	28	8	28	8	...	...	...	...	...	...	...
56	LYALLPUR.	ALL RELIGIONS ...	26,690	25,278	1,412	11,797	11,430	367	11,428	367	2	...	1,606	1,489	117	856	112
57		0—10 ...	368	281	87	171	162	9	162	9	...	...	26	4	22	3	22
58		10—15 ...	2,117	1,926	191	1,119	1,078	41	1,078	41	...	...	92	60	32	14	32
59		15—20 ...	2,980	2,761	219	1,882	1,327	55	1,326	55	1	...	147	128	19	53	19
60		20 and over ...	21,225	20,310	915	9,125	8,863	262	8,862	262	1	...	1,341	1,297	44	786	39
61		HINDU ...	10,569	10,138	431	3,318	3,287	31	3,285	31	2	...	1,437	1,323	114	764	109
62		0—10 ...	141	98	44	61	60	1	60	1	...	...	25	4	21	3	21
63		10—15 ...	672	603	69	291	287	4	287	4	...	...	89	58	31	14	31
64		15—20 ...	1,125	1,042	83	384	378	6	377	6	1	...	131	112	19	43	19
65		20 and over ...	8,631	8,395	236	2,582	2,562	20	2,561	20	1	...	1,192	1,149	43	704	38

EDUCATION (BY RELIGION AND AGE).

DISTRICTS AND STATES—*continued.*

LITERATE IN VERNACULAR.																				
HINDI.				PUNJABI.													OTHERS.			
Lande or Mahajani.		*Others.*		*Total.*			*Gurmukhi.*		*Lande or Mahajani.*		*Nagri.*		*Tankri.*		*Persian.*					
Males.	Females.	Males.	Females.	Persons.	Males.	Females.	Males.	Females.	Males.	Females.	Males.	Females.	Males.	Females.	Males.	Females.	Persons.	Males.	Females.	Serial No.
18	19	20	21	22	23	24	25	26	27	28	29	30	31	32	33	34	35	36	37	
10	..	...	...	132	132	...	6	..	126	...	...	...	...	...	...	...	...	...	...	1
...	...	...	...	...	...	...	...	...	...	...	...	...	...	...	...	...	...	...	...	2
1	...	...	...	5	5	...	...	...	5	...	...	...	...	...	...	...	...	...	...	3
...	...	...	...	7	7	...	1	...	6	...	...	...	...	...	...	...	...	...	...	4
9	...	...	...	120	120	...	5	...	115	...	...	...	...	...	...	...	...	...	...	5
...	..	...	...	...	...	...	...	...	...	...	...	...	...	...	...	...	...	...	...	6
...	...	...	...	...	...	...	..	...	...	...	...	...	...	...	...	...	...	...	...	7
...	-	...	...	...	...	...	...	...	...	...	...	...	...	...	...	...	...	...	...	8
...	...	...	..	...	...	...	...	...	...	...	...	...	...	...	...	...	...	...	...	9
...	...	...	..	...	...	...	...	...	...	...	...	...	...	...	...	...	...	...	...	10
...	..	...	...	5,849	5,634	215	822	174	5,185	31	125	10	...	...	2	...	...	...	...	11
...	...	...	..	37	24	13	6	8	18	4	...	1	...	...	...	...	...	...	...	12
...	...	...	-	255	210	45	20	35	186	5	4	5	...	...	...	...	...	...	...	13
...	...	...	...	498	466	32	22	26	437	5	7	1	...	...	...	...	...	...	...	14
...	...	...	...	5,059	4,934	125	274	105	4,544	17	114	3	...	...	2	...	...	...	...	15
...	...	...	...	4,968	4,838	130	194	91	4,519	29	124	10	...	...	1	...	...	...	...	16
...	...	...	...	28	19	9	4	4	15	4	...	1	...	...	...	...	...	...	...	17
...	...	...	...	216	185	34	10	21	171	5	4	5	...	...	...	...	...	...	...	18
...	...	...	...	426	404	22	11	16	386	5	7	1	...	...	...	...	...	...	...	19
...	...	...	...	4,298	4,230	68	169	50	3,947	15	113	3	...	...	1	...	...	...	...	20
...	...	...	...	753	668	85	125	83	542	2	1	...	...	...	...	...	...	...	...	21
...	...	...	...	9	5	4	2	4	3	...	...	...	...	...	...	...	...	...	...	22
...		...	...	38	24	14	10	14	14	...	...	...	...	...	...	...	...	...	...	23
...	...	...	...	68	58	10	11	10	47	...	...	...	...	...	...	...	...	...	...	24
...	...	...		638	581	57	102	55	478	2	1	...	...	...	...	...	...	...	...	25
...	...	...	...	121	121	...	2	...	118	...	...	...	...	...	1	...	...	...	...	26
...	...	...	...	...	...	...	...	...	...	...	...	...	...	...	...	...	...	...	...	27
...	...	...	...	1	1	...	...	...	1	...	...	...	...	...	...	...	...	...	...	28
...	...	...	...	4	4	...	...	...	4	...	...	...	...	...	...	...	...	...	...	29
...	...	...	...	116	116	...	2	...	113	...	...	...	...	...	1	...	...	...	...	30
241	2	...	...	10,636	9,937	699	2,364	514	7,279	77	274	108	...	...	20	...	6	4	2	31
3	...	...	...	108	74	84	45	24	29	...	...	10	...	...	...	...	...	...	...	32
3	...	...	...	742	599	143	250	106	337	3	12	34	...	...	...	...	1	...	1	33
17	1	...	...	930	801	129	245	94	536	12	19	23	...	...	1	...	1	1	...	34
218	1	...	...	8,856	8,468	388	1,824	290	6,377	62	243	41	...	...	19	...	4	3	1	35
102	...	...	...	4,695	4,318	377	504	227	3,549	53	265	97	...	...	...	...	1	1	...	36
2	...	...	...	39	21	18	4	8	17	...	...	10	...	...	...	...	...	...	...	37
...	...	...	...	306	222	84	49	54	164	1	9	29	...	...	...	...	...	...	...	38
7	...	...	...	299	229	70	38	40	174	9	17	21	...	...	...	...	...	...	...	39
93	...	...	...	4,051	3,846	205	413	125	3,194	43	239	37	...	...	...	...	1	1	...	40
136	...	...	...	5,776	5,455	321	1,841	286	3,607	24	7	11	...	...	...	...	1	1	...	41
1	...	...	...	69	53	16	41	16	12	...	...	...	...	...	...	...	...	...	...	42
3	...	...	...	435	376	59	201	52	172	2	3	5	...	...	...	...	...	...	...	43
10	...	...	...	623	564	59	205	54	357	3	2	2	...	...	...	...	...	...	...	44
122	...	...	...	4,649	4,462	187	1,394	164	3,066	19	2	4	...	...	...	...	1	1	...	45
3	2	...	...	161	160	1	15	1	123	...	2	...	...	...	20	...	1	1	...	46
...	...	...	...	...	...	...	...	...	...	...	...	...	...	...	...	...	...	...	...	47
...	...	...	...	1	1	...	...	...	1	...	...	...	...	...	...	...	...	...	...	48
...	1	...	...	8	8	...	2	...	5	...	...	...	...	...	1	...	1	1	...	49
3	1	...	...	152	151	1	13	1	117	...	2	...	...	...	19	...	...	...	...	50
...	...	...	...	3	3	...	3	...	...	...	...	...	...	...	...	...	...	...	...	51
...	..	...	...	...	...	...	...	...	...	...	...	...	...	...	...	...	...	...	...	52
...	...	...	...	...	...	...	...	...	...	...	...	...	...	...	...	...	...	...	...	53
...	...	...	...	...	...	...	..	..	...	...	...	...	...	...	...	...	...	...	...	54
...	...	...	...	3	3	...	3	...	...	...	...	...	...	...	...	...	...	...	...	55
633	5	...	...	13,280	12,352	928	6,278	857	5,655	28	391	43	18	...	10	...	7	7	...	56
1	...	...	...	171	115	56	91	51	22	...	2	5	...	...	...	...	...	...	...	57
46	...	...	...	906	785	118	522	111	254	3	10	4	...	...	2	...	...	...	...	58
75	...	...	...	1,451	1,306	145	745	136	548	2	10	7	3	...	...	...	...	...	...	59
511	5	...	...	10,752	10,143	609	4,920	559	4,831	23	369	27	15	...	8	...	7	7	...	60
559	5	...	...	5,807	5,521	286	1,219	229	3,942	15	339	42	18	...	3	...	7	7	...	61
1	...	...	...	55	34	21	13	16	9	...	2	5	...	...	...	...	...	...	...	62
44	...	...	...	292	258	34	77	28	173	2	7	4	...	...	1	...	...	...	...	63
69	...	...	...	619	552	58	159	52	380	...	10	6	3	...	...	...	...	...	...	64
445	5	...	...	4,850	4,677	173	970	133	3,370	13	320	27	15	...	2	...	7	7	...	65

APPENDIX TO IMPERIAL TABLE VIII.—

PART B.—DETAILS FOR

Serial No.	District or State.	Religion and Age.	Literate in Vernacular. Total. Persons.	Total. Males.	Total. Females.	Urdu. Total. Persons.	Urdu. Total. Males.	Urdu. Total. Females.	Urdu. Persian. Males.	Urdu. Persian. Females.	Urdu. Others. Males.	Urdu. Others. Females.	Hindi. Total. Persons.	Hindi. Total. Males.	Hindi. Total. Females.	Hindi. Nagri. Males.	Hindi. Nagri. Females.
	1	2	3	4	5	6	7	8	9	10	11	12	13	14	15	16	17
1	LYALLPUR.	SIKH ...	9,599	8,944	655	2,163	2,150	13	2,150	13	...	...	142	139	3	87	3
2		0—10 ...	146	110	36	29	29	...	28	...	...	...	1	...	1	...	1
3		10—15 ...	896	810	86	286	285	1	285	1	...	...	2	1	1	...	1
4		15—20 ...	1,144	1,055	89	295	292	3	292	3	...	...	15	15	...	10	...
5		20 and over ...	7,413	6,969	444	1,553	1,544	9	1,544	9	...	...	124	123	1	77	1
6		MUHAMMADAN ...	6,210	5,965	245	6,031	5,787	244	5,787	244	...	...	17	17	...	4	...
7		0—10 ...	79	71	8	79	71	8	71	8	...	...	...	...	...	...	...
8		10—15 ...	531	500	31	524	493	31	493	31	...	...	1	1	...	...	...
9		15—20 ...	674	639	35	669	634	35	634	35	...	...	...	...	...	...	...
10		20 and over ...	4,926	4,755	171	4,759	4,589	170	4,589	170	...	...	16	16	...	4	...
11		CHRISTIAN ...	261	186	75	261	186	75	186	75	...	...	...	...	...	...	...
12		0—10 ...	2	2	...	2	2	...	2	...	...	...	...	...	...	...	...
13		10—15 ...	16	12	4	16	12	4	12	4	...	...	...	...	...	...	...
14		15—20 ...	32	22	10	32	22	10	22	10	...	...	...	...	...	...	...
15		20 and over ...	211	150	61	211	150	61	150	61	...	...	...	...	...	...	...
16	JHANG.	ALL RELIGIONS ...	20,545	19,660	885	5,672	5,598	74	5,598	74	...	...	970	923	47	294	39
17		0—10 ...	142	105	37	44	40	4	40	4	...	...	10	6	4	5	4
18		10—15 ...	1,378	1,249	129	652	644	8	644	8	...	...	40	33	7	9	7
19		15—20 ...	2,320	2,150	170	817	799	18	799	18	...	...	111	106	5	47	3
20		20 and over ...	16,705	16,156	549	4,159	4,115	44	4,115	44	...	...	809	778	31	233	25
21		HINDU ...	13,331	12,689	642	2,182	2,152	30	2,152	30	...	...	891	845	46	292	39
22		0—10 ...	100	73	27	31	31	...	31	...	...	...	9	5	4	4	4
23		10—15 ...	897	793	104	340	334	6	334	6	...	...	37	30	7	9	7
24		15—20 ...	1,548	1,425	123	386	379	7	379	7	...	...	107	102	5	47	8
25		20 and over ...	10,786	10,398	388	1,425	1,408	17	1,408	17	...	...	738	708	30	232	25
26		SIKH ...	3,718	3,519	199	356	354	2	354	2	...	...	70	69	1	2	...
27		0—10 ...	32	26	6	3	3	...	3	...	...	...	1	1	...	1	...
28		10—15 ...	222	199	23	57	57	...	57	...	...	...	3	3	...	...	...
29		15—20 ...	369	333	36	47	47	...	47	...	...	...	4	4	...	...	...
30		20 and over ...	3,095	2,961	134	249	247	2	247	2	...	...	62	61	1	1	...
31		MUHAMMADAN ...	3,490	3,446	44	3,128	3,086	42	3,086	42	...	...	9	9	...	...	...
32		0—10 ...	10	6	4	10	6	4	6	4	...	...	...	...	...	...	...
33		10—15 ...	258	256	2	254	252	2	252	2	...	...	...	...	...	...	...
34		15—20 ...	403	392	11	384	373	11	373	11	...	...	...	...	...	...	...
35		20 and over ...	2,819	2,792	27	2,480	2,455	25	2,455	25	...	...	9	9	...	...	...
36	MULTAN.	ALL RELIGIONS ...	38,390	36,968	1,422	15,608	15,249	359	15,224	356	25	3	11,960	11,404	556	967	487
37		0—10 ...	524	424	100	221	202	19	202	19	...	...	220	162	58	63	57
38		10—15 ...	2,866	2,635	231	1,585	1,555	30	1,555	30	...	...	761	629	132	47	125
39		15—20 ...	4,038	3,826	212	1,979	1,937	42	1,930	42	7	...	1,125	1,037	88	109	77
40		20 and over ...	30,962	30,083	879	11,823	11,555	268	11,537	265	18	3	9,854	9,576	278	748	228
41		HINDU ...	24,109	23,252	857	5,412	5,346	66	5,321	64	25	2	11,346	10,815	531	901	466
42		0—10 ...	359	297	62	106	106	...	106	...	...	...	213	157	56	61	55
43		10—15 ...	1,870	1,698	172	780	776	4	776	4	...	...	737	606	131	46	124
44		15—20 ...	2,584	2,438	146	901	887	14	880	14	7	...	1,067	983	84	103	73
45		20 and over ...	19,296	18,819	477	3,625	3,577	48	3,559	46	18	2	9,329	9,069	260	691	214
46		SIKH ...	4,664	4,419	245	886	870	16	870	16	...	...	437	424	13	43	13
47		0—10 ...	61	44	17	17	16	1	16	1	...	...	3	2	1	1	1
48		10—15 ...	303	272	31	132	130	2	130	2	...	...	13	12	1	...	1
49		15—20 ...	478	447	31	129	128	1	128	1	...	...	40	38	2	3	2
50		20 and over ...	3,822	3,656	166	608	596	12	596	12	...	...	381	372	9	39	9
51		MUHAMMADAN ...	9,301	9,083	218	9,141	8,936	205	8,936	205	...	...	78	75	3	8	...
52		0—10 ...	86	77	9	85	77	8	77	8	...	...	...	...	...	...	...
53		10—15 ...	662	641	21	658	638	20	638	20	...	...	2	2	...	...	...
54		15—20 ...	942	921	21	933	914	19	914	19	...	...	4	4	...	1	...
55		20 and over ...	7,611	7,444	167	7,465	7,307	158	7,307	158	...	...	72	69	3	7	...
56		CHRISTIAN ...	154	78	76	144	72	72	72	71	...	1	8	4	4	4	4
57		0—10 ...	13	3	10	13	3	10	3	10	...	...	...	...	...	...	...
58		10—15 ...	11	7	4	11	7	4	7	4	...	...	...	...	...	...	...
59		15—20 ...	17	7	10	14	6	8	6	8	...	...	3	1	2	1	2
60		20 and over ...	113	61	52	106	56	50	56	49	...	1	5	3	2	3	2
61	MUZAFFARGARH.	ALL RELIGIONS ...	21,276	20,740	536	8,618	8,518	100	8,507	100	11	...	189	127	62	127	41
62		0—10 ...	228	201	27	118	111	7	111	7	...	...	6	6	...	6	...
63		10—15 ...	1,721	1,632	89	1,074	1,058	16	1,058	16	...	...	24	9	15	9	12
64		15—20 ...	2,244	2,154	90	1,083	1,070	13	1,070	13	...	...	25	7	18	7	15
65		20 and over ...	17,083	16,753	330	6,343	6,279	64	6,268	64	11	...	134	105	29	105	14

EDUCATION (BY RELIGION AND AGE).

DISTRICTS AND STATES—*continued.*

LITERATE IN VERNACULAR.																				
HINDI.				PUNJABI.													OTHERS.			
Lande or Mahajani.		*Others.*		*Total.*			*Gurmukhi.*		*Lande or Mahajani.*		*Nagri.*		*Tankri.*		*Persian.*					
Males.	Females.	Males.	Females.	Persons.	Males.	Females.	Males.	Females.	Males.	Females.	Males.	Females.	Males.	Females.	Males.	Females.	Persons.	Males.	Females.	Serial No.
18	19	20	21	22	23	24	25	26	27	28	29	30	31	32	33	34	35	36	37	
52	...	...	...	7,294	6,655	639	4,997	626	1,612	13	45	...	...	...	1	...	...	...	...	1
...	...	...	...	116	81	35	78	35	3	...	...	...	...	...	...	...	...	...	...	2
1	...	...	...	608	524	84	444	83	76	1	3	...	...	...	1	...	...	...	...	3
5	...	...	...	834	748	86	583	84	165	2	...	...	...	...	...	...	...	...	...	4
46	...	...	...	5,736	5,302	434	3,892	424	1,368	10	42	...	...	...	...	...	...	...	...	5
13	...	...	...	162	161	1	61	1	88	...	6	...	...	...	6	...	...	...	...	6
...	...	...	...	...	...	...	...	...	...	...	...	...	...	...	...	...	...	...	...	7
1	...	...	...	6	6	...	1	...	5	...	...	...	...	...	...	...	...	...	...	8
...	...	...	...	5	5	...	3	...	2	...	...	...	...	...	...	...	...	...	...	9
12	...	...	...	151	150	1	57	1	81	...	6	...	...	...	6	...	...	...	...	10
...	...	...	...	...	...	...	...	...	...	...	...	...	...	...	...	...	...	...	...	11
...	...	...	...	...	...	...	...	...	...	...	...	...	...	...	...	...	...	...	...	12
...	...	...	...	...	...	...	...	...	...	...	...	...	...	...	...	...	...	...	...	13
...	...	...	...	...	...	...	...	...	...	...	...	...	...	...	...	...	...	...	...	14
...	...	...	...	...	...	...	...	...	...	...	...	...	...	...	...	...	...	...	...	15
629	8	...	...	13,903	13,139	764	1,801	640	10,886	109	277	14	174	1	1	...	...	...	...	16
1	...	...	...	88	59	29	36	21	23	6	...	1	...	1	...	...	...	...	...	17
24	...	...	...	686	572	114	188	107	355	5	17	2	12	...	...	...	...	...	...	18
59	2	...	...	1,392	1,245	147	155	139	1,056	7	24	1	10	...	...	...	...	...	...	19
545	6	...	...	11,737	11,263	474	1,422	373	9,452	91	236	10	152	...	1	...	...	...	...	20
553	7	...	...	10,258	9,692	566	1,038	455	8,218	96	276	14	160	1	...	...	...	...	...	21
1	...	...	...	60	37	23	22	16	15	5	...	1	...	1	...	...	...	...	...	22
21	...	...	...	520	429	91	103	84	297	5	17	2	12	...	...	...	...	...	...	23
55	2	...	...	1,055	944	111	80	105	831	5	24	1	9	...	...	...	...	...	...	24
476	5	...	...	8,623	8,282	341	838	250	7,075	81	235	10	139	...	...	...	...	...	...	25
67	1	...	...	3,292	3,096	196	763	184	2,319	12	1	...	13	...	...	...	...	...	...	26
...	...	...	...	28	22	6	14	5	8	1	...	...	...	...	...	...	...	...	...	27
3	...	...	...	162	139	23	85	23	54	...	...	...	...	...	...	...	...	...	...	28
4	...	...	...	318	282	36	75	34	206	2	...	...	1	...	...	...	...	...	...	29
60	1	...	...	2,784	2,653	131	589	122	2,051	9	1	...	12	...	...	...	...	...	...	30
9	...	...	...	353	351	2	...	1	349	1	...	...	1	...	1	...	...	...	...	31
...	...	...	...	...	...	...	...	...	...	...	...	...	...	...	...	...	...	...	...	32
...	...	...	...	4	4	...	...	...	4	...	...	...	...	...	...	...	...	...	...	33
...	...	...	...	19	19	...	...	...	19	...	...	...	...	...	...	...	...	...	...	34
9	...	...	...	330	328	2	...	1	326	1	...	...	1	...	1	...	...	...	...	35
10,437	69	...	...	10,770	10,284	486	1,852	421	7,854	51	507	12	67	...	4	2	52	31	21	36
99	1	...	...	82	60	22	27	20	32	...	...	...	1	...	...	2	1	...	1	37
582	7	...	...	512	446	66	126	56	314	5	5	5	1	...	...	...	8	5	3	38
828	11	...	...	980	852	78	196	68	630	8	20	2	6	...	...	...	4	...	4	39
8,828	50	...	...	9,246	8,926	320	1,503	277	6,878	38	482	5	59	...	4	...	39	26	13	40
9,914	65	...	...	7,348	7,088	260	751	217	5,792	29	487	12	58	...	...	2	3	3	...	41
96	1	...	...	40	34	6	9	4	24	...	...	...	1	...	...	2	...	...	...	42
560	7	...	...	353	316	37	77	28	233	4	5	5	1	...	...	...	...	...	...	43
880	11	...	...	616	568	48	68	42	474	4	20	2	6	...	...	...	...	...	...	44
8,378	46	...	...	6,339	6,170	169	597	143	5,061	21	462	5	50	...	...	...	3	3	...	45
381	...	...	...	3,341	3,125	216	1,090	201	2,002	15	20	...	9	...	4	...	...	...	...	46
1	...	...	...	41	26	15	18	15	8	...	...	...	...	...	...	...	...	...	...	47
12	...	...	...	158	130	28	49	28	81	...	...	...	...	...	...	...	...	...	...	48
85	...	...	...	309	281	28	127	26	154	2	...	...	...	...	...	...	...	...	...	49
833	...	...	...	2,833	2,688	145	896	132	1,759	13	20	...	9	...	4	...	...	...	...	50
67	3	...	...	81	71	10	11	3	60	7	...	...	...	...	...	...	1	1	...	51
...	...	...	...	1	...	1	...	1	...	...	...	...	...	...	...	...	...	...	...	52
2	...	...	...	1	...	1	...	...	...	1	...	...	...	...	...	...	1	1	...	53
3	...	...	...	5	3	2	1	...	2	2	...	...	...	...	...	...	...	...	...	54
62	3	...	...	74	68	6	10	2	58	4	...	...	...	...	...	...	...	...	...	55
...	...	...	...	...	...	...	...	...	...	...	...	...	...	...	...	...	2	2	...	56
...	...	...	...	...	...	...	...	...	...	...	...	...	...	...	...	...	...	...	...	57
...	...	...	...	...	...	...	...	...	...	...	...	...	...	...	...	...	...	...	...	58
...	...	...	...	...	...	...	...	...	...	...	...	...	...	...	...	...	...	...	...	59
...	...	...	...	...	...	...	...	...	...	...	...	...	...	...	...	...	2	2	...	60
...	21	...	...	12,464	12,093	371	355	220	11,432	29	306	122	...	...	...	...	5	2	3	61
...	...	...	...	104	84	20	4	6	79	3	1	11	...	...	...	...	...	...	...	62
...	3	...	...	623	565	58	19	28	527	1	19	29	...	...	...	...	...	...	...	63
...	8	...	...	1,136	1,077	59	88	35	1,026	12	15	12	...	...	...	...	...	...	...	64
...	15	...	...	10,601	10,367	234	296	151	9,800	13	271	70	...	...	...	...	5	2	3	65

APPENDIX TO IMPERIAL TABLE VIII.—
PART B.—DETAILS FOR

Serial No.	District or State.	Religion and age.	Literate in Vernacular. Total. Persons.	Total. Males.	Total. Females.	Urdu. Total. Persons.	Urdu. Total. Males.	Urdu. Total. Females.	Urdu. Persian. Males.	Urdu. Persian. Females.	Urdu. Others. Males.	Urdu. Others. Females.	Hindi. Total. Persons.	Hindi. Total. Males.	Hindi. Total. Females.	Hindi. Nagri. Males.	Hindi. Nagri. Females.
	1	2	3	4	5	6	7	8	9	10	11	12	13	14	15	16	17
1	MUZAFFARGARH.	HINDU ...	15,019	14,636	383	3,030	3,019	11	3,008	11	11	...	186	126	60	126	39
2		0—10 ...	153	137	16	57	56	1	56	1	...	...	6	6	...	6	...
3		10—15 ...	1,041	976	65	437	434	3	434	3	...	...	22	9	13	9	10
4		15—20 ...	1,547	1,480	67	452	451	1	451	1	...	...	25	7	18	7	15
5		20 and over ...	12,278	12,043	235	2,084	2,078	6	2,067	6	11	...	133	104	29	104	14
6		SIKH ...	765	706	59	202	201	1	201	1	...	...	2	...	2	...	2
7		0—10 ...	17	12	5	3	3		3		...	...		...		...	
8		10—15 ...	88	72	11	41	41	...	41	...	...	...	...	...	...	...	...
9		15—20 ...	85	74	11	25	25	...	25	...	...	...	2	...	2	...	2
10		20 and over ...	580	548	32	133	132	1	132	1	...	...	...	...	...	...	...
11		MUHAMMADAN ...	5,481	5,391	90	5,382	5,294	88	5,294	88	...	...	...	...	...	...	...
12		0—10 ...	56	50	6	56	50	6	50	6	...	...	...	...	...	...	...
13		10—15 ...	597	584	13	596	583	13	583	13	...	...	...	...	...	...	...
14		15—20 ...	612	600	12	606	594	12	594	12	...	...	...	...	...	...	...
15		20 and over ...	4,216	4,157	59	4,124	4,067	57	4,067	57	...	...	...	...	...	...	...
16	DERA GHAZI KHAN.	ALL RELIGIONS ...	14,126	13,841	285	6,197	6,121	76	6,121	76	...	...	6,407	6,233	174	174	99
17		0—10 ..	130	106	24	80	69	11	69	11	...	...	47	36	11	...	6
18		10—15 ...	1,158	1,099	59	756	749	7	749	7	...	...	339	295	44	11	32
19		15—20 ...	1,588	1,541	47	863	855	8	855	8	...	...	566	532	34	25	22
20		20 and over ...	11,250	11,095	155	4,498	4,448	50	4,448	50	...	...	5,455	5,370	85	138	39
21		HINDU ...	9,884	9,660	224	2,101	2,080	21	2,080	21	...	...	6,297	6,124	173	171	99
22		0—10 ...	73	55	18	28	23	5	23	5	...	...	43	32	11	...	6
23		10—15 ...	751	697	54	357	354	3	354	3	...	...	334	290	44	11	32
24		15—20 ...	1,059	1,019	40	348	346	2	346	2	...	...	557	523	34	24	22
25		20 and over ...	8,001	7,889	112	1,368	1,357	11	1,357	11	...	...	5,363	5,279	84	136	39
26		SIKH ...	96	89	7	29	28	1	28	1	...	...	40	39	1	1	...
27		0—10 ..	2	2	...	...	...	...	...	...	...	...	1	1	...	...	...
28		10—15 ...	12	11	1	6	6	...	6	...	...	...	3	3	...	...	...
29		15—20 ...	16	15	1	6	6	...	6	...	...	...	5	5	...	...	...
30		20 and over ...	66	61	5	17	16	1	16	1	...	...	31	30	1	1	...
31		MUHAMMADAN ...	4,118	4,073	45	4,046	4,001	45	4,001	45	...	...	63	63	...	...	...
32		0—10 ...	54	48	6	52	46	6	46	6	...	...	2	2	...	...	...
33		10—15 ...	395	391	4	393	389	4	389	4	...	...	2	2	...	...	...
34		15—20 ...	510	505	5	507	502	5	502	5	...	...	3	3	...	...	...
35		20 and over ...	3,159	3,129	30	3,094	3,064	30	3,064	30	...	...	56	56	...	...	...
36	LOHARU.	ALL RELIGIONS ...	267	258	9	74	65	9	65	8	...	1	193	193	...	129	...
37		0—10 ...	3	2	1	2	1	1	1	1	...	...	1	1	...	1	...
38		10—15 ...	8	6	2	7	5	2	5	2	...	...	1	1	...	1	...
39		15—20 ...	31	30	1	11	10	1	10	1	...	...	20	20	...	12	...
40		20 and over ...	225	220	5	54	49	5	49	4	...	1	171	171	...	115	...
41		HINDU ...	198	198	...	15	15	...	15	...	...	...	183	188	...	119	...
42		0—10 ...	1	1	...	...	...	...	...	...	...	...	1	1	...	1	...
43		10—15 ...	1	1	...	...	...	...	...	...	...	...	1	1	...	1	...
44		15—20 ...	17	17	...	1	1	...	1	...	...	...	16	18	...	8	...
45		20 and over ...	179	179	...	14	14	...	14	...	...	...	165	165	...	109	...
46		MUHAMMADAN ...	63	54	9	58	49	9	49	8	...	1	5	5	...	5	...
47		0—10 ...	2	1	1	2	1	1	1	1	...	...	...	...	...	...	...
48		10—15 ...	7	5	2	7	5	2	5	2	...	...	...	...	...	...	...
49		15—20 ...	11	10	1	10	9	1	9	1	...	...	1	1	...	1	...
50		20 and over ...	43	38	5	39	34	5	34	4	...	1	4	4	...	4	...
51	DUJANA.	ALL RELIGIONS ...	561	549	12	313	304	9	243	7	61	2	248	245	3	89	1
52		0—10 ...	2	2	...	1	1	...	1	...	...	...	1	1	...	...	...
53		10—15 ...	46	45	1	28	28	...	23	...	5	...	18	17	1	3	1
54		15—20 ..	99	98	1	68	67	1	60	...	7	1	31	31	...	11	...
55		20 and over ...	414	404	10	216	208	8	159	7	49	1	198	196	2	75	...
56		HINDU ...	417	412	5	169	167	2	107	...	60	2	248	245	3	89	1
57		0—10 ...	1	1	...	...	...	...	...	...	...	...	1	1	...	...	...
58		10—15 ...	39	38	1	21	21	...	16	...	5	...	18	17	1	3	1
59		15—20	75	74	1	44	43	1	37	...	6	1	31	31	...	11	...
60		20 and over ...	302	299	3	104	103	1	54	...	49	1	198	196	2	75	...
61		MUHAMMADAN ...	144	137	7	144	137	7	136	7	1	...	...	...	...	...	...
62		0—10 ...	1	1	...	1	1	...	1	...	...	...	...	...	...	...	...
63		10—15 ...	7	7	...	7	7	...	7	...	...	...	...	...	...	...	...
64		15—20 ...	24	24	...	24	24	...	23	...	1	...	...	...	...	...	...
65		20 and over ...	112	105	7	112	105	7	105	7	...	...	...	...	...	...	...

EDUCATION (BY RELIGION AND AGE).

DISTRICTS AND STATES—*continued.*

LITERATE IN VERNACULAR.																				
HINDI.				PUNJABI.														OTHERS.		
Lande or Mahajani.		*Others.*		*Total.*			*Gurmukhi.*		*Lande or Mahajani.*		*Nagri.*		*Tankri.*		*Persian.*					
Males.	Females.	Males.	Females.	Persons.	Males.	Females.	Males.	Females.	Males.	Females.	Males.	Females.	Males.	Females.	Males.	Females.	Persons.	Males.	Females.	Serial No.
18	19	20	21	22	23	24	25	26	27	28	29	30	31	32	33	34	35	36	37	
...	21	...	...	11,803	11,491	312	252	174	10,937	24	302	114	...	...	...	...	...	...	...	1
...	...	...	...	90	75	15	1	5	74	2	...	8	...	...	...	...	...	...	...	2
...	3	...	...	582	533	49	11	20	506	1	16	28	...	...	...	...	...	...	...	3
...	3	...	...	1,070	1,022	48	26	26	981	10	15	12	...	...	...	...	...	...	...	4
...	15	...	...	10,061	9,861	200	214	123	9,376	11	271	66	...	...	...	...	...	...	...	5
...	...	...	...	561	505	56	100	46	401	3	4	7	...	...	...	...	...	...	...	6
...	...	...	...	14	9	5	3	1	5	1	1	3	...	...	...	...	...	...	...	7
...	...	...	...	40	31	9	8	8	20	...	3	1	...	...	...	...	...	...	...	8
...	...	...	...	60	49	11	9	9	40	2	...	...	...	...	...	...	...	...	...	9
...	...	...	...	447	416	31	80	28	336	...	...	3	...	...	...	...	...	...	...	10
...	...	...	...	98	96	2	2	...	94	2	...	...	...	...	...	...	1	1	...	11
...	...	...	...	...	...	...	...	...	...	...	...	...	...	...	...	...	...	...	...	12
...	...	...	...	1	1	...	...	...	1	...	...	...	...	...	...	...	...	...	...	13
...	...	...	...	6	6	...	1	...	5	...	...	...	...	...	...	...	...	...	...	14
...	...	...	...	91	89	2	1	...	88	2	...	...	...	...	...	...	1	1	...	15
6,059	75	...	...	1,522	1,487	35	32	27	1,439	8	16	...	...	...	...	...	...	...	...	16
36	5	...	...	3	1	2	1	1	...	1	...	...	...	...	...	...	...	...	...	17
284	12	...	...	63	55	8	2	7	53	1	...	...	...	...	...	...	...	...	...	18
507	12	...	...	159	154	5	2	4	150	1	2	...	...	...	...	...	...	...	...	19
5,232	46	...	...	1,297	1,277	20	27	15	1,236	5	14	...	...	...	...	...	...	...	...	20
5,953	74	...	...	1,486	1,456	30	13	22	1,427	8	16	...	...	...	...	...	...	...	...	21
32	5	...	...	2	...	2	...	1	...	1	...	...	...	...	...	...	...	...	...	22
279	12	...	...	60	53	7	1	6	52	1	...	...	...	...	...	...	...	...	...	23
499	12	...	...	154	150	4	1	3	147	1	2	...	...	...	...	...	...	...	...	24
5,143	45	...	...	1,270	1,253	17	11	12	1,228	5	14	...	...	...	...	...	...	...	...	25
38	1	...	...	27	22	5	18	5	4	...	...	...	...	...	...	...	...	...	...	26
1	...	...	...	1	1	...	1	...	...	...	...	...	...	...	...	...	...	...	...	27
3	...	...	...	3	2	1	1	1	1	...	...	...	...	...	...	...	...	...	...	28
5	...	...	...	5	4	1	1	1	3	...	...	...	...	...	...	...	...	...	...	29
29	1	...	...	18	15	3	15	3	...	...	...	...	...	...	...	...	...	...	...	30
63	...	...	...	9	9	...	1	...	8	...	...	...	...	...	...	...	...	...	...	31
2	...	...	...	...	...	...	...	...	...	...	...	...	...	...	...	...	...	...	...	32
2	...	...	...	...	...	...	...	...	...	...	...	...	...	...	...	...	...	...	...	33
3	...	...	...	...	...	...	...	...	...	...	...	...	...	...	...	...	...	...	...	34
56	...	...	...	9	9	...	1	...	8	...	...	...	...	...	...	...	...	...	...	35
64	...	...	...	...	...	...	...	...	...	...	...	...	...	...	...	...	...	...	...	36
...	...	...	...	...	...	...	...	...	...	...	...	...	...	...	...	...	...	...	...	37
8	...	...	...	...	...	...	...	...	...	...	...	...	...	...	...	...	...	...	...	38
56	...	...	...	...	...	...	...	...	...	...	...	...	...	...	...	...	...	...	...	39
...	...	...	...	...	...	...	...	...	...	...	...	...	...	...	...	...	...	...	...	40
64	...	...	...	...	...	...	...	...	...	...	...	...	...	...	...	...	...	...	...	41
...	...	...	...	...	...	...	...	...	...	...	...	...	...	...	...	...	...	...	...	42
8	...	...	...	...	...	...	...	...	...	...	...	...	...	...	...	...	...	...	...	43
56	...	...	...	...	...	...	...	...	...	...	...	...	...	...	...	...	...	...	...	44
...	...	...	...	...	...	...	...	...	...	...	...	...	...	...	...	...	...	...	...	45
...	...	...	...	...	...	...	...	...	...	...	...	...	...	...	...	...	...	...	...	46
...	...	...	...	...	...	...	...	...	...	...	...	...	...	...	...	...	...	...	...	47
...	...	...	...	...	...	...	...	...	...	...	...	...	...	...	...	...	...	...	...	48
...	...	...	...	...	...	...	...	...	...	...	...	...	...	...	...	...	...	...	...	49
...	...	...	...	...	...	...	...	...	...	...	...	...	...	...	...	...	...	...	...	50
156	2	...	...	...	...	...	...	...	...	...	...	...	...	...	...	...	...	...	...	51
1	...	...	...	...	...	...	...	...	...	...	...	...	...	...	...	...	...	...	...	52
14	...	...	...	...	...	...	...	...	...	...	...	...	...	...	...	...	...	...	...	53
20	...	...	...	...	...	...	...	...	...	...	...	...	...	...	...	...	...	...	...	54
121	2	...	...	...	...	...	...	...	...	...	...	...	...	...	...	...	...	...	...	55
156	2	...	...	...	...	...	...	...	...	...	...	...	...	...	...	...	...	...	...	56
1	...	...	...	...	...	...	...	...	...	...	...	...	...	...	...	...	...	...	...	57
14	...	...	...	...	...	...	...	...	...	...	...	...	...	...	...	...	...	...	...	58
20	...	...	...	...	...	...	...	...	...	...	...	...	...	...	...	...	...	...	...	59
121	2	...	...	...	...	...	...	...	...	...	...	...	...	...	...	...	...	...	...	60
...	...	...	...	...	...	...	...	...	...	...	...	...	...	...	...	...	...	...	...	61
...	...	...	...	...	...	...	...	...	...	...	...	...	...	...	...	...	...	...	...	62
...	...	...	...	...	...	...	...	...	...	...	...	...	...	...	...	...	...	...	...	63
...	...	...	...	...	...	...	...	...	...	...	...	...	...	...	...	...	...	...	...	64
...	...	...	...	...	...	...	...	...	...	...	...	...	...	...	...	...	...	...	...	65

APPENDIX TO IMPERIAL TABLE VIII.—

PART B.—DETAILS FOR

Serial No.	District or State.	Religion and Age.	Literate in Vernacular. Total. Persons.	Total. Males.	Total Females.	Urdu. Total. Persons.	Urdu. Total. Males.	Urdu. Total. Females.	Urdu. Persian. Males.	Urdu. Persian. Females.	Urdu. Others. Males.	Urdu. Others. Females.	Hindi. Total. Persons.	Hindi. Total. Males.	Hindi. Total. Females.	Hindi. Nagri. Males.	Hindi. Nagri. Females.
	1	2	3	4	5	6	7	8	9	10	11	12	13	14	15	16	17
1	PATAUDI.	ALL RELIGIONS ...	559	541	18	507	495	12	218	6	277	6	52	46	6	24	6
2		0—10 ...	5	4	1	5	4	1	1	1	3	...	...	...	...	...	...
3		10—15 ...	39	38	1	35	34	1	22	...	12	1	4	4	...	2	...
4		15—20 ...	49	46	3	44	44	...	24	...	20	...	5	2	3	...	3
5		20 and over ...	466	453	13	423	413	10	171	5	242	5	43	40	3	22	3
6		HINDU ...	418	406	12	388	381	7	104	1	277	6	30	25	5	9	5
7		0—10 ...	3	3	...	3	3	...	...	...	3	...	...	...	...	...	...
8		10—15 ...	29	28	1	27	26	1	14	...	12	1	2	2	...	...	...
9		15—20 ...	34	31	3	31	31	...	11	...	20	...	3	...	3	...	3
10		20 and over ...	352	344	8	327	321	6	79	1	242	5	25	23	2	9	2
11		MUHAMMADAN	112	107	5	112	107	5	107	5	...	...	...	...	...	...	...
12		0—10 ...	1	...	1	1	...	1	...	1	...	...	...	...	...	...	...
13		10—15 ...	6	6	...	6	6	...	6	...	...	...	...	...	...	...	...
14		15—20 ...	13	13	...	13	13	...	13	...	...	...	...	...	...	...	...
15		20 and over ...	92	88	4	92	88	4	88	4	...	...	...	...	...	...	...
16	KALSIA.	ALL RELIGIONS ...	1,634	1,553	81	559	549	10	479	5	70	5	812	761	51	154	26
17		0—10 ..	5	5	...	3	3	...	3	...	...	...	2	2	...	...	...
18		10—15 ...	88	83	5	36	36	...	35	...	1	...	34	30	4	8	4
19		15—20 ...	147	137	10	70	68	2	65	2	3	...	63	57	6	15	4
20		20 and over ...	1,394	1,328	66	450	442	8	376	3	66	5	713	672	41	131	18
21		HINDU ..	1,023	983	40	300	292	8	235	3	57	5	664	633	31	153	24
22		0—10 ...	5	5	...	3	3	...	3	...	...	...	2	2	...	...	...
23		10—15 ...	60	56	4	24	24	...	24	...	...	...	32	28	4	8	4
24		15—20 ...	109	104	5	45	45	...	42	...	3	...	60	56	4	15	4
25		20 and over ...	849	818	31	228	220	8	166	3	54	5	570	547	23	130	16
26		SIKH ...	353	314	39	61	61	...	49	...	12	...	97	77	20	1	2
27		0—10 ...	...	...	...	...	...	...	...	...	...	...	...	...	...	...	...
28		10—15 ...	17	16	1	3	3	...	2	...	1	...	...	...	...	...	...
29		15—20 ...	13	10	3	1	1	...	1	...	...	...	2	...	2	...	...
30		20 and over ...	323	288	35	57	57	...	46	...	11	...	95	77	18	1	2
31		MUHAMMADAN ...	232	231	1	184	183	1	183	1	...	...	39	39	...	...	...
32		0—10 ...	...	...	...	...	...	...	...	...	...	...	...	...	...	...	...
33		10—15 ...	11	11	...	9	9	...	9	...	...	...	2	2	...	...	...
34		15—20 ...	22	21	1	21	20	1	20	1	...	...	1	1	...	...	...
35		20 and over ...	199	199	...	154	154	...	154	...	...	...	36	36	...	...	...
36	NAHAN.	ALL RELIGIONS ...	3,785	3,566	219	895	860	35	860	28	...	7	2,747	2,577	170	2,188	164
37		0—10 ...	38	21	17	15	11	4	11	4	...	...	21	9	12	5	12
38		10—15 ...	181	156	25	94	91	3	91	3	...	...	78	56	22	39	20
39		15—20 ...	271	242	29	102	95	7	95	5	...	2	158	136	22	104	22
40		20 and over ...	3,295	3,147	148	684	663	21	663	16	...	5	2,490	2,376	114	2,040	110
41		HINDU ...	3,505	3,312	193	708	686	22	686	15	...	7	2,719	2,556	163	2,178	159
42		0—10 ...	30	17	13	9	7	2	7	2	...	...	19	9	10	5	10
43		10—15 ...	163	139	24	86	84	2	84	2	...	...	76	54	22	39	20
44		15—20 ...	246	219	27	83	78	5	78	3	...	2	157	135	22	103	22
45		20 and over ...	3,066	2,937	129	530	517	13	517	8	...	5	2,467	2,358	109	2,031	107
46		SIKH ...	84	72	12	22	21	1	21	1	...	...	7	2	5	2	3
47		0—10 ...	2	1	1	1	1	...	1	...	...	...	1	...	1	...	1
48		10—15 ...	3	3	...	...	...	...	...	...	...	...	...	...	...	...	...
49		15—20 ...	11	11	...	5	5	...	5	...	...	...	1	1	...	1	...
50		20 and over ...	68	57	11	16	15	1	15	1	...	...	5	1	4	1	2
51		MUHAMMADAN ...	169	157	12	149	138	11	138	11	...	...	10	9	1	8	1
52		0—10 ...	2	...	2	2	...	2	...	2	...	...	...	...	...	...	...
53		10—15 ...	11	10	1	6	5	1	5	1	...	...	...	...	...	...	...
54		15—20 ...	13	11	2	13	11	2	11	2	...	...	...	...	...	...	...
55		20 and over ...	143	136	7	128	122	6	122	6	...	...	10	9	1	8	1
56	JABBAL.	ALL RELIGIONS ...	399	370	29	131	131	...	123	...	8	...	236	207	29	207	29
57		0—10 ...	...	...	...	...	...	...	...	...	...	...	...	...	...	...	...
58		10—15 ...	1	...	1	...	...	...	...	...	...	...	1	...	1	...	1
59		15—20 ...	49	45	4	34	34	...	34	...	...	...	15	11	4	11	4
60		20 and over ...	349	325	24	97	97	...	89	...	8	...	220	196	24	196	24
61		HINDU ...	399	370	29	131	131	...	123	...	8	...	236	207	29	207	29
62		0—10 ...	...	...	...	...	...	...	...	...	...	...	...	...	...	...	...
63		10—15 ...	1	...	1	...	...	...	...	...	...	...	1	...	1	...	1
64		15—20 ...	49	45	4	34	34	...	34	...	...	...	15	11	4	11	4
65		20 and over ...	349	325	24	97	97	...	89	...	8	...	220	196	24	196	24

EDUCATION (BY RELIGION AND AGE).

DISTRICTS AND STATES—*continued.*

LITERATE IN VERNACULAR.																				
HINDI.				PUNJABI.														OTHERS.		
Lande or Mahajani.		*Others.*		*Total.*			*Gurmukhi.*		*Lande or Mahajani.*		*Nagri.*		*Tankri.*		*Persian.*					
Males.	Females.	Males.	Females.	Persons.	Males.	Females.	Males.	Females.	Males.	Females.	Males.	Females.	Males.	Females.	Males.	Females.	Persons.	Males.	Females.	Serial No.
18	19	20	21	22	23	24	25	26	27	28	29	30	31	32	33	34	35	36	37	
22	...	...	...	...	...	...	...	...	...	...	...	...	...	...	...	...	...	...	...	1
...	...	...	...	...	...	...	...	...	...	...	...	...	...	...	...	...	...	...	...	2
2	...	...	...	...	...	...	...	...	...	...	...	...	...	...	...	...	...	...	...	3
2	...	...	...	...	...	...	...	...	...	...	...	...	...	...	...	...	...	...	...	4
18	...	...	...	...	...	...	...	...	...	...	...	...	...	...	...	...	...	...	...	5
16	...	...	...	...	...	...	...	...	...	...	...	...	...	...	...	...	...	...	...	6
...	...	...	...	...	...	...	...	...	...	...	...	...	...	...	...	...	...	...	...	7
2	...	...	...	...	...	...	...	...	...	...	...	...	...	...	...	...	...	...	...	8
...	...	...	...	...	...	...	...	...	...	...	...	...	...	...	...	...	...	...	...	9
14	...	...	...	...	...	...	...	...	...	...	...	...	...	...	...	...	...	...	...	10
...	...	...	...	...	...	...	...	...	...	...	...	...	...	...	...	...	...	...	...	11
...	...	...	...	...	...	...	...	...	...	...	...	...	...	...	...	...	...	...	...	12
...	...	...	...	...	...	...	...	...	...	...	...	...	...	...	...	...	...	...	...	13
...	...	...	...	...	...	...	...	...	...	...	...	...	...	...	...	...	...	...	...	14
...	...	...	...	...	...	...	...	...	...	...	...	...	...	...	...	...	...	...	...	15
483	6	174	19	263	243	20	201	20	25	...	13	...	...	...	4	...	...	...	...	16
2	...	...	...	...	...	...	...	...	...	...	...	...	...	...	...	...	...	...	...	17
13	...	9	...	18	17	1	15	1	2	...	...	...	...	...	...	...	...	...	...	18
34	...	8	2	14	12	2	9	2	1	...	2	...	...	...	...	...	...	...	...	19
384	6	157	17	231	214	17	177	17	22	...	11	...	...	...	4	...	...	...	...	20
409	6	71	1	59	58	1	21	1	24	...	13	...	...	...	...	...	...	...	...	21
2	...	...	...	...	...	...	...	...	...	...	...	...	...	...	...	...	...	...	...	22
13	...	7	...	4	4	...	2	...	2	...	...	...	...	...	...	...	...	...	...	23
34	...	7	...	4	3	1	...	1	1	...	2	...	...	...	...	...	...	...	...	24
360	6	57	1	51	51	...	19	...	21	...	11	...	...	...	...	...	...	...	...	25
6	...	70	18	195	176	19	174	19	1	...	...	...	...	...	1	...	...	...	...	26
...	...	...	...	...	...	...	...	...	...	...	...	...	...	...	...	...	...	...	...	27
...	...	...	...	14	13	1	13	1	...	...	...	...	...	...	...	...	...	...	...	28
...	...	...	2	10	9	1	9	1	...	...	...	...	...	...	...	...	...	...	...	29
6	...	70	16	171	154	17	152	17	1	...	...	...	...	...	1	...	...	...	...	30
6	...	33	...	9	9	...	6	...	...	...	...	...	...	...	3	...	...	...	...	31
...	...	...	...	...	...	...	...	...	...	...	...	...	...	...	...	...	...	...	...	32
...	...	2	...	...	...	...	...	...	...	...	...	...	...	...	...	...	...	...	...	33
...	...	1	...	...	...	...	...	...	...	...	...	...	...	...	...	...	...	...	...	34
6	...	30	...	9	9	...	6	...	...	...	...	...	...	...	3	...	...	...	...	35
389	4	...	2	139	125	14	72	6	...	...	3	7	50	1	...	...	4	4	...	36
4	...	...	...	2	1	1	...	...	...	...	1	1	...	...	...	...	...	...	...	37
17	2	...	...	9	9	...	4	...	...	...	...	...	5	...	...	...	...	...	...	38
32	...	...	...	11	11	...	6	...	...	...	...	...	5	...	...	...	...	...	...	39
336	2	...	2	117	104	13	62	6	...	...	2	6	40	1	...	...	4	4	...	40
378	4	...	...	78	70	8	22	1	...	...	3	7	45	...	...	...	...	...	...	41
4	...	...	...	2	1	1	...	...	...	...	1	1	...	...	...	...	...	...	...	42
15	2	...	...	1	1	...	1	...	...	...	...	...	...	...	...	...	...	...	...	43
32	...	...	...	6	6	...	1	...	...	...	...	...	5	...	...	...	...	...	...	44
327	2	...	...	69	62	7	20	1	...	...	2	6	40	...	...	...	...	...	...	45
...	...	...	2	55	49	6	49	5	...	...	...	...	...	1	...	...	...	...	...	46
...	...	...	...	...	...	...	...	...	...	...	...	...	...	...	...	...	...	...	...	47
...	...	...	...	3	3	...	3	...	...	...	...	...	...	...	...	...	...	...	...	48
...	...	...	...	5	5	...	5	...	...	...	...	...	...	...	...	...	...	...	...	49
...	...	...	2	47	41	6	41	5	...	...	...	...	...	1	...	...	...	...	...	50
1	...	...	...	6	6	...	1	...	...	...	...	...	5	...	...	...	4	4	...	51
...	...	...	...	5	5	...	...	...	...	...	...	...	...	...	...	...	...	...	...	52
...	...	...	...	...	...	...	...	...	...	...	...	...	5	...	...	...	...	...	...	53
...	...	...	...	...	...	...	...	...	...	...	...	...	...	...	...	...	...	...	...	54
1	...	...	...	1	1	...	1	...	...	...	...	...	...	...	...	...	4	4	...	55
...	...	...	...	32	32	...	...	...	...	...	...	...	32	...	...	...	...	...	...	56
...	...	...	...	...	...	...	...	...	...	...	...	...	...	...	...	...	...	...	...	57
...	...	...	...	...	...	...	...	...	...	...	...	...	...	...	...	...	...	...	...	58
...	...	...	...	...	...	...	...	...	...	...	...	...	...	...	...	...	...	...	...	59
...	...	...	...	32	32	...	...	...	...	...	...	...	32	...	...	...	...	...	...	60
...	...	...	...	32	32	...	...	...	...	...	...	...	32	...	...	...	...	...	...	61
...	...	...	...	...	...	...	...	...	...	...	...	...	...	...	...	...	...	...	...	62
...	...	...	...	...	...	...	...	...	...	...	...	...	...	...	...	...	...	...	...	63
...	...	...	...	...	...	...	...	...	...	...	...	...	...	...	...	...	...	...	...	64
...	...	...	...	32	32	...	...	...	...	...	...	...	32	...	...	...	...	...	...	65

APPENDIX TO IMPERIAL TABLE VIII.—

PART B.—DETAILS FOR

Serial No.	District or State.	Religion and Age.	Literate in Vernacular. Total. Persons.	Total. Males.	Total. Females.	Urdu. Total. Persons.	Urdu. Total. Males.	Urdu. Total. Females.	Urdu. Persian. Males.	Urdu. Persian. Females.	Urdu. Others. Males.	Urdu. Others. Females.	Hindi. Total. Persons.	Hindi. Total. Males.	Hindi. Total. Females.	Hindi. Nagri. Males.	Hindi. Nagri. Females.
	1	2	3	4	5	6	7	8	9	10	11	12	13	14	15	16	17
1	Bashahr.	ALL RELIGIONS ...	2,037	1,984	53	769	762	7	757	7	5	...	976	947	29	529	25
2		0—10 ...	15	13	2	4	4	...	4	...	...	...	6	5	1	2	1
3		10—15 ...	89	88	1	59	59	...	54	...	5	...	28	27	1	23	1
4		15—20 ...	188	185	3	111	111	...	111	...	...	...	63	61	2	39	2
5		20 and over ...	1,745	1,698	47	595	588	7	588	7	...	...	879	854	25	485	21
6		HINDU ...	1,904	1,871	33	739	736	3	731	3	5	...	976	947	29	529	25
7		0—10 ...	13	12	1	4	4	...	4	...	...	...	6	5	1	2	1
8		10—15 ...	87	86	1	57	57	...	52	...	5	...	28	27	1	23	1
9		15—20 ...	182	179	3	107	107	...	107	...	...	...	63	61	2	39	2
10		20 and over ...	1,622	1,594	28	571	568	3	568	3	...	...	879	854	25	465	21
11		MUHAMMADAN ...	17	16	1	17	16	1	16	1	...	...	...	...	...	...	...
12		0—10 ...	...	...	...	...	...	...	...	...	...	...	...	...	...	...	...
13		10—15 ...	2	2	...	2	2	...	2	...	...	...	...	...	...	...	...
14		15—20 ...	3	3	...	3	3	...	3	...	...	...	...	...	...	...	...
15		20 and over ...	12	11	1	12	11	1	11	1	...	...	...	...	...	...	...
16	Keonthal.	ALL RELIGIONS ...	1,102	1,034	68	321	316	5	316	2	...	3	699	638	61	638	61
17		0—10 ...	8	3	5	3	1	2	1	...	...	2	5	2	3	2	3
18		10—15 ...	81	76	5	30	30	...	30	...	...	...	47	43	4	43	4
19		15—20 ...	122	114	8	44	43	1	43	1	...	...	73	66	7	66	7
20		20 and over ...	891	841	50	244	242	2	242	1	...	1	574	527	47	527	47
21		HINDU ...	984	922	62	215	215	...	215	...	...	...	698	637	61	637	61
22		0—10 ...	6	3	3	1	1	...	1	...	...	...	5	2	3	2	3
23		10—15 ...	72	67	5	21	21	...	21	...	...	...	47	43	4	43	4
24		15—20 ...	111	104	7	33	33	...	33	...	...	...	73	66	7	66	7
25		20 and over ...	795	748	47	160	160	...	160	...	...	...	573	526	47	526	47
26		MUHAMMADAN ...	96	94	2	95	93	2	93	2	...	...	1	1	...	1	...
27		0—10 ...	...	...	...	...	...	...	...	...	...	...	...	...	...	...	...
28		10—15 ...	7	7	...	7	7	...	7	...	...	...	...	...	...	...	...
29		15—20 ...	11	10	1	11	10	1	10	1	...	...	...	...	...	...	..
30		20 and over ...	78	77	1	77	76	1	76	1	...	...	1	1	...	1	...
31	Baghal.	ALL RELIGIONS ...	987	962	25	220	216	4	216	...	...	4	11	11	...	11	...
32		0—10 ...	...	...	...	...	...	...	...	...	...	...	...	...	...	...	...
33		10—15 ...	46	43	3	8	6	2	6	...	...	2	...	...	...	...	...
34		15—20 ...	73	70	3	13	11	2	11	...	...	2	2	2	...	2	...
35		20 and over ...	868	849	19	199	199	...	199	...	...	...	9	9	...	9	...
36		HINDU ...	973	950	23	209	205	4	205	...	...	4	11	11	...	11	...
37		0—10 ...	...	...	...	...	...	...	...	...	...	..	...	...	...	...	...
38		10—15 ...	45	43	2	8	6	2	6	...	...	2	...	...	...	...	...
39		15—20 ...	78	70	8	13	11	2	11	...	...	2	2	2	...	2	...
40		20 and over ...	855	837	18	188	188	...	188	...	...	...	9	9	...	9	...
41	Bilaspur.	ALL RELIGIONS ...	1,637	1,612	25	237	237	...	237	...	...	...	827	807	20	605	17
42		0—10 ...	6	6	...	3	3	...	3	...	...	...	3	3	...	3	...
43		10—15 ...	119	114	5	52	52	...	52	...	...	...	50	46	4	38	4
44		15—20 ...	148	143	5	58	58	...	58	...	...	...	51	48	3	34	3
45		20 and over ...	1,364	1,349	15	124	124	...	124	...	...	...	723	710	13	530	10
46		HINDU ...	1,606	1,581	25	224	224	...	224	...	...	...	826	806	20	604	17
47		0—10 ...	5	5	...	2	2	...	2	...	...	...	3	3	...	3	...
48		10—15 ...	117	112	5	51	51	...	51	...	..	...	50	46	4	38	4
49		15—20 ...	145	140	5	56	56	...	56	..	...	...	51	48	3	34	3
50		20 and over ...	1,339	1,324	15	115	115	...	115	...	...	...	732	709	13	529	10
51		MUHAMMADAN ...	8	8	...	6	6	...	6	...	...	...	...	...	...	...	...
52		0—10 ...	...	...	...	...	...	...	...	...	...	...	...	...	...	...	...
53		10—15 ...	1	1	...	1	1	...	1	...	...	...	...	...	...	...	...
54		15—20 ...	...	...	...	...	...	...	...	...	...	...	...	...	...	...	...
55		20 and over ...	7	7	...	5	5	...	5	...	...	...	...	...	...	...	...
56	Nalagarh.	ALL RELIGIONS ...	1,111	1,082	29	176	172	4	172	4	...	...	173	169	4	169	4
57		0—10 ...	...	...	...	...	...	...	...	...	...	...	...	...	...	...	...
58		10—15 ...	39	39	...	5	5	...	5	...	...	...	5	5	...	5	...
59		15—20 ...	105	95	10	33	31	2	31	2	...	...	11	9	2	9	2
60		20 and over ...	967	948	19	138	136	2	136	2	...	...	157	155	2	155	2
61		HINDU ...	915	895	20	97	97	...	97	...	...	...	122	119	3	119	3
62		0—10 ...	...	...	...	...	...	...	...	...	...	...	...	...	...	..	...
63		10—15 ...	31	31	...	5	5	...	5	...	...	...	4	4	...	4	...
64		15—20 ...	76	69	7	14	14	...	14	...	...	...	6	5	1	5	1
65		20 and over ...	808	795	13	78	78	...	78	...	...	...	112	110	2	110	2

EDUCATION (BY RELIGION AND AGE).

DISTRICTS AND STATES—*continued*.

LITERATE IN VERNACULAR.																				
HINDI.				PUNJABI.													OTHERS.			
Lande or Mahajani.		*Others.*		*Total.*			*Gurmukhi.*		*Lande or Mahajani.*		*Nagri.*		*Tankri.*		*Persian.*					
Males.	Females.	Males.	Females.	Persons.	Males.	Females.	Males.	Females.	Males.	Females.	Males.	Females.	Males.	Females.	Males.	Females.	Persons.	Males.	Females.	Serial No.
18	19	20	21	22	23	24	25	26	27	28	29	30	31	32	33	34	35	36	37	
418	4	...	...	87	86	1	3	1	83	...	...	...	...	...	...	...	205	189	16	1
3	...	...	...	...	...	...	...	...	...	...	...	...	...	...	...	...	5	4	1	2
4	...	...	...	...	...	...	...	...	...	...	...	...	...	...	...	...	2	2	...	3
22	...	...	...	...	...	...	...	...	...	...	...	...	...	...	...	...	14	13	1	4
369	4	...	...	87	86	1	3	1	83	...	...	...	...	...	...	...	184	170	14	5
418	4	...	...	84	84	...	1	...	83	...	...	...	...	...	...	...	105	104	1	6
3	...	...	...	...	...	...	...	...	...	...	...	...	...	...	...	...	3	3	...	7
4	...	...	...	...	...	...	...	...	...	...	...	...	...	...	...	...	2	2	...	8
22	...	...	...	...	...	...	...	...	...	...	...	...	...	...	...	...	12	11	1	9
389	4	...	...	84	84	...	1	...	83	...	...	...	...	...	...	...	88	88	...	10
...	...	...	...	...	...	...	...	...	...	...	...	...	...	...	...	...	...	...	...	11
...	...	...	...	...	...	...	...	...	...	...	...	...	...	...	...	...	...	...	...	12
...	...	...	...	...	...	...	...	...	...	...	...	...	...	...	...	...	...	...	...	13
...	...	...	...	...	...	...	...	...	...	...	...	...	...	...	...	...	...	...	...	14
...	...	...	...	...	...	...	...	...	...	...	...	...	...	...	...	...	...	...	...	15
...	...	...	...	82	80	2	15	2	...	...	2	...	63	...	...	...	...	...	...	16
...	...	...	...	...	...	...	...	...	...	...	...	...	...	...	...	...	...	...	...	17
...	...	...	...	4	3	1	1	1	...	...	...	...	2	...	...	...	...	...	...	18
...	...	...	...	5	5	...	1	...	...	...	...	...	4	...	...	...	...	...	...	19
...	...	...	...	73	72	1	13	1	...	...	2	...	57	...	...	...	...	...	...	20
...	...	...	...	71	70	1	7	1	...	...	...	...	63	...	...	...	...	...	...	21
...	...	...	...	...	...	...	...	...	...	...	...	...	...	...	...	...	...	...	...	22
...	...	...	...	4	3	1	1	1	...	...	...	...	2	...	...	...	...	...	...	23
...	...	...	...	5	5	...	1	...	...	...	...	...	4	...	...	...	...	...	...	24
...	...	...	...	62	62	...	5	...	...	...	...	...	57	...	...	...	...	...	...	25
...	...	...	...	...	...	...	...	...	...	...	...	...	...	...	...	...	...	...	...	26
...	...	...	...	...	...	...	...	...	...	...	...	...	...	...	...	...	...	...	...	27
...	...	...	...	...	...	...	...	...	...	...	...	...	...	...	...	...	...	...	...	28
...	...	...	...	...	...	...	...	...	...	...	...	...	...	...	...	...	...	...	...	29
...	...	...	...	...	...	...	...	...	...	...	...	...	...	...	...	...	...	...	...	30
...	...	...	...	755	735	21	2	2	733	18	...	1	...	...	...	...	...	...	...	31
...	...	...	...	...	...	...	...	...	...	...	...	...	...	...	...	...	...	...	...	32
...	...	...	...	38	37	1	...	1	37	...	...	...	...	...	...	...	...	...	...	33
...	...	...	...	58	57	1	...	...	57	1	...	...	...	...	...	...	...	...	...	34
...	...	...	...	660	641	19	2	1	639	17	...	1	...	...	...	...	...	...	...	35
...	...	...	...	753	734	19	1	...	733	18	..	1	...	...	...	...	...	...	...	36
...	...	...	...	...	...	...	...	...	...	...	...	...	...	...	...	...	...	...	...	37
...	...	...	...	37	37	...	...	...	37	...	...	...	...	...	...	...	...	...	...	38
...	...	...	...	58	57	1	...	...	57	1	...	...	...	...	...	...	...	...	...	39
...	...	...	...	658	640	18	1	...	639	17	...	1	...	...	...	...	...	...	...	40
197	3	5	...	573	568	5	166	1	3	...	53	...	346	4	...	...	...	...	...	41
...	...	...	...	...	...	..	...	...	...	...	...	...	...	...	...	...	...	...	...	42
8	..	...	..	17	16	1	6	...	...	...	...	...	10	1	...	...	...	...	...	43
13	..	1	...	39	37	2	11	1	...	...	5	...	21	1	...	...	...	...	...	44
178	3	4	...	517	515	2	149	...	3	...	48	...	315	2	...	...	...	...	...	45
197	3	5	..	556	551	5	149	1	3	...	53	...	346	4	...	...	...	...	...	46
...	...	...	...	...	...	...	...	...	...	...	...	...	...	...	...	...	...	...	...	47
8	...	...	...	13	15	1	5	...	...	...	...	...	10	1	...	...	...	...	...	48
13	...	1	...	38	36	2	10	1	...	...	5	...	21	1	...	...	...	...	...	49
176	3	4	...	502	500	2	134	...	3	...	48	...	315	2	...	...	...	...	...	50
...	...	...	...	2	2	...	2	...	...	...	...	...	...	...	...	...	...	...	...	51
...	...	...	...	...	...	...	...	...	...	...	...	...	...	...	...	...	...	...	...	52
...	...	...	...	...	...	...	...	...	...	...	...	...	...	...	...	...	...	...	...	53
...	...	...	...	...	...	...	...	...	...	...	...	...	...	...	...	...	...	...	...	54
...	...	...	...	2	2	...	2	...	...	...	...	...	...	...	...	...	...	...	...	55
...	...	...	...	762	741	21	140	6	145	...	383	15	79	...	14	...	...	...	...	56
...	...	...	...	...	...	...	...	...	...	...	...	...	...	...	...	...	...	...	...	57
...	...	...	...	29	29	...	7	...	2	...	14	...	2	...	4	...	...	...	...	58
...	...	...	...	61	55	6	12	1	8	...	26	5	4	...	10	...	...	...	...	59
...	...	...	...	672	657	15	121	5	140	...	323	10	73	...	...	...	...	...	..	60
...	...	...	..	698	679	17	83	2	142	...	388	15	71	...	14	...	...	...	...	61
...	...	...	...	...	...	...	..	...	...	...	...	...	...	...	...	...	...	...	...	62
...	...	...	...	22	22	..	...	...	2	...	14	...	2	...	4	...	...	...	...	63
...	...	..	...	56	50	6	7	1	3	...	26	5	4	...	10	...	...	...	...	64
...	...	...	...	618	607	11	82	1	137	...	323	10	65	...	...	...	...	...	..	65

APPENDIX TO IMPERIAL TABLE VIII.—
PART B.—DETAILS FOR

Serial No.	District or State.	Religion and Age.	Literate in Vernacular. Total. Persons.	Males.	Females.	Urdu. Total. Persons.	Males.	Females.	Urdu. Persian. Males.	Females.	Urdu. Others. Males.	Females.	Hindi. Total. Persons.	Males.	Females.	Hindi. Nagri. Males.	Females.
	1	2	3	4	5	6	7	8	9	10	11	12	13	14	15	16	17
1	NALAGARH.	SIKH ...	70	67	3	14	14	...	14	...	...	...	4	4	...	4	...
2		0—10 ...	...	...	...	...	...	...	...	...	...	...	...	...	...	...	...
3		10—15 ...	7	7	...	...	...	...	...	...	...	...	...	...	...	...	...
4		15—20 ...	8	8	...	3	3	...	3	...	...	...	...	...	...	...	...
5		20 and over ...	55	52	3	11	11	...	11	...	...	...	4	4	...	4	...
6		JAIN ...	59	56	3	9	8	1	8	1	...	...	42	41	1	41	1
7		0—10 ...	...	...	...	...	...	...	...	...	...	...	...	...	...	...	...
8		10—15 ...	1	1	...	...	...	...	...	...	...	...	1	1	...	1	...
9		15—20 ...	11	9	2	6	5	1	5	1	...	...	5	4	1	4	1
10		20 and over ...	47	46	1	3	3	...	3	...	...	...	36	36	...	36	...
11		MUHAMMADAN ...	63	62	1	52	51	1	51	1	...	...	5	5	...	5	...
12		0—10 ...	...	...	...	...	...	...	...	...	...	...	...	...	...	...	...
13		10—15 ...	...	...	...	...	...	...	...	...	...	...	...	...	...	...	...
14		15—20 ...	9	9	...	9	9	...	9	...	...	...	...	...	...	...	...
15		20 and over ...	54	53	1	43	42	1	42	1	...	...	5	5	...	5	...
16	SIMLA MINOR HILL STATES.	ALL RELIGIONS ...	2,474	2,332	142	520	512	8	510	8	2	...	1,843	1,710	133	1,608	133
17		0—10 ...	23	20	3	9	9	...	9	...	...	...	14	11	3	11	3
18		10—15 ...	152	138	14	69	68	1	68	1	...	...	82	69	13	58	13
19		15—20 ...	255	232	23	77	76	1	76	1	...	...	174	152	22	139	22
20		20 and over ...	2,044	1,942	102	365	359	6	357	6	2	...	1,573	1,478	95	1,400	95
21		HINDU ...	2,354	2,218	136	432	428	4	426	4	2	...	1,830	1,698	132	1,596	132
22		0—10 ...	23	20	3	9	9	...	9	...	...	...	14	11	3	11	3
23		10—15 ...	146	134	14	65	64	1	64	1	...	...	82	69	13	58	13
24		15—20 ...	248	225	23	72	71	1	71	1	...	...	174	152	22	139	22
25		20 and over ...	1,935	1,839	96	286	284	2	282	2	2	...	1,560	1,466	94	1,388	94
26		SIKH ...	39	37	2	12	12	...	12	...	...	...	8	7	1	7	1
27		0—10 ...	...	...	...	...	...	...	...	...	...	...	...	...	...	...	...
28		10—15 ...	3	3	...	3	3	...	3	...	...	...	...	...	...	...	...
29		15—20 ...	2	2	...	...	...	...	...	...	...	...	...	...	...	...	...
30		20 and over ...	34	32	2	9	9	...	9	...	...	...	8	7	1	7	1
31		MUHAMMADAN ...	74	73	1	69	68	1	68	1	...	...	5	5	...	5	...
32		0—10 ...	...	...	...	...	...	...	...	...	...	...	...	...	...	...	...
33		10—15 ...	1	1	...	1	1	...	1	...	...	...	...	...	...	...	...
34		15—20 ...	4	4	...	4	4	...	4	...	...	...	...	...	...	...	...
35		20 and over ...	69	68	1	64	63	1	63	1	...	...	5	5	...	5	...
36	MANDI.	ALL RELIGIONS ...	3,144	3,003	141	326	321	5	321	5	...	...	20	12	8	12	5
37		0—10 ...	9	7	2	1	1	...	1	...	...	...	1	1	...	1	...
38		10—15 ...	146	132	14	33	33	...	33	...	...	...	2	1	1	1	...
39		15—20 ...	272	253	19	67	65	2	65	2	...	...	1	...	1	...	1
40		20 and over ...	2,717	2,611	106	225	222	3	222	3	...	...	16	10	6	10	4
41		HINDU ...	3,088	2,949	139	283	279	4	279	4	...	...	17	10	7	10	4
42		0—10 ...	9	7	2	1	1	...	1	...	...	...	1	1	...	1	...
43		10—15 ...	145	131	14	32	32	...	32	...	...	...	2	1	1	1	...
44		15—20 ...	267	248	19	63	61	2	61	2	...	...	1	...	1	...	1
45		20 and over ...	2,667	2,563	104	187	185	2	185	2	...	...	13	8	5	8	3
46		MUHAMMADAN ...	42	41	1	37	36	1	36	1	...	...	...	...	...	...	...
47		0—10 ...	...	...	...	...	...	...	...	...	...	...	...	...	...	...	...
48		10—15 ...	1	1	...	1	1	...	1	...	...	...	...	...	...	...	...
49		15—20 ...	4	4	...	3	3	...	3	...	...	...	...	...	...	...	...
50		20 and over ...	37	36	1	33	32	1	32	1	...	...	...	...	...	...	...
51	SUKET.	ALL RELIGIONS ...	1,269	1,242	27	95	95	...	95	...	...	...	60	60	...	60	...
52		0—10 ...	4	4	...	...	...	...	...	...	...	...	...	...	...	...	...
53		10—15 ...	46	42	4	7	7	...	7	...	...	...	...	...	...	...	...
54		15—20 ...	112	107	5	13	13	...	13	...	...	...	...	...	...	...	...
55		20 and over ...	1,107	1,089	18	75	75	...	75	...	...	...	60	60	...	60	...
56		HINDU ...	1,242	1,217	25	76	76	...	76	...	...	...	60	60	...	60	...
57		0—10 ...	4	4	...	...	...	...	...	...	...	...	...	...	...	...	...
58		10—15 ...	46	42	4	7	7	...	7	...	...	...	...	...	...	...	...
59		15—20 ...	110	105	5	11	11	...	11	...	...	...	...	...	...	...	...
60		20 and over ...	1,082	1,066	16	58	58	...	58	...	...	...	60	60	...	60	...
61		MUHAMMADAN ...	18	18	...	16	16	...	16	...	...	...	...	...	...	...	...
62		0—10 ...	...	...	...	...	...	...	...	...	...	...	...	...	...	...	...
63		10—15 ...	...	...	...	...	...	...	...	...	...	...	...	...	...	...	...
64		15—20 ...	2	2	...	2	2	...	2	...	...	...	...	...	...	...	...
65		20 and over ...	16	16	...	14	14	...	14	...	...	...	...	...	...	...	...

EDUCATION (BY RELIGION AND AGE).

DISTRICTS AND STATES—*continued.*

LITERATE IN VERNACULAR.																				
HINDI.				PUNJABI.														OTHERS.		
Lande or Mahajani.		*Others.*		*Total.*			*Gurmukhi.*		*Lande or Mahajani.*		*Nagri.*		*Tankri.*		*Persian.*					
Males.	Females.	Males.	Females.	Persons.	Males.	Females.	Males.	Females.	Males.	Females.	Males.	Females.	Males.	Females.	Males.	Females.	Persons.	Males.	Females.	Serial No.
18	19	20	21	22	23	24	25	26	27	28	29	30	31	32	33	34	35	36	37	
...	...	...	...	52	49	3	49	3	...	...	...	...	...	...	...	...	...	...	...	1
...	...	...	...	...	...	...	...	...	...	...	...	...	...	...	...	...	...	...	...	2
...	...	...	...	7	7	...	7	...	...	...	...	...	...	...	...	...	...	...	...	3
...	...	...	...	5	5	...	5	...	...	...	...	...	...	...	...	...	...	...	...	4
...	...	...	...	40	37	3	37	3	...	...	...	...	...	...	...	...	...	...	...	5
...	...	...	...	8	7	1	...	1	...	...	...	...	7	...	...	...	...	...	...	6
...	...	...	...	...	...	...	...	...	...	...	...	...	...	...	...	...	...	...	...	7
...	...	...	...	...	...	...	...	...	...	...	...	...	...	...	...	...	...	...	...	8
...	...	...	...	...	...	...	...	...	...	...	...	...	...	...	...	...	...	...	...	9
...	...	...	...	8	7	1	...	1	...	...	...	...	7	...	...	...	...	...	...	10
...	...	...	...	6	6	...	2	...	3	...	...	...	1	...	...	...	...	...	...	11
...	...	...	...	...	...	...	...	...	...	...	...	...	...	...	...	...	...	...	...	12
...	...	...	...	...	...	...	...	...	...	...	...	...	...	...	...	...	...	...	...	13
...	...	...	...	...	...	...	...	...	...	...	...	...	...	...	...	...	...	...	...	14
...	...	...	...	6	6	...	2	...	3	...	...	...	1	...	...	...	...	...	...	15
97	...	5	...	107	106	1	77	1	12	...	1	...	16	...	...	...	4	4	...	16
...	...	...	...	...	...	...	...	...	...	...	...	...	...	...	...	...	...	...	...	17
11	...	...	...	1	1	...	1	...	...	...	...	...	...	...	...	...	...	...	...	18
13	...	...	...	4	4	...	4	...	...	...	...	...	...	...	...	...	...	...	...	19
78	...	5	...	102	101	1	72	1	12	...	1	...	16	...	...	...	4	4	...	20
97	...	5	...	88	88	...	59	...	12	...	1	...	16	...	...	...	4	4	...	21
...	...	...	...	...	...	...	...	...	...	...	...	...	...	...	...	...	...	...	...	22
11	...	...	...	1	1	...	1	...	...	...	...	...	...	...	...	...	...	...	...	23
13	...	...	...	2	2	...	2	...	...	...	...	...	...	...	...	...	...	...	...	24
78	...	5	...	85	85	...	56	...	12	...	1	...	16	...	...	...	4	4	...	25
...	...	...	...	19	18	1	18	1	...	...	...	...	...	...	...	...	...	...	...	26
...	...	...	...	...	...	...	...	...	...	...	...	...	...	...	...	...	...	...	...	27
...	...	...	...	...	...	...	...	...	...	...	...	...	...	...	...	...	...	...	...	28
...	...	...	...	2	2	...	2	...	...	...	...	...	...	...	...	...	...	...	...	29
...	...	...	...	17	16	1	16	1	...	...	...	...	...	...	...	...	...	...	...	30
...	...	...	...	...	...	...	...	...	...	...	...	...	...	...	...	...	...	...	...	31
...	...	...	...	...	...	...	...	...	...	...	...	...	...	...	...	...	...	...	...	32
...	...	...	...	...	...	...	...	...	...	...	...	...	...	...	...	...	...	...	...	33
...	...	...	...	...	...	...	...	...	...	...	...	...	...	...	...	...	...	...	...	34
...	...	...	...	...	...	...	...	...	...	...	...	...	...	...	...	...	...	...	...	35
...	8	...	...	2,797	2,669	128	51	...	16	...	425	36	2,177	92	...	...	1	1	...	36
...	...	...	...	7	5	2	...	...	...	...	...	2	5	...	...	...	...	...	...	37
...	1	...	...	111	98	13	...	...	1	...	23	3	74	10	...	...	...	...	...	38
...	...	...	...	203	187	16	2	...	1	...	29	6	155	10	...	...	1	1	...	39
...	2	...	...	2,476	2,379	97	49	...	14	...	373	25	1,943	72	...	...	...	...	...	40
...	8	...	...	2,788	2,660	128	46	...	16	...	425	36	2,173	92	...	...	...	...	...	41
...	...	...	...	7	5	2	...	...	...	...	...	2	5	...	...	...	...	...	...	42
...	1	...	...	111	98	13	...	...	1	...	23	3	74	10	...	...	...	...	...	43
...	...	...	...	203	187	16	2	...	1	...	29	6	155	10	...	...	...	...	...	44
...	2	...	...	2,487	2,370	97	44	...	14	...	373	25	1,939	72	...	...	...	...	...	45
...	...	...	...	4	4	...	...	...	...	...	...	...	4	...	...	...	1	1	...	46
...	...	...	...	...	...	...	...	...	...	...	...	...	...	...	...	...	...	...	...	47
...	...	...	...	...	...	...	...	...	...	...	...	...	...	...	...	...	...	...	...	48
...	...	...	...	...	...	...	...	...	...	...	...	...	...	...	...	...	1	1	...	49
...	...	...	...	4	4	...	...	...	...	...	...	...	4	...	...	...	...	...	...	50
...	...	...	...	1,114	1,087	27	11	2	4	...	428	...	644	25	...	...	...	...	...	51
...	...	...	...	4	4	...	...	...	...	...	4	...	...	...	...	...	...	...	...	52
...	...	...	...	89	35	4	...	...	...	...	19	...	16	4	...	...	...	...	...	53
...	...	...	...	99	94	5	...	...	...	...	47	...	47	5	...	...	...	...	...	54
...	...	...	...	972	954	18	11	2	4	...	358	...	581	16	...	...	...	...	...	55
...	...	...	...	1,106	1,081	25	8	...	3	...	428	...	642	25	...	...	...	...	...	56
...	...	...	...	4	4	...	...	...	...	...	4	...	...	...	...	...	...	...	...	57
...	...	...	...	89	35	4	...	...	...	...	19	...	16	4	...	...	...	...	...	58
...	...	...	...	99	94	5	...	...	...	...	47	...	47	5	...	...	...	...	...	59
...	...	...	...	964	948	16	8	...	3	...	358	...	579	16	...	...	...	...	...	60
...	...	...	...	2	2	...	...	...	...	...	...	...	2	...	...	...	...	...	...	61
...	...	...	...	...	...	...	...	...	...	...	...	...	...	...	...	...	...	...	...	62
...	...	...	...	...	...	...	...	...	...	...	...	...	...	...	...	...	...	...	...	63
...	...	...	...	...	...	...	...	...	...	...	...	...	...	...	...	...	...	...	...	64
...	...	...	...	2	2	...	...	...	...	...	...	...	2	...	...	...	...	...	...	65

APPENDIX TO IMPERIAL TABLE VIII.—
PART B.—DETAILS FOR

Serial No.	District or State.	Religion and Age.	Literate in Vernacular. Total. Persons.	Total. Males.	Total. Females.	Urdu. Total. Persons.	Urdu. Total. Males.	Urdu. Total. Females.	Urdu. Persian. Males.	Urdu. Persian. Females.	Urdu. Others. Males.	Urdu. Others. Females.	Hindi. Total. Persons.	Hindi. Total. Males.	Hindi. Total. Females.	Hindi. Nagri. Males.	Hindi. Nagri. Females.
	1	2	3	4	5	6	7	8	9	10	11	12	13	14	15	16	17
1	KAPURTHALA.	ALL RELIGIONS ...	10,462	9,853	609	5,596	5,425	171	5,424	170	1	1	433	331	102	289	102
2		0—10 ...	153	119	34	90	84	6	84	6	...	...	9	2	7	2	7
3		10—15 ...	962	803	79	687	666	21	666	21	...	...	26	15	11	15	11
4		15—20 ...	1,206	1,113	93	764	733	31	733	31	...	...	69	53	16	48	16
5		20 and over ...	8,121	7,718	403	4,055	3,942	113	3,941	112	1	1	329	261	68	224	68
6		HINDU ...	4,952	4,683	269	2,225	2,199	26	2,198	26	1	...	423	323	100	288	100
7		0—10 ...	70	54	16	40	40	...	40	...	..	...	9	2	7	2	7
8		10—15 ...	471	433	38	317	314	3	314	3	...	...	25	15	10	15	10
9		15—20 ...	590	551	39	321	318	3	318	3	...	...	69	53	16	48	16
10		20 and over ...	3,821	3,645	176	1,547	1,527	20	1,526	20	1	...	320	253	67	221	67
11		SIKH ...	2,716	2,506	210	701	682	19	682	19	...	...	6	5	1	2	1
12		0—10 ...	51	38	13	19	18	1	18	1	...	...	...	...	...	...	...
13		10—15 ...	258	222	26	122	118	4	118	4	...	...	1	...	1	...	1
14		15—20 ...	271	243	28	113	111	2	111	2	...	...	...	...	...	...	...
15		20 and over ...	2,136	1,993	143	447	435	12	435	12	...	...	5	5	...	2	...
16		MUHAMMADAN ...	2,715	2,593	122	2,641	2,519	122	2,519	122	...	...	...	...	...	...	...
17		0—10 ...	32	27	5	31	26	5	26	5	...	...	...	...	...	...	...
18		10—15 ...	248	234	14	244	230	14	230	14	...	...	...	...	...	...	...
19		15—20 ...	337	312	25	325	300	25	300	25	...	...	...	...	...	...	...
20		20 and over ...	2,098	2,020	78	2,041	1,963	78	1,963	78	...	...	...	...	...	...	...
21	MALER KOTLA.	ALL RELIGIONS ...	3,386	3,200	186	1,420	1,309	111	1,286	110	23	1	408	396	12	71	1
22		0—10 ...	40	35	5	29	25	4	25	4	...	...	4	4	...	...	...
23		10—15 ...	161	161	20	99	86	13	86	13	...	...	9	7	2	1	1
24		15—20 ...	403	373	30	216	199	17	199	17	...	...	40	37	3	9	...
25		20 and over ...	2,762	2,681	131	1,076	999	77	976	76	23	1	355	348	7	61	...
26		HINDU ...	1,455	1,402	53	364	356	8	343	8	13	...	275	269	6	63	...
27		0—10 ...	18	18	...	11	11	...	11	...	...	...	4	4	...	...	...
28		10—15 ...	73	68	5	31	31	...	31	...	...	...	5	4	1	1	...
29		15—20 ...	181	167	14	73	69	4	69	4	...	...	26	24	2	8	...
30		20 and over ...	1,183	1,149	34	249	245	4	232	4	13	...	240	237	3	54	...
31		SIKH ...	641	625	16	67	67	...	59	...	8	...	...	...	...	...	...
32		0—10 ...	4	3	1	...	...	...	...	...	...	...	...	...	...	...	...
33		10—15 ...	39	38	1	5	5	...	5	...	...	...	...	...	...	...	...
34		15—20 ...	53	52	1	6	6	...	6	...	...	...	...	...	...	...	...
35		20 and over ...	545	532	13	56	56	...	48	...	8	...	...	...	...	...	...
36		JAIN ...	276	264	12	36	36	...	35	...	1	...	128	122	6	4	1
37		0—10 ...	...	...	...	...	...	...	...	...	...	...	...	...	...	...	...
38		10—15 ...	9	8	1	4	4	...	4	...	...	...	4	3	1	...	1
39		15—20 ...	29	27	2	6	6	...	6	...	...	...	13	12	1	...	...
40		20 and over ...	238	229	9	26	26	...	25	...	1	...	111	107	4	4	...
41		MUHAMMADAN ...	1,014	909	105	953	850	103	849	102	1	1	5	5	...	4	...
42		0—10 ...	18	14	4	18	14	4	14	4	...	...	...	...	...	...	...
43		10—15 ...	60	47	13	59	46	13	46	13	...	...	...	...	...	...	...
44		15—20 ...	140	127	13	131	118	13	118	13	...	...	1	1	...	1	...
45		20 and over ...	796	721	75	745	672	73	671	72	1	1	4	4	...	3	...
46	FARIDKOT.	ALL RELIGIONS ...	5,016	4,961	55	1,240	1,239	1	1,239	1	...	...	606	589	17	149	17
47		0—10 ...	4	1	3	...	...	...	...	...	...	...	2	...	2	...	2
48		10—15 ...	228	224	4	100	100	...	100	...	...	...	24	22	2	5	2
49		15—20 ...	569	557	12	168	168	...	168	...	...	...	88	85	3	15	3
50		20 and over ...	4,215	4,179	36	972	971	1	971	1	...	...	492	482	10	129	10
51		HINDU ...	2,624	2,594	30	503	502	1	502	1	...	...	572	559	13	147	13
52		0—10 ...	3	...	3	...	...	...	...	...	...	...	2	...	2	...	2
53		10—15 ...	125	121	4	35	35	...	35	...	...	...	24	22	2	5	2
54		15—20 ...	308	303	5	56	56	...	56	...	...	...	80	77	3	15	3
55		20 and over ...	2,188	2,170	18	412	411	1	411	1	...	...	466	460	6	127	6
56		SIKH ...	1,812	1,791	21	332	332	...	332	...	...	...	8	8	...	1	...
57		0—10 ...	1	1	...	...	...	...	...	...	...	...	...	...	...	...	...
58		10—15 ...	95	95	...	59	59	...	59	...	...	...	...	...	...	...	...
59		15—20 ...	188	181	7	65	65	...	65	...	...	...	3	3	...	...	...
60		20 and over ...	1,528	1,514	14	208	208	...	208	...	...	...	5	5	...	1	...
61		JAIN ...	140	136	4	20	20	...	20	...	...	...	21	17	4	...	4
62		0—10 ...	...	...	...	...	...	...	...	...	...	...	...	...	...	...	...
63		10—15 ...	2	2	...	...	...	...	...	...	...	...	...	...	...	...	...
64		15—20 ...	22	22	...	1	1	...	1	...	...	...	4	4	...	...	...
65		20 and over ...	116	112	4	19	19	...	19	...	...	...	17	13	4	...	4

EDUCATION (BY RELIGION AND AGE).

DISTRICTS AND STATES—*continued.*

LITERATE IN VERNACULAR.																				
HINDI.				PUNJABI.													OTHERS.			
Lande or Mahajani.		*Others.*		*Total.*			*Gurmukhi.*		*Lande or Mahajani.*		*Nagri.*		*Tankri*		*Persian.*					
Males.	Females.	Males.	Females.	Persons.	Males.	Females.	Males.	Females.	Males.	Females.	Males.	Females.	Males.	Females.	Males.	Females.	Persons.	Males.	Females.	Serial No.
18	19	20	21	22	23	24	25	26	27	28	29	30	31	32	33	34	35	36	37	
42	...	...	...	4,428	4,093	335	2,531	276	1,219	7	319	50	...	...	24	2	5	4	1	1
...	...	...	...	54	33	21	25	20	5	...	3	1	...	...	...	...	...	...	...	2
...	...	...	...	269	222	47	129	34	70	2	21	11	...	...	2	...	...	...	...	3
5	...	...	...	373	327	46	180	34	96	2	42	10	...	...	9	...	...	...	...	4
37	...	...	...	3,732	3,511	221	2,197	188	1,048	3	253	28	...	...	13	2	5	4	1	5
37	...	...	...	2,303	2,160	143	750	88	1,074	6	316	47	...	...	20	2	1	1	...	6
...	...	...	...	21	12	9	4	8	5	...	3	1	...	...	...	...	...	...	...	7
...	...	...	...	129	104	25	19	14	62	1	21	10	...	...	2	...	...	...	...	8
5	...	...	...	200	180	20	49	9	84	2	42	9	...	...	5	...	...	...	...	9
32	...	...	...	1,953	1,864	89	678	57	923	8	250	27	...	...	13	2	1	1	...	10
3	...	...	...	2,009	1,819	190	1,738	187	80	1	1	2	...	...	...	...	...	...	...	11
...	...	...	...	32	20	12	20	12	...	...	...	...	...	...	...	...	...	...	...	12
...	...	...	...	135	114	21	107	20	7	1	...	...	...	...	...	...	...	...	...	13
...	...	...	...	158	132	26	125	25	7	...	...	1	...	...	...	...	...	...	...	14
3	...	...	...	1,684	1,553	131	1,486	130	66	...	1	1	...	...	...	...	...	...	...	15
...	...	...	...	71	71	...	43	...	23	...	1	...	...	...	4	...	3	3	...	16
...	...	...	...	1	1	...	1	...	...	...	...	...	...	...	...	...	...	...	...	17
...	...	...	...	4	4	...	3	...	1	...	...	...	...	...	...	...	...	...	...	18
...	...	...	...	12	12	...	6	...	2	...	...	...	...	...	4	...	...	...	...	19
...	...	...	...	54	54	...	33	...	20	...	1	...	...	...	...	...	3	3	...	20
325	11	...	...	1,558	1,495	63	788	30	583	13	151	20	...	...	23	...	...	...	...	21
4	...	...	...	7	6	1	3	1	1	...	2	...	...	...	...	...	...	...	...	22
6	1	...	...	73	68	5	45	3	15	...	7	2	...	...	1	...	...	...	...	23
28	3	...	...	147	137	10	72	4	61	2	3	4	...	...	1	...	...	...	...	24
287	7	...	...	1,331	1,284	47	668	22	456	11	139	14	...	...	21	...	...	...	...	25
206	6	...	...	816	777	39	246	16	371	8	144	15	...	...	16	...	...	...	...	26
4	...	...	...	3	3	...	...	...	1	...	2	...	...	...	...	...	...	...	...	27
3	1	...	...	37	33	4	11	2	14	...	7	2	...	...	1	...	...	...	...	28
16	2	...	...	82	74	8	24	4	47	...	3	4	...	...	...	...	...	...	...	29
183	3	...	...	694	667	27	211	10	309	8	132	9	...	...	15	...	...	...	...	30
...	...	...	...	574	558	16	521	13	35	3	2	...	...	...	...	...	...	...	...	31
...	...	...	...	4	3	1	3	1	...	...	...	...	...	...	...	...	...	...	...	32
...	...	...	...	34	33	1	32	1	1	...	...	...	...	...	...	...	...	...	...	33
...	...	...	...	47	46	1	45	...	1	1	...	...	...	...	...	...	...	...	...	34
...	...	...	...	489	476	13	441	11	38	2	2	...	...	...	...	...	...	...	...	35
118	5	...	...	112	106	6	2	1	101	1	3	4	...	...	...	...	...	...	...	36
...	...	...	...	...	...	...	...	...	...	...	...	...	...	...	...	...	...	...	...	37
3	...	...	...	1	1	...	1	...	...	...	...	...	...	...	...	...	...	...	...	38
12	1	...	...	10	9	1	...	...	9	1	...	...	...	...	...	...	...	...	...	39
103	4	...	...	101	96	5	1	1	92	...	3	4	...	...	...	...	...	...	...	40
1	...	...	...	56	54	2	19	...	26	1	2	1	...	...	7	...	...	...	...	41
...	...	...	...	...	...	...	...	...	...	...	...	...	...	...	...	...	...	...	...	42
...	...	...	...	1	1	...	1	...	...	...	...	...	...	...	...	...	...	...	...	43
...	...	...	...	8	8	...	3	...	4	...	...	...	...	...	1	...	...	...	...	44
1	...	...	...	47	45	2	15	...	22	1	2	1	...	...	6	...	...	...	...	45
440	...	...	...	3,163	3,126	37	1,774	36	1,193	...	152	1	...	...	7	...	7	7	...	46
...	...	...	...	2	1	1	1	1	...	...	...	...	...	...	...	...	...	...	...	47
17	...	...	...	104	102	2	48	2	49	...	5	...	...	...	...	...	...	...	...	48
70	...	...	...	312	303	9	145	9	148	...	10	...	...	...	...	...	1	1	...	49
353	...	...	...	2,745	2,720	25	1,580	24	996	...	137	1	...	...	7	...	6	6	...	50
412	...	...	...	1,549	1,533	16	370	15	1,013	...	147	1	...	...	3	...	...	...	...	51
...	...	...	...	1	...	1	...	1	...	...	...	...	...	...	...	...	...	...	...	52
17	...	...	...	66	64	2	15	2	45	...	4	...	...	...	...	...	...	...	...	53
62	...	...	...	172	170	2	88	2	123	...	9	...	...	...	...	...	...	...	...	54
333	...	...	...	1,310	1,299	11	317	10	845	...	134	1	...	...	3	...	...	...	...	55
7	...	...	...	1,472	1,451	21	1,361	21	82	...	4	...	...	...	4	...	...	...	...	56
...	...	...	...	1	1	...	1	...	...	...	...	...	...	...	...	...	...	...	...	57
...	...	...	...	36	36	...	33	...	2	...	1	...	...	...	...	...	...	...	...	58
3	...	...	...	120	113	7	102	7	11	...	...	...	...	...	...	...	...	...	...	59
4	...	...	...	1,315	1,301	14	1,225	14	69	...	3	...	...	...	4	...	...	...	...	60
17	...	...	...	92	92	...	2	...	89	...	1	...	...	...	...	...	7	7	...	61
...	...	...	...	...	...	...	...	...	...	...	...	...	...	...	...	...	...	...	...	62
...	...	...	...	2	2	...	...	...	2	...	...	...	...	...	...	...	...	...	...	63
4	...	...	...	16	16	...	1	...	14	...	1	...	...	...	...	...	1	1	...	64
13	...	...	...	74	74	...	1	...	73	...	...	...	...	...	...	...	6	6	...	65

APPENDIX TO IMPERIAL TABLE VIII.—
PART B.—DETAILS FOR

Serial No.	District or State.	Religion and Age.	Literate in Vernacular. Total. Persons.	Total. Males.	Total. Females.	Urdu. Total. Persons.	Urdu. Total. Males.	Urdu. Total. Females.	Urdu. Persian. Males.	Urdu. Persian. Females.	Urdu. Others. Males.	Urdu. Others. Females.	Hindi. Total. Persons.	Hindi. Total. Males.	Hindi. Total. Females.	Hindi. Nagri. Males.	Hindi. Nagri. Females.
	1	2	3	4	5	6	7	8	9	10	11	12	13	14	15	16	17
1	FARIDKOT.	MUHAMMADAN ...	440	440	...	385	385	...	385	...	...	...	5	5	...	1	...
2		0—10 ...	...	...	...	...	...	...	...	...	...	...	...	...	...	...	...
3		10—15 ...	6	6	...	6	6	...	6	...	...	...	...	...	...	...	...
4		15—20 ...	51	51	...	46	46	...	46	...	...	...	1	1	...	...	...
5		20 and over ...	383	383	...	333	333	...	333	...	...	...	4	4	...	1	...
6	CHAMBA.	ALL RELIGIONS ...	2,479	2,403	76	454	434	20	434	20	...	...	784	748	36	652	36
7		0—10 ...	...	...	...	...	...	...	...	...	...	...	...	...	...	...	...
8		10—15 ...	104	99	5	38	36	2	36	2	...	...	29	26	3	26	3
9		15—20 ...	174	160	14	69	65	4	65	4	...	...	39	33	6	32	6
10		20 and over ...	2,201	2,144	57	347	333	14	333	14	...	...	716	689	27	594	27
11		HINDU ...	2,256	2,202	54	297	293	4	293	4	...	...	770	734	36	638	36
12		0—10 ...	...	...	...	...	...	...	...	...	...	...	...	...	...	...	...
13		10—15 ...	92	89	3	26	26	...	26	...	...	...	29	26	3	26	3
14		15—20 ...	149	140	9	47	46	1	46	1	...	...	39	33	6	32	6
15		20 and over ...	2,015	1,973	42	224	221	3	221	3	...	...	702	675	27	580	27
16		MUHAMMADAN ...	151	144	7	124	117	7	117	7	...	...	4	4	...	4	...
17		0—10 ...	...	...	...	...	...	...	...	...	...	...	...	...	...	...	...
18		10—15 ...	9	8	1	9	8	1	8	1	...	...	...	...	...	...	...
19		15—20 ...	20	17	3	19	16	3	16	3	...	...	...	...	...	...	...
20		20 and over ...	122	119	3	96	93	3	93	3	...	...	4	4	...	4	...
21	PATIALA.	ALL RELIGIONS ...	51,100	49,053	2,047	14,660	14,246	414	14,168	404	78	10	5,355	5,118	237	3,732	232
22		0—10 ...	344	278	66	128	122	6	121	6	1	—	43	33	10	18	10
23		10—15 ...	2,598	2,395	203	1,177	1,146	31	1,144	31	2	...	293	259	34	170	34
24		15—20 ...	5,687	5,344	343	2,180	2,111	69	2,109	67	2	2	557	508	49	361	48
25		20 and over ...	42,471	41,036	1,435	11,175	10,867	308	10,794	300	73	8	4,462	4,318	144	3,183	140
26		HINDU ...	29,757	28,883	874	7,061	6,958	103	6,890	97	68	6	5,036	4,803	233	3,564	228
27		0—10 ...	168	143	25	68	68	...	67	...	1	...	41	31	10	17	10
28		10—15 ...	1,553	1,446	107	605	598	7	596	7	2	...	269	237	32	163	32
29		15—20 ...	3,532	3,366	166	1,094	1,080	14	1,078	13	2	1	502	453	49	338	48
30		20 and over ...	24,504	23,928	576	5,294	5,212	82	5,149	77	63	5	4,224	4,082	142	3,046	138
31		SIKH ...	14,567	13,729	838	2,193	2,178	15	2,168	15	10	...	134	133	1	79	1
32		0—10 ...	139	105	34	28	28	...	28	...	...	...	...	...	...	...	...
33		10—15 ...	643	580	63	226	226	...	226	...	...	...	11	11	...	3	...
34		15—20 ...	1,344	1,221	123	401	398	3	398	3	...	...	33	33	...	10	...
35		20 and over ...	12,441	11,823	618	1,538	1,526	12	1,516	12	10	...	90	89	1	66	1
36		JAIN ...	790	774	16	112	109	3	109	2	...	1	155	152	3	69	3
37		0—10 ...	4	4	...	2	2	...	2	...	...	...	2	2	...	1	...
38		10—15 ...	55	50	5	22	21	1	21	1	...	...	13	11	2	4	2
39		15—20 ...	90	89	1	16	16	...	16	...	...	...	20	20	...	11	...
40		20 and over ...	641	631	10	72	70	2	70	1	...	1	120	119	1	53	1
41		MUHAMMADAN ...	5,862	5,584	278	5,194	4,934	260	4,934	260	...	...	29	29	...	19	...
42		0—10 ...	28	22	6	25	20	5	20	5	...	...	...	...	...	...	...
43		10—15 ...	343	317	26	320	299	21	299	21	...	...	...	...	...	...	...
44		15—20 ...	702	655	47	653	607	46	607	46	...	...	1	1	...	1	...
45		20 and over ...	4,789	4,590	199	4,196	4,008	188	4,008	188	...	...	28	28	...	18	...
46		CHRISTIAN ...	111	73	38	96	63	33	63	30	...	3	1	1	...	1	...
47		0—10 ...	5	4	1	5	4	1	4	1	...	...	...	...	...	...	...
48		10—15 ...	4	2	2	4	2	2	2	2	...	...	...	...	...	...	...
49		15—20 ...	17	11	6	14	8	6	8	5	...	1	1	1	...	1	...
50		20 and over ...	85	56	29	73	49	24	49	22	...	2	...	...	...	...	...
51	JIND.	ALL RELIGIONS ...	6,791	6,569	222	1,928	1,903	25	1,902	25	1	...	3,653	3,542	111	1,156	107
52		0—10 ...	32	22	10	9	9	...	9	...	...	...	15	10	5	5	4
53		10—15 ...	327	304	23	176	173	3	173	3	...	...	123	109	14	86	14
54		15—20 ...	774	723	51	304	296	8	296	8	...	...	383	356	27	91	27
55		20 and over ...	5,658	5,520	138	1,439	1,425	14	1,424	14	1	...	3,132	3,067	65	1,024	62
56		HINDU ...	4,732	4,616	116	1,095	1,090	5	1,090	5	...	...	3,478	3,374	104	1,135	100
57		0—10 ...	20	15	5	5	5	...	5	...	...	...	15	10	5	5	4
58		10—15 ...	230	216	14	110	110	...	110	...	...	...	117	104	13	85	13
59		15—20 ...	572	545	27	192	190	2	190	2	...	...	368	344	24	90	24
60		20 and over ...	3,910	3,840	70	788	785	3	785	3	...	...	2,978	2,916	62	1,005	59
61		SIKH ...	1,195	1,116	79	170	170	...	170	...	...	...	14	14	...	2	...
62		0—10 ...	9	4	5	1	1	...	1	...	...	...	...	...	...	...	...
63		10—15 ...	50	45	5	25	25	...	25	...	...	...	...	...	...	...	...
64		15—20 ...	106	91	15	33	33	...	33	...	...	...	...	...	...	...	...
65		20 and over ...	1,030	976	54	111	111	...	111	...	...	...	14	14	...	2	...

EDUCATION (BY RELIGION AND AGE).

DISTRICTS AND STATES—*continued.*

LITERATE IN VERNACULAR.																				
HINDI.				PUNJABI.													OTHERS.			
Lande or Mahájani.		*Others.*		*Total.*			*Gurmukhi.*		*Lande or Mahájani.*		*Nágri.*		*Tankri.*		*Persian.*					
Males.	Females.	Males.	Females.	Persons.	Males.	Females.	Males.	Females.	Males.	Females.	Males.	Females.	Males.	Females.	Males.	Females.	Persons.	Males.	Females.	Serial No.
18	19	20	21	22	23	24	25	26	27	28	29	30	31	32	33	34	35	36	37	
4	...	...	...	50	50	...	41	...	9	...	...	...	...	...	...	...	...	...	...	1
...	...	...	...	...	...	...	...	...	...	...	...	...	...	...	...	...	...	...	...	2
...	...	...	...	...	...	...	...	...	...	...	...	...	...	...	...	...	...	...	...	3
1	...	...	...	4	4	...	4	...	...	...	...	...	...	...	...	...	...	...	...	4
3	...	...	...	46	46	...	37	...	9	...	...	...	...	...	...	...	...	...	...	5
96	...	...	...	1,241	1,221	20	59	13	6	...	13	...	1,143	7	...	...	...	...	...	6
...	...	...	...	...	...	...	...	...	...	...	...	...	...	...	...	...	...	...	...	7
...	...	...	...	37	37	...	1	...	...	...	...	...	36	...	...	...	...	...	...	8
1	...	...	...	66	62	4	...	4	...	...	...	...	62	...	...	...	...	...	...	9
95	...	...	...	1,138	1,122	16	58	9	6	...	13	...	1,045	7	...	...	...	...	...	10
96	...	...	...	1,189	1,175	14	40	7	6	...	13	...	1,116	7	...	...	...	...	...	11
...	...	...	...	...	...	...	...	...	...	...	...	...	...	...	...	...	...	...	...	12
...	...	...	...	37	37	...	1	...	...	...	...	...	36	...	...	...	...	...	...	13
1	...	...	...	63	61	2	...	2	...	...	...	...	61	...	...	...	...	...	...	14
95	...	...	...	1,089	1,077	12	39	5	6	...	13	...	1,019	7	...	...	...	...	...	15
...	...	...	...	23	23	...	..	...	...	...	...	...	23	...	...	...	...	...	...	16
...	...	...	...	...	...	...	...	...	...	...	...	...	...	...	...	...	...	...	...	17
...	...	...	...	...	...	...	...	...	...	...	...	...	...	...	...	...	...	...	...	18
...	...	...	...	1	1	...	...	...	...	...	...	...	1	...	...	...	...	...	...	19
...	...	...	...	22	22	...	...	...	...	...	...	...	22	...	...	...	...	...	...	20
1,358	5	28	...	31,043	29,656	1,387	12,227	941	14,137	69	2,846	363	38	...	408	14	42	33	9	21
15	...	...	...	173	123	50	83	38	25	3	12	8	1	...	2	1	...	...	...	22
89	...	...	...	1,125	987	138	364	79	475	10	104	46	2	...	42	3	3	3	...	23
147	1	...	...	2,945	2,722	223	899	143	1,501	12	261	68	7	...	54	...	5	3	2	24
1,107	4	28	...	26,800	25,824	976	10,881	681	12,136	44	2,469	241	28	...	310	10	34	27	7	25
1,211	5	28	...	17,634	17,101	533	1,746	131	12,511	63	2,711	339	37	...	96	...	25	21	5	26
14	...	...	...	59	44	15	7	6	24	1	12	8	1	...	...	...	...	...	...	27
74	...	...	...	676	608	68	51	15	436	10	101	43	2	...	18	...	3	3	...	28
115	1	...	...	1,932	1,831	101	167	22	1,389	12	255	67	6	...	14	...	4	2	2	29
1,008	4	28	...	14,967	14,618	349	1,521	88	10,662	40	2,343	221	28	...	64	...	19	16	3	30
54	...	...	...	12,240	11,418	822	10,239	805	960	5	102	11	1	...	116	1	...	...	...	31
...	...	...	...	111	77	34	76	32	1	2	...	...	...	...	...	...	...	...	...	32
8	...	...	...	406	343	63	308	62	18	...	3	1	...	...	14	...	...	...	...	33
23	...	...	...	910	790	120	715	120	52	...	5	...	1	...	17	...	...	...	...	34
23	...	...	...	10,813	10,208	605	9,140	591	889	3	94	10	...	...	85	1	...	...	...	35
83	...	...	...	523	513	10	2	...	501	...	7	10	...	...	3	..	...	...	...	36
1	...	...	...	...	...	...	...	...	...	...	...	...	...	...	...	...	...	...	...	37
7	...	...	...	20	18	2	...	...	17	...	...	2	...	...	1	...	...	...	...	38
9	...	...	...	54	53	1	...	...	52	...	1	1	...	...	...	...	...	...	...	39
66	...	...	...	449	442	7	2	...	432	...	6	7	...	...	2	...	...	...	...	40
10	...	...	...	635	617	18	234	3	165	1	26	1	...	...	192	13	4	4	...	41
...	...	...	...	3	2	1	...	...	...	...	...	...	...	...	2	1	...	...	...	42
...	...	...	...	23	18	5	5	2	4	...	...	...	...	...	9	3	...	...	...	43
...	...	...	...	48	47	1	17	1	8	...	...	...	...	...	22	...	...	...	...	44
10	...	...	...	561	550	11	212	...	153	1	26	1	...	...	159	9	4	4	...	45
...	...	...	...	11	7	4	6	2	...	...	...	2	...	...	1	...	3	2	1	46
...	...	...	...	...	...	...	...	...	...	...	...	...	...	...	...	...	...	...	...	47
...	...	...	...	...	...	...	...	...	...	...	...	...	...	...	...	...	...	...	...	48
...	...	...	...	1	1	...	...	...	...	...	...	...	...	...	1	...	1	1	...	49
...	...	...	...	10	6	4	6	2	...	...	...	2	...	...	...	...	2	1	1	50
2,383	2	3	2	1,210	1,124	86	1,123	86	...	...	...	...	1	...	...	...	...	...	...	51
4	1	1	...	8	3	5	3	5	...	...	...	...	...	...	...	...	...	...	...	52
73	...	...	...	28	22	6	22	6	...	...	...	...	...	...	...	...	...	...	...	53
265	...	...	...	87	71	16	71	16	...	...	...	...	...	...	...	...	...	...	...	54
2,041	1	2	2	1,087	1,028	59	1,027	59	...	...	...	...	1	...	...	...	...	...	...	55
2,236	2	3	2	159	152	7	151	7	...	...	...	...	1	...	...	...	...	...	...	56
4	1	1	...	...	...	...	...	...	...	...	...	...	...	...	...	...	...	...	...	57
69	...	...	...	3	2	1	2	1	...	...	...	...	...	...	...	...	...	...	...	58
254	...	...	...	12	11	1	11	1	...	...	...	...	...	...	...	...	...	...	...	59
1,909	1	2	2	144	139	5	138	5	...	...	...	...	1	...	...	...	...	...	...	60
12	...	...	...	1,011	932	79	932	79	...	...	...	...	...	...	...	...	...	...	...	61
...	...	...	...	8	3	5	3	5	...	...	...	...	...	...	...	...	...	...	...	62
...	...	...	...	25	20	5	20	5	...	...	...	...	...	...	...	...	...	...	...	63
...	...	...	...	73	58	15	58	15	...	...	...	...	...	...	...	...	...	...	...	64
12	...	...	...	905	851	54	851	54	...	...	...	...	...	...	...	...	...	...	...	65

APPENDIX TO IMPERIAL TABLE VIII.—

PART B.—DETAILS FOR

Serial No.	District or State.	Religion and age.	Literate in Vernacular. Total. Persons.	Total. Males.	Total. Females.	Urdu. Total. Persons.	Urdu. Total. Males.	Urdu. Total. Females.	Urdu. Persian. Males.	Urdu. Persian. Females.	Urdu. Others. Males.	Urdu. Others. Females.	Hindi. Total. Persons.	Hindi. Total. Males.	Hindi. Total. Females.	Hindi. Nagri. Males.	Hindi. Nagri. Females.
	1	2	3	4	5	6	7	8	9	10	11	12	13	14	15	16	17
1	Jind.	JAIN ...	231	224	7	80	80	...	80	...	...	...	151	144	7	18	7
2		0—10 ...	1	1	...	1	1	...	1	...	...	...	...	...	...	...	...
3		10—15 ...	21	20	1	15	15	...	15	...	...	...	6	5	1	1	1
4		15—20 ...	28	25	3	14	14	...	14	...	...	...	14	11	3	1	3
5		20 and over ...	181	178	3	50	50	...	50	...	...	...	131	128	3	16	3
6		MUHAMMADAN ...	616	607	9	566	557	9	557	9	...	...	10	10	...	1	...
7		0—10 ...	2	2	...	2	2	...	2	...	...	...	...	...	...	...	...
8		10—15 ...	24	22	2	24	22	2	22	2	...	...	...	...	...	...	...
9		15—20 ...	64	62	2	61	59	2	59	2	...	...	1	1	...	...	...
10		20 and over ...	526	521	5	479	474	5	474	5	...	...	9	9	...	1	...
11		CHRISTIAN ...	17	6	11	17	6	11	5	11	1	...	...	...	...	...	...
12		0—10 ...	...	...	...	...	...	...	...	...	...	...	...	...	...	...	...
13		10—15 ...	2	1	1	2	1	1	1	1	...	...	...	...	...	...	...
14		15—20 ...	4	...	4	4	...	4	...	4	...	...	...	...	...	...	...
15		20 and over ...	11	5	6	11	5	6	4	6	1	...	...	...	...	...	...
16	Nabha.	ALL RELIGIONS ...	7,138	6,840	298	1,546	1,506	40	1,493	39	13	1	1,114	1,100	14	479	7
17		0—10 ...	43	33	10	15	10	5	10	5	...	...	5	5	...	1	...
18		10—15 ...	327	308	19	102	100	2	98	2	2	...	55	53	2	14	...
19		15—20 ...	750	711	39	198	193	5	193	5	...	...	129	126	3	42	2
20		20 and over ...	6,018	5,788	230	1,231	1,203	28	1,192	27	11	1	925	916	9	422	5
21		HINDU ...	4,393	4,298	95	901	888	13	882	13	6	...	1,080	1,066	14	474	7
22		0—10 ...	20	18	2	7	6	1	6	1	...	...	4	4	...	1	...
23		10—15 ...	202	198	4	61	61	...	61	...	...	...	55	53	2	14	...
24		15—20 ...	517	504	13	126	124	2	124	2	...	...	125	122	3	42	2
25		20 and over ...	3,654	3,578	76	707	697	10	681	10	6	...	896	887	9	417	5
26		SIKH ...	2,116	1,982	134	249	239	10	238	9	1	1	23	23	...	...	...
27		0—10 ...	16	11	5	2	1	1	1	1	...	...	...	...	...	...	...
28		10—15 ...	95	85	10	23	22	1	22	1	...	...	...	...	...	...	...
29		15—20 ...	173	154	19	34	33	1	33	1	...	...	2	2	...	...	...
30		20 and over ...	1,832	1,732	100	190	183	7	182	6	1	1	21	21	...	...	...
31		JAIN ...	67	57	10	14	14	...	14	...	...	...	...	...	...	...	...
32		0—10 ...	...	...	...	...	...	...	...	...	...	...	...	...	...	...	...
33		10—15 ...	6	6	...	2	2	...	2	...	...	...	...	...	...	...	...
34		15—20 ...	9	9	...	...	...	...	...	...	...	...	...	...	...	...	...
35		20 and over ...	52	42	10	12	12	...	12	...	...	...	...	...	...	...	...
36		MUHAMMADAN ...	562	503	59	382	365	17	359	17	6	...	11	11	...	5	...
37		0—10 ...	7	4	3	6	3	3	3	3	...	...	1	1	...	...	...
38		10—15 ...	24	19	5	16	15	1	13	1	2	...	...	...	...	...	...
39		15—20 ...	51	44	7	38	36	2	36	2	...	...	2	2	...	...	...
40		20 and over ...	480	436	44	322	311	11	307	11	4	...	8	8	...	5	...
41	Bahawalpur.	ALL RELIGIONS ...	16,255	15,671	584	6,434	6,212	222	6,208	222	4	...	6,643	6,447	196	715	67
42		0—10 ...	292	249	43	129	111	18	111	18	...	...	120	104	16	6	...
43		10—15 ...	1,038	971	62	526	503	23	501	23	2	...	340	323	17	46	9
44		15—20 ...	1,396	1,323	73	608	576	32	576	32	...	...	554	529	25	60	11
45		20 and over ...	13,534	13,128	406	5,171	5,022	149	5,020	149	2	...	5,629	5,491	138	603	47
46		HINDU ...	11,272	10,867	405	2,047	1,983	64	1,983	64	...	...	6,357	6,166	191	693	67
47		0—10 ...	189	162	27	51	46	5	46	5	...	...	97	83	14	3	...
48		10—15 ...	626	572	54	191	176	15	176	15	...	...	277	260	17	44	9
49		15—20 ...	910	860	50	239	228	11	228	11	...	...	455	430	25	57	11
50		20 and over ...	9,547	9,273	274	1,566	1,533	33	1,533	33	...	...	5,528	5,393	135	589	47
51		SIKH ...	491	471	20	132	129	3	129	3	...	...	63	62	1	7	...
52		0—10 ...	5	4	1	3	3	...	3	...	...	...	...	...	...	...	...
53		10—15 ...	17	17	...	8	8	...	8	...	...	...	...	...	...	...	...
54		15—20 ...	47	45	2	25	25	...	25	...	...	...	5	5	...	1	...
55		20 and over ...	422	405	17	96	93	3	93	3	...	...	58	57	1	6	...
56		MUHAMMADAN ...	4,452	4,306	146	4,230	4,084	146	4,084	146	...	...	208	208	...	6	...
57		0—10 ...	92	79	13	74	61	13	61	13	...	...	18	18	...	...	...
58		10—15 ...	388	380	8	325	317	8	317	8	...	...	63	63	...	2	...
59		15—20 ...	436	416	20	341	321	20	321	20	...	...	94	94	...	2	...
60		20 and over ...	3,536	3,431	105	3,490	3,385	105	3,385	105	...	...	33	33	...	2	...
61		CHRISTIAN ...	36	23	13	23	14	9	12	9	2	...	13	9	4	8	...
62		0—10 ...	6	4	2	1	1	...	1	...	...	...	6	3	2	3	...
63		10—15 ...	2	2	...	2	2	...	...	...	2	...	...	...	...	...	...
64		15—20 ...	3	2	1	3	2	1	2	1	...	...	...	...	...	...	...
65		20 and over ...	25	15	10	17	9	8	9	8	...	...	8	6	2	5	...

EDUCATION (BY RELIGION AND AGE).

DISTRICTS AND STATES—*concluded.*

LITERATE IN VERNACULAR.																				
Hindi.				Punjabi.													Others.			
Lande or Mahájani.		*Others.*		*Total.*			*Gurmukhi.*		*Lande or Mahájani.*		*Nágri.*		*Tankri.*		*Persian.*					
Males.	Females.	Males.	Females.	Persons.	Males.	Females.	Males.	Females.	Males.	Females.	Males.	Females.	Males.	Females.	Males.	Females.	Persons.	Males.	Females.	Serial No.
18	19	20	21	22	23	24	25	26	27	28	29	30	31	32	33	34	35	36	37	
126	...	...	...	...	...	...	...	...	...	...	...	...	...	...	...	...	...	...	...	1
...	...	...	...	...	...	...	...	...	...	...	...	...	...	...	...	...	...	...	...	2
4	...	...	...	...	...	...	...	...	...	...	...	...	...	...	...	...	...	...	...	3
10	...	...	...	...	...	...	...	...	...	...	...	...	...	...	...	...	...	...	...	4
112	...	...	...	...	...	...	...	...	...	...	...	...	...	...	...	...	...	...	...	5
9	...	...	...	40	40	...	40	...	...	...	...	...	...	...	...	...	...	...	...	6
...	...	...	...	...	...	...	...	...	...	...	...	...	...	...	...	...	...	...	...	7
...	...	...	...	...	...	...	...	...	...	...	...	...	...	...	...	...	...	...	...	8
1	...	...	...	2	2	...	2	...	...	...	...	...	...	...	...	...	...	...	...	9
8	...	...	...	38	38	...	38	...	...	...	...	...	...	...	...	...	...	...	...	10
...	...	...	...	...	...	...	...	...	...	...	...	...	...	...	...	...	...	...	...	11
...	...	...	...	...	...	...	...	...	...	...	...	...	...	...	...	...	...	...	...	12
...	...	...	...	...	...	...	...	...	...	...	...	...	...	...	...	...	...	...	...	13
...	...	...	...	...	...	...	...	...	...	...	...	...	...	...	...	...	...	...	...	14
...	...	...	...	...	...	...	...	...	...	...	...	...	...	...	...	...	...	...	...	15
586	7	35	...	4,478	4,234	244	2,024	182	1,580	26	249	25	225	9	156	2	...	...	...	16
4	...	...	...	23	18	5	9	4	7	1	1	...	1	...	...	...	...	...	...	17
35	2	4	...	170	155	15	73	13	55	1	10	1	8	...	9	...	...	...	...	18
77	1	7	...	423	392	31	139	25	179	1	28	2	19	2	27	1	...	...	...	19
470	4	24	...	3,862	3,669	193	1,803	140	1,339	23	210	22	197	7	120	1	...	...	...	20
557	7	35	...	2,412	2,344	68	395	21	1,444	26	235	14	193	6	77	1	...	...	...	21
3	...	...	...	9	8	1	...	...	6	1	1	...	1	...	...	...	...	...	...	22
35	2	4	...	86	84	2	14	...	49	1	10	1	7	...	4	...	...	...	...	23
73	1	7	...	286	258	8	38	3	164	1	28	2	18	2	10	...	...	...	...	24
446	4	24	...	2,051	1,994	57	343	18	1,225	23	196	11	167	4	63	1	...	...	...	25
23	...	...	...	1,844	1,720	124	1,578	121	70	...	8	2	15	...	49	1	...	...	...	26
...	...	...	...	14	10	4	9	4	1	...	...	...	...	...	...	...	...	...	...	27
...	...	...	...	72	63	9	58	9	3	...	...	...	...	...	2	...	...	...	...	28
2	...	...	...	137	119	18	99	17	5	...	...	...	...	...	15	1	...	...	...	29
21	...	...	...	1,621	1,528	93	1,412	91	61	...	8	2	15	...	32	...	...	...	...	30
...	...	...	...	53	43	10	1	2	34	...	2	8	5	...	1	...	...	...	...	31
...	...	...	...	...	...	...	...	...	...	...	...	...	...	...	...	...	...	...	...	32
...	...	...	...	4	4	...	...	...	3	...	...	...	1	...	...	...	...	...	...	33
...	...	...	...	9	9	...	...	...	7	...	...	...	1	...	1	...	...	...	...	34
...	...	...	...	40	30	10	1	2	24	...	2	8	3	...	...	...	...	...	...	35
6	...	...	...	169	127	42	50	38	32	...	4	1	12	3	29	...	...	...	...	36
1	...	...	...	...	...	...	...	...	...	...	...	...	...	...	...	...	...	...	...	37
...	...	...	...	8	4	4	1	4	...	...	...	...	...	...	3	...	...	...	...	38
2	...	...	...	11	6	5	2	5	3	...	...	...	...	...	1	...	...	...	...	39
3	...	...	...	150	117	33	47	29	29	...	4	1	12	3	25	...	...	...	...	40
5,732	129	...	...	3,166	3,000	166	649	90	2,266	75	60	1	25	...	...	...	12	12	...	41
98	16	...	...	43	34	9	10	5	24	4	...	...	...	...	...	...	...	...	...	42
277	8	...	...	167	145	22	36	12	106	10	3	...	...	...	...	...	...	...	...	43
469	14	...	...	234	218	16	59	10	153	6	6	...	...	...	...	...	...	...	...	44
4,888	91	...	...	2,722	2,603	119	544	63	1,983	55	51	1	25	...	...	...	12	12	...	45
5,473	124	...	...	2,868	2,718	150	429	79	2,204	70	60	1	25	...	...	...	...	...	...	46
80	14	...	...	41	33	8	9	4	24	4	...	...	...	...	...	...	...	...	...	47
216	8	...	...	158	136	22	27	12	106	10	3	...	...	...	...	...	...	...	...	48
373	14	...	...	216	202	14	47	9	149	5	6	...	...	...	...	...	...	...	...	49
4,804	88	...	...	2,453	2,347	106	346	54	1,925	51	51	1	25	...	...	...	...	...	...	50
55	1	...	...	294	278	16	220	11	58	5	...	...	...	...	...	...	2	2	...	51
...	...	...	...	2	1	1	1	1	...	...	...	...	...	...	...	...	...	...	...	52
...	...	...	...	9	9	...	9	...	...	...	...	...	...	...	...	...	...	...	...	53
4	...	...	...	17	15	2	12	1	3	1	...	...	...	...	...	...	...	...	...	54
51	1	...	...	266	253	13	198	9	55	4	...	...	...	...	...	...	2	2	...	55
202	...	...	...	4	4	...	...	...	4	...	...	...	...	...	...	...	10	10	...	56
18	...	...	...	...	...	...	...	...	...	...	...	...	...	...	...	...	...	...	...	57
61	...	...	...	...	...	...	...	...	...	...	...	...	...	...	...	...	...	...	...	58
92	...	...	...	1	1	...	...	...	1	...	...	...	...	...	...	...	...	...	...	59
31	...	...	...	3	3	...	...	...	3	...	...	...	...	...	...	...	10	10	...	60
1	4	...	...	...	...	...	...	...	...	...	...	...	...	...	...	...	...	...	...	61
...	2	...	...	...	...	...	...	...	...	...	...	...	...	...	...	...	...	...	...	62
...	...	...	...	...	...	...	...	...	...	...	...	...	...	...	...	...	...	...	...	63
...	...	...	...	...	...	...	...	...	...	...	...	...	...	...	...	...	...	...	...	64
1	2	...	...	...	...	...	...	...	...	...	...	...	...	...	...	...	...	...	...	65

APPENDIX TO IMPERIAL TABLE VIII.—

PART C.—DETAILS FOR

Serial No.	City or Town.	Religion and age.	Literate in Vernacular. Total. Persons.	Total. Males.	Total. Females.	Urdu. Total. Persons.	Urdu. Total. Males.	Urdu. Total. Females.	Urdu. Persian. Males.	Urdu. Persian. Females.	Urdu. Others. Males.	Urdu. Others. Females.	Hindi. Total. Persons.	Hindi. Total. Males.	Hindi. Total. Females.	Hindi. Nagri. Males.	Hindi. Nagri. Females.
	1	2	3	4	5	6	7	8	9	10	11	12	13	14	15	16	17
1	DELHI.	ALL RELIGIONS ...	26,153	23,014	3,139	14,342	12,884	1,458	12,746	1,370	138	88	10,198	8,664	1,534	6,650	1,397
2		0—10 ...	551	352	199	314	240	74	237	71	3	3	223	107	116	90	107
3		10—15 ...	2,233	1,772	461	1,454	1,223	231	1,210	221	13	10	727	512	215	402	194
4		15—20 ...	3,208	2,679	529	1,888	1,618	270	1,606	249	12	21	1,178	935	243	718	218
5		20 and over ...	20,161	18,211	1,950	10,686	9,808	888	9,693	829	110	54	8,070	7,110	960	5,433	877
6		HINDU ...	14,931	13,155	1,776	5,289	4,998	291	4,882	214	116	77	9,080	7,704	1,376	6,034	1,289
7		0—10 ...	326	198	128	114	101	13	98	11	3	2	201	93	108	79	100
8		10—15 ...	1,239	991	248	540	504	36	491	26	13	10	651	452	199	368	180
9		15—20 ...	1,810	1,518	292	682	625	57	613	41	12	16	1,065	843	222	659	201
10		20 and over ...	11,556	10,448	1,108	3,953	3,768	185	3,680	136	88	49	7,163	6,316	847	4,928	788
11		SIKH ...	1,081	1,047	34	166	144	22	139	22	5	...	20	18	2	13	2
12		0—10 ...	2	1	1	2	1	1	1	1	...	...	...	...	...	...	...
13		10—15 ...	9	6	3	7	4	3	4	3	...	...	...	...	...	...	...
14		15—20 ...	76	73	3	18	15	3	15	3	...	...	2	2	...	2	...
15		20 and over ...	994	967	27	139	124	15	119	15	5	...	18	16	2	11	2
16		JAIN ...	1,352	1,201	151	390	376	14	376	14	...	...	949	814	135	511	114
17		0—10 ...	24	15	9	6	4	2	4	2	...	...	18	11	7	11	7
18		10—15 ...	108	90	18	35	33	2	33	2	...	...	73	57	16	40	14
19		15—20 ...	143	122	21	41	38	3	38	3	...	...	99	82	17	55	17
20		20 and over ...	1,077	974	103	308	301	7	301	7	...	...	759	664	95	405	76
21		MUHAMMADAN ...	8,037	7,206	831	7,886	7,057	829	7,041	823	16	6	83	81	2	64	2
22		0—10 ...	141	115	26	140	114	26	114	25	...	1	1	1	...	...	...
23		10—15 ...	716	608	108	716	608	108	608	108	...	...	...	...	...	...	...
24		15—20 ...	1,030	898	132	1,021	889	132	889	130	...	2	1	1	...	...	...
25		20 and over ...	6,150	5,585	565	6,009	5,446	563	5,430	560	16	3	81	79	2	64	2
26		CHRISTIAN ...	700	372	328	599	302	297	301	292	1	5	61	42	19	23	10
27		0—10 ...	56	22	34	52	20	32	20	32	...	...	3	2	1	...	...
28		10—15 ...	159	76	83	156	74	82	74	82	...	...	2	2	...	...	...
29		15—20 ...	146	67	79	126	51	75	51	72	...	3	11	7	4	2	1
30		20 and over ...	339	207	132	265	157	108	156	106	1	2	45	31	14	21	9
31	LAHORE.	ALL RELIGIONS ...	42,371	34,263	8,108	29,837	25,383	4,454	25,234	4,434	149	20	7,869	5,230	2,639	3,588	2,277
32		0—10 ...	1,468	877	591	973	639	334	637	334	2	...	417	195	222	143	169
33		10—15 ...	5,215	3,379	1,836	3,537	2,416	1,121	2,414	1,116	2	5	1,190	629	561	488	491
34		15—20 ...	7,858	5,482	2,376	5,360	4,057	1,303	4,022	1,299	35	4	1,617	825	792	700	686
35		20 and over ...	27,830	24,525	3,305	19,967	18,271	1,696	18,161	1,686	110	11	4,645	3,581	1,064	2,257	931
36		HINDU ...	22,639	17,033	5,606	12,866	10,802	2,064	10,673	2,058	129	6	7,697	5,079	2,618	3,498	2,256
37		0—10 ...	807	408	399	329	183	146	183	146	...	...	414	194	220	142	167
38		10—15 ...	3,251	1,809	1,442	1,843	1,097	746	1,097	743	...	3	1,143	584	559	486	489
39		15—20 ...	5,213	3,198	2,015	3,072	2,107	965	2,078	962	29	3	1,601	813	788	690	682
40		20 and over ...	13,368	11,618	1,750	7,622	7,415	207	7,315	207	100	...	4,539	3,488	1,051	2,180	918
41		SIKH ...	4,067	3,917	150	1,602	1,477	125	1,477	120	...	5	40	40	...	...	...
42		0—10 ...	22	7	15	22	7	15	7	15	...	...	...	...	...	...	...
43		10—15 ...	345	330	15	98	90	8	90	8	...	...	40	40	...	...	...
44		15—20 ...	480	440	40	162	130	32	130	32	...	...	...	...	...	...	...
45		20 and over ...	3,220	3,140	80	1,320	1,250	70	1,250	65	...	5	...	...	...	...	...
46		JAIN ...	185	167	18	114	109	5	109	5	...	...	59	46	13	83	13
47		0—10 ...	8	5	3	6	5	1	5	1	...	...	2	...	2	...	2
48		10—15 ...	12	9	3	10	8	2	8	2	...	...	1	...	1	...	1
49		15—20 ...	39	34	5	25	24	1	24	1	...	...	14	10	4	9	4
50		20 and over ...	126	119	7	78	72	1	72	1	...	...	42	36	6	24	6
51		MUHAMMADAN ...	14,848	12,764	2,079	14,761	12,704	2,057	12,685	2,050	19	7	38	37	1	31	1
52		0—10 ...	577	419	158	575	417	158	415	158	2	...	1	1	...	1	...
53		10—15 ...	1,506	1,181	325	1,498	1,179	319	1,177	317	2	2	2	2	...	1	...
54		15—20 ...	1,976	1,721	255	1,969	1,717	252	1,711	252	6	...	1	1	...	...	...
55		20 and over ...	10,784	9,443	1,341	10,719	9,391	1,328	9,382	1,323	9	5	34	33	1	29	1
56		CHRISTIAN ...	514	305	209	479	279	200	278	198	1	2	27	20	7	20	7
57		0—10 ...	41	27	14	41	27	14	27	14	...	...	...	...	...	...	...
58		10—15 ...	86	42	44	85	42	43	42	43	...	...	1	...	1	...	1
59		15—20 ...	133	80	53	132	79	53	79	52	...	1	1	1	...	1	...
60		20 and over ...	254	156	98	221	131	90	130	89	1	1	25	19	6	19	6
61	AMRITSAR.	ALL RELIGIONS ...	17,959	16,187	1,772	8,793	8,143	650	8,140	650	3	...	4,181	3,856	825	3,813	825
62		0—10 ...	404	335	69	220	205	15	205	15	...	...	69	48	21	47	21
63		10—15 ...	1,613	1,364	249	965	839	126	839	126	...	...	266	211	55	208	55
64		15—20 ...	2,350	2,093	257	1,353	1,228	125	1,227	125	1	...	387	334	53	326	53
65		20 and over ...	13,592	12,395	1,197	6,255	5,871	384	5,869	384	2	...	3,459	3,203	196	3,232	196

EDUCATION (BY RELIGION AND AGE).

CITIES AND SELECTED TOWNS.

LITERATE IN VERNACULAR.																				
HINDI.				PUNJABI.													OTHERS.			
Lande or Mahajani.		*Others.*		*Total.*			*Gurmukhi.*		*Lande or Mahajani.*		*Nagri.*		*Tankri.*		*Persian.*					
Males.	Females.	Males.	Females.	Persons.	Males.	Females.	Males.	Females.	Males.	Females.	Males.	Females.	Males.	Females.	Males.	Females.	Persons.	Males.	Females.	Serial No.
18	19	20	21	22	23	24	25	26	27	28	29	30	31	32	33	34	35	36	37	
1,600	83	414	54	847	816	31	805	13	5	1	4	17	...	...	2	...	766	650	116	1
11	5	6	4	1	1	...	1	...	...	...	...	...	...	...	...	...	13	4	9	2
83	13	20	8	2	2	...	2	...	...	...	...	...	...	...	...	...	50	35	15	3
191	17	26	7	53	51	2	51	2	...	...	...	...	...	...	...	...	89	75	14	4
1,315	48	362	35	791	762	29	751	11	5	1	4	17	...	...	2	...	614	536	78	5
1,360	62	310	45	50	29	21	25	3	...	1	4	17	...	...	...	...	512	424	88	6
11	6	3	3	1	1	...	1	...	...	...	...	...	...	...	...	...	10	8	7	7
72	11	12	8	1	1	...	1	...	...	...	...	...	...	...	...	...	47	34	13	8
167	17	17	4	3	1	2	1	2	...	...	...	...	...	...	...	...	60	49	11	9
1,110	29	278	30	45	26	19	22	1	...	1	4	17	...	...	...	...	395	338	57	10
...	...	5	...	797	787	10	780	10	5	...	...	...	...	...	2	...	98	98	...	11
...	...	...	...	...	...	...	...	...	...	...	...	...	...	...	...	...	...	...	...	12
...	...	...	...	1	1	...	1	...	...	...	...	...	...	...	...	...	1	1	...	13
...	...	...	...	50	50	...	50	...	...	...	...	...	...	...	...	...	6	6	...	14
...	...	5	...	746	736	10	729	10	5	...	...	...	...	...	2	...	91	91	...	15
238	21	65	...	...	...	...	...	...	...	...	...	...	...	...	...	...	13	11	2	16
...	...	...	...	...	...	...	...	...	...	...	...	...	...	...	...	...	...	...	...	17
11	2	6	...	...	...	...	...	...	...	...	...	...	...	...	...	...	...	...	...	18
23	...	4	...	...	...	...	...	...	...	...	...	...	...	...	...	...	3	2	1	19
204	19	55	...	...	...	...	...	...	...	...	...	...	...	...	...	...	10	9	1	20
2	...	15	...	...	...	...	...	...	...	...	...	...	...	...	...	...	68	68	...	21
...	...	1	...	...	...	...	...	...	...	...	...	...	...	...	...	...	...	...	...	22
...	...	...	...	...	...	...	...	...	...	...	...	...	...	...	...	...	...	...	...	23
1	...	...	...	...	...	...	...	...	...	...	...	...	...	...	...	...	8	8	...	24
1	...	14	...	...	...	...	...	...	...	...	...	...	...	...	...	...	60	60	...	25
...	...	19	9	...	...	...	...	...	...	...	...	...	...	...	...	...	40	28	12	26
...	...	2	1	...	...	...	...	...	...	...	...	...	...	...	...	...	1	...	1	27
...	...	2	...	...	...	...	...	...	...	...	...	...	...	...	...	...	1	...	1	28
...	...	5	3	...	...	...	...	...	...	...	...	...	...	...	...	...	9	9	...	29
...	...	10	5	...	...	...	...	...	...	...	...	...	...	...	...	...	29	19	10	30
1,640	362	2	...	4,561	3,589	972	2,845	587	429	126	258	231	1	8	56	20	104	61	43	31
52	53	...	...	65	32	33	8	15	21	...	3	18	...	...	...	...	13	11	2	32
189	70	2	...	479	329	150	243	69	44	32	42	49	...	...	...	...	9	5	4	33
125	106	...	...	864	591	273	433	169	115	32	43	44	...	8	...	20	17	9	8	34
1,324	133	...	...	3,153	2,637	516	2,161	334	249	62	170	120	1	...	56	...	65	36	29	35
1,581	362	...	...	2,076	1,152	924	425	549	419	116	257	231	1	8	50	20	...	...	...	36
52	53	...	...	64	31	33	8	15	20	...	3	16	...	...	...	...	...	...	...	37
98	70	...	...	265	128	137	42	61	44	27	42	49	...	...	...	...	...	...	...	38
123	106	...	...	540	278	262	122	160	113	30	43	44	...	8	...	20	...	...	...	39
1,308	133	...	...	1,207	715	492	253	313	242	59	169	120	1	...	50	...	...	...	...	40
40	...	...	...	2,425	2,400	25	2,400	25	...	...	...	...	...	...	...	...	...	...	...	41
...	...	...	...	...	...	...	...	...	...	...	...	...	...	...	...	...	...	...	...	42
40	...	...	...	207	200	7	200	7	...	...	...	...	...	...	...	...	...	...	...	43
...	...	...	...	318	310	8	310	8	...	...	...	...	...	...	...	...	...	...	...	44
...	...	...	...	1,900	1,890	10	1,890	10	...	...	...	...	...	...	...	...	...	...	...	45
13	...	...	...	5	5	...	5	...	...	...	...	...	...	...	...	...	7	7	...	46
...	...	...	...	...	...	...	...	...	...	...	...	...	...	...	...	...	...	...	...	47
...	...	...	...	1	1	...	1	...	...	...	...	...	...	...	...	...	...	...	...	48
1	...	...	...	...	...	...	...	...	...	...	...	...	...	...	...	...	...	...	...	49
12	...	...	...	4	4	...	4	...	...	...	...	...	...	...	...	...	7	7	...	50
6	...	...	...	44	23	21	6	11	10	10	1	...	...	...	6	...	...	...	...	51
...	...	...	...	1	1	...	...	...	1	...	...	...	...	...	...	...	...	...	...	52
1	...	...	...	6	...	6	...	1	...	5	...	...	...	...	...	...	...	...	...	53
1	...	...	...	6	3	3	1	1	2	2	...	...	...	...	...	...	...	...	...	54
4	...	...	...	31	19	12	5	9	7	3	1	...	...	...	6	...	...	...	...	55
...	...	...	...	7	5	2	5	2	...	...	...	...	...	...	...	...	1	1	...	56
...	...	...	...	...	...	...	...	...	...	...	...	...	...	...	...	...	...	...	...	57
...	...	...	...	...	...	...	...	...	...	...	...	...	...	...	...	...	...	...	...	58
...	...	...	...	...	...	...	...	...	...	...	...	...	...	...	...	...	...	...	...	59
...	...	...	...	7	5	2	5	2	...	...	...	...	...	...	...	...	1	1	...	60
48	...	...	...	4,959	4,171	788	2,697	716	1,394	68	80	4	...	...	...	...	26	17	9	61
1	...	...	...	113	81	32	58	28	27	4	1	...	...	...	...	...	2	1	1	62
3	...	...	...	380	314	66	211	55	101	11	2	...	...	...	...	...	2	...	2	63
8	...	...	...	610	531	79	273	66	256	12	2	1	...	...	...	...	...	...	...	64
31	...	...	...	3,856	3,245	611	2,160	567	1,010	41	75	3	...	...	...	...	22	16	6	65

APPENDIX TO IMPERIAL TABLE VIII.—

PART C.—DETAILS FOR

Serial No.	City or Town.	Religion and age.	Literate in Vernacular.														
			Total.			Urdu. Total.			Urdu. Persian.		Urdu. Others.		Hindi. Total.			Hindi. Nagri.	
			Persons.	Males.	Females.	Persons.	Males.	Females.	Males.	Females.	Males.	Females.	Persons.	Males.	Females.	Males.	Females.
	1	2	3	4	5	6	7	8	9	10	11	12	13	14	15	16	17
1	AMRITSAR—concluded.	HINDU ...	8,915	8,222	693	3,027	2,929	98	2,929	98	...	...	3,662	3,354	308	3,312	308
2		0—10 ...	210	181	29	102	101	1	101	1	...	...	63	45	18	44	18
3		10—15 ...	664	560	104	253	241	12	241	12	...	...	239	186	53	188	53
4		15—20 ...	1,248	1,143	105	554	539	15	539	15	...	...	328	277	51	270	51
5		20 and over ...	6,793	6,338	455	2,118	2,048	70	2,048	70	...	...	3,032	2,846	186	2,815	186
6		SIKH ...	4,175	3,655	520	1,068	1,055	13	1,055	13	...	...	476	461	15	461	15
7		0—10 ...	94	69	25	21	21	...	21	...	...	...	6	3	3	3	3
8		10—15 ...	348	318	30	122	121	1	121	1	...	...	24	22	2	22	2
9		15—20 ...	455	412	43	156	153	3	153	3	...	...	58	56	2	56	2
10		20 and over ...	3,278	2,856	422	769	760	9	760	9	...	...	388	380	8	380	8
11		JAIN ...	149	142	7	43	42	1	42	1	...	...	26	24	2	24	2
12		0—10 ...	8	8	...	2	2	...	2	...	...	...	...	...	...	...	...
13		10—15 ...	19	19	...	13	13	...	13	...	...	...	1	1	...	1	...
14		15—20 ...	1	...	1	...	...	...	...	...	...	...	...	...	...	...	...
15		20 and over ...	126	120	6	28	27	1	27	1	...	...	25	23	2	23	2
16		MUHAMMADAN ...	4,469	4,070	399	4,432	4,036	396	4,033	396	3	...	16	16	...	15	...
17		0—10 ...	81	77	4	81	77	4	77	4	...	...	...	...	...	...	...
18		10—15 ...	533	459	74	530	456	74	456	74	...	...	2	2	...	2	...
19		15—20 ...	596	530	66	594	528	66	527	66	1	...	1	1	...	...	...
20		20 and over ...	3,259	3,004	255	3,227	2,975	252	2,973	252	2	...	13	13	...	13	...
21		CHRISTIAN ...	224	80	144	220	79	141	79	141	...	...	1	1	...	1	...
22		0—10 ...	14	4	10	14	4	10	4	10	...	...	...	...	...	...	...
23		10—15 ...	47	8	39	47	8	39	8	39	...	...	...	...	...	...	...
24		15—20 ...	50	8	42	49	8	41	8	41	...	...	...	...	...	...	...
25		20 and over ...	113	60	53	110	59	51	59	51	...	...	1	1	...	1	...
26	MULTAN.	ALL RELIGIONS ...	13,049	12,028	1,021	6,118	5,847	271	5,832	270	15	1	4,976	4,458	518	673	466
27		0—10 ...	289	198	91	122	104	18	104	18	...	...	138	80	58	15	57
28		10—15 ...	1,203	1,030	173	674	655	19	655	19	...	...	443	316	127	40	122
29		15—20 ...	1,675	1,526	149	948	915	33	909	33	6	...	569	487	82	93	72
30		20 and over ...	9,852	9,274	608	4,374	4,178	201	4,164	200	9	1	3,826	3,575	251	525	215
31		HINDU ...	8,649	7,962	687	2,699	2,647	52	2,632	52	15	...	4,776	4,272	504	627	454
32		0—10 ...	207	146	61	66	66	...	66	...	...	...	131	75	56	13	55
33		10—15 ...	865	721	144	390	387	3	387	3	...	...	427	301	126	39	121
34		15—20 ...	1,181	1,066	115	554	542	12	538	12	6	...	545	466	79	89	69
35		20 and over ...	6,396	6,029	367	1,689	1,652	37	1,643	37	9	...	3,673	3,430	243	486	209
36		SIKH ...	1,034	945	89	231	224	7	224	7	...	...	85	80	5	80	5
37		0—10 ...	28	18	10	8	7	1	7	1	...	...	3	2	1	1	1
38		10—15 ...	68	58	10	32	32	...	32	...	...	...	6	5	1	...	1
39		15—20 ...	122	116	7	41	41	...	41	...	...	...	10	9	1	2	1
40		20 and over ...	816	754	62	150	144	6	144	6	...	...	66	64	2	27	2
41		MUHAMMADAN ...	3,059	2,915	144	3,026	2,886	140	2,886	140	...	...	18	17	1	2	...
42		0—10 ...	36	28	8	35	28	7	28	7	...	...	...	...	...	...	...
43		10—15 ...	239	227	12	237	225	12	225	12	...	...	1	1	...	...	...
44		15—20 ...	338	325	13	337	324	13	324	13	...	...	...	...	...	...	...
45		20 and over ...	2,446	2,335	111	2,417	2,309	108	2,309	108	...	...	17	16	1	2	...
46		CHRISTIAN ...	149	73	76	139	67	72	67	71	...	1	8	4	4	4	4
47		0—10 ...	13	3	10	13	3	10	3	10	...	...	...	...	...	...	...
48		10—15 ...	11	7	4	11	7	4	7	4	...	...	...	...	...	...	...
49		15—20 ..	17	7	10	14	6	8	6	8	...	...	3	1	2	1	2
50		20 and over ...	108	56	52	101	51	50	51	49	...	1	5	3	2	3	2
51	RAWALPINDI.	ALL RELIGIONS ...	11,895	10,035	1,860	6,182	5,840	342	5,838	339	2	3	1,971	1,776	195	1,727	192
52		0—10 ...	394	252	142	198	176	22	176	22	...	...	29	7	22	7	22
53		10—15 ...	1,362	1,060	302	830	780	50	780	50	...	...	108	74	34	72	33
54		15—20 ...	1,920	1,610	310	1,184	1,132	52	1,132	52	...	...	177	148	29	140	29
55		20 and over ...	8,219	7,113	1,106	3,970	3,752	218	3,750	215	2	3	1,657	1,547	110	1,508	108
56		HINDU ...	6,144	5,286	858	2,497	2,439	58	2,439	58	...	...	1,758	1,585	173	1,547	170
57		0—10 ...	194	124	70	97	90	7	90	7	...	...	29	7	22	7	22
58		10—15 ...	646	512	134	392	387	5	387	5	...	...	96	64	32	62	31
59		15—20 ...	982	833	149	569	559	10	559	10	...	...	150	129	21	126	21
60		20 and over ...	4,322	3,817	505	1,439	1,403	36	1,403	36	...	...	1,483	1,385	98	1,352	96
61		SIKH ...	2,385	1,697	688	693	675	18	675	18	...	...	64	59	5	59	5
62		0—10 ...	124	66	58	26	24	2	24	2	...	...	...	...	...	...	...
63		10—15 ...	392	269	123	137	131	6	131	6	...	...	6	5	1	5	1
64		15—20 ...	442	331	111	156	154	2	154	2	...	...	10	8	2	8	2
65		20 and over ...	1,427	1,031	396	374	366	8	366	8	...	...	48	46	2	46	2

EDUCATION (BY RELIGION AND AGE).

CITIES AND SELECTED TOWNS—*continued.*

LITERATE IN VERNACULAR.																				
HINDI.				PUNJABI.													OTHERS.			
Lande or Mahajani.		Others.		Total.			Gurmukhi.		Lande or Mahajani.		Nagri.		Tankri.		Persian.					
Males.	Females.	Males.	Females.	Persons.	Males.	Females.	Males.	Females.	Males.	Females.	Males.	Females.	Males.	Females.	Males.	Females.	Persons.	Males.	Females.	Serial No.
18	19	20	21	22	23	24	25	26	27	28	29	30	31	32	33	34	35	36	37	
42	...	...	...	2,225	1,939	286	726	239	1,161	46	52	1	...	...	...	...	1	...	1	1
1	...	...	...	45	35	10	11	8	24	2	...	...	...	...	...	...	...	...	...	2
3	...	...	...	172	133	39	51	32	82	7	...	...	...	...	...	...	...	...	...	3
7	...	...	...	366	327	39	88	32	237	6	2	1	...	...	...	...	...	...	...	4
31	...	...	...	1,642	1,444	198	576	167	818	31	50	...	...	...	...	...	1	...	1	5
...	...	...	...	2,631	2,139	492	1,940	473	185	19	14	...	...	...	...	...	...	...	...	6
...	...	...	...	67	45	22	42	20	3	2	...	...	...	...	...	...	...	...	...	7
...	...	...	...	202	175	27	160	23	14	4	1	...	...	...	...	...	...	...	...	8
...	...	...	...	241	203	38	185	33	18	5	...	...	...	...	...	...	...	...	...	9
...	...	...	...	2,121	1,716	405	1,553	397	150	8	13	...	...	...	...	...	...	...	...	10
...	...	...	...	80	76	4	19	...	44	2	13	2	...	...	...	...	...	...	...	11
...	...	...	...	1	1	...	...	...	...	...	1	...	...	...	...	...	...	...	...	12
...	...	...	...	5	5	...	...	...	4	...	1	...	...	...	...	...	...	...	...	13
...	...	...	...	1	...	1	...	...	...	1	...	...	...	...	...	...	...	...	...	14
...	...	...	...	73	70	3	19	...	40	1	11	2	...	...	...	...	...	...	...	15
1	...	...	...	20	17	3	12	2	4	1	1	...	...	...	...	...	1	1	...	16
...	...	...	...	...	...	...	...	...	...	...	...	...	...	...	...	...	...	...	...	17
...	...	...	...	1	1	...	...	...	1	...	...	...	...	...	...	...	...	...	...	18
1	...	...	...	1	1	...	...	...	1	...	...	...	...	...	...	...	...	...	...	19
...	...	...	...	18	15	3	12	2	2	1	1	...	...	...	...	...	1	1	...	20
...	...	...	...	3	...	3	...	2	...	...	...	1	...	...	...	...	...	...	...	21
...	...	...	...	...	...	...	...	...	...	...	...	...	...	...	...	...	...	...	...	22
...	...	...	...	...	...	...	...	...	...	...	...	...	...	...	...	...	...	...	...	23
...	...	...	...	1	...	1	...	1	...	...	...	...	...	...	...	...	...	...	...	24
...	...	...	...	2	...	2	...	1	...	...	...	1	...	...	...	...	...	...	...	25
3,785	52	...	...	1,906	1,695	211	955	209	205	...	473	...	58	...	4	2	49	28	21	26
65	1	...	...	28	14	14	13	12	...	...	...	...	1	...	...	2	1	...	1	27
276	5	...	...	78	54	24	48	24	4	...	1	...	1	...	...	...	8	5	3	28
394	10	...	...	154	124	30	95	30	8	...	15	...	6	...	...	...	4	...	4	29
3,050	36	...	...	1,646	1,503	143	799	143	193	...	457	...	50	...	4	...	36	23	13	30
2,645	50	...	...	1,174	1,043	131	315	129	198	...	472	...	58	...	...	2	...	...	...	31
62	1	...	...	10	5	5	4	3	...	...	...	...	1	...	...	2	...	...	...	32
262	5	...	...	48	33	15	27	15	4	...	1	...	1	...	...	...	...	...	...	33
377	10	...	...	82	58	24	30	24	7	...	15	...	6	...	...	...	...	...	...	34
2,944	34	...	...	1,034	947	87	254	87	187	...	456	...	50	...	...	...	...	...	...	35
50	...	...	...	718	641	77	634	77	2	...	1	...	...	...	4	...	...	...	...	36
1	...	...	...	17	9	8	9	8	...	...	...	...	...	...	...	...	...	...	...	37
5	...	...	...	30	21	9	21	9	...	...	...	...	...	...	...	...	...	...	...	38
7	...	...	...	71	65	6	65	6	...	...	...	...	...	...	...	...	...	...	...	39
37	...	...	...	600	546	54	539	54	2	...	1	...	...	...	4	...	...	...	...	40
15	1	...	...	14	11	3	6	3	5	...	...	...	...	...	...	...	1	1	...	41
...	...	...	...	1	...	1	...	1	...	...	...	...	...	...	...	...	...	...	...	42
1	...	...	...	...	...	...	...	...	...	...	...	...	...	...	...	...	1	1	...	43
...	...	...	...	1	1	...	...	...	1	...	...	...	...	...	...	...	...	...	...	44
14	1	...	...	12	10	2	6	2	4	...	...	...	...	...	...	...	...	...	...	45
...	...	...	...	...	...	...	...	...	...	...	...	...	...	...	...	...	2	2	...	46
...	...	...	...	...	...	...	...	...	...	...	...	...	...	...	...	...	...	...	...	47
...	...	...	...	...	...	...	...	...	...	...	...	...	...	...	...	...	...	...	...	48
...	...	...	...	...	...	...	...	...	...	...	...	...	...	...	...	...	...	...	...	49
...	...	...	...	...	...	...	...	...	...	...	...	...	...	...	...	...	2	2	...	50
49	3	...	...	3,606	2,323	1,283	1,780	1,257	378	7	74	18	91	1	...	...	136	96	40	51
...	...	...	...	166	69	97	60	95	5	1	3	1	1	...	...	...	1	...	1	52
2	1	...	...	413	202	211	178	205	15	1	9	5	...	...	...	...	11	4	7	53
8	...	...	...	547	322	225	249	221	60	2	7	2	6	...	...	...	12	8	4	54
39	2	...	...	2,480	1,730	750	1,293	736	298	3	55	10	84	1	...	...	112	84	28	55
38	3	...	...	1,792	1,192	600	856	586	226	2	51	12	59	...	...	...	97	70	27	56
...	...	...	...	68	27	41	18	39	5	1	3	1	1	...	...	...	...	...	...	57
2	1	...	...	150	57	93	45	89	8	...	4	4	...	...	...	...	8	4	4	58
3	...	...	...	252	138	114	85	113	47	...	1	1	5	...	...	...	11	7	4	59
33	2	...	...	1,322	970	352	708	345	166	1	43	6	58	...	...	...	78	59	19	60
...	...	...	...	1,628	963	665	912	663	43	2	...	...	8	...	...	...	...	...	...	61
...	...	...	...	98	42	56	42	56	...	...	...	...	...	...	...	...	...	...	...	62
...	...	...	...	249	133	116	138	116	...	...	...	...	...	...	...	...	...	...	...	63
...	...	...	...	276	169	107	163	105	5	2	...	...	1	...	...	...	...	...	...	64
...	...	...	...	1,005	619	386	574	386	38	...	...	...	7	...	...	...	...	...	...	65

APPENDIX TO IMPERIAL TABLE VIII.—

PART C.—DETAILS FOR

Serial No.	City Town.	Religion and Age.	Literate in Vernacular.														
			Total.			Urdu.							Hindi.				
						Total.			Persian.		Others.		Total.			Nagri.	
			Persons.	Males.	Females.	Persons.	Males.	Females.	Males.	Females.	Males.	Females.	Persons.	Males.	Females.	Males.	Females.
	1	2	3	4	5	6	7	8	9	10	11	12	13	14	15	16	17
1	RAWALPINDI—concluded.	JAIN ...	338	321	17	85	85	...	85	...	...	...	87	80	7	69	7
2		0—10 ...	1	1	...	1	1	...	1	...	...	...	...	...	...	...	...
3		10—15 ...	37	34	3	17	17	...	17	...	...	...	6	5	1	5	1
4		15—20 ...	44	38	6	14	14	...	14	...	...	...	15	10	5	5	5
5		20 and over ...	256	248	8	53	53	...	53	...	...	...	66	65	1	59	1
6		MUHAMMADAN ...	2,753	2,547	206	2,710	2,512	198	2,512	198	...	...	38	35	3	35	3
7		0—10 ...	62	50	12	62	50	12	50	12	...	...	...	...	...	...	...
8		10—15 ...	268	233	35	268	233	35	233	35	...	...	...	...	...	...	...
9		15—20 ...	426	392	34	424	392	32	392	32	...	...	...	...	...	...	...
10		20 and over ...	1,997	1,872	125	1,956	1,837	119	1,837	119	...	...	38	35	3	35	3
11		CHRISTIAN ...	231	156	75	189	125	64	123	61	2	3	24	17	7	17	7
12		0—10 ...	12	11	1	12	11	1	11	1	...	...	...	...	...	...	...
13		10—15 ...	16	12	4	16	12	4	12	4	...	...	...	...	...	...	...
14		15—20 ...	26	16	10	21	13	8	13	8	...	...	2	1	1	1	1
15		20 and over ...	177	117	60	140	89	51	87	48	2	3	22	16	6	16	6
16	AMBALLA.	ALL RELIGIONS ...	8,728	8,109	619	5,788	5,356	432	4,679	319	677	113	1,658	1,507	151	405	70
17		0—10 ...	114	87	27	103	77	26	71	17	6	9	8	7	1	...	...
18		10—15 ...	620	527	93	524	457	67	416	48	41	19	67	43	24	...	13
19		15—20 ...	1,091	987	104	826	750	76	688	54	62	22	134	109	25	...	19
20		20 and over ...	6,903	6,508	395	4,335	4,072	263	3,504	200	568	63	1,449	1,348	101	405	38
21		HINDU ...	4,319	4,005	314	2,706	2,540	166	2,022	75	518	91	1,500	1,359	141	398	67
22		0—10 ...	56	47	9	50	42	8	38	...	4	8	5	4	1	...	...
23		10—15 ...	348	300	48	275	252	23	217	8	35	15	61	37	24	...	13
24		15—20 ...	541	486	55	414	383	31	338	13	45	18	116	92	24	...	18
25		20 and over ...	3,374	3,172	202	1,967	1,863	104	1,429	54	434	50	1,318	1,226	92	398	36
26		SIKH ...	1,392	1,340	52	217	197	20	174	4	23	16	26	23	3	2	...
27		0—10 ...	4	3	1	2	1	1	1	...	...	1	...	...	...	...	...
28		10—15 ...	43	38	5	26	22	4	22	...	...	4	...	...	...	...	...
29		15—20 ...	152	145	7	32	28	4	28	...	...	4	2	2	...	...	...
30		20 and over ...	1,193	1,154	39	157	146	11	123	4	23	7	24	21	3	2	...
31		JAIN ...	346	330	16	244	235	9	107	7	128	2	100	93	7	...	5
32		0—10 ...	6	6	...	3	3	...	1	...	2	...	3	3	...	...	...
33		10—15 ...	24	24	...	18	18	...	12	...	6	...	6	6	...	...	...
34		15—20 ...	48	47	1	33	33	...	17	...	16	...	15	14	1	...	1
35		20 and over ...	268	253	15	190	181	9	77	7	104	2	76	70	6	...	2
36		MUHAMMADAN ...	2,534	2,335	199	2,496	2,297	199	2,297	199	...	...	25	25	...	2	...
37		0—10 ...	47	30	17	47	30	17	30	17	...	...	...	...	...	...	...
38		10—15 ...	200	161	39	200	161	39	161	39	...	...	...	...	...	...	...
39		15—20 ...	331	296	35	330	295	35	295	35	...	...	...	...	...	...	...
40		20 and over ...	1,956	1,848	108	1,919	1,811	108	1,811	108	...	...	25	25	...	2	...
41		CHRISTIAN ...	134	96	38	122	84	38	76	34	8	4	7	7	...	3	...
42		0—10 ...	1	1	...	1	1	...	1	...	...	...	...	...	...	...	...
43		10—15 ...	5	4	1	5	4	1	4	1	...	...	...	...	...	...	...
44		15—20 ...	19	13	6	17	11	6	10	6	1	...	1	1	...	...	...
45		20 and over ...	109	78	31	99	68	31	61	27	7	4	6	6	...	3	...
46	JULLUNDUR.	ALL RELIGIONS ...	5,620	4,996	624	2,973	2,812	161	2,812	161	...	...	539	398	141	280	139
47		0—10 ...	79	70	9	55	51	4	51	4	...	...	5	1	4	...	4
48		10—15 ...	603	488	115	359	335	24	335	24	...	...	108	81	27	67	27
49		15—20 ...	1,206	1,059	147	709	683	26	683	26	...	...	141	99	42	75	42
50		20 and over ...	3,732	3,379	353	1,850	1,743	107	1,743	107	...	...	285	217	68	138	66
51		HINDU ...	2,653	2,267	386	1,165	1,143	22	1,143	22	...	...	484	357	127	264	125
52		0—10 ...	21	17	4	9	9	...	9	...	...	...	4	...	4	...	4
53		10—15 ...	401	320	81	182	182	...	182	...	...	...	103	80	23	67	23
54		15—20 ...	758	654	104	398	395	3	395	3	...	...	135	95	40	74	40
55		20 and over ...	1,473	1,276	197	576	557	19	557	19	...	...	242	182	60	123	58
56		SIKH ...	1,323	1,240	83	284	280	4	280	4	...	...	9	8	1	4	1
57		0—10 ...	16	15	1	7	7	...	7	...	...	...	...	...	...	...	...
58		10—15 ...	56	47	9	36	34	2	34	2	...	...	1	...	1	...	1
59		15—20 ...	216	198	18	91	90	1	90	1	...	...	2	2	...	1	...
60		20 and over ...	1,035	980	55	150	149	1	149	1	...	...	6	6	...	3	...
61		MUHAMMADAN ...	1,438	1,324	114	1,406	1,297	109	1,297	109	...	...	8	8	...	5	...
62		0—10 ...	36	33	3	35	32	3	32	3	...	...	1	1	...	...	...
63		10—15 ...	128	110	18	128	110	18	110	18	...	...	...	...	...	...	...
64		15—20 ...	202	182	20	200	181	19	181	19	...	...	...	...	...	...	...
65		20 and over ...	1,072	999	73	1,048	974	69	974	69	...	...	7	7	...	5	...

EDUCATION (BY RELIGION AND AGE)·
CITIES AND SELECTED TOWNS—*continued.*

LITERATE IN VERNACULAR.																				
HINDI.				PUNJABI.														OTHERS.		
Lande or Mahajani.		*Others.*		*Total.*			*Gurmukhi.*		*Lande or Mahajani.*		*Nagri.*		*Tankri.*		*Persian.*					
Males.	Females.	Males.	Females.	Persons.	Males.	Females.	Males.	Females.	Males.	Females.	Males.	Females.	Males.	Females.	Males.	Females.	Persons.	Males.	Females.	Serial No.
18	19	20	21	22	23	24	25	26	27	28	29	30	31	32	33	34	35	36	37	
11	...	...	...	166	156	10	...	...	109	3	23	6	24	1	...	...	...	...	...	1
...	...	...	...	...	...	...	...	...	...	...	...	...	...	...	...	...	...	...	...	2
...	...	...	...	14	12	2	...	...	7	1	5	1	...	...	...	...	...	...	...	3
5	...	...	..	15	14	1	...	...	8	...	6	1	...	...	...	...	...	...	...	4
6	...	..	...	137	130	7	...	...	94	2	12	4	24	1	...	...	...	...	...	5
...	...	...	...	5	...	5	...	5	...	...	...	...	...	...	...	...	...	...	...	6
...	...	...	...	...	...	...	...	...	...	...	...	...	...	...	...	...	...	...	..	7
...	...	...	...	...	...	...	...	...	...	...	...	...	...	...	...	...	...	...	...	8
...	...	...	...	2	...	2	...	2	...	...	...	...	...	...	...	...	...	...	...	9
...	...	...	...	3	...	3	...	3	...	...	...	...	...	...	...	...	...	...	...	10
...	...	...	...	15	12	3	12	3	...	...	...	...	...	...	...	...	3	2	1	11
...	...	...	...	...	...	...	...	...	...	...	...	...	...	...	...	...	...	...	..	12
...	...	...	...	...	...	..	...	...	...	...	...	...	...	...	...	...	...	...	...	13
...	...	...	...	2	1	1	1	1	...	...	...	...	...	...	...	...	1	1	...	14
...	...	...	...	13	11	2	11	2	...	...	...	...	...	...	...	...	2	1	1	15
1,091	81	11	...	1,259	1,223	36	1,213	35	1	...	1	..	...	...	8	...	23	23	...	16
7	1	...	...	3	3	...	3	...	...	...	...	...	...	...	...	...	...	...	...	17
43	11	...	...	29	27	2	27	2	...	...	...	...	...	...	...	...	...	...	...	18
109	6	...	...	128	125	3	124	3	...	...	...	...	...	...	1	...	3	3	...	19
932	63	11	...	1,099	1,068	31	1,059	31	1	...	1	...	...	...	7	...	20	20	...	20
961	74	...	...	94	87	7	86	7	1	...	...	...	...	...	...	...	19	19	...	21
4	1	..	...	1	1	...	1	...	...	...	...	...	...	...	...	...	...	...	...	22
37	11	...	...	12	11	1	11	1	...	...	...	...	...	...	...	...	...	...	...	23
92	6	...	...	8	8	...	8	...	...	...	...	...	...	...	...	...	3	3	...	24
828	56	...	...	73	67	6	66	6	1	...	...	...	...	...	...	...	16	16	...	25
10	3	11	...	1,148	1,119	29	1,118	29	...	...	...	...	...	...	1	...	1	1	...	26
...	...	...	..	2	2	...	2	...	...	...	...	...	...	...	...	...	...	...	...	27
...	...	...	...	17	16	1	16	1	...	...	...	...	...	...	...	...	...	...	...	28
2	...	...	...	118	115	3	115	3	...	...	...	...	...	...	...	...	...	...	...	29
8	3	11	...	1,011	986	25	985	25	...	...	...	...	...	...	1	...	1	1	...	30
93	4	...	...	2	2	...	...	...	...	...	...	...	...	...	2	...	...	...	...	31
3	..	...	...	...	...	...	...	...	...	...	...	...	...	...	...	...	...	...	...	32
6	...	...	...	...	...	...	...	...	...	...	...	...	...	...	...	...	...	...	...	33
14	...	...	...	...	...	...	...	...	...	...	...	...	...	...	...	...	...	...	...	34
70	4	...	...	2	2	...	...	...	...	...	...	...	...	...	2	...	...	...	...	35
23	...	...	...	11	11	...	6	...	...	...	1	...	...	...	4	...	2	2	...	36
...	..	...	...	...	...	...	...	...	...	...	...	...	...	...	...	...	...	...	...	37
...	...	...	...	...	...	...	...	...	...	...	...	...	...	...	...	...	...	...	...	38
...	...	...	...	1	1	...	...	...	...	...	...	...	...	...	1	...	...	...	...	39
23	...	...	...	10	10	...	6	...	...	..	1	...	...	...	3	...	2	2	...	40
4	...	...	...	4	4	...	3	...	...	...	...	...	...	...	1	...	1	1	...	41
...	...	...	...	...	...	...	...	...	...	...	...	...	...	...	...	...	...	...	...	42
...	...	...	...	...	...	...	...	...	...	...	...	...	...	...	...	...	...	...	...	43
1	...	...	...	1	1	...	1	...	...	...	...	...	...	...	...	...	...	...	...	44
3	...	...	...	3	3	...	2	...	...	...	...	...	...	...	1	...	1	1	...	45
118	2	...	...	2,087	1,772	315	1,030	105	557	8	185	202	...	...	...	...	21	14	7	46
1	...	...	...	19	18	1	8	1	4	...	6	...	...	...	...	...	...	...	...	47
14	...	...	...	136	72	64	18	10	44	4	10	50	...	...	...	...	...	...	...	48
24	...	...	...	355	277	78	120	18	84	1	73	59	...	...	..	...	1	...	1	49
79	2	...	...	1,577	1,405	172	884	76	425	3	96	93	...	...	...	...	20	14	6	50
93	2	...	...	996	761	235	85	80	503	6	173	199	...	...	...	...	8	6	2	51
...	...	...	...	8	8	...	...	...	2	...	6	...	...	...	...	...	...	...	..	52
13	...	...	...	116	58	58	7	4	43	4	8	50	...	...	...	...	...	...	...	53
21	...	...	...	225	164	61	14	2	78	...	72	59	...	...	...	...	...	...	...	54
59	2	...	...	647	531	116	64	24	380	2	87	90	...	...	...	...	8	6	2	55
4	...	...	...	1,030	952	78	942	75	1	1	9	2	...	...	...	...	..	...	...	56
...	...	...	...	9	8	1	8	1	...	...	...	...	...	...	...	...	...	...	...	57
...	...	...	...	19	13	6	11	6	...	...	2	...	...	...	...	...	...	...	...	58
1	...	...	...	123	106	17	105	16	1	1	...	...	...	...	...	...	...	...	...	59
3	...	...	...	879	825	54	818	52	...	...	7	2	...	...	...	...	...	...	...	60
3	...	...	...	12	12	...	3	...	8	...	1	...	...	..	...	...	12	7	5	61
1	...	..	...	...	...	...	...	...	...	...	...	...	...	...	...	...	...	...	...	62
...	...	..	...	...	...	...	...	...	...	...	...	...	...	...	...	...	...	...	...	63
...	...	...	..	1	1	...	1	...	...	...	...	...	...	...	...	...	1	...	1	64
2	...	...	...	11	11	...	2	...	8	...	1	...	...	...	...	...	11	7	4	65

APPENDIX TO IMPERIAL TABLE VIII.—

PART C.—DETAIL FOR

Serial No.	City or Town.	Religion and Age.	Literate in Vernacular. Total. Persons.	Total. Males.	Total. Females.	Urdu. Total. Persons.	Urdu. Total. Males.	Urdu. Total. Females.	Urdu. Persian. Males.	Urdu. Persian. Females.	Urdu. Others. Males.	Urdu. Others. Females.	Hindi. Total. Persons.	Hindi. Total. Males.	Hindi. Total. Females.	Hindi. Nagri. Males.	Hindi. Nagri. Females.
	1	2	3	4	5	6	7	8	9	10	11	12	13	14	15	16	17
1	JULLUNDUR.	CHRISTIAN ...	67	44	23	68	40	23	40	23	...	...	2	2	...	2	...
2		0—10 ...	1	...	1	1	...	1	...	1	...	...	...	...	...	...	...
3		10—15 ...	9	5	4	9	5	4	5	4	...	...	...	...	...	...	...
4		15—20 ...	9	7	2	9	7	2	7	2	...	...	...	...	...	...	...
5		20 and over ...	48	32	16	44	28	16	28	16	...	...	2	2	...	2	...
6	SIALKOT.	ALL RELIGIONS ...	7,322	6,524	798	4,674	4,337	337	4,332	337	5	...	1,079	931	148	794	146
7		0—10 ...	189	148	41	125	114	11	114	11	...	...	35	26	9	25	9
8		10—15 ...	872	725	147	665	613	52	613	52	...	...	110	72	38	69	38
9		15—20 ...	1,099	972	127	834	777	57	777	57	...	...	150	130	20	121	19
10		20 and over ...	5,162	4,679	483	3,050	2,833	217	2,828	217	5	...	784	703	81	579	80
11		HINDU ...	2,388	2,095	293	1,399	1,379	20	1,374	20	5	...	667	532	135	531	135
12		0—10 ...	68	53	15	31	30	1	30	1	...	...	30	21	9	21	9
13		10—15 ...	328	264	64	214	211	3	211	3	...	...	89	53	36	53	36
14		15—20 ...	378	343	35	254	252	2	252	2	...	...	96	81	15	81	15
15		20 and over ...	1,614	1,435	179	900	886	14	881	14	5	...	452	377	75	376	75
16		SIKH ...	1,786	1,598	188	396	388	8	388	8	...	...	266	257	9	257	9
17		0—10 ...	39	23	16	13	13	...	13	...	...	...	4	4	...	4	...
18		10—15 ...	126	92	34	46	45	1	45	1	...	...	18	16	2	16	2
19		15—20 ...	244	207	37	128	126	2	126	2	...	...	40	36	4	36	4
20		20 and over ...	1,377	1,276	101	209	204	5	204	5	...	...	204	201	3	201	3
21		JAIN ...	312	306	6	55	55	...	55	...	...	...	141	137	4	4	2
22		0—10 ...	3	3	...	2	2	...	2	...	...	...	1	1	...	...	...
23		10—15 ...	20	19	1	7	7	...	7	...	...	...	3	3	...	...	...
24		15—20 ...	46	44	2	21	21	...	21	...	...	...	14	13	1	4	...
25		20 and over ...	243	240	3	25	25	...	25	...	...	...	123	120	3	...	2
26		MUHAMMADAN ...	2,747	2,452	295	2,742	2,447	295	2,447	295	...	...	5	5	...	2	...
27		0—10 ...	76	67	9	76	67	9	67	9	...	...	...	...	...	...	...
28		10—15 ...	390	344	46	390	344	46	344	46	...	...	...	...	...	...	...
29		15—20 ...	412	366	46	412	366	46	366	46	...	...	...	...	...	...	...
30		20 and over ...	1,869	1,675	194	1,864	1,670	194	1,670	194	...	...	5	5	...	2	...
31		CHRISTIAN ...	82	68	14	82	68	14	68	14	...	...	...	...	...	...	...
32		0—10 ...	3	2	1	3	2	1	2	1	...	...	...	...	...	...	...
33		10—15 ...	8	6	2	8	6	2	6	2	...	...	...	...	...	...	...
34		15—20 ...	19	12	7	19	12	7	12	7	...	...	...	...	...	...	...
35		20 and over ...	52	48	4	52	48	4	48	4	...	...	...	...	...	...	...
36	FEROZEPORE.	ALL RELIGIONS ...	7,645	6,456	1,189	3,664	3,327	337	3,327	335	...	2	2,369	1,932	437	1,703	428
37		0—10 ...	345	163	182	118	90	28	90	28	...	...	127	61	66	59	66
38		10—15 ...	795	543	252	396	350	46	350	46	...	...	228	139	89	127	88
39		15—20 ...	962	762	200	482	433	49	433	49	...	...	297	213	84	192	83
40		20 and over ...	5,543	4,988	555	2,668	2,454	214	2,454	212	...	2	1,717	1,519	198	1,325	191
41		HINDU ...	4,205	3,656	549	1,536	1,469	67	1,469	67	...	...	2,183	1,773	410	1,570	405
42		0—10 ...	182	110	72	56	51	5	51	5	...	...	119	54	65	52	65
43		10—15 ...	441	336	105	198	185	13	185	13	...	...	218	131	87	119	86
44		15—20 ...	539	442	97	198	194	4	194	4	...	...	274	195	79	176	79
45		20 and over ...	3,043	2,768	275	1,084	1,039	45	1,039	45	...	...	1,572	1,393	179	1,223	175
46		SIKH ...	1,284	940	344	182	169	13	169	13	...	...	40	39	1	38	1
47		0—10 ...	102	17	85	5	5	...	5	...	...	...	5	5	...	5	...
48		10—15 ...	174	62	112	28	28	...	28	...	...	...	...	...	...	...	...
49		15—20 ...	154	101	53	38	34	4	34	4	...	...	7	7	...	7	...
50		20 and over ...	854	760	94	111	102	9	102	9	...	...	28	27	1	26	1
51		JAIN ...	187	155	32	73	67	6	67	6	...	...	107	82	25	65	22
52		0—10 ...	8	5	3	4	3	1	3	1	...	...	3	2	1	2	1
53		10—15 ...	19	16	3	11	10	1	10	1	...	...	8	6	2	6	2
54		15—20 ...	22	17	5	6	8	...	6	...	...	...	16	11	5	9	4
55		20 and over ...	138	117	21	52	48	4	48	4	...	...	80	63	17	48	15
56		MUHAMMADAN ...	1,845	1,617	228	1,787	1,560	227	1,560	227	...	...	37	36	1	29	...
57		0—10 ...	51	29	22	51	29	22	29	22	...	...	...	...	...	...	...
58		10—15 ...	154	124	30	152	122	30	122	30	...	...	2	2	...	2	...
59		15—20 ...	225	188	37	223	186	37	186	37	...	...	...	...	...	...	...
60		20 and over ...	1,415	1,276	139	1,361	1,223	138	1,223	138	...	...	35	34	1	27	...
61		CHRISTIAN ...	110	78	32	82	60	22	60	20	...	2	1	1	...	1	...
62		0—10 ...	2	2	...	2	2	...	2	...	...	...	...	...	...	...	...
63		10—15 ...	7	5	2	7	5	2	5	2	...	...	...	...	...	...	...
64		15—20 ...	21	14	7	17	13	4	13	4	...	...	...	...	...	...	...
65		20 and over ...	80	57	23	56	40	16	40	14	...	2	1	1	...	1	...

EDUCATION (BY RELIGION AND AGE).

CITIES AND SELECTED TOWNS—*concluded.*

LITERATE IN VERNACULAR.																				
HINDI.				PUNJABI.													OTHERS.			
Lande or Mahajani.		*Others.*		*Total.*			*Gurmukhi.*		*Lande or Mahajani.*		*Nagri.*		*Tankri.*		*Persian.*					
Males.	Females.	Males.	Females.	Persons.	Males.	Females.	Males.	Females.	Males.	Females.	Males.	Females.	Males.	Females.	Males.	Females.	Persons.	Males.	Females.	Serial No.
18	19	20	21	22	23	24	25	26	27	28	29	30	31	32	33	34	35	36	37	
...	...	...	...	1	1	...	...	...	...	...	1	...	...	...	.	...	1	1	...	1
...	...	...	...	...	...	...	...	...	...	...	...	...	...	...	...	...	...	...	...	2
...	...	...	...	...	...	...	...	...	...	...	...	...	...	...	...	...	...	...	...	3
...	...	...	...	...	...	...	...	...	...	...	...	...	...	...	...	...	...	...	...	4
...	...	...	...	1	1	...	...	...	...	...	1	...	...	...	...	...	1	1	...	5
137	2	...	...	1,562	1,251	311	997	307	133	3	121	1	...	...	...	...	7	5	2	6
1	...	...	...	29	8	21	7	21	...	...	1	...	...	...	...	...	...	...	...	7
3	...	...	...	97	40	57	31	56	3	...	6	1	...	...	...	...	...	...	...	8
9	1	...	...	115	65	50	46	50	7	...	12	...	...	...	...	...	...	...	...	9
124	1	...	...	1,321	1,138	183	913	180	123	3	102	...	...	...	...	...	7	5	2	10
1	...	...	...	322	184	138	86	135	42	3	56	...	...	...	...	...	...	...	...	11
...	...	...	...	7	2	5	1	5	...	...	1	...	...	...	...	...	...	...	...	12
...	...	...	...	25	...	25	...	25	...	...	...	...	...	...	...	...	...	...	...	13
...	...	...	...	28	10	18	7	18	1	...	2	...	...	...	...	...	...	...	...	14
1	...	...	...	262	172	90	78	87	41	3	53	...	...	...	...	...	...	...	...	15
...	...	...	...	1,124	953	171	910	171	43	...	...	...	...	...	...	...	...	...	...	16
...	...	...	...	22	6	16	6	16	...	...	...	...	...	...	...	...	...	...	...	17
...	...	...	...	62	31	31	21	31	...	...	...	...	...	...	...	...	...	...	...	18
...	...	...	...	76	45	31	39	31	6	...	...	...	...	...	...	...	...	...	...	19
...	...	...	...	964	871	93	834	93	37	...	...	...	...	...	...	...	...	...	...	20
133	2	...	...	116	114	2	1	1	48	...	65	1	...	...	...	...	...	...	...	21
1	...	...	...	...	...	...	...	...	...	...	...	...	...	...	...	...	...	...	...	22
3	...	...	...	10	9	1	...	...	3	...	6	1	...	...	...	...	...	...	...	23
9	1	...	...	11	10	1	...	1	...	...	10	...	...	...	...	...	...	...	...	24
120	1	...	...	95	95	...	1	...	45	...	49	...	...	...	...	...	...	...	...	25
3	...	...	...	...	...	...	...	...	...	...	...	...	...	...	...	...	...	...	...	26
...	...	...	...	...	...	...	...	...	...	...	...	...	...	...	...	...	...	...	...	27
...	...	...	...	...	...	...	...	...	...	...	...	...	...	...	...	...	...	...	...	28
...	...	...	...	...	...	...	...	...	...	...	...	...	...	...	...	...	...	...	...	29
3	...	...	...	...	...	...	...	...	...	...	...	...	...	...	...	...	...	...	...	30
...	...	...	...	...	...	...	...	...	...	...	...	...	...	...	...	...	...	...	...	31
...	...	...	...	...	...	...	...	...	...	...	...	...	...	...	...	...	...	...	...	32
...	...	...	...	...	...	...	...	...	...	...	...	...	...	...	...	...	...	...	...	33
...	...	...	...	...	...	...	...	...	...	...	...	...	...	...	...	...	...	...	...	34
...	...	...	...	...	...	...	...	...	...	...	...	...	...	...	...	...	...	...	...	35
229	9	...	...	1,601	1,188	413	884	406	295	3	9	3	...	1	...	...	11	9	2	36
2	...	...	...	100	12	88	11	87	...	...	1	1	...	...	...	...	...	...	...	37
12	1	...	...	171	54	117	39	116	15	...	...	...	...	1	...	...	...	...	...	38
21	1	...	...	182	116	66	76	64	39	2	1	...	...	...	...	...	1	...	1	39
194	7	...	...	1,148	1,006	142	758	139	241	1	7	2	...	...	...	...	10	9	1	40
203	5	...	...	486	414	72	132	67	277	3	5	1	...	1	...	...	...	...	...	41
2	...	...	...	7	5	2	4	2	...	...	1	...	...	...	...	...	...	...	...	42
12	1	...	...	25	20	5	5	4	15	...	...	...	...	1	...	...	...	...	...	43
19	...	...	...	67	53	14	16	12	36	2	1	...	...	...	...	...	...	...	...	44
170	4	...	...	387	336	51	107	49	226	1	3	1	...	...	...	...	...	...	...	45
1	...	...	...	1,062	732	330	729	330	2	...	1	...	...	...	...	...	...	...	...	46
...	...	...	...	92	7	85	7	85	...	...	...	...	...	...	...	...	...	...	...	47
...	...	...	...	146	34	112	34	112	...	...	...	...	...	...	...	...	...	...	...	48
...	...	...	...	109	60	49	59	49	1	...	...	...	...	...	...	...	...	...	...	49
1	...	...	...	715	631	84	629	84	1	...	1	...	...	...	...	...	...	...	...	50
17	3	...	...	7	6	1	...	...	6	...	...	1	...	...	...	...	...	...	...	51
...	...	...	...	1	...	1	...	...	...	...	...	1	...	...	...	...	...	...	...	52
...	...	...	...	...	...	...	...	...	...	...	...	...	...	...	...	...	...	...	...	53
2	1	...	...	...	...	...	...	...	...	...	...	...	...	...	...	...	...	...	...	54
15	2	...	...	6	6	...	...	...	6	...	...	...	...	...	...	...	...	...	...	55
7	1	...	...	19	19	...	7	...	10	...	2	...	...	...	...	...	2	2	...	56
...	...	...	...	...	...	...	...	...	...	...	...	...	...	...	...	...	...	...	...	57
...	...	...	...	...	...	...	...	...	...	...	...	...	...	...	...	...	...	...	...	58
...	...	...	...	2	2	...	...	...	2	...	...	...	...	...	...	...	...	...	...	59
7	1	...	...	17	17	...	7	...	8	...	2	...	...	...	...	...	2	2	...	60
...	...	...	...	27	17	10	16	9	...	...	1	1	...	...	...	...	...	...	...	61
...	...	...	...	...	...	...	...	...	...	...	...	...	...	...	...	...	...	...	...	62
...	...	...	...	...	...	...	...	...	...	...	...	...	...	...	...	...	...	...	...	63
...	...	...	...	4	1	3	1	3	...	...	...	...	...	...	...	...	...	...	...	64
...	...	...	...	23	16	7	15	6	...	...	1	1	...	...	...	...	...	...	...	65

APPENDIX TO IMPERIAL TABLE IX.

EDUCATION BY CASTES IN CERTAIN SECTS, FOR SELECTED DISTRICTS.

1. This table has been prepared according to Census Commissioner's instructions contained in his Nos. 1227 and 1255, dated the 25th August 1911, and 29th August 1911, respectively, and shows for certain districts, the castes of Aryas, Brahmos and the followers of Dev Dharm, together with the extent of literacy in each (*vide* para. 4, Title page of Imperial Table IX).

2. The districts selected are those where the followers of these sects are found in considerable strength.

3. Only 40 Sikhs have returned themselves as Aryas and 22 as Brahmos in these districts. They have not, therefore, been included in the figures shown in this table.

4. Castes returning less than 10 persons have been grouped under "others."

APPENDIX TO IMPERIAL TABLE IX.—EDUCATION BY

1. ARYA.

Serial No.	Caste.	Locality.	Population. Total. Persons.	Total. Males.	Total. Females.	Literate. Persons.	Literate. Males.	Literate. Females.	Illiterate. Persons.	Illiterate. Males.	Illiterate. Females.	Literate in English. Persons.	Literate in English. Males.	Literate in English. Females.
	1	2	3	4	5	6	7	8	9	10	11	12	13	14
1	TOTAL	...	82,488	47,125	35,363	13,666	10,853	2,813	68,822	36,272	32,550	3,301	3,169	132
2	AHÍR ...	TOTAL ...	96	57	39	20	18	2	76	39	37	2	2	...
3		Hissar ...	17	14	3	4	4	...	13	10	3	1	1	...
4		Delhi ...	64	34	30	10	10	...	54	24	30	1	1	...
5		Hoshiarpur ...	1	1	...	...	...	...	1	1	...	...	...	...
6		Jullundur ...	14	8	6	6	4	2	8	4	4	...	...	...
7	ARORÁ ...	TOTAL ...	10,547	6,211	4,336	3,613	2,884	729	6,934	3,327	3,607	929	902	27
8		Hissar ...	66	39	27	5	5	...	61	34	27	...	...	...
9		Kangra ...	13	8	5	7	5	2	6	3	3	1	1	...
10		Hoshiarpur ...	15	5	10	6	4	2	9	1	8	1	1	...
11		Jullundur ...	36	20	16	20	12	8	16	8	8	1	1	...
12		Lahore ...	1,876	1,242	634	576	453	123	1,300	789	511	151	147	4
13		Amritsar ...	445	260	185	218	171	47	227	89	138	64	62	2
14		Gurdaspur ...	152	85	67	43	35	8	109	50	59	7	7	...
15		Sialkot ...	1,081	602	479	203	176	27	878	426	452	18	17	1
16		Gujranwala ...	909	560	349	361	303	58	548	257	291	80	80	...
17		Gujrat ...	173	74	99	56	52	4	117	22	95	24	24	...
18		Shahpur ...	904	523	381	407	308	99	497	215	282	63	59	4
19		Lyallpur ...	1,561	933	628	402	330	72	1,159	603	556	114	107	7
20		Multan ...	2,601	1,424	1,177	969	727	242	1,632	697	935	296	287	9
21		Muzaffargarh ...	715	436	279	340	303	37	375	133	242	109	109	...
22	BAIRÁGI ...	TOTAL ...	19	14	5	2	2	...	17	12	5	2	2	...
23		Delhi ...	17	12	5	1	1	...	16	11	5	1	1	...
24		Hoshiarpur ...	2	2	...	1	1	...	1	1	...	1	1	...
25	BANIÁ — Aggarwál	TOTAL ...	1,983	1,164	819	474	402	72	1,509	762	747	109	107	2
26		Hissar ...	309	184	125	105	83	22	204	101	103	21	20	1
27		Delhi ...	609	300	209	111	105	6	398	195	203	33	33	...
28		Karnal ...	574	322	252	86	80	6	488	242	246	23	23	...
29		Hoshiarpur ...	47	35	12	22	22	...	25	13	12	3	3	...
30		Jullundur ...	76	42	34	35	20	15	41	22	19	...	...	...
31		Lahore ...	208	133	75	53	41	12	155	92	63	18	17	1
32		Amritsar ...	7	5	2	2	2	...	5	3	2	...	...	...
33		Gurdaspur ...	91	50	41	48	38	10	43	12	31	9	9	...
34		Sialkot ...	118	68	50	7	7	...	111	61	50	1	1	...
35		Gujranwala ...	34	20	14	4	3	1	30	17	13	...	...	...
36		Gujrat ...	10	5	5	1	1	...	9	4	5	1	1	...
37	BANIÁ — Unspecified	TOTAL ...	45	23	22	12	10	2	33	13	20	3	3	...
38		Kangra ...	1	1	...	1	1	...	...	...	...	1	1	...
39		Hoshiarpur ...	8	3	5	3	2	1	5	1	4	1	1	...
40		Jullundur ...	10	5	5	2	1	1	8	4	4	...	...	...
41		Lahore ...	3	2	1	1	1	...	2	1	1	...	...	...
42		Gurdaspur ...	22	12	10	5	5	...	17	7	10	1	1	...
43		Gujranwala ...	1	...	1	...	...	...	1	...	1	...	...	...
44	BHÁT ...	TOTAL ...	11	8	3	2	2	...	9	6	3	...	...	...
45		Amritsar ...	8	8	...	2	2	...	6	6	...	...	...	...
46		Gurdaspur ...	3	...	3	...	...	...	3	...	3	...	...	...
47	BHÁTIÁ ...	TOTAL ...	64	31	33	8	7	1	56	24	32	1	1	...
48		Jullundur ...	6	3	3	2	1	1	4	2	2	...	...	...
49		Lahore ...	12	7	5	1	1	...	11	6	5	...	...	...
50		Amritsar ...	9	...	9	...	...	...	9	...	9	...	...	...
51		Gujranwala ...	20	13	7	2	2	...	18	11	7	1	1	...
52		Gujrat ...	17	8	9	3	3	...	14	5	9	...	...	...
53	BRÁHMAN ...	TOTAL ...	7,240	4,139	3,101	2,077	1,672	405	5,163	2,467	2,696	502	481	21
54		Hissar ...	168	97	71	48	35	13	120	62	58	16	16	...
55		Delhi ...	314	196	118	75	71	4	239	125	114	31	81	...
56		Karnal ...	118	72	46	12	9	3	106	63	43	4	4	...
57		Kangra ...	599	315	284	71	60	11	528	255	273	15	15	...
58		Hoshiarpur ...	506	300	206	274	199	75	232	101	131	87	86	1
59		Jullundur ...	262	152	110	92	68	24	170	84	86	11	10	1
60		Lahore ...	1,271	805	466	222	167	55	1,049	638	411	72	66	6
61		Amritsar ...	333	191	142	168	112	56	165	79	86	33	28	5
62		Gurdaspur ...	1,071	609	462	363	319	44	708	290	418	66	66	...
63		Sialkot ...	1,108	597	511	251	234	17	857	363	494	36	36	...
64		Gujranwala ...	810	483	327	268	219	49	542	264	278	53	53	...
65		Gujrat ...	237	93	144	71	65	6	166	28	138	32	32	...
66		Shahpur ...	164	90	74	68	49	19	96	41	55	19	18	1
67		Lyallpur ...	204	84	120	58	36	22	146	48	98	15	13	2
68		Multan ...	40	30	10	23	17	6	17	13	4	10	5	5
69		Muzaffargarh ...	35	25	10	13	12	1	22	13	9	2	2	...

CASTES IN CERTAIN SECTS, FOR SELECTED DISTRICTS.

ARYA—*continued.*

Serial No.	Caste.	Locality.	Population. Total. Persons.	Males.	Females.	Literate. Persons.	Males.	Females.	Illiterate. Persons.	Males.	Females.	Literate in English. Persons.	Males.	Females.
	1	2	3	4	5	6	7	8	9	10	11	12	13	14
1	CHAMÁR ...	TOTAL ...	311	154	157	6	6	...	305	148	157	1	1	...
2		Hissar ...	32	16	16	4	4	...	28	12	16	...	...	...
3		Kangra ...	231	113	118	...	...	...	231	113	118	...	...	...
4		Hoshiarpur ...	21	9	12	1	1	...	20	8	12	...	...	...
5		Lahore ...	6	4	2	...	...	...	6	4	2	...	...	...
6		Amritsar ...	7	4	3	1	1	...	6	3	3	1	1	...
7		Sialkot ...	11	5	6	...	...	...	11	5	6	...	...	...
8		Gujrat ...	3	3	...	..	...	...	3	3	...	...	...	...
9	CHHÍMBÁ ...	TOTAL ...	68	42	26	10	9	1	58	33	25	3	3	..
10		Hissar ...	1	1	...	1	1	...	...	...	...	...	...	...
11		Kangra ...	21	10	11	1	1	...	20	9	11	1	1	...
12		Hoshiarpur ...	12	9	3	5	5	...	7	4	3	1	1	...
13		Jullundur ...	16	9	7	3	2	1	13	7	6	1	1	...
14		Lahore ...	8	5	3	...	...	...	8	5	3	...	...	...
15		Amritsar ...	5	3	2	...	...	...	5	3	2	...	...	...
16		Gurdaspur ...	5	5	...	...	...	...	5	5	...	...	...	...
17	DÁGI AND KOLI.	TOTAL ...	67	32	35	1	1	...	66	31	35	...	...	...
18		Delhi ...	9	6	3	...	...	...	9	6	3	...	...	...
19		Kangra ...	58	26	32	1	1	...	57	25	32	...	...	...
20	DHOBI ...	TOTAL ...	33	28	5	...	...	...	33	28	5	...	...	...
21		Delhi ...	15	14	1	...	...	...	15	14	1	...	...	...
22		Karnal ...	1	1	...	...	...	...	1	1	...	...	...	...
23		Jullundur ..	17	13	4	...	...	...	17	13	4	...	...	...
24	DUMNÁ ...	Kangra ...	94	50	44	...	...	...	94	50	44	...	...	...
25	GADARIÁ ...	Delhi ...	30	19	11	1	1	...	29	18	11	1	1	...
26	GHIRATH ...	TOTAL ...	41	30	11	11	10	1	30	20	10	5	5	...
27		Kangra ...	23	15	8	4	4	...	19	11	8	3	3	...
28		Hoshiarpur ...	18	15	3	7	6	1	11	9	2	2	2	...
29	GUJJAR ...	TOTAL ...	69	39	30	...	...	...	69	39	30	...	...	...
30		Hissar ...	2	2	...	...	...	...	2	2	...	...	...	...
31		Delhi ...	42	25	17	...	...	...	42	25	17	...	...	...
32		Karnal ...	18	9	9	...	..	...	18	9	9	...	...	...
33		Kangra ...	6	2	4	...	...	...	6	2	4	...	...	...
34		Gujrat ...	1	1	...	...	...	...	1	1	...	...	...	...
35	JAT ...	TOTAL ...	9,203	5,057	4,146	305	292	13	8,898	4,765	4,133	35	35	...
36		Hissar ...	2,402	1,345	1,057	97	93	4	2,305	1,252	1,053	8	8	...
37		Delhi ...	2,274	1,209	1,065	38	38	...	2,236	1,171	1,065	4	4	...
38		Karnal ...	2,110	1,147	963	13	13	...	2,097	1,134	963	1	1	...
39		Kangra ...	4	3	1	2	2	...	2	1	1	2	2	...
40		Hoshiarpur ...	78	49	29	21	17	4	57	32	25	10	10	...
41		Jullundur ...	9	6	3	1	1	...	8	5	3	...	...	...
42		Lahore ...	207	150	57	11	11	...	196	139	57	3	3	...
43		Amritsar ...	15	9	6	9	7	2	6	2	4	1	1	...
44		Gurdaspur ...	313	190	123	13	12	1	300	178	122	1	1	...
45		Sialkot ...	1,588	823	765	64	62	2	1,524	761	763	3	3	...
46		Gujranwala ...	187	113	74	34	34	...	153	79	74	2	2	...
47		Gujrat ...	16	13	3	2	2	...	14	11	3	...	...	...
48	JHÍNWAR ...	TOTAL ...	471	282	189	65	62	3	406	220	186	9	9	...
49		Delhi ...	24	18	6	4	4	...	20	14	6	...	...	...
50		Hoshiarpur ...	28	11	17	3	3	...	25	8	17	...	...	...
51		Jullundur ...	22	8	14	2	2	...	20	6	14	...	...	...
52		Lahore ...	28	16	12	9	9	...	19	7	12	3	3	...
53		Amritsar ...	35	23	12	11	10	1	24	13	11	3	3	...
54		Gurdaspur ...	130	82	48	11	11	...	119	71	48	...	...	...
55		Sialkot ...	118	67	51	22	20	2	96	47	49	2	2	...
56		Gujranwala ..	50	34	16	1	1	...	49	33	16	1	1	...
57		Gujrat ...	36	23	13	2	2	...	34	21	13	...	...	...
58	JOGI ...	TOTAL ...	21	21	...	1	1	...	20	20	...	...	...	...
59		Hissar ...	2	2	...	1	1	...	1	1	...	...	...	...
60		Gurdaspur ...	11	11	...	...	...	...	11	11	...	...	...	...
61		Gujranwala ...	8	8	...	...	...	...	8	8	...	...	...	...
62	JULÁHÁ ...	TOTAL ...	625	354	271	8	8	..	617	346	271	2	2	...
63		Delhi ...	3	3	...	...	...	.	3	3	...	...	...	...
64		Kangra ...	176	84	92	...	...	..	176	84	92	...	...	...
65		Hoshiarpur ...	226	145	81	6	6	...	220	139	81	2	2	...
66		Gujrat ...	220	122	98	2	2	...	218	120	98	...	...	...

APPENDIX TO IMPERIAL TABLE IX.—EDUCATION BY

ARYA—*continued.*

Serial No.	Caste.	Locality.	Population.									Literate in English.		
			Total.			Literate.			Illiterate.					
			Persons.	Males.	Females.	Persons.	Males.	Females.	Persons.	Males.	Females.	Persons.	Males.	Females.
	1	2	3	4	5	6	7	8	9	10	11	12	13	14
1	KALÁL ...	TOTAL ...	319	167	152	103	77	26	216	90	126	22	20	2
2		Hissar ...	12	7	5	8	6	2	4	1	3	2	2	...
3		Delhi ...	7	4	3	...	...	...	7	4	3	...	..	...
4		Karnal ...	55	27	28	4	4	...	51	23	28	1	1	...
5		Kangra ...	7	5	2	4	4	...	3	1	2	3	3	...
6		Hoshiarpur ...	168	87	81	75	55	20	93	32	61	14	12	2
7		Jullundur ...	32	16	16	9	5	4	23	11	12	1	1	...
8		Lahore ...	16	9	7	1	1	...	15	8	7	...	...	...
9		Amritsar ...	10	6	4	...	...	...	10	6	4	...	...	...
10		Gurdaspur ...	12	6	6	2	2	...	10	4	6	1	1	...
11	KAMBOH ...	TOTAL ...	122	65	57	6	6	...	116	59	57	...	...	...
12		Karnal ...	117	63	54	5	5	...	112	58	54	...	...	...
13		Jullundur ...	5	2	3	1	1	...	4	1	3	...	...	...
14	KÁYASTH ...	TOTAL ...	337	205	132	129	113	16	208	92	116	45	45	...
15		Hissar ...	35	24	11	22	16	6	13	8	5	11	11	...
16		Delhi ...	227	138	89	77	75	2	150	63	87	29	29	...
17		Karnal ...	8	8	...	4	4	...	4	4	...	3	3	...
18		Hoshiarpur ...	16	7	9	10	5	5	6	2	4	...	...	...
19		Jullundur ...	10	5	5	6	3	3	4	2	2	...	...	...
20		Lahore ...	37	20	17	8	8	...	29	12	17	1	1	...
21		Gurdaspur ...	4	3	1	2	2	...	2	1	1	1	1	...
22	KHATRÍ ...	TOTAL ...	17,237	10,389	6,848	5,212	4,021	1,191	12,025	6,368	5,657	1,353	1,278	75
23		Hissar ...	110	69	41	49	38	11	61	31	30	22	22	...
24		Delhi ...	325	191	134	114	100	14	211	91	120	54	54	...
25		Karnal ...	71	36	35	16	11	5	55	25	30	4	4	...
26		Kangra ...	137	85	52	58	50	8	79	35	44	25	25	...
27		Hoshiarpur ...	903	546	357	422	327	95	481	219	262	124	121	3
28		Jullundur ...	1,746	1,027	719	252	139	113	1,494	888	606	36	24	12
29		Lahore ...	4,571	3,124	1,447	1,008	704	304	3,563	2,420	1,143	219	206	13
30		Amritsar ...	1,604	914	690	555	430	125	1,049	484	565	128	118	10
31		Gurdaspur ...	984	533	451	392	301	91	592	232	360	97	95	2
32		Sialkot ...	2,505	1,389	1,116	613	547	66	1,892	842	1,050	89	89	...
33		Gujranwala ...	1,136	663	473	440	383	57	696	280	416	132	131	1
34		Gujrat ...	837	487	350	315	307	8	522	180	342	118	118	...
35		Shahpur ...	963	560	403	392	301	91	571	259	312	131	117	14
36		Lyallpur ...	601	397	204	190	155	35	411	242	169	53	49	4
37		Multan ...	617	297	320	333	178	155	284	119	165	97	82	15
38		Muzaffargarh ...	127	71	56	63	50	13	64	21	43	24	23	1
39	KUMHÁR ...	TOTAL ...	313	197	116	18	17	1	295	180	115	5	5	...
40		Hissar ...	66	44	22	4	4	...	62	40	22	2	2	...
41		Delhi ...	19	17	2	...	...	...	19	17	2	...	...	...
42		Hoshiarpur ...	19	19	...	6	6	...	13	13	...	3	3	...
43		Jullundur ...	15	13	2	6	6	...	9	7	2	...	...	...
44		Lahore ...	3	1	2	...	...	...	3	1	2	...	.	...
45		Amritsar ...	7	4	3	1	...	1	6	4	2	...	...	...
46		Gurdaspur ...	95	48	47	1	1	...	94	47	47	...	...	...
47		Sialkot ...	56	29	27	...	...	...	56	29	27	...	...	...
48		Gujranwala ...	30	19	11	...	...	...	30	19	11	...	...	...
49		Gujrat ...	3	3	...	...	...	...	3	3	...	...	...	...
50	LOHÁR ...	TOTAL ...	42	24	18	6	4	2	36	20	16	1	1	...
51		Hissar ...	1	...	1	...	...	...	1	...	1	...	...	...
52		Kangra ...	31	18	13	2	2	...	29	16	13	1	1	...
53		Hoshiarpur ...	8	5	3	4	2	2	4	3	1	...	...	...
54		Jullundur ...	2	1	1	...	...	...	2	1	1	...	...	...
55	MAHÁJAN ...	TOTAL ...	108	74	34	54	50	4	54	24	30	23	23	...
56		Kangra ...	68	47	21	42	38	4	26	9	17	20	20	...
57		Lahore ...	4	3	1	2	2	...	2	1	1	...	...	...
58		Sialkot ...	35	23	12	9	9	...	26	14	12	2	2	...
59		Gujrat ...	1	1	...	1	1	...	...	...	...	1	1	...
60	MAHTON ...	Hoshiarpur ...	29	16	13	7	1	6	22	15	7	1	1	...
61	MÁLI ...	TOTAL ...	116	72	44	8	8	...	108	64	44	...	..	...
62		Hissar ...	9	9	...	1	1	...	8	8	...	...	...	...
63		Delhi ...	93	53	40	4	4	...	89	49	40	...	...	...
64		Karnal ...	14	10	4	3	3	...	11	7	4	...	...	...
65	MEGH ...	TOTAL ...	22,115	12,120	9,995	111	111	...	22,004	12,009	9,995	...	...	...
66		Lahore ...	3	2	1	...	...	...	3	2	1	...	...	...
67		Gurdaspur ...	1	1	...	...	...	...	1	1	...	...	...	...
68		Sialkot ...	21,107	11,565	9,542	109	109	...	20,998	11,456	9,542	...	...	...
69		Gujrat ...	1,004	552	452	2	2	...	1,002	550	452	...	...	...
70	MINÁ ...	Delhi ...	19	12	7	...	...	...	19	12	7	...	...	...

CASTES IN CERTAIN SECTS, FOR SELECTED DISTRICTS—*continued.*

ARYA—*continued.*

Serial No.	Caste.	Locality.	Population. Total. Persons.	Total. Males.	Total. Females.	Literate. Persons.	Literate. Males.	Literate. Females.	Illiterate. Persons.	Illiterate. Males.	Illiterate. Females.	Literate in English. Persons.	Literate in English. Males.	Literate in English. Females.
	1	2	3	4	5	6	7	8	9	10	11	12	13	14
1	NÁI ...	TOTAL ...	98	58	40	12	10	2	86	48	38	3	3	...
2		*Hissar* ...	*9*	4	5	1	1	...	8	3	5	...	...	...
3		Delhi ...	*13*	6	7	...	...	...	13	6	7	...	...	...
4		Karnal ...	*2*	2	...	1	1	...	1	1	...	...	...	...
5		Kangra ...	*14*	8	6	1	1	...	13	7	6	...	...	...
6		Hoshiarpur ...	*28*	21	7	6	5	1	22	16	6	3	3	...
7		Jullundur ...	*16*	9	7	2	1	1	14	8	6	...	...	...
8		Gurdaspur ...	*16*	8	8	1	1	...	15	7	8	...	...	...
9	OD ...	TOTAL ...	5,102	2,778	2,324	542	339	203	4,560	2,439	2,121	46	43	3
10		Shahpur ...	*174*	90	84	53	31	22	121	59	62	2	2	...
11		Lyallpur ...	*409*	238	171	88	49	39	321	189	132	4	3	1
12		Multan ...	*3,289*	1,838	1,451	317	198	119	2,972	1,640	1,332	34	32	2
13		Muzaffargarh ...	*1,230*	612	618	84	61	23	1,146	551	595	6	6	...
14	BÁJ ...	TOTAL ...	13	9	4	5	3	2	8	6	2	1	1	...
15		Jullundur ...	*12*	8	4	5	3	2	7	5	2	1	1	...
16		Karnal ...	*1*	1	...	...	...	...	1	1	...	...	...	...
17	RÁJPUT ...	TOTAL ...	2,403	1,458	945	421	373	48	1,982	1,085	897	120	118	2
18		Hissar ...	*237*	105	132	19	17	2	218	88	130	1	1	...
19		Delhi ...	*552*	349	203	43	42	1	509	307	202	15	15	...
20		Karnal ...	*114*	66	48	4	4	...	110	62	48	1	1	...
21		Kangra ...	*134*	79	55	38	34	4	96	45	51	16	16	...
22		Hoshiarpur ...	*201*	120	81	109	86	23	92	34	58	44	42	2
23		Jullundur ...	*287*	154	133	52	37	15	235	117	118	...	...	...
24		Lahore ...	*227*	168	59	11	11	...	216	157	59	4	4	...
25		Amritsar ...	*101*	58	43	24	24	...	77	34	43	7	7	...
26		Gurdaspur ...	*448*	294	154	103	100	3	345	194	151	24	24	...
27		Gujranwala ...	*90*	57	33	15	15	...	75	42	33	6	6	...
28		Gujrat ...	*12*	8	4	3	3	...	9	5	4	2	2	...
29	RÁTHÍ ...	Kangra ...	*589*	278	311	3	2	1	586	276	310	...	...	...
30	ROUB ...	Karnal ...	*246*	144	102	3	3	...	243	141	102	2	2	...
31	SAINI ...	TOTAL ...	301	185	116	67	57	10	234	128	106	23	23	...
32		Delhi ...	*86*	42	44	9	9	...	77	33	44	2	2	...
33		Kangra ...	*6*	4	2	4	4	...	2	...	2	2	2	...
34		Hoshiarpur ...	*208*	188	70	54	44	10	154	94	60	19	19	...
35		Jullundur ...	*1*	1	...	...	...	...	1	1	...	...	...	...
36	SÚD ...	TOTAL ...	306	189	117	111	78	33	195	111	84	20	20	...
37		Delhi ...	*3*	3	...	1	1	...	2	2	...	1	1	...
38		Kangra ...	*26*	18	8	20	16	4	6	2	4	9	9	...
39		Hoshiarpur ...	*30*	21	9	14	11	3	16	10	6	5	5	...
40		Jullundur ...	*197*	109	88	61	35	26	136	74	62	3	3	...
41		Amritsar ...	*50*	38	12	15	15	...	35	23	12	2	2	...
42	SUNÁR ...	TOTAL ...	1,009	575	434	184	148	36	825	427	398	25	25	...
43		Hissar ...	*24*	12	12	4	4	...	20	8	12	...	...	...
44		Delhi ...	*54*	30	24	2	2	...	52	28	24	...	...	...
45		Karnal ...	*15*	8	7	...	...	...	15	8	7	...	...	...
46		Hoshiarpur ...	*206*	129	77	50	25	25	156	104	52	6	6	...
47		Jullundur ...	*28*	16	12	5	5	...	23	11	12	...	...	...
48		Lahore ...	*60*	31	29	20	17	3	40	14	26	3	3	...
49		Amritsar ...	*141*	77	64	17	17	...	124	60	64	1	1	...
50		Gurdaspur ...	*145*	73	72	25	22	3	120	51	69	1	1	...
51		Sialkot ...	*92*	50	42	20	16	4	72	34	38	2	2	...
52		Gujranwala ...	*208*	131	77	29	28	1	179	103	76	1	1	...
53		Gujrat ...	*36*	18	18	12	12	...	24	6	18	11	11	...
54	TARKHÁN ...	TOTAL ...	553	311	242	42	39	3	511	272	239	7	7	...
55		Hissar ...	*2*	2	...	...	...	...	2	2	...	...	...	...
56		Delhi ...	*28*	17	11	4	4	...	24	13	11	...	...	...
57		Karnal ...	*6*	5	1	1	1	...	5	4	1	...	...	...
58		Kangra ...	*20*	11	9	2	1	1	18	10	8	1	1	...
59		Hoshiarpur ...	*21*	16	5	4	4	...	17	12	5	2	2	...
60		Jullundur ...	*50*	34	16	6	6	...	44	28	16	...	...	...
61		Lahore ...	*15*	7	8	2	2	...	13	5	8	1	1	...
62		Amritsar ...	*3*	1	2	1	...	1	2	1	1	...	...	...
63		Gurdaspur ...	*271*	153	118	15	15	...	256	138	118	1	1	...
64		Sialkot ...	*88*	42	46	4	4	...	84	38	46	...	...	...
65		Gujranwala ...	*41*	18	23	1	...	1	40	18	22	...	...	...
66		Gujrat ...	*8*	5	3	2	2	...	6	3	3	2	2	...

APPENDIX TO IMPERIAL TABLE IX.—EDUCATION BY

ARYA—*concluded.*

Serial No.	Caste.	Locality.	Population. Total. Persons.	Total. Males.	Total. Females.	Literate. Persons.	Literate. Males.	Literate. Females.	Illiterate. Persons.	Illiterate. Males.	Illiterate. Females.	Literate in English. Persons.	Literate in English. Males.	Literate in English. Females.
	1	2	3	4	5	6	7	8	9	10	11	12	13	14
1	*OTHERS ...	TOTAL ...	73	44	29	6	6	...	67	38	29	...	..	...
2		Hissar ...	2	2	...	...	...	...	2	2	...	...	...	...
3		Delhi ...	38	23	15	...	...	...	38	23	15	...	...	...
4		Kangra ...	14	8	6	5	5	...	9	3	6	...	...	..
5		Hoshiarpur ...	1	1	...	1	1	...	...	...	...	...	...	...
6		Jullundur ...	5	1	4	...	...	...	5	1	4	...	...	...
7		Amritsar ...	6	4	2	...	...	...	6	4	2	...	...	...
8		Siálkot ...	3	3	...	...	...	...	3	3	...	...	...	...
9		Gujrat ...	4	2	2	...	...	...	4	2	2	...	...	...

* *Detail of Others.*—Agári males 3, Báhti male 1, females 3, Báwariá males 2, Bhábrá males 2, Bhanjrá female 1, Bharbhunjá males 4, females 3, Dhának females 2, Faqir males 3, females 2, Gosáin males 3, females 2, Gurkhá (unspecified) male 1, Jogí Ráwal males 3, Kanet males 3, females 4, Mochi males 2, females 2, Sangtarásh male 1, Minor Castes males 16, females 10.

2. BRAHMO.

Serial No.	Caste.	Locality.	Total. Persons.	Total. Males.	Total. Females.	Literate. Persons.	Literate. Males.	Literate. Females.	Illiterate. Persons.	Illiterate. Males.	Illiterate. Females.	Literate in English. Persons.	Literate in English. Males.	Literate in English. Females.
1	TOTAL	...	627	353	274	235	193	42	392	160	232	82	69	13
2	ARORÁ ...	TOTAL ...	126	70	56	52	38	14	74	32	42	9	8	1
3		Ferozepore ...	6	3	3	2	2	...	4	1	3	...	...	...
4		Lahore ...	51	26	25	17	12	5	34	14	20	5	4	1
5		Gurdaspur ...	5	1	4	1	...	1	4	1	3	...	...	...
6		Shahpur ...	51	33	18	25	19	6	26	14	12	4	4	...
7		Montgomery ...	9	3	6	4	2	2	5	1	4	...	...	...
8		Lyallpur ...	4	4	...	3	3	...	1	1	...	...	...	...
9	BÁNIÁ (AGGARWÁL).	TOTAL ...	20	10	10	3	2	1	17	8	9	1	1	...
10		Hoshiarpur ...	11	6	5	...	...	...	11	6	5	...	...	...
11		Ferozepore ...	7	4	3	2	2	...	5	2	3	1	1	..
12		Gurdaspur ...	2	...	2	1	...	1	1	...	1	...	...	...
13	BRÁHMAN ...	TOTAL ...	236	135	101	99	84	15	137	51	86	36	32	4
14		Delhi ...	29	16	13	17	11	6	12	5	7	14	10	4
15		Simla ...	14	7	7	6	4	2	8	3	5	2	2	...
16		Lahore ...	79	53	26	32	29	3	47	24	23	13	13	...
17		Amritsar ...	36	18	18	13	11	2	23	7	16	2	2	...
18		Gurdaspur ...	34	19	15	16	14	2	18	5	13	5	5	...
19		Rawalpindi ...	42	21	21	14	14	...	28	7	21	...	...	...
20		Montgomery ...	2	1	1	1	1	...	1	...	1	...	...	...
21	KALÁL ...	TOTAL ...	22	12	10	2	2	...	20	10	10	1	1	...
22		Hoshiarpur ...	15	8	7	2	2	...	13	6	7	1	1	..
23		Lahore ...	7	4	3	...	...	...	7	4	3	...	...	...
24	KHATRÍ ...	TOTAL ...	171	94	77	60	50	10	111	44	67	29	21	8
25		Lahore ...	61	30	31	20	18	2	41	12	29	12	6	6
26		Amritsar ...	18	12	6	10	8	2	8	4	4	4	3	1
27		Gurdaspur ...	53	31	22	11	10	1	42	21	21	7	7	...
28		Gujrat ...	6	2	4	2	...	2	4	2	2	1	...	1
29		Shahpur ...	22	11	11	10	8	2	12	3	9	3	3	...
30		Montgomery ...	5	2	3	2	1	1	3	1	2	..	...	...
31		Lyallpur ...	6	6	...	5	5	...	1	1	...	2	2	...
32	RÁJPUT ...	TOTAL ...	11	8	3	3	3	...	8	5	3	...	...	...
33		Ferozepore ...	4	3	1	2	2	...	2	1	1	...	...	...
34		Lahore ...	6	4	2	...	...	...	6	4	2	...	...	...
35		Gurdaspur ...	1	1	...	1	1	...	...	...	...	...	...	...
36	SUNÁR ...	TOTAL ..	23	17	6	11	10	1	12	7	5	4	4	...
37		Lahore ...	5	3	2	2	2	...	3	1	2	1	1	...
38		Gurdaspur ...	12	10	2	6	6	...	6	4	2	2	2	...
39		Gujrat ...	6	4	2	3	2	1	3	2	1	1	1	...
40	†OTHERS ...	TOTAL ...	18	7	11	5	4	1	13	3	10	2	2	...
41		Lahore ...	3	2	1	...	...	...	3	2	1	...	...	...
42		Gurdaspur ...	11	5	6	4	4	...	7	1	6	2	2	...
43		Lyallpur ...	4	...	4	1	...	1	3	...	3	...	...	...

† *Detail of Others.*—Jat males 2, females 4, Jhinwar males 2, female 1, Tarkhán males 3, females 6.

CASTES IN CERTAIN SECTS, FOR SELECTED DISTRICTS—*concluded.*

3. DEV DHARM.

Serial No	Caste.	Locality.	Population. Total. Persons.	Total. Males.	Total. Females.	Literate. Persons.	Literate. Males.	Literate. Females.	Illiterate. Persons.	Illiterate. Males.	Illiterate. Females.	Literate in English. Persons.	Literate in English. Males.	Literate in English. Females.
	1	2	3	4	5	6	7	8	9	10	11	12	13	14
1	**TOTAL**	...	**2,317**	**1,321**	**996**	**426**	**323**	**103**	**1,891**	**998**	**893**	**68**	**62**	**6**
2	ARORÁ ...	TOTAL ...	**337**	**186**	**151**	**168**	**126**	**42**	**169**	**60**	**109**	**26**	**23**	**3**
3		Ferozepore ...	*237*	128	109	132	94	38	105	34	71	17	15	2
4		Lyallpur ...	*100*	58	42	36	32	4	64	26	38	9	8	1
5	BÁNIÁ (AGGARWÁL.)	TOTAL ...	**53**	**17**	**36**	**21**	**9**	**12**	**32**	**8**	**24**	**4**	**2**	**2**
6		Delhi ..	*2*	...	2	...	...	...	2	...	2	...	...	...
7		Hoshiarpur ...	*2*	...	2	...	...	...	2	...	2	...	...	...
8		Ferozepore ...	*49*	17	32	21	9	12	28	8	20	4	2	2
9	BRÁHMAN ...	TOTAL ...	**142**	**80**	**62**	**58**	**42**	**16**	**84**	**38**	**46**	**5**	**5**	...
10		Simla ...	*13*	13	...	6	6	...	7	7	..	...	...	...
11		Hoshiarpur ...	*34*	23	11	7	5	2	27	18	9	1	1	...
12		Ferozepore ...	*55*	25	30	28	19	9	27	6	21	2	2	...
13		Lyallpur ...	*40*	19	21	17	12	5	23	7	16	2	2	...
14	CHAMÁR ...	TOTAL ...	**670**	**401**	**269**	**4**	**4**	...	**666**	**397**	**269**	...	...	...
15		Simla ...	*2*	...	2	...	...	...	2	...	2	...	...	...
16		Hoshiarpur ...	*578*	344	234	4	4	...	574	340	234	...	...	...
17		Kapurthala State	*90*	57	33	...	...	...	90	57	33	...	...	...
18	DÁGI AND KOLI.	Simla	*37*	19	18	...	...	...	37	19	18	...	...	...
19	DHOBI	Simla ...	*15*	12	3	...	...	...	15	12	3	...	...	...
20	JAT ...	TOTAL ...	**269**	**150**	**119**	**23**	**20**	**3**	**246**	**130**	**116**	**5**	**5**	...
21		Hoshiarpur ...	*119*	68	51	4	3	1	115	65	50	...	...	...
22		Ferozepore ...	*4*	3	1	1	1	...	3	2	1	...	...	...
23		Lyallpur ...	*50*	28	22	14	12	2	36	16	20	5	5	...
24		Kapurthala State	*96*	51	45	4	4	...	92	47	45	...	...	...
25	KANET ...	Simla ...	*36*	18	18	6	4	2	30	14	16	...	...	...
26	KHATRÍ ...	TOTAL ...	**209**	**117**	**92**	**104**	**83**	**21**	**105**	**34**	**71**	**18**	**17**	**1**
27		Delhi ...	*10*	2	8	5	2	3	5	...	5	2	2	...
28		Ferozepore ...	*141*	78	63	67	53	14	74	25	49	13	12	1
29		Lyallpur ...	*58*	37	21	32	28	4	26	9	17	3	3	..
30	KUMHÁR ...	TOTAL ...	**34**	**19**	**15**	**2**	...	**2**	**32**	**19**	**13**	...	...	...
31		Simla ...	*9*	5	4	2	...	2	7	5	2	..	...	...
32		Hoshiarpur ...	*25*	14	11	...	...	...	25	14	11	...	...	...
33	LOHÁR ...	TOTAL ...	**20**	**14**	**6**	...	...	...	**20**	**14**	**6**	...	...	...
34		Simla ...	*6*	6	...	...	...	...	6	6	...	...	...	...
35		Hoshiarpur ...	*14*	8	6	...	...	...	14	8	6	...	...	...
36	MIRÁSI ...	TOTAL ...	**17**	**10**	**7**	...	...	...	**17**	**10**	**7**	...	...	...
37		Simla ...	*4*	...	4	...	...	...	4	...	4	...	...	...
38		Hoshiarpur ...	*13*	10	3	..	...	...	13	10	3	...	...	..
39	NÁI ...	Hoshiarpur ...	*14*	7	7	...	...	...	14	7	7	...	...	...
40	NÁIK ...	Delhi ...	*353*	191	162	3	3	...	350	188	162	...	...	...
41	RÁJPUT ...	TOTAL ...	**23**	**20**	**3**	**9**	**8**	**1**	**14**	**12**	**2**	**4**	**4**	...
42		Delhi ...	*1*	...	1	...	...	...	1	...	1	...	...	...
43		Simla ...	*17*	17	...	6	6	...	11	11	...	4	4	...
44		Hoshiarpur ...	*5*	3	2	3	2	1	2	1	1	...	...	...
45	SUNÁR ...	TOTAL ..	**22**	**13**	**9**	...	...	...	**22**	**13**	**9**	...	...	...
46		Hoshiarpur ...	*5*	2	3	...	...	...	5	2	3	...	...	...
47		Kapurthala State	*17*	11	6	...	...	...	17	11	6	...	...	...
48	TARKHÁN ...	TOTAL ...	**37**	**25**	**12**	**25**	**21**	**4**	**12**	**4**	**8**	**6**	**6**	...
49		Hoshiarpur ...	*2*	2	...	1	1	...	1	1	...	...	...	...
50		Ferozepore ...	*35*	23	12	24	20	4	11	3	8	6	6	...
51	*OTHERS ...	TOTAL ...	**29**	**22**	**7**	**3**	**3**	...	**26**	**19**	**7**	...	...	...
52		Delhi ...	*4*	4	...	...	...	...	4	4	...	...	...	...
53		Simla ...	*18*	12	6	2	2	...	16	10	6	...	...	...
54		Hoshiarpur ...	7	6	1	1	1	...	6	5	1	...	...	...

* *Detail of Others.*—Báhti male 1, Bairági male 1, Bhát males 3, Chanál females 2, Ghirath males 2, Jaiswárá males 6, Jhínwar male 1, female 1, Juláhá malo 1, females 4, Kurmi males 2, Mochí males 3, Sarerá males 2.

APPENDIX TO IMPERIAL TABLE XIII.

SUB-CASTES OF CERTAIN SELECTED CASTES.

1. This table has been prepared under the orders of the Punjab Government for the following 15 castes:—

Aggarwál, Ahir, Awán, Biloch, Brahman, Chuhrá, Faqir, Ját, Khatri, Lohár, Máchhi, Mussalli (including Kutáná), Rájput, Sheikh and Sunár.

2. The total strength of each caste, with detail by religion, has been given at the beginning.

3. The letter immediately following the name of each Sub-caste denotes the religion, thus:—

H=Hindu, S=Sikh, J=Jain, B=Buddhist, M=Muhammadan.

4. The following signs have been used for indicating the locality in which the Sub-castes are met with in considerable numbers:—

P=Punjab, B=British Territory, S=Native States, D=Delhi Division, J=Jullundur Division, L=Lahore Division, R=Rawalpindi Division, M=Multan Division.

1 = Hissar District.	19 = Shahpur District.	36 = Bashahr State.
2 = Rohtak ,,	20 = Jhelum ,,	37 = Keonthal ,,
3 = Gurgaon ,,	21 = Rawalpindi ,,	38 = Baghal ,,
4 = Delhi ,,	22 = Attock ,,	39 = Bilaspur ,,
5 = Karnal ,,	23 = Mianwali ,,	40 = Nalagarh ,,
6 = Ambala ,,	24 = Montgomery ,,	41 = Simla Minor Hill States.
7 = Simla ,,	25 = Lyallpur ,,	42 = Mandi State.
8 = Kangra ,,	26 = Jhang ,,	43 = Suket ,,
9 = Hoshiarpur ,,	27 = Multan ,,	44 = Kapurthala ,,
10 = Jullundur ,,	28 = Muzaffargarh ,,	45 = Maler Kotla ,,
11 = Ludhiana ,,	29 = Dera Ghazi Khan ,,	46 = Faridkot ,,
12 = Ferozepore ,,	30 = Loharu State.	47 = Chamba ,,
13 = Lahore ,,	31 = Dujana ,,	48 = Patiala ,,
14 = Amritsar ,,	32 = Pataudi ,,	49 = Jind ,,
15 = Gurdaspur ,,	33 = Kalsia ,,	50 = Nabha ,,
16 = Sialkot ,,	34 = Nahan ,,	51 = Bahawalpur ,,
17 = Gujranwala ,,	35 = Jubbal ,,	
18 = Gujrat ,,		

5. Sub-castes returning not more than 10 persons have been grouped together under the head "Minor" with a footnote giving the detail of such sub-castes with the strength of each. To economise space, the locality has not been noted in case of the "Minor" and "Unspecified" sub-castes.

6. The compilation of this table has been one of extreme difficulty owing to the obscurity of an immense proportion of the terms used. The names of sub-castes were carelessly written by the Enumerators, some of whom did not know how to spell the words. The copyists cared equally little about the accuracy of the spelling. The sorting was the third stage at which the names were read anyhow and put down according to the opinion of the operator. Tabulation was the first operation at which a rational rendering of the entries was undertaken. Such mistakes as were detected owing to the personal knowledge of the staff from myself down to the compilers were corrected after reference to slips, or where necessary, to the Enumeration books. Lists of all doubtful sub-caste entries were then sent to the Tahsils of Enumeration and the correct spellings obtained from the Tahsildars in triple character (Roman, Persian and Nagri). Nevertheless considering the enormous number of the sub-castes and the low paid clerks through whose hands the record has passed repeatedly, numerous meaningless entries must have escaped notice. I have corrected the names where I could be certain of an error but have not attempted more for fear of erring on the opposite side. I contemplated circulating the complete lists of sub-castes to Districts for criticism, but have had to give up the idea as it would have caused inordinate delay. I therefore prefix the Table with my apologies for such mistakes of spelling as may have crept in.

Aggarwal 373,622 { H. 340,768; S. 1,929; M. 10; J. 30,904; B. 11 }

Names of Sub-Castes.		Persons.	Locality.
Ahran ...	H	2,612	D. 21, 48
Amin ...	H	68	4
	J	25	3
Bachhal ...	H	68	2, 5, 6
Bades ...	H	48	1
Báhal ...	H	38	2, 10
Bains ...	H	13	13, 21, 39
Bajáwat ...	H	74	4
Báiá ...	H	12	11, 24
Balewál ...	J	16	4
Bandal ...	H	832	1, 2, 4, 12, 49
Bandes ...	H	1,465	D. 11
Bánsal ...	H	35,272	D. J. 48, 49, 50, 51
	S	268	1, 48, 51
	J	971	D. 45, 48, 49, 50
Bánsar ...	H	19	6, 12
Baqál ...	H	92	41
	M	1	44
	J	13	4
Bárá Saini ...	H	173	3, 4
Barhiá ...	H	39	1, 3
Báriwál ...	H	28	3, 12
Barjat ...	J	14	1
Básal ...	H	78	9, 11, 17
	J	16	12
Básrá ...	H	23	4, 11
Basti ...	H	26	5, 6
Báwalia ...	H	454	25, 50
Bhanwasiá ...	H	8	9
	J	6	3
Bharat ...	H	29	6, 16
Bhárgo ...	H	467	2
Bográ ...	H	88	50
Chagal ...	H	52	45
Chandni ...	H	14	12, 13
Chendal ..	H	452	1, 3, 6, 11, 12, 51
	S	2	5, 50
	J	491	1, 5, 6
Chhoti Saran	H	429	5, 6
Charási ...	H	14	12, 17
Dassá ...	H	1,628	D. 13, 32, 44
	J	27	4, 5
Dassar ...	H	35	4, 16
	J	4	13
Desi ...	H	358	1, 5, 33
	S	4	33.
Dhosar ...	H	32	12, 16. 24
	S	3	12
Gandoiá ...	H	103	3
Gar (Gargoti)	H	51,763	L. 1, 2, 9, 10, 11, 31, 45, 46, 48, 49, 50
	S	685	11, 48, 50
	J	3,111	1, 6, 11, 33, 45, 46, 48, 49
Garag ...	H	40,144	D. J. 30, 34
	S	19	6, 12
	J	6,714	D. J. 32, 33, 34
Gargon ...	H	113	33
Gariwál ...	H	13	11
Gátá ...	H	219	6, 24
	S	2	6
Ger ...	H	12,498	5, 6, 12, 15
	S	93	6, 12
	J	1,169	5, 12, 45
Ghar ...	H	434	4, 9, 13, 44
	J	1	25
Gharakh ...	H	11	11
Ghas ...	H	143	6, 9
Gil	H	96	6, 45, 51
	J	15	45
Godhá ...	H	19	12, 16
	J	14	3

Names of Sub-Castes.		Persons.	Locality.
Goil ...	H	52,339	D. 12, 48, 49, 50
	S	141	1, 12, 48, 50
	J	6,346	D. 10, 11, 48, 49
Gol ...	H	6,362	J. 1, 2, 3, 4, 5
	S	5	11, 12, 46
	J	41	11, 44, 45
Golár ...	H	97	12
Goliá ...	H	157	2, 4
Goriá ...	H	72	4, 7, 9
Gosal ...	H	1,647	6, 11, 45
	S	4	11
	J	50	45
Guru ...	H	13	4, 11
	J	2	4
Hari ...	H	32	1, 8
Higal ...	H	20	11
Iran ...	H	465	3, 5, 12, 30, 46
	J	10	3
Jaini ...	H	8	27
	J	10	21, 25
Jándar ...	H	101	5, 16, 44
Jángal ...	H	183	2, 5
Jasarwál ...	H	3,307	13
	J	158	3, 4
Jaswárá ...	H	14	11, 14, 44
Jendal ...	H	11,244	1, 4, 5, 48, 50
	S	85	11, 12, 48, 50
	J	378	11, 45, 48
Jindiál ...	H	369	4, 10, 12, 5.
Josni ..	H	12	11
Kágal ...	H	43	12
Kajlas ...	H	95	5
Kálá ...	J	12	1
Kalas ...	H	13	11, 12, 33
	S	10	12
Kalri ...	H	28	51
Kandiárí ...	H	40	12
Kánjal ...	H	552	1, 2, 4, 5, 12, 45
	J	5	45
Kánshal ...	H	4,456	5, 48, 49, 50
	S	2	50
	J	21	11, 48
Kapal ...	H	50	5, 6, 12, 27
Karab ...	H	38	15, 44
Kariwál ...	H	9	4, 11
	S	49	12
Kasal ...	H	1,673	D. 11, 12, 31, 32, 45
	J	185	3, 6
Kasandan ...	H	42	6
Kashap ...	H	73	1, 2, 3, 4, 7, 12
Khandelwál	H	509	3, 12
	J	249	3, 9
Kochaliá ...	H	20	2, 3
Koban ...	H	23	16
Koil ...	H	54	11, 12, 51
	J	6	3
Konchal ...	H	737	4
Lohiá ...	H	123	3
Máhar ...	H	29	2, 12, 22, 30
Mahesri ...	H	251	10, 12, 50
	J	9	3
Mahurá ...	H	2,195	3, 12
Majlas ...	H	42	5
Mansani ...	H	87	12
Manal ...	H	177	2
Mandal ...	H	206	3, 13, 51
Mangal ...	H	5,332	J. 3, 4, 5, 48, 49
	S	42	48
	J	195	3, 4, 48
Manglas ...	H	12	6
Mansal ...	H	608	5, 14, 16, 20, 30
Mánsari ...	H	12	7, 13, 42
	J	4	4
Márári ...	H	231	6, 17
	S	2	21
Matár ...	H	242	9, 13, 30, 31
Matin ...	H	24	16
Matosari ...	H	13	16

Names of Sub-Castes.		Persons.	Locality.
Megal ...	H	448	1, 12, 48
	S	1	48
Mehmi ...	H	12	18
Mesan ...	H	13	45
Mil ...	H	71	6, 11, 51
	S	4	12
Miri ...	H	19	9
Mital ...	H	22,226	1, 4, 5, 9, 10, 11, 48, 49, 50
	S	166	12, 48, 50
	J	4,266	4, 5, 6, 48, 49
Mitlas ...	H	17	6, 33
	J	13	33
Mitras ...	H	20	5, 34
Nágar ...	H	168	3
Náhar ...	H	12	3
Nángal ...	H	64	3
	J	95	5
Narek ...	H	37	15
Ochhal ...	H	14	1, 2, 5
Orás ...	H	30	5
Oswál ...	H	112	4, 12
Párasnáth ...	H	15	5
Pasrili ...	H	13	51
Patel ...	H	41	4
Rájá Sháhi ...	H	3	2
	J	11	4
Rastgi ...	H	1,510	3, 4, 32
	J	8	4
Saghar ...	H	55	10, 11, 12
Sahal ...	H	62	34
Saigal ...	H	1,727	1, 5, 10, 12, 16, 18, 45, 46
	S	1	10
	J	748	1, 10, 12, 24, 45
Saiti ...	H	2	2
	J	24	1
Sándal ...	H	30	5, 6, 9, 44
Sangal ...	H	41,089	D. J. 31, 45, 46, 48, 49
	S	192	12, 48, 50
	J	2,843	D. 12, 48, 49
Sangraji ...	H	16	12, 44
	J	1	12
Saralia ...	H	35	25, 30, 40
Saráogi ...	H	39	16
	J	230	4
Sil .	H	42	2
Sirimál ...	J	41	4
Sital ...	H	603	4, 11, 25, 48
	S	2	5
	J	29	5, 13, 48
Sohiná ...	J	23	4
Táil ...	H	2,423	D. 10, 12, 48, 49
	J	107	4, 48, 49
Tál ...	H	130	2, 4, 5
Tamoli ...	H	45	1
Tatle ...	H	13,197	11, 12, 25, 30
	J	1	14
Thákar ...	J	65	4
Thal ...	H	7	10
	J	8	44
Vaish ...	H	1,153	4, 11, 13, 24, 27
	S	1	12
	J	178	4, 21, 45
Vaishno ...	H	64	2, 6, 27, 28
	J	2	42
Vásal ...	H	1,865	10, 12, 15, 46
	S	25	12
Vátis ...	H	15	12
*Minor ...	H	429	
	S	2	
	M	2	
	J	61	
Unspecified ...	H	7,818	
	S	119	
	M	7	
	J	1,862	
	B	11	

* DETAIL OF MINOR.

Agrúl 2, Alsiwál 2, Amar 1, Anchal 3, Astál 6, Atarji 4, Aus 1, Bahádar 1, Bahti 4, Bairági 1, Bajái 6, Bákhar 2, Bálak 4, Band 9, Bandhra 7, Basán 10, Basli 6, Batká 1, Bator 2, Bedwán 3, Beniwál 7, Bhantá 6, Bhatáru 5, Bishan 10, Bol 2, Bopáni 1, Brahman 2, Chamiá 1, Chandi 1, Chandrawál 2, Chhatri 8, Chopré 5, Dágar 6, Dawálu 4, Degammar 10, Dhaiá 1, Dhami 3, Dhangol 3, Dháriwál 7, Dharmi 2, Dhowán 1, Dodáti 3, Dogré 2, Duli 2, Gandhal 2, Gani 8, Garaj 1, Gárlesan 2, Gogalgogar 4, Golgawá 1, Gorin 7, Gorká 1, Gorpál 2, Gungal 9, Handáshi 1, Hans 3, Hirat 4, Hugti 2, Jande 2, Jáoli 1, Jariâ 5, Ját 1, Jedar 4, Jiasia 7, Jindan 2, Jindu 9, Jotiá 2, Jotshi 2, Kabai 1, Káchhal 4, Kaihgal 3, Kalari 4, Kalejá 2, Kanáje 1, Kans 1, Kapur 5, Karan 1, Kartádhári 2, Kaswál 1, Káthwál 1, Kátián 4, Kaushak 5, Kesarwáli 4, Khatri 2, Khokhar 2, Kochak 2, Kori 1, Lagál 2, Láli 3, Lánolia 1, Lothi 1, Mádin 4, Mahod 1, Makar 4, Mánaktálá 4, Manglá 2, Masgal 3, Matrodiá 2, Mehtar 2, Mohrá 8, Motal 3, Nái 3, Nánakpanthi 1, Nandáuri 9, Nandoi 2, Naraínwál 7, Natorá 1, Ogre 1, Pal 1, Panár 3, Pandáre 1, Patri 1, Pauniá 1, Phulerái 2, Qanauji 4, Rájbans 9, Rájput 10, Rájkumár 6, Rorá 5, Sádhu Jaini 6, Sandiá 1, Sangoti 6, Sankarwál 1, Sanwál 3, Sarál 1, Sársiwál 8, Sársut 8, Satnágar 9, Segar 2, Shakardár 5, Sián 8, Sigan 5, Sikáyta 4, Siláwatyá 2, Síripadh 2, Sohiná 1, Soti 1, Táhad 1, Tor 2, Uchhat 2, Vaisí 5, and Vánsal 8.

SUB-CASTES OF CERTAIN SELECTED CASTES.

Names of Sub-Castes.		Persons.	Locality.
Ahir		208,594	H. 205,631 S. 836 M. 2,626 J. 1
Abhiryá ...	H	46	2, 12
Ahiri ..	H	38	18, 26, 51
	M	15	23, 26
Ajarwáh ...	H	11	4
Ajnasi ...	H	15	5
Alpariá ...	H	240	1, 4, 46
	S	2	12
Árwál ...	H	6	21
	S	3	49
	M	17	21
Ataryá ...	H	127	1, 14, 15
Bachhowáli	H	9	45, 50
	S	15	50
Bachhwáriá ...	H	236	1, 12, 30, 46
Badhowál ...	H	71	1, 4
Bágariá ...	H	36	2, 12
Bajwáliá ...	H	112	2, 5, 12, 13
Bákwál ...	H	65	2, 12
Balásiá ...	H	16	1
Bálbans ...	H	65	5
Balewál ...	H	28	2, 12
Bálwán ...	H	469	1, 2
Banoli ..	H	14	1, 5, 13
Bánerá ...	H	14	46
Bansi ...	H	11	44
Bánswál ...	H	22	1
Barái .	H	139	1, 27, 44
Barálá ...	H	55	1, 6
Báswarán ...	H	68	2
Bhagoriá ...	H	83	1, 2, 3, 4, 12
Bhagwári ...	H	44	1, 12
Bhálkhá ..	H	76	2, 4
Bhankariá ..	H	97	1, 4, 12
Bhátiá ...	H	62	1, 2, 3, 6, 12
	M	65	1, 6, 19, 27
Bhil ...	H	401	3, 5
Bhunklán ...	H	12	1
Bhusáriá ..	H	278	2, 4, 6
Botar ...	H	17	46
Chakná ..	H	200	1, 2, 49, 50, 51
Chandáil ...	H	14	50
	S	1	50
Chandáná ...	H	73	1, 2
Channsháb ...	H	20	12
Charkhiá ...	H	34	2, 46
Chatarbansi	H	138	4
Chatosiá ..	H	114	1, 2
Chauhán ...	H	79	1, 3, 12
	S	2	12
	M	1	26
Chhonkar ...	H	14	3
Chhosiá ...	H	169	1, 2, 12
Choprá ...	H	14	5
Churá ...	H	593	1, 2, 3, 4, 12, 13
Dahiá ...	H	265	1, 2, 3, 5
Dáhir ...	H	149	2, 12, 46
	M	1	27
Dalál ...	H	17	2
Dántar ..	H	99	1, 2, 3, 5, 12
Dárán ...	H	38	1, 2
Dáriwál ...	H	35	2
Daswálgrámi	H	27	4
Dátir ...	H	102	1, 34
	S	3	49
	M	31	27
Dátle ...	H	13	4
Dátriá ...	H	41	1, 3
Devá ...	H	167	1, 2, 3, 12, 34
Dhábar ...	H	476	1, 12
	S	4	49
Dhák Puchh...	H	18	5
Dhákwál ...	H	38	5
Dhánilá ...	H	56	1, 12, 50
	S	6	6
Dhanudiá ...	H	22	1, 46
Dhanwál ...	H	44	1, 12, 30
Dharan ...	H	11	3
Dharma ...	H	36	12
Dhátri ...	H	19	2, 4
Dhiyá ...	H	17	4
Dhodhilá ...	H	26	1, 2, 12
Dholán ...	H	11	2
	M	2	27
Dholiwál ...	H	51	1, 4, 12
Dhundálá ...	H	51	2, 12, 14
Dhorá ...	H	71	4
Dogar ...	H	954	D. 12, 30, 46
	M	1	21
Dohi ...	H	70	1
Dosádá ...	H	372	1, 2, 12, 30, 34
Dandak ...	H	76	2
Gadariá ...	H	75	7, 12, 13, 14, 30
Gandwál ...	H	136	1, 2, 12
Gangá ...	M	26	19
Gangáwái ...	H	130	1, 4
Gathwál ...	H	120	2
	S	1	11
Gawálá ...	H	969	L. 2, 3, 6, 7, 18, 19, 21, 44
	S	4	48
	M	6	10
Gawál Bansi	H	4,370	B. 34, 44, 48, 49, 50, 51
	S	39	14, 48
	M	6	14
Gawáliá ...	H	61	50
Gawáns ...	H	20	4, 12
Gharu ...	H	140	2, 3
Gharwál ...	H	182	1, 2, 4, 21
	M	1	21
Ghatwál ...	H	118	1, 2
Ghogar ...	H	24	1, 2, 12, 24
Ghoriá ...	H	39	1, 6, 12
Ghosiá ...	H	80	2, 4, 32
	M	164	21
Goliá ...	H	35	1, 4
Gomi ...	H	15	1
Gujar ...	H	60	10, 14, 27
Gulgáran ...	H	48	1, 2
Gurál ...	H	14	27, 32
Gurbansi ...	H	25	4, 5
Gwál Ratan	H	32	21
Hamál ...	H	53	1, 2, 4
Handwál ...	H	19	1, 2
Harbali ...	H	42	2, 46
	S	4	5
Hári ...	H	12	2, 12
Harkhá ...	H	21	2
Jádam ..	H	296	1, 2, 4, 5, 12, 30
	S	1	1
Jádu Bansi ...	H	145,800	D. 12, 31, 33, 48, 49, 50
	S	58	14, 48
	M	9	3, 48
Jádwál ...	H	33	12
Jágariá ...	H	15	30
Jágu ...	H	14	1
Jájam ...	H	26	1, 2, 12
Janjariá ...	H	204	4
	M	1	47
Jaráh ...	H	13	1, 2
Jásal ...	H	12	1, 25
Jat ...	H	6	12
	M	462	19, 23, 27
Játrá ...	H	17	1, 2
	S	1	5
Jausiá ...	H	14	1, 30
Jhagruliá ...	H	325	1, 2, 3, 4
Jharoiá ...	H	77	1, 3, 30
Jharudiá ...	H	589	1, 2
Jharwál ...	H	475	2, 4, 13
Kabirá ...	H	34	1
Kakráliá ...	H	72	12, 46
Kákudiá ...	H	43	2, 25, 30
Kaláliá ...	H	73	1, 3, 5
	S	15	49
	M	12	21
Kalál Satti ...	H	102	1, 6
Kalgán ...	H	410	1, 2
Kandál ...	H	125	1, 2, 4
Kángar ...	H	313	1, 2, 3, 4, 6, 12
Kánkasi ...	H	412	1, 2, 4, 5
	S	15	5
Karáná ...	H	276	2, 3, 6
Karanwál ...	H	62	2
Karerá ...	H	54	1, 5, 11, 49
Kásab ...	H	58	4, 5, 12, 13, 21, 25
Kásan ...	H	67	17, 30
Káth ...	H	1,235	1, 2
Kawáriá ...	H	241	1, 2, 4, 6, 12, 13, 30
Kenwán ...	H	58	2, 4, 10
Khalád ...	H	190	1, 2, 12, 15
Khaliár ...	H	133	1, 2, 5, 18
Khandwál ...	H	43	1, 2, 3, 12, 32
Khanwál ...	H	68	1, 2, 12
Khároliá ...	H	120	1, 2, 3, 12
	S	4	12
Khárotiá ...	H	14	12
Kharwál ...	H	188	1, 2, 34
Khátodiá ...	H	1,016	1, 2, 3, 12
Khodal ...	H	66	1, 7
Khokhariá ...	H	36	2, 4
	M	23	26
Kholá ...	H	674	1, 2, 3, 4, 5, 12, 46
Khosá ...	H	801	1, 2, 4, 12
Khoshi ...	H	130	1, 2, 12, 49
Kinwál ...	H	113	2
Kondal ...	H	64	1, 7
	M	5	27
Kosaliá ...	H	3,776	2, 4, 12, 30, 48
	M	1	12
Kotlá ...	H	24	2, 4
Krishan Bansi	H	74	1, 4, 21
Lachhiwál ...	H	30	5
Lagániá ...	H	155	1, 2, 3, 12
Lákhi ...	H	14	4
Lámbá ...	H	536	1, 2, 3, 4
Lániá ...	H	55	2
Lápán ...	H	17	30
Lodi ...	H	21	12, 16
Luniwál ...	H	28	5
Madáriá ...	H	14	2, 4
Madhanwál ...	H	68	4
Mahlá ...	H	142	2, 4, 11, 32
Mahtá ...	H	219	1, 2, 4, 12, 46
	M	56	27
Mákrá ...	H	18	1, 12, 30
Malián ...	H	48	1, 4, 16
Mamlá ...	H	18	4
Mándas ...	H	16	4
Mandhar ...	H	75	2, 5, 19
Manmál ...	H	88	2
Mekhwál ...	H	108	13
Mohal ...	H	64	1
Mohmál ...	H	140	1
Mohni ...	H	97	1, 3
Mula ...	H	20	2, 5
Nagláriá ...	H	71	2, 12
Nágrál ...	H	14	2, 13, 16
Náhariá ...	H	99	1, 2, 3
Nái ...	H	25	1, 4
Nand Bansi	H	17,672	D. L. 12, 32, 48, 49, 50
	S	69	48
Nandsi ...	H	15	46
Nanwál ...	H	60	2, 4, 12, 46
	S	3	5
Nirbálá ...	H	99	2, 4
Nirbán ...	H	305	2, 4, 5, 12, 31
Notidál ...	H	138	2
Nunwál ...	H	38	2, 5
Pachariá ...	H	49	1, 2, 3
Pachhwál ...	H	117	2, 4, 30
Panár ...	H	28	1, 7, 12
Panwáliá ...	H	17	12, 51
Peswál ...	H	11	1, 2, 6, 31
Pawár ...	H	36	1, 4, 51
Phaparwál ...	H	48	1
Puniá ...	H	183	1
Purbiá ...	H	13	12, 13, 15, 16, 27
	M	2	25
Rábar ...	H	41	1, 2, 4, 12
	S	1	10
Raghu Bansi	H	83	5, 6, 12, 15, 50
Ráj Bansi ...	H	17	10, 17, 45
Rájput ...	H	2	12, 24
	S	5	15
	M	114	19
Ráthu ...	H	11	2
Ráwji ...	H	36	12, 16
Rorwál ...	H	75	1, 4
Ságariá ...	H	54	1, 12, 13
Samalwál ...	H	186	1, 2, 12

Names of Sub-Castes.		Persons.	Locality.
Sanádiá ...	H	460	2, 4, 12, 32
Sangálfa ...	H	133	1, 2, 4, 30
Sánkliá ...	H	20	2
Sansáriá ...	H	600	1, 2, 3, 4, 12, 30
Sánp ...	H	1,388	D. 12, 25, 30, 46, 49
	S	2	49
Sarswál ...	H	27	2, 12, 31
Satoriá ...	H	246	1, 4, 30
Sepra ...	H	13	11
Solangia ...	H	151	1, 2, 5, 16
	S	1	50
Sultáni ...	H	160	1, 2, 3, 4, 5, 12, 30
Suraj Bansi	H	149	3, 4, 5, 6, 21
Tagániá ...	H	120	1, 2
Tarbhán ...	H	383	4
Tátlá ...	H	127	1, 50
Tawáliá ...	H	41	1, 2, 32
Tedia ...	H	37	2
Thakaria ...	H	439	1, 2, 4, 5
Thokrán ...	H	326	1, 2, 3, 4, 12, 46
Tundak ...	H	245	1, 2
Tur ...	H	15	4, 11, 12
	M	2	25
Tutiwál ...	H	19	2
Uhodewál ...	H	43	1
Ulmá ..	M	23	19
* Minor ...	H	1,046	
	S	16	
	M	41	
Unspecified	H	3,986	
	S	61	
	M	1,539	
	J	1	

* DETAIL OF MINOR.

Adwál 2, Aggarwál 10, Ahirwál 5, Ajainwál 1, Akariyá 7, Akholá 9, Andoriá 4, Aráin 2, Ardoke 2, Atharwál 10, Athwál 9, Auj 5, Bádhná 7, Bagat 2, Bágri 10, Balwáni 1, Bamráliá 10, Band Bansi 8, Bangeliá 10, Bangrál 5, Banolí 7, Bárgar 5, Barkerá 5, Barni 1, Basáwal 6, Básor 1, Bathoriá 2, Báwaniá 4, Bhabálá 1, Bhábrá 10, Bhádur 7, Bhagráin 1, Bhandlá 10, Bhangri 4, Bhárdwáj 9, Bhat 10, Bhátak 4, Bhatáriá 3, Bhatoni 3, Bhogar 3, Bhoghát 3, Bhorá 6, Bhowinwál 10, Bishpál 3, Bodná 4, Botiá 3, Bráriá 9, Chadhar 1, Cháhar 1, Chakári 5, Chandar Bansi 4, Chándiá 8, Chandor 1, Chandráwal 1, Changri 8, Chárni 6, Chaudhri 2, Choliá 1, Dádu-Bansi 8, Dádu-Panthi 4, Dahmi 3, Dahriá 7, Dáirá 4, Dalá 8, Dargariá 1, Dasá 5, Dasghar 7, Deswál 2, Deviá 4, Dewal 4, Dhab 4, Dhakaná 5, Dhandal 4, Dhark 1, Diál 6, Diná 3, Dindár 2, Gandoniá 6, Gawáliá Lewán 9, Ghoti 7, Gogiá 3, Goil 7, Golas 1, Gomán 8, Goslá 8, Handiá 4, Hánsi 5, Harwanwál 1, Hindustáni 3, Jádu-Panthi 3, Jagáwasi 3, Jagráo 1, Jagráná 5, Jain-Panthi 2, Jaiswárá 3, Jawási 9, Joia 1, Jomli 3, Juláha 1, Juniá 10, Kahnár 5, Kaholi 2, Kalániá 7, Kanghá 2, Kankráli 1, Kánt 8, Kanwár 9, Karidá 1, Karpál 1, Kasumi 4, Katárwál 6, Khanná 4, Khatti 10, Kirkiá 8, Kori 8, Koska 1, Ladhá 9, Lákán 10, Lakhiár 9, Láwáh 4, Lunia 7, Madhán 10, Maiwal 8, Makki 1, Maláisi 6, Malgán 3, Malláh 6, Málswál 10, Mámán 2, Mandwan 2, Mánoriá 10, Marob 1, Maroriá 1, Masonia 9, Moman 4, Mugbalia 10, Mukhia 10, Nadhá 10, Nádiná 9, Nagáleni 3, Námar 8, Nár 1, Nathoriá 5, Nodhak 10, Panál 10, Parswál 10, Patwár 1, Phagwári 10, Qázi 10, Rai Bansi 9, Rájá 10, Rájoke 9, Rájoriá 10, Rám Dási 4, Ramiá 9, Rangan 10, Rawás 6, Sádh 9, Sadhán 10, Sáhi 2, Sáhor 10, Saidi 9, Sais 2, Saligá 8, Sangal 7, Sanghá 9, Sanoriá 6, Sanwre 1, Sarang 8, Sarsona 10, Sarwin 9, Shab 7, Sháhzádá 10, Sial 1, Silá 9, Sodágar 10, Sodiwál 8, Soglá 10, Somráh 3, Sankot 10, Takáli 8, Támlá 7, Tandoli 9, Tánk 3, Tarkhoni 9, Tátotá 8, Thal 10, Tokas 10, Tuhwál 5, Tulsia 7, Untwál 10 and Zamindár 10.

Awan 425,931 ... M. 425,931.

Names of Sub-Castes.		Persons.	Locality.
Abshi ...	M	14	20
Abwál ...	M	324	20, 22
Achhiál ...	M	96	21, 23
Achhrál ...	M	2,365	R. 15, 25, 51
Adál ...	M	40	20
Adhe ...	M	12	21
Adyál ...	M	15	20
Aghwán ...	M	40	13
Agrál ...	M	599	21, 22
Ahir ..	M	669	20, 21, 22
Ahmadál ...	M	63	18
Ahmader ...	M	148	22
Ajrál ...	M	502	20, 22, 25
Ajre ...	M	12	22
Ajwál ...	M	86	20, 27
Akbarál ...	M	37	19
Aklál ..	M	148	22
Aliál ...	M	183	22
Aliyási ...	M	47	22
Amirkhel ...	M	20	21
Amrál ...	M	984	20, 21, 22
Anotrá ...	M	39	21
Ansári ...	M	19	51
Aráin ...	M	118	12, 23, 51
Armár ...	M	11	19
Arwán ...	M	268	18, 22
Asirál ...	M	16	15
Asmáilkhel ...	M	70	23
Asnál ...	M	27	20
Aspanál ...	M	52	22
Atwál ...	M	877	19, 21, 22
Awánkhel ...	M	844	20, 26, 51
Azmál ...	M	48	19, 22
Babar ..	M	209	13, 22
Bábká ...	M	717	22
Babkál ...	M	2,042	22
Bachál ...	M	36	19
Bache ...	M	16	21
Badán ...	M	34	20, 27
Badhau ...	M	74	18, 25
Badhiál ...	M	7,730	19, 20, 22, 25, 26
Badhwál ...	M	1,677	15, 18, 20, 27, 51
Bagdial ...	M	4,516	22
Bághá ...	M	248	19, 20, 22, 44
Baghwál ...	M	913	16, 22, 23
Bagiál ...	M	35	22
Bagwál ...	M	2,299	10, 16, 18, 21, 25
Báhmiá ...	M	71	10, 12
Báhn ...	M	84	10, 51
Bái ...	M	665	22
Bájrá ...	M	362	16, 20
Bajrál ...	M	155	22
Bajwál ...	M	35	20, 22
Bakhshiál ...	M	181	19, 20, 22
Bakiál ...	M	331	21
Bakrál ...	M	405	19, 20, 21, 22
Bálá ...	M	93	19, 22
Balál ...	M	30	22
Balfáori ...	M	24	22
Baloh ...	M	15	20, 27
Balorá ...	M	120	29, 51
Balwál ...	M	3,394	18, 22
Bambi ...	M	22	25
Bamiál ...	M	25	21
Báná ...	M	22	9, 19, 20
Bandiál ...	M	167	20, 21, 23
Bángi ...	M	15	19, 22
Bangiál ...	M	79	16, 21
Bángra ...	M	23	8
Barán ...	M	96	18, 21, 22
Bargál ..	M	17	9, 22
Barhál ...	M	220	19, 22
Barmál ...	M	302	20, 21, 22
Barniál ...	M	18	21
Barthál ...	M	1,102	20, 22, 23
Barwál ...	M	90	13, 19, 22, 23
Baryál ...	M	1,213	20, 22
Baryár ...	M	458	22, 23
Básal ...	M	62	22
Bashriál ...	M	165	22
Battá ...	M	12	51
Báwre ...	M	11	20
Bebrá ...	M	43	22
Bhadwál ...	M	60	23, 28
Bhagtál ...	M	586	22
Bhagwál ...	M	3,103	16, 18, 19, 20, 23
Bhakriál ...	M	156	22
Bhalwál ...	M	682	22
Bhamtál ...	M	90	22
Bhanb ...	M	141	22, 23
Bhaniwál ...	M	177	44
Bharmál ...	M	540	20, 22
Bharochi ...	M	14	18
Bharthál ...	M	379	19, 20, 22, 23
Bhárti ...	M	28	20
Bhat ...	M	478	9, 18, 22
Bhatál ...	M	56	19
Bhátra ...	M	21	19
Bhatti ...	M	643	17, 18, 19, 21, 51
Bhawál ...	M	48	19, 23
Bhidel ...	M	307	22, 25
Bhimb ...	M	65	19
Bhin ...	M	120	19, 20
Bhochari ...	M	69	19, 20, 22
Bhogi ...	M	30	23
Bhojál ...	M	389	20, 22
Bhoriwál ...	M	12	22
Bhularwál ...	M	33	20
Bhusin ...	M	113	19
Bhuttá ...	M	441	21, 22, 23, 51
Bhuttar ...	M	323	13, 22, 23
Biddar ...	M	2,134	15, 16, 17, 20, 21, 22
Biloch ...	M	160	15, 21, 22
Biyál ...	M	24	22
Bok ...	M	27	23
Burákhel ...	M	45	22, 25
Chabal ...	M	14	18
Chadhar ...	M	43	22
Chakiál ...	M	18	18
Chakwál ...	M	717	22, 27
Chanáwar ...	M	26	24
Chand ...	M	1,232	16, 17, 21, 24, 51
Chandán ...	M	12	19
Chander ...	M	206	18, 20
Chandhar ...	M	409	17, 19, 27
Chandol ...	M	47	18, 22
Chandor ...	M	1,274	9, 20, 22
Chandrál ...	M	379	22
Chandrán ...	M	52	18
Changál ...	M	38	22
Chanwál ...	M	204	16, 23, 25
Charál ...	M	754	17, 21
Charkál ...	M	22	22
Chasú ...	M	79	19
Chatiál ...	M	55	22
Chatwáliá ...	M	495	9, 20, 22
Chauhán ...	M	3,836	J. L. R. 48, 51
Chechi ...	M	4,402	20, 22
Chháila ...	M	239	20
Chhán ...	M	2,276	16, 19, 20, 21
Chhángondal	M	428	18
Chhiná ...	M	375	16
Chhuttá ...	M	17	23
Choghattá ...	M	87	19, 23, 27, 51
Chotál ...	M	64	20, 23
Chotar	M	30	20
Chuchá ...	M	11	23
Chuggal ...	M	34	18, 20
Chubarial ...	M	62	20
Churigar ...	M	11	25
Chutiál ...	M	16	23

Names of Sub-Castes.	Persons.	Locality.
Dábi ... M	257	22, 23
Dábrá ... M	163	20, 21, 22, 23
Dag ... M	71	19
Dagwál ... M	30	14
Dál ... M	87	20
Daliál ... M	120	19, 22
Daloi ... M	261	22
Damiál ... M	62	23
Dand ... M	239	19, 22
Dandukhel ... M	22	23
Dángar ... M	30	20
Danti ... M	18	19
Darahoti ... M	76	22
Daraich ... M	62	22
Darhál ... M	1,498	19, 20, 22, 23, 25
Dariál ... M	1,896	21, 22, 23
Darsál ... M	363	22, 23
Daryá ... M	101	22, 23
Darzi ... M	25	21, 23, 24
Dath ... M	38	19
Deál ... M	830	19, 20
Derá ... M	11	19
Desi ... M	28	23
Dhádi ... M	24	21, 24
Dhagiál ... M	99	22
Dhál ... M	97	12, 20, 51
Dhale ... M	30	23, 25, 27
Dhamiál ... M	185	19, 20, 21, 22
Dhamrál ... M	263	20, 23
Dhán ... M	16	22
Dhaniá ... M	18	19
Dhanwál ... M	114	20, 22
Dharál ... M	4,564	19, 22, 51
Dháriwál ... M	1,457	13, 22, 23
Dheglá ... M	597	16
Dhingle ... M	129	18
Dhodi ... M	650	21, 22, 23
Dhogwál ... M	45	20
Dholi ... M	361	15, 19, 21, 22, 24
Dhorá ... M	245	20, 22
Dhundwál ... M	363	21, 22
Didár ... M	33	19
Dinwál ... M	21	18
Dosá ... M	19	51
Dográ ... M	42	18, 19, 20, 22
Dole ... M	13	11, 24
Dora ... M	73	19, 22
Dudhán ... M	63	19, 20
Dudiál ... M	15	19
Dudu ... M	107	22
Dudwál ... M	49	20, 21
Duliál ... M	31	22
Faqir ... M	69	19, 21, 22, 51
Fatah Mamdál M	122	22
Gabirá ... M	12	20
Gadiál ... M	256	22
Gajiál ... M	207	23
Gajjá ... M	12	20
Gakhar ... M	157	16, 20, 22
Galiál ... M	132	21
Galmál ... M	100	22
Gandal ... M	397	10, 16, 21, 22
Gándhi ... M	138	21, 22
Gang ... M	2,129	16, 22, 27
Gangál ... M	2,953	20, 21, 22, 25
Gangi ... M	33	18
Ganiál ... M	250	22
Ganirá ... M	81	23
Garjál ... M	126	22, 23
Garog ... M	39	22
Gat ... M	63	22
Gatnál ... M	836	22
Gatooh ... M	11	20
Gelál ... M	106	23
Gelán ... M	13	10, 19
Gelár ... M	22	13, 16
Gewárá ... M	91	13, 16, 17
Ghalli ... M	1,124	10, 16, 18, 25
Ghaniá ... M	52	23, 27, 29
Gharáná ... M	27	18
Gharsiál ... M	35	22
Ghawál ... M	51	19, 22, 25
Ghebe ... M	37	16, 17, 19, 27
Ghi ... M	135	16, 23
Ghial ... M	27	19
Ghog ... M	247	23
Ghogar ... M	29	22
Ghornái ... M	100	22
Ghosi ... M	48	22, 26
Ghotrá ... M	58	20, 22
Giloi ... M	16	23
Gibál ... M	91	22
Godre ... M	53	10, 19
Gogbri ... M	153	22, 25, 27
Gokhiál ... M	908	22
Golái ... M	11	18, 51
Golre ... M	5,063	10, 15, 18, 20, 21, 22
Gomrál ... M	244	8, 27
Gondal ... M	1,579	19, 20, 21, 22
Gondar ... M	18	51
Gorái ... M	179	R. 51
Goral ... M	11	25
Goráre ... M	3,519	16, 17, 18, 19, 20
Gorsá ... M	27	22, 25
Gori ... M	141	18, 19, 23
Gorwárá ... M	181	13, 22
Gotre ... M	78	13, 16, 20
Guár ... M	50	22
Guggiál ... M	119	22, 23, 24
Gulgán ... M	21	11, 14, 17
Guliáni ... M	11	29
Gulkan ... M	211	44
Gul Mohamdán ... M	89	22
Gulsháhi ... M	5,306	10, 15, 21, 25, 44
Hadrál ... M	90	22, 23
Háfizi ... M	13	19
Haider ... M	37	20
Hajjám ... M	35	21
Hakmál ... M	1,108	22, 23
Hamar ... M	41	25
Hamun ... M	743	22
Haujrá ... M	47	21
Háns ... M	38	9, 10, 27
Harpál ... M	1,041	10, 16, 21, 22
Hasanwál ... M	68	18
Hásilá ... M	103	22
Határ ... M	724	16, 20, 22
Hazrál ... M	14	29
Hicharwál ... M	33	26
Hulohál ... M	318	23
Jadhál ... M	331	23
Jáfrál ... M	130	22
Jagar ... M	18	9, 12
Jaggan ... M	44	18
Jaggi ... M	1,186	21
Jagrál ... M	40	24
Jagtole ... M	88	9
Jagwál ... M	218	19, 20, 21
Jahál ... M	475	21
Jahángiri ... M	358	17, 20, 22, 23
Jakhar ... M	241	22
Jálap ... M	57	21
Jálbhatti ... M	47	23
Jamál ... M	690	19, 20, 22, 24
Jámdáni ... M	31	19
Jamwál ... M	508	20, 22
Jand ... M	2,644	10, 16, 20, 22
Jandán ... M	11	19
Jandiál ... M	245	18, 19, 20, 21
Jandli ... M	54	19
Jandrál ... M	98	22
Jandrán ... M	374	19, 20
Jang ... M	48	23
Jangáli ... M	877	22
Jánglá ... M	296	20, 21, 22
Jangwál ... M	11	23
Janjrál ... M	40	19
Janjuá ... M	216	19, 20, 22
Janwál ... M	139	22, 23
Jaráh ... M	75	19, 20, 21, 22
Jás ... M	29	20
Jaspál ... M	135	20, 22, 24
Jessu ... M	86	19
Jaswál ... M	588	18, 19, 22
Jat ... M	636	14, 20, 22, 29, 51
Jatálá ... M	1,129	19, 21, 23, 25
Jatmál ... M	117	22
Jatoi ... M	84	19, 27
Jhajar ... M	21	19, 20
Jhallar ... M	189	19, 20
Jhalungrá ... M	42	19, 20, 22
Jhammat ... M	1,121	17, 18, 20, 22, 23
Jhán ... M	40	4, 19
Jháttá ... M	683	18, 20, 22
Jhukan ... M	53	20
Jial ... M	23	21
Jodri ... M	303	21, 22
Jogi ... M	14	13, 27
Johd ... M	212	22, 51
Joi ... M	76	19, 23
Jojál ... M	12	25
Jondu ... M	13	22
Jorá ... M	228	19, 22, 23
Jothiál ... M	144	22
Joyá ... M	48	24, 27
Joyál ... M	676	22
Juláhá ... M	64	22
Jutál ... M	39	19, 22
Juthá ... M	97	19, 21
Kabíal ... M	181	20, 23
Kadhwál ... M	97	22
Kadiál ... M	104	22, 25
Kadir ... M	101	22
Kahut ... M	1,001	12, 22
Kakar ... M	75	20, 21, 22
Kakwál ... M	46	23
Kalál ... M	57	17, 18, 22
Kalár ... M	1,675	19, 22
Kalgán ... M	6,819	R. 11, 13, 16
Kaliál ... M	1,170	19, 20, 21, 22
Kalián ... M	81	11, 20, 22
Kaliár ... M	44	23, 25, 27
Kalkai ... M	26	16, 19
Kallá ... M	185	20, 22
Kallu .. M	223	23, 25
Kalol ... M	59	9, 51
Kalwál ... M	34	19, 51
Kamboh ... M	42	14, 20, 27
Kamená ... M	25	19
Kamlál ... M	197	22
Kamrál ... M	116	21, 51
Kandán ... M	1,235	19, 23
Kandi ... M	18	22
Kandiál ... M	353	19, 20
Kandrál ... M	66	22
Kanerá ... M	17	23
Kang ... M	57	20, 22, 23
Kangar ... M	48	14, 19
Kaniál ... M	456	20, 21, 22, 27
Kánjan ... M	397	18, 22, 27
Karchoni ... M	164	9
Karin ... M	179	19, 21, 22
Karmali Khel M	15	23
Karog ... M	168	19, 20, 25
Karsiál ... M	1,151	18, 22, 23
Karwál ... M	20	11, 20, 22
Kasar ... M	154	20, 21, 22
Kashmiri ... M	21	18, 20, 21
Kasián ... M	336	22
Kasrákhel ... M	17	51
Kaswál ... M	111	19, 22
Katán ... M	23	20
Katiál ... M	41	21, 22, 27
Katoni ... M	19	20
Katwál ... M	153	16, 20, 22, 23
Kawál ... M	439	20, 22
Keori ... M	1,270	19, 22, 27
Khachar ... M	28	11, 21
Khaddi ... M	140	25
Khágán ... M	27	19
Khairal ... M	140	18, 22, 23
Khakan ... M	36	20, 25
Khalál ... M	94	20, 22
Khalán ... M	2,317	17, 20, 22
Khalandar ... M	15	19
Khalqál ... M	490	20, 22
Kháli ... M	26	51
Khámre ... M	717	16, 17, 19
Khandar ... M	135	19, 22
Khange ... M	23	20
Khánke ... M	56	24
Kháprá ... M	190	16
Kharáná ... M	4,748	16, 17, 18, 19, 20
Khattar ... M	2,875	16, 19, 21, 22, 25
Kheri ... M	55	22
Khetrián ... M	13	51
Khichi ... M	166	19, 22, 23
Khishatband M	24	29
Khoi ... M	507	23
Khokhar ... M	5,770	20, 21, 22
Khottá ... M	14	19
Khowári ... M	324	20, 22, 34

Names of Sub-Castes.	Persons.	Locality.	Names of Sub-Castes.	Persons.	Locality.	Names of Sub-Castes.	Persons.	Locality.
Khushmamdál M	252	22	Moklá ... M	11	19	Ropar ... M	733	16, 22
Kochi ... M	73	22	Mongar ... M	395	16, 22	Borá ... M	547	20, 22, 23
Kokárá ... M	800	21, 22	Mughal ... M	61	22	Sabwál ... M	137	18, 23
Korá ... M	87	22	Mullán .. M	18	22	Sabzál ... M	79	22
Kotlá ... M	8,960	19, 20, 21, 22	Mund ... M	3,487	22, 23	Sadál ... M	67	19
Kurtáná ... M	28	22, 24	Mundiál ... M	34	22	Sadhá ... M	136	9
Ladhál ... M	482	20, 22, 23	Murid Khel... M	19	22	Sadhál ... M	23	22
Ladhwál ... M	130	13, 20, 22	Mussalli ... M	206	22, 23	Sadiál ... M	280	20, 22
Ladiál ... M	59	19, 22	Nabiál ... M	17	20	Sádiq ... M	57	10, 20, 25
Lakhiál ... M	24	9, 19	Nagiál ... M	377	20, 21, 22	Sadkál ... M	7,009	R. 27
Lakwál ... M	157	11	Nagrál ... M	90	21	Sadkár .. M	76	20, 24
Langáh ... M	246	19, 16, 21	Nahar ... M	19	51	Sadoke ... M	16	25
Langariál ... M	16	18	Nái ... M	46	21, 22, 23	Sadwál ... M	530	22
Lár .. M	50	51	Naij ... M	11	19	Saefer ... M	68	19
Lashkariál ... M	13	22	Nainwál ... M	28	10, 19	Saghál ... M	374	23
Lodhrá ... M	1,095	19, 22	Nakpál ... M	11	21	Saghrál ... M	4,819	22, 23, 28
Lohár ... M	348	20, 21, 22	Nánakshâhi... M	20	9	Ságí ... M	117	9, 22
Loni ... M	15	19	Náru ... M	248	18, 25	Sagiál ... M	129	21
Lund ... M	194	20, 22	Natál ... M	1,981	22, 23	Sagwál ... M	827	19, 22, 23
Máchhi ... M	18	22, 23	Natwál ... M	1,429	9, 10, 11	Sahál ... M	24	16, 22
Madá ... M	33	22, 24	Nazir Khel ... M	147	22	Sahotrá ... M	655	20, 21, 22, 51
Madháni ... M	437	18	Niál ... M	92	20	Saidai ... M	22	9, 13
Madhwál ... M	5,423	19, 20, 22, 23, 51	Niká ... M	11	19	Sailu ... M	352	23
Madoká ... M	33	24	Nonerá ... M	541	51	Sajál ... M	29	22
Madrá .. M	67	18, 19, 22	Nun ... M	23	20, 22	Sajrál ... M	33	23
Maghi ... M	17	22	Nurál ... M	39	18, 19	Sajwál ... M	15	22
Magiál ... M	39	22	Nuriál ... M	269	22	Sakrál ... M	145	22
Mahlá ... M	217	19, 20, 21	Obhechar ... M	14	51	Saláhi ... M	434	16, 22
Máhar ... M	584	20, 21, 22	Opar ... M	62	20	Salár ... M	1,359	22, 23
Máhi ... M	69	19, 22	Othi ... M	146	23, 24	Saltál ... M	227	22
Mahtá ... M	23	19, 23	Pakhrál ... M	25	22	Salwáná ... M	55	19, 20
Majwál ... M	94	18, 19	Páli ... M	69	22, 23	Samál ... M	266	22, 23
Makhan ... M	201	20, 21	Pallá Khel ... M	73	23	Samel ... M	30	22
Makhniál ... M	77	21	Pándi ... M	21	19, 22	Samrál ... M	90	19, 22
Makhrál ... M	13	20	Pandwán ... M	44	22	Samsiál ... M	1,681	22, 23
Makiál ... M	66	19	Paniál ... M	95	20, 21	Samthál ... M	18	22
Malak ... M	3,999	17, 18, 20, 25	Panjhuthá ... M	623	19, 22	Samwál ... M	75	22
Malál ... M	38	22	Panjwál ... M	155	18, 21	Sanádhá ... M	20	19, 20
Maláná ... M	163	20, 23, 51	Panwár ... M	131	24, 27, 51	Sánd ... M	184	23, 25
Maliál ... M	697	R. 27	Páoli ... M	29	27, 28	Sandá ... M	36	12, 27
Malwár ... M	463	23	Papin ... M	958	21, 22, 26	Sandrál ... M	90	22, 25
Mamdál ... M	912	19, 22	Parhál ... M	414	19, 20, 22	Sandráná ... M	170	21, 22
Mamnál ... M	19	19, 22	Parwál ... M	129	19, 22, 23	Sanger ... M	21	10
Mandiál ... M	822	19, 21	Pásián ... M	88	21	Sangwál ... M	140	20, 23
Mandu ... M	52	10, 19	Pasrál ... M	23	22, 25	Sángrá ... M	56	23, 27
Mángáná ... M	29	22	Paswál ... M	24	19, 23	Sanochi ... M	40	22
Mangar ... M	69	16, 22	Pathán ... M	82	20, 22	Saráj Khel ... M	17	22
Mar ... M	161	19, 20, 22	Phakrál ... M	24	19	Sardwál ... M	110	18, 22
Marhál ... M	388	9, 21, 24, 27	Phalerun ... M	24	13, 18	Sariál ... M	427	20, 22
Marhán ... M	15	18	Pharwál ... M	128	20	Sarkhwál ... M	123	19
Marhatta ... M	19	22	Pheráh ... M	106	22, 23	Saroiá .. M	493	13, 16, 22
Mariká ... M	206	24, 25	Phulbahri ... M	11	22	Sarwál ... M	493	20, 22
Marján ... M	919	10, 16, 18, 25	Phulial ... M	43	22	Satpál ... M	85	22, 23
Markhál ... M	197	22	Pirkál ... M	20	22	Sengá ... M	166	19
Martáná ... M	20	24	Poin-min ... M	25	18	Setál ... M	153	22
Marwál ... M	64	19	Pothwári ... M	107	22	Seti ... M	40	22
Maswál ... M	23	19, 22	Qalandar ... M	68	17, 19, 20	Shádi Khel ... M	71	23
Mashándi ... M	17	19	Qalbi ... M	34	13, 22, 23, 26	Sháfli ... M	12	19
Máshki ... M	13	13	Qázi ... M	139	13, 22, 23	Sháhmamdál M	33	22
Mashwál ... M	42	22	Qureshi ... M	3,519	J. L. R.	Sháhri ... M	25	22
Masmarál ... M	32	19	Qutabshâhi ... M	76,538	B.	Shaliál ... M	27	22, 23
Mathin ... M	35	20	Quthál ... M	15	20, 22	Sháni ... M	25	19
Matiál ... M	454	21, 22	Rachhi ... M	53	19, 22	Sharomatál ... M	124	19
Matkál ... M	123	22	Ráhi ... M	144	23	Sheikh ... M	131	18, 19
Matwál ... M	56	20	Ráhiál ... M	46	20	Sherál ... M	66	22
Mehr ... M	27	22	Rahmiál ... M	40	19	Siál ... M	726	2, 19, 22, 23
Mekan ... M	289	20, 22	Rájá ... M	11	22, 23	Silárhál ... M	14	14
Memál ... M	196	22	Rajál ... M	160	21, 22, 23	Sindhi ... M	35	13
Mendwál ... M	540	22, 23, 25	Raján ... M	5,858	20, 22	Sindhu .. M	186	25
Mengwál ... M	611	R. 51	Rájput ... M	166	L. 18, 25	Sípràl ... M	236	22
Meo ... M	16	10	Rakwál ... M	60	19, 23	Sodán ... M	859	21, 22
Miál ... M	2,491	19, 21, 22	Ramiál ... M	155	9	Sodrá ... M	64	20, 22
Miáná ... M	244	19, 20, 22, 24	Ramnál ... M	91	20, 22	Soe ... M	45	14
Mirá Khel ... M	128	19	Ramtál ... M	25	23	Sogan ... M	185	16, 22
Mirási ... M	42	21, 22, 23	Rán ... M	146	16, 22	Sohál ... M	41	16, 18, 23
Mirdhá ... M	84	19, 20	Randiál ... M	85	19, 22	Sohná ... M	13	22
Mirzál ... M	534	22	Ranghar ... M	98	18, 20, 22	Sukhál ... M	281	22, 51
Misri Khel ... M	15	22, 27	Ránjhá ... M	198	22	Sultátál ... M	32	22
Mochi ... M	196	22	Ratiál ... M	18	22, 27	Sunárá .. M	61	23
Modh ... M	11	24	Raushnál ... M	297	19, 22	Tabárá .. M	30	29
Modhuwál ... M	70	2, 51	Ráwal ... M	43	19, 22	Táhi ... M	25	23
Mohd. Khel M	45	23	Ráwan ... M	11	25	Talhi ... M	90	17, 22
Mohd. Shâhi M	64	20, 23	Raziál ... M	72	22	Tallar ... M	37	20, 21
Moháná ... M	15	23, 23	Rehán ... M	2,039	19, 20, 22, 25, 51	Tamboli ... M	14	21
Mohár ... M	94	22	Reri ... M	559	22	Támrá ... M	175	22
Mohiál ... M	207	20, 22, 23	Riál ... M	160	22	Tanáoli ... M	17	22
			Roli ... M	25	25	Tándá ... M	67	20

SUB-CASTES OF CERTAIN SELECTED CASTES—*continued.*

Names of Sub-Castes.	Persons.	Locality.	Names of Sub-Castes.	Persons.	Locality.	Names of Sub-Castes.	Persons	Locality.
Tanwál ... M	16	21	Tindá ... M	16	22	Vadbál ... M	409	16, 21, 22
Tareli ... M	25	51	Tiwáná ... M	18	25	Vahind ... M	88	19
Tarer ... M	5,000	21,22, 23, 25	Toba ... M	52	51	Vaina ... M	200	22
Tari ... M	108	22	Tugwál ... M	46	9, 22	Vali Khel ... M	14	23
Turkhan ... M	29	21, 25	Turkmán ... M	49	22	Valote ... M	22	13
Tatál ... M	124	21	Tutiál ... M	98	22	Vathela ... M	23	20
Tátri ... M	32	16, 22	Uchar ... M	63	23	Vethá .. M	66	22
Thag ... M	15	22	Udál ... M	68	22	Wazir ... M	19	22
Tharáne ... M	11	25	Ujrál ... M	863	22	Yaqubál ... M	29	22
Thathiár ... M	31	23	Ulemá ... M	47	19, 23.	Zahriá .. M	19	23
Thatiál ... M	220	20, 21	Ulvi ... M	79	10, 51	Zingál ... M	60	21
Thim ... M	220	22	Utar Khel ... M	288	23, 25, 29	Minor* ... M	1,273	
Thor ... M	180	22	Utrán . M	52	22	Unspecified... M	80,000	

*DETAIL OF MINOR.

Abarwál 3, Achhrán 7, Ádham 2, Ádrá 2, Afridi 10, Ahán 5, Akhwál 1, Álam Sháhi 2, Aliyás Khel 2, Altmash 6, Alwál 9, Anbiál 2, Andheri 2, Anhariál 2, Anwál 8, Ardál 1, Arwál 2, Aryai 3, Aslámke 6, Atrál 2, Badhwá 7, Badrai 6, Bafindá 5, Bageli 2, Bághbán 10, Bagral 2, Bahádar Sháhi 8, Bahishti 4, Bahu Khel 1, Baiswál 1, Bajár 3, Bájwá 6, Bakhtiár 1, Bakki 8, Bakwál 9, Balandi 4, Balar 4, Báli 4, Bamin 7, Bángar 1, Banjrá 2, Banpál 8, Barál 7, Baroká 9, Basharati 2, Batán 9, Batiál 4, Báwla 3, Báz Khel 8, Bhabá 6, Bhábra 10, Bhad 9, Bhágot 1, Bháli 4, Bhalle 3, Bhanbri 1, Bhándu 3, Bhangal 2, Bhará 3, Bháris 2, Bhatiárah 1, Bhatla 6, Bhirth 7, Bhori 2, Bhumál 1, Boli 4, Busrál 9, Chachrál 1, Cháki 1, Chaknál 1, Chálap 1, Chamán 9, Chamrang 6, Chanan 4, Chapál 7, Chaprál 2, Charohá 1, Chatbá 1, Chhabu 9, Chhatá Khel 1, Chhorá 2, Chishti 6, Chohal 2, Chokarwál 9, Dáduwál 3, Dágrá 6, Dábál 2, Dalwál 1, Dáriwál 6, Daryán 2, Deri 2, Desal 10, Dhakar 9, Dhalán 1, Dhánsi Khel 3, Dhándal 2, Dhangi 4, Dhund 2, Dindár 3, Dohar 4, Dohiál 3, Drámi 7, Dugrá 1, Duzi 1, Fatehsál 7, Gag 2, Galar 1, Gamáu 4, Ganjul 8, Gaupál 2, Gegan 10, Ghorwál 4, Gijnot 2, Gilán 7, Gogan 2, Gondái 7, Got 1, Gowáliá 1, Gujar 1, Gujrál 4, Habal 3, Hafzál 1, Haji Abdál 1, Hakamwái 2, Hali 1, Hamrál 3, Hamsheráh 4, Hazrat Sháhi 4, Isharpál 1, Jagrál 9, Jáli 5, Jaláhál 1, Jandá 9, Jander 6, Jáni 2, Jarmál 4, Jatpál 3, Jhábri 8, Jhaggar 10, Jher 7, Jochhál 2, Jogiál 3, Joli 2, Joruwál 10, Kachhlál 1, Kahmolj 8, Kajiál 1, Kakezai 1, Kakiál 5, Kakku 6, Kalán 8, Kalbáli 1, Káliá 1, Kalochi 3, Kamial 2, Kanglál 9, Kanoi 10, Karmoká 1, Katobil 6, Khás 2, Khobálá 1, Khojá 4, Khotre 1, Khurji 6, Kirán 1, Kochrá 4, Kodál 1, Kokar 5, Kolar 3, Láhori 4, Lak 5, Lakdári 1, Lalhi 6, Lálli 5, Larki 1, Latáká 1, Liliári 2, Lodhi 6, Luqmáni 4, Maghwán 5, Makhdum 9, Malakshábi 5, Máli Khel 7, Mandár 2, Mandhál 5, Mandu Khel 6, Mansan 5, Marar 5, Marát 2, Márkandi 1, Matái 2, Matrál 7, Mehrchads 10, Men 5, Minhás 2, Mirdhár 8, Moglá 6, Mohla 8, Moth 6, Moti 6, Muhammad Dariál 2, Mundre 5, Munshi 1, Musá 3, Nádri 4, Nain 3, Nakál 8, Nanál 8, Narolá 1, Narwán 7, Nase 3, Nathi 4, Niázi 3, Nunári 9, Nur Khel 6, Páchá Khel 4, Padhál 2, Padwál 8, Pajwál 1, Pame 6, Pandár 2, Panjábi 1, Paráchá 2, Parhár 1, Pathwál 10, Phabrál 1, Phaliál 3, Phákre 3, Piráin 4, Qázi 2, Rabábi 2, Rachhá 7, Rájwál 1, Rándá 2, Ransial 1, Rasul Sháhi 9, Rátanpál 2, Rawshi 7, Rere 6, Ropál 2, Rukná Khel 1, Sadhák 1, Ságar 1, Sahirá 1, Sáhotá 1, Sáhu 4, Sáhu Khel 8, Saidwál 7, Sakál 4, Saláná 8, Salgan 8, Samun 2, Sándal 7, Sándrai 3, Sankiá 5, Sanoriá 5, Sauwán 3, Saprá 2, Saráná 10, Sarhál 6, Sarkál 10, Sarpál 6, Sarur 8, Sarwári 1, Sawál 10, Sawáriá 1, Sebkál 5, Seki 3, Sethi 3, Shah Madár 2, Shárak 10, Shatál 3, Shekhu Khel 10, Siáuon 1, Sodhan 3, Sogi 7, Sudh 2, Tablar 2, Takhail 5, Takoch 5, Talogar 6, Tanwári 7, Táru 7, Taryál 10, Thaloja 3, Thápal 1, Thár 1, Tila 1, Tur 7, Ubhál 3, Ujlál 10, Uthnál 7, Vagrán 3, Valázáq 2, Varyáh 2, Vathárah 10, Wajhoke 7, Warhán 1, Wighál 6, Wirk 2, Zamindár 4, Zarál 4, Zargar 1.

Biloch 532,499 ... M. 532,499

Names of Sub-Castes.	Persons.	Locality.
Abáskhel ... M	17	27
Abdáli ... M	25	51
Achkáni ... M	31	51
Admáni ... M	89	19
Afgháni ... M	57	5, 29
Ahir ... M	18	25, 29
Ahjáni ... M	40	51
Ahmadáni ... M	5,981	1, 27, 29, 51
Aisháni ... M	160	13, 27, 29
Akháni ... M	21	51
Aláhdádi ... M	88	19, 24, 26
Alkáni .. M	237	10, 29
Altiáni ... M	2,091	19, 26, 29
Allikhel . M	58	19, 25
Almáni ... M	4,115	M. 19
Amdáni ... M	3,569	19, 27, 29, 51
And ... M	293	5, 14, 18, 20, 44
Angrá ... M	20	19, 28
Angwáni ... M	15	27
Ansári ... M	258	19, 27, 29, 51
Arvar ... M	43	27
Aspáni ... M	135	19, 51
Asráni ... M	62	29
Awán ... M	150	16, 27
Bábá ... M	43	51
Babáduri ... M	25	24
Bábar ... M	156	19, 20, 27, 29
Bacháni .. M	71	19
Badáni ... M	332	29, 51
Badhái ... M	28	19, 24
Badhwáná ... M	653	18, 19, 29
Badoi .. M	106	29
Badráni ... M	34	29
Bagár ... M	72	19, 29
Bagdádi ... M	53	25
Bagdar ... M	57	24
Bagháni ... M	2,006	19, 29
Baghwáni ... M	489	29
Baginni ... M	41	19
Bagláni ... M	15	51

Names of Sub-Castes.	Persons.	Locality.
Bagráná ... M	49	29
Báhi ... M	42	1, 27
Bakhbári ... M	51	19
Bákhri ... M	54	19
Balábre ... M	13	6
Balgháni ... M	853	29
Bamáni ... M	11	28
Bándar Chhik M	12	27
Bandráni ... M	60	19
Banjárá ... M	60	6, 13
Bánjh ... M	14	19
Barámi ... M	178	27, 29, 51
Báre ... M	481	26
Bargáh .. M	20	19
Bariáni ... M	2,639	18, 19
Bariás ... M	20	13
Barrá .. M	13	25
Barráni ... M	401	26, 29
Barwár ... M	19	19
Batáni ... M	71	29
Batwáni ... M	161	51
Bázigar ... M	293	29, 50
Beg ... M	79	29
Bhalrun ... M	25	13
Bhand ... M	1,955	19, 27, 29, 51
Bhandár ... M	53	13, 14, 19
Bhandwáni ... M	443	29
Bhangálá ... M	24	27
Bhángi ... M	26	24
Bhanjri ... M	142	4, 26, 48
Bharáni ... M	290	19, 27
Bharár ... M	62	13
Bharat ... M	127	51
Bhároiá .. M	46	51
Bhatti ... M	1,581	1, 13, 17, 19, 24, 25, 48, 51
Bhatti Khokhár. M	12	19
Bhawáni ... M	16	51
Bhiári ... M	28	5, 51
Bhilká ... M	165	51

Names of Sub-Castes.	Persons.	Locality.
Bhobrá ... M	217	24
Bhoiáná ... M	20	13, 19
Bhubat ... M	47	1, 12
Bhúd ... M	61	26, 27, 29
Bhudáná ... M	42	19
Bhuttá ... M	9[illegible]	48
Bijwáni ... M	[illegible]5	29
Biliáni ... M	69	29
Bilocháni ... M	27	29
Birmáni ... M	1[illegible]4	28
Birohi ... M	127	29
Bohári ... M	72	25
Boláki ... M	11	29
Boláni ... M	11	29
Brind ... M	10,345	27
Budh ... M	2[illegible]9	24, 25
Bukh ... M	557	25
Bukhári ... M	23	50
Bulá ... M	340	19, 29
Buráni ... M	80	29
Buzdár ... M	16,633	28, 29
Cháohá ... M	13	29
Chadhar ... M	239	19, 26
Chakráni ... M	111	27, 29
Chándia ... M	28,509	1, 2, 0, 13, 18, 27, 28, 51
Chang ... M	360	19, 26, 27, 29
Changwápi ... M	1,299	29
Chanttar ... M	269	25 29
Chanwáni ... M	14	29
Chárá ... M	46	51
Chassiáni ... M	17	51
Chatthá ... M	100	48
Chaughattá ... M	46	13, 19, 24
Chauhán ... M	288	2, 12, 19, 27, 47
Chelári ... M	15	11
Chharimár ... M	27	19
Chishti ... M	18	19, 27, 51
Chokhani ... M	15	51
Churigar ... M	12	24
Dadpotrá ... M	19	28

Names of Sub-Castes.		Persons.	Locality.
Dadwáni	... M	422	29
Dábá	... M	338	24, 27
Dakhná	... M	27	27
Damrá	... M	14	48
Damráná	... M	120	29
Dandáni	... M	33	51
Dandná	... M	128	28, 29
Dandwáni	.. M	131	29
Dangwáni	... M	30	29
Dankáni	... M	11	26
Darhiwat	... M	257	14
Darishak	... M	5,121	28, 29
Darkháni	... M	262	29
Daryái	... M	44	25, 51
Dashtáini	... M	18	29
Dasti	... M	7,578	27, 29
Dewat	... M	186	17, 19, 25
Dewat Khel	... M	18	19
Dhakor	... M	32	24
Dhol	... M	80	23, 26, 27
Dhowál	... M	100	19
Diá	... M	49	24
Digantkhel	... M	48	25
Dolá	... M	15	5
Dolá Bhatti	... M	21	5
Doláni	... M	1,098	29, 51
Donegi	... M	85	29
Dor	... M	416	28
Dosá	... M	18	19
Downá	... M	256	27, 29
Duráni	... M	201	23, 27, 28
Dutáni	... M	119	29, 51
Faqir	... M	23	27
Fardáni	... M	23	29
Farosh	... M	18	29
Fasháni	... M	13	51
Firozi	... M	454	25, 26
Gabol	... M	476	51
Gadgor	... M	28	24, 25
Gádhi	... M	3,690	M. 19, 23, 27
Gagráni	... M	17	51
Gándi	... M	38	18, 24, 51
Gangáni	... M	135	29
Ganj	... M	423	19, 27, 51
Gapol	... M	7,023	27, 28
Garwáhán	... M	47	28
Gashkori	... M	6,501	18, 24, 28, 51
Gasurá	... M	22	27
Gawáráh	... M	186	1, 51
Ghabesar	... M	16	24
Ghaleja	... M	78	51
Ghanád	... M	133	28
Gháru	... M	102	26
Ghazláni	... M	1,637	28, 29, 50
Gholá	... M	1,004	29, 51
Ghoráli	... M	457	24
Ghoriwál	... M	13	15, 27
Ghouri	... M	381	27, 49
Ghulámáni	... M	504	29, 51
Ghumráni	... M	111	13, 15, 29
Giloi	... M	354	27, 29
Gohar	... M	192	28
Gond	... M	47	1, 23
Gondal	... M	206	13, 28
Gopáng	... M	33,436	27, 28, 29, 51
Gopang Kári	M	13	4
Goráh	.. M	93	27, 28, 29
Gorganj	... M	1,014	29, 51
Gorsá	... M	331	23
Gujar	... M	78	27, 29
Gulfád	... M	1,376	29
Gulkiálá	... M	456	27
Gurcháni	... M	5,390	29
Gurdli	... M	29	24
Gurmáni	... M	8,619	18, 23, 28
Guroni	... M	209	4, 17
Gurzwani	... M	276	29
Hadwár	... M	104	28, 29
Haidáni	... M	42	23, 28
Hajáni	... M	3,557	27, 29
Hajbani	... M	415	29
Hajláni	... M	103	29
Haláni	... M	196	28
Halásari	... M	205	5
Hamáná	... M	18	51
Hamdáni	... M	503	M.
Handáná	... M	34	26
Hanjáli	... M	235	26
Háns	... M	14	19, 26, 27
Harjáná	... M	25	29
Harkáni	... M	17	27
Hasnáni	... M	78	19, 26
Hasti	... M	19	29
Hindwáni	... M	50	27, 29, 51
Hinjrá	... M	11	27
Hir	... M	24	17, 27
Hot	... M	8,518	D. R. M.
Hotwâni	... M	120	28, 29
Isákheli	... M	18	19
Isáni	... M	159	29
Ismáiliá	... M	19	3
Itbáni	... M	21	29
Jaggil	... M	19	29
Jagiáni	... M	816	27, 29
Jagwáni	... M	82	28, 29
Jaitaj	... M	11	24
Jajiáli	... M	25	29
Jajiáná	.. M	82	29
Jajwáni	... M	945	28, 29
Jakál	... M	28	26
Jákhri	... M	17	3, 18
Jaláláni	... M	858	3, 29
Jaliáni	... M	767	26, 29
Jalig	... M	235	12, 24, 25
Jalmáná	... M	17	25
Jamáni	... M	492	25, 51
Jamlálá	... M	37	24, 25
Janwáni	... M	63	29
Janak	... M	181	51
Jandi	... M	754	13, 24, 27
Jandwáni	... M	357	29, 51
Jangláná	... M	109	19, 25, 27
Janjoli	... M	58	13
Janjuá	... M	30	17
Janoá	... M	63	48, 50
Jarrá	... M	189	13, 51
Jarwár	... M	1,878	29
Jashkáni	... M	1,862	26, 27, 28, 29, 51
Jasmáni	... M	19	29
Jassáni	... M	25	29
Jatáni	... M	8,293	17, 19, 26, 29, 51
Jatoi	... M	25,022	M. 11, 13, 20, 33, 51
Jatra	... M	41	26
Jatt	... M	1,176	13, 20, 24, 27
Jhagwáni	... M	26	29
Jhakkar	... M	124	20, 24
Jhandi	... M	220	5, 6, 11, 13
Jhirkál	... M	18	29
Joi	... M	75	13, 23, 25
Joláni	... M	290	28, 29
Jugáni	... M	17	51
Jughláni	... M	132	24
Kabáhi	... M	1,008	2, 3
Kabira	... M	17	24, 26
Kabjáni	... M	267	23, 29
Kaláchi	... M	5,344	M. 48, 51
Kalál	... M	60	11, 13, 18, 29
Kaler	... M	464	29, 51
Kalhorá	... M	41	29
Kaliáni	... M	427	10, 14, 29
Kaliár	... M	508	10, 14, 17, 26
Kalmág	... M	50	13, 27
Kaloi	... M	25	2
Kálru	... M	671	13, 17, 18, 20, 29
Kamáni	... M	25	10, 29, 31
Kámláni	... M	40	29
Kandáni	... M	24	28
Kanerá	... M	17	27
Kang	... M	50	29, 51
Kangmáni	... M	47	28, 29
Kankori	... M	89	2
Karai	... M	1,053	4, 49
Karáli	... M	435	5, 10, 13, 17, 21, 26
Karáni	... M	2,011	19, 29
Karbárá	... M	126	25
Karmáná	... M	1,049	12, 13, 17, 25
Karnák	... M	44	13
Karnáli	... M	896	13, 25, 51
Karori	... M	19	25
Karoti	... M	76	22
Karyán	... M	60	48
Kashmiri	... M	56	25, 26
Kasráni	... M	241	20, 24, 28, 29
Kassar	... M	44	20, 24
Katak	... M	18	2
Katáni	... M	297	24, 27
Katpál	.. M	14	24, 27
Kawári	... M	389	13, 20, 26, 31
Kawázi	... M	239	20
Khái	... M	86	1, 4, 22
Khak	... M	11	51
Khálti	... M	264	51
Khalung	... M	13	29
Khanai	.. M	257	29
Khandwáni	.. M	1,818	26, 27, 28
Khántak	... M	18	29
Kharái	... M	330	17, 26, 29
Kharás	... M	191	28, 29
Khári	... M	114	24
Kharkháni	... M	44	29
Kharl	... M	267	24, 26
Khatrán	... M	326	27, 28, 29
Kheri	... M	30	2, 27
Khichi	... M	21	13, 27, 51
Khijáni	... M	14	25
Khizri	... M	101	26
Khokhar	... M	198	16, 17, 26
Khole	... M	11	12
Khori	.. M	104	12, 51
Khosá	... M	23,495	14, 28, 29, 51
Khosak	... M	14	24
Khoth	... M	25	28
Khurásáni	... M	14	4
Kicháni	... M	146	26, 29
Koháli	... M	600	2, 18
Kohán	... M	95	2, 13
Korái	... M	5,671	M. 3, 12, 19, 51
Kore	... M	42	14, 51
Kukrá	... M	28	25
Kulkali	... M	42	29
Kurtani	... M	250	29
Kushak	... M	4,753	25, 26, 27, 28
Kushári	... M	63	13, 26, 51
Ladwáni	... M	428	5, 29
Lag	.. M	11	24, 48
Lagai	... M	14	27
Laghári	... M	11,383	19, 23, 24, 28, 29
Lahar	... M	35	25
Lajhári	... M	143	1
Lálbegi	... M	47	27
Lalhani	... M	703	25
Lalwáni	... M	25	28
Langáh	... M	598	12, 28, 29, 51
Langràná	... M	101	26, 29
Lanjwáni	... M	233	29
Lár	... M	70	24, 51
Larkáne	... M	21	51
Lashkari	... M	1,033	23, 27, 28
Lishári	.. M	24,775	M. 2, 3, 19, 49, 51
Lodáni	... M	32	29, 51
Lodhre	... M	4,207	16, 17, 26, 27
Lohari	... M	11	51
Lohráná	... M	64	23, 29
Lorái	... M	866	51
Lori	... M	340	24, 29, 51
Ludhiáni	... M	14	26
Lukáni	... M	769	29
Lund	.. M	6,475	29
Machhráni	.. M	203	29
Madári	... M	237	26
Madráni	... M	342	23
Madwána	... M	90	19
Magal	. M	60	12, 17, 51
Magassi	... M	819	27, 28, 29, 51
Maggi	... M	277	23
Magráni	... M	15	51
Máhani	.. M	36	27, 51
Máhar	.. M	167	18, 24, 29
Mahár	... M	291	13, 29
Mahon	... M	179	24, 51
Mahtam	... M	88	29
Mahurkand	... M	13	28
Majosi	... M	39	29
Malki	... M	89	13, 51
Mamar	... M	313	26, 27
Mamdáni	... M	1,343	23, 51
Mandráni	... M	68	19, 29

SUB-CASTES OF CERTAIN SELECTED CASTES—*continued.*

Names of Sub-Castes.		Persons.	Locality.
Mandwáia	... M	1,223	28
Mángir	... M	111	23
Mangláni	... M	58	29, 51
Manbás	... M	27	12, 13
Manjwáni	... M	850	19, 25, 29
Maráni	... M	112	24, 51
Marári	.. M	637	13, 24
Mardáná	... M	57	25, 51
Markand	... M	345	23, 27
Marrái	... M	978	26, 28, 29
Marri	... M	734	19, 28
Marrmáni	... M	126	29
Márth	... M	584	24, 25, 27, 29
Mashori	... M	3,047	28, 29, 51
Mastoi	... M	5,306	19, 27, 29, 51
Mateli	... M	240	17
Matrá	... M	52	28
Matwál	... M	35	27
Mazári	... M	12,618	26, 29, 51
Mengláná	... M	37	25
Miáni	.. M	173	23, 29
Millanbás	... M	115	24, 27
Mirdádi	... M	65	24
Mirzai	... M	71	12, 27
Mirzani	... M	1,358	27, 29, 51
Misgáni	... M	66	29
Missan	... M	68	24, 29
Miswáni	... M	108	29
Mita	... M	63	20, 24, 25
Mitor	... M	23	27, 51
Mitwáni	... M	194	29
Modher	... M	27	25
Mohil	... M	63	27
Mughal	... M	29	18, 19, 21
Mughláni	... M	616	12, 29
Mukimáná	... M	242	25
Mulkáni	... M	3,514	12, 19, 28, 29
Multáni	... M	208	13, 29, 48, 49
Muráni	... M	4,271	27, 29, 51
Murdáni	... M	48	29
Musáni	... M	163	29, 51
Naduáni	... M	158	29
Nagarpál	... M	37	13
Náhar	... M	60	29
Najári	... M	38	48
Namurdi	... M	75	29
Nángri	... M	604	29
Nunkani	... M	24	29
Nashári	... M	2,652	19, 26, 46, 48, 50
Nathwáni	... M	491	29
Naul	... M	18	27, 29
Nazli	... M	12	19
Niáni	... M	27	29
Nirmán	... M	11	49
Nirwáni	... M	75	29
Nisháhdi	... M	188	12
Noháni	... M	239	28, 51
Nonári	... M	39	12, 25, 27
Nosháhi	... M	14	23
Nosherá	... M	251	27
Nuráni	... M	899	23, 29
Nuri	... M	66	19, 27
Nusráni	... M	47	29
Nutkáni	.. M	2,827	27, 28, 29, 51
Orkháni	... M	18	29
Pachár	... M	570	28, 29, 51
Pakhiwárá	... M	67	27, 29
Paliál	... M	12	19
Palotráná	... M	13	25
Panwár	... M	102	13, 14, 24, 26
Parái	... M	153	17, 51
Parihár	... M	900	19, 24, 26
Pariwar	.. M	16	51
Parkáná	... M	37	26, 27
Parozáni	... M	90	29
Pasháwari	... M	18	13, 48
Passoi	... M	561	12, 24, 25
Passoli	.. M	47	13, 46
Pathal	... M	30	17
Pathán	... M	63	2, 13, 17, 27
Pathár	... M	52	13, 46
Patoi	... M	12	29
Pawár	... M	57	5, 13, 48
Phaleli	... M	324	51
Phirwáni	... M	749	29
Phor	... M	70	24
Pitafi	... M	6,593	23, 24, 26, 27, 28
Pohár	... M	12	48
Poi	... M	482	12, 24
Pokhan	... M	11	12
Pushá	... M	179	27, 51
Qádiri	... M	111	20
Qalandar	... M	93	13, 27
Qandráni	... M	145	4, 19, 29
Qarái	... M	201	1, 11, 12, 13
Qásmi	... M	130	27, 29
Qesráni	... M	14,348	29
Qureshi	... M	139	1, 13, 20, 48
Rabbáni	... M	28	29
Rági	... M	57	25, 26
Raháni	... M	41	27
Rahmáni	.. M	26	51
Rajháni	... M	59	23, 29
Rakhshiáni	... M	54	29
Rangdi	... M	21	15, 19
Rangerá	... M	853	19, 23, 27, 28, 29
Rangilá	... M	66	28
Ráthor	... M	28	29, 51
Rawáni	... M	16	26
Rikhijá	... M	19	24
Rind	... M	36,209	D. M. 12, 13, 17, 19, 22, 23, 51.
Rindwáni	... M	61	26, 27, 28, 29
Ronat	... M	15	13
Roswáni	... M	23	28
Ruke	... M	20	13, 14
Rustamáni	... M	232	29
Sábki	... M	1,098	26, 27, 29
Sadkáni	... M	135	19, 28, 29
Sadráj	... M	15	24
Saghráni	... M	19	27
Sagi	... M	18	19
Saháran	.. M	30	29
Sabján Bhakri	M	72	3
Sablá	... M	13	25
Sahotre	... M	127	24
Saírijh	... M	560	2
Sakhiáni	... M	4,837	M. 23, 51
Sakhráni	... M	19	29
Sakni	... M	22	19, 25
Saládhiáná	... M	79	27
Salián	... M	97	26
Sallári	... M	441	28
Salotre	... M	88	24
Samáni	... M	29	27, 51
Samáth	... M	188	1, 27
Samiá	... M	30	1, 25
Samijá	... M	235	1, 2
Sanáwán	... M	30	5
Sandhilá	... M	75	13, 24
Sándi	... M	44	13, 19, 23
Sandoráni	... M	27	19, 27
Sangri	... M	67	51
Sanjráni	... M	3,040	27, 29, 51
Sankáni	... M	35	29
Sánoni	... M	59	23
Sapiál	... M	35	20, 29
Saráhi	... M	351	2, 16, 29
Saráni	... M	3,650	13, 23, 29
Sárbán	... M	33	23, 25, 26
Sargáná	... M	2,114	20, 25, 27, 28, 29
Sarjanáh	... M	13	13
Sarori	... M	13	13
Sarwán	... M	147	9, 10, 16, 33
Satwári	... M	82	27
Sawánri	... M	48	29
Sech	... M	71	24, 48
Shaddáni	... M	135	29, 51
Shádi	... M	33	27
Shábi Khel	M	108	19
Sháhwáni	... M	982	27, 28, 29
Shakláni	... M	832	29, 51
Shákri	... M	41	26, 27
Shaláli	... M	32	19, 29
Shalwáni	... M	44	23
Shame	... M	75	29
Shar	... M	2,338	29, 51
Shári	... M	40	17, 19, 27
Sharmáni	... M	35	29
Shekháni	... M	116	27, 28, 29, 51
Shiháni	... M	211	27, 29
Shujrá	... M	221	3, 27, 28, 29
Shukráni	... M	216	23, 28, 51
Shutarbán	... M	25	6, 10
Siál	... M	84	13, 25, 27
Silári	... M	132	28, 29
Silkáni	... M	20	29
Sindhi	... M	27	20, 27
Sobki	... M	503	28
Sográ	... M	26	23
Sobi	... M	111	12, 17, 19
Sohláh	... M	682	17
Sombar	... M	25	25
Sopráni	... M	11	28
Sori	... M	78	29, 48
Sotrá	... M	34	20, 23
Subráni	... M	1,303	25, 29, 51
Sulemáni	... M	207	23, 29
Sumrá	... M	32	27, 29
Sundari	... M	21	29, 46
Surái	... M	19	24
Táhar	... M	135	19, 29
Tálpur	... M	969	29
Tandwáni	... M	706	28, 29
Tanur	... M	65	29, 48
Tanwári	... M	447	24, 25, 26
Tar	... M	431	12, 25
Tarat	... M	100	28
Tátári	... M	194	19, 26, 27, 28
Tatkáni	... M	83	28
Tawári	... M	39	13, 24, 26, 28
Thagáni	... M	192	27, 28
Thakri	... M	17	29
Thalláni	... M	289	28
Thamráni	... M	23	51
Thir	... M	41	29
Thotá	... M	40	22
Timar	... M	45	25
Tiráni	... M	150	17, 51
Tor	... M	245	2, 24
Toráni	... M	456	23, 29
Ulmáni	... M	822	25, 27, 29
Umráni	... M	32	28, 51
Ushmáni	... M	16	29
Vadáni	... M	1,116	29
Vággá	... M	40	19, 28, 29
Váh	... M	378	17
Vais	... M	44	19
Variáh	... M	17	17, 27, 51
Vasir	... M	78	27
Vaswáni	... M	83	29
Vedádi	... M	219	28
Vijhi	... M	16	27
Virk	... M	39	12, 19, 24
Wangariál	... M	12	23
Yákiáni	... M	109	29
Yalghári	... M	22	49
Zahráni	... M	160	29
Zangi	... M	55	19, 23
Zangiláni	... M	48	29
Zangizá	... M	430	19, 26
Zangrezi	... M	143	23, 29
Zardáná	... M	16	19
Zarbáni	... M	196	23, 29
Zarkáni	... M	125	23
Zindá	... M	742	25
Ziwál	... M	43	29
Zor	... M	473	29
Zuráni	... M	345	19, 23, 29
* Minor	... M	1,790	
Unspecified	M	23,032	

*** DETAIL OF MINOR.**

Abási 8, Abi 8, Adhári 2, Ajráni 10, Ajwáni 1, Akarni 1, Alláni 1, Allar 2, Alpáná 10, Anand 6, Anári 6, Anda 2, Andar 4, Andoi 2, Arab 6, Arandi 1, Arháni 6, Arjang 6, Arkáni 5, Armáni 8, Asbej 2, Asbrái 3, Asháqáni 1, Askori 2, Aubár 4, Autráh 10, Bábru 1, Bachiáná 9, Badári 1, Baggá 8, Baghrábi 6, Bahádnri 10, Bajáni 5, Bakhal 5, Bakháná 3, Baklámrá 1, Bálak 1, Baloi 10,

DETAIL OF MINOR—*concluded.*

Bandálo 2, Bandan 6, Bandochi 1, Bangli 6, Banie 7, Bánki 1, Banmár 1, Bans 2, Brás 6, Baril 8, Baroj 1, Basi 2, Bátli 3, Bhadráni 7, Bhadwál 3, Bharái 5, Bharkál 5, Bharkat 7, Bhát 4, Bhatiárá 6, Bhawál 10, Bhiráwán 2, Bhuchrá 10, Bhular 1, Bhundlá 2, Bindwáni 5, Bisiári 1, Bohelá 8, Bokhiá 4, Bolar 1, Boráná 6, Brái 2, Buchhári 1, Búkser 1, Bulhái 1, Bumki 5, Bumzádi 5, Chabáná 7, Chachiána 2, Chagráni 1, Chaine 3, Chakáti 1, Chalang 1, Chaláni 4, Chámble 1, Chanan 1, Chanar 3, Chanári 4, Chanáwar 5, Chándká 6, Chandra 4, Changál 6, Changerá 1, Chaniál 5, Chhájrá 2, Chhandi 1, Chharmáni 4, Chohbá 8, Chokhrá 8, Chondi 1, Chuliáni 1, Chuthiáni 1, Dádar 2, Dághi 3, Dalil 1, Dáná 6, Daph 4, Darkhe 1, Dareshop Jámle 4, Darsang 8, Dási 2, Daspáná 4, Dhádi 6, Dhag 8, Dhakshori 4, Dhaku 2, Dhalwáni 1, Dhamráh 7, Dhándlá 3, Dhani 6, Dholgi 3, Dhon 4, Dhori 2, Diáni 5, Dig 5, Dogre 2, Doltáná 2, Doura 1, Dorá 1, Dub 4, Falghani 1, Farári 4, Fatuki 1, Galli 3, Gandrá 1, Gang 1, Gangorásál 6, Garláti 3, Garnái. 5, Gawáni 2, Ghalláni 3, Ghalu 8, Ghání 5, Giáná 2, Gil 7, Giljáná 10, Giráni 8, Godárá 4, Golle 10, Gos 2, Gotá 1, Gujráti 1, Gurgáni 10, Gurbáni 2, Hakwáni 3, Hámshirá 9, Haqáni 4, Hari 10, Harni 6, Harwál 1, Hasal 8, Hedri 6, Holá 3, Hoshá 1, Jafláni 3, Jafri 2, Jaliál 7, Jalok 1, Jalp 4, Jalpáni 9, Jamáláni 2, Jandá 4, Jandráne 4, Jáng 1, Japal 10, Jardárlánd 4, Jatiá 3, Jatráni 1, Jhálá 2, Jhamat 4, Jhanj 2, Jhánwla 9, Jhattál 2; Jindpál 3, Johná 1, Jolá 5, Kadhár 10, Kajwáni 2, Kakhurzai 2, Káli 4, Kaliál 1, Kalláli 6, Kamál 1, Kemangar 7, Kámrá 4, Kanjáli 2, Karamshábi 8, Karánsi 2, Karáru 3, Karlu 3, Karwál 8, Kásmáni 2, Kaunchi 1, Kayánki 4, Khágá 9, Khákwáni 6, Kharách 1, Khatrá Jamáti 4, Khos Khel 7, Kinjur 5, Koras 2, Kormi 6, Kundi 5, Kunj 5, Labáná 4, Ládeki 2, Ladhar 1, Lábori 2, Lahun 1, Lakhirá 3, Lakhni 5, Lalgáná 8, Langas 6, Langrál 4, Langráná 10, Láni 1, Lathá 5, Lawán 4, Lohách 10, Lohde 5, Lohrind 2, Lons 1, Madhorá 3, Madmá 2, Mágar 6, Magwáná 5, Mahájri 1, Mahráin 2, Mahroa 2, Mabrok 2, Mahtar 6, Makál 3, Makári 1, Makki 5, Makwál 2, Maliár 1, Malláh 1, Malot 7, Mamdia 2, Manákhábi 8, Mandás 3, Mánde 4, Mandláni 10, Mangankári 1, Mangori 6, Manjothán 1, Maqiná 6, Maráhi 9, Marsháni 1, Maslá Kháni 1, Mastáná 2, Máthrás 9, Megal 1, Mekan 7, Men 3, Mezi 1, Miráná 2, Mirási 6, Mir Káliáz 1, Missar 4, Mohan 5, Mokal 4, Mokwál 5, Mujáeá 5, Mulláná 5, Muqeemáláh 6, Musalmán Khel 1, Mussalli 8, Nadmáni 9, Nagori 2, Nakái 2, Nakámi 1, Nakráni 1, Namdári 7, Nanár 3, Naudwáki 6, Naráin 4, Nasráná 4, Nazámaná 7, Niázi 9, Nidári 3, Nilá 1, Niládi 3, Ninri 3, Nodmár 5, Non 7, Nurwandá 3, Och 2, Odewál 2, Ojhá 10, Or 4, Orak 1, Orzi 1, Pacháli 2, Pachháni 5, Paká 1, Pakri 9, Paliána 5, Palonbá 4, Panáhi 9, Pandá 6, Panthi 2, Pardi 2, Parohá 5, Parori 2, Pathwárá 10, Phochrá 7, Pilkáná 10, Pirshábi 10, Popal 9, Porá 6, Qáim Kháni 3, Qaltái 7, Qutabshábi 8, Qutbáni 3, Ráf 3, Rahejá 2, Rajáni 5, Rájar 1, Rájput 1, Ráju 2, Rajwáná 10, Rakháná 3, Rangáni 8, Rangi 2, Ratanpál 10, Riás 8, Rindal 1, Rohelá 8, Roli 6, Romiá 1, Ror 6, Sabil 1, Sabzáni 6, Sábzkhái 2, Sadhal 6, Sadhar 1, Ságar 1, Saggál 1, Saggiáni 6, Sáhi 4, Sáhot 1, Sáhri 1, Sáhu 10, Saidáni 3, Saidur 8, Saini 6, Samdáná 1, Sanáhal 1, Sángi 10, Sangiáná 2, Sanjháni 6, Sanjoi 4, Sanwani 2, Sapráh 10, Saráj 10, Sarási 8, Sarrán 4, Sátole 4, Satti 3, Shadwálá 8, Sháhbázi 2, Shanárá 8, Shanir 1, Sharf 1, Sheroi 8, Sheryáná 8, Shohán 2, Siád 4, Siládi 5, Sinár 1, Sipand 4, Sobi 2, Sodhi 4, Sohat 2, Sokiál 3, Solgi 5, Sorági 1, Sot 2, Sotterá 8, Sultáni 8, Sumin 2, Sundewáne 1, Tab 1, Tabráni 8, Tabun 8, Talwár 4, Tánk 2, Tannoi 10, Targáni 4, Tarili 3, Tarkáli 8, Tarkháni 4, Tárki 8, Tárráná 2, Tarrin 7, Tatlá 3, Tattwál 7, Thaile 5, Thalál 2, Tham 1, Thámal 1, Tháni 2, Thári 4, Thatiyár 1, Tifláni 1, Tij 1, Tiwáná 7, Topwál 2, Udáthi 6, Udháni 5, Ughá 2, Ujle 2, Uráni 6, Vachhal 3, Vádi 1, Vahgrá 5, Váhi 10, Vakyár 1, Vánd 2, Vardhy 1, Varghá 8, Varshi 10, Vasi 1, Vasli 4, Vattu 7, Venis 3, Vijhár 3, Wiljáni 1, Yúsafzai 1, Zakáni 3, Zan 1, Zargari 1, Zarmadáni 1.

Names of Sub-Castes.		Persons.	Locality.
Brahman 1,017,743	H.	1,008,315	
	S.	9,065	
	M.	324	
	J.	35	
	B.	4	
Abal ...	H	11	24
Abi ...	H	52	19, 24
Abri ...	H	142	15, 42
Acháraj ...	H	8,802	P
	S	62	13, 22, 48
	M	2	6
Achárajwadáji	H	16	15
Achária ...	H	28	8, 9
Achit ...	H	47	9, 15, 34
Ádam ...	H	16	9
Adgaur ...	H	142	9, 11, 12, 16, 25, 30
Adhal ...	H	56	9, 15
Adhrál ...	H	51	19, 20
Adpál ...	H	504	13, 15, 17
Aganhotri ...	H	936	5, 9, 10, 27, 28
Aganpotrá ...	H	12	23
Agant ...	H	64	9, 13, 34
Agarwál ...	H	34	11, 12, 25
Agnoi ...	H	39	24, 39
	S	1	15
Agphak ...	H	67	11, 44
Agrásbi ...	H	28	41
Ahir ...	H	27	11, 23
Ahlupotrá ...	H	29	29
Ahri ...	H	142	9, 14, 15
Ain ...	S	155	20, 21
Ajan ...	H	21	11, 12, 17, 24
	S	5	9
Ajli ...	H	20	19
Akhluti ...	H	174	9, 15, 39
Akori ...	H	16	9
Alsi ...	H	58	9, 10, 11
Alspál ...	H	33	9, 25
Amar ...	H	86	9
Amiál ...	H	203	5, 24, 42
Amiri ...	H	180	9, 11
Anbri ...	H	48	34, 41
Andauriá ...	H	73	1, 25, 30
Andi ...	H	48	10, 21, 24
	S	14	14, 17
Andke ...	H	11	13, 51
Angal ...	H	57	13, 33
Angresh ..	H	278	5, 9, 11, 34, 39, 41
Anotrá ...	H	61	4, 15, 34
Anpál ...	H	33	12, 24, 41
Arági ...	H	115	9, 42
Ari ...	H	498	9, 15, 44

Names of Sub-Castes.		Persons.	Locality.
Arjan ..	H	151	14, 15
Aryá ...	H	13	9
Asandhar ...	H	21	10, 11
Asar ...	H	429	19, 21, 25
	S	76	13, 21
Asdhir ...	H	69	12, 14
Asgotre ...	H	77	15
Ashart ..	H	111	20
Ashtán ...	H	12	11
Aslá ...	H	11	9
Aspál ...	H	104	14, 25
Asri ...	H	57	9, 11, 15
Atatri ...	H	132	12, 16, 37
Athbáns ...	H	13	11, 14
Áti ...	H	60	21, 45
Atlas ...	H	43	10, 33, 41
Atri ...	H	41	8, 11
Atrosh ...	H	38	1, 34
	S	25	4
Attar ...	H	819	9, 15, 34, 41, 47
Átwál ...	H	102	9, 14
Auj ...	H	43	4, 13, 15
	S	4	44
Austi ...	H	528	8, 14, 15, 17, 24
Autpal ...	H	231	9, 13
Awáhin ...	H	24	11, 14
Awásti ...	H	127	42
Babar ...	H	13	14, 45
Bábarwál ...	H	15	1
Báchhal ...	H	15	47
Badal ...	H	62	8, 9, 14, 47
Badanji ...	H	42	9, 15, 47
Badgotre ...	H	40	1, 15, 17
Badhá ...	H	48	8
Badiál ...	H	196	9, 15, 16, 42, 47
Badrál ...	H	21	20
Badri ...	H	99	11, 12, 14, 15
Badwáji ...	H	13	17, 18
Bagá ...	H	135	9, 17, 18, 19, 26, 27, 42
Bagdán ...	H	110	47
Baghiál ...	H	43	15, 23
Boglor ...	H	80	18
Bagoli ...	H	97	32, 41, 47
Bagrant ...	H	38	12, 15, 47
Bagrár ...	H	20	27, 47
Bagroliá ...	H	12	47
Báhri ...	H	621	9, 15, 18, 21, 24, 42
Bairági ...	H	93	9, 11, 12, 42, 47
Baján ...	H	14	36
Bajat ...	H	12	47

Names of Sub-Castes.		Persons.	Locality.
Bajhas ...	H	45	5, 11, 33
Bajrá ...	H	195	8, 9, 11, 15, 16, 18, 21
	M	25	8
Bakhlál ...	H	11	9
Bakhre ...	H	19	9, 27, 47
Bál ...	H	49	9, 15
Baláloch ...	H	120	15, 47
Bálán ...	H	81	4, 47
Balásar ...	H	101	9, 14, 37
Baldewáji ...	H	291	9, 47
Balgo ...	H	66	14, 18, 47
Báli ...	H	836	8, 9, 14, 18, 21, 25, 26, 27, 44
Balián ...	H	113	15, 47
Balori ...	H	107	14, 17, 25, 45
Balwás ...	H	99	18
Bambotri ...	H	108	15, 47
Bamiál ...	H	17	47
Bamnoli ...	H	29	41
Bamri ...	H	117	9, 27, 41
Banás ...	H	26	15, 19
Bandair ...	H	78	9, 11, 16
Bandhotre ...	H	93	15
Bándi ...	H	70	9, 18, 21, 41
Bando ...	H	48	11, 15, 21
Bangáli ...	H	93	4, 6, 23, 42
Bango ...	H	26	9, 42, 45
Báni ...	H	38	10, 15, 39
Bannotrá ...	H	170	9, 15, 16
Banon ...	H	18	25, 47
Banot ...	H	649	9, 11, 14, 15, 39
Bans ...	H	182	4, 5, 11, 17, 18, 42, 44
Bánsali ...	H	47	44, 47
Bansi ...	H	29	9, 15, 25
Bánto ...	H	55	39
Banwáli ...	H	57	47
Banwári ...	H	287	42
Bárad ...	H	61	8, 42, 47
Barahrú ...	H	26	8
Baráng ...	H	11	10, 24
Barar ...	H	147	9, 10, 15, 42, 47
Barás ...	H	107	15, 47
Barat ...	H	32	12, 47
Bardán ...	H	15	47
Barer ...	H	22	15, 42
Bariál ...	H	64	15, 16, 47
Bariwán ...	H	442	42
Bárkar ...	H	12	14, 45, 47
Bárli ...	H	878	9, 10, 12, 14
Bármi ...	H	224	15, 16, 19, 28, 47

Names of Sub-Castes.		Persons.	Locality.
Bárná ...	H	22	15, 44
Baroliá ...	H	52	42
Barsá ...	H	242	9, 15, 47
Bartbál ...	H	17	18, 43
Baryá ...	H	27	18
	S	1	44
Basand ...	H	16	14, 25
Basat Koni ...	H	413	4, 9, 17
Bashisht ...	H	1,515	3, 10, 12, 34, 39, 41, 47
Bási ...	H	157	9
Basmobatri ...	H	34	15
Basotari ...	H	105	15, 47
Basrá ...	H	327	9, 15, 41
Bastar ...	H	27	15
Batán ...	H	83	9, 15, 42
Batanjan ...	H	24	14, 44
Batási ...	H	23	9
Bathli ...	H	30	9, 10
Bathwári ...	H	25	8, 15, 16
Batiálo ...	H	12	47
Batorá ...	H	446	14, 17, 18, 27, 43
Báwá ...	H	42	2, 14
Báwaliá ...	H	13	3
Bedi ...	H	913	8, 15, 17, 39
Bhábrá ...	H	71	7, 13, 24, 25
Bhagan ...	H	25	44
Bhagat ...	H	97	9, 24, 45
	S	1	9
Bhagdite ...	H	51	47
Bhági ...	H	686	J. L. 18, 44
Bhagiál ...	H	114	21
Bhagirthi ...	H	102	8, 14
Bhaglál ...	H	18	25, 47
Bhagotre ..	H	142	15
Bhagwál ...	H	298	15, 17, 39, 47
Bhagwati ...	H	71	47
Bhái ...	H	219	15, 42
Bhákar ...	H	122	J. 14, 15
Bhákhri ...	H	500	9, 10, 17, 18
Bhal ...	H	469	14, 15, 19, 42
Bhále ...	H	159	10, 14, 24, 45
Bhalgn ...	H	119	12, 14, 20
Bhalotre ...	H	57	15
Bhan ...	H	80	11, 15, 47
Bhánbásar ...	H	201	12, 14, 16, 17, 18, 21
Bhánbhákar ...	H	418	16
Bhandále ...	H	28	15, 18
Bhandár ...	H	86	11
Bhandotare ...	H	21	39
Bhangre ...	H	40	10, 18, 25, 45
Bhanot ...	H	426	9, 11, 15, 25, 44
Bhanotri ...	H	513	15, 17, 25, 43
Bhárámal ...	H	21	9, 45, 47
Bharán ...	H	52	47
Bharande ...	H	58	14
Bharbhákar	H	600	9, 11, 18, 25
Bhárdawáj ...	H	27,659	P.
	S	101	9, 10, 12, 13, 18
Bhardwáre ...	H	475	8, 9
Bharg ...	H	22	27, 44, 47
Bhárgo ...	H	416	J. 3, 14, 15, 27, 28, 49
Bháriá ...	H	19	9, 11
Bhariwál ...	H	20	12
Bhárj ...	H	167	9, 15, 19, 45
Bhárthi ...	H	62	14, 19, 21, 24
Bharwáh ...	H	40	9, 47
Bharwák ...	H	22	11
Bhát ...	H	3,761	J. R. M. 14, 42, 47, 50
	S	20	9, 44
	M	5	50
Bhathár ...	H	174	8, 9, 15, 44
Bhatori ...	H	457	9, 14, 18, 27, 42
Bhátrá ...	H	323	9, 25
Bhawákar ...	H	255	11, 44, 45
	S	2	44
Bhawáliá ...	H	19	9, 45
Bhoi ...	H	55	15, 44
Bhojál ...	H	96	10, 14, 42, 47
Bhojki ...	H	114	8, 9, 12, 26, 28
Bhojpotrá ...	H	350	17, 19, 23, 24
Bhola ...	H	27	11, 21
Bhonkre ...	H	95	39
Bhot ...	H	207	9, 11, 19, 24

Names of Sub-Castes.		Persons.	Locality.
Bhotar ...	H	38	39
Bhotha ...	H	40	27, 34
Bhotin ...	H	29	27, 29
Bhotrá ...	H	60	12, 14
Bhuchal ...	H	30	11, 42
Bhupál ...	H	26	17, 45
Bhushan ..	H	21	18
Biáhá ...	H	93	14
Biás ...	H	790	D. 11, 48, 49, 51
Bikrami ...	H	19	7
Bishnu ...	H	41	8, 12, 14, 41
Bobak ...	H	20	47
Bobi ...	H	41	11, 16, 39, 41
Bodeg ...	H	12	47
Bohákar ...	H	89	9, 10, 27
Bonaj ...	H	16	14, 19
Borát ...	H	11	47
Bot ...	H	370	42, 47
Botháliá ...	H	14	47
Brahm Bhat	H	87	51
Brahm Chári	H	102	8, 11, 14, 19, 47
Brahmi ...	H	222	10, 11, 12, 13, 15, 23
Bujhru ...	H	296	8
Búnjái ...	U	1,003	10, 13, 14, 15, 18
Chabarmán ...	H	38	12, 21, 25
Chábiá ...	H	56	10, 14, 18
Chabrin ...	H	613	39
Chadar ...	H	38	21, 47
Chagal ...	H	15	15
Chagotre ...	H	164	15, 29
Chaldak ...	H	12	47
Chalgo ...	H	258	39, 42
Chaloi ...	H	21	46
Chalotrá ...	H	31	15, 47
Chanan ...	H	412	L. 18, 21, 24, 25, 42
Chanchi ...	H	142	18, 42
Chándaná ...	H	56	19, 23
Chándi ...	H	115	15, 27, 37, 47
Chandiál ...	H	39	42
	S	17	21
Chandni ...	H	43	19
Chandrás ...	H	13	17, 41, 47
Chapchút ...	H	879	11, 12
Chárang ...	H	53	11, 47
Charwá ...	H	43	42
Chatarchot ...	H	89	17, 19, 26, 45
	S	5	11
Chaterá ...	H	55	9, 34, 42
Chator ...	H	177	42
Chhabrá ...	H	119	9, 15, 19
Chhábron ...	H	39	47
Chhall ...	H	15	15
Chhanchhan	H	36	17, 18
Chhangar ...	H	66	9, 17
Chhári ...	H	64	8, 47
Chheli ...	H	19	18, 20
Chher ...	H	108	8, 15, 45
Chhibi ...	H	61	5, 8, 20
Chhoti Saran	H	14	5
Chichar ...	H	24	18, 19, 29
Chitar Gupt ...	H	308	10, 13, 34
Chobe ...	H	51	1, 4, 32, 34
	S	27	18
Chobiá ...	H	184	3, 50
Chobrá ...	H	18	4
Chohán ...	H	42	11, 12, 25
Choli ...	H	66	20, 29
	S	2	12
Cholrá ...	H	17	15
Chonbatu ...	H	20	47
Chorásiá ...	H	3,346	1, 2, 3, 4, 5, 49, 50
Chori ...	H	39	29
Chuni ...	H	220	19, 21, 23, 25, 27
Churáwan ...	H	18	24, 27
Dabgar ...	H	78	9, 14
Daboli ...	H	770	7, 19, 47
Dag ...	H	225	14
Dági ...	H	24	9, 11, 23
	S	5	19
Dagor ...	H	145	9, 15, 19
Dagotar ...	H	65	18, 21
	S	3	14, 21
Dáhre ...	H	11	16, 18

Names of Sub-Castes.		Persons.	Locality.
Dahu ..	H	15	42
Dáimá ...	H	226	1
Dákar ...	H	58	9, 29
Dakaut ...	H	6,890	P.
	S	305	21, 22, 24, 48
	M	267	6, 19, 48, 50
Dakshani ...	H	24	4, 5
Dálá ...	H	412	9
Dalwál ...	H	127	14, 18, 21
Damáru ...	H	13	47
Damde ...	H	20	15
Dandáli ...	H	48	17, 47
Dandwáni ...	H	18	15
Daner ...	H	53	9, 10
Dangot ...	U	167	20, 21
Dárá ...	H	46	14, 15
Darangwál ...	H	14	42
Daráni ...	H	36	14, 19, 47
Dareri ...	H	15	11, 26, 42
Dárko ..	H	15	42
Darotri ...	H	14	15, 17, 42
Darwál ...	H	17	42
Dasri ...	H	13	2, 6, 19
Dassá ...	H	138	5, 33, 49
Daswán ...	H	30	42
Datta ...	H	451	J. L. 18, 19, 20, 25, 26, 51
	S	89	14, 16, 17, 18, 25
Dawá ...	H	51	9, 15, 19, 42
Degan ...	H	426	L. 11, 45, 47
	S	16	18, 25
Deghat ...	H	16	11, 14
Deogawan ...	H	1,047	14
Deopál ...	H	38	12, 20, 29
Deosar ...	H	244	14
Desi ...	H	104	2, 11, 33
Devi Sár Sut	H	89	15, 17
Dhágá ...	H	63	9, 12
Dhaki ...	H	70	26, 27
Dhakni ...	H	9	25
	S	54	16
Dhalwál ...	H	60	8, 15
Dhami ...	H	528	9, 10, 11, 12, 14, 15, 16, 19, 26, 30, 45, 51
	S	15	9, 15
Dhamrá ...	H	64	39
Dhandi ...	H	59	14, 15
Dhani ...	H	215	24, 25, 27
	S	1	11
Dhannar ...	H	70	11, 23, 26
Dhánpotrá ...	H	39	23, 28, 42
Dhanatar ...	H	21	19
Dhará ...	H	111	11, 12, 21, 47
Dhári ..	H	150	11, 14, 15, 19, 42
	S̃	8	19
Dharmátar ...	H	15	36
Dharni ...	H	162	8, 11, 14, 16, 17, 19
Dharokára ...	H	102	3
	S	5	18
Dhoi ...	H	275	9, 27, 42
	S	3	17
Dhosar ...	H	181	14, 15, 25
Dhotar ...	H	414	4, 10, 11, 15
Diárru ...	H	11	41
Dikh Chat ...	J	1	11
Dobbági ...	S	35	12
Dodá ...	H	105	11, 14, 42, 47
Dogal ...	H	121	11
Dográ ...	H	1,051	J. 14, 15, 16, 18, 25, 27, 39, 41, 42
	S	6	14
Dohrá ...	H	19	8, 25
Doi ...	H	95	9, 11, 15, 37
Doj ...	H	12	8
Dolar ...	H	615	14, 19
	S	10	14
	M	1	14
Doli ...	H	91	15, 16, 42
Dophar ...	H	26	26
Dori ...	H	113	9, 15
Dosar ...	H	845	15
Dotar ...	H	24	47
Dur ...	H	47	15, 19
	S	1	14

APPENDIX TO IMPERIAL TABLE XIII.

Names of Sub-Castes.		Persons.	Locality.
Eri ...	H	216	9
Fagin ...	H	17	27
Gádá ...	H	162	8, 14, 33, 42, 43
Gaheri ...	H	27	1, 8, 13
Galotre ...	H	45	15, 47
Gandal ..	H	139	9, 15, 27, 45
	S	5	17
Gandár ...	H	138	9, 24, 27
Gandhar ...	H	1,239	M. 12, 15, 19, 23
Gandi ...	H	191	11, 14, 17, 47
	S	8	10
Gandir ...	H	265	11, 14, 18, 27
Gandi Sársut	H	18	15
Gandri ...	H	111	11
Gane ...	H	104	14, 42
Gangá ...	H	210	9, 12, 13, 14, 24
Gangotre ..	H	49	8, 14, 17, 47
Gangwáni ...	H	29	7, 15
Ganotre ...	H	35	15, 28
Gárá ...	H	72	6, 15, 29, 47
Garg ...	H	4,743	4, 7, 8, 9, 15, 39, 40, 41, 47
	S	13	9
Garri ...	H	80	15, 19, 47
Gáte ...	H	38	6, 34
Gaur ...	H	361,322	P.
	S	381	4, 6, 9, 12, 13, 14, 17, 22, 25, 48
	J	3	11, 14, 25
Gauri ...	H	116	15, 18, 42
Ghag ...	H	16	42, 47
Ghamdoli ...	H	77	42
Ghand ...	H	38	17
Ghangár ...	H	681	14, 15, 19, 29
Ghariál ...	H	654	39
Gharot ...	H	25	42
Gharoujá ...	H	12	47
Ghatwáriá ...	H	273	3, 15, 42
Ghichand ...	H	43	14
Gidar ...	H	31	24, 26
Godar ...	H	284	16, 47
Gohani ...	H	12	6, 47
Gokal ...	H	16	11, 43, 47
Gol ...	H	69	8, 25, 42
	S	5	17
Gondi ...	H	53	9, 14, 47
Gondwál ...	H	34	24, 42
Gopál ...	H	115	9, 11, 14, 15
Gorái ...	H	43	41
Gormáli ...	H	36	33
Gotam ...	H	6,690	D. J. L. 19, 20, 24, 34, 36, 37, 39, 41, 42, 47
Gujráti ...	H	8,952	D. J. L. 21, 26, 33, 42, 47, 48, 50
	S	2	14
	M	3	6
Gurder ...	H	20	27, 45
Guriá ...	H	126	14, 15, 42
Guruwáli ...	H	19	15
Gusáin ...	H	711	L. R. M. 8, 12, 41, 47
	S	1	14
Hais ...	H	67	14, 15, 45
Haisar ...	H	178	14, 26, 42
Hami ...	H	18	11
Hamlogo ...	H	16	47
Hanojá ...	H	20	20
Hansti ...	H	77	19, 24
Harappu ...	H	15	24
Hardowári ...	H	22	47
Harichandoiá	H	46	15, 45
	S	16	21
Harmahesh	H	12	12
Hars ..	H	47	11, 42, 47
Harsiál ...	H	23	42
Harwáki ...	H	23	14, 17, 18, 47
Hirá ...	H	18	24, 47
Husaini ...	H	31	19, 29, 47
	S	4	24
	M	10	24, 29
Isar ...	H	73	18
	S	2	14
Jáble ...	H	52	47
Jágá ...	H	17	3
Jagná ...	H	28	14, 28
Jagran ...	H	89	27
Jaichandi ...	H	396	11, 12, 15, 45
Jaihotar ...	H	51	15
Jaili ...	H	61	25
Jaini ...	H	38	25, 47
Jajori ...	H	48	1, 9
Jajwál ...	H	29	11
Jakan ...	H	26	47
Jali ...	H	93	11, 15, 17
	S	1	12
Jálpot ...	H	179	9, 11, 12, 15
Jamotre ...	H	23	15, 47
Jamráon ...	H	60	42
Jamwál ...	H	56	8, 14, 15, 47
Jangan ...	H	408	16, 19, 24, 26, 42
Jángar ...	H	89	15, 47
Jangi ...	H	159	15, 19, 47
Janjuá ...	H	415	17, 18, 37
Jankar ...	H	73	14
Jarál ...	H	20	15, 41
Járun ...	H	30	15, 47
	S	1	10
Jas ...	S	22	26
Jashál ...	H	27	21, 47
Jaspál ...	H	26	42, 47
Jasrá ...	H	187	9, 14, 16
Jatálá ...	H	87	18, 27, 28
	S	1	12
Jatli ...	H	572	M. 12
Jatli Sársut	H	21	23, 26
Jatti ...	H	365	14, 15, 19, 24, 51
Jawáni ...	H	165	47
Jeki ...	H	11	47
Jhagan ...	H	178	12, 14, 24, 25
	S	2	14
Jhagar ...	H	86	9, 12
Jhakáhar ...	H	23	18, 47
Jhakrotiá ...	H	15	47
Jhalotre ...	H	21	9, 47
Jogi ...	H	71	11, 27, 47
Jokháyat ...	H	166	39
Joli ...	H	33	11
Jor Kor ...	H	18	2, 47
Joshi ...	H	1,687	L. 9, 11, 20, 25, 51
	S	19	17, 44
Josin ...	H	13	16
Joti ...	H	322	9, 14, 19, 21
Jotshi ...	H	485	J. 3, 15
	S	9	14
Junglan ...	H	18	47
Kablus ...	S	19	44
Kaibal ...	H	11	18, 21, 24
Kaisham ...	H	168	34
Kaisth ...	H	59	11, 20, 47
Kajlie ...	H	29	17
Kajroliá ...	S	17	15
Kákar ...	H	397	9, 18, 23, 26, 47
Kake ...	H	71	19
Káhal ...	H	35	24
Kalan ...	H	527	12, 16, 18, 42
Kálar ...	H	258	9, 25, 51
Káliá ...	H	4,508	L. 10, 11, 18, 26, 41, 47
	S	38	14
Kalit ...	H	20	47
Kálkech ...	H	15	14
Kallu ...	H	154	9, 29, 41, 42
Kámalián ...	H	13	47
Kamre ...	H	117	24, 26, 42
Kánas ...	H	63	9, 19
Kandal ...	H	109	9, 37, 47
Kandewál ...	H	1,939	1, 17
Kandhár ...	H	95	15, 16, 27
Kandi ...	H	51	19, 45, 47
	S	1	12
Kandri ...	H	157	9, 14, 15, 17
	S	3	15
Kangáliá ...	H	45	18, 42
Kangar ...	H	75	15, 47
Kangásair ...	H	37	15
Káne ...	H	17	9
Kanjorá ...	H	150	16, 18, 37, 42
Kank ...	H	38	8
Kánkubj ...	H	341	4, 8, 49
Kanopotre ...	H	19	28
Kanwál ...	H	71	42
Kapuri ...	H	276	9, 19, 27
Kárang ...	H	11	12
Karar ...	H	111	15, 39
Kariál ...	H	311	21, 42
	S	2	9
Karmál ...	H	64	14
Káshab ...	H	2,065	J. 4, 14, 15, 41, 42, 47
	S	11	14
Kashmiri ...	H	895	J. R. 14, 42, 47
	S	25	14
Kasir ...	H	60	14, 15, 42, 45
Kástián ...	H	40	47
Káthpál ...	H	508	M. 15, 19
Katiálu ...	H	48	42
Kátitán ...	H	39	47
Katoi ...	H	50	42, 47
Katwál ...	H	301	15, 39, 42
Kaul ...	H	31	14, 19
Kaunsal ...	H	117	36, 45
Kaushash ...	H	447	3, 4, 5, 12
Kawár ...	H	47	11, 27
Khádariá ...	H	36	12
Khadián ...	H	108	42
Khadri ...	H	325	15, 25
Khajia ...	H	47	9
Khajurá ...	H	1,503	2, 9, 15, 39
	S	12	15
Khal ...	H	16	42
Khaledu ...	H	27	47
Khalli ...	H	194	47
Khandar ...	H	288	9, 14, 42
	S	5	14
Khandelwál	H	764	3, 12, 30, 41, 49
Khandorá ...	H	112	15, 27
Khanhkátu	H	14	47
Khar ...	H	34	15
Kharia ...	H	117	27, 47
Kharral ...	H	159	20, 42
Kharre ...	H	102	47
Kharwál ...	H	56	8
Khatri ...	H	101	8, 15, 16
Khorjá ...	H	42	15
Kishanwári	H	13	47
Kochas ...	H	34	1
Kodri ...	H	334	41
Kohrpál ...	H	95	14, 17
Kokarne ...	H	30	24, 34
Kor ...	H	36	15, 19, 25
	S	3	33
Kosh ...	H	235	11, 15, 16, 19, 34
Koshak ...	H	114	4, 34
Koshál ...	H	1,946	J. 5, 14, 15, 34, 39, 47
	S	29	14
Kotal ...	H	47	42
Kotaliál ...	H	12	47
Kothli ...	H	50	47
Kotri ...	H	58	9, 24, 51
Kotwál ...	H	63	41
Kundal ...	H	194	7, 8, 34, 42
Kundari ...	H	18	14
Kushál ...	H	19	27, 41
Ladhar ...	H	286	14, 15, 25, 4[illegible], 47
	M	4	14
Lagotre ...	H	39	14, 15
Lagwál ..	H	70	42
Láhar ...	H	41	11, 14, 25
Láhori ...	H	206	12, 14, 41, 47
	S	1	9
Láhri ...	H	14	17, 41
Laie ...	H	160	11, 18, 19, 27
	S	28	15
Lake ...	H	32	15, 28, 42
Lakhanpál	H	1,839	L. M. 10, 42
	S	7	18
Lakhere ...	H	11	47
Lali ...	H	86	12, 16, 27
Lálibachá ...	H	11	29
Lálotrá ...	H	95	15, 16, 29
Lalri ...	H	148	15, 19, 23
Lám ...	H	30	26
Lándáh ...	H	11	42
Langáh ...	H	108	47
Lauji ...	H	16	41
Lánthe ...	H	17	11

Names of Sub-Castes.		Persons.	Locality.
Lát ...	H	82	9
Látbi ...	H	70	28, 47
Látti ...	H	71	14, 30, 42
Lin ...	H	26	9
Lodbi ...	H	42	8
Lodián ...	H	44	42
Lohár ...	H	21	47
Lohárich ...	H	17	47
Lor ...	H	408	15, 17, 26
Lotre ...	H	16	16
Machan ...	H	30	15
Madáre ...	H	46	10
Madárijá ...	H	23	17, 41
Mádho ...	H	81	11, 14, 42
Madwál ...	H	87	42
Mahán Brahman.	H	876	2, 5, 9, 49, 51
Mahantá ...	H	179	9
Mahbi ...	H	42	11, 41
Mahlwál ...	H	22	42
Maholá ...	H	122	19, 26,
Mahrirái ...	H	17	27
Mahtiái ...	H	737	9, 16, 17
Maidár ...	H	294	15, 16
Majhorí ...	H	24	42
Makarzátu ...	H	39	47
Makhi ...	H	82	9, 26
Makhíál ...	H	12	47
Máldeo ...	H	25	10
Maleri ...	H	82	15, 42
Mandab ...	H	13	42
Mandar ...	H	605	L. 34, 42, 47
	S	12	14, 15
Mandoliá ...	H	17	8, 47
Mangal ...	H	49	8
Manglern ...	H	23	47
Maniás ...	H	228	14, 23, 27
Manojá ...	H	17	18, 45
Marar ...	H	124	15, 47
Maráthu ...	H	28	47
Marchar ...	H	28	19, 45
Marcheti ...	H	27	16, 47
Marhattá ...	H	11	50
Márkande ...	H	876	8, 12, 47
	S	3	12
Mármandre	H	17	47
Maror ...	H	67	9
Máski ...	H	18	37
Mátri ...	H	19	21, 41
Megal ...	H	58	11, 17, 25, 41
Mesi ...	H	151	14, 17
Milanhána ...	H	50	16, 29
Minjál ...	H	69	9, 17, 29
Missar ...	H	823	8, 9, 15, 18, 19
Mitar ...	H	174	15, 19, 25
Mithu ...	H	159	14
Mohan ...	H	182	10, 14, 15, 19
Mohtá ...	H	249	3, 15, 17
	S	18	12
Mohyál ...	H	8,395	10, 14, 20, 26, 48
	S	310	20, 22, 33
Mojal ...	H	2,212	16, 18, 19, 22, 25
	S	43	18
Molá ...	H	25	24, 25, 29
Montár ...	H	156	15, 47
Mor ...	H	35	26
Mose ...	H	17	24
Motál ...	H	41	6, 15, 29, 36, 41
Mudgal ...	H	242	3, 9, 50
Mundri ...	H	15	15, 47
Munge ...	H	793	9, 14, 15, 26, 29, 47
Munnan ...	H	149	17, 45
Nábhá ...	H	191	14, 15, 16, 19
Nade ...	H	95	42
Nágar ...	H	30	2, 8, 12
Nágpál ...	H	68	14
Nágu ...	H	74	9, 17, 27, 47
Nágwál ...	H	52	4, 8
	S	14	4, 5
Náias ...	H	115	42
Nainsain ...	H	32	47
Nánakshúhi	H	195	12, 14
Napárá ...	H	14	42
Nárad ...	H	65	15
Náraj ...	H	205	9, 18, 45
	S	15	18
Naranjan ...	H	18	45
Naroe ...	H	20	13
Nashándá ...	H	18	11
Nawábir ...	H	37	14, 47
Nekan ...	H	61	15, 33, 47
Obansh ...	H	14	17
Ocbi ...	H	12	14, 19
Odepál ...	H	84	14, 17, 47
Ogur ...	H	316	4, 11
Ojhá ...	H	268	11, 19, 23, 26
Oji ...	H	41	8, 17, 21
Opádiá ...	H	52	3, 12, 34
Oshal ...	H	25	14
Osi ...	H	226	14, 47
Osni ...	H	194	14, 15
Otrá ...	H	41	14, 16, 47
Pacháhdu ...	H	13	47
Padál ...	H	222	9, 15, 21, 34
Pádhe ...	H	386	8, 10, 42, 47
Pagotre ...	H	13	17
Páhal ...	H	14	9, 11
Páhri ...	H	129	20, 39, 42
Pál ...	H	67	9, 10, 14, 25, 26
Palang ...	H	188	10, 39, 44, 47
Palásar ...	H	92	9, 14, 16, 39, 41
Palástar ...	H	77	18, 39, 47
Palgo ...	H	28	44
Páli ...	H	151	9, 14, 15, 44
Pálliwál ...	H	115	3, 4
Pambno ...	H	88	26, 28
Pandáre ...	H	50	8, 15, 27
Pánde ...	H	822	J, 15, 21, 44, 47
	S	32	12, 17, 20, 21
Pándhá ...	H	869	8, 9, 16, 19, 25, 50
	M	1	50
Pándi ...	H	241	11, 12, 14, 16, 42
	S	2	15
Pandit ...	H	712	8, 9, 13, 15, 42
Pandotar ...	H	54	9, 42, 47
Pani ...	H	19	15, 19, 25
Panj ...	H	252	11, 15, 28, 25, 44
Panjál ...	H	291	9, 11, 14, 47
Panjkhandi	H	12	12
Panjpál ...	H	129	8, 11, 25, 47
Panotar ...	H	34	11, 15, 47
Panwár ...	H	68	15, 19, 41, 42
Paráoh ...	H	30	8
Paránchi ...	H	36	13, 26, 42
Parandná ...	H	78	25, 26
Parángol ...	H	21	15, 26, 44
Parásar ...	H	1,814	J. L. 26, 44, 45
	S	13	9, 10, 45
Parbál ...	H	107	18, 25, 44, 47
Parhár ...	H	15	12, 47
Pári ...	H	321	12, 14, 25, 39
Parichi ...	H	62	14, 17, 24, 27
Párikh ...	H	1,336	1, 3, 12, 49
Parohat ...	H	738	8, 14, 21, 30, 42
Paroj ...	H	191	15
Pásak ...	H	47	15, 45
Pasáman ...	H	136	14, 25, 51
Pátak ...	H	985	9, 11, 15, 26, 39
Patán ...	H	57	9, 14, 42
Patgále ...	H	79	9, 11, 47
Pather ...	H	13	15, 45
Patiál ...	H	222	9, 15, 47
Patiári ...	H	32	9, 15, 21, 51
Patrijá ...	H	25	17
Pattu ...	H	57	15, 18, 44, 45
Patwárá ...	H	86	14, 15, 39, 42
	S	10	14
Perulo ...	H	23	3, 9
Phágan ...	H	192	10, 26, 47
Phagohrá ...	H	27	39
Phákar ...	H	11	19, 28
Phalle ...	H	382	12, 15, 24, 39
	S	8	12
Phami ...	H	147	9, 10, 11, 39
Phándi ...	H	19	9, 26, 28, 45
Pharánt ...	H	14	45, 51
Pháthi ...	H	36	14
Phatre ...	H	15	18
Phore ...	H	60	15, 19, 45
Pipálwá ...	H	16	30
Poj ...	H	106	11, 12, 14
Ponch ...	H	763	L. 4, 21, 26
Poziáli ...	H	11	47
Pujári ...	H	302	8, 12, 15, 47
Punjá ...	H	58	9, 14, 20, 24
	S	9	17
Purang ...	H	57	10
Purbiá ...	H	64	15
Puri ...	H	40	11, 12, 25
	S	1	14
Pushkarná ...	H	2,986	M. 18, 19, 23
	S	11	23, 26
Qananji ...	H	1,858	D. L. 25, 49
	S	14	14, 49
Rábrá ...	H	309	12, 19, 24, 26
	S	2	25
Ráhi ...	H	257	15, 16, 45
Rahin ...	H	171	9, 15, 18, 21
	S	24	14, 15, 21
Rái ...	H	524	11, 15, 19, 21
	S	10	20
Raini ...	H	229	15, 47
Rájghát ...	H	25	11
Rájhi ...	H	39	11, 15, 44
Rájiál ...	H	97	14, 25, 45
Rajolie ...	H	345	47
Rájput ...	H	17	25
Rakhána ...	H	24	26, 45
Rakhari ...	H	17	8
Rakhesar ...	H	102	8
Rakhotre ...	H	95	17, 42, 47
Rákhshash ...	H	11	13
Rámánandi	H	61	10, 21, 24, 25, 41
	S	1	12
Rámde ...	H	115	19, 21, 44, 45
Rámdev ...	H	142	M. 14, 19, 23
	S	10	14, 18
Ramdhiá ...	H	28	4, 17
Rámgarhie ...	S	12	4
Rámpál ...	H	285	14, 21
Randlor ...	H	82	11, 47
Rangá ...	H	35	11, 24, 25, 45
Rángotre ...	H	34	9, 51
Ráni ...	H	391	9, 10, 14, 27, 47
Ranpál ...	H	238	L. 8, 12, 19
	S	3	12
Rasbál ...	H	101	10, 14, 42
Rasgotre ...	H	15	47
Rasi ...	H	90	9, 21, 27
	S	12	17, 21
Ratan ...	H	347	9, 15, 24, 39, 42
...	S	11	9
Ratan bhárdwáj.	H	189	8, 9
Ratanpál ...	H	1,144	L. 9, 44, 47
	S	6	20, 44
Rathi ...	H	261	9, 13, 17, 21
Ráthor ...	H	13	15, 25
	S	16	24, 27
Ratiwál ...	H	70	12
Ratnágar ...	H	25	47
Reopotra ...	H	18	47
Rigvedi ...	H	14	3
Rikhi ...	H	527	12, 14, 16, 17, 45
	S	16	14
Rithál ...	H	801	4, 21, 39
	S	11	21
Rohát ...	H	19	8
Rohtia ...	H	29	12, 27
Rojhá ...	H	37	19, 27
Rophlo ...	H	22	47
Rosti ...	H	213	15, 47
Rumál ...	H	64	45, 47
Rupál ...	H	275	10, 11, 13, 27, 45
Sabál ...	H	42	7, 9, 14
Sabjpál ...	H	294	10, 11, 25, 45
Sabotrá ...	H	117	15
Sabrili ...	H	33	3, 47
Sachde ...	H	14	21, 25
Sadála ...	H	23	7, 23, 42
Sadátai ...	H	69	15
Sadathe ...	H	27	15
Sadgal ...	H	184	9
Sádh ...	H	4	7, 14
Sadhan ...	H	80	15, 39, 47
	S	4	21
Sadhár ...	H	347	12, 16, 21, 24
	S	7	13, 17
Sadhri ...	H	39	9, 16, 21
Sadi ...	H	266	9, 11, 15, 16, 21
Safan ...	H	16	47
Sagal ...	H	97	11, 12, 15, 21, 27
Sagar ...	H	24	7, 11

Names of Sub-Castes.		Persons.	Locality.
Saghar ...	H	59	10, 20, 25
Sagotri ...	H	107	12, 15, 16, 21, 36
Saháran ...	H	98	15, 18, 20, 25
	S	4	18
Sahgal ...	H	303	9, 14, 24, 38
	S	1	10
Sahgan ...	H	95	21
Sahjpál ...	H	379	12
Sahlotri ...	H	55	16
Sahlpál ...	H	49	9, 11, 12, 45
Sahmotre ...	H	88	15
Sahotar ...	H	288	9, 15, 18, 26, 39
Saidar ...	H	15	12
	S	9	13
Saidu ...	H	82	15
Sair ...	H	24	15, 24
Sajgotre ...	H	28	15
Sakal ...	H	243	11, 16, 41, 45
Sakhi ...	H	199	9, 16, 26, 28
	S	1	10
Sakhiál ...	H	640	39
Sakráo ...	H	11	42
Salang ...	H	24	15
Sálbában ...	H	778	11, 14, 15, 25, 42
	S	8	18
Salmoi ...	H	708	9, 39, 47
Salori ...	H	70	15, 42, 47
Salotri ...	H	13	16, 17
Sámipotra ...	H	47	9, 17, 18, 23
Samláhi ..	H	42	42
Samsáhi ...	H	57	9, 42
Sámyál ...	H	11	25
Sanádh ...	H	556	3, 4, 10, 12, 14, 20, 49
Sanál ...	H	69	1, 11, 15, 26
Sanár ...	H	25	11, 45
Sándá ...	H	175	9, 10, 14, 23
Sándal ...	H	1,527	J.L. 35, 37, 41, 47
	S	17	9, 17, 21, 26
Sande ...	H	62	12, 14, 15, 28
Sándel ...	H	814	7, 9, 19, 37, 42
Sándesi ...	H	119	4, 5, 14
Sandeur Joshi	H	14	39
Sandhar ...	H	402	9, 11, 15, 19, 45, 47
	S	1	24
Sandiálu ...	H	32	47
Sandoliá ...	H	94	30
Sandrál ...	H	304	16, 27, 46
Sándras ...	H	138	3, 12, 15, 31, 34
	S	1	25
Sang ...	H	20	24, 25, 51
Sangar ...	H	434	9, 11, 19, 39, 44
	S	2	9, 11
Sángart ...	H	92	3, 44, 47
Saugotre ...	H	324	15, 16, 18, 48
Saugrál ...	H	156	11, 12, 18, 41, 47
Sanhiároo ...	H	18	39
Saniási ...	H	410	8, 12, 18, 21
	S	3	21
Sankrinú ...	H	22	47
Sanotrá ...	H	82	12, 14, 15, 25, 27
Sans ...	H	109	9, 14, 21, 37
	S	84	21
Sanupál ...	H	121	5, 15, 39, 48
Sánwati ...	H	81	11, 23, 29
	S	5	29
Sapnál ...	H	174	14, 15, 45, 47
Sar ...	H	95	15, 19, 45
Sarái ...	H	117	9, 15, 25, 47
	S	5	15
Sarál ...	H	59	15, 41, 47
Sáran ...	H	164	15, 17, 18, 25
Sárandar ...	H	57	14, 25, 41, 51
Sárang ...	H	63	19, 23, 26
Sáras ...	H	2,287	11, 15, 16, 47
	S	1	16
Sarbándi ...	H	12	11, 47
Sarbliá ...	H	13	23, 26, 47
Sardhiá ...	H	206	11, 25, 45, 47
Sardhiál ...	H	11	39
Saregu ...	H	22	39, 41
Sargol ...	H	52	15, 47
	S	3	25
Sárh ...	H	154	9, 24, 26, 43
Sari ...	H	170	9, 11, 15, 45
Saríli ...	H	204	16, 17, 18, 28, 45
Sarkandi ...	H	30	15, 47
Sárle ...	H	19	25
Sarnítu ...	H	37	47
Saroiá ...	H	59	2, 19, 25, 28, 47
Saroliá ...	H	29	12
Saror ...	H	94	9, 11, 15, 45
Sarotri ...	H	41	9, 15, 47
Sarpatti ...	H	11	11, 18, 45
Sarsán ...	H	48	10
Sárswál ..	H	73	12, 15, 24
Sársut ...	H	351,649	P
	S	3,975	J. L. R. 56, 25, 26, 33, 44, 48, 49, 50
	M	4	14, 50
Sárd ...	H	329	10, 11, 15, 44, 45
Sarví ..	H	76	11, 12
Sarwán ...	H	40	4, 11, 14, 15, 47
Sárwání ..	H	14	29, 47
Sarwariá ...	H	163	4, 6, 21, 24
Sás ...	H	24	21, 26, 46
Sásan ...	H	258	10, 18, 21, 25
Satán ...	H	27	9, 14, 45
Satár ...	H	101	9, 26, 27
Sathi ...	H	286	15, 21, 27
	S	1	20
Satiál ...	H	33	9, 12, 20, 47
Satpál ...	H	61	19, 23, 26, 47
Satrá ...	H	23	15, 24, 36
Satwáh ...	H	21	18
Satwál ...	H	30	9, 19, 27
Sáwál ...	H	71	11, 39
Sawáni ...	H	617	9, 12, 27, 28, 29
	S	1	14
Sáwíli ...	H	201	9, 15, 27, 42, 44
...	S	1	51
Sehám ...	H	26	18
Seku ..	H	63	41
Seli ...	H	469	10, 11, 15, 44
Sem ...	H	112	19
Ser ...	H	23	15, 44
Sethi ...	H	221	15, 26, 27, 45
Sewán ...	H	23	9
Sháhpotrá ...	H	27	9, 28, 29
Shálupotrá	H	13	19, 24
Shámol ...	H	139	27
Shámpotrá	H	118	19, 23, 26, 27
Shankar ...	H	31	14, 47
Shánt ...	H	75	15, 16
Sher ...	H	67	8
Shogal ...	H	24	14, 15
Shoriá ...	H	158	2, 3, 9, 10, 12, 14, 25, 44
Shukal ...	H	650	9, 12, 17, 18, 42
Sidhár ...	H	173	10, 12, 14, 17, 45
	S	2	45
Sígan ...	H	56	26
Sindhiá ...	H	77	47
Sindhu ...	H	20	8, 12, 25, 26
Sir ...	H	11	11
Sirikhand ...	H	101	9, 15, 47
Sírmál ...	H	63	14
Sodán ...	H	741	9, 12, 16, 21
	S	7	16, 18
Sodári ...	H	34	15, 21
	S	86	21
Sodhi ...	H	62	14, 47
	S	7	14
Sohán ...	H	26	14, 16
Sohl ...	H	13	9, 34, 42
Sokal ...	H	121	15, 22, 47
Sokar ...	H	18	23
Sokhi ...	H	32	15, 45, 47
Solete ...	H	183	39
Son ..	H	20	15
Sonái ...	H	19	19, 47
Sonki ...	H	102	14, 15, 18, 47
Sonklá ...	H	13	42
Sopli ...	H	28	11, 15
Soti ...	H	1,033	9, 11, 14, 29
	S	2	12
Sotrá ...	H	102	14, 15, 16, 24, 25
	S	8	21
Sotrak ...	H	109	23, 24, 26, 28
Sotre ...	H	70	15, 18, 39
Suárna ...	H	25	9
Súdan ...	H	264	19, 20, 21, 23
	S	84	9, 21
Sundar ...	H	31	12, 14, 25
Suraj ...	H	93	7, 8, 9, 17, 41
Suri ...	H	283	11, 14, 15, 16, 1
	S	4	18
Swán ...	H	784	18, 19, 27, 28
Tabári ...	H	30	12, 14, 47
Tabat ...	H	25	14, 34
Tagáh ...	H	505	2, 3, 4, 26
Tágbit ...	H	13	10
	S	1	11
Tagnáit ...	H	55	8, 9
Tágu ...	H	132	5
Tah ...	H	520	9, 11, 12, 15, 44
		43	9, 11, 25
Tabní ...	H	182	12
Táik ...	H	114	9, 15, 27
	S	4	27
Táit ...	H	21	14
Tajpál ...	H	45	9, 12, 25, 51
Takarwál ...	H	201	39
Takhná ...	H	30	10, 16, 44
Takmio ...	H	23	15
Taknet ...	H	181	8, 9, 10, 16
Takoriá ..	H	51	15, 30, 42
Takri ...	H	25	9, 42
Talári ...	H	12	47
Talhan ...	H	113	9, 19, 27
Talbogo ...	H	41	42
Talni ...	H	125	14, 18, 26, 44
Talori ...	H	54	19
Talwári ...	H	24	9, 11, 24, 42
	S	2	11
Tamaryál ...	H	35	47
Tamoli ...	H	20	47
Tand ...	H	19	12, 27
Tandni ...	H	175	11, 29, 44, 47
Tángar ...	H	21	9, 16
Tanghát ...	H	162	9
Tánk ...	H	59	14, 27, 41
Tannan ...	H	234	9, 11, 14
Tanoja ...	H	9	9
	S	25	18
Tapariál ...	H	14	4, 7
Tapásar ...	H	61	14, 16
Tár ..	H	38	10, 14
Tárá ...	H	74	14, 16, 19, 21
Tarangrá ...	H	18	47
Tarbeni ...	H	36	14, 15, 43, 47
Targálá ...	H	39	14
Tarhárch ...	H	361	15, 47
Tári ...	H	71	16, 19, 28
Tariál ...	H	92	15, 18, 47
Tariár ...	H	22	15
Tarkáli ...	H	84	14, 16
Tarkhá ...	H	470	11, 19, 24, 26, 27
Tawári ...	H	309	9, 11, 16, 27, 51
	S	1	11
Tej ...	H	18	15
Tejpál ...	H	451	9, 14, 15, 18
Teká ...	H	82	5
Teli Rájá ...	H	5	29
	S	12	27, 29
Tewári ...	H	130	10, 13, 24, 27
Thákar ...	H	295	9, 14, 15, 24, 51
	S	7	14
Tháli ...	H	45	9, 14, 34, 51
Thaman ...	H	71	11, 14, 38
Thamdái ...	H	16	14
Thami ...	H	18	11, 26
Thandár ...	H	30	9
Thanik ...	H	11	9, 24
Thatbrán ...	H	40	47
Tolá ...	H	202	10, 11, 14, 15, 19
Torá ...	H	117	9, 15, 26
Tuniál ...	H	25	47
Turi ...	H	21	8, 12
Uchal ..	H	18	18, 26
Udási ...	H	91	9, 14, 42
	S	3	12, 14
Upáhde ...	H	333	43
Upál ...	H	12	9, 14
Utriál ...	H	178	15
Uttam ...	H	65	17, 18, 21
	S	7	21
Vabdwá ...	H	32	12, 13
Vadá ...	H	44	11, 12, 14, 21
	S	3	21
Vahárá ...	H	58	19
Vaink ...	H	44	19, 24

Names of Sub-Castes.		Persons.	Locality.	Names of Sub-Castes.		Persons.	Locality.	Names of Sub-Castes.		Persons.	Locality.
Vais ...	H	142	15, 19, 23, 27	Vasand ...	H	34	24, 25	Yodhin ...	H	15	47
	S	2	15	Vasdev ...	H	1,440	9, 14, 15, 16, 44	Minor* ...	H	1,871	
Vaisno ...	H	67	10, 15	Vasti ...	H	197	14, 16, 17, 25		S	63	
	S	15	17		S	4	12, 15		M	1	
Valáli ...	H	25	10, 25, 28	Váwal ...	H	38	26	Unspecified ...	H	61,442	
	S	2	10	Vedwá ...	H	200	17, 18, 24, 25		S	2,118	
Vals ...	H	29	14, 25, 44		S	4	25		M	1	
Vanj ...	H	44	14, 21, 25	Vegi ...	H	27	12, 25		J	31	
Váole ...	H	26	44		S	3	12		B	4	
Varmi ...	H	28	2, 29, 51	Vid ...	H	258	13, 15, 16, 26				
Varsu ...	H	21	15, 16, 21		S	3	18, 19				

***DETAIL OF MINOR.**

Abbeb 3, Abdhia 3, Ablish 3, Áchkaru 8, Adrich 1, Aghar 3, Agtari 6, Ahauns 9, Ajrá 6, Akhoti 8, Akri 9, Alstar 1, Alwási 6, Amak 9, Amáli 1, Amial Kash 4, Amri 5, Anand 2, Anant Phat 1, Andal 5, Ankrans 4, Ararpopo 1, Arichiú 5, Arni 2, Arotrá 9, Ársi 10, Arsti 1, Áryal 10, Asnád 4, Asni 1, Asttrá 8, Atarmál 8, Athán 4, Auban 1, Auli 1, Aungal 1, Awáhil 9, Awaidá 8, Bachbiál 2, Badakh 6, Badam 5, Badháti 8, Baishno 10, Bákari 9, Bakhs 7, Baksál 2, Bálmik 3, Baloj 3, Banwái 3, Baráriá 5, Barchháli 7, Bargám 1, Bariákál 10, Bariákár 6, Barwáne 4, Basáhará 8, Basjain 10, Batriji 2, Berami 5, Beriar 2, Bhabák 1, Bhaini 9, Bhainiwál 3, Bhalkán 1, Bhának 5, Bhánar 5, Bharmore 1, Bharthari 3, Bhasant 2, Bhateru 3, Bhokli 6, Bholá 7, Bholmáli 1, Bhoman Paliú 1, Bishán Nágri 2, Biskarná 6, Bisni 3, Brahm Bhojá 1, Burthi 1, Chabgi 4, Cháche 7, Chakar 8, Chakrá 3, Chaldrách 7, Chand 3, Chániál 2, Charotari 1, Chawál 10, Chhakan 10, Cholán 5, Chosi 3, Dabdie 8, Dabnar 5, Dabor 2, Dádal 9, Dádaliá 5, Dádhlá 10, Dadwál 2, Dagthaliá 1, Dahdaham 2, Dákhiál 2, Dalore 8, Dandwálá 6, Dángmár 3, Darhán 1, Darbáwá 3, Dardariá 8, Dargade 1, Dárkhbáj 9, Darshani 4, Dasti 4, Datmál 4, Degam 5, Deori 4, Dhadwán 4, Dhagarwál 6, Dhagiáre 9, Dhájorliá 3, Dhal 9, Dhangu 4, Dhaul 7, Dherbáli 2, Diámbrá 4, Die 1, Diná 3, Dith 7, Dudrái 4, Dunial 7, Eman 1, English 4, Fatlián 9, Gadáhar 10, Gadiwál 7, Gagre 1, Gaindá 5, Gálián 8, Gandwái 10, Ganj 1, Garbh 8, Gawál Bans 10, Ghalogaro 7, Ghamal 2, Ghasnli 7, Ghiman 10, Gidaz 3, Gilá 8, Golshán 9, Gorádayán 1, Gotre 6, Granthi 3, Gubtá 1, Gújar 5, Gurniál 9, Gursiál 2, Hál 1, Hálwi 1, Hamsain 2, Handdilu 5, Harnál 8, Hathkári 7, Humán 10, Indaurá 3, Jabak 1, Jadwáni 5, Jágarwál 3, Jagpál 1, Jagthalia 4, Jahar 2, Jaiwál 6, Jakál 7, Jamás 4, Jamhuriá 5, Jamná Dási 1, Jamrá 2, Jand 1, Jangpál 3, Janrá 5, Jartál 2, Jat Karn 1, Jesni 3, Jhalmariá 2, Jhangsain 7, Jhári 6, Jhároliá 2, Jhontaru 1, Jogián 3, Johriá 7, Jokatár 1, Jor 1, Jori 9, Káchhwál 5, Kachráyá 7, Kachwá 6, Káhangari 4, Kábie 8, Kail 1, Kál 2, Kalanbi 5, Kalhánch 8, Kaljáníá 1, Kallikalá 3, Kalnás 1, Kalsi 1, Kandwál 5, Kánkar 2, Kanotre 9, Kánphatá 10, Kantrián 1, Kasandarbi 1, Kasiá 8, Katiári 2, Katorná 5, Kelukbariá 8, Kespotrá 6, Khangabar 5, Khattá 7, Khekpotrá 1, Khojia 4, Khotká 6, Khuriá 8, Kiriá 1, Konthi 8, Koran 1, Kothiálú 10, Kothián 10, Kotmiál 5, Kunb 2, Kung 3, Ladá 3, Lagái 1, Lagan 4, Lakhim 1, Lalgát 8, Lalin 1, Lalmoná 9, Lamián 2, Lánge 7, Langot 2, Láthari 5, Láwen 1, Lewá 1, Loiál 3, Lunj 8, Macharwál 7, Machhándar 6, Machu 2, Madáhar 7, Maháráshtar 2, Mahárwál 3, Mahesar 3, Makan 1, Makhnotre 5, Malkáne 1, Mamre 9, Mán 2, Mandhál 10, Mandhon 10, Manmahesh 2, Manon 4, Marái 8, Marháls 8, Marindá 1, Mehtá 8, Mihánpanthi 3, Mohdá 8, Mulhid 1, Murli 5, Nadewálie 3, Nadiálu 1, Nágetu 1, Náhku 6, Najumi 8, Nárá 6, Nardankhu 3, Naumuslim 1, Natiwál 1, Nirmitrá 1, Nobak 5, Obbi 9, Odhá 4, Odij 1, Odmiri 2, Oklal 8, Ovinhál 3, Pachhiálu 6, Padhár 4, Paghiál 2, Paldhan 3, Palnál 8, Palru 7, Panan 2, Pandáhar 5, Pandhotre 2, Pandroliá 9, Pándwáin 2, Panjgaur 2, Panjurái 10, Párakpandá 9, Parmin 7, Parsbar 4, Parsrám 2, Pasbopotrá 1, Pásti 6, Pathári 10, Phán Pansi 8, Phánphákar 1, Phatwariá 3, Pinjar 1, Popu 3, Posal 4, Punman 1, Purán 2, Qawál 1, Radwál 10, Ragú 9, Ráibbat 8, Rájpái 3, Rájprohat 1, Rajún 6, Rakhpál 2, Ranito 2, Ratpal 1, Ráwaru 9, Razadha 1, Regau 3, Rith 3, Rokiná 7, Rukanhotre 2, Sabáyá 3, Sabdá 4, Sabwáyá 2, Sában 1, Sahárni 3, Sáhdú 2, Sáini 8, Sáins 3, Sajjan 1, Sakhwár 6, Sakiwák 6, Sakral 4, Sakrúr 5, Salan 2, Salánon 5, Samáli 1, Samotra 2, Sandlas 2, Sangal 5, Sangat 1, Sanijál 1, Sanoliá 4, Sántwáhi 3, Sapánwal 8, Sapolia 8, Sarankari 7, Sarbar 3, Sargandi 2, Sarmotrá 3, Saroj 7, Sarothápú 4, Sarsi 9, Sárth 1, Satoh 4, Satwáli 1, Saú 1, Sawárá 10, Sazák 6, Seondá 2, Sewak 6, Shangarpotra 1, Shaniwál 1, Shanwári 2, Sharmá 2, Sheokaran 2, Shebu 8, Shiriu Shisbti 7, Shohal 2, Siániá 5, Siási 9, Sihat 1, Siltán 2, Singi 1, Sirithiákar 1, Sitla 7, Sogunián 1, Sojbi 3, Somebans 2, Sondal 2, Song 2, Songtháli 7, Sudbhatiá 6, Sudh 1, Suráni 3, Surisari 1, Surjwál 9, Taháke 8, Tágan 8, Taggar 8, Tébie 7, Tahmchat 1, Tainto 4, Táku 9, Talorá 3, Talwár 6, Tamiálu 9, Tamizá 9, Tarandi 9, Taraugrit 10, Tarkh 8, Tarkhadi 6, Tarthián 2, Thakarná 9, Thalián 10, Tháthi 1, Tin 4, Tindoliá 2, Toke 1, Toi 10, Torak 2, Tori 2, Tosárá 1, Tunak 10, Tupál 5, Ud 1, Udhkáru 6, Udyál 1, Ujba 1, Uparpá 1, Upnain 5, Uppal 8, Uthál 8, Utrádhi 1, Vádhle 6, Vasgi 6, Váttu 1, Vedáni 3, Vedpatra 7, Vegashe 9, Vedpanthi 7.

Chuhra 925,535 { H. 789,857; S. 51,549; M. 84,128; J. 1 }

Names of Sub-Castes.		Persons.	Locality.
Abwiál ...	H	168	9, 44
	S	39	9, 12
Achal ...	H	40	1
Adalwál ...	H	239	9, 15
Achháwa ...	H	197	9, 10, 14, 25
Adhirwál ...	H	60	4
Adiwál ...	H	2,455	1, 6, 10, 25, 46, 48
	S	901	1, 12, 14, 25, 48
	M	72	12, 13
Adlál ...	H	19	1
Adrál ...	M	54	12
Adwál ...	H	954	11, 13
	M	17	13, 21
Ahír ...	H	107	1, 6, 11
	S	4	6
	M	1	25
Ahmal ...	H	65	11
Ajníwál ...	H	1,423	3, 4, 32, 51
Ákál ...	H	11	5
Alwál ..	H	69	3, 5
Amal ...	H	12	9, 25
Anant ...	H	5	44
	M	58	4
Andal ...	H	20	2
Andlú ...	H	458	13, 15, 25
	M	2	14
Andwál ...	H	17	1
	M	21	13
Aniwál ...	H	60	4
Anjin ...	H	19	14, 27
Anjinwál ...	H	236	4
Anod Lál ...	H	12	4
Answál ...	H	106	1, 4
Anwál ...	H	150	8, 15, 48, 50
Anwat ...	H	37	1
Aráin ...	M	48	51
Asal ...	H	352	5, 6, 50
Asíwál ...	H	3	48
	S	87	12, 14
	M	7	51
Aspál ...	H	10	50
	S	16	50
Astolia ...	H	13	3
Atal ...	H	277	8, 9, 10
Atáwalí ...	H	6	1, 2
	S	4	14
	M	20	27
Athwál ...	H	12,868	L. 1, 2, 3, 25, 46, 48
	S	1,289	9, 12, 14, 25, 48
	M	1,520	12, 13, 24, 25
Atí ...	S	101	48
Átú ...	H	19	9, 10, 46
Audí ...	H	34	15
	S	2	13
	M	7	13
Aujhwál ..	H	11	2
Aulakh ...	H	22	25, 48
	S	48	48
Aur ...	H	21	18
	S	55	25
	M	3	13
Autal ...	H	183	9, 10, 48
Awán ...	H	239	4, 16, 25
	M	14	12, 13, 16, 25
Áwí ...	H	99	25
Bábá ...	H	1,213	1, 6, 7, 17
	S	49	12
	M	4	17
Babar ...	H	125	16, 17
	S	1	48
Bablar ...	H	89	25
Báchhal ...	H	29	3, 48
Bádal ...	H	217	3, 11, 14, 48
	M	18	24
Badárí ...	H	385	13
Badban ...	H	38	1
Badhál ...	H	61	2, 17, 25
	M	7	16, 25
Badhán ...	H	22	5, 8, 44, 48
Badbará ...	H	43	17
Badídan ...	H	103	5, 16 48

Names of Sub-Castes.		Persons.	Locality.
Badlána	H	333	4, 6
Badwál	H	108	4, 48
Badwán	H	11	48
Bagal	H	16	2, 6
Bágán	H	135	5, 6, 10, 11
	S	6	6
Bagar	H	584	5, 10
Bágaria	H	566	2, 5, 10, 11, 25
	M	28	13
Bagarní	H	107	50
	S	21	50
Bághí	H	75	16, 25, 44
Bágrí	H	4,956	1, 2, 4, 14, 25, 48
	S	110	11, 14, 25, 48
	M	86	25
Báhú	H	25	6
	S	6	10
Báí	H	34	9, 13. 20
Baid	H	155	5, 9
	M	1	16
Baigan	H	29	25
Baimwál	H	11	3
Baios	H	556	8, 9, 10, 11, 14, 44, 48
	S	44	48
	M	5	10
Bairágí	H	1	25
	M	14	14
Bajálgohar	H	25	4
Bájothá	H	15	44
Bájwáh	H	689	14, 15
	S	8	14
	M	9	16, 25
Bakhará	H	84	3, 49
Bál	H	120	1, 48
	S	12	2 14
Balamín	H	25	9
Balan	H	22	9
Balang	H	113	48
Bálar	H	2	11
	S	9	25
	M	13	16
Bálásháhi	H	44	6, 15, 27
	M	59	28, 29, 51
Baldhán	H	55	1, 4
Baldí	M	18	13
Balgohar	H	414	2, 3, 4
Balkím	H	25	24
	S	1	23
	M	46	12, 16, 17
Balí	H	22	5, 6
	M	13	24
Bálmán	H	22	9, 11
Balmí	H	273	25
Bálmíkí	H	1,019	3,6, 9, 14, 15, 48
	S	36	48
	M	12	15, 25
Balmúí	H	298	15, 16, 46, 48
	S	2	16
	M	26	13
Balowáli	M	111	13
Balpawár	H	13	2
Balrán	H	168	1, 2
	M	8	27
Bálú	H	5,005	5, 9, 10, 11, 25, 48, 49, 50
	S	1,837	6, 11, 25, 48, 50
	M	3	11
Balúná	H	37	4, 11, 48
	S	1	12
Bamak	H	104	6
Bámani	H	67	9, 48
	S	9	50
Bánáí	H	45	5, 10, 31
Banak	H	308	4, 5, 9, 25
Band	H	151	2
Bandál	H	123	9, 16, 25, 48
	S	38	48
	M	39	24
Bandar	H	281	13. 14, 15, 16
Bandárá	H	20	5, 14
	M	11	16
Bandgal	H	34	2, 25
Bandíja	H	411	14
Bandní	H	25	9
Bangálí	H	226	6, 9, 11, 48, 51
	S	68	11, 48
Bangar	H	65	5, 6, 11
	S	23	6, 11
Banghá	H	66	48
Bangri	H	837	5, 6, 11, 48
	S	90	48
Banián	H	40	4
Banjal	S	70	11
Banji	H	85	9, 44
Báns	H	533	6, 9, 25, 44
	S	59	6, 14
	M	19	13
Bansí	H	68	9
	S	107	14
Banswál	H	189	2, 5, 15, 48, 50
Banún	H	94	1
	M	8	47
Banwál	H	145	5, 6, 49
Banwárí	H	13	11
Barahman	H	145	8, 10, 15, 31
Baráich	H	436	9, 10
	S	105	48
Barak	H	46	5, 6, 24
	M	23	13
Baránjí	M	17	25
Barar	H	290	5, 6, 10, 48
	M	25	16, 25
Barat	H	497	1, 24
	S	8	1, 5, 25
	M	2	15
Bardár	H	18	9, 13
Barde	H	29	22
Barengí	H	40	25
Barbál	H	11	1
Barhichlát	H	325	5
	M	5	17, 25
Barí	H	32	21, 26, 39, 40
Bariáh	H	24	48
	S	106	48
	M	59	13, 48
Bariál	H	25	17
Barlán	H	235	1, 2, 4, 5, 49
Barme	S	45	48
Barogá	H	141	48
	S	120	48
Barohí	H	372	1, 2, 6, 48
	M	3	25
Bartária	H	11	4
Barth	H	1,111	16, 17
	M	9	25
Barwálí	H	71	9, 10, 25
	M	56	23
Baryár	H	27	17
	M	102	13, 25
Basí	H	17	5, 9, 16
Basír	H	39	8, 15
	M	9	13
Basrái	H	243	14
	S	16	14
Batil	S	3	10
	M	3	45
Batoí	H	477	3, 10, 16
	S	6	9, 25
Batwá	S	27	48
Batwál	H	142	4
Bátwárí	H	16	9, 17
	S	1	9
	M	56	13
Batyálá	H	53	4
Báwar	H	411	1, 25, 48
	M	30	13
Bechení	H	30	10
Bed	H	5,637	1, 2, 5, 6, 11, 48, 49
	S	307	48
Bedal	H	35	1, 5
Bedlan	H	2,048	1, 2, 4, 5, 50
	S	28	50
Begántí	H	34	50
Begí	H	27	1
Belá	H	170	5, 48
	S	5	45
Beníwál	H	100	48
	S	2	48
	M	4	48
Berán	H	77	9
Bhábhí	H	65	9
	M	20	27
Bhadá	H	25	1, 49
	M	37	19
Bhádar	H	726	1, 5, 13, 48
	M	134	13, 25
Bhadaur	H	22	48
Bhade	H	233	18, 48
	M	4	13
Bhadiár	H	517	1, 9, 16, 17
Bhadlán	H	1,835	1, 2, 5, 6, 48
	S	1	48
Bhadmár	H	18	15
Bhádon	H	13	48
	S	9	48
Bhadpál	H	17	48
Bhadro	H	182	13, 48
	S	22	48
	M	41	25
Bhagá Bhatti	H	390	6
	S	3	6
Bhagái	H	260	10
Bhagáni	H	795	1, 5, 10, 11, 14
	S	60	11, 25, 48
	M	1	25
Bhagátte	H	258	6, 14, 44, 48
Bhágú	H	297	1, 6, 13, 15, 25
Bhagwán	H	44	4, 17, 25
Bhagwária	H	22	25
Bhagwati	H	17	3
	S	3	48
Bhainswál	H	99	3, 7, 48
	S	2	48
	M	4	17
Bhajdí	H	11	10
Bhajúmal	H	37	10
Bhakar	H	201	1, 5, 17, 25, 46
	S	11	25
Bhakarke	H	331	25, 46, 49, 51
	S	29	11, 12, 50
Bhakhorke	H	398	48
Bhál	H	131	2, 3, 4
Bhalá	H	85	4, 5, 48
Bhalán	H	131	1, 31, 40
	M	154	13, 20, 26
Bhalar	H	124	3, 16, 25
	M	7	25
Bhalráh	H	64	2
Bhalrwán	H	58	1, 2
Bhamak	H	348	5, 6, 11
	S	3	6, 33
Bhandar	H	3	18
	S	2	17, 25
	M	24	13, 17, 25
Bhandí	H	15	16
Bhangán	H	478	5. 6, 25, 48
	S	458	25, 48
Bhangar	H	199	4, 9, 10, 25
Bhangí	H	611	1, 7, 21, 22, 37, 51
	M	10	13, 27
Bhangú	H	720	5, 9, 11, 12, 13, 14, 48
	S	35	11
Bhaní	H	29	11
Bhank	H	1,098	1, 5, 48
	S	23	48
Bhanwál	H	882	3, 4, 5
Bhár	H	107	5, 13, 15
	M	6	24, 25
Bhárá	H	196	3, 48
	S	16	48
Bharáchí	H	31	1, 27
Bharáí	H	13	6
Bharandar	H	149	3
Bhárí	H	120	5, 12
Bhariál	H	434	12, 17
	M	29	13
Bhark	H	19	25
Bharmár	H	35	1, 14
Bhart	H	441	1, 13, 16, 48
	S	137	48
	M	38	13, 27
Bharwáhá	H	109	9, 10
Bharwái	H	33	10
Bharwál	H	37	2, 5, 24, 48, 49
	M	1	25
Bhasiál	H	12	9
Bhasorí	H	26	5, 19

Names of Sub-Castes.		Persons.	Locality.
Bhat	H	648	1, 5, 14, 25, 31
	S	3	2
Bhatáí ...	H	62	21
	S	9	11
Bhatal ...	H	56	50
Bhatan ...	H	12	2, 25
Bhatar ...	H	70	13
	M	2	13
Bhatiárá ...	H	36	50
Bhatík ...	H	59	6
Bhat Khokar	H	22	25
Bhatti ...	H	28,266	J. L. 1, 6, 24, 25, 44, 46, 48, 50
	S	1,648	12, 13, 14, 25, 48, 50
	M	8,278	L. 12, 24, 25, 27, 29, 51
Bhatwál ...	H	382	1, 2, 4, 5, 17
	M	2	13
Bhawál ...	H	19	1, 48
	M	4	19, 21
Bhawár ...	H	54	1, 9
Bhím ...	H	1,747	10, 13, 14, 19
	S	36	11
	M	15	19, 27
Bhohál ...	H	70	1, 14
Bhokar ...	H	151	2, 3, 15
	M	3	13
Bholang ...	H	242	6
Bholgar ...	H	11	32
Bholí ...	H	62	1, 11, 32
Bhonárí ...	H	17	48
Bhondí ...	H	12	9, 46
Bhonk ...	H	22	49
Bhorat ...	H	97	1, 11, 12, 13
	M	29	12, 14
Bhorí ...	H	1,498	3, 4, 17, 48
Bhosar ...	H	119	9, 13
Bhotí ...	H	492	16, 25
	M	28	16
Bhotrá ...	H	35	6, 11, 19
Bhugáyan ...	H	164	48
	S	224	48
Bhullar ...	H	150	4, 13, 46, 48
	S	65	12, 48
	M	8	4
Bhunchak	H	597	1, 48, 49
	S	5	48
Bhuniár ...	H	70	2, 4
Bhúp ...	H	3	48
	S	8	18
Bhusarí ...	H	12	25
Bhuttá ...	H	1,690	1, 4, 5, 10, 13, 16, 18, 19, 48.
	S	1	48
	M	396	13, 16, 25
Bilgan ...	H	227	25, 48
Bimlak ...	H	16	9
Bír ...	H	26	2, 5
Bishisht ...	H	24	10
Bobak ...	H	137	1, 6
Bodri ...	H	14	1
Bohán ...	H	146	4, 5, 12, 13, 25
Bohat ...	H	4,791	1, 2, 3, 6, 13, 32, 49
	M	3	25
Bohná ...	H	123	2
Bolgí ...	M	14	13
Boli Barhál	H	17	21
Boná ...	H	74	9
	S	11	9
Borath ...	H	2,272	13, 19, 51
	M	181	13, 19
Boriá ...	H	79	4, 25
	S	59	25
Ború ...	H	24	4
	M	9	16
Bot ...	H	5,002	1, 4, 5, 10, 12, 14, 15, 25
	S	107	15, 16, 25
	M	199	13, 25
Botri ...	H	6	9
	M	24	13
Burat ...	H	567	1, 2, 4, 25
	M	583	1, 13, 16, 17
Chabri ...	H	47	12
	S	10	6, 11
Chachláná ...	H	12	3
Chachodiá ...	H	29	50
	S	81	50
Chachohán ...	H	13	5
Chachotar ...	H	226	44
Chadariá ...	H	24	2, 12
	M	83	17, 25
Chaddá ...	H	811	17, 14, 16, 21
	M	17	13
Chajá ...	H	3	6
	M	41	28
Chajloliá ...	H	25	3
Chajohar ...	H	22	9
Chaliání ...	H	90	6, 10
Chaloriá ...	H	15	1, 12, 30, 50
Chamrú ...	H	12	10
Chanáhate ...	H	33	1
Chanál ...	H	2,300	5, 6, 9, 11, 13, 48
	M	11	25
Chanan ...	H	65	10, 11
	M	2	27
Chanár ...	H	26	17
	M	12	25
Chand ...	M	28	13, 28, 29
Chandál ...	H	3,634	1, 2, 3, 4, 6, 7, 25, 49
	S	7	48
	M	3	24
Chandán	H	187	4, 7
	M	38	29
Chándiá	H	98	5, 48
	S	8	11
	M	77	15, 25
Chandol ...	H	1,041	3, 25, 48
Chandrí ...	H	35	14
Chandú ...	H	3	49
	M	36	28
Changál ...	H	17	2
	M	10	28
Changari ...	H	260	3, 9, 28
	M	14	28, 29
Chángrá ...	M	11	29
Chaní ...	M	36	28
Chanjar ...	H	25	5, 24
	M	1	13
Chánor ...	H	743	2, 3, 12, 32, 49
Chantalí ...	H	13	6
Chánwariá ...	H	797	1, 2, 3, 4, 5, 27, 48
Charáman ...	H	11	9
Cháran ...	H	184	2, 3, 6, 49, 51
Cháriá ...	H	48	5
	M	6	51
Chariáná ...	H	16	4
Chasianá ...	H	17	6, 48
Chatálí ...	H	61	6, 49
Chatan ...	H	18	12
Chatar Sen ...	H	270	50
	S	133	50
Cháwaliá ...	H	27	48
	S	2	11, 12
Chedá ..	H	3,412	13, 14, 15, 19, 25, 44
	S	74	14, 15
	M	48	13, 16
Chhachhodar	H	108	2, 44
Chhachrík	H	52	48
Chhag ...	S	17	12
Chhagotar ...	H	20	16
Chhágre ...	H	17	48
Chháhá ...	H	46	17, 48
Chhaj ...	H	21	48
	S	10	48
Chhajohar ...	H	44	10, 48
	S	285	11, 48
Chhájork ...	H	104	6
Chhání ...	H	2	6
	M	25	17
Chhapríband	H	18,095	9, 10, 12, 14, 15, 17, 19, 25, 48
	S	767	9, 11, 14, 25, 48
	M	1,466	12, 13, 16, 24, 25
Chhárkotal ...	H	28	3
Chhatar ...	H	20	25, 44
	M	29	14, 17
Chhochhate ...	H	11	48
Chholia ...	H	691	5, 48
	S	2	48
Chhopá ...	H	113	14
Chhopar ...	H	52	44
Chhorí ...	H	176	2, 4, 17, 51
	S	5	13, 27
	M	366	28
Chhotrál ...	H	15	25
Chhotrí ...	H	161	5, 10, 11, 17
	M	6	13
Chhuriband ...	H	189	48
	S	482	48
Chobaliá ...	H	22	50
Chogatta ...	H	471	12, 13, 16, 17, 25
	S	10	13
	M	63	13, 24
Chohán ...	H	9,248	B. 46, 48, 49
	S	1,473	1, 12, 48, 50
	M	577	12, 13, 17, 25, 27, 28
Chohrí ...	H	1,249	6, 19, 27
	S	16	14
	M	15	26
Chohriá ...	H	641	2, 4, 5, 49
	S	5	25
	M	35	25
Cholí ...	H	3	8
	M	17	29
Chonch ...	H	13	1
Chonkar ...	H	26	3
Chonpar ...	H	610	5
Chophalá ...	H	35	3
Chopra ...	H	215	2, 18
Chotále ...	H	105	3
Chotiá ...	H	114	17, 40
	M	9	16
Chotra ...	H	11	8
Choyá ...	H	31	27
	S	3	14
	M	3	51
Chujand ...	H	11	48
Chumár ...	H	33	5, 48
Chuthe ...	H	13	48
Dábarwán ...	H	13	2, 24
Dabgohar ..	H	806	3
Dabri ...	H	11	2, 21
	S	1	48
Dadháns ...	H	149	2, 10
Dádhari ...	H	661	10, 12, 25
	S	48	12, 14, 25
Dádí ...	H	2	13, 15
	S	30	1, 14, 15
	M	11	25
Dádrí ...	H	669	9, 11, 25, 26
	S	4	11
	M	6	25
Daganj ...	H	144	12, 32
Dágar ...	H	46	1, 2, 9, 17
Dagech ...	H	94	48
Dábrá ...	H	15	3, 9
	S	1	3
Dajwál ...	H	14	48
Dáka ...	H	12	2
Dakád ...	H	48	3
Dákhal ...	H	31	10, 48
Dalalot ...	H	133	4, 5, 14, 21
Dalgach ...	H	2,590	2, 3, 4
Dalganj ...	H	2,112	1, 2, 36, 45
	S	3	6
Dalhiáp ...	H	85	12
Dalhor ...	H	373	5, 6, 14
Dali ...	H	88	12, 17
Dálín ...	H	21	11
Dálo ...	H	23	10
	S	15	48
Dalor ...	H	174	5, 6, 12
Daleoz ...	H	78	3
Dálwán ...	H	21	2
Damáne ...	H	441	1, 6, 8, 10, 48, 49
	S	146	48, 49
Danbálá ...	H	15	25
Dáng ...	H	11	4
Dangal ...	H	13	3, 10, 19
Dangí ...	H	49	1, 2, 25
	M	6	13
Dargat ...	H	30	2, 3, 9
Darholí ...	H	37	48
Dári ...	H	174	10, 12, 25
	S	1	25
	M	161	25

Names of Sub-Castes.		Persons.	Locality.
Dáriá ...	H	35	10, 12
Dart ...	H	63	13
Dasánbar ...	H	46	11
Dásbar ...	H	51	6, 9
	S	3	9
Dashní ...	H	35	16
Dásiá ...	H	17	48
Dasnáyal ...	H	22	48
Dáwarí ...	H	206	9, 12
Dedimál ...	H	12	44
Dekhná ...	H	11	4, 51
Desi ...	H	30	4
Deswál ...	H	55	5, 48
Devlá ...	H	27	2
	S	4	14
	M	46	14
Dhabgan ...	H	15	48
	S	2	48
Dhadwál ...	H	39	46
Dháí ...	H	681	9, 13, 26, 44
Dhágá ...	H	203	1, 4, 9, 13, 49
Dhakán ...	H	72	1, 2, 3, 5, 32
Dhakas ...	H	15	2
Dhakíra ...	H	62	24
Dhakka ...	H	960	2, 3, 4, 19, 31
Dhakojá ...	H	31	3
Dhákri ...	H	43	3
Dhál ...	H	24	1, 4
Dhalar ...	H	75	2, 6, 25, 48
Dhálí ...	H	16	9, 46, 48
Dháliwál ...	H	6,091	1, 2, 10, 11, 12, 46, 50
Dhálo ...	H	10	15
	S	1	17
	M	1	13
Dhalor ...	H	670	1, 2, 4, 49
Dhamai ...	H	18	24
Dhamáni ...	H	67	3, 50
Dhamgat ...	H	29	5, 12
Dhammán ...	H	86	9, 25
Dhán ...	H	35	11, 18
	S	48	12, 25
	M	1	18
Dhának ...	H	158	2, 44, 51
Dhandhora ...	H	15	12
Dhandri ...	H	11	9
Dhángar ...	H	34	12
Dhange ...	H	436	4, 5, 25
	M	139	25
Dhaní ...	H	76	3, 5, 14
	M	6	13
Dhankal ...	H	41	1, 7, 32
Dhankor ...	H	14	5, 6
Dhánku ...	H	130	2, 3, 7
Dhanwal ...	H	168	2, 13, 17, 45
Dhap ...	H	3,067	10, 11, 12, 13, 25, 48
	S	216	6, 9, 10, 12, 13
	M	1	17
Dhápar ...	H	90	26
Dhar ...	H	205	9, 17, 25, 40
	M	830	19, 24, 28, 29
Dharijá ...	H	25	7, 20, 48
	M	22	16, 24
Dháríwál ...	H	5,061	2, 11, 12, 13, 14, 35, 48
	S	3,040	6, 9, 11, 12, 25, 48
	M	51	13, 25
Dharoke ...	H	12	3
	S	21	25
Dharí ...	H	545	10, 13, 25, 48
	S	17	48
Dhát ...	H	81	9, 10, 11
Dháwal ...	H	264	2, 5, 6, 9, 12
Dhawán ...	H	42	48
	S	91	48
Dhí ...	H	1	15
	M	60	13, 28
Dhiá ...	H	153	4, 6, 24
Dhillon ...	H	107	1, 2, 4, 50, 51
	S	2	11, 17
	M	17	25
Dhirán ...	H	15	9, 29
Dhobganj ...	H	111	2, 4
Dhochand ...	H	13	3
Dhodí ...	H	184	12, 13, 17, 24, 25
	S	7	51
	M	72	13, 13, 24, 51
Dhoibhans ...	H	18	12
Dhoká ...	M	31	24
Dhol ...	H	93	5, 48, 49
	M	1	12
Dholír ...	H	90	5, 16
	M	12	25
Dhon ...	H	25	25, 44, 49
Dhonchak ...	H	39	5, 32
	S	15	11, 48
Dhondhor ...	H	58	1, 27
Dhor ...	H	1,316	1, 2, 4, 5, 48, 51
	S	19	48, 49
	M	3	12, 24
Dhosar ...	H	28	18, 25
	M	12	13, 16
Dhotí ...	H	25	12, 15, 25
Dhottari ...	H	43	1, 16, 46, 48
	S	2	9, 48
Dhúmar ...	H	24	4
Did ...	H	132	48
Dìgá ...	H	36	2, 5
Digach ...	H	124	2
Dilganj ...	H	200	48
Dilor ..	H	181	4, 5
Díndár ...	M	55	1, 12, 28, 29
Dindsá ...	H	13	48
	S	34	48
Diwat ...	H	512	48
Dobdárí ...	H	38	9
Dode ...	H	44	6, 48
	S	2	48
Dodhári ...	H	23	11, 25
Dogal ...	H	209	2, 4, 7, 12
Doglit ...	H	82	2
Dogra ...	H	16	3, 5, 13, 15
Dohri ...	H	123	2, 5, 14
Dohwál ...	H	28	3
Dolganj ...	H	2,296	2, 4, 5, 31, 49
Dolgat ...	H	824	1, 2, 4, 5, 49, 51
Dolhor ...	H	113	5
Domrá ...	H	56	5
Dosánbar ...	H	11	49
Dasrá ...	H	21	5, 14
Dúm ...	H	51	11, 27
Dumná ...	H	89	10
Faqir ...	H	156	10, 12, 13, 16, 25
	S	1	12
	M	17	13, 16
Farukhábádí	H	263	16
Fiqrádodsi ...	H	15	5, 13
Gachal ...	H	11	25
Gáchhan ...	H	30	3, 7, 48
Gachlet ...	H	110	9
Gáchli ...	H	300	6, 9, 10, 40
	S	11	1, 46
Gadará ...	H	130	1, 6, 9, 25
Gáddu ...	H	17	11
	S	11	11
	M	13	12
Gadhar ...	H	21	5, 45
	S	1	5
	M	1	13
Gaddi ...	H	106	22, 25
	S	17	25, 44
Gádi ...	H	6	6, 48
	S	5	50
Gagalsan ...	H	12	5
Gágat ...	H	988	1, 5, 6, 12, 21, 49, 50
	S	27	45, 50
Gagnaje ...	H	26	48.
Gagrá ...	H	138	5, 12, 25, 32, 50
	S	42	25
	M	35	25
Gáhro ...	H	46	16
Gaichand ...	H	727	2, 4, 51
Gaihlá ...	S	39	48
Gájle ...	H	57	48
Gájui ...	H	8	9
	S	6	9
Gajri ...	H	146	15, 48
Gákri ...	H	108	6
Galan ...	H	40	1, 5, 16
	M	7	13, 16
Galiáná ...	H	296	2, 4, 6, 48
	S	71	11, 12, 13, 14, 25
Galit ...	H	21	1, 4, 15
Galjari ...	H	112	5
Galot ...	H	239	4, 5, 7, 9
Gamiá ...	H	54	6, 10
Gandar ...	H	30	12, 15, 28
	S	9	25
	M	26	28
Gandárá ...	H	262	2, 3, 6, 17
	S	8	11
	M	208	12, 13, 25
Gandhári ...	H	22	1, 25
	M	2	12, 13
Gandhu ...	H	81	16
Gangábáhra	H	122	2, 3
Gangápuri ...	H	83	3
Gangi ...	H	43	1, 9
Gángri ...	M	13	25
Gár ...	H	10	9, 24, 28
	S	47	12, 13, 14, 25
Garari ...	H	11	12, 24
	M	8	24
Gardwál ...	H	22	11
Gári ...	H	43	5
Gariálá ...	H	83	7
Gariwál ...	H	13	2, 25
	M	15	25
Garjí ...	H	18	6
Garsu ...	H	648	17
Gáru ...	H	243	44
Gásar ...	H	218	15, 45
	S	31	14
Gatálá ...	H	12	50
Gawárá ...	H	12	2, 5, 24
Geli ...	H	137	9, 16, 17
Goo ...	H	38	10
Gerre ...	H	6	48, 51
	S	163	48
Ghádri ...	H	27	3, 6
	S	31	6, 12, 14
Ghágat ...	H	742	1, 9, 48
	S	164	48
Ghagli ...	H	193	5
Gháí ...	H	988	6, 9, 10, 15, 25, 44
	M	1	15
Ghajotar ...	H	17	2
Ghakhán ...	M	18	17
Ghál ...	H	22	2, 9, 12, 15
	S	1	45
Ghalan ...	H	53	1, 2, 3
Gháli ...	H	24	2, 10, 25
	S	27	6, 9, 11
Ghamáni ...	H	15	49
Ghan ...	H	685	14, 17, 48
	M	50	13, 14
Gháná ...	H	12	9
Ghanaure ...	H	74	48
	S	10	48
Ghánián ...	H	45	10, 25
Ghanír ...	H	245	9, 10, 12, 17
Ghar ...	H	3,861	1, 9, 11, 12, 13, 14, 15, 24, 25, 44, 48
	S	130	9, 11, 12, 25
	M	84	13, 17, 18, 25
Ghárá ...	H	683	5, 6, 11
	M	350	13, 15, 28, 29
Ghardháliwál	H	23	12
Ghárau ...	H	37	14
Gháru ...	H	25,850	2, 5, 9, 10, 11, 12, 13, 24, 25, 37, 44, 46, 48, 49, 51
	S	2,549	11, 12, 25, 46, 48, 51
	M	4,018	12, 13, 19, 24, 25, 29, 51
Ghas ...	H	33	11, 12, 25
Ghaseri ...	H	1,994	6, 9, 10, 11, 14, 25
	S	4	12
	M	21	13, 15
Ghashtar ...	H	295	6, 25
Ghássi ...	H	135	9, 11, 16
Ghatorá ...	H	116	3, 6
Ghatti ...	H	357	1, 9, 10, 51
	M	1	25
Ghatuke ...	H	118	25
Gher ...	S	37	25
Ghisar ...	H	207	1, 44
Ghobat ...	H	16	2

SUB-CASTES OF CERTAIN SELECTED CASTES—*continued.*

Names of Sub-Castes.		Persons.	Locality.
Ghogli ...	H	176	1, 3, 4, 24
Ghol ...	H	231	6, 14
Ghontal ...	H	12	13
Ghor ...	H	1,165	1, 6, 8, 11, 25, 27, 39, 45, 48
	S	40	6, 9, 15, 51
	M	80	13, 16
Ghosá ...	H	383	2, 6, 10
	S	20	12
Ghular ...	H	40	5
Ghumman ...	H	269	9, 14, 44, 48
	S	36	48
	M	2	13
Ghundi ...	H	34	48
Ghussar ...	H	7,042	6, 7, 9, 10, 11, 12, 13, 14, 15, 17, 19, 25, 44, 46, 48, 49
	S	105	14, 25, 48
	M	17	13, 17
Giáji ...	H	189	11, 24, 40
Giárá ...	H	62	1
	M	80	24
Gil ...	H	67,433	J. L. M. 1, 4, 6, 7, 18, 19, 20, 22, 44, 45, 46, 48, 49, 50, 51
	S	4,341	L. 2, 6, 9, 11, 12, 25, 44, 48, 49, 50, 51
	M	5,692	12, 13, 14, 17, 18, 20, 21, 24, 25, 51
Gilganj ...	H	162	2
Godálá ...	H	136	1, 2, 3
Godar ...	H	12	27
Gogalhá ...	H	305	1, 2, 3, 20
Gogariá ...	H	229	1, 48
	S	42	48
Gobál ...	H	18	49
Gohar ...	H	744	1, 15, 19, 51
Goharlit ...	H	28	3
Gohátsi ...	H	88	3
Goiá ...	H	12	27
	M	21	24
Gojráni ...	H	13	9, 21
	M	1	17
Golar ...	H	85	1, 11, 14, 45
	M	7	14
Golit ...	H	92	9
Gondi ...	H	115	17
	M	300	28, 29
Gonji ...	H	13	10, 14, 20
Gopi ...	H	25	28, 47
Gorái ...	H	15	16
	M	1	18
Goráliá ...	H	14	2, 3
	M	71	13, 17
Gordiálá ...	H	293	7
Gori ...	H	486	1, 4, 5, 6, 11, 12, 13, 16, 17, 44, 49
	S	68	13, 25
	M	319	12, 13
Gorní Rattan	H	81	12
Gosal ...	H	100	1, 8, 12, 46, 50
	S	4	50
	M	24	13
Gugal ...	H	25	50
Guleria ...	H	19	4
Hadáliá ...	H	26	4
Hadilan ...	H	204	3
Hadphor ...	H	14	48
Hajám ...	H	67	14, 44
Hajor ...	H	658	15
Hálan ...	H	348	8, 9, 14
	S	3	14
Hamiq ...	H	15	48
Handár ...	S	62	11, 25
Handa ...	H	108	25
Hanoi ...	H	61	14
Háns ...	H	9,778	J. L. 1, 6, 19, 21, 24, 25, 44, 45, 46, 48, 50, 51
	S	342	4, 11, 12, 14, 15, 17, 25, 48, 50
Háns ...	M	444	12, 13, 14, 18, 21, 24, 25, 28, 29
Hánshori ...	H	33	3
Hardari ...	H	19	25
Hari ...	H	628	5, 15, 25
Hariál ...	H	57	5, 17, 44
	M	29	19
Hark ...	H	62	11
Harojá ...	H	34	50
Hutwál ...	H	245	3, 5, 12
Hazuri ...	S	11	11, 27
Hindhlán ...	H	22	4
Hinjrái ...	H	83	12, 14, 17, 25
	S	17	11, 14
	M	88	13, 16, 17, 24
Hír ...	H	103	8, 9, 12, 13, 27
	S	77	48
	M	9	18
Hirdewál ...	H	16	48
Hiroliá ...	H	48	3
Hodá ...	H	68	4, 8, 14, 49
Hoi ...	H	10	10
	S	79	13
Hons ...	H	777	17
	M	15	19, 25
Horá ...	H	130	2, 4
Hot ...	H	92	7, 9, 13, 15, 51
	S	10	6, 25, 51
	M	54	13, 14
Hotrá ...	H	48	10, 15
	M	70	24
Jabá ...	H	1,942	5, 6, 13, 15
Jabrá ...	S	84	11
Jadi ...	H	55	12
Jádon ...	H	120	4, 25
Jádri ...	H	62	3
Jadusakar ...	H	17	8, 12
Jáfar ...	M	21	27
Jagdeo Panwár.	H	30	48
Jaghá ...	H	13	1, 12
	M	4	14, 25
Jaj ...	H	419	6, 44
	S	67	11
	M	12	25
Jajhúmar ...	H	450	1, 12, 48
Jajotar ...	H	132	1, 4, 49
	S	101	9, 49
	M	9	27
Jaklán ...	H	16	39
Jal ...	H	31	4, 48
Jalab ...	H	15	4
Jaláli ...	H	116	5, 6
	M	10	12
Jále ...	H	45	1, 50
	S	39	48
Jal Sakandar	H	13	25
Jamdowál ...	H	25	2, 4, 8
Janáli ...	H	20	5
	S	26	25
	M	19	19
Jandál ...	H	376	2, 5, 12, 15, 31, 48
	S	15	48
	M	63	13, 29
Jandi ...	H	126	2, 6, 44
	S	4	5
	M	7	13, 25
Jandráni ...	M	44	28
Jandre ...	H	29	48
	S	4	48
Jánglá ...	H	500	2, 3, 4, 29
Jáni ...	H	32	48
	S	3	48
Janjuá	H	63	2, 9, 25, 45
	S	2	24
	M	7	9, 13, 25
Janjuhan ..	H	566	5, 9
	S	1	24
	M	4	25, 28, 29
Janjohar ...	H	171	5, 7, 11, 15
	S	3	24
Janjutar ...	H	2,049	5, 6, 13, 14, 17, 25
	S	9	9, 15, 24
	M	48	15, 25, 27
Januin ...	M	38	28, 29
Janur ...	H	12	2
Janwál ...	H	17	10, 48
	S	1	48
Jánwár ...	H	53	1, 2, 4, 30
Jatái ...	H	50	4, 5, 8, 25
	S	4	25, 37
	M	5	2, 25
Járiá ...	H	43	4, 8
Jasi ...	H	107	46
	S	2	14
	M	64	27
Jassar ...	H	10	14, 45
	M	3	29
Jaswál ...	H	29	5, 6, 8
Jat ...	H	66	6, 9
	M	50	16, 29
Jatálá ...	H	76	4, 9, 45
Jatáná ...	H	87	48
	S	42	48
Jatiá ...	H	8	5
	M	25	25
Jatrálá ...	H	65	25
Játtu ...	H	29	6, 49
Jaure ...	H	36	48
Jawái ...	H	87	12
Jáwal ...	H	41	4, 5
	M	21	28
Jawán ...	H	26	6, 11
	M	16	28
Jhabá ...	H	30	29
	S	5	24
Jhae ...	H	24	19
	M	12	28
Jhajohar ...	H	346	1, 2, 5, 9, 12, 25, 44
Jhajotor ...	H	2,333	1, 4, 5, 9, 10, 14, 19, 25, 44
	S	16	14, 25
Jhán ...	H	12	15, 51
	S	77	11
	M	2	20
Jhanb ...	M	22	16
Jhandli ...	H	11	9
Jhanjoj ...	H	9	11, 12
	M	2	15
Jhánsi ...	H	50	6, 48
Jhár ...	H	81	1
Jholar ...	H	20	48
	S	27	48
Jhonch ...	H	89	1, 5, 6, 49
	S	2	49
Jhunji ...	H	19	48
	S	10	48
Jital ...	H	15	24
Jobá ...	H	10	4
	M	81	28
Johri ...	H	29	7
Joia ...	H	2,327	12, 16, 17, 25, 26
	S	595	24, 47
	M	2,457	12, 24, 25, 26, 27
Jokal ...	H	227	14
Joniá ...	H	48	17
	S	1	14
Jumak ...	H	27	48
Kabar ...	H	175	3, 5, 44
Kachhwái ...	H	170	3, 5, 12
	S	1	25
Kadmári ...	H	29	11, 44
Kaháru ...	H	481	4, 6, 12, 13, 45, 50
	S	17	6, 50
	M	15	12
Káhi ...	H	31	9
Kakar ...	H	204	5, 9, 19, 50, 51
	M	24	4, 17
Kakhni ...	H	46	10
Kákrá ...	H	4,555	D. 11, 12, 15, 25, 48
	S	267	1, 2, 5, 6, 12, 45, 48
	M	121	28, 29
Kaláloi ...	H	70	5, 9
Kalban ...	H	100	49
	S	3	49
Kalorá ...	H	120	12, 16, 17, 48
	S	1	12
Káli ...	H	42	11, 14, 25
	M	54	27

Names of Sub-Castes.		Persons.	Locality.
Káliá ...	H	157	2, 4, 12, 15, 48
	M	36	28, 29
Kaliáni ...	H	19,400	J. L. 1, 2, 4, 5, 6, 19, 22, 24 to 27, 29, 40, 44 to 46, 48, 50, 51
	S	2,145	6, 11, 12, 13, 14, 18, 19, 24 to 26, 33, 45, 47, 48, 50
	M	1,090	11, 12, 13, 15, 16, 24, 27, 47
Kaliáras ...	H	557	10, 12, 43
Kaliáru ...	H	91	44
Káliwál ...	H	52	3, 17, 51
Kalni ...	H	19	21, 26. 48
	S	1	19
Kaloniá ...	H	1,651	6, 25
	M	12	17
Kalotá ...	H	18	44
Kals ...	H	15	11, 12
Kalsrá ...	H	11	5, 15
Kámá ...	H	26	11, 48
Kambob ...	H	14	5
	S	1	14
	M	7	24, 27
Kamon ...	H	34	5, 17, 40
Kamprá ...	H	42	2, 25
Kanári ...	H	248	12, 13, 16, 17, 25, 49
Kanchan ...	H	49	2, 17, 48
Kandále ...	H	64	21, 25
Kandárá ...	H	6,715	1, 3 to 6, 10, 12 to 14, 16, 17, 19, 21, 25, 26, 28, 46, 49 to 51
	S	58	6, 11, 25, 50
	M	937	17, 25
Kandháná ...	H	32	44
Kandhári ...	H	444	1, 2, 12, 14, 25, 51
	S	2	14
	M	51	12, 25, 27
Kondi ...	H	21	3, 11
	M	1	13
Kandiál ...	H	651	L. 25, 48
Kandiáná ...	H	89	12, 14, 48
	S	13	10
Kandiári ...	H	4,130	12, 13, 15, 17, 24, 48
	S	73	6, 12, 14, 24. 48
	M	683	13, 16, 28, 29
Kandiwál ...	H	45	2, 9, 50
	M	3	16
Kandwáre ...	H	795	48
	S	1,238	48
	M	14	16
Kang ...	H	76	4, 6, 12, 48
	S	3	48
	M	13	16
Kangrá ...	H	445	2, 4, 5, 48
	S	7	24, 48
Kankwál ...	H	22	48
Kanotri ...	H	14	10, 45
Kánwár ...	H	103	25
	S	2	14
Kará ...	H	48	1, 9, 12
	S	10	12
	M	3	11, 12
Karáliá ...	H	25	2, 12
Karárá ...	H	61	10, 12
Kardiánán ...	H	31	4
Kariáná ...	H	20	10, 12
	S	14	14
Karosiá ...	H	97	3, 4
	M	36	17
Karpál ...	H	21	19
Kaser ...	H	128	3, 15, 25
	S	2	1
	M	12	25
Káshab ...	H	150	14, 24, 25
Kasimári Kaj	H	119	14, 15, 17
	M	16	16, 21
Katab ...	H	35	5, 21
Kátak ...	H	271	5, 6
Katári ...	H	241	4, 6, 8, 10, 12, 28, 45, 48
Kathwál ...	H	37	11
Kati ...	H	15	18
Kattalodi ...	H	6	48
	S	5	48
Kattu ...	H	24	25
Kaurán ...	H	13	48
Káyat ...	H	33	48
Kesar ...	H	218	44
Keyáru ...	H	48	48
Khabrá ...	H	309	15, 16
Khachi ...	M	35	16
Khadwárá ...	H	398	12
Khagar ...	H	27	2, 9, 44
Khalot ...	H	12	9
	S	1	24
	M	5	25
Khálsá ...	H	17	14
	S	4	11, 48
Khambán ...	H	23	3
Kháná ...	H	175	6, 16, 27
	S	1	24
	M	1	27
Khande ...	S	22	48
Khandiárá ...	H	89	3
	S	1	24
	M	227	12, 13, 17
Khanwál ...	H	68	3
	M	16	13
Khárá ...	H	1,042	1, 4, 11 to 15
	S	2	48
	M	6	13, 25
Kharal ...	H	196	3, 13, 17, 48
	S	18	14, 24, 47
	M	90	13, 25, 27
Kharáliá ...	H	418	3, 12
Kharári ...	H	12	21, 44
Khardinmal	H	40	2, 44
Khari ...	H	13	3, 45
	M	2	12, 13
Kháriá ...	H	85	9, 51
Kharod ...	H	12	48
Kháru ...	H	1,735	13, 17, 25, 44
	S	85	13, 14, 45
	M	677	4, 14
Kharwá ...	H	20	3
Kharwál ...	H	47	6
Khasáni ...	H	20	9
Khasrá ...	H	20	10, 48
Khatáná ...	H	18	26
Khatar ...	H	173	9, 16
Khatik ...	H	109	5, 6
Khatri ...	H	46	10, 12, 16
Khatti ...	H	36	8, 12
Khodi ...	H	133	25
	S	1	18
	M	2	16
Khokhar ...	H	12,980	L. 1, 4, 6, 12 to 15, 17 to 19, 21, 22, 25 to 28, 45, 46, 48, 50
	S	680	L. 24, 25, 47
	M	4,178	11 to 15, 17, 19, 21, 23, 25, 27 to 29, 47
Kholar ...	H	333	1, 17, 26
	S	1	45
	M	4	47
Kholi ...	H	21	5, 25, 51
	S	13	11, 12
Khonje ...	H	431	14, 15, 17, 18, 21, 25
	S	9	18
	M	64	16
Khori ...	H	73	6
	S	2	25
Khosá ...	H	165	4, 10
	S	4	25, 46
	M	4	15, 47
Khosar ...	H	3,878	1, 3, 13, 14, 17, 48
	S	37	11, 14, 47
Khote ...	H	56	48
	S	27	48
Khotre ...	H	27	21, 48
	S	20	14, 15
Koli ...	H	8	10, 21, 50
	M	62	12, 13
Korá ...	H	37	13, 25, 48
	S	1	47
Koral ...	H	111	14, 17
Kortáná ...	H	348	16, 17, 18, 24, 25
	S	388	12, 24
	M	887	27
Kotar ...	H	57	4, 5, 6
Labáná ...	H	50	30
Lád ...	H	28	48
	S	47	48
Ladarpatti ...	H	30	16
	M	104	17
Ladhar ...	H	4,719	4, 9, 10, 12, 14 to 16, 24 to 26, 44, 46, 48, 50
	S	527	L. 25, 48
	M	935	12 to 14, 16, 20, 21, 25, 27, 47
Lador ...	H	13,196	4, 13, 14, 15
	S	4	46
	M	259	13
Ladu ...	H	108	9, 13, 21
	S	5	9, 44
	M	4	17
Lagania ...	H	31	9
Lagor ...	H	515	15
	S	12	12
Lágru ...	S	26	48
Láhru ...	H	5,514	D. L. 8, 9, 10, 12, 14, 15, 17, 18, 24, 25, 44
	S	20	5, 9, 11, 48
	M	218	13, 24, 27, 47
Lakh ...	H	91	1, 4, 12
	S	20	5
	M	21	13, 29
Lakhan ...	H	26	2, 13, 51
	M	44	27, 28, 29
Lakhar ...	H	212	7, 49.
	M	81	25
Lakhírá ...	M	39	13, 17
Lalá ...	H	9	9
	M	2	13
Laláriá ...	H	12	50
Lálbegi ...	H	1,267	J. 5, 13, 15, 16, 18, 19, 21, 27, 29, 37, 43, 48, 51
	S	60	9, 41, 48
	M	196	4, 16, 28, 29, 47
Lalli ...	H	251	14, 44
	M	2	17
Landá ...	M	15	13, 25
Langáh ...	H	19	1, 3, 15
Langar ...	H	11	15, 49
	M	14	25, 29
Lár ...	H	186	12, 15
	M	93	12
Lasámri ...	H	39	5
Latobrá ...	H	42	48
Latoi ...	H	52	9, 13, 15
Latra ...	H	16	3
Lattu ...	H	7	48
	S	225	48
Legi ...	H	37	1, 16, 18
Lik ...	H	91	48
	S	14	48
Lodhri ...	H	3,122	17
Lodi ...	H	24	5, 48
Lodimariá ...	H	16	9, 13, 21
Lohál ...	H	96	3, 5, 10
Lohan ...	H	110	2, 5, 48
Lohár ...	H	2,271	3, 5, 50
Lohat ...	H	3,388	1 to 6, 11, 46, 48, 50
	S	838	48
Lohirá ...	H	12	4, 27
Lohtiá ...	H	18	12
Loi ...	H	43	5, 9 10
Lokar ...	H	123	2
Loli ...	H	33	5, 12, 44
Longie ...	H	21	9, 21
Loniá ...	H	58	12, 44
Lont ...	H	16	25

SUB-CASTES OF CERTAIN SELECTED CASTES—*continued.*

Names of Sub-Castes.		Persons.	Locality.
Lorat ...	H	725	2, 13, 17, 18
	M	29	1, 13, 25
Lot ...	H	2,248	1, 2, 5, 12, 13, 17, 21, 24 to 26, 44, 49
	S	10	11, 46, 51
	M	331	13, 21, 24, 25
Lothri ...	H	124	5, 13, 50
	M	5	13
Machal ...	H	1,246	3, 4, 5, 6, 48
	M	62	4
Madá ...	H	20	1, 5, 13
Madal ...	H	22	5, 26
	M	75	13, 24
Mádar ...	H	81	1, 16, 24, 51
	M	137	25
Madári ...	H	12	12, 13
Maderi ...	H	13	50
Madhar ...	H	626	12, 19, 25, 26
	M	270	12, 25, 26
Mádhi ...	H	28	1, 19, 24
	M	39	25
Mádhil ...	H	36	I
Madhrán ..	H	45	4
Magrá ...	H	114	6, 10
Magú ...	H	124	44
Máhal ...	H	448	4, 10, 12, 14
Mahháná ...	H	9	15, 18
	M	3	18
Mahandal ...	H	795	4, 12
Mahande ...	H	41	12
Mahans ...	H	151	6, 17
	M	38	13, 17, 25
Máhar ...	H	248	5, 6, 12
	S	14	6, 11
	M	144	25
Máhdar ...	H	14	12, 17
Mahiwál ...	H	29	1, 25, 48
Máhlá ...	H	50	15
Mahore ...	H	9	8, 48
	S	239	11, 48
Mahotá ...	H	623	13, 14, 25
	M	13	17
Máhri ...	H	48	3, 4
Mahroliá ...	H	274	3, 4
Mahtá ...	H	11	48
Mahtniwál ..	H	29	2, 40
Máji ...	H	5	44
	M	45	17, 25
Makhyáná ...	H	56	9, 48
	S	69	48
Makiáni ...	H	27	9
	S	2	11
Makre ...	H	3	10, 44
	M	62	16
Mal ...	H	15	25
Malái ...	H	66	9, 49, 50
	M	11	24
Malak ...	H	222	4, 5, 7, 13
Malan ...	H	79	3, 6, 9, 17
	S	16	11, 25
	M	37	27
Malará ...	H	11	4
Malháná ...	H	45	45
Máli ...	H	1	48
	S	11	48
Malkiet ...	H	115	3, 12, 27
Malkját ...	H	2	25
	M	9	17, 25
Malotrá ...	H	256	13, 16, 17, 25
	M	20	13
Málú ...	H	245	12, 14, 44, 46
Maman ...	H	361	15, 16
	S	27	15
	M	37	13, 25
Mán ...	H	800	10, 12, 46, 48, 50
	S	326	48, 51
	M	3	12
Mánasi ...	H	4	48
	S	25	48
	M	94	13, 16
Mand ...	H	38	5, 10
Mandáhar ...	H	11	48
Mandal ...	H	665	3, 4, 11, 48
Mandar ...	H	74	1, 44
	S	6	48
Mandi ...	H	49	12, 44
	M	8	3, 13
Mandoiá ...	H	129	1, 25
Mandwál ...	H	62	2, 50
Mangá ...	S	93	48
Mangáhiá ...	H	94	48
	S	49	48
Mangal ...	H	36	12, 48
Mángat ...	H	42	11, 48
Mangú ...	H	150	3, 11
Mangwáli ...	H	182	4, 5, 51
Manhárá ...	H	55	24, 51
Maniár ...	S	51	12, 14, 25
Manji ...	H	461	9, 10, 14, 44
	S	38	14
Manjohar ...	H	11	1
Manon ...	H	13	12
Manwál ...	H	75	4, 5
Marar ...	H	35	10, 50
	S	22	50
Maráre ...	H	12	48
	S	21	48
Marási ...	H	84	14, 17, 25
	M	19	13, 18
Marauch ...	H	41	48
Máre ...	H	7	48
	S	7	48
Marhatá ...	H	96	6, 9, 12
Maroi ...	H	76	12, 48
	M	5	21, 25
Márolfá ...	H	73	12
Marwáná ...	H	60	9, 25
	M	6	47
Masur ...	H	18	12
Matah ...	H	47	9, 48
Matándal ...	H	23	48
Matar ...	H	50	10, 14
	M	2	13
Mathárú ...	H	27	12
Mathode ...	H	210	48
	S	87	48
Matoi ...	H	2,103	10, 15, 16, 17
Matori ...	H	61	50
	S	23	50
Matti ...	H	457	6, 9, 13, 18
	S	20	11, 12, 25
Mattú ...	H	26,669	L. R. I. 5, 6, 9, 11, 25, 44, 45, 46, 48
	S	1,608	L. except (16), 6, 11, 12, 25, 45, 48
	M	1,497	L. 18, 19, 25
Mazhabi ...	H	51	13, 15, 21, 27
	S	451	7, 12, 13, 14, 50, 51
	M	6	12, 19, 24
Meái ...	H	12	12
Medá ...	H	255	1, 12, 47
Meho ...	H	36	1, 5
Mehtar ...	H	365	6, 10, 12, 27
	S	2	9
Memi ...	H	22	45
Metho ...	H	603	7, 9, 49, 50
Meti ...	H	18	5, 24, 44
Mochra ...	H	85	15
Modiáne ...	H	2	11
	S	106	48
Mohal ...	H	51	1, 4, 21, 49
	S	1	12
Moháná ...	H	119	5, 12, 19, 21
	S	12	15
Mohni ...	H	18	8, 10, 48
	S	4	13
Mohrá ...	H	7	14, 48
Mokhar ...	H	44	2, 4
Moki ...	H	7	19
	M	20	12
Momál ...	H	9	24
	S	2	25
Moman ...	H	86	44
	S	1	10
	M	237	16, 25
Momi ...	H	1,279	10, 12, 15, 25, 44
	S	7	25
	M	4	12
Monái ...	H	143	10, 21, 25
Mondi ...	H	38	9, 25, 48
	S	29	13, 15, 45
Mong ...	H	60	5, 12, 25
Mor ...	H	22	21, 28
	M	114	28, 29
Motá ...	H	501	14, 44
	S	279	14, 25
	M	14	2
Moth ...	H	24	28
Moti ...	H	742	13, 15, 17, 25
	M	163	13, 16, 25
Motú ...	H	1,405	9, 13, 17
	M	48	17
Mughal ...	H	72	1, 12
	M	19	13
Multáni ...	H	10	12, 16
	M	5	25
Munj ...	H	322	12, 16
Musalmán ...	M	82	12, 24, 27
Mussalli ...	H	4	2, 24
	M	42	13, 15, 16, 27
Nachchar ...	H	75	12
Nadámá ...	H	17	3
Nádar ...	H	35	16, 17
Nagar ...	H	15	10
Nág ...	H	36	2
	M	2	14
Nagáhiá ...	H	13	8, 48
Nágre ...	H	12	15, 25, 48
	M	2	25
Náhal ...	H	341	10, 12, 13, 44
Nahaliwál ...	H	41	8
Náhar ...	H	11,563	J. L. 1, 6, 19, 25, 44, 46, 48, 49, 50, 51
	S	501	17, 25, 48, 50
	M	76	12, 15, 16, 21
Nahár ...	H	2	5
	S	163	13, 14
	M	26	25
Náhi ...	H	22	9, 13, 20
Nahoti ...	H	17	50
Nákal ...	H	50	2, 25
Naki ...	H	23	25
Námi ...	H	12	12, 15, 50
Nának ...	H	106	3, 7, 12
Nanar ...	S	25	12
Nanátián ...	H	52	6
Nandpál ...	H	34	3, 4, 9
	M	1	13
Nár ...	H	231	9, 10, 14, 27, 44
	S	28	3, 15
	M	3	13
Náranwál ...	H	60	5
Narnáliá ...	H	67	3, 5, 6
Narnattu ...	H	30	3, 6
	S	4	3
Nároi ...	H	25	5
Nárú ...	H	482	11, 12, 25
	S	88	3, 12, 14
	M	59	12, 25
Nárwálke ...	H	27	17
Nathú ...	H	12	49
Nanmuslam ...	M	45	13, 15, 16, 25
Naunár ...	H	301	2, 44
Nek ...	H	84	13, 48
	S	2	48
Newál ...	H	22	2, 4
Nunári ...	M	43	24
Odhán ...	H	16	1
Pábá ...	H	31	26
	M	443	24, 25, 28, 29
Pádal ...	H	25	44
Padhári ...	H	110	2
	M	1	16
Padi ...	H	60	10
Padmán ...	H	46	48
Pagániyán ...	H	344	10, 11, 48, 49
	S	13	48
Páhil ...	H	536	5
Pahmál ...	H	30	3
	S	1	9
Páji ...	H	33	48
Pále ...	H	22	8, 11, 48
	S	1	48
Pakhár ...	H	2	12
	M	92	28, 29
Paliár ...	H	335	14
	M	3	29
Pálo ...	H	5	13, 14
	M	9	25

Names of Sub-Castes.		Persons.	Locality.
Pálon ...	H	126	8, 9, 11
Pamán ...	H	14	10
Pambi ...	H	254	8, 10, 11
Pandás ...	H	217	17, 26, 28, 29
	M	243	28, 29
Pandhán ...	H	47	25
	S	149	14, 25
Pandbár ...	H	91	16
Pandit ...	H	576	13, 17, 24, 25, 27
	M	894	13, 24, 25, 28, 29
Pandwál ...	H	41	4
Pánfye ...	H	13	48
Panjali ...	H	46	9, 12
Panji ...	H	118	9, 14, 15, 25
	S	1	9
	M	7	12
Panjotá ...	H	12	11
Panjwerá ...	M	42	12
Pannú ...	H	1,222	6, 9
Panven ...	H	13	50
Panwál ...	H	295	6, 24, 48
	S	3	48
Panwár ...	H	1,935	1, 3, 5, 12, 24, 48, 50
	S	15	48
	M	94	24, 27
Papmin ...	H	49	10
Paráe ...	H	482	5, 10, 13, 28, 44
Párchá ...	H	716	D. except (6, 7), 9, 17
	S	4	46
Parchal ...	H	30	2, 25
Parchi ...	H	665	4, 5, 17
Parhál ...	H	56	17, 25
	M	46	25
Parhár ...	H	2,095	M. except (28, 29), 11, 13, 17
	M	1,445	M. except (26), 9, 51
Parmáni ...	H	11	10
Pármir ...	H	32	13
Parochá ...	H	870	6, 37, 48, 49
	S	47	48
Paroiá ...	M	12	25
Parwári ...	H	54	9, 15, 25
Pási ...	H	78	10, 17, 48, 50
	M	4	24
Pasoli ...	H	57	20, 25
Pátak ...	H	16	11
Patál ...	H	15	9, 25
Pathán ...	H	1,013	11, 12, 13, 16, 17, 24, 40
	M	304	12, 13, 24, 25
Pathán-gori ...	H	25	12
Patti ...	H	348	9, 10, 13, 25
	S	5	12, 48
Paunpanhár	H	376	12, 40
Paunpatiála	H	19	13
Pawál ...	H	591	1, 2, 5
Páwal ...	H	148	1, 5
Páwan ...	H	56	1, 5, 6, 10, 44
Pawár ...	H	154	1, 5, 6, 10, 44
	S	17	2, 6
	M	116	12, 13, 24, 25
Páwli ...	H	168	2, 5, 9
Phadar ...	S	118	12
Phágrá ...	H	35	48
Phalrán ...	H	29	4
Phalwál ...	H	109	1, 3, 11
	S	2	46
Phaphiál ..	H	83	4, 20
Phartá ...	H	14	13
Pharwáli ...	H	71	9, 10
Pholik ...	H	96	48
Phor ...	H	45	1, 9, 44
Pogháníál ...	H	31	1, 25
Pohái ...	H	114	16, 48
Pohwál ...	H	87	49
Pori ...	H	20	15, 17
Purbiá ...	H	44	24, 50
Rachhariá ...	H	17	9
Rafiq ...	H	19	12
Raggan ...	M	62	28, 29
Raghar ...	H	11	4, 19
Rahár ...	H	32	1, 25
	M	131	1, 13, 29
Rahilá ...	H	48	9
	M	1[illegible]	2, 7
Rahl ...	H	24	5, 9
	M	89	24
Ráhwál ...	H	25	1, 2, 4
	S	48	50
	M	2	13
Rájpút ...	H	72	4, 10, 13
	M	1	27
Rajwáliá ...	H	13	2, 19, 27
Rajwar ...	H	104	3
Rakhrái ...	S	14	11
Ramál ...	H	13	11
Ramáná ...	H	50	49
	S	1	48
	M	13	29
Rámdási ...	H	108	10, 14, 19, 21
	S	12	13, 15
	M	77	51
Ramri ...	H	28	12, 49
Randháwe ...	H	2,736	L. 3, 5, 11, 12, 25, 26, 44, 46, 49, 50
	S	250	13, 14, 48, 50
	M	79	13, 25
Rangar ...	H	82	17
	M	9	47
Rangrethá ...	S	16	10, 33
Rangrú ...	H	13	48, 50
	S	14	48, 50
Rangú ...	H	175	25
	S	1	11
Ránjhá ...	H	156	16
Ranwál ...	H	69	14
	M	16	25
Rápar ...	H	69	5
Raswál ...	H	31	17, 48
Ratá ...	H	161	4, 5
	M	2	25
Rathorá ...	H	1	48
	S	19	48
Rathwál ...	H	1,673	9, 17, 19
	M	32	12, 16
Ratiál ...	H	13	9, 44
	M	21	13, 24
Ratikhokhar	H	182	12, 13, 16, 17
	M	8	12, 27
Ratti ...	H	2,595	L. M. 1, 9, 10, 12, 21, 22, 48
	S	178	11, 25, 48
	M	901	13, 16, 17, 19, 20, 24, 25, 27, 28, 29
Ratwál ...	H	111	13, 16, 17, 24, 29
	M	5	25
Redlán ...	H	937	2, 4, 50
Rerwál ...	H	31	2, 4
Rohlá ...	H	98	12, 14
	M	12	13, 17
Rohti ..	H	49	48
Roj ...	H	12	48
	M	115	25
Ropal ...	H	13	49
Ror ...	S	56	48
Rúnjwán ...	H	24	4, 13
Sab ...	H	252	15, 25, 44
	S	8	15
Sabha ...	H	1,152	13, 44
	M	15	15
Sábir ...	H	20	12
Sachhi ...	H	14	10, 25
Sadáh ...	H	101	25, 44, 46
Sadái ...	H	18	11
Sadáná ...	H	11	11
Sadhare ...	H	364	12, 14, 17
	M	3	25
Sagar ...	H	45	9, 19, 44
	M	1	25
Sagoná ...	S	37	48
Sagoti ...	H	18	12, 46, 49
Sahal ...	H	4	48
	S	6	48
	M	6	12, 20
Saháli ...	H	9	12
	M	38	13, 17
Sáhar ...	H	45	17
Sabáwan ...	M	19	25
Sáhdá ...	H	11	13, 15
Sáhi ...	H	127	50
	S	1	48
	M	1	14
Sahiti ...	H	388	6, 19
Sáhnsi ...	H	16	2, 20, 50
	M	18	25, 27
Sahoná ...	H	11	12, 15, 17
Sahote ...	H	21,942	J. except (8), L. except(17), 1, 2, 25, 44, 46, 48, 49, 50
	S	2,964	11, 12, 14, 25, 51
	M	73	13, 16, 19, 25
Sahs ...	H	169	3
Sahúlhat ...	H	20	2, 19
Sahúntrá ...	H	8,882	1, 2, 4, 8, 12, 13, 17, 21, 26, 44, 51
	S	40	11, 13, 14, 25
	M	2,327	1, 12, 13, 16, 17, 25
Sajji ...	H	7	14
	S	40	48
Saju ...	M	11	12
Sakáliá ...	H	1	25
	M	184	13
Sakará ...	H	38	27
Sakhá ...	H	11	12
Salá ...	H	63	1, 2
Salahrá ...	H	27	13, 24
	M	3	13
Salaun ...	H	54	9, 46, 48
	S	10	14, 15, 25
Salhotrá ...	H	1,397	12, 21, 25
	S	7	9, 12, 17
	M	72	19, 24
Sali ...	H	394	14, 15
Salkáhi ...	H	15	4, 32
Salkotrá ...	H	37	9, 16
Sálri ...	S	34	11
Sámal ...	H	79	11, 25
Samarli ...	H	14	5, 6, 9
Sambar ...	H	18	2, 4, 16
Samor ...	M	12	16
Samrád ...	H	5	12
	S	7	9, 11
San ...	H	619	5, 12
	S	69	15, 48
	M	7	13
Sanáthir ...	H	11	12
Sambhati ...	H	44	10
Sandá ...	H	116	1, 4, 9, 26
	M	8	27
Sándal ...	H	147	6, 15, 17, 49
	S	26	25
	M	2	25
Sándar ...	H	780	1, 6, 13, 25, 26
	M	246	23, 24, 25
Sandhi ...	H	3,532	2, 4, 9, 10, 11, 26, 44
	S	306	48
	M	171	13, 17, 19
Sangal ...	H	32	1, 3, 10, 12
Sangaliá ...	H	61	48
Sangar ...	H	1,330	1, 4, 6, 48, 51
	S	532	5, 6, 25, 48
	M	7	11
Sánghari ...	H	181	1, 10, 12
Sángi ...	H	89	2, 11
	S	4	2
	M	27	51
Sángiá ...	H	30	51
Sangotri ...	H	9	14
	S	8	11
Sangwáliá ...	H	304	3
Sangwán ...	H	256	3, 4
	M	1	4
Sanoti ...	H	551	14, 16
Sanotra ...	H	493	1, 14, 15
	S	29	25
	M	875	14, 16, 17, 25
Sanswál ...	H	67	1, 3, 6
Sant ...	H	117	1, 6, 10, 44
	M	4	13
Santáil ...	H	25	44
Santrá ...	H	11	13, 27
	S	67	45
	M	41	13, 27
Sap ...	H	189	16, 25
Sapat ...	H	1	13
	M	20	25, 29

SUB-CASTES OF CERTAIN SELECTED CASTES—*continued.*

Names of Sub-Castes.		Persons.	Locality.
Saplí	... H	20	12
Sarai	... H	435	12, 13, 14, 15
	S	50	12, 25
	M	54	17, 24
Sarak	... H	12	48
Saral	... H	11	3
Sáran	... H	94	12, 16, 17
Saráni	... H	129	3, 5
Sárao	... H	92	48, 49
	S	263	48
	M	60	13
Sáras	... H	1,420	1, 2, 3, 4, 12, 13
	M	16	25
Sarbatti	... H	1,596	10, 12, 44, 46
	M	44	12, 25
Sárdon	... H	31	2, 9
Sardbá	... H	146	2
Sardi	... H	361	1, 2, 15, 44
Sareta	... H	174	48
Sargohar	... H	171	3
Sári	... H	99	2, 15, 16
	S	9	11, 12, 25
	M	8	25
Sáriá	... M	19	13
Sarín	... H	527	1, 5, 6, 9, 46, 50
	S	244	1, 2, 6, 50
Sarinwál	... H	302	48
Sárman	... H	16	4, 6
Sarnitti	... H	34	1
Saroe	... H	1,485	1, 5, 12, 13, 17, 48
	S	467	48
	M	145	12, 13, 25
Saroh	... H	46	13
Saroiá	... H	1,409	1, 5, 12, 13, 17, 48
	S	6	48, 49
	M	484	12, 13, 25
Saroja	... S	80	48
Sarota	... H	1,062	1, 3, 12, 24, 48
	S	346	48
Sársal	... H	56	2, 5, 11, 21
	S	1	6
Sársar	... H	2,346	D. except (6, 7), 24, 25, 48
	S	230	48
	M	200	24, 25
Sársut	... H	243	5, 6, 9, 11
Sarswál	... H	2,947	D. except (7), 49, 51
	S	8	6, 25, 46
Sarth	... H	164	1, 25
Sartiá	... H	242	12
Sarwál	... H	176	3, 5, 6, 48
Sárwán	... H	912	2, 4, 12, 32, 47, 51
Saryá	... H	7	48
	S	20	48
Sáserá	... H	21	9, 11, 32
Sasi	... H	51	1, 2, 5, 9
Saswál	... H	543	2, 4, 5
Satal	... H	16	2
	M	17	28
Sátan	... H	22	19, 24
	M	8	13
Sathn	... H	366	10, 11, 12
	M	22	16
Satiwál	... H	36	2, 16
Satri	... H	285	8, 12, 21, 27, 32
	M	270	22, 25, 29
Sáwan	... H	43	1, 5, 12
	S	2	25
Sawári	... H	64	2, 14
Sedí	... H	118	5, 10
Seli	... H	333	10, 17
	M	52	13
Seniwat	... H	15	3
Seoni	... H	515	10, 12
	M	9	4
Sertiá	... H	181	50
	M	158	13
Shábi	... H	17	15
Shári	... H	31	45
Shekh	... H	35	14, 25
	S	2	14
	M	20	27
Shérgil	... H	643	10, 12, 13, 25
	S	12	25
	M	9	25
Shir	... H	18	15, 25
Siái	... H	39	6, 9
Siál	... H	480	17, 24
	M	45	17, 24, 25
Siánbar	... H	35	15
Sidhar	... H	15	1, 13
Sidhu	... H	3,898	1, 9, 12, 46, 48
	S	831	12, 13, 48, 50
	M	2,433	13, 17
Siháná	... H	81	7
Sihumár	... H	103	47
	S	68	47
Sijoi	... H	36	10
Sikhan	... H	119	6, 14, 46
	S	19	25, 45, 46
Sikhú	... H	228	12
Sinámár	... H	80	5, 12
Sindhu	... H	18,906	L. except (16), 1, 9, 10, 11, 24, 25, 44, 46, 50
	S	774	12, 13, 14, 25, 48
	M	526	12, 13, 17, 25
Sinswál	... H	39	48
Sinti	... H	18	1
Siotri	... H	135	24
Sit	... H	18	10
Sitár	... H	37	1
Sodan	... H	13	4, 5
Sode	... H	3,598	1, 5, 6, 32
	M	1	24
Sohal	... H	30	1, 3, 15, 26
Sohanpandhár	H	841	9, 17
	S	3	12, 13
	M	151	12, 13, 16
Sohi	... H	3	19
	S	12	11, 25
	M	1	13
Sohná	... H	99	6, 9, 19
	S	57	12, 14, 48
Sohni	... H	2,294	6, 7, 14, 15
	S	100	14, 15, 25
	M	40	13
Sohriá	... H	31	2, 15
	M	4	13
Soi	... H	406	2, 10, 17, 21, 47
	S	4	45
Soiá	... H	170	10, 14, 15
	M	1	12
Somnáth	... H	24	15
Sonhári	... H	6	11
	M	7	13
Soni	... H	44	11, 25
	M	1	16
Sonibatiár	... H	462	12, 25, 46
	M	619	13, 17
Soni Bhandár	H	1,056	16, 17, 27
	M	276	13, 19, 25
Soni Bhandiál	H	1,540	13, 14, 17, 25
	M	46	12, 16, 24
Sonita	... H	28	1, 15
Sonpanhál	... M	303	13, 16
Sosani	... H	462	1, 2, 15, 48
	S	3	48
Sosri	... H	23	6
Sota	... H	150	5, 12, 15, 16
	M	75	24, 25
Sotani	... H	99	11, 17
Sotha	... H	273	1, 2, 5, 10
Soti Bharáh	... H	109	25
Sotra	... H	2,978	13, 18, 24, 25
	S	8	12, 13, 21
	M	150	4, 12, 24
Sotri	... H	1,012	13
	M	196	25, 27
Sud	... H	287	9
Sukhan	... H	146	48
	S	13	48
Sulemán	... H	26	4
Sumhi	... H	11	25
Sunián	... H	75	1, 12, 48
	M	8	1, 51
Sunni	H	134	10, 14
	S	8	11, 12, 21
Sutra	... H	52	48
Tahim	... H	27	12, 24
	M	17	13, 25
Tahote	... H	108	25, 44
Tahur	... H	77	1, 2, 12
Tahurán	... H	26	2
Tajoli	... H	53	3
	M	32	25
Ták	... H	4,673	1, 2, 17, 25
	M	2	13
Tákhi	... H	25	1
Takso	... H	335	19
Tal	... H	7	11, 48
	M	12	25
Taliáná	... H	61	9, 10
Talor	... H	78	6
Tamni	... H	11	26
	S	3	11
	M	1,042	13
Tánji	... H	58	9, 48
Tánk	... H	5,319	D. except (7), 10, 11, 21, 49
	S	5	2
	M	1	13
Tanká	... H	54	44
Tant	... H	17	1, 5
Tanwár	... H	104	3
Tap	... H	46	10, 16, 25, 48
Tará	... H	3	5, 8
	M	13	17
Tarál	... H	62	4
Tarbán	... H	5	8, 12
	S	6	12
	M	85	13
Tarmián	... H	25	1, 16
Tasahar	... H	1,546	4, 5
Tashám	... H	49	2, 4
Tatli	... H	42	19, 24
	S	5	11
	M	11	13, 24
Taur	... H	12	48
	S	5	11, 48
	M	5	13
Teji	... H	1,974	10, 12, 13, 25, 46
	S	61	48
	M	855	12, 13, 24, 25
Tejie	... H	306	13, 14
	M	8	13
Teli	... H	38	12, 14, 27
	M	2	13
Tháp	... H	980	J. except (8), 15, 44
	S	2	25
Thatal	... H	15	24
Thind	... H	25	50
	S	6	48
Thora	... H	21	51
Thori	... H	96	1, 6, 10, 51
	M	50	12, 51
Thothwál	... H	161	2, 9
Tindalwál	... H	12	48
	S	2	48
Tode	... H	71	48
Túr	... H	86	25
	M	16	4, 10, 12
Ude	... H	733	12
Udewál	... H	462	48, 50
	S	11	50
Untwál	... H	952	1, 2, 6, 9, 48
Uppál	... H	24	50
	S	4	13
Utal	... H	173	11
Uthwal	... H	217	50
	S	4	50
Vadhaki	... H	14	12
Vadhwá	... H	55	10
Vágri	... H	76	13, 24, 26
	M	154	24, 25
Vaháh	... H	228	25
Váhan	... H	16	12, 44
	M	20	24, 27
Váhi	... H	94	2, 10, 27
Váich	... H	15	9, 14
Vains	... H	31	16, 25
Váiras	... M	18	29
Váldhia	... H	28	9
	M	2	25
Valotiá	... M	84	29
Vangra	... H	20	12
Variáh	... H	64	11, 12, 17, 25
	M	29	12, 13, 21, 27
Varián	... M	29	24

Names of Sub-Castes.	Persons.	Locality.	Names of Sub-Castes.	Persons.	Locality.	Names of Sub-Castes.	Persons.	Locality.
Varwál ... M	11	25	Vedi ... H	81	10, 12, 46	*Minor ... H	2,999	
Vasir ... M	45	13, 24	S	1	25	S	316	
Vátal ... H	210	16, 17, 18, 19, 47	Vedu ... H	24	11	M	328	
M	128	16, 17, 18	S	1	12	Unspecified ... H	112,878	
Vattu ... H	42	12, 13, 25, 51	Virk ... H	322	12, 13, 14, 17	S	4,886	
M	14	12, 13, 25	M	20	13	M	17,249	
						J	1	

*** DETAIL OF MINOR.**

Ábi 5, Abláe 3, Ablú 2, Adarní 4, Ader 1, Adháp 8, Ádiál 10, Adráe 2, Agáhi 7, Agarwál 9, Agwání 2, Airlán 1, Ajiál 2, Ajráti 5, Aloma 1, Alpa 1, Alwán 1, Alyás 6, Amáni 1, Amín 2, Amráwál 10, Amrúke 1, Andási 6, Andgal 2, Angre 1, Ankwál 1, Anmal 1, Anni 4, Anpat 8, Apoj 5, Ari 2, Arjanwál 3, Arlál 2, Aroja 1, Arwále 3, Arwání 1, Ashman 1, Asnáni 4, Asoda 4, Athore 2, Atwár 7, Aujál 10, Awál 5, Bábiá 1, Babne 5, Badan 9, Badháláí 1, Badher 2, Badhwál 10, Badla 1, Badoja 8, Badrak 1, Badtán 7, Bagoche 6, Bagwál 1, Bahlar 2, Báhri 1, Bájí 1, Bakální 2, Bakánia 9, Bakhwání 6, Baknáth 8, Bakostar 1, Bákrí 2, Balánia 1, Baldáe 2, Bálebán 1, Bálgoya 1, Balkat 1, Balkí 6, Balote 4, Balparia 1, Balta 3, Balwin 3, Balyání 1, Bamal Johar 5, Bambú 3, Bamotrí 3, Bán 7, Bandhwár 8, Bandoklí 2, Banjwára 4, Banotí 6, Bargújar 4, Barhár 3, Barokh 2, Baráya 7, Bardhala 2, Barjí 2, Baroche 3, Barote 1, Barsí 8, Barsmdhar 1, Barwán 8, Bashárí 2, Basmár 1, Batária 5, Bataur 6, Batián 2, Batsarí 1, Báwalí 8, Bawáne 10, Bedí 6, Bedra 1, Belang 7, Belotri 1, Bepál 9, Beraj 7, Betgohta 1, Bhábre 6, Bháí 2, Bhak 9, Bhalwál 2, Bhamal 3, Bhambar 9, Bhamí 8, Bhamra 1, Bhandál 5, Bhandárí 2, Bhanghnáth 1, Bharanda 3, Bhardán 1, Bhárdawájí 1, Bharlán 2, Bharmál 9, Bharola 1, Bhárú 7, Bháwna 6, Bhawánd 5, Bhigása 3, Bhoi 4, Bhojrak 1, Bhokal 2, Bhol 6, Bholmán 5, Bhonthe 1, Bhornálí 1, Bhos 9, Bhúkal 2, Bhúlálan 2, Bhúmán 5, Bhúmás 1, Bhúnde 3, Bhúpál 1, Bhuteli 6, Bigal 1, Bijáltí 1, Birbal 4, Bíyás 9, Bodí 4, Bohrí 4, Bonid 3, Borak 2, Boriband 3, Bosiya 1, Brah 9, Búja 1, Bunianí 1, Búrákhal 2, Chadál 1, Chador 3, Chagorí 1, Cháhal 5, Chakal 1, Chakan 3, Chakoria 6, Chakrádí 1, Chaláne 3, Chalohar 3, Chamaria 2, Chamia 7, Chandál 1, Chandarma 1, Chándlí 4, Chandna 8, Chandohar 1, Chandohí 2, Chandrál 2, Chang 5, Changáníye 3, Changon 8, Chanjotri 7, Charál 2, Charámal 1, Chárgotie 2, Charoi 1, Charsáín 1, Charswál 1, Chat 1, Chhábre 4, Chhabrú 2, Chhachhárú 5, Chhajal 7, Chhajrú 7, Chháleti 5, Chhanjhari 6, Chhára 6, Chharália 7, Chhatanda 2, Chháwan 1, Chhigat 1, Chho 1, Chhote 1, Chhúmat 1, Chímí 1, Chirimár 3, Chitoria 6, Chohta 5, Choja 3, Chokra 1, Chonbar 6, Chopli 1, Chorián 1, Chúkate 7, Chutrál 2, Dágas 2, Dagjága 4, Dagji 5, Dahgarí 2, Dabi 2, Daier 3, Dáig 5, Dakanj 6, Dákar 3, Dákati 10, Dakolia 3, Dalální 3, Daldí 1, Dalgan 1, Daljotra 5, Dalkotra 10, Damal 5, Dandíwál 1, Dánejap 1, Dangar 1, Dantú 2, Dapoch 8, Dardoí 1, Darmrája 1, Darna 1, Darvesh 1, Darya 8, Darzí 5, Dasathra 6, Datrol 5, Daulká 1, Dawál 9, Dawání 2, Dega 3, Degána 8, Degpár 2, Degta 2, Dehíya 7, Dekohí 1, Dem 6, Deráman 5, Deyáe 1, Dháb 2, Dhádania 5, Dhají 2, Dhajwál 1, Dhakád 5, Dhakiás 6, Dhámmi 1, Dhanda 9, Dhanga Pawár 6, Dhangohar 3, Dhanj 5, Dhanoe 2, Dhánsar 3, Dharálí 2, Dharanjí 1, Dhargán 1, Dhargotri 2, Dhátar 2, Dhaten 3, Dhaulán 5, Dhaun 3, Dher 1, Dhingat 8, Dhogar 4, Dhogse 10, Dhokad 2, Dholak 1, Dholikhokhar 2, Dhonkal 2, Dhontra 7, Dhúlewána 1, Dhundra 1, Dígat 5, Dikan 2, Dikhárú 6, Díwálá 9, Dodas 8, Dokhána 1, Dokbar 1, Domande 4, Donáli 2, Dorí 10, Doria 10, Dosnáj 2, Dota 1, Dúsra 1, Faráhí 2, Farwáín 2, Fattú 2, Gabi 2, Gabirá 1, Gachrá 1, Gadiaji 2, Gadlán 4, Gádri 4, Gágá 10, Gagathana 1, Gagián 9, Gagna 1, Gagrán 1, Gágwán 3, Gaidar 2, Gaigi 4, Gáji 4, Gajlet 9, Gajutan 6, Galál 9, Galántá 5, Gálar 9, Galgawári 4, Galhore 5, Gali 7, Galirá 1, Galoniá 2, Galre 2, Galsí 7, Gan 1, Gandár 6, Gandi 5, Gandlál 6, Gandli 3, Gangál 8, Gangarabri 2, Gangasari 1, Gángiá 4, Gangotri 2, Gangriá 1, Gangwáni 3, Ganso 1, Gaphar 5, Gardáliá 1, Gárt 5, Garte 2, Gárwán 5, Gáshak 8, Gatáru 10, Gathárá 1, Gatoi 1, Gaur Brahman Khákrub 6, Gawáliá 7, Ghagar 8, Ghalli 1, Ghamárchandi 9, Ghanchalá 2, Ghamirá 7, Ghamniá 3, Ghanáti 1, Ghandsi 1, Ghaniár 4, Gharot 4, Gharwalá 6, Ghírath 1, Ghomare 4, Ghomarya 4, Ghonsal 2, Ghoriwáh 8, Ghosanwál 1, Ghowará 4, Godbalá 7, Godhi 4, Gogá 8, Gogach 1, Gogal 1, Gogamalía 7, Gogri 7, Gojgiá 4, Goje 1, Gokhá 4, Goli 8, Gomal 2, Gomir 3, Gon 5, Gonah 9, Gonsá 1, Gopáhar 1, Gopáng 6, Goram 1, Gorgal 1, Goriál 1, Gorimal 1, Gorkha 4, Gorsiá 1, Gosh 10, Got 8, Gujar 6, Gulábdási 1, Gurg 1, Gurmaki 3, Gurne 8, Guryaná 3, Haderán 2, Hádi 1, Hadiál 1, Hadlál 1, Hadriá 1, Hagán 2, Hakmáre 2, Haktan 10, Halálkhor 5, Haliáná 2, Hamdáni 6, Hamman 6, Hamní 5, Hánd 1, Hándo 1, Hangá 4, Hanir 2, Hánji 6, Hanswál 6, Hardwárá 5, Hargan 3, Harhár 2, Hariti 1, Harnáwe 4, Harochi 9, Harswál 6, Hartkhokhar 1, Haru 8, Harwáji 2, Hatti 2, Hatton 1, Hele 2, Hindal 3, Hirháni 1, Hiwa 2, Hos 7, Hoski 6, Hatre 4, Hukma 2, Huseni 2, Jabal 2, Jadúrá 5, Jagáne 5, Jagot 2, Jalghori 8, Jalhore 10, Jalyár 2, Jamásage 1, Janádar 4, Janáhar 1, Janglá 3, Jangrá 4, Janjan 1, Jankaná 5, Janoi 9, Janole 10, Jaraliá 10, Jarwáná 3, Jatále 3, Jáwal 6, Jawándhe 3, Jawáre 9, Jawáse 2, Jedhar 4, Jhájar 7, Jhajotá 3, Jhandhál 5, Jhokar 1, Jhokhá 1, Jhongar 4, Jhotre 3, Jiná 7, Johá 8, Jogi 1, Johal 1, Jokanke 2, Jonare 3, Jonch 1, Jondar 4, Jondi 10, Jonji 5, Jorán 2, Joribhatti 3, Joriki 5, Josh 2, Jotra 8, Kábans 1, Kachan 10, Kachli 7, Kachháre 4, Kachhwe 2, Kachnawe 1, Kadhári 8, Kagáe 1, Kágat 2, Kághal 3, Kabir 8, Káith 1, Kakariá 2, Kalábán 8, Kalank 6, Kaliáli 6, Kalit 1, Kalji 3, Kalotá 5, Kalsán 3, Kalsiá 4, Kálthe 1, Kamrú 9, Kampora 1, Kandolá 10, Kandri 2, Kangwál 2, Kankot 9, Kánsal 6, Kansi 8, Kantori 7, Kapar 7, Kaptál 2, Kapuri 5, Karáhú 1, Karban 5, Kard 3, Karil 1, Kariál 4, Karkoria 1, Karnál 8, Kartari 1, Karyáo 1, Káshab 1, Kashira 5, Kasrota 10, Káswal 5, Katle 1, Katwar 5, Kesi 1, Khakhaná 3, Khal 5, Khanak 5, Khani 2, Kharoki 1, Khatánwári 1, Khawáli 2, Khawári 3, Khesri 4, Khish 1, Khokhala 1, Khokrae 4, Khoprá 4, Kirat 5, Kohávati 1, Korsi 2, Kort 5, Kosarni 2, Kot 7, Kotal 5, Kuldesi 1, Kungáhe 1, Ládwál 5, Lágat 6, Lakhárá 6, Lakhiáná 3, Lakhpatti 2, Lakhrá 4, Lálán 2, Lálaryá 2, Lálra 2, Lálú 1, Lánbá 1, Lang 9, Lánsar 1, Laryán 7, Lás 1, Latmár 2, Latti 1, Láwat 1, Lesrá 1, Liakarob 10, Librangi 9, Loriá 4, Luná 1, Meadharrán 1, Mádi 9, Mághi 2, Magnobir 4, Magu 3, Mabans 1, Máhar 2, Máhi 1, Mahioná 1, Máhli 7, Mabmia 3, Makhána 3, Makher 7, Makhi 3, Makhotre 2, Mako 5, Malang 2, Malgár 1, Málgoná 1, Maloti 7, Malpura 6, Málre 1, Málsi 2, Malwar 6, Mamak 4, Mámai 7, Manárwál 7, Manás 2, Mangoliá 5, Mangwáná 4, Maniáre 1, Manai 6, Maráchá 1, Máraná 3, Maráti 3, Mare 5, Marghe 2, Mariáli 5, Markand 5, Martoi 1, Masand 5, Matarwál 6, Mathiáni 1, Mawákhá 3, Megni 8, Mewáti 10, Mezwál 3, Mirg 1, Mohni 8, Mohri 5, Mohte 5, Molchand 1, Moli 1, Momibeg 6, Munjdháriá 3, Musi 1, Nágriá 6, Náhab 2, Nábaná 10, Náhothiá 1, Náhran 9, Nabre 2, Nahtál 10, Náich 1, Naibrije 6, Náikbádshábi 2, Nakir 2, Námimanár 1, Naná 6, Nánakpanthi 8, Nandáliá 5, Nandwi 1, Nángá 2, Nángli 6, Nangpál 7, Nánki 1, Nansá 1, Náráh 3, Narán 10, Nári 5, Narkat 6, Narlái 3, Narlál 10, Narnáli 7, Násia 1, Natri 1, Natyái 2, Náwdháwá 2, Negi 4, Nihang 8, Niharman 8, Nil 10, Nimán 6, Nir 5, Nirákárí 2, Nosáhar 1, Nosáhiká 8, Notak 2, Nothná 7, Nuniyán 3, Oditwár 3, Pábsain 6, Pachur 1, Padesi 1, Pádhe 1, Pagháne 9, Págopáni 3, Pagul 8, Páhote 7, Pakániá 9, Pakhidás 2, Palambi 2, Pálde 1, Palirwál 2, Pálon 3, Pálwi 6, Pambari 2, Pami 1, Panab 9, Pandháre 4, Pandwári 1, Panet 4, Panhár 10, Panjábi 7, Panjethá 1, Panjohar 3, Pánpal 1, Pánsur 9, Pantálie 1, Páposh 8, Parail 4, Paránd 1, Pardári 2, Pardiá 1, Parmákhokhar 2, Parsan 10, Parseháwe 1, Párshá 5, Páro 1, Pásal 1, Patharchohán 3, Pathwál 1, Patráe 2, Pátre 2, Patrur 8, Patun 1, Paunbandiál 2, Páwen 1, Payán 7, Phagwáná 2, Pháil 8, Phalgan 3, Phalrá 1, Phami 2, Phand 3, Phank 4, Phankár 1, Phar 2, Pharwál 9, Phikan 2, Pholarwán 1, Photak 1, Pinons 7, Piplán 1, Piriban 2, Pohari 2, Poská 3, Pubri 3, Punián 7, Purji 3, Rádhadat 1, Radiwál 7, Ráhal 2, Rái 6, Rái Dás 2, Rájal 6, Rájanwál 5, Rájewál 2, Rájmoto 1, Rajotá 4, Rájrá 1, Rakshpál 7, Rál 1, Rámsar 1, Rándal 8, Randálán 9, Ráng 5, Ranganá 1, Rangbar 9, Rangroliá 4, Rangroti 1, Rangwári 1, Rar 4, Rasoti 7, Ratan 3, Ráthor 6, Rawán 1,Ráwri 10, Rekhi 7, Relokatar 7, Rihan 10, Rochandi 4, Rolu 1, Ropilá 1, Sabri 6, Sachni 4, Sadeli 10, Sadhan 1, Sadiqi 3, Sagáre 3, Sagi 5, Sagini 4, Sagwáni 1, Sahádi 4, Sahli 4, Sáhmal 4, Sahnár 1, Saholi 4, Sahwárá 9, Sajan 8, Sajark 10, Sajju 6, Sajli 6, Sakhná 6, Sakariá 1, Sakriban 5, Salári 2, Salatin 2, Salláh 2, Salpat 1, Salsat 2, Salwán 1, Samak 9, Saman 9, Sambo 1, Samgari 2, Samti 2, Sanáli 7, Sanámal 1, Sanátal 3, Sanduriá 5, Sandhore 4, Sándíwál 3, Sangáyan 4, Sanginá 3, Sangu 5, Sanipat 9, Sanjal 1, Sankalás 3, Sáns 1, Sánsas 4, Sanski 1, Sansona 5, Sánuriá 4, Sapádhá 1, Sapal 1, Sapar 3, Sárában 2, Saráo 1, Saraut 1, Sarbangi 2, Sarchohán 9, Sarháni 4, Sarhwál 4, Sarinwál 2, Sarkal 6, Sarkandi 3, Sárli 4, Sárochi 1, Sársar 6, Sarson 9, Sarswáni 2, Sarwáh 10, Sarware 1, Saunsal 9, Segal 2, Sekri 6, Seti 1, Shaboke 2, Shám 2, Shashgor 5, Shadhá 8, Sián 6, Sikári 2, Sikhu 3, Silwál 10, Simár 1, Sindal 3, Singal 6, Singu 8, Sink 2, Sispál 7, Siyáná 7, Sodhari 10, Sogáni 10, Sohan 9, Sorbandi 3, Sotá 4, Sukar 3, Sumra 1, Surá 6, Surja 4, Suthwál 1, Tabanmár 2, Tádar 3, Táhmiál 4, Tábrá 1, Tabriá 3, Tajutri 3, Tákar 2, Tálimál 3, Talipargál 10, Tallá 2, Támochar 1, Tanan 1, Tandol 3, Tangar 1, Tángari 1, Takálá 10, Tarájar 1, Taráng 6, Taranjwá 1, Tárar 8, Tardás 6, Tári 4, Tarkhán 3, Taror 3, Tasámrá 6, Tathar 2, Taunkrá 4, Tellan 1, Tes 9, Thad 1, Thagári 7, Thaj 3, Thak 2, Thakar 1, Thandliá 2, Thánewál 3, Tharal 2, Thathmak 7, Tholor 10, Thori 3, Thotha 1, Tit 1, Titri 3, Toánál 3, Tolkhe 1, Torná 4, Tun 8, Udási 10, Ugal 1, Undar 1, Vachhal 3, Vadotre 1, Vajun 1, Vál 1, Valáná 6, Valu 3, Varáich 7, Varkaloi 3, Varki 1, Vasián 9, Vazirpuri 3, Vech 4, Ves 2, Vidwán 9, Vikhu 8, Voghe 5.

SUB-CASTES OF CERTAIN SELECTED CASTES—*continued.*

Names of Sub-Castes.		Persons.	Locality.
Faqir		279,722	H. 30,561; S. 16,103; M 232,978; J. 80
Abásí ...	M	23	16, 37
Abdáli ...	M	53	8, 13, 14
Abrá ...	M	13	16
Achnít ...	H	167	9, 11, 44
	S	52	1, 9, 10, 11, 13
Afgán ...	M	155	15, 27
Agrúl ...	H	24	5, 9, 14, 44, 45
'Abdi ...	S	3	45
	M	11	1
Ahír ...	H	5	1
	M	67	16, 25, 26
Ahmadí ...	M	15	2, 11
Aibzai ..	M	22	17
Aipanthi ...	H	14	1
Ajiál ...	H	15	4, 9
Akálí ...	S	36	9, 44, 48
	M	5	26
Almast Sáhib	M	26	10
Amámshábí	H	3	1, 9
	M	59	3, 8, 12, 19, 25
Amír ...	M	30	16, 28
Amlí ...	M	12	3, 15
Angadnámi	H	148	6
Ansári ...	M	80	19, 27, 51
Apárí ...	M	21	16
Apárnáthí ...	H	15	8
Aráín ...	M	51	16, 17, 45
Arbí ...	M	175	28, 29
A'rifshábí ...	M	32	4, 14
A'shqán ...	M	39	2, 49
Áskari ...	M	25	3, 12, 45
Atal ...	H	24	11
	M	21	9, 12
Atlas ...	H	19	9, 11
Atmal ...	M	13	3
Augar ...	H	220	1, 5, 8, 9, 10, 13, 42
	S	1	12
	M	231	13
Augarnathí ...	H	34	50
	S	35	50
Aulakh ...	H	1	15
	M	72	13, 14, 16
Awán ...	H	12	8, 11, 13
	S	7	11
	M	1,483	L. R. M. 8, 9, 46, 51
Azl ...	M	20	17, 25
Badan ...	H	1	10
	M	10	11, 23
Baddú ...	H	3	8
	M	19	6, 8
Bad-gujar ...	S	8	11
	M	42	1, 3
Bád-kan ...	M	14	49
Badri ...	M	31	19, 26
Bagál ...	H	7	1
	M	31	8, 11, 15, 16
Bágariá ...	H	1	1
	M	47	14, 16, 20, 44
Bagdádi ...	M	56	2, 26
Bagorná ...	M	12	1
Bains ...	H	89	9, 15, 51
	M	491	L. 19, 24, 29
Bairágí ...	H	3,316	J. R. M. 13, 15, 50, 51
	S	125	12, 14, 25, 50
	M	2	13, 22
Bájwá ...	H	10	11
	M	438	L. 25
Bal ...	H	20	1, 3, 5
	S	2	11
	M	8	15, 16, 25
Balgán ...	M	20	16
Balím ...	H	4	11, 14
	M	259	5, 11, 16, 25
Bálke ...	S	3	12
	M	17	11, 17
Balorí ...	M	27	13, 28, 39
Bálut ...	H	25	3
Baná ...	M	13	16
Bándí ...	H	1	11
	S	5	11
	M	209	2, 11, 16
Bangálí ...	H	115	11, 40
	M	100	8, 11, 51
Bánkí ...	H	2	1
	M	21	1
Bánwá ...	H	66	5, 11
	M	10,389	D. 9, 11, 12, 32, 33, 45, 48, 49, 50
Bappar ...	M	29	51
Bárá ...	H	3	14
	S	14	25
	M	58	1, 15, 25, 40
Bráich ...	M	903	2, 18, 25, 44
Barán ...	H	2	1
	M	24	9, 15
Barar ...	H	5	1
	M	41	15, 17, 18, 28, 51
Barkhá ...	M	14	9
Barlás ...	M	31	13, 25
Barwále ...	M	69	9, 16, 17, 25
Baryár ...	M	87	16, 17
Basrá ...	H	1	10
	M	153	11, 12, 15, 16, 17
Basrái ...	M	56	16, 17, 25
Báth ...	M	81	16, 17
Batrí ...	H	1	27
	S	7	21, 44
	M	37	13, 16
Batt ...	H	5	45
	M	326	11, 16, 26
Báwá ...	H	112	13, 23, 51
	S	1	50
	M	26	16, 45
Báwariá ...	H	4	12
	M	127	6, 11
Bázígar ...	M	56	27, 42
Bedi ...	H	14	13, 44
	S	19	13, 26
	M	14	11
Began ...	H	1	27
	S	25	25
	M	10	18, 25, 28
Bewán ...	S	17	11
	M	1	17
Bbadal ...	H	5	29
	M	74	14, 17
Bhágí ...	M	12	16, 25
Bhagwáná ...	M	36	11, 29, 51
Bháí ...	S	44	10
Bhákrí ...	S	1	45
	M	89	8, 11, 12, 13, 15, 44
Bhanb ...	H	40	12
	M	9	45
Bhánde ...	H	5	14
	S	13	51
	M	47	23, 25, 51
Bhangu ...	M	40	12
Bhánmatí ...	H	12	1, 9
Bharáf ...	H	1	11
	M	44	12, 14, 17
Bhárdwáj ...	H	20	8, 9, 12
	S	1	44
	M	3	17
Bhárthí ...	H	62	1, 21, 26, 27
	S	1	45
Bhátre ...	H	26	10
Bhatt ...	H	49	27, 28, 45
	M	35	13, 15, 24, 27, 29
Bhattí ...	H	22	5, 11, 12
	S	5	11
	M	12,591	L. M. 1, 8, 9, 12, 44, 51
Bhirrá ...	M	16	1, 25
Bholá ...	M	66	9, 10, 14, 44
Bhorí ...	H	25	13
	M	27	9
Bhullar ...	M	69	15, 16, 17, 44
Bhutta ...	M	625	L. 11, 20, 26, 27
Bilbhana ...	M	13	3, 18, 24
Biloch ...	M	308	11, 16, 19, 20, 21, 24, 25, 27, 51
Bishanswamí	H	23	1, 5, 8, 9, 10, 14
Bodla ...	H	17	1, 9, 12
	S	1	9
	M	110	6, 12, 13, 15, 17, 18, 19, 21
Bohar ...	H	6	1, 27
	M	34	6, 9, 12, 14, 16, 18, 25, 33
Bothana ...	M	18	27
Brahman ...	H	24	2, 27, 28
Brahmchárí ...	H	59	J. 13, 14, 15, 26, 28, 33, 48
	S	12	12
Bukhárí ...	M	303	L. 9, 11, 25, 26, 44, 49, 51
Bustaní ...	M	30	13, 24
Chadhar ...	M	715	17, 18, 19, 20, 24, 25, 26, 27
Chátil ...	M	326	1, 13, 17, 25, 26, 45, 51
Chamri ...	H	1	10
	M	12	26
Chanan ...	M	58	9, 51
Chanawar ...	M	16	51
Chand ...	H	5	11
	M	6	19, 24, 34
Chandal ...	H	20	12, 40, 51
	M	59	6, 8, 9, 13, 40
Chander ...	H	5	12, 25
	M	217	1, 13, 16, 17, 26, 28
Chandíla ...	M	44	8, 9
Chaugar ...	M	91	13, 16, 28
Chapre ...	H	17	11, 27, 45
	M	164	9, 12, 14, 44
Chárak ...	H	11	13
Charandási ...	H	101	1, 3, 5, 11, 48, 49
	S	7	4, 49
	M	4	10
Chator ...	M	82	27, 29
Chaudri ...	M	52	6, 27, 51
Chauhán ...	H	157	3, 8, 42, 43, 51
	S	1	12
	M	3,718	D. J. L. M. 18, 19, 44, 45, 49, 51
Cháwlí ...	M	149	6, 24, 25, 27, 51
Chetrámi ...	M	12	17, 25
Chhab ...	H	3	15
	M	79	11, 15, 18, 21
Chhallar ...	M	15	25
Chharimár ...	M	98	11, 12, 24
Chhattar ...	M	79	9, 11, 16, 17, 18
Chhínbá ...	M	377	14, 15, 17, 19, 25, 26
Chirimár ...	H	1	2
	M	18	6, 10
Chishtí ...	M	8,326	P. except 35, 36, 37, 41
Choí ...	M	68	10, 17
Chotia ...	M	35	8, 12, 18
Chugatta ...	M	273	9, 10, 12, 13, 15, 16, 17, 18, 25, 27
Chubra ...	H	6	14, 15
	M	11	10, 16, 24
Dadrae ...	M	40	10, 16, 19
Dádúpanthí	H	459	1, 2, 5, 9, 11, 12, 13, 14, 48, 49, 50
	S	39	10, 12, 48
	M	8	19, 28
Dafiá ...	M	11	50
Dalwán-kám	M	58	5, 13, 33, 43, 45
Dán ...	H	5	9, 14
	M	18	13, 16, 51
Dandí ...	H	11	8
Dángráh ...	M	54	9, 12, 25, 27
Dánje ...	M	33	25, 26
Daríjá ...	M	15	8, 9, 27
Darnáth ...	M	14	15
Darshaní ...	H	21	2, 8, 49
	M	52	1, 10, 16, 17
Darvesh ...	H	19	1, 2, 14
	M	924	L. 1, 8, 10, 11, 43, 44, 51
Dátáshábí ...	H	23	42
	M	13	15, 44
Daurká ...	M	11	51
Dawál ...	H	4	11
	M	113	5, 10, 25, 28
Deswálí ...	M	16	5, 6
Dhakkú ...	M	38	51
Dhalíwál ...	H	8	8
	S	18	12
	M	201	10, 11, 12, 18, 44
Dhamani ...	M	45	12, 13, 14, 17
Dhamrá ...	M	110	21, 26, 27, 50

Names of Sub-Castes.		Persons.	Locality.
Dharár ...	H	11	1
	M	33	9, 12, 17, 28
Dháríwál ...	H	1	1
	M	326	8, 10, 13, 15, 16, 17, 25
Dhaul ...	M	37	14, 17, 27, 51
Dhaunkal ...	M	44	3
Dhillon ...	H	1	33
	S	2	25
	M	731	L. 25, 46
Dhobí ...	M	32	10, 26, 27
Dhodí ...	M	774	M. 1, 9, 10, 13, 15, 17, 46, 51
Dhor ...	M	11	14, 25
Dhúnd ...	H	1	11
	M	53	8, 9, 21
Dhundiá ...	J	20	48, 50
Díndár ...	H	1	9
	M	56	16, 26, 27, 28, 51
Díng ...	M	36	9, 14, 27
Díwáná ...	H	301	12, 13, 45, 48, 49, 50
	S	568	10, 12, 45, 48, 49, 50
	M	16	9, 14
Díwará ...	H	5	11, 45
	S	3	1
	M	13	13, 16, 28
Doáng ...	M	63	9
Dográ ...	H	12	11
	M	243	1, 9, 10, 12, 13, 16, 17, 18, 23, 25
Dúdh-dhárí...	H	24	1
	M	12	9, 18, 24
Dúndal ...	H	2	1
	M	9	1, 21
Faqírsháhí ...	H	17	51
	M	233	19
Fárúqí ...	M	49	23, 28
Fazalsháhi ...	M	13	11, 15
Gadágar ...	H	16	2, 27
	S	2	12
	M	92	8, 13, 25
Gadariá ...	M	56	1, 8
Gadhí ...	H	29	2, 11
	S	2	6
	M	26	15, 18
Gadí-naráin...	M	13	44, 45
Gagar ...	M	269	L. 26, 51
Gaidrí ...	H	22	12, 51
	M	13	13, 26, 34
Gakkhar ...	M	370	15, 16, 17, 25
Galotar ...	M	16	26
Gandárá ...	H	1	1
	M	13	9, 10
Gandu ...	H	3	11
	M	9	16
Gang ...	M	13	11, 15, 17
Gar ...	H	14	5, 51
	M	11	8
Gáríwál ...	H	107	21
	S	3	9, 10
	M	6	12, 17
Garíbdásí ...	H	221	2, 5, 6, 48
	S	41	10, 12, 48
Gashkori ...	M	40	6, 28, 44
Gaur ...	H	7	2
	M	12	1, 39
Gaurí ...	H	194	8, 9
	S	2	45
	M	683	L. 1, 8, 51
Gaznawí ...	M	52	1
Ghakar ...	M	108	17, 18, 19
Ghalote ...	M	18	11
Ghamman ...	M	294	16, 17, 18, 25
Ghaní ...	M	48	10, 16, 51
Ghariáli ...	H	5	5, 45
	M	172	16, 27, 28
Ghorewáhá ...	M	551	10, 11, 25, 44
Ghumhár ...	M	52	14, 15, 25
Gil ...	H	11	1, 5, 16
	S	1	13
	M	1,074	L. 12, 25, 27
Gíláni ...	M	119	12, 15, 25, 28
Gilgo ...	H	23	51
	M	55	17, 26
Girí ...	H	468	5, 6, 8, 12
	S	7	13
	M	82	28

Names of Sub-Castes.		Persons.	Locality.
Gondal ...	H	8	6, 42
	M	1,166	L. M. 3, 18, 51
Goráiá ...	M	452	9, 14, 15, 16
Gorakhnáth ...	H	43	6, 12, 13, 19
	M	5	9
Gormáná ...	M	15	2, 11
Gornang ...	M	44	27
Gosáín ...	H	590	1, 5, 12, 50
	S	5	1, 6, 11, 50
	M	2	9, 19
Granthí ...	H	8	11
	S	36	4, 9, 14
Gujar ...	H	9	2, 27
	M	54	9, 13, 15, 28
Gujrátí ...	H	16	8
	M	1	8
Guláḃdásí ...	H	41	1, 9, 13
	S	66	12, 13, 48
Gurjmár ...	M	464	J. L. 24, 46, 48
Haidrí ...	M	13	L. 19
Hajanwálá ...	M	28	19, 45
Hamdí ...	M	18	4, 16, 18
Handal ...	M	30	51
Hans ...	M	15	1
Háns ...	H	1	9
	M	195	13, 15, 24, 28
Háral ...	H	21	27
	S	2	11, 12
	M	119	16, 17, 44
Hinjrá ...	S	8	11
	M	304	16, 17, 24, 26
Hír ...	H	6	25
	S	1	25
	M	32	17, 23, 24
Hot ...	M	57	28
Husaini ...	S	1	13
	M	313	J. 14, 16, 16
Ichhánathi ...	H	13	1
Jad ...	H	9	9
	M	5	17
Jafri ...	H	17	1, 22
	M	28	14, 16, 33
Jainmi ...	M	14	12, 14, 18
Jajak ...	H	57	27, 51
	M	26	8, 17, 44
Jajohan ...	M	23	27
Jalálí ...	H	6	1, 4, 9
	M	8,412	B. 44, 48, 49, 50
Jali ...	H	2	12
	M	30	8, 51
Jalip ...	M	72	17, 18, 33
Jamáli ...	M	56	50
Jamún ...	M	11	9
Jandal ...	M	66	10, 13, 17, 51
	J	1	15
Jandír ...	M	144	16, 26, 28, 29
Jandrán ...	M	96	13
Jangam-jogí...	H	81	12, 20, 29
	M	49	14, 25
Janjuá ...	H	2	50
	M	1,006	16, 17, 18, 21
Jarmál ...	H	6	11, 47,
	M	9	8, 9, 10, 18
Jasiál ...	S	2	11
	M	77	8, 10, 18, 25
Jaswál ...	M	17	16, 17
Ját ...	H	5	1, 9
	M	390	L. 8, 9, 10
Jatásháhí ...	H	2	1, 5
	M	10	8, 10, 18
Jatoi ...	M	88	25, 27, 28
Jaun ...	M	32	13, 25
Jhakar ...	M	66	12, 15, 28
Jhamat ...	M	48	8, 20, 26
Jhatwál ...	M	12	16
Jholíchak ...	H	21	27
	M	92	24, 25, 26
Jíláni ...	H	2	9
	M	155	9, 10, 12, 13
Jindásháhí ...	H	6	3, 9
	M	13	3, 19
Jíwán ...	M	19	15, 25, 40
Jogí ...	H	809	M. 13, 21, 50, 51
	S	9	50
	M	666	R. 19, 27, 50
Jogí-Ráwal ...	H	132	51
	M	257	51
Johar ...	M	26	25

Names of Sub-Castes.		Persons.	Locality.
Joiá ...	H	4	12
	M	1,026	M. 1, 13, 15, 17
Joriye ...	H	6	27, 45
	M	46	15, 19
Kabírpanthí...	H	38	1, 2, 5, 12
Káchhi ...	M	92	25
Kachhwáyá ...	M	157	5, 15
Kahár ...	M	17	51
Kahl ...	H	9	1, 12, 45
	M	58	10, 15, 51
Káhlon ...	M	67	14, 15
Káisth ...	H	1	51
	M	164	15, 16
Kakezaí ...	M	31	8, 14, 18
Kakrelí ...	S	2	9
	M	39	8, 13, 18
Kakuáná ...	M	22	25
Kalál ...	H	5	8
	M	826	12, 24, 25, 27
Kaler ...	M	107	16, 25, 29
Kalhorá ...	H	3	12, 26
	S	4	11
	M	294	9, 24, 26, 28
Kaliáná ...	H	3	6, 26
	M	14	9
Kálíposh ...	M	860	6, 10, 48, 50
Kalorá ...	M	19	27
Kálu ...	M	31	16, 25
Kamángar ...	M	13	15
Kamboh ...	M	24	16, 19
Kandi ...	H	4	5, 9, 45
	S	3	44
	M	14	25, 51
Kánju ...	M	164	16, 19, 25
Kankar ...	H	1	12
	M	138	3, 16, 25
Kanpárá ...	H	153	2, 5, 13
Kánwán ..	M	50	26, 27
Kapur-khatrí	M	45	9
Karmsháhí ...	M	18	14, 19, 44
Karwal ...	H	8	1
	M	136	3, 12, 14 22
Kashmírí ...	H	2	8
	M	138	15, 16, 25
Kasboh ...	M	14	15
Kasiál ...	M	112	11, 15
Katárí ...	H	40	1, 4
	S	5	17
	M	50	1, 11, 13, 15
Káthwál ...	H	5	1
	M	16	1, 2, 21
Kátib ...	M	11	16
Khákí ...	M	76	21, 27, 28
Khalang ...	M	31	29
Khalífá ...	M	13	16
Khalwárá ...	M	12	50
Khámbrá ...	M	39	16, 25
Khanálídás ...	M	38	21, 27
Khangrí ...	M	26	27, 29
Kharáliá ...	H	6	2
	S	6	12
	M	199	12, 13, 18, 44
Kharl ...	M	390	16, 17, 24, 26
Khatiál ...	M	84	27, 51
Khere ...	H	1	1
	S	1	20
	M	289	14, 15, 23
Khichi ...	M	162	24, 26, 27, 51
Khohár ...	H	1	27
	M	23	13, 24, 29
Khojá ...	H	8	24, 25
	M	107	23, 29, 51
Khokhar ..	H	90	43
	M	6,291	J. L. M.
Khotgar ...	S	2	45
	M	53	11, 12, 15
Khwájá ...	M	139	13, 51
Kingarí ...	M	68	29, 51
Kíral ...	H	1	11
	S	2	13
	M	59	1, 18, 25
Koriá ...	M	20	28
Kukárá ...	S	1	17
	M	386	12, 17, 24, 27
Kunjídár ...	M	22	28
Kurtáná ...	M	22	51
Labáná ...	M	16	11

Names of Sub-Castes.		Persons.	Locality.
Ladhar ...	H	10	9
	S	13	6, 25
	M	131	12, 16, 17, 44
Ladhiáná ...	M	32	26
Láesan ...	H	12	9
Lakeshí ...	M	11	26
Lákho ...	M	34	27
Lálbegí ...	M	141	16, 28
Lalerá ...	M	42	17
Lál Husain ...	M	31	19, 22
Láli ...	M	56	1, 14, 25
Langáh ...	H	13	51
	M	992	L. M. 44, 51
Lángrí ...	M	12	25
Langriál ...	M	109	10, 16, 25
Lár ...	M	171	25, 27, 28, 51
Lodí ...	H	3	45
	S	2	9
	M	314	9, 10, 12, 44
Lohán ...	M	18	12, 15
Lohár ...	H	8	27
	M	21	10, 15
Lol ...	M	21	27
Londí ...	M	130	10, 13, 42
Loníwál ...	H	6	1
	M	10	18, 47
Lorí ...	M	129	28
Lotí ...	H	4	9
	M	50	10
Ludhar ...	H	12	14
	M	250	16, 17, 29
Madárí ...	H	51	2, 3, 45
	M	64,768	P. except 35, 36, 37, 41
Madho-Lál Husain.	M	32	9, 13
Mahbúbshahí	M	54	26
Mahesh ...	M	33	15, 25
Máhí ...	H	3	45
	S	3	11
	M	73	8, 16, 17
Máhígír ...	M	133	11, 14, 15, 16
Majáwar ...	M	3,318	17, 25, 26, 29
Makhanshahí	M	246	27, 28, 29
Makhdumání	M	14	19
Makhdumshahí	M	435	25, 26, 51
Makhianá ...	M	79	24, 26, 51
Maláh ...	S	4	51
	M	27	10, 15, 25
Malak ...	M	191	12, 13, 16, 18
Maláná ...	M	152	26, 27, 28, 51
Malang ...	H	11	51
	S	1	1
	M	2,797	J. 27, 46, 48
Malanhás ...	H	1	10
	M	61	25
Malká ...	M	76	15, 16, 28
Malotre ...	M	69	16
Malwáná ...	M	72	26
Mamerá ...	M	25	26, 27
Mán ...	M	38	26, 49
Manante ...	H	16	9
Mándí ...	H	6	44
	S	2	12
	M	127	1, 10, 12, 16
Mangrá ...	M	23	51
Mangrál ...	M	37	21
Manhás ...	H	7	1, 27, 51
	M	1,354	L. 6, 8, 22
Manj ...	M	1,057	9, 10, 11, 42
Manj-bhattí ...	M	16	15
Mánjhu ...	M	86	1, 19, 27, 31
Maral ...	M	105	19, 28, 51
Marár ...	M	44	17, 25
Marás ...	M	212	9, 10, 15, 25
Marí ...	H	4	2, 51
	S	1	12
	M	21	11, 27
Marthá ...	H	1	2
	S	4	5, 24
	M	36	17, 19, 26
Mashahdí ...	H	3	45
	M	37	12, 26, 51
Mathrás ...	H	6	14, 44
	M	187	9, 14, 18, 44
Maulá ...	S	1	27
	M	58	2, 3, 16, 25
Maulá-Dastgír	M	24	24
Maulá Husain	H	2	27
	M	13	12, 51
Mazhabí ...	H	21	13, 14
Mekan ...	M	53	17, 19, 20
Miáná ...	H	28	16
	M	24	5, 26, 28
Miánsáhib ...	H	9	12
	S	8	44
Mirásí ...	H	3	24
	M	244	8, 9, 27, 51
Mítlá ...	M	74	15, 16, 28
Mochí ...	M	113	28, 51
Modí ...	M	11	6
Mohal ...	M	90	8, 24, 51
Moman ...	M	19	26
Mughal ...	M	2,474	L. 10, 21, 25
Mughal-barlás	M	16	17
Mughlání ...	M	754	9, 17, 18, 44
Muhammadí	M	30	5, 6, 16
Muqímshahí	M	144	9, 10, 12, 44
Muridá ...	M	26	26
Mussalí ...	M	45	16, 17
Mustaqím-shahí.	M	17	17, 50
Nagáí ...	H	24	1, 2, 9
	S	1	9
	M	57	11, 16, 17
Nagárchí ...	H	5	1
	S	2	1
	M	33	1, 13, 26
Naggle ...	M	17	9
Náhar ...	M	38	9
Najumí ...	M	13	9
Námdhárí ...	S	28	13, 27
Nánakpanthí	H	69	3, 10, 12
	S	75	9, 27, 50
	M	53	11, 24, 25
Nángá ...	H	35	1, 3, 5, 9
	S	34	5, 9, 33
	M	249	16, 24, 26
Nangpál ...	M	48	21
Naqshbandí ...	H	6	50
	M	443	L. 6, 9, 48
Nárá ...	M	906	J. 15, 16, 17
Naráiní ...	H	4	12
	M	130	6, 44, 50
Nárdí ...	M	12	44
Náru ...	S	16	5, 11
	M	142	16, 25
Nat ...	M	78	16, 27
Náth ...	H	119	1, 5, 12, 14
	S	1	50
	M	90	8, 15, 51
Naumuslim ...	M	15	13, 16, 44
Naurangshahí	M	57	27
Naushahí ...	H	5	25
	S	2	14
	M	7,116	B. 44, 46, 48, 50
Nazámí ...	M	24	29
Niází ...	M	175	10, 12, 19, 51
Nihang ...	H	4	1, 9, 10
	S	116	6, 9, 12, 18
Níkokárá ...	M	260	20, 25, 26
Nirankárí ...	H	115	5, 26, 48, 50
	S	130	14, 21, 48
	M	9	1, 3
Nirmalá ...	H	189	4, 9, 12, 14
	S	1,680	9, 12, 14, 44, 48
	M	16	14, 25
Nitiánand ...	H	89	1, 50
	M	17	25
Núrí ...	M	71	24, 27
Ojan ...	M	74	51
Pákrahmání ...	M	17	44
Pakrí ...	M	14	9
Pandit ...	M	26	16, 25, 27
Pangá ...	H	4	12
	M	36	2, 3, 15, 27
Panjetá ...	M	12	16
Pánmri ...	H	33	12
Panwár ...	H	9	25, 27, 51
	S	1	12
	M	435	1, 25, 27, 51
Páolí ...	M	14	10, 24
Parhár ...	M	196	24, 27, 28, 29
Parmhans ...	H	8	3
	S	1	50
	M	2	51
Pársái ...	M	62	28
Paswál ...	M	20	2, 11, 16, 45
Pathán ...	M	1,698	J. R. L. M. 44, 51
Patwá ...	M	61	9
Pawár ...	H	10	1, 5
	M	344	9, 15, 16, 25
Phiphrá ...	H	3	19
	M	340	10, 16, 17, 24
Pír ...	M	29	16, 24, 25
Poslá ...	M	43	12, 20, 28
Pothohárí ...	M	56	15
Práin ...	M	35	27
Púrí ...	H	396	1, 4, 5, 9, 12
	S	3	9
	M	51	15, 16, 26, 46
Qádrí ...	H	57	50
	M	6,726	B. 44, 48, 50
Qalandar ...	H	8	49
	M	3,456	3, 5, 13, 19, 24
Qandhárí ...	H	19	1
	M	21	43
Qází ...	M	110	26, 27, 28
Qureshí ...	M	2,685	J. L. M. 1, 6, 44
Rághubansí ...	M	40	1, 2, 51
Rájá ...	H	4	9
	S	2	10
	M	30	10, 13, 27, 44
Rájáshahí ...	M	21	9, 15
Rájpál ...	M	11	1, 10, 21, 47
Rájput ...	M	1,239	J. L. 18, 25, 44
Rámádat ...	H	442	1, 50
	S	1	50
Rámánandí ...	H	241	9, 12, 13, 14, 45
Rámdásí ...	H	108	1, 2, 12, 25
	S	101	11, 12, 27
	M	1	12
Rámke ...	H	17	9, 12
Ramle ...	H	22	29
Rammál ...	H	26	31
	S	1	20
	M	39	13
Rán ...	M	46	16, 19, 25, 51
Randháwá ...	H	15	2, 12
	S	5	11, 12, 14
	M	302	L. 8, 20, 25
Rángráh ...	H	1	2
	M	144	9, 14, 17, 25
Ránjhá ...	M	256	15, 19, 17, 28
Ráshá ...	M	21	8
Ratannáth ...	H	36	9
Ráthal ...	M	29	16
Ráthor ...	H	18	51
	M	16	9
Ráwal ...	H	39	2, 8, 50
	M	69	8, 12, 13, 16
Ráwalpír ...	H	16	33, 51
Rodí ...	H	5	1, 10
	M	66	1, 24, 44, 51
Sábariá ...	H	2	26
	M	66	3, 6, 10, 14
Sádh ...	H	2,982	L. 12, 13, 46, 48
	S	2,175	L. 10, 24, 46
	M	57	16, 19, 26
	J	11	5, 12
Sádh-faqír ...	H	50	13
Sádh-jogí ...	H	19	13
Sádh-nirmala	S	53	17
Sádh-saniásí ...	H	12	13
	S	1	42
Sádh-suthrá ...	H	53	13
Sádhu ...	H	765	4, 10, 16, 18, 39
	S	90	15, 18, 20
	J	4	40
Sádh-udásí ...	H	37	17
Sadí ...	H	5	9
	S	25	25, 26
	M	11	13, 18, 50
Ságí ...	H	1	33
	S	10	6
	M	64	9, 16, 19
Sabáwan ...	H	8	1
	S	17	44
	M	54	13, 16
Sabota ...	M	138	16, 17, 24, 28
Saidártái ...	M	58	1, 10, 17, 18

APPENDIX TO IMPERIAL TABLE XIII.—

Names of Sub-Castes.		Persons.	Locality.	Names of Sub-Castes.		Persons.	Locality.	Names of Sub-Castes.		Persons.	Locality.
Sailání ...	H	1	1	Sháhí ...	H	13	26	Táhar ...	H	1	44
	M	10	21, 45		S	16	10, 44		M	44	9, 13, 19
Saini ...	M	11	9, 19		M	66	4, 10, 16, 17	Tahím ...	H	4	8
Sakhárí ...	H	8	2	Sháh Madár ...	H	5	5, 44		M	70	16, 24, 25, 27
	M	10	16		S	1	25	Tajrá ...	H	13	11
Salehriá ...	H	4	9, 27		M	6,878	J. L. 1, 25, 45	Tánbrí ...	H	3	2
	M	318	15, 16, 17, 25	Sheikh ...	M	383	M. 10, 14, 16		M	58	12, 15, 25, 41
Salotre ...	M	39	1, 15, 18, 19	Sheikh-háshmí	M	89	15, 17, 18, 28	Tanur ...	H	11	1, 34
Samande ...	H	20	20, 44	Shámí ...	H	1,873	1, 2, 43, 48		M	357	1, 12, 28
	M	217	10, 27, 28, 51		S	2	19	Tárar ...	H	1	21
Samrái ...	M	22	10		M	18	19		M	296	16, 17, 19, 25
Samráná ...	H	2	2, 26	Shamsí ...	M	24	27, 51	Telí-thakar ...	H	34	27
	M	58	14, 17, 25, 27	Shibnáth ...	H	14	1, 9, 11, 44		M	25	6, 11, 16, 25
Sanádá ...	H	1	27		S	1	9	Thákrí ...	M	17	9
	S	137	44	Shídí ...	M	73	13, 28, 45, 51	Thamsháhí ...	M	60	11, 19, 25
	M	84	9, 12	Siál ...	M	313	15, 24, 26, 51	Tur ...	H	5	8, 12
Sandal ...	H	19	43	Siddíqí ...	M	86	1, 2, 27, 29		M	871	J. 1, 5, 16, 17
Sangatsabhá	H	7	12, 44	Sikhú ...	M	58	17, 19	Uchchat ...	H	33	5, 12
	S	10	10, 12, 44	Silkhí ...	M	13	1		S	18	9, 25
	M	1	16	Síndhar ...	M	40	9	Udásí ...	H	3,465	P. except 35
	J	7	44	Sindhu ...	H	68	9, 12, 13, 16		S	8,644	P. except 2, 7, 30, 31, 32, 35, 36, 37, 38, 41, 43, 47
Sangráh ...	H	1	1		S	80	10, 12				
	M	155	5, 18, 28, 44		M	2,178	L. 25, 29, 44				
Saniásí ...	H	5,020	B. 44, 49, 51	Sínmár ...	M	73	10, 26, 28				
	S	143	12, 14, 15, 48	Siprái ...	H	2	9		M	37	12, 13
	M	185	14, 19, 27		M	255	16, 17, 25. 20, 27		J	5	10
Saniásigirí ...	H	18	10	Sirichand ...	H	18	11	Ulmái ...	M	18	17, 26
Sant ...	H	19	1	Soharwardí ...	S	1	10	Upárnáth ...	H	132	1
Sapal ...	H	2	2		M	32	17, 18, 46	Uppal ...	H	8	11
	M	72	17, 18, 25	Somrá ...	M	90	17		M	111	9, 14, 44
Sarál ...	H	37	12, 27, 51	Soní ...	M	80	16, 20	Vagan ...	M	14	27
	S	1	11	Soyal ...	H	4	12, 51	Vahan ..	M	185	26, 51
	M	53	10, 27, 44		S	7	10	Vaidántí ...	H	1	8
Sarárí ...	M	147	12, 17, 20, 26		M	245	13, 17, 25, 27		M	86	16, 17, 25
Sarbhangí ...	H	43	3, 6, 49	Subáhkhezí ...	M	118	33	Vaishno ...	H	43	1, 9, 44
	S	12	11, 48	Sufí ...	S	1	9		S	2	9
	M	5	8, 9		M	209	3, 5, 9, 10, 45	Válot ...	M	29	27
Sargáná ...	M	36	16	Sulemání ...	M	16	2, 16	Vangar ...	M	11	51
Sárwán ...	H	19	12, 51	Sundarnagr ...	H	15	12	Variáh ..	H	1	9
	M	53	16, 19, 34	Sundarsháhí	S	10	13, 14		S	35	50
Sárwangi ...	H	17	1, 2, 3, 5		M	9	6		M	225	J. L. 25, 26
	M	10	11	Surajbansí ...	H	6	12, 20, 33	Vasír ...	M	22	24
Sarwi ...	H	28	1, 27		M	5	14	Vehá ...	M	230	51
Satdhárí ...	H	8	9	Surastí ...	H	30	5, 25, 51	Virk ...	M	302	16, 17, 27
	M	20	8		M	7	13, 51	Yalgár ...	M	79	1
Satsáhibá ...	H	10	5, 60	Surí ...	M	111	9, 10, 14, 26	Yusafzaí ...	M	33	6, 11
	S	4	48, 49	Sutbrá ...	H	234	12, 13, 14, 24	Ziudápír ...	M	25	17, 45
Sawántí ...	M	82	9, 15		S	75	10, 22, 24	Minor* ...	H	382	
Sayad ...	M	185	1, 12, 11, 45		M	64	13, 24, 51		S	105	
Sewápanthí ...	H	37	19, 23, 26, 28	Suthrásháhí ...	H	52	12, 26, 48		M	1,137	
	S	71	19, 26, 27		S	86	48	Unspecified ...	H	2,597	
	M	47	19, 45		M	5	48		S	793	
Shahábi-gaurí	M	41	24, 34, 45	Swámí ...	H	287	50		M	18,823	
Sháhgadá ...	M	85	8, 9, 14	Tabqáí ...	M	25	3		J	32	

*DETAIL OF MINOR.

Abhiágat 6, Abrais 1, Abuljar 1, Achhráná 2, Adál 4, Afríd 8, Aghoriá 4, Agníhotrí 8, Aiwáí 8, Alifzí 1, Ali Mohammad 1, Alírá 3, Alkh 7, Allah 1, Almík-sáhib 1, Amardásí 1, Ambáráí 4, Amrotí 4, Anandí 10, Angosháh 3, Antál 6, Antrí 6, Anujá 6, Ará 7, Arthí 2, Ashok 6, Aslí 5, Atú 6, Aujít 1, Aukárnáthí 5, Auliá 1, Aurar 3, Aure 8, Auspál 1, Awankárí 7, Bábá 6, Bachít 2, Bad-goriá 2, Badmán 3, Badohe 10, Bage 10, Bagote 7, Bahiál 1, Baid 3, Baidáwat 4, Bákarmangal 1, Bakarmár 1, Bakwáná 3, Bálázaí 2, Bálbasuá 10, Bamrení 8, Bandechá 5, Bangá 5, Bániá 8, Banjárá 7, Banmáuas 1, Bánslá 6, Bánwál 4, Banwátab 6, Baráq 6, Barelí 1, Baríd 6, Barkbá 4, Barmansháhí 4, Bárwí 10, Báwá-kálu 2, Bechak 3, Bedhár 1, Behlolsháhí 8, Beldár 1, Belí 2, Bhábre 8, Bhagírthí 1, Bhagtí 5, Bhagwál 2, Bhagwánpurí 6, Bhaje 3, Bhalál 7, Bhale 3, Bhandárí 2, Bhandiál 3, Bhangrá 6, Bhanot 5, Bháonáth 4, Bhatrá-Telí 7, Bhatríje 4, Bhígam 3, Bhíngam 7, Bhojkí 4, Bhokabe 9, Bholi 7, Boholsí 7. Bhorbhosiá 2, Bhuchchar 2, Bhúríwála 9, Biás 2, Bihágan 7, Bikhárí 1, Birájá 4, Bodí 6, Bohat 8, Boká 6, Bopárái 8, Brahmbans 1, Brahmdhári 8, Brahmsáhí 4, Brahmvástí 1, Bukansháhí 6, Chakrání 1, Chamarwá 8, Chándíwále 6, Chanor 1, Chatie 2, Cháwle 2, Chhabíldás 1, Chishtiá 8, Choie 9, Chokbá 2, Chorále 7, Dadí 8, Dadpotra 9, Dádugarh 1, Dadwaí 9, Dáhí 5, Dáhrá 2, Dáiá 8, Dákaut 1, Dakhnáwál 2, Dakhne 7, Dalálí 10, Dámgí 8, Damodrí 3, Dandesar 8, Darbán 7, Dargáhí 1, Darkbán 2. Darmál 1, Dasádh 8, Des 6, Dev 1, Devnandí 7, Dhágar 6, Dhakpuj 9, Dham 4, Dhámí 7, Dhandke 8, Dhandolá 1, Dhamiál 3, Dharche 6, Dhasí 5, Dhaun 1, Dhindsá 2, Dhíngrá 2, Dhodrí 10, Dhot 10, Dhotí-mandá 1, Dhotrá 10, Diálnáthí 1, Dínápanthi 1, Dírath 8, Dítarwál 1, Díwat 4, Dokhar 4, Dolat 4, Droch 5, Farídı 6, Galkálá 3, Gamániá 3, Gandá 9, Gangárás 2, Garhán 9, Gariálí 4, Garím 1, Garm-chár 4, Garnár 4, Garwáh 1, Gaur-beri 1, Gawáliá 1, Gawánsí 2, Ghalar 8, Gharál 1, Ghattí 5, Ghísapanthi 1, Ghorcharhe 6, Gobindsingh 2, Gogí 7, Goháliá 5, Gof 1, Goil 1, Gopírái 8, Gosal 4, Gulábsháhí 6, Gurbakhsh 8, Gurjí 1, Guru 8, Habíbsháhí 9, Hafízí 6, Hajám 7, Hamdání 10, Hamzá 2, Hangam 2, Harchand 3, Háru 9, Háshmí 10, Hawárzí 5, Holá 4, Imámí 8, Imámjafar 1, Isrám 8, Jadugar 2, Jágá 1, Jakharwá 6, Jalálí-malang 6, Jaloke 2, Jamwal 3, Jándí 2, Janhal 4, Janjusháhí 3, Jánsháhí 5, Jástar 1, Ját-gil 5, Jathol 8, Jhabel 4, Jhám 3, Jhanbar 2, Jhanjre 6, Jhar 6, Jodh 7, Jotshi 3, Kachání 5, Kákrí 9, Kálíe-brahman 3, Káluká 1, Kálwán 9, Kauaute 8, Kánbar 6, Kandal 7, Kandráná 3, Kandúrí 5, Kunere 1, Káre 8, Karmán 4, Kásam-mái 10, Kathá 8, Katoch 9, Káwá 3, Khajwál 10, Khálsá 10, Khamál 6, Khángí 2, Khatrí 7, Khiljí 4, Kiál 5, Koshal 1, Ladhmán 5, Lahoriá 2, Lakh 8, Lal-hussain 1, Lassan 1, Láthí 4, Latre 2, Lodhrá 2, Lohám 6, Lonbárí 2, Luchá 8, Máchhí 4, Madáhar 6, Magní 4, Magotrí 6, Magrál 3, Mahant 7, Máher 3, Máhi-sáhib 5, Máh-jal 5, Mahmísháh 7, Mair 2, Málí 10, Maliál 8, Malí-sayad 2. Malodí 1, Manan 1, Manbhád 5, Mangal 4, Mangásrá 3, Mauiárá 3, Manol 4, Maroch 8, Maserí 2, Masror 8, Mast 10, Mathrás 1, Mator 4, Mehra 4, Mekh 8, Mele 1, Miánálí 6, Mítal 8, Mohání 5, Momí 1, Mor 8, Mullán 2, Multání 8, Murlí 8, Nágarsháhí 10, Nand 4, Nepálí 5, Niárí 9, Nonárí 8, Olag 4, Páliá 2, Parhár 1, Parkayá 8, Parmalái 4, Parmánandi 3, Parsutí 7, Pattí 2, Payá 1, Phamman 7, Phíká 6, Phosar 8, Pushkarná 1, Qásam 1, Radhnáth 4, Rámánandí 6, Rámráyá 2, Rasulsháhí 5, Rishi 2, Ruhání 5, Sádh-rámdásiá 1, Sagwál 6, Saif-rahmání 6, Sakandrí 6, Sarájí 1, Sardípiá 6, Sársudh 5, Sarupiá 9, Satmon 1, Shekh-galoí 5, Singh-sabhiá 9, Sodhbans 1, Sonkhiá 4, Sultáni 4, Tárak 6, Telí-rájá 2, Torí 5, Udásí-nanaksháhí 5, Ulví 3, Uradnáth 9, Vidiárthí 1.

SUB-CASTES OF CERTAIN SELECTED CASTES—*continued.*

Names of Sub-Castes.		Persons.	Locality.
Jat		4,956,536	H 1,057,932
			S 1,619,408
			M 2,279,158
			J 38
Abahá ...	M	35	12, 23
Abáliání ...	M	49	51
Abdáli ...	M	115	8, 28
Abhál ...	S	18	10
Abí ...	M	519	7, 17, 27, 29, 50
Abráh ...	H	108	8, 11, 14
	M	592	8, 13, 18, 19, 26, 28, 51
Abrí ...	H	14	16
	S	2	51
	M	1,125	27, 28, 29, 51
Abrín ...	M	277	51
Achahá ...	M	269	29, 51
Achhál ...	H	659	6, 11, 14, 25
	S	59	1, 48
	M	308	15, 20, 23, 24, 51
Achláná ...	M	118	28
Aohrá ...	H	36	12, 13
	M	531	9, 10, 15, 16, 18, 19, 25
Achrál ...	M	19	19
Ad ..	M	212	13, 17, 29
Adái ...	H	1	12
	M	57	12
Adan ...	H	88	4
Adarkar	S	11	48
Adham ...	H	46	19
Adhárí ...	H	5	11, 25
	S	3	5
	M	72	13, 23
Adhí ...	H	17	9, 11
	S	6	48
	M	13	12, 27
Adhíán ...	H	18	9, 19
	M	499	26, 27, 29, 51
Adhrá ...	H	3	1, 10
	M	223	27, 28, 29
Adhwál ...	H	697	4, 9, 12, 13, 14, 25
	S	5	9
	M	288	13, 18, 27, 28 44, 46
Adláná ...	M	61	51
Admál ...	H	9	9
	S	64	6
	M	20	16, 51
Adní ...	H	14	2
	M	1	25
Adoháná ...	M	1,327	27, 28
Adolí ...	M	55	28
Agálí ...	H	15	3, 25
	M	113	25, 28
Agar ...	M	118	12, 15, 19, 25, 26, 28
Agarwál ...	H	84	1, 9, 10, 12, 15, 27
	S	2	11
	M	160	1, 10, 13, 27, 28
Agbíán ...	H	45	6
	M	13	27
Agwál ...	M	18	11, 14
Ahál ...	H	15	2, 15
	S	269	9, 11, 12
	M	10	15, 27
Ahand ...	M	18	25
Ahang ...	M	201	24
Ahir ...	H	1,509	6, 9, 11, 12, 13, 15, 16, 24, 43, 46, 51
	S	1,143	9, 12, 14, 16, 17, 19, 27, 45
	M	2,647	9, 10, 12, 14, 16, 18, 19, 23, 24, 25, 27, 29, 44
Ahláwat ...	H	7,473	1, 3, 4, 12, 19, 31, 39, 49, 51
	S	9	5
	M	26	2, 4
Ahler	M	33	9
Ahlúwáliá ...	H	5	10, 48
	S	132	10, 12, 13, 17, 51
	M	3	10
Ábúláná ...	H	7,534	4
Ahwá ...	M	17	14, 24
Ai ...	H	65	4
Aidoo	S	31	48
Aidwál	S	20	42
Ajaká ...	M	59	19
Ajáli ...	H	4	10
	S	26	44
	M	9	25, 26
Ajarái ...	M	79	15, 27, 44, 50
Ajhál ...	M	59	20, 24
Ajli ...	H	1	44
	S	1,134	44
	M	25	11, 17, 51
Ajrá ...	H	17	31
	S	306	10, 25
	M	276	14, 20, 27, 29
Ajrál ...	H	2	9
	M	15	20
Ajwál	H	15	2
	M	6	27
Akáli ...	H	2	9, 18
	S	28	48, 50
Akar ...	H	52	9, 10, 25, 48
	S	248	6, 9, 25, 48
	M	18	11
Akerá ...	H	103	6
	M	239	23, 25, 26
Akhrá	S	1	26
	M	272	13, 16, 26
Ako ...	M	47	28
Akor ...	M	22	51
Alada ...	H	12	19
	S	4	3
	M	4	15
Alán ...	H	3	49
	S	1	13
	M	29	11
Alekí ...	S	8	27
	M	3	14
Alí ...	M	1,497	9, 12, 17, 19, 24, 26
Aliálí ...	H	28	1
Alkorá ...	S	43	16
Alo ...	H	1	27
	M	180	10, 22
Aloní ...	H	33	10, 11, 51
	S	19	11
	M	122	10, 11, 25, 26, 48
Alpá ...	S	26	25
	M	221	26, 27
Alpiál ...	M	88	20
Alsí ...	H	1	49
	M	36	11, 26
Altá ...	M	486	23
Alvi ...	S	11	2, 15
	M	633	25, 27
Alwál ...	H	228	9, 10, 30
	M	61	6, 14, 23
Alwár ...	H	2	30
	M	182	9, 29, 51
Amán ...	H	2	25
	S	17	12, 25, 27
	M	7	13
Amár ...	S	4	19, 48
	M	78	17, 26
Amiál ...	H	2	15, 49
	S	20	9
Amir ...	H	60	2, 12, 27
	S	10	40
	M	130	19, 25, 26, 29
Amrál ...	M	138	18, 20, 25
Amwáná ...	M	111	27
Anál ...	H	90	1, 2
	S	2	49
	M	110	2
Anáná ...	H	47	1, 33, 39, 48
	M	396	24, 27, 48, 51
Anandí ...	H	1	10
	M	66	18
Anárá ...	H	63	28
Anbarí ...	H	26	16
	M	16	12, 19
Anbhál ..	H	3	9
	M	29	18
Anchaláná ...	H	3	2, 9
	S	20	12, 48
And ...	S	2	10
	M	37	12, 13
Andar ...	H	41	1, 16, 25
	S	6	5, 25
	M	641	17, 19, 26, 27, 28, 29, 51
Andhí ...	H	157	8, 15, 16
	S	41	9, 10, 13, 19, 25
	M	32	11, 51
Andlo ...	S	24	9
Ando ...	H	354	6
	M	21	16
Andolá ...	M	23	14, 15, 27
Angar ...	S	6	27
	M	61	51
Angí ...	H	2	19, 24
	S	23	12
Aniá ...	S	3	9
	M	228	16
Anjal ...	S	180	9, 11, 13, 47
	M	54	9, 11
Anjan ...	H	140	2, 3
	S	87	11
Anjatr ...	M	47	16, 19
Anjbái ...	M	96	51
Ankaráh ...	H	30	16
Anli ...	H	91	3
Anojah ...	M	31	27
Anotrá ...	M	838	23
Ansári ...	M	654	24, 25, 27, 29,
Anrám ...	H	82	1
Antál ...	H	5,671	2, 4, 6, 9, 33, 48, 49
	S	1,347	5, 6, 25, 39, 48
	M	716	2, 3, 4, 5, 6, 24, 48
Antar ...	M	2,365	23, 27
Antwál ...	H	37	2, 48
	S	7	48
Annái ...	M	3,105	28
Anwál ...	H	94	9
	S	14	9, 10, 34
	M	167	9, 13, 19, 26, 27
Anwán ...	H	165	1, 12
	S	20	12
	M	173	16, 28
Apár ...	H	3	8
	M	14	9
Ar ...	H	22	2, 49
	S	2	9
	M	216	10, 17, 25, 28
Arab ...	S	84	10
	M	112	6, 17, 27, 29
Aráín ...	H	277	9, 11
	S	128	9, 11, 13, 25
	M	2,492	9, 12, 13, 23, 26, 27, 29, 51
Arak ...	H	433	9, 10, 25, 39, 48, 50
	S	255	9, 48, 50
	M	54	10, 25, 44, 49
Aránjá ...	H	14	10
	S	3	10
Arar ...	H	3	1, 10
	S	61	10, 16
	M	1,858	19, 20, 24, 26
Arawí ...	M	48	27
Arbál ...	H	65	6
	M	16	20, 27
Arbání ...	S	15	25
Arbí ...	H	12	10, 47
	M	1,119	11, 25, 26, 28, 29
Ardhádhí ...	S	46	9, 19, 25, 45
	M	3	11
Argan ...	S	11	9
	M	10	27, 46
Arí ...	H	18	11
	M	124	9, 24
Ariách ...	H	14	11
	S	126	11
	M	22	11
Aríká ...	M	45	23
Arjí ...	S	1	9
	M	55	24, 27
Arkal ...	H	24	9
Arkhar ...	H	180	10
	M	8	16, 28

Names of Sub-Castes.		Persons.	Locality.
Armal ...	M	50	29
Armáni ...	M	11	10, 23
Arní ...	M	72	11, 29
Arora ...	H	2	9
	S	43	9,11
	M	1,511	17, 20, 21, 23,25, 26, 27
Aroríkhel ...	M	34	23
Aru ...	H	48	1, 11, 48
	S	12	44, 48
	M	26	11, 48
Arwál ...	S	4	19
	M	169	19, 27
Arwídogar ...	M	82	16
Áryá ...	H	3	2
	M	625	13, 20, 27, 51
As ...	M	14	18
Asal ...	S	8	13
	M	143	12, 13, 17
Asám ...	M	27	28
Asar ...	H	153	9, 16
	S	1	25
	M	1,911	19, 23, 25, 27, 28
Asboni ...	M	67	51
Ashtál ...	M	99	51
Asf ...	M	569	17, 19, 25
Asír ...	M	289	28
Askhará ...	S	17	17
Aslí ...	M	28	13, 18, 19,
Aso ...	M	205	16, 17 25, 26
Aspál ...	H	7	1, 12, 24
	S	94	12, 48, 50
	M	18	17, 48
Asrám ...	M	1,158	23, 25, 28, 51
Astar ...	M	628	16, 18, 19, 26
Astoráh ...	H	68	16
Aswál ...	H	3	2, 16
	M	19	4, 17
Atákh ...	M	837	23
Atal ...	H	766	8, 9, 11,39
	S	712	11, 25
	M	322	5, 11, 13, 18
Atar ...	H	8	47, 48
	S	4	25
	M	107	21, 25, 27, 29
Ataráh ...	H	401	28
Atarkhel ...	M	31	25
Atarmá ...	S	15	48
Athán ...	H	76	4
	S	2	9
	M	1,080	27, 29
Athwál ..	H	237	1, 8, 9, 10, 15, 25, 44, 49
	S	2,463	9, 10, 13, 16, 17, 18, 44, 49
	M	3,850	L. M, 10, 12, 44, 51
Atián ...	H	1	10
	S	6	27
	M	19	9
Atrá ...	H	1	8
	M	2,162	19, 26, 28, 51
Atran ...	H	4	48
	M	500	51
Atreawáchál	H	151	4
Attar ...	S	1	10
	M	981	17, 23, 24, 25, 51
Atwál ...	H	103	1, 6, 9, 10, 39
	S	582	11, 19, 25, 51
	M	37	6, 9, 19
Atwán ...	S	4	48
	M	12	9, 10, 46
Atwár ...	H	11	48
	S	1	10
	M	746	9, 17, 29, 48, 51
Augar ...	S	364	48
Augh ...	M	266	18
Augrá ...	H	1	24
	S	96	9, 48
	M	1,331	19, 23, 26, 28, 29
Aujale ...	H	154	1, 8, 11, 39, 49
	S	1,452	20, 49
	M	962	9, 13, 27, 28, 49, 51
Aujaryá ...	H	27	49
	M	16	49
Aujhanrá ...	M	705	16
Auki ...	H	1	33
	M	18	19
Aulá ...	H	21	48
	S	7	48
Aulakh ...	H	1,158	1, 9, 10, 15, 17, 44, 48, 50
	S	12,673	J. 1, 4, 5, 16, 17 24, 25, 27, 48, 49, 50
	M	4,486	15, 16, 17, 23, 24, 28, 29, 50
Aulhán ...	H	13	2, 12
	S	170	9
	M	74	27, 46
Aumáli ...	S	32	20
Aunak ...	H	12	9
Aunchalá ...	S	2	48
	M	80	51
Aunjha ...	M	64	51
Aur ...	H	12	8
Autará ...	M	1,912	28
Awal ...	H	21	1, 9, 13
	S	5	4, 25, 48
	M	80	10, 20, 46
Awán ...	H	47	8, 10, 16, 44
	S	73	6, 13, 27
	M	21,098	L. R. M. 12, 44, 51
Awár ...	M	1,108	9, 19, 23, 26
Awármal ...	H	92	4
Ayar ...	S	106	9, 17, 25, 51
	M	151	19, 27
Bábá ...	H	78	5
Bábal ...	H	392	2, 5, 30
	S	134	2, 5, 11
	M	23	12, 17
Babarwán ...	S	14	5
Bábbar ...	H	3	5
	S	9	6
	M	5,257	29
Bábeki ...	M	16	17
Bábhar ...	M	82	17, 27
Babranak ...	S	22	25
Báchal ...	H	1,027	1, 5, 6, 16, 48
	S	404	6, 33, 48
	M	63	6
Báchar ...	H	529	1, 2, 6, 10, 16
	S	510	11
	M	35	5, 10, 15
Bachárái ...	H	136	1, 4
Bachrí ...	H	814	1, 2, 5, 10
	S	298	10
Báchhí ...	H	37	48
	M	1	48
Bachiá ...	H	229	1, 5
	S	187	6, 14
Bachtá ...	S	626	48
Bád ...	H	77	1, 10, 27, 44
	S	290	10, 15
	M	4	15
Badái ...	S	22	5, 22
Badal ...	H	70	1, 6, 32, 50
	S	325	6, 9, 12, 25, 44, 50
	M	25	6, 10, 14, 41, 50
Badaljí ...	H	14	6
	S	103	5, 12, 45
Badalsí ...	H	170	6
Badán ...	H	495	1, 2, 5, 6, 15, 48
	S	414	5, 6, 11
	M	1,814	9, 18
Badániá ...	H	429	1, 2, 5
Badár ...	H	571	1, 2, 10, 34
	S	461	5, 44
	M	134	15
Badartiá ...	H	2	48
	S	292	48
	M	21	48
Badbral ...	S	38	48
Bado ...	H	210	11, 25
	S	135	1, 9, 25
	M	2	13
Badech ...	H	47	48
	S	1,176	48
	M	10	48
Bad Gújar ...	H	1,605	2, 3, 4, 5, 30, 48
	S	1	48
Badh ...	H	1	1
	S	1	6
	M	17	17, 51
Badháí ...	H	15	1
	S	14	6, 33
	M	19	17
Badhál ...	H	84	1, 2, 50
	S	1,070	50
	M	209	17, 22
Badhan ...	H	216	5, 10, 17, 30, 48, 49
	S	84	10
	M	424	5, 10, 21, 27
Badhár ...	H	199	1, 2, 5, 48
	S	41	25, 48
	M	251	17
Badhí ...	H	1	2
	S	14	6, 25
	M	23	6, 23
Badhián ...	H	23	4, 5, 39
Badhna ...	H	15	3, 5
Badhor ...	H	16	2
	S	2	27
	M	86	27
Badhráo ...	S	39	6
Badhú ...	H	5	5
	M	171	15, 17
Badhwár ...	H	150	2, 4, 49
Badiálí ...	M	1,173	6, 21
Badkar ...	H	2	7
	M	86	6, 23
Bádle ...	S	38	6, 25
Badrá ...	H	24	5
	M	15	6, 27
Badsará ...	H	684	1, 2, 3, 48, 49
Badwál ...	H	123	1, 6, 30, 49, 50,
	S	43	12, 24, 44, 49 50
	M	2,406	14, 23, 28, 51
Badwán ...	M	44	6
Bagáh ..	S	11	8
	M	502	2, 27
Bagáná ...	S	28	27
Bágar ...	H	85	48
	S	599	48
	M	21	48
Bagbálol ...	S	159	6
Baghbán ...	H	50	5
Bághe ..	H	2,913	1, 4, 5, 6, 8, 9, 25, 48
	S	314	6, 48
	M	25	6
Bághwá ...	M	15	14, 17
Bágí ...	H	43	5, 6, 10
	S	2	48
	M	2,900	14, 17, 27
Bagír ...	H	99	1, 12
	S	5	5
Bagojáí ...	M	46	10, 14
Bagrá ...	H	550	5, 10, 13, 32
	M	2	14
Bagráhtí ...	H	378	1, 17
	M	21	44
Bágrí ...	H	1,109	1, 2, 6, 10, 12, 25, 33, 45, 49, 51
	S	1,532	6, 10, 12, 25, 44, 45, 49, 50
	M	18,070	15, 16, 18, 27, 44
Bagsarwá ...	H	109	1, 2
Bagwál ...	H	7	14
	M	514	14, 21, 27
Bahál ...	H	2,027	1, 2, 4, 5, 10, 31, 48
	S	1,251	5, 9, 10, 17, 26
	M	16	8
Báhan ...	H	135	1, 3, 4
	S	1	45
Báhar ...	H	371	1, 9, 49
	S	1,036	8, 11, 12
	M	753	3, 15, 27, 51
Báhe ...	S	184	48
Bahráwal ...	H	873	1
Báhrí ...	H	43	1, 14,49
	S	34	44, 45
	M	1,868	29, 51

SUB-CASTES OF CERTAIN SELECTED CASTES—*continued.*

Names of Sub-Castes.		Persons.	Locality.
Báí ...	H	2	6
	S	164	16
	M	867	10, 27, 28
Baigal ...	S	43	48
Bains ...	H	2,133	10, 11, 13, 17, 39, 40, 43, 44, 48, 50
	S	9,286	7, 8, 9, 10, 16, 25, 34, 48, 49
	M	1,515	5, 9, 10, 15, 48
Bairí ...	H	1	48
	S	669	48
	M	9	48
Bajá ...	H	42	1
	M	7	45
Bajál ...	H	10	15, 41
	S	52	1, 5
Bájan ...	H	67	1, 2, 5
	S	29	6, 27
Bajárí ...	H	1,419	1, 2, 4, 5, 40, 48
	S	146	10, 45, 48
	M	295	23, 26, 48
Bajant ...	H	59	48
Bajho ...	H	1,751	1, 14, 16, 25
	S	1,419	25
	M	9	14
Bají ...	H	63	1, 2, 4, 30
	M	101	15, 26
Bajíra ...	H	38	2
Bajohal ...	H	63	38
Bajon ...	H	311	1, 6, 48
	S	89	2, 6, 25, 48
	M	176	26
Bajran ...	H	56	30
	S	4	24
	M	265	2, 9, 27
Bájre ...	H	88	10, 25, 48
	S	95	27, 48
	M	644	48
Bájwá ...	H	6,065	4, 5, 6, 9, 10, 17, 20, 39, 44, 48, 50
	S	13,650	5, 6, 10, 12, 15, 16, 17, 19, 20, 24, 25, 44, 48, 49, 50
	M	6,956	L. 1, 6, 10, 23, 27
Bajwál ...	H	19	51
	S	35	24, 44
	M	43	14, 44
Bakhár ...	H	93	10, 16
	M	161	28
Bakrál ...	H	2	10
	S	7	6
	M	73	28, 51
Bákrí ...	H	522	6
	M	403	23, 27
Bal ...	H	947	5, 6, 10, 11, 14, 15, 16, 17, 44, 46
	S	3,912	1, 5, 6, 10, 11, 12, 16, 17, 19, 25, 48
	M	714	5, 8, 11, 14, 15, 17, 44, 46, 48
Bálá ...	H	2,237	1, 2, 25, 50
	S	161	1, 6, 26, 50
	M	202	14, 17, 20, 46
Baláde ...	H	303	1, 48
Balágal ...	S	201	6
Balágat ...	H	117	6
	M	15	6
Balágan ..	M	199	6
Baláhar ...	H	1,931	2, 4, 5, 39, 49
	S	17	49
Baláhí ...	H	2	41
	S	3	1
	M	16	14, 27, 44
Bálak ...	H	83	4, 10, 44
	M	121	23, 26
Balál ...	H	20	4 5, 49
	S	4	45
	M	232	14, 23, 28
Bálán ...	H	938	2, 3, 4, 5, 6, 10, 30, 48
	S	248	10, 48, 49
	M	458	6, 9, 26, 44
Balang ...	H	1,695	5, 11 15, 16, 48, 50
	S	2,316	6, 11, 25, 45, 48
Balaserí ...	H	618	2, 4
Balát ...	H	26	6
Baldián ...	H	12	48
	S	7	48
Balgar ...	H	67	15, 17, 39
	S	15	17
	M	292	15, 17
Balhorí ...	H	334	2, 6
	S	5	33
	M	103	6, 51
Bálí ...	H	685	1, 3, 6, 27
	S	84	6, 12, 45
	M	702	23, 26, 27, 28
Bálián ...	H	592	4, 5, 6, 10, 33
	M	43	10, 27
Bálmhí ...	M	15	26
Balo ...	H	206	1, 10, 49
	S	91	49
	M	90	17, 49
Baloch ...	M	167	20, 24
Baloda ...	H	107	48
Balrán ...	H	12	1
Balre ...	H	11	1, 5, 33, 44, 46
	S	164	44, 48
	M	6	48
Balsarí ...	H	64	6
	S	236	6
Balwán ...	H	236	1, 3
	S	2	6
	M	4,741	20, 29
Bámal ...	H	19	1
	S	145	1, 27
	M	10	17
Bamariyá ...	H	20	48
Banal ...	H	36	3
Banáná ...	H	5	1, 40
	S	29	1, 6, 22, 29
Banás ...	H	418	1, 5, 15, 39
	S	12	4, 33
	M	1,017	4, 10, 15, 21
Banchharí ...	H	46	1, 3, 44
Bandáh ...	H	2,808	1
	M	109	27
Bandal ...	H	107	6, 16, 45
	S	1,819	1, 6, 9, 10, 44, 46, 48, 49
	M	968	9, 10, 14, 15, 28, 48
Bandan ...	H	128	1
	M	9	14
Bandar ...	H	688	10, 15, 16, 17, 44, 48
	S	2,289	17, 23, 48, 49
	M	5,703	9, 10, 14, 15, 16, 17, 20, 23, 44, 48, 51
Bandhejí ...	H	45	17, 46
	S	11	17, 20
	M	1,466	14
Bandhíro ...	M	15	6
Bandí ...	H	48	6, 10, 33
	S	6	6
	M	38	10, 27
Bandíchá ...	H	544	11, 16, 45, 50
	S	137	49, 50
	M	5	17
Bándo ...	H	14	1, 5
	S	133	50
	M	12	15
Bándoí ...	H	1,159	2
	S	53	6
Bandol ...	H	27	5, 39
Bandrol ...	M	13	23
Bandsál ...	H	527	2, 6, 45
Bang ...	H	241	2, 33, 45
	S	14	50
	M	99	6, 14, 50
Bangalá ...	H	2,657	2, 9, 33, 46, 48
	S	272	27, 48
	M	16	23, 46
Bángar ...	H	3,773	2, 5, 16, 29, 48
	S	148	5, 6, 44, 48
	M	448	9, 27
Bángat ...	H	1	31
	S	63	11
Bángí ...	H	187	2, 10, 15
	M	275	26, 27
Bangiál ...	H	383	1, 16, 18
	M	586	18
Bangorí ...	H	79	1, 30
Bangrída ...	H	164	2, 30, 49
Bángrilá ...	H	56	1, 3
	S	51	10
Bángrú ...	H	44	48
	S	55	48
Bangú ...	H	47	13, 34
	S	1,818	9
	M	654	9, 11, 27
Bánhal ...	H	82	48
Bánhoá ...	H	322	48
	S	2	48
Banhwál ...	H	311	3
	M	10	5, 15
Bániá ...	H	183	1, 2, 5, 6, 10, 15, 40, 42
	S	78	5, 12
	M	29	1, 15
Baniál ...	H	405	1, 2, 5, 6
	S	13	6
Banidár ...	H	1	49
	S	427	25
	M	140	17
Banídat ...	H	48	1
Banídí ...	H	93	1, 30
Bánil ...	H	148	1
Banírá ...	H	11	7, 30
	M	290	14, 15, 27
Banís ...	S	18	4
Baníwál ...	H	3,721	1, 2, 3, 8, 12, 30, 45, 48, 49, 50
	S	2,521	1, 13, 14, 34, 45, 48, 49
	M	1,266	1, 28
Banjan ...	H	82	12
	S	8	4
Banjárá ...	H	193	1, 27
Banjí ...	M	42	15
Banjútá ...	H	96	1, 24
Bankián ...	H	84	4, 6
	M	1,620	16, 17
Báno ...	H	195	1, 2, 5, 6, 14
	S	594	1, 10, 44, 48
Bánon ...	H	299	49
	M	280	17
Bánowáliá ...	H	24	5, 30
Bánoyá ...	H	31	48
Bans ...	H	18	6
	S	1,097	6
	M	432	48
Bánsal ...	H	1,671	1, 5, 6, 12, 14, 33, 39, 48, 49
	S	1,679	5, 6, 9, 10, 48, 49, 51
	M	89	6
Bansanwál ...	H	541	1, 5, 6, 49
	S	67	1, 5, 6
Bánsarí ...	H	116	5, 6, 48
	S	239	6, 48
	M	403	27
Bánsí ...	H	142	48
	S	847	48
Bansráo ...	H	99	48
	S	233	48
Banswár ...	H	1,640	1, 5
Bánte ..	H	1	48
	S	1,400	48, 51
	M	70	10
Banthán ...	H	10	39
	S	21	51
Banwála ...	H	310	48
	S	1	48
Banwán ...	H	1,610	48
	S	81	48
	M	8	14, 48
Bára ...	H	2,527	1, 2, 4, 5, 12, 30
	S	207	1, 10
	M	1,073	15, 17, 26, 27, 51
Bareg ...	H	110	1, 10, 45
	S	127	10, 12, 33
	M	21	10, 14
Baráh ...	H	168	1, 2, 6
	S	108	10, 16
	M	773	51
Baráich ...	H	577	10, 44, 45, 48, 50
	S	975	12, 44, 45, 48, 50
	M	60	45, 48, 50

Names of Sub-Castes.		Persons.	Locality.
Barak ...	H	773	1, 2, 4, 10, 39
	S	268	9, 25, 45
Barál ...	H	226	1, 2, 11, 12, 33, 35, 48
	S	6	42, 45
	M	1,257	11, 23, 26, 27, 48
Baran ...	H	121	1, 5, 44, 48
		7,070	44, 48
	M	1,718	17, 23, 28, 44
Barang ...	H	761	1, 5, 6, 10, 44, 45, 50
	S	1,314	1, 10, 44, 45, 50
	M	348	1, 6, 43, 44, 50
Barár ...	H	276	1, 15, 48
	S	758	9, 16, 48
	M	1,815	15, 23, 26, 27, 28
Barára ...	H	47	1, 48
	S	4	48
	M	465	15, 17, 26, 51
Barchan ...	H	21	4, 5
	M	2	6
Bardáí ...	H	637	1, 4
Bardal ...	H	13	1, 3
Bardán ...	H	14	5
Bardár ...	M	460	18
Bargán ...	H	50	48
Bargí ...	H	189	6, 33
	S	8	33
	M	32	5, 23
Bárhar ...	H	16	45
	M	126	14, 23
Barhat ...	H	8	1, 2
	M	53	17
Báriá ...	H	1,513	1, 5, 44, 48
	S	1,165	1, 12, 48
	M	654	9, 11, 14, 16, 23, 44, 48
Bariál ...	H	17	17, 20
	S	1	20
	M	657	14, 17, 20, 23, 26
Barián ...	H	28	1, 20
	S	110	6, 10, 43
	M	265	17, 20
Barjiá ...	H	24	2, 5
	S	6	5
Barjiál ...	M	62	20
Bark ...	H	619	2, 11, 44
	S	411	5, 6, 9, 44
	M	303	1, 10, 26
Barkasí ...	H	19	1
Barkát ...	H	26	1, 48
	S	106	6
	M	2	20
Barkhán ...	S	43	48
Barmá ...	H	110	32
	M	1	14
Bárne ...	S	17	5
Baroch ...	H	146	6
	M	55	27
Baroda ...	H	11	48
Baroge ...	M	596	14, 23
Barolá ...	H	1	2
	M	558	6, 10, 27
Baror ...	H	923	5
	S	56	17
Barota ...	M	215	51
Barsání ...	M	57	6, 26, 46
Barsarí ...	H	77	2
	M	24	11
Bart ...	H	20	50
	S	80	50
	M	217	26, 50
Barwála ...	H	73	14
	S	1	48
	M	236	13, 14, 48
Barwí ...	H	1,217	D. 44, 48
	S	849	9, 27, 48
	M	70	48
Baryár ...	S	79	48
	M	22	20
Bassh wál ...	H	9	1, 2
	S	4	6, 34
Basain ...	H	93	4, 14, 25
Básal ...	H	28	1, 5
Básan ...	S	295	14
	M	976	5, 26
Basátí ...	H	287	3, 5, 6, 33, 34, 45, 48
	S	1,609	6, 11, 25, 33, 48
	M	196	6, 23, 48
Basdá ...	S	16	5
Baser ...	H	152	1, 2, 4, 10
	S	22	10, 44
	M	1,048	26, 27, 40
Basethá ...	H	90	5, 40
Basgal ...	H	8	6
	S	5	48
Basí ...	H	779	5, 10, 25, 45, 46, 48
	S	3,642	1, 6, 10, 11, 12, 25, 45, 50
	M	115	6, 13, 26, 44
Basiál ...	H	222	4, 11, 46
	M	14	14
Básíní ...	M	203	10
Baskí ...	H	30	12
	S	587	12
Basor ...	H	22	2
	S	12	5
	M	172	12, 27
Basrá ...	H	857	10, 16, 17, 42, 44
	S	3,307	5, 10, 11, 14, 15, 16, 17, 19, 44
	M	4,417	1, 9, 10, 14, 15, 16, 17, 18, 44, 46
Baswál ...	H	47	1
	S	6	21
	M	3	20
Bat ...	H	353	8, 15
	S	177	5, 6, 33
	M	279	9, 14, 27, 44
Bátar ..	H	234	4, 5
	S	31	1
	M	21	5, 10, 26
Báṭh ...	H	2,442	6, 9, 10, 17, 24, 45, 46, 48, 50
	S	4,724	6, 9, 10, 11, 15, 16, 17, 20, 24, 27, 45, 48, 50
	M	3,550	9, 13, 14, 16, 17, 23, 26, 27, 46
Baṭhiár ...	H	37	1, 4, 44
	M	304	15, 27, 45
Batiál ...	H	814	9
	S	1,429	1, 5, 11, 50
	M	219	14, 50, 51
Baṭoe ...	H	3	48
	S	624	48
	M	32	48
Batráí ...	H	3	38, 50
	S	6	50
	M	16	50
Baṭwál ...	H	1,896	2, 15
	S	28	20, 36
	M	1,182	1, 14, 20, 27, 28
Batwár ...	H	1	2
	S	12	48
	M	114	48
Báwaliá ..	S	191	5
Báware ...	H	555	1, 2, 4, 15, 17, 30
	S	210	12, 17, 44
	M	1,141	17, 26, 44, 51
Báyal ...	H	1	5
	S	440	25
Báyar ...	M	231	17, 27
Bedan ...	H	438	5, 39, 48
	S	6	48
Bedechí ...	S	297	10
Bedhá ...	H	348	1
Bedwán ...	H	163	1, 5, 33, 48
	S	569	33, 48
	M	1,976	48
Begí Ráe ...	H	1	44
	S	6	1
	M	32	17, 44
Begnál ...	H	104	1
Ber ...	H	478	12, 27, 50
	M	3,048	9, 10, 17, 27, 50
Besrí ...	H	42	33
	S	159	25
Bhábí ..	H	45	48
Bhábíú ...	H	182	1, 5, 12
	S	36	51
	M	190	20, 23, 27
Bhábra ...	H	1,067	1, 46
	S	2	24
	M	2,560	15, 17, 27
Bhadah ...	M	254	26, 51
Bhadál ...	H	48	5
Bhadlál ...	H	484	1, 10
	S	1	48
	M	564	6, 17, 27
Bhádon ...	H	690	1, 12
	M	6	1
Bhádrí ...	S	185	5, 48
	M	552	15, 17
Bhadro ...	H	1	30
	S	531	1, 12
	M	118	1, 20, 27
Bhagáí ...	H	509	3
Bhagat ...	H	1,146	1, 9, 20, 48
	S	5	44, 48
	M	1,062	4, 16, 17, 20, 27, 28, 48
Bhagiál ...	H	17	39, 49
	M	149	17, 27
Bhágna ...	H	199	1, 5
	S	3	44
Bhagor ...	H	4,654	1, 2, 3, 4, 10, 44, 46, 49
	S	256	1, 9, 10, 24
	M	397	27, 46
Bhágú ...	H	660	1, 7, 14, 16, 33
	S	1,550	1, 12, 17, 24, 25, 33, 48
	M	163	1, 15, 27, 51
Bhagwál	M	12	48
Bhagwat ...	H	116	4, 48
	S	5	4, 48
	M	55	15, 27
Bháiá ...	M	13	51
Bhail ...	H	2	46
	S	17	11
Bhainíwál ...	H	775	1, 5
Bhaje ...	H	25	5
	M	121	1, 23, 27, 51
Bhajwál ...	H	33	24, 48
Bháká ...	H	3	48
	S	4	48
	M	41	6, 10
Bhákar ...	H	400	1, 2, 27, 30, 46, 48, 49
	S	8	6, 20, 44
	M	1,343	6, 20, 51
Bhakaria ...	H	11	1
	S	11	17
	M	12	20
Bhakarwál ...	H	26	10
	M	2,480	20, 51
Bhál ...	H	855	1, 2, 5, 6, 14, 46
	S	145	10, 24, 34, 44
	M	263	17, 26, 27
Bhaláha ...	H	24	1
	M	310	17
Bhálak ...	M	28	20
Bhalán ...	H	216	4, 6, 48
	S	88	48, 49
	M	321	5, 9, 27, 48
Bhalar ...	H	307	5
	S	444	6, 25
	M	105	4, 5
Bhalonka ...	H	55	1
Bhalot ...	H	77	2, 5
	S	94	1
Bhálotiá ...	H	139	1, 12, 30
	S	7	6
	M	242	11
Bhalúriyá ...	H	115	48
Bhalwán ...	H	7	1, 2
	M	25	2
Bham ...	M	74	10, 14, 23, 26
Bhamáí ...	H	28	1, 33
Bhamál ...	H	9	1
	S	3	1
	M	1	22
Bhammar ...	H	6	48
	S	32	6, 15, 48
	M	95	17
Bhan ...	H	344	1, 11, 12, 44
	S	298	1, 20, 44
	M	363	1, 12, 20, 44
Bhanb ...	M	1,452	23

SUB-CASTES OF CERTAIN SELECTED CASTES—*continued.*

Names of Sub-Castes.		Persons.	Locality.
Bháubar ...	H	54	48
	S	2	48
Bhanbare ...	H	90	49
Bhandar ...	H	185	5, 6
Bhandwá ...	H	26	6
	M	1,299	13, 14, 20, 46
Bhangar ...	H	297	1, 2, 10, 17, 31
	S	618	6, 9, 10, 11, 12, 25, 34, 50
	M	1,206	6, 10, 17, 23, 28
Bhangí ...	H	40	5, 6, 25, 45, 49
	S	36	12, 24, 44
	M	61	26
Bhangiál ...	H	444	5, 10
	M	1,349	20
Bhangú ...	H	798	5, 10, 46, 48, 49, 50
	S	6,464	1, 4, 5, 6, 10, 11, 12, 15, 16, 19, 45, 48, 49, 50, 51
	M	1,827	10, 15, 17, 18, 26, 46, 48
Bhangwálí ...	H	18	30
	S	28	44
	M	3	6
Bhangiáu ...	H	444	48
	M	1,349	48
Bhankaryá ...	H	287	1, 3, 4, 5
	M	256	51
Bhánkú ...	M	28	1
Bháno ...	H	1,126	1, 2, 12
	S	3	1
	M	324	28
Bhanolí ...	H	999	1, 10, 48
	S	1,471	10, 48
	M	115	48
Bhánoriya ...	H	2	48
	S	294	48
	M	21	48
Bhánri ...	H	4	48
	S	15	48
Bhanswál ...	H	1,207	1, 2, 3, 4, 5, 12
	S	80	5, 12
	M	6	26
Bhanwár ...	H	208	1, 2, 3, 4, 10, 15, 33
	S	111	1, 10
	M	37	5, 17
Bháo ...	H	25	48
	S	21	48
Bhápoṭ ...	H	53	48
Bhar ...	H	306	1, 19, 34
	S	86	1, 48
	M	137	17, 51
Bhára ...	H	334	1, 2, 3, 10, 48
	S	846	9, 44, 48
	M	470	6, 10, 17, 20, 26, 40, 42, 48
Bharán ...	H	8,980	1
	S	2	5
	M	142	10, 23
Bharánjí ...	S	169	10
	M	1	20
Bharáo ...	M	33	48
Bhárdwáj ...	H	7	14, 39
	S	267	25
Bharg ...	S	130	6
Bhárí ...	H	243	1, 24, 48
	S	55	48, 51
	M	253	14, 23, 26
Bharkú ...	S	11	48
Bharle ...	H	53	21
	S	25	26, 42, 48
	M	79	25, 26
Bharmán ...	M	23	26, 33
Bharmár ...	S	74	11
Bharnwál ...	H	55	1, 4, 30
Bharocha ...	S	487	6
	M	86	17, 51
Bharog ...	M	89	26
Bharwána ...	H	263	1
	M	448	17, 20, 26, 51
Bhas ...	H	14	15, 30
	S	44	10
	M	637	14, 20
Bhat ...	H	17	2, 27, 30
	S	3,322	12, 13, 14, 48
	M	1,292	6, 9, 20, 26, 28, 44, 48, 51
Bhátan ...	H	105	1, 2, 6
	S	2	48
	M	850	33, 50, 48
Bhaṭere ...	H	365	8, 14
	M	252	17, 51
Bhaṭhal ...	H	385	6, 10, 33, 39, 48
	S	2,120	6, 10, 24, 39, 48
	M	333	10, 26, 46, 47, 48
Bhaṭhan ...	H	86	5, 48
	S	114	48
Bhátiá ...	S	22	48
Bhaṭoí ...	M	419	11
Bhaṭrárí ...	H	18	1, 41
	M	369	51
Bhaṭṭewad ...	H	216	15, 16
	S	1,507	14, 15, 17, 25
	M	3,731	14, 15, 16, 51
Bhaṭṭewál ...	H	662	1, 2, 4, 5
	S	19	5, 14
	M	1,026	9, 51
Bhaṭṭí ...	H	1,483	1, 5, 6, 10, 12, 13, 16, 17, 25, 33, 44, 48, 49, 50, 51
	S	2,189	1, 6, 10, 11, 14, 15, 17, 18, 19, 20, 24, 25, 33, 48, 50
	M	41,529	P. except (3, 4, 9, 23, 24, 25, 44, 46, 48, 49 50, 51)
Bháṭú ...	H	122	48
	S	3	48
	M	633	27, 51
Bhawálí ...	H	7	48
	S	32	48
Bhawán ...	M	508	23, 26
Bhawániá ...	H	9	48, 49
	S	53	48, 49
	M	582	27
Bháyal ...	H	575	48
	S	178	48
Bhechar ...	M	1,516	23
Bhede ...	H	311	48
	M	11	48
Bhero ...	H	20	1, 10
	S	5	10, 33
Bhíl ...	H	10	1, 34
	S	4	1
	M	373	23
Bhindí ...	M	64	11
Bhod ...	H	62	4, 49
	S	68	38
	M	359	23
Bhodwál ...	M	268	23, 26
Bhogal ...	H	38	2, 48
	S	277	10, 45, 48
	M	2	48
Bhogar ...	H	16	5
	S	2	6
Bhogat ...	H	541	2, 31
	M	1,262	27
Bhoiál ...	H	11	14
	S	283	7, 10, 12, 26
Bhojia ...	M	11	17
Bhojkí ...	H	9	48
	S	1	48
	M	1	48
Bhok ...	H	17	10
	S	300	10
	M	872	10, 11, 18, 23, 26
Bhokan ...	H	27	10, 30
Bhokáre ...	H	381	1, 5, 33
	S	26	33
	M	225	10, 23
Bhokat ...	H	350	4, 5
Bhokhal ...	M	96	23
Bhokre ...	H	381	48
	S	26	48
	M	225	48
Bholá ...	H	328	2, 9, 49
	S	224	9, 51
	M	439	14, 17, 20, 27, 44, 51
Bholiá ...	H	95	1, 49
Bholí Ráe ...	H	4	6
	S	47	5, 45
	M	172	11
Bhoman ...	H	14	48
	M	4	48
Bhon ...	S	49	6, 10
	M	7,010	17, 18
Bhondá ...	H	11	2, 49
	S	30	5, 45, 49
	M	764	14, 17, 28
Bhondiál ...	S	215	6
Bhoniá ...	H	67	6
Bhonkar ...	H	71	2, 49
	M	53	23
Bhor ...	H	1,199	2, 4, 5, 6, 10, 31, 48
	S	161	6, 48, 50
	M	491	9, 16
Bhosan ...	M	127	10, 11, 17
Bhosariá ...	S	49	6, 17, 24
	M	49	17
Bhot ...	H	644	5, 10, 49
	S	1,063	5, 10, 14
	M	584	10, 17, 23, 49
Bhoṭián ...	H	466	27 50
	S	4	20, 50
	M	170	20
Bhullar ...	H	1,107	10, 11, 44, 45, 46, 48, 50
	S	24,983	J. L. 1, 19, 20, 33, 45, 47, 48, 49, 50, 51
	M	4,358	1, 6, 11, 12, 13, 14, 16, 17, 23, 27, 29, 44, 45, 48, 49, 50, 51
Bhúndal ...	S	14	48
Bhundher ...	S	24	48
Bhunsalá ...	M	26	48
Bhuṭṭá ...	H	291	10, 17, 48, 50,
	S	1,349	9, 14, 48, 50
	M	16,772	14, 16, 17, 18, 20, 23, 28, 29, 46, 48, 51
Bhuṭṭar ...	H	1,283	11, 46, 49
	S	2,098	1, 11, 14, 27, 38, 49
	M	2,526	L. 12, 22, 23, 46, 50
Biáno ..	S	9	5
	M	291	1
Bijná ..	M	14	49
Bilon ...	H	182	5
Birk ...	H	77	11, 44, 48
	S	4,618	10, 11, 12, 45, 48, 49
	M	9,738	27, 48, 50
Birm ...	M	32	48
Bírwál ...	H	1,019	1, 3, 5
Bisálí ...	H	116	51
Bíshnoí ...	H	186	12, 48
Bobak ...	H	1	5
	M	285	14, 15, 17, 51
Bodáh ...	H	34	30
	S	19	51
	M	965	28
Bodí ...	H	100	30
	S	8	27
Bodlá ...	S	57	48
Boh ...	H	249	4, 5, 15, 49
	S	382	5, 10, 12, 15, 51
	M	2,669	17, 27, 25, 51
Boháti ...	H	11	48
Bole ...	H	719	5, 12, 48, 49
	S	1,031	18, 48
	M	1,349	5, 10, 14, 15, 27, 28, 44, 48
Bolo ...	H	77	6, 7, 10
	S	3	5
	M	35	1
Boním ...	M	769	12, 27
Bonkal ...	H	124	48
	S	1	48
	M	1	46
Bonsre ...	H	128	5
Bopá Rái ...	H	1,767	9, 10, 15, 45, 46, 48, 50
	S	7,458	11, 14, 15, 17, 45, 48, 49, 50
	M	1,779	10, 13, 14, 15, 17, 27, 51
Bor ...	S	457	6, 11, 38
	M	6	17, 46

Names of Sub-Castes.		Persons.	Locality.
Borák ...	H	16	33
	S	2	33
	M	4	33
Bore ...	H	3,186	1, 5, 10, 33, 48
	S	1,396	1, 10, 15, 48, 49
	M	120	3, 14, 15, 48, 49
Boríwál ...	H	66	14
	S	502	10
Brahman ...	H	819	1, 2, 4, 10, 49
Brahmi ...	H	9	15, 24
	S	10	10, 48
	M	453	11, 48
Brijiá ...	H	11	5
Búṇṭí ...	S	7	48
	M	10	48
Chách ...	H	6	18, 25
	S	8	18
	M	1,408	18, 19, 20
Chachákar ...	M	775	27
Cháchal ...	H	30	48
	S	9	48
Cháchar ...	H	365	1, 2, 3, 9, 30
	M	3,324	13, 16, 20, 26, 27, 28, 29, 51
Chachhán ...	H	132	1
	M	733	19, 26, 28, 29,
Chadá ...	H	69	18
	S	86	6
	M	477	L. 20, 29
Chadhán ...	H	108	6
	M	9	9
Chadhár ...	H	160	6, 8, 9, 13, 17
	S	45	6
	M	17,748	12, 13, 14, 17, 18, 23 to 26, 29, 51
Chágal ...	H	6	16
	S	653	6
	M	485	9
Chábar ...	H	567	49
	S	6	49
	M	656	51
Cháhari ...	H	1,388	1 to 5, 9, 10, 12
	S	3,895	9, 10, 11, 14
	M	3,007	6, 25, 28
Chábil ...	H	12,234	D. J. L. 20, 31, 39, 45, 49, 50
	S	17,579	L. 1, 4 to 7, 9, 12, 18, 19, 20, 25, 33, 44 to 46, 49, 50, 51
	M	6,914	L. 1, 6, 9, 19, 24, 25, 27, 44, 46, 49, 51
Chahurwál ...	S	13	51
Chaji ...	H	109	9, 38
	S	888	9, 10, 11, 25, 45
	M	981	25, 27, 29
Chakal ...	H	121	6
	S	44	6
Chakrál ...	M	40	19
Chakrí Khel	M	35	23
Chala ...	H	2	33
	M	37	19
Chamal ...	H	24	4, 33
	S	2	14
	M	509	21, 27
Chamiál ...	S	10	6, 10
	M	653	13, 15, 20
Chamkate ...	H	122	16
	M	20	16
Chaná ...	M	69	23, 27, 29, 51
Chanáb ...	H	2	15
	S	2,146	14, 15
Chanan ...	H	193	15, 27
	M	3	18
Chanayá ...	M	55	12
Chanchal ...	H	90	6
Chand ...	H	176	1, 12, 19, 51
	S	115	10, 17, 25, 49
	M	7,694	12, 13, 16, 25, 26, 27
Chandáliá ...	H	34	6
	M	43	12
Chandan ...	H	4	6
	M	4,100	19, 24
Chandarasiá	H	15	4
Chander ...	H	16	2, 49
	M	612	17
Chandiál ...	S	11	51
	M	1	42
Chandor ...	H	70	8, 10, 16
	S	37	12, 16, 17
	M	549	11, 16, 26
Chandrán ...	H	16	2, 49
Chandrár ...	M	24	24, 51
Chandu ...	M	64	27
Chandwáná ...	M	179	19, 51
Cháne ..	H	109	2, 3, 10, 12
	S	670	5, 12, 25, 46
	M	1,123	28, 29
Chang ...	H	196	11
	M	7	10
Changrí ...	H	253	4, 9, 10, 12, 25, 45
	S	673	5, 9 to 13, 45, 46
	M	3,570	M. 9, 12, 13, 17, 18, 19, 23, 44, 46
Changu ...	S	231	6
Channár ...	M	87	23, 26
Chapál ..	H	83	5
	S	30	12, 45, 46
	M	10	10
Chapparwál ...	H	15	12
Charáin ...	H	34	4
Charál ...	H	74	1, 2, 25, 33
	S	48	25
	M	364	13, 18, 20, 25, 27, 29
Cháregar ...	M	15	23
Chariá ...	H	1179	1
Charmará ...	M	51	26
Chárni ...	M	17	12
Charsatí ...	H	6	12
	M	430	51
Chartor ...	M	21	6, 14
Cháru ...	M	54	23
Chasá ...	M	80	16
Chashho ...	M	42	26
Chashmá ...	M	48	13, 26
Chasmí ...	S	67	6
Chaspál ...	M	502	18
Chat ...	S	11	51
	M	55	19, 25
Chatak ...	H	492	4
Chatal ...	S	4	6
	M	113	26
Chatar ...	H	183	1, 4, 9, 10, 12
	S	174	6, 9, 14, 15, 27
	M	1,911	9, 13, 15, 19, 20, 25, 26, 28
Chateri ...	H	33	2, 6, 9
Chatiál ...	M	15	11
Chattarwál ...	H	28	30, 51
Chatthá ...	H	564	5, 8, 10, 12, 16, 17, 33, 44
...	S	2,105	1, 6, 9, 10, 12, 13, 14, 17, 18, 25, 34, 49
...	M	4,667	13, 15 to 21, 25, 26, 27, 28, 44
Chaughatta ...	H	105	16
	S	53	16
	M	4,201	M. 13, 17, 18, 19, 23, 51
Chauhán ...	H	5,313	L. 1, 2, 6, 25, 30, 33, 45, 49
	S	1,422	1, 12, 18, 25, 33, 46, 49
	M	8,213	6, 13, 17, 18, 19, 23, 27, 28, 29, 33
Chávak ...	M	54	27
Cháwalá ...	H	10	9, 12, 17
	S	40	3, 6, 25
	M	517	12, 27, 28, 46
Chedi ...	H	44	8, 10
	M	531	1, 18, 20, 27, 29
Chehallá ...	M	231	23
Chell ...	M	16	26
Cheniá ...	H	8	6
	M	151	16
Chhab ...	H	61	17
	S	44	25
	M	341	23, 28
Chhacherok ...	H	73	6
Chháchharyá	H	13	9
Chhag ...	H	8	11
	S	340	11
Chháhá ...	H	163	1, 9
	M	383	51
Chháharwál ...	H	179	1
Chhajechám	M	62	26, 48
Chhajír ...	H	117	1
Chhalá ...	H	11	6
	S	916	6, 9
	M	60	26
Chhami ...	H	44	8, 17
	S	134	9, 17, 19
	M	28	6, 13, 23
Chhán ...	H	253	2, 9, 18, 25
	S	277	12, 15, 16, 27
	M	3,415	13, 16, 20, 27
Chhand ...	M	51	16
Chhangal ...	M	38	9
Chharwál ...	H	14	49
	S	382	19, 46
Chhathá ...	M	184	18
Chhewah ...	M	15	23
Chhiál ...	H	191	1, 2, 5
	S	117	1, 14
	M	322	15, 20
Chhillar ...	H	1,512	2
Chhimba ...	H	32	16
	S	792	12, 19
	M	2,075	11, 17, 18
Chhiná ...	H	265	10, 11, 12, 15, 45
	S	3,266	1, 10, 11, 13, 15, 25, 44
	M	19,135	L. M. 11, 23, 44
Chhod ...	H	19	1
Chhoriá ...	H	20	2, 12
	S	4	51
	M	629	12
Chhoto ...	H	16	2
	S	5	4
	M	145	1, 13
Chhunerái ...	H	57	6
Chiá ...	M	496	23
Chichá ...	M	1,467	13, 18
Chikárá ..	H	2,079	2, 4, 5, 11, 12
	S	443	5, 9, 11, 44
	M	868	4, 11, 27, 29, 44, 51
Chilar ...	H	152	49
Chilkí ...	H	15	2
Chimá ...	H	3,793	J. L. 18, 19, 25, 45, 50
	S	10,828	J. L. 5, 19, 25, 33, 44, 49, 50, 51
	M	17,632	L. 12, 18, 19, 20, 21, 25 to 28, 44, 46, 50
Chimár ...	H	134	2, 13, 45
	S	108	1, 10, 18, 35
	M	1,030	13, 18, 24, 25, 27, 28
Chináwah ...	M	146	28
Chishti ...	M	112	17, 23, 26
Chohang ...	H	14	9
...	S	14	15
Chohar ...	H	300	2
...	S	15	1, 12
...	M	1	13
Chokar ...	H	408	2, 10, 12, 30, 33, 42, 44
	S	1,668	6, 10, 12, 25, 44
...	M	4,191	11, 14, 25
Cholakh ...	M	31	19
Choli ...	H	410	1, 5, 9, 39
	S	2	12
	M	65	29
Choná ...	H	15	1
Chondráni ...	H	1,044	2
	M	49	23
Chong	H	359	9, 10, 50
	S	663	1, 9, 12, 13, 49, 50
	M	29	10, 46
Chopal ...	H	7	2
	M	5	18

SUB-CASTES OF CERTAIN SELECTED CASTES—*continued.*

Names of Sub-Castes.		Persons.	Locality.
Chopre	H	160	1, 3, 49
	S	255	11, 46
	M	12	6, 9
Choráne	H	24	3, 12
	M	40	11, 26
Chorang	H	54	1
Chorás	H	69	9, 19
	M	1,438	13, 17, 27, 44
Chozan	H	17	9
	M	511	28, 51
Chuchak	M	26	18
Chughwál	M	37	23
Chuki	M	214	51
Chunia	M	17	9, 12
	S	20	1
Chura	H	24	8, 51
	M	32	8
Churwáhah	M	38	12
Chutiá	S	16	46, 50
	M	462	12
Dabbo	H	61	39
	S	25	25
	M	191	20, 24, 26, 29
Dabdál	H	1,315	1, 5, 6, 48
	S	28	5, 49
	M	173	1, 5, 48
Dábdár	M	288	28
Dábhojá	S	1	12
	M	67	19
Dabír	H	71	5, 44
	S	18	5, 14, 48
	M	3	10, 19
Dablán	H	198	49
Dablí	H	66	48
	S	5	48
	M	22	19, 44
Dabot	H	1,171	2, 12
	M	26	25
Dádá	H	36	18, 33
	M	146	9, 28
Dadál	M	24	18
Dadán	H	88	1, 8
	S	14	1, 48
	M	34	1
Daddí	H	1	44
	S	144	6, 9
	M	24	9, 15
Dádoná	H	254	6
	M	40	29
Dádpotra	M	404	27, 29
Dádrá	H	3	30
	S	16	16
	M	303	6, 10, 11, 26
Dádram	H	11	1, 25
Dáduka	H	55	1
	M	211	26, 27
Dadyál	H	14	12, 30
	S	1	10
	M	29	10, 25
Dág	S	59	6, 11
	M	440	27, 29
Dágal	S	4	9
	M	285	16, 17, 18, 19
Dagán	H	17	2, 5
Dágar	H	9,694	1, 2, 3, 4, 5, 30, 32, 49
	S	160	10, 15
	M	363	13, 14, 16, 27
Daggi	H	14	2, 3
	M	3	15
Dagh	M	12	17, 25
Dagharwál	H	44	1
Dagrá	H	19	1, 12
	M	144	16
Dáhá	H	14	25
	M	2,370	8, 28, 29
Dáhal	H	335	1, 2, 9
	M	6	4, 20
Dáhar	H	144	6, 7
	S	220	10
	M	4,391	M except (25), 11, 16, 17, 20, 29, 50
Dahdes	H	9	18
	M	95	28
Dahegi	M	37	11
Dáhíl	H	366	1, 9, 12
	S	65	5, 9, 25
Dahír	H	10	12
	S	411	16
	M	250	19, 24
Dáhlí	H	277	1, 9, 13
Dáhoi	H	26	9
Dahráiá	H	3	34
	M	18	29
Dáiá	H	2	25
	S	298	9
	M	161	27, 29
Dailwáh	H	450	48
	S	138	25
Dáit	S	4	20, 48
	M	20	20
Dájwán	H	39	1, 25
	M	72	25, 29
Dáká	H	161	1, 9
	S	12	4, 9
	M	908	11, 12, 16, 26, 27
Dákar	H	198	1, 4, 5
	M	24	28
Dákhal	M	84	13, 26
Dakhaná	H	14	12
	S	1	6
	M	1,700	28, 29, 51
Dakwár	S	18	48
Dál	H	25	2, 46
	S	31	12, 48
	M	1,002	10, 26, 27, 28, 29, 51
Daláh	H	53	1, 2
	S	2	14
	M	182	17, 29
Dálaka	H	7	1
	M	79	17
Dalál	H	15,331	1, 2, 3, 4, 5, 16, 21, 31, 48, 49
	S	108	1, 9, 16
	M	83	2, 5, 19, 21
Dalán	H	51	1, 5, 28
	S	140	24
	M	483	16, 17, 18, 19, 46
Dalar	H	11	25
	S	6	6, 12
	M	55	20, 29
Dalerá	H	4	10
	S	499	25
Dalewál	H	14	1, 48
	M	147	15, 44
Dálgi	H	680	48
	S	54	48
	M	8	48
Dalla	H	212	1, 9, 18, 48
	S	1,200	6, 10, 17, 48
	M	2,168	16, 17, 24, 26, 27, 28
Daloi	H	7	48
	S	15	12
Dalot	M	167	9, 18, 44
Dalt	S	238	12, 14, 15
Dalwá	H	57	1, 6
Damal	H	723	2, 3, 4, 5, 48
	S	540	9, 10, 12, 48
	M	57	19, 21
Damán	H	6	48
	S	20	15, 48, 51
	M	5	13, 44
Damára	H	114	48
	S	5	21, 48
	M	331	22, 28
Damás	H	8,458	2, 3, 4, 5, 49
	M	50	2, 3, 29
Damb	M	102	26
Dáná	H	2	25, 45
	S	23	1
	M	95	17, 19, 20
Dándá	H	1,846	1, 5, 7, 12, 34, 48
	S	113	5, 6, 25, 48
	M	34	1, 10, 48
Dandal	H	81	5, 14, 29, 44
	M	180	17, 20, 26, 27, 29, 49
Dandalwál	H	9	5, 24
	M	16	26
Dándar	H	11	2, 12
	S	122	12, 13
	M	552	17, 27
Dandasá	H	114	2, 5
Dandíwál	H	1,362	1, 30, 32, 49
	S	1,055	1, 5, 12, 15, 46, 48
	M	6	11, 46
Dándmán	H	1	33
	S	14	5, 49
Dandolí	H	45	1, 6, 24, 48
Dandor	S	39	9
	M	43	29
Dandu	H	13	18
	S	4	47
	M	4	13
Dang	H	819	1, 2, 5, 9, 30, 49
	S	24	12, 19
	M	276	14, 17, 18, 19, 26, 51
Dangal	H	37	1, 4
	S	5	14
	M	38	11
Dangar	H	33	30
	S	88	6, 9, 10, 14, 16, 27
	M	1,189	13, 24, 27, 29, 51
Dániá	H	9	1
	S	23	9, 14
	M	325	14, 28
Daniál	M	423	4, 12, 21, 24
Dáníwál	H	8	3
	M	4,581	20
Dánorá	S	5	9
	M	11	18
Dáns	H	152	3, 48
	S	8	48
	M	105	48
Dansar	M	105	16
Danterwál	H	411	48
	M	10	9, 25
Danwáná	H	10	1
	M	176	28, 29
Dapoti	H	279	48
Dapta	H	14	48
Dár	H	127	1, 12, 18, 48
	S	130	14, 48
	M	1,368	14, 16, 27, 47
Daráian	H	4,390	48
	S	236	48
Darájh	H	8	1, 48
	S	33	48
	M	2,165	16, 17, 26, 29
Daral	H	675	4, 31
	S	8	13
	M	147	10, 19, 23, 28
Daram	H	71	49
	M	30	28
Daráná	H	101	2, 3, 48
	S	55	48
	M	123	1, 48
Darang	H	19	5
	S	4	13
	M	2,330	18, 20, 23, 27, 28
Darhan	H	60	1, 16, 30, 39
Dariá	H	42	2, 9, 25
	S	175	16
	M	307	9, 12, 51
Darka	H	142	1, 9, 16, 48
	S	221	1, 9, 25, 48
	M	10	29
Darkará	H	2	48
	S	11	48
Darochí	H	13	16
	M	284	17, 44
Darsi	H	5	10, 12
	S	37	25
	M	594	16, 19, 27, 29
Daruna	H	8	12
	M	6	13, 17
Darwál	H	44	1, 10
	M	75	19, 50
Darwán	S	1	29
	M	12	48,
Daryái	S	11	10
	M	214	19, 29
Dasádal	H	15	8
	S	2	48
Dasiál	H	9	12
	S	33	1, 13, 27
	M	21	11, 16
Dasrát	H	8	8, 48
	M	258	18, 29

Names of Sub-Castes.		Persons.	Locality.
Dassíwál ...	H	293	4, 11, 12, 25,
Datarlí ...	H	17	2
	S	27	9
	M	125	29
Datas ...	H	261	4
Dathwán ...	H	64	2, 5
	S	8	13, 16
	M	6	20
Dati ...	M	42	13, 18
Datoná ...	S	48	48
	M	30	16
Datrá ...	H	48	9, 30
Daurá ...	H	18	30, 45
Dawál ..	H	71	11, 12
	S	50	6, 9, 11, 18
	M	148	14
Dawáná ...	M	1,291	6, 19, 27
Dawári ...	H	71	12, 18
	S	50	48
	M	148	11, 16, 17
Dáyá ...	H	1,184	1, 5, 27
	S	41	9
	M	121	23, 27, 28
Debái ...	H	79	9, 10
	S	6	6
	M	50	1, 10, 12
Dedah ...	H	69	8
	S	33	10
	M	210	10, 27, 28
Dedar ...	H	5	1
	S	8	6
Dedwál ...	H	1	45
	S	1,449	1, 30, 49
Deg ...	H	42	1, 12
	S	10	4, 7
	M	55	2, 8
Degar ...	H	17	2, 9
	S	16	9
	M	34	27
Dehiá ...	H	16,637	2, 3, 4, 5, 11, 25, 49
	S	77	5, 10, 48, 49
	M	92	4, 9, 12, 28
Dehmí ...	H	1	8
	M	52	9
Dehr ...	H	1	9
	S	44	25
	M	143	9, 19, 27
Del ...	H	18	25
	S	101	9
	M	533	11, 12
Delon ..	H	49	8, 12, 34
Demáni ...	H	2	48
	M	955	29
Den ...	H	1,372	1, 49
	M	3	29
Dendí ...	H	306	16, 17, 25
	S	72	25, 30, 48
	M	223	23, 29
Dendwál ...	H	34	1
Dengri ...	H	11	9
Deoli ...	H	9	11
	S	1,635	11, 48
Deorá ...	H	38	1
	M	7	13
Deotá ...	S	70	16
	M	38	1, 29, 44
Der ...	H	538	16
	S	1	17
	M	557	15, 19, 26, 29
Dersa ...	H	72	6
	S	8	48
Desi ...	H	24	8, 9
	S	450	9, 25, 48
	M	512	9, 10, 12, 19, 23, 29
Deswál ...	H	9,624	D. except (7) 8, 31, 33, 48
	S	98	5, 48
	M	507	2, 5, 18, 27
Det ..	H	6	9, 44
	M	898	19, 28
Dev ...	H	725	6, 9, 10, 13, 16, 17, 40, 49
	S	4,770	1, 6, 9, 10, 12, 14, 16, 17, 49
	M	1,679	L. 12, 19, 49
Deval ...	H	113	4, 5, 44, 45, 48
	S	3,544	10, 11, 12, 15, 17, 30, 48, 50
	M	1,226	9, 10 12, 15, 17, 48
Devar ...	H	29	4, 9
	S	16	25
	M	49	9, 29
Dewá ...	H	16	9, 10, 12, 44
	S	202	19
	M	38	19, 48
Dewán ...	H	2	49
	S	282	12
	M	226	10, 18, 20, 49
Dewat ...	S	8	12
	M	69	9, 19
Dhá ...	H	38	9, 10
	S	189	9, 25
	M	3,603	15, 24, 26, 51
Dhabbí ...	H	1	44
	S	191	9
	M	134	13, 19, 29
Dhábbn ...	M	63	17
Dhadá ...	H	38	8, 9
	S	169	9, 15, 33, 40
	M	558	10, 11, 17, 26
Dhaddar ...	M	247	23
Dháddi ...	H	15	5, 10, 18, 29
	S	89	10, 12, 24, 27
	M	1,388	13, 16, 17, 24, 28
Dhadherá ...	S	21	10, 17
	M	841	13, 17, 18, 27, 28
Dhágá ...	H	28	25
	S	372	6, 9
Dhágal ...	M	57	17
Dhaggarí ...	H	251	1, 6, 9, 51
	S	324	5, 25
	M	1	45
Dhágí ..	H	6	9
	S	48	44
	M	40	23
Dháháli ...	H	79	1
Dhái ...	H	1,009	4, 5, 6, 10, 21, 49
	S	494	6, 9, 12, 44
	M	84	13, 27
Dhaind ...	H	29	48
	S	1	48
Dháíwál ..	S	131	11, 12
Dháj ...	S	30	10, 17
	M	784	27, 51
Dháká ...	H	3,181	1, 2, 4, 12, 49
	S	8	1, 48
	M	2,682	19, 25, 51
Dhákal ...	H	386	1, 2, 12, 30
	M	188	24
Dhakalíwál ...	H	56	1, 49
	S	643	49
Dhákan ...	H	11	1, 2, 12
	M	10	14
Dhákar ...	H	695	2, 4, 5, 31, 43
	M	12	26
Dhákki ..	H	35	4, 51
	M	147	26
Dháku ...	H	79	1, 2, 24, 48
	S	6	24, 48
	M	833	9, 17, 24
Dhal ...	H	5,587	1, 2, 5, 8, 9, 18
	S	1,014	1, 10, 18, 46
	M	147	13, 25, 26
Dhálam ...	M	65	9, 13
Dhalán ...	H	1,131	8, 10, 45, 48
	S	1,635	9 to 12, 24, 44, 48
Dhálans ...	H	32	3
Dhaláti ...	S	19	1, 9
	M	60	33
Dhaler ...	M	29	19
Dhallu ...	H	1,834	1, 9, 16, 47, 51
	S	5,361	9, 12, 19, 27
	M	5,099	13, 16, 17, 19, 23, 27, 48
Dhalwál ...	H	1,745	J. 1, 2, 25, 45, 46, 50
	S	35,343	J. 1, 14, 44, 45, 50, 51
	M	561	10, 11, 14, 46, 50
Dhalwán ...	H	121	2, 8, 9, 30
	S	425	3, 25
	M	445	5, 12, 13, 14, 25
Dham ...	H	51	2, 4, 10, 44
	S	55	8, 10, 14, 48
	M	26	11, 13, 21
Dhamál ...	H	66	1, 12, 13
	S	11	6
	M	103	5, 9, 42, 47
Dhamán ...	H	66	4, 25
	S	53	10, 14, 19, 48
	M	13	23, 26, 27, 29
Dhamar ..	H	18	4
	M	1,258	M. 23
Dhámi ...	H	723	8, 9, 10, 16, 44
	S	975	6, 10, 44, 45
	M	9	10, 17
Dhamiál ...	H	41	1, 13
	S	712	6, 45
	M	1,595	14, 19, 21
Dhamián ...	H	19	6, 9, 50
	S	42	20, 51
	M	10	9
Dhamrái ...	H	28	4, 8, 47
	M	305	19, 51
Dhan ...	H	421	5, 9, 14
	S	788	1, 12, 44, 46
	M	28	9, 13, 14
Dhanda ...	H	2,362	1, 3, 6, 10, 48, 49
	S	6,907	6, 10, 19, 48
	M	742	18, 28, 44, 48
Dhándal ...	H	173	1, 9, 17, 33, 39
	S	219	9, 10, 44, 48
	M	1,687	14, 15, 16, 27, 28, 29
Dhándarie ...	H	48	50
	S	677	13, 45, 50,
	M	187	9, 50
Dhandás ...	H	18	48
	S	417	10, 17, 25, 48
	M	50	48
Dhandholá ..	H	1,410	1
	S	577	48
Dhándí ...	H	1,290	1, 2, 3, 5, 8, 9, 50
	S	431	11, 12, 14, 19, 45, 48
	M	187	10, 12, 19, 27, 44
Dhandiál ...	H	365	1, 10, 48
	S	305	34, 48
	M	18	10
Dhandoi ...	S	632	6, 12, 25
	M	844	51
Dhandol ...	H	99	2, 45
	S	9	44
	M	321	10, 16, 29
Dhándu ...	H	13	6
Dhandwál ...	H	2,187	10, 44, 48, 50
	S	4,452	12, 14, 45, 48
	M	268	15, 28, 48
Dhandwár ...	H	28	44
	S	4	45
Dhanerá ...	S	12	51
	M	179	6
Dhangá ...	H	5	12, 16
	S	256	12
	M	364	11, 14, 24, 27
Dhangar ...	H	455	1, 4, 50
	S	432	6, 48, 50
	M	207	27, 50
Dhángrián ...	H	41	9
Dháni ...	H	1,222	3, 5, 6, 9, 25
	S	26	1, 12, 13, 27
	M	79	13, 14, 19
Dhániwál ...	H	872	6, 9, 33
	S	527	5, 9, 12, 33
	M	176	6, 21, 26, 33
Dhankar ...	H	6,466	2, 3, 4, 5, 48, 49
	S	11	2, 48
	M	45	2
Dhanoí ...	H	164	5, 10, 12, 45
	S	2,650	10, 11, 12, 13, 14, 45, 48
	M	408	16, 17, 51
Dhánon ...	H	144	9
	M	106	11, 24, 28
Dhanpál ...	M	218	12, 18
Dhansí ...	H	445	42, 44, 48, 49
	S	1,067	9, 48
	M	102	29, 48
Dhanu ...	S	467	48
Dhánun ...	M	16	18

SUB-CASTES OF CERTAIN SELECTED CASTES—*continued.*

Names of Sub-Castes.		Persons.	Locality.
Dhanwá ...	H	9	25
	S	1,931	1, 11, 48, 49, 50
Dhanwáliá ...	H	10	12, 19, 27
	M	21	9, 46
Dharán ...	H	276	1, 5, 12, 49
	S	5	12
	M	30	26
Dhárar ...	S	2	19
	M	2,027	9, 16, 17, 18, 27
Dhárie ...	H	356	2, 9, 10, 25, 33
	S	1,267	6, 9, 14, 17, 27, 40, 49
	M	1,524	6, 11, 14, 19, 23, 27
Dháríwál ...	H	3,529	D. except (7), 8, 9, 12, 16, 17, 20, 40, 48, 49
	S	29,930	L. 1, 6, 12, 19, 25, 34, 48, 51
	M	3,939	L. 6, 11, 19, 20, 24, 25, 27, 45, 48, 49
Dháríwán ...	H	8	8
	M	4	8
Dhariyá ...	M	717	14, 23, 24, 28, 51
Dháriyál ...	H	5	8
	M	124	11, 26
Dhárli ...	H	103	9
	M	3	24
Dháru ...	H	131	6, 9, 26
	M	13	24
Dharrá ...	S	7	44, 51
	M	1,074	51
Dháru ...	H	260	1, 8, 12
	S	15	9
	M	513	18, 44
Dharwái ...	H	50	1, 12
	M	24	17
Dharwál ...	H	564	1, 4, 6, 9, 11
	S	996	46
	M	247	1, 26
Dhás ...	H	56	1, 44
	S	10	44
Dhássi ...	H	46	9, 11
	S	47	9, 12
	M	559	14, 15
Dhat ...	H	377	9, 10
	S	457	9, 10, 11, 27
	M	376	23, 28
Dhatíwál ...	H	537	1, 3, 49
	S	19	49
	M	3	49
Dhatre ...	H	4	5
	S	11	13, 25
	M	49	13, 26
Dhátun ...	H	28	1
	S	146	9, 25
Dháwal ...	H	339	6, 44
	S	245	12, 24, 25
	M	41	11,
Dháwi ...	H	205	8, 9, 16, 19, 48
	S	1,809	1, 7, 9, 10, 48
	M	304	10, 11, 29, 48
Dháyá ...	H	141	2
	S	1	44
Dháyal ...	H	38	48
	M	2	48
Dhayán ...	H	28	1
	S	1,418	44
Dheru ...	H	583	2, 4, 9, 10, 12, 17
	S	869	1, 10, 14, 16, 25
	M	461	14, 24, 27, 44
Dheti ...	H	45	9
Dhetrí ...	H	147	9
Dhi ...	H	6,586	2
	S	116	9
	M	74	27, 29
Dhil ...	H	79	2, 3, 5, 19
	S	9	20, 33, 40
	M	288	16, 26
Dhillon ...	H	7,096	1, 10, 11, 16, 30, 48
	S	41,405	L. 1, 6, 10, 11, 12, 24, 45, 48, 49
	M	7,506	1, 10, 11, 15, 17, 28, 48
Dhím ...	H	22	12, 25, 44
	S	9	20
	M	753	16, 17, 18, 20
Dhíndsá ...	H	1,823	6, 10, 11, 16, 45
	S	3,897	1, 5, 10, 11, 16, 45, 49
	M	163	17, 18, 49
Dhingá ...	H	2	45
	M	948	15, 16, 17, 19, 45
Dhingar ...	H	554	3, 9
	M	248	17, 19, 27
Dhiní ...	H	11	9
	M	2	15
Dhirk ...	M	39	12
Dhírwál ...	H	42	30
Dho ...	H	338	1, 9, 11, 25, 48
	S	420	1, 6, 25, 48
	M	81	19, 48
Dhobí ...	H	152	5, 6
	S	815	5, 6
	M	698	19, 27, 44
Dhochak ...	H	360	1, 5, 6, 49
	S	3	6
	M	374	17, 29
Dhodál ...	H	6	1
	M	143	17, 24
Dhodi ...	H	109	25, 30, 33, 40
	S	93	1, 16, 25
	M	7,193	12, 18, 19, 23, 28, 51
Dhogá ...	H	5	9, 27
	S	76	10, 20
	M	15	9, 24
Dhogal ...	H	7	1, 12
	M	16	14
Dhogar ...	H	12	6, 16
	S	7	48
	M	1	20
Dhogi ...	H	11	9, 42
	S	66	9, 44
Dhoi ...	H	41	5, 8, 50
	S	505	6, 14, 25, 50
	M	37	14, 25, 45
Dhokiá ...	H	187	1, 2, 12
	M	59	23
Dholán ...	H	146	4, 5, 25, 48
	S	670	11
	M	128	11
Dholar ...	S	5	13
	M	101	18, 29, 44
Dholia ...	H	1,201	1, 5, 6, 8, 27, 48, 49
	S	300	6, 9, 12, 16, 20, 48
	M	10,643	12, 16, 18, 19, 20, 28, 29, 48,
Dholiár ...	H	11	42
Dhon ...	H	700	4, 5, 6, 12, 15, 49
	S	13,032	6, 14, 15, 25, 48, 49
	M	1,062	14, 19, 23, 28
Dhond ...	H	60	1, 4,
	M	275	17, 20, 24, 27
Dhonoi ...	H	41	8, 16
	S	4	17
	M	5	12
Dhonta ...	S	5	9
Dhor ...	H	49	1, 3, 6, 13
	M	822	17, 19, 27, 28
Dhosi ...	S	184	11, 12, 46
	M	4	9
Dhot ...	H	438	9, 44, 48
	S	1,351	9, 13, 44, 48
	M	668	9, 15
Dhotar ...	H	206	10, 17
	S	1,365	10, 17, 25, 44
	M	2,012	9, 17, 18, 19, 28
Dhoyá ...	H	29	6
	M	8	17
Dhude ...	H	84	12, 50
	S	343	25, 46
	M	12	44
Dhullar ...	H	824	49
	S	2	49
	M	23	46
Dhum ...	H	16	1
	S	256	50
	M	11	17
Dhuná ...	M	228	1, 27
Dhundálá ...	H	13	6, 25
	S	46	5, 25
	M	1	11
Día ...	H	135	1, 4, 49
	S	10	1
	M	274	24, 29
Diál ...	H	1,731	9, 10, 30, 39
	S	1,325	6, 9, 10, 48
	M	357	11, 19, 28, 29
Dián ...	M	87	28
Díbá ...	H	32	1
	S	65	48
Dída ...	H	89	9
	S	97	1
	M	15	27
Dídaráh ...	H	18	1, 12, 25
	S	132	25
Dídwál ...	H	155	1, 6, 9, 49
	S	51	9
Didwán ...	S	12	48
Dighra ...	H	7	13
	S	1	10
	M	5	11
Dílho ...	H	15	1, 9
	S	104	1
	M	2	19
Dilli ...	H	30	9
	S	287	11
	M	15	9, 18
Díngrí ...	H	70	9, 10
	S	59	9, 10
	M	1,385	18, 26, 28
Dípál ...	M	845	27
Díthiwál ...	S	42	1
Díwál ...	H	28	10, 12, 25
	S	68	9, 50
	M	280	11, 26, 29, 50
Diyár ...	H	245	9
	M	1	10
Dod ...	H	1,749	40, 47
	S	128	16, 25, 48
	M	1,242	6, 10, 20, 29
Dodál ...	H	70	1, 2, 6
	M	84	18, 20
Dodániá ...	H	206	2
Dodhá ...	H	48	10, 12, 15
	M	65	17, 18
Dodwál ...	H	64	1
	S	518	10, 14
	M	103	11, 14
Dogal ...	S	6	10, 14, 17
	M	944	9, 17, 44, 45
Dogar ...	H	251	1, 18, 31, 48
	S	1,701	15
	M	1,548	11, 17, 28, 51
Dogi ...	H	14	1, 12
	M	48	28
Dohal ...	H	20	2, 24
	S	37	13, 24
	M	81	27, 29
Dohán ...	H	3,333	1, 2, 3, 5,
	S	5	6, 15
	M	549	2, 18, 28
Dohar ...	H	7	11, 18
	S	17	9, 19
	M	993	13, 23, 24, 29
Dohtar ...	H	3	5
	S	80	13
	M	272	24, 28, 29
Doí ...	M	229	14, 29
Doká ...	H	9	9
	S	7	12
	M	40	17, 20, 26, 51
Dokar ...	H	15	2, 31
	M	220	51
Dolak ...	H	2	4
	S	51	10, 48
	M	74	17, 21, 29
Dolam ...	S	1	14
	M	82	28, 42
Dolar ...	H	32	1, 14
	M	3	13
Dolat ...	H	602	1, 5, 6, 14, 48
	S	1,984	1, 6, 9, 14, 48, 50, 51
	M	328	9, 10, 17, 24, 44
Dolí ...	H	189	11
	S	76	10, 17
	M	38	17, 20, 24

Names of Sub-Castes.		Persons.	Locality.
Dolín ...	H	530	10
	M	3	11
Domarí ...	H	1	7
	M	90	15, 28
Domrál ...	M	335	19, 28, 51
Don ...	H	28	2, 5
	S	104	10, 44
	M	95	15, 27
Dong ...	H	34	6
	S	2	47
	M	24	29, 34
Dorái ...	H	15	1, 17
	S	23	15, 17, 44
	M	450	18, 17, 23
Doráná ...	H	40	1, 4
	M	17	27
Doru ...	H	66	11, 18, 25
	S	23	13, 18
	M	775	1, 9, 19, 20, 28, 29
Dosádh ...	H	121	1, 2, 12
	M	10	1
Dosái ...	S	45	9, 15
	M	21	17
Dosárá ...	H	1	2
	M	119	28
Dosláh ...	H	8	1, 12
	S	43	12
Dotáshara ...	M	19	29
Duj ...	H	37	1, 9, 15
	M	8	17
Dusáhi ...	H	18	1
Dusánjh ...	H	113	9, 10, 44, 48
	S	2,461	9, 10, 14, 25, 48
	M	12	14, 29
Esráh ...	M	35	29
Faqír ...	H	7	2, 8
Farásh ...	M	260	20, 29
Farndal ...	H	99	3
Fojdár ...	H	18	3
Gabará ...	H	11	8, 25
	S	4	14
	M	223	25
Gábhír ...	H	19	21
	M	1	27
Gabír ...	H	54	5
	M	5	28
Gadá ...	H	105	1, 4, 5
	S	76	14
	M	83	28
Gadábá ...	H	51	1
	M	48	27, 51
Gadán ...	H	23	5
Gádar ...	H	7,469	1
	S	43	1, 25
	M	455	25, 26, 27, 28
Gádaráh ...	H	291	2, 12, 25, 49
	M	316	14, 24
Gadare ...	H	1,028	D. 30
	S	238	6, 14, 21
	M	2,129	M. 19, 46, 51
Gáddí ...	H	6	2
	M	117	9, 11, 25, 27, 28
Gadhí ...	H	28	8
	S	4	19
	M	604	9, 17, 18, 28, 29
Gadhwál ...	H	1,155	1, 2, 4, 12
	M	535	20, 24, 25
Gádrán ...	H	66	5
Gádre ...	H	95	4, 10, 25, 48
	S	978	12, 25, 48
	M	2,071	9, 10, 11, 15, 17, 25, 27, 48
Gadwál ...	H	19	2, 8, 12
	M	328	27
Gág ...	S	2	10
	M	290	17
Gagáí ...	M	24	14, 24
Gagal ...	H	20	8
	M	225	23
Gáganí ...	H	3	8
	M	287	24, 51
Gágar ...	H	52	1, 9
	S	10	14, 27
	M	878	16, 19, 20, 25, 27, 29, 51
Gagarí ...	H	33	5, 27, 42
	S	50	44
	M	803	16, 23, 25, 27, 51
Gágat ...	H	109	5
	M	86	23
Gáhí ...	H	62	8
	M	333	19, 27
Gáhín ...	H	14	5
	S	1	20
	M	37	24
Gahlan ...	H	3,393	5
	S	2	12
	M	6	17
Gáhún ...	M	13	18
Gailú ...	H	11	6
Gainá ...	H	42	12, 19
Gáír ...	S	22	9
	M	1	14
Gajoriá ...	H	19	48
	S	1	48
Gajrú ...	H	42	1, 8, 25
	S	4	27
	M	604	10, 18, 19, 20, 26
Gákbal ...	H	57	9, 10
	S	607	8, 10
	M	104	14, 19, 29
Gakhar ...	H	1	16
	S	18	10, 15
	M	1,425	10, 14 to 21, 25, 26, 29
Gál ...	H	7	18
	S	36	9, 22, 28, 50
	M	223	13, 28, 29, 45
Galál ...	H	12	5, 44
	S	1	6
	M	7	29, 51
Galan ...	H	57	1, 6
	S	2	13
Galant ...	H	180	50
Gálárí ...	H	180	5, 8, 48
	S	53	6, 13, 48
	M	42	10, 17, 48
Galaru ...	H	126	5, 34
	S	7	18
	M	196	27, 28, 29
Gale ...	H	1	9
	S	5	9
	M	1,498	28
Galgal ...	H	5	48
	S	41	48
	M	68	19, 26
Galbat ...	H	255	4, 49
	S	22	10
Galiá ...	H	891	1, 2, 4
Galiál ...	S	34	9, 10
Galián ...	H	82	3, 5, 48
	M	36	25
Galkálá ...	M	30	51
Galotar ...	H	83	6, 9
	S	44	13, 44
	M	967	17, 19, 25, 26, 27, 51
Galtí ...	H	30	1
	S	93	6
Gálú ...	H	19	8
	S	12	6, 25
	M	445	6, 23, 25, 29
Galuwál ...	S	539	6, 12, 13
	M	8	9
Gamal ...	H	14	13
	M	107	27
Gan ...	H	7	5
	M	49	51
Gandal ...	H	382	6, 8, 9, 13, 15
	S	8	9, 10
	M	24,169	6, 13, 14, 18, 27
Gandan ...	M	108	9, 25
Gandáre ...	S	275	5, 9, 12, 13
	M	82	3, 11, 13, 14, 25, 51
Gandás ...	H	521	1, 2, 3, 5, 32, 48, 49
	M	55	28
Gandhá ...	H	185	44
	M	2	25
Gandhan ...	H	15	8
Gandhár ...	H	30	11
	S	1	45
Gandhase ...	H	133	8
Gándhi ...	H	385	5, 8, 9, 33, 48
	S	45	9, 24
	M	97	15, 20
Gandhú ...	H	1,349	5, 11, 25, 33, 48, 50
	S	7,388	1, 6, 9, 25, 48, 49, 50
	M	795	5, 11, 16, 48, 50
Gandiá ...	H	262	1, 4, 5, 8, 9, 18
	S	1,967	1, 8, 9, 11, 13, 19, 25, 26, 45
	M	73	11, 28, 29
Gandoh ...	H	13	40
	M	66	51
Gandwále ...	S	26	9
	M	4	51
Gang ...	H	269	8, 9, 13, 15, 25, 45
	S	484	5, 9, 11, 12, 13, 17, 25, 51
	M	1,681	9, 11, 12, 17 to 21, 27, 51
Gangán ...	H	347	5, 25
	S	302	5, 14, 25, 48
	M	2,232	11, 17, 18, 20, 25, 51
Gangar ...	H	18	5
	S	59	5, 12
	M	348	14, 23, 25, 26, 51
Gangas ...	H	4,492	1, 2, 3, 5, 30
	S	140	9, 25
	M	1	3
Gagoní ...	S	1,280	6, 48
	M	1	11
Gangoti ...	H	13	9
	M	8	17
Gangra ...	M	151	17, 28
Gangráwat ...	S	64	12
	M	30	17
Gangu Sháhí	H	50	1
	S	5	13
	M	19	1
Gangwálí ..	H	220	2, 18
	S	30	15
Ganírá ..	S	3	9, 13, 45
	M	57	25, 27, 28
Ganjá ...	H	2	5
	M	138	19, 20, 27, 29
Ganjál ...	S	14	18
	M	160	19, 21, 23, 24
Ganjar ...	H	4	8
	M	850	19, 26
Ganráí ...	M	37	23, 24
Ganwárí ...	M	160	13, 15, 23, 27, 29, 51
Gáohar ...	H	134	13
	M	12	11
Gárá ...	H	171	2, 5, 8
	S	33	5, 45
	M	819	M. 17
Garáiá ...	H	378	13, 44
	S	1	44
	M	563	13, 24, 27
Garálí ...	H	520	2, 6, 9, 31, 45, 48
	S	380	9, 14, 15, 21, 45, 48
	M	59	13, 14, 21, 24
Garalwál ...	H	4	12
	S	1,608	9, 11
	M	965	11
Garan Bhawál	H	88	9
	M	146	28
Garang ...	S	40	48
Garárí ...	H	412	1, 59
	S	55	5, 9
	M	208	10, 27
Garbál ...	H	70	4
	S	27	15
Garchí ...	H	717	6, 9, 10, 11, 25
	S	52	9
	M	1,054	23
Gárd ...	H	217	1, 49
	M	61	19, 27
Gardan ...	H	1,169	1, 2, 25
	S	6	21
	M	185	19, 51
Gardána ...	H	237	1
	M	46	15, 17, 51
Gardezí ...	H	2	5
	M	10	17

SUB-CASTES OF CERTAIN SELECTED CASTES—*continued.*

Names of Sub-Castes.		Persons.	Locality.
Gardiá ...	H	80	9
	M	4	22
Garewál ...	H	5,520	8, 9,10,11,12,18, 25, 33,45, 48,49
	S	22,408	J. 2,3,4, 6,17,19, 25,33, 45,46, 49
	M	1,158	6, 10, 17, 18, 24, 25, 29, 48
Garg ...	H	28	3
	S	163	6, 9
Gargas ...	H	4	6, 48
	S	14	13, 48
	M	34	16, 29
Garí ...	S	101	9, 44
	M	2	19
Gári ...	H	91	2, 19
	M	189	23
Gariál ...	H	137	3, 11
	S	70	5, 9, 10
Garídal ...	M	20	24, 25
Gariwá ...	H	2	10, 25
	M	360	6, 25
Garjáne ...	H	27	48
	S	33	48
	M	10	48
Garje ...	H	36	9, 45, 48
	S	346	5, 48
	M	61	6, 29
Garlú ..	H	6	8, 25
	S	89	25
	M	72	6, 9, 11,25
Garmál ...	S	18	25
Garnú ...	H	48	1, 25
Garoh ...	H	25	1, 8
	M	3	19, 24
Garola ...	H	1	10
	M	55	24, 46
Garoní ...	S	85	25
Garot ...	H	956	4
Garpál ...	H	30	4, 9
	S	5	23
Garsá ...	H	102	1, 2, 4, 48
	S	17	48
	M	16	48
Garsotí ...	H	29	1, 4
Gart ...	H	477	4
Garur ...	H	28	45
	S	54	5, 26
	M	109	25, 28
Garwál ...	H	626	1, 3, 6,13, 25, 48
	S	2,613	25, 44
	M	524	11, 19, 25, 27, 28, 29
Garwán ...	H	90	6, 13
	S	87	6, 9
	M	817	16, 17, 24, 28, 29
Garyál ...	S	10	47
	M	2	18
Gás ...	H	88	5
	M	8	28
Gasolá ...	H	17	2, 12
	S	13	6, 45
	M	502	24, 27, 29, 51
Gaṭ ...	H	206	1
	S	48	27
	M	164	24, 28, 29
Gatána ...	H	2	13
	S	2	14
	M	7	18
Gathál ...	H	128	1, 2, 31
	M	74	18, 25
Gathwál ...	H	2,565	1, 2, 4
	S	11	6
	M	10	12, 49
Gatía ...	H	3	2
	S	42	50
Gatiál ...	H	242	8, 30, 33, 34
	M	28	5, 10, 24
Gatola ...	H	56	4, 48
	S	7	1
Gatwálí ...	H	33	4, 12, 33
	S	9	13
	M	9	5
Gaur ...	H	54	12
	M	7	24
Gaurí ..	H	271	2, 11
	S	12	6, 12
	M	25	27

Names of Sub-Castes.		Persons.	Locality.
Gáwá ...	S	2	6
	M	387	28
Gawálbansi ...	H	25	4, 16
	M	793	18, 19, 25, 51
Gáwandí ...	H	11	5
	M	601	24, 25, 26, 27
Gawáriá ...	H	423	1, 3, 4, 25
	S	1,026	9, 15, 25
	M	342	14, 17, 26, 27
Gázárí ...	S	54	9
	M	12	11
Gelí ...	H	1	9
	M	30	20
Gerí ...	H	2	12
	M	6	17
Geríwál ...	H	111	49
	S	223	49
	M	1	49
Ghabál ...	H	6	12
	M	137	26
Ghadarí ...	H	19	8
	M	70	27
Ghág ...	S	462	10, 14, 44
	M	593	9, 10, 13, 25, 26, 27
Ghágará ...	S	24	10
	M	1,239	17, 19, 20, 23,26
Ghagiá ...	H	17	2, 19
	S	143	24
	M	189	20, 21, 25, 44
Ghágori ...	S	1	16
	M	67	23
Ghái ...	M	160	19, 23, 24, 28
Ghakar ...	S	9	6, 25
	M	485	M. 13, 19
Ghal ...	H	68	1, 5, 9
	S	208	9, 10, 16, 46
	M	168	16, 22, 24, 28, 29
Ghalán ...	H	93	4, 5, 9, 10
	S	522	M. 10, 13
	M	91	10, 23, 25
Ghaloṭ ...	H	350	1, 2, 3, 4
	S	1	33
	M	101	20
Ghalú ...	H	18	1, 9, 47, 49
	S	65	5, 9, 20, 27, 49
	M	6,348	M. 13, 18, 19, 23, 51
Ghalwání ...	S	1	12
	M	301	27
Ghamál ...	H	35	1
	S	2,166	46
	M	33	13, 16
Ghamí ...	H	12	1
	S	2	6, 10
	M	16	16
Ghamíl ...	H	83	16
	S	2	1
Ghán ...	H	15	8, 25
	S	15	9, 10
	M	41	19, 28
Ghandílá ...	H	29	9, 11
	M	1,267	19, 51
Ghandú ...	H	16	25
	S	426	11, 33
	M	407	9, 25, 29
Ghanghas ...	H	725	2, 5, 6, 48
	S	720	11, 13, 48
	M	363	28, 51
Ghaní ...	H	1	5
	M	341	29, 51
Ghankí ...	H	11	11
	M	489	24, 29, 51
Ghans ...	M	2,519	6, 51
Ghanṭa ...	H	2	11
	M	114	1, 9, 51
Ghanṭwál ...	H	14	5
	M	4	17
Gharán ...	H	15	15
	S	1,022	5, 15, 27
	M	428	28, 29
Gharar ...	H	517	5, 48
	S	95	48
Gharaṭ ...	H	23	12, 25
	S	12	45
	M	338	26, 27
Ghariál ...	H	64	5
	M	355	16, 23, 26

Names of Sub-Castes.		Persons.	Locality.
Gharir ...	H	189	5
Ghariwál ...	H	34	5, 12, 50
	S	125	13, 51
	M	629	23, 28
Gharola ...	H	21	24, 33
Gharthi ...	H	2	10
	S	81	24
	M	711	17, 20, 50
Gharú ...	H	42	2, 12, 16
	S	5	25, 51
	M	680	6, 19, 23, 25, 28, 51
Gharuní ...	H	12	9
	M	18	25
Gharwál ...	H	110	48
	S	93	17, 20, 45, 48
	M	319	11, 19, 26, 27
Ghás ...	H	41	1, 2
	S	5	6
	M	8	9
Ghasár ..	H	22	2
Ghaṭírá ...	S	69	46
	M	2	14
Ghatwál ...	H	22,461	1, 2, 4, 5, 6, 8, 27
	S	656	4
	M	25	17
Ghatwán ...	H	93	1
Ghawál ...	H	983	1
	S	9	10, 27
	M	1,616	9, 23, 29
Ghawás ...	S	30	13, 50
	M	3	11
Ghelí ...	H	96	2, 12
	S	2	10
	M	52	19, 25, 27
Ghí ...	H	4	5, 12
	S	22	25
	M	158	12, 15, 25
Ghirt ...	H	21	1
	S	4	19
	M	2	9
Ghogarí ...	H	94	2, 48, 49
	S	1	48
	M	209	12, 17
Gholá ...	H	26	2, 4, 9, 12
	M	189	12, 16, 18
Ghonge ...	H	15	1, 5, 48
	S	223	9, 10
	M	118	20, 48, 51
Ghoní ...	H	4	12
	S	1	9
	M	70	26
Ghorí ...	H	272	1, 2, 5, 9, 45, 50
	S	10	9, 33
	M	614	4, 5, 15, 19, 25, 29, 42, 51
Ghosa ...	H	1,263	1, 11, 19, 30
	S	95	25
	M	94	5, 16
Ghotá ...	H	41	1
	M	237	23
Ghotál ...	H	745	5
Ghúlá ...	H	2	12
	S	43	46
	M	336	11, 23, 28, 29, 42
Ghulárí ...	H	1	11
	S	9	49
	M	3	15
Ghumman ...	H	5,497	6, 15, 16, 17, 19, 48
	S	14,735	11, 15, 16, 17, 25, 48
	M	10,859	15, 16, 17, 19, 24, 25, 48
Ghuna ...	H	5	4
	S	75	9, 12
	M	6	15, 27
Ghuwálá ...	H	113	6
	M	41	13, 27
Giál ...	H	39	6
	M	226	19, 25, 27
Gián ...	S	5	12
	M	121	29
Gidar ...	H	34	8, 48
	S	1	13
	M	10	29

Names of Sub-Castes.		Persons.	Locality.
Gigari ...	H	158	8
Gil ...	H	9,810	J. L. M. 1. 2, 6, 19, 20, 33, 34, 39 to 46, 48 to 51
	S	110,424	B. 33, 34, 44 to 51
	M	25,146	B. 33, 36, 41, 44 to 51
Gilák ...	M	295	51
Giláni ...	H	27	2, 12, 34
	S	58	48
	M	26	8, 16, 25
Gild ...	H	164	2
	M	317	2
Gilt ...	H	1,902	2, 3, 30
	S	1	14
	M	28	2, 13, 19
Girí ...	H	60	12, 13
	S	9	16
	M	4,552	16, 28
Gírjá ...	H	138	9, 39
	S	390	9, 10
Gobatí ...	H	13	5
	M	353	27, 29
Gobí ...	H	114	10
Gobrá ...	H	16	10
	S	2	19
Gocha ...	H	7	47
	S	6	47
Godâ ...	H	75	4, 5
	S	4	44
	M	11	19
Godal ...	H	17	2, 4
	S	1	19
	M	251	11, 23
Godálíá ...	H	222	6, 9
Godamyán ...	H	152	48
Godar ...	H	140	2, 3, 5, 19, 25, 51
Godárá ...	H	2,122	2, 5, 11, 12, 25, 48, 51
	S	887	1, 10, 48, 51
	M	733	1, 18, 25, 27, 29, 44, 48, 51
Godaria ...	H	271	2, 49
	S	49	10, 49
	M	181	12, 25, 51
Godáwarí ...	H	27	2
Godhá ...	H	11	2
	S	9	1
Godíá ...	H	42	2, 4
	S	3	25
Godlái ...	M	43	29
Gogaí ...	H	12	2
	S	1	1
	M	486	17, 19, 25, 27, 29, 44
Gogarí ...	M	53	25, 27
Gohar ...	H	19	25, 48
	S	24	24, 25, 48
	M	142	19, 27, 51
Gohari ...	S	39	9, 50
	M	8	20
Gohat ...	H	2,275	1, 6
	S	51	1
	M	43	6
Gohíá ...	H	72	4, 5
	M	30	23
Gohil ...	H	42	1
	S	17	12
Gohlán ...	H	3	5, 47
	M	44	23
Goil ...	H	49	5, 12
	S	3	49
	M	34	12
Goímán ...	M	26	5, 11
Goind ...	H	766	11, 49
	M	407	26
Gojá ...	H	2	25, 49
	S	9	14, 19, 51
	M	754	5, 12, 23, 26, 27, 29, 51
Gojrál ...	H	57	4
	M	1	15
Gokhá ...	M	17	10, 51
Golá ...	H	6,907	1, 2, 3, 4, 5, 18, 25, 49
	S	22	1, 14, 39
	M	473	4, 9, 16, 29, 51
Golána ..	S	62	9
Golar ...	H	5	10
	S	2	5
	M	50	13, 17, 20, 29
Goliár ...	S	77	12
	M	2	13
Golohorí	M	21	12
Gomala	H	25	9, 12
	S	8	10, 25
	M	63	5, 15
Gomárí ...	H	7	1
	S	5	12
Gond ...	S	1	10
	M	107	29
Gondál ...	H	61	9, 14, 16
	S	131	8, 13, 15, 25, 48
	M	37,630	M. 4, 10, 11, 15, 16, 17, 19, 21
Gondal ...	H	75	20, 46
	S	69	14
	M	7,031	8, 12, 14, 20, 28, 44, 46
Gondar ...	H	3	49
	S	85	12, 49
	M	27	11
Gondárí ...	H	79	4, 12
	S	144	12
Gondí ...	H	22	5, 9, 10
	M	249	15, 17, 19, 24, 29, 46
Gondwál ...	H	185	2, 46
	M	6	14, 46
Goní ...	H	211	5
	S	17	8
Gonin ...	S	6	12
	M	15	20
Gopál ...	H	2	13
	S	6	6, 27
	M	79	26, 28
Gopírái ...	H	50	1, 5, 12
	S	315	6, 11, 12, 13, 14, 16
	M	510	16, 17, 24, 25, 26, 27, 51
Gopraní	M	499	25, 27
Gor ...	H	401	1, 2, 5, 9
	M	183	17, 19, 27, 28
Gorábí ...	H	19	9, 16, 25
	S	2	14, 19
	M	1,137	10, 14, 16, 25, 27, 28
Goráe ...	H	116	1, 10
	S	73	10, 14
	M	847	9, 19, 26, 29, 51
Goráha ...	H	406	2, 15, 17
	S	4,012	15, 17
	M	1,570	19, 24, 25, 28, 29, 44
Gorál ...	H	23	10
	M	40	11, 13
Gorán ...	H	13	11
	S	400	11, 48
Goran ...	H	193	2, 14
	S	64	11, 13, 27, 43
	M	96	11, 14, 29
Goráná ...	H	6	18
	S	2	25
	M	193	13, 19
Goras ...	M	114	13, 19, 24, 25
Gorátah ...	H	73	2
	M	11	25
Gorawál ...	H	100	2, 3
	S	367	11, 48
	M	2	48
Goraya ...	H	255	2, 12
Gorchhá ...	H	3	6, 11
	S	36	11
	M	138	19, 26
Gorgì ...	H	22	1, 9
	S	15	6
	M	186	9, 23, 26
Gorí ...	H	89	9, 10, 12, 51
	S	97	5, 10, 17
	M	1,002	L. M. 9, 10, 19, 23
Goriá ..	H	1,437	9, 10, 12, 14, 15, 16, 19, 24
	S	2,696	14, 16, 17, 25
	M	7,097	J. 14, 17, 19, 20,
Gorjap ...	H	240	48
	S	28	48
Gorliá ...	H	119	1, 42
	S	26	9, 24
	M	13	17
Gorú ...	H	9	12
	S	4	10
	M	3	17
Gorún ...	S	254	11
Gorúwál ...	H	26	49
Gorwán ...	H	8	1
	M	19	14
Gos ...	H	7	5, 8, 33
	S	49	15, 14
	M	36	11, 12, 27
Gosal ...	H	141	1, 13, 15, 25, 48
	S	3,508	5, 6, 10, 11, 13, 14, 15, 20, 25, 45, 46, 49
	M	432	12, 27, 28, 48
Gosain ...	H	8	12, 51
	M	82	27, 28
Gosil ...	H	1	25
	S	82	11, 33
	M	104	27 28
Got ...	H	46	1, 5, 12
	M	1,117	28
Gotaná ...	H	23	12, 38
Goṭerá ...	H	19	5, 25
	M	4	13, 19
Gotewál ...	S	41	47
Gowálíá ...	H	12	46
	S	24	5
Gowárá ...	H	397	4, 6, 27, 50
	S	161	50
	M	72	25, 50
Gral ...	H	130	9
	S	22	9
	M	2	14
Gujar ...	H	133	1, 12, 14, 24, 46
	S	163	12, 25
	M	3,653	10, 13, 17, 18, 19, 20, 24 to 28, 51
Gujaru ...	M	21	6, 27
Gujjrál ...	H	16	27
	S	13	17, 19
	M	1,020	20, 27
Gular ...	H	46	4
	S	40	15
	M	192	25, 27
Gulchí ...	H	2	11
	S	81	11
Guleriga ...	H	31	48
	M	1	48
Gulí ...	H	148	6, 9
	M	13	27
Guliál ...	H	524	4, 6
	S	1	50
	M	103	27, 50
Gulsher ...	H	91	8, 44
	S	146	44, 48
	M	272	6, 14, 27
Gundá ...	S	85	11
	M	301	23, 27
Gur ...	H	188	49
	S	8	49
Guralwál ...	H	7	6, 12
	S	5	34
	M	114	12, 18
Gurám ...	H	215	50
	S	684	13, 50
	M	89	10
Gurgí ...	M	15	12
Gurgaur ...	H	48	48
	S	51	48
Gurma ...	H	199	48, 50
	S	1,519	48, 49, 50
	M	48	48
Gursa ...	H	167	2
Gursál ...	S	36	6
	M	5	6
Guru ...	H	4	6
	S	196	6, 17, 49
	M	159	19

SUB-CASTES OF CERTAIN SELECTED CASTES—*continued*.

Names of Sub-Castes.		Persons.	Locality.
Gurú Nanak	S	71	18
	M	123	17, 29
Hachhar ...	H	1	18
	S	42	5, 16
	M	5	29
Haddirá ...	M	374	28, 29
Hadol ...	H	487	11, 16, 25
	S	852	6, 11, 12, 14, 16
	M	89	12, 13, 14
Hadwál ...	H	3	5, 25, 46
	S	45	25, 44
	M	38	17, 21
Haiál ...	H	17	27
	M	2	21
Hál ...	H	12	8
	M	75	12, 16, 20
Haláwat ...	H	85	1, 4, 9, 14
	S	2	45
Halch ...	M	119	20, 28
Haldar ...	M	81	23, 26
Hálgarmál ...	M	255	26
Háli ...	H	36	4, 8, 19, 25
	S	1,136	4, 12, 14, 16
	M	157	19, 23, 29, 51
Halir ...	H	1	5
	S	5	41
	M	181	11, 17, 23, 29
Hallá ...	H	16	4, 34
	S	4	12
	M	208	29
Hallál ...	H	10	1
	S	152	15
Hallar ...	M	107	19, 23
Halti ...	H	29	9, 44, 48
	M	76	23, 29
Halwál ...	H	749	5, 6, 9, 10
	S	170	4, 15
	M	38	51
Halwán ...	H	17	1, 25, 48
	M	40	5, 16, 29
Halyat ...	H	81	8
	S	59	9
Hamdáni ...	H	139	6
	S	1	9
Hamige ...	H	63	11
Hamirá ...	H	1	12
	S	1	10
	M	113	1, 29
Hamman ...	H	2	25
	M	318	11, 23, 27, 28
Hamoká ...	M	132	19
Hamrán ..	M	27	25, 27
Hamsar ..	M	105	23
Hamshiráh ...	H	4	47
	S	1	6
	M	481	29, 50
Hamzá ...	M	14	27
Hán ...	H	5	8, 25
	M	46	17
Hanchani ...	M	128	27
Hand ...	S	64	9, 11, 12
	M	62	13, 16, 24
Handál ...	H	195	5, 9, 12, 15, 19, 25, 46
	S	673	12,14,27,38,46, 48
	M	287	17, 21,22, 24, 27
Hándi	H	9	17
	S	111	6, 50, 51
	M	18	50
Handrái ...	S	50	48
Hangá ...	S	1,479	11, 14, 17
	M	467	23, 24
Hangál ...	H	4	9
	S	58	12, 13
	M	182	16, 17
Hangú ...	H	31	8, 17, 34
	S	12	25, 44
	M	2,989	12, 14, 18, 28
Hanháns ...	M	51	13, 14
Hanj ...	M	60	28
Hanjlá ..	H	2	11
	M	185	9, 21, 25
Hanjúl ...	H	12	19
Hanri ...	H	2	9
	S	51	12
	M	127	27
Háns ...	H	2,714	4, 6, 8, 10, 11, 15, 44, 48, 50
	S	1,786	6, 11, 12, 15, 25, 38, 45, 46, 48, 49, 50
	M	4,019	M. 1, 12, 14, 17, 19, 48, 50, 51
Hánsi ..	M	691	23
Hansláh ...	H	54	4, 8, 9, 11
	S	61	25
	M	1,199	27, 28, 29, 51
Hanslin ...	H	3	13, 25
	S	17	10, 25
	M	111	9, 10, 19, 26, 29
Hansrái ...	H	1	25
	S	448	6, 11, 12
	M	318	27, 29
Hanswál	M	262	27
Hanswáni	H	79	8
	M	152	12, 27
Hará ...	H	571	9, 11, 44, 50
	S	438	16, 49, 50
	M	504	9, 11, 19, 21, 23, 27, 28, 50
Haráich ...	H	104	8, 9, 11
	S	184	9, 11
	M	42	26
Haráji ...	H	4	11
	S	1	12
	M	19	24
Harák ...	H	107	9, 18, 46
	S	59	9
	M	37	16, 19, 39
Haráng ...	H	6	25
	S	11	12, 25
	M	548	19, 28, 29, 46
Harar ...	H	18	15
	S	9	9
	M	194	9, 17, 27, 28, 51
Hardawár ...	H	19	8
	S	6	8, 9
	M	508	12
Hardil ...	H	1	19
	S	55	46
	M	1	18
Hardol ...	H	1	48
	S	31	5
	M	84	1, 13, 28
Háre ...	H	168	5, 9, 40, 45
	S	11	5, 19, 25, 40
	M	113	9, 19, 23, 40
Hargan	H	2	48
	S	29	48
	M	16	23, 26
Hariá ...	H	840	5, 9, 11, 12, 16, 44, 48
	S	776	11, 12, 16, 48
	M	282	11, 19, 29, 44, 48
Hariál ...	H	18	6, 19, 25
	S	256	15, 25, 46
	M	5,036	12, 13, 26, 27, 48
Hariáná ...	S	2	9
	M	472	29
Hariár ...	M	156	23
Hariharwán ...	H	22	51
Harjá ..	M	74	26, 29
Harkár ...	S	1	11
	M	159	11, 18, 27
Harkhel ...	M	33	27
Hárti ...	S	117	1, 11
	M	364	11, 24, 28
Harná ...	H	19	9, 10, 48
	S	1	25
	M	67	9, 22, 24, 28, 48
Harnán ...	M	40	24, 29
Harnari ...	H	3	10
	S	16	15
	M	2	13
Harnáwá ...	H	11	2, 21
Hárni ...	H	2	1
	M	58	10, 23, 24
Harnwál ...	H	145	1, 13
Haroká ...	M	24	16
Harpál ..	M	22	11, 17, 27
Harrad ...	M	325	16, 18
Harrái ...	H	1,101	1, 8, 16
	S	21	1
	M	697	20, 26
Harrál ...	H	100	16, 48
	S	56	16, 45
	M	3,945	16, 17, 20, 27
Harrárá ...	H	1	19
	S	18	5
	M	98	16, 17
Harsáli ...	H	45	6, 24, 30, 48
	S	27	1
	M	363	18, 49, 51
Harwádi ...	S	19	4, 5, 44
Harwáh ...	S	4	13
	M	75	23
Harwálá ...	H	8	16, 19
	M	4	17, 19
Harwán ...	M	1,201	18, 24
Hasni ...	H	76	46
	S	1,075	46
	M	461	20, 24, 26, 27
Hathár ...	S	74	9, 25
	M	285	9, 18, 26, 27, 48, 51
Hatiár ...	H	15	10
	S	102	19, 25
	M	831	19, 21, 27
Hatin ...	H	1	9
	M	212	10, 27
Hatli ...	H	38	6
	M	142	51
Hattá ...	H	118	4, 8
	S	102	1, 6, 9, 10
	M	831	11, 19, 20,24,25, 26
Hattol ...	H	83	8, 16
	M	227	19, 20, 23, 51
Hawá ...	H	528	2, 6
	M	19	28
Hawáná ...	S	3	26
	M	2	24
Hazárá ...	H	144	6
	M	2	23
Her ...	H	4,872	J. 16, 17, 18,25, 34, 39, 42, 45, 46, 49
	S	6,601	6, 10, 11, 12,13, 15, 25, 44, 46, 48, 49
	M	5,644	J. L. M. 18, 19, 34, 44, 48
Heri ...	H	30	1, 27, 38
	S	30	20
	M	271	24
Hesri ...	H	45	2, 38
	M	44	18, 19
Hidan ...	M	294	17, 23
Hidrás ...	M	105	19
Higu ...	H	27	1
	S	49	25, 51
Hijrale ...	M	1,038	18, 26
Hill ...	H	14	9, 34
	S	48	11, 25
	M	1,509	15, 23, 28, 29
Hillan ...	H	11	10
	M	10	29, 45
Hilor ...	S	3,797	9
	M	10	13, 44
Him ...	H	32	10
	S	14	16
	M	2	23
Hindín ...	H	2	24
	S	12	9, 25
	M	305	19, 27, 29
Hinjár ...	H	902	11, 12
	S	1,588	9, 10
	M	4,341	9, 13, 16, 17, 20
Hinjrá ...	H	716	5, 9, 15, 16, 17, 25, 46,49
	S	1,017	3, 13, 16,18, 19, 24, 25, 46,48, 49
	M	5,462	12, 13, 15, 17,18, 19,20, 24, 26, 28, 46, 48
Hinjrál ...	H	1	19
	S	261	12
	M	1,270	13, 24
Hinora ...	H	13	5, 9, 25, 27
	S	259	25
	M	58	19

Names of Sub-Castes.		Persons.	Locality.
Hitri ...	H	97	9
	S	14	9
	M	3	11
Hodá ...	H	7,579	1, 2, 3, 4, 5, 9, 12, 46
	S	297	4, 9, 49
	M	8	5, 44
Hodál ...	H	187	1, 9
	M	2	27
Hodár ...	M	777	16, 21, 27
Hogar ...	H	7	1
	M	1,448	16, 17, 18, 27
Hoi ...	H	71	10
	S	7	9, 12
	M	149	19, 27, 28
Holi ...	H	123	2, 16
	S	24	12, 15, 25
	M	652	17, 26, 27, 28
Honá ...	H	15	25
	S	11	10
	M	383	14, 16, 27
Horá ...	H	402	5, 9, 12, 15, 47
	M	552	9, 11, 20, 27
Hot ...	H	27	5
	S	3	9
	M	80	13, 19, 28, 29
Hothe ...	H	81	1, 9, 16, 44
	S	144	6, 19 25
	M	39	9, 14, 19, 44
Hujjhan ...	S	30	13
	M	935	17, 19, 24, 29
Húndal ...	S	136	13
Indrar ...	M	241	28
Isákhel ...	M	13	29
Isar ...	M	17	16, 17
Isázai ...	M	12	17
Ithwál ...	H	1	28
	S	23	15
Jabar ...	H	367	1, 9, 16
	S	106	15, 40
	M	396	18, 25, 27, 28
Jabo ...	H	268	9, 45
	M	4	17
Jadal ...	M	249	13
Jádam ...	H	49	4
Jadari ...	H	1	12
	M	103	17, 51
Jádh ...	M	160	51
Jáda ...	H	2	10, 12
	S	142	44, 45, 46
	M	209	15, 46
Jádú Bansi ...	H	831	3
Jádúrán ...	H	480	4
	M	85	20
Jag ...	H	77	4
	M	1,703	17, 18, 19, 24, 27
Jagal ...	H	18	12, 48
	S	18	48
	M	80	13, 19
Jagan ...	H	295	48, 50
	S	41	48
Jagará ...	H	391	4, 5, 15, 48
	M	14	1, 12, 46
Jagi ...	S	38	50
	M	59	24
Jagíáná ..	H	32	2, 5, 44
	S	1	44
	M	50	5, 28
Jaglán ...	H	3,286	2, 4, 5, 49
	S	32	5
	M	25	1, 5
Jagupál ...	H	88	10, 44
	S	671	9, 15, 44
Jahái ...	H	19	50
	S	12	51
Jáhal ...	H	928	2, 4, 5, 15, 24, 25, 31, 39, 48
	S	1,203	5, 6, 9, 10, 12, 15, 25, 48
	M	740	8, 10, 11. 12, 19, 25, 28, 48,
Jaháli ...	M	242	27
Jahángiri ...	H	4	40
	M	83	27
Jahmi ...	H	291	10, 11
	S	29	6
	M	95	11, 16, 17
Jaid ...	S	21	49
Jail ...	H	10	6
	M	36	44
Jaipál ...	M	63	12
Jaj ...	H	1,824	1, 9, 10, 25, 44
	S	673	5, 9, 10, 11, 25, 44
	M	434	9, 11, 17, 29, 51
Jáján ...	S	15	48
Jajohán ...	H	5	48
	S	16	48
	M	763	12, 27
Jajotre ...	H	19	16
Jajrán ..	H	16	5
Jajwán ...	H	32	6
	S	31	6
Jákhal ...	H	190	50
	S	2	50
Jákhar ...	H	9,024	D. 9, 11, 12, 19, 30, 31, 49, 50
	S	492	1, 4, 8, 12, 19, 25, 44, 49, 51
	M	1,670	5, 16, 19, 23, 27, 28, 29, 51
Jal ...	H	91	2, 9, 10
	S	299	9, 10, 12, 44
	M	28	9, 10, 17, 18
Jaláli ...	M	882	11, 23
Jaláni ..	S	19	29
	M	38	25
Jálap ...	M	276	16, 17, 18, 20, 21
Jáli ...	H	24	12, 13, 51
	M	2	18
Jalorán ...	S	105	6
	M	117	26
Jalroi ...	H	35	32
Jaluhán ...	M	1,642	19, 29
Jalukh ...	M	179	17, 24
Jám ...	H	3	9, 11
	S	4	10
	M	1,444	17, 18, 19, 26, 27, 28, 29, 51
Jámal ...	S	31	12, 24
	M	504	16, 19, 20, 29, 51
Jamat ...	M	1,094	9, 10, 16, 17, 25, 26, 27, 29, 51
Jamik ...	H	105	48
	S	283	48
Jammún ...	H	521	1, 12, 25, 48
	S	491	12, 25, 48
	M	2,784	16, 18, 23, 24, 27, 28, 46, 51
Jamrá ...	S	651	14
Jamud ...	M	352	27
Jáná ...	H	10	12, 15
	S	1,326	12, 14, 46
	M	232	6, 9, 10, 21, 28
Janari ...	M	62	51
Jándal ...	H	272	1, 5, 12, 45
	S	11	5, 49
	M	280	6, 10, 24, 25, 27, 28, 44
Jander ...	H	36	8, 10, 17
	S	284	9, 10, 11, 16, 25
	M	1,674	10, 13, 16, 26, 28, 29, 44
Jándi ...	H	79	9, 11, 44, 45
	S	1,075	5, 6, 10, 12, 44, 49
	M	1,212	9, 10, 15, 17, 18, 25, 27, 44, 48
Jandrál ...	H	3	47
	M	618	30
Jandrán ...	H	22	5, 13, 16
	M	454	10, 16, 17, 19, 21, 26, 27, 28, 51
Jáng ...	H	93	1
Jangá ...	H	1,501	4, 48, 49
	S	64	9
	M	1,508	19, 48
Jangál ...	H	137	1, 4, 8, 9, 15, 45
	S	1,305	9, 15, 20
	M	2,296	20, 26, 27, 28, 29, 51
Jangál ...	H	576	3, 6
	S	1	8
Jángar ...	S	243	6
	M	9	13
Jánglá ...	M	21	51
Jángoriá ...	H	10	8, 24
	M	30	24
Jánj ...	H	13	10, 40, 41, 48
	S	1,688	2, 48
	M	3,572	15, 25, 26, 48
Janjuá ...	H	195	5, 49
	S	12	12, 16, 19
	M	483	16, 25, 26, 44, 51
Janjúl ...	H	53	21
	S	3	8
Jánkará ...	H	54	4, 49
	M	279	27
Janará ...	H	185	40, 48
	S	1,164	48
	M	224	48
Jantari ...	H	4	9, 12
	S	8	12, 15, 45
	M	65	24, 26
Janwár ...	M	12	26
Japá ...	M	266	26
Japák ...	H	10	11, 19
	S	1	19
Jar ...	H	3	10, 12
	S	132	1, 10, 12
	M	1,829	M. 19, 23, 51
Járá ...	H	215	3, 30
	S	393	1, 10
	M	2,141	19, 20, 26, 27, 28, 29
Jarál ...	H	87	15, 16, 19, 24
	S	1	15
Jarán ...	H	1,865	48
	S	1,887	2, 4, 48
	M	3	48
Jargá ...	M	17	17
Jarki ...	M	165	13, 17, 25, 26
Jaroiá ...	H	210	1, 5, 31
	S	5	12
Jarolá ...	H	62	48
	S	7	48
	M	421	M 51
Jaryá ...	H	305	5, 12, 48
	S	309	48
Jase ...	H	19	48
	S	18	6, 48
	M	9	11, 48
Jasid ...	H	6	9
	S	131	9
Jaskol ...	M	257	16
Jaslin ...	H	18	6
Jasota ...	H	11	15
Jaspál ...	H	13	9, 12
	S	378	9, 11, 12
	M	686	10, 15, 18, 19, 20, 44
Jassar ...	H	107	9, 44, 48, 50
	S	1,363	9, 11, 13, 16, 48, 49, 50
	M	225	9, 11, 16, 18, 19, 48
Jastar ...	H	15	6, 11
	S	249	6, 9
	M	23	11
Jaswál ...	H	28	48, 50
	S	56	12, 48, 50
	M	62	48
Jaswárá ...	H	191	14, 16, 18, 25, 51
	M	11	13, 17
Jatálá ...	H	5	10
	S	33	12, 13
	M	491	1, 10, 17, 21 26
Jatáná ...	H	839	1, 5, 6, 48, 49
	S	2,025	9, 12, 48, 49, 50, 51
	M	176	1, 5, 48
Jathi ...	S	111	1
Jatbol ...	M	454	13, 23
Játi ...	H	295	4, 8, 11, 12
	S	24	5, 6, 9, 12
	M	92	10, 15, 16, 27
Jatoi ...	H	80	16
	S	329	16, 49
	M	2,449	10, 13, 16, 20, 27, 28
Jatol ...	S	227	25, 48
	M	1,328	20, 21, 26, 48
Jatolia ...	H	11	12, 30
	M	151	12, 51

SUB-CASTES OF CERTAIN SELECTED CASTES—*continued.*

Names of Sub-Castes.		Persons.	Locality.
Jator ...	H	104	1, 3, 9
	S	91	12, 15, 20, 45
	M	349	6, 9, 10, 24, 27
Jaṭráná ...	H	1,380	1, 2, 3, 4, 34 49
	S	46	6, 40
Jatsar ...	S	36	12, 46
	M	30	10
Játu ...	H	286	6, 18, 27, 29
	S	427	6, 10, 14, 27, 29
	M	4,031	12, 16, 18, 19, 20, 23, 25, 26, 27, 28, 51
Jaṭuji ...	S	60	10
	M	40	27
Jaṭwál ...	H	61	2, 5, 8, 17, 30
	S	93	6, 17
	M	98	9, 10, 17, 29
Jawán ...	S	149	11
	M	98	29
Jawand ...	H	14	11, 15, 48
	S	701	45, 48, 49
	M	163	9, 11, 20, 48
Jawára ...	H	79	8, 11, 12, 15
	S	681	14, 15, 17
	M	830	13, 17, 27, 29
Jhadal ...	H	9	10
	S	8	9
Jhadar ...	H	3	9
	S	201	14
	M	87	9, 13, 17
Jhadu ...	M	11	26
Jhagal ...	H	5	5
	S	135	12, 18
	M	257	10, 13, 18, 24, 29
Jhagan ...	M	65	27
Jhagrán ...	H	56	2
Jháj ...	H	689	3, 9, 10, 11
	S	700	9, 11, 19
	M	346	11, 13, 16, 17, 26, 29, 44
Jhajáhan	H	9	5
	S	9	5, 33
	M	565	26, 28, 51
Jhajar ...	H	120	30
	S	36	1, 12, 19
	M	1,786	11, 27, 28
Jhaji ...	S	7	51
	M	168	16
Jhájra ...	H	466	2, 3, 12, 33
	S	3	12
	M	231	15, 28, 51
Jhajú ...	H	2	48
	S	147	48
	M	50	48
Jhakkar ...	H	2,550	1, 3, 25, 32, 49
	S	61	10, 12
	M	2,432	M. 11, 16, 20, 51
Jhála ...	S	42	9, 13
	M	384	17, 19, 20, 26, 29
Jhalan ...	H	4	29, 51
	M	91	51
Jhali ...	H	650	6, 10, 11, 12, 45, 50
	S	1,410	10, 11, 12, 19, 20, 25, 45, 50
	M	686	10, 11, 19, 26, 27, 28, 29
Jhale ...	M	75	26
Jhaman ...	M	241	12, 51
Jhammat ...	S	51	10, 45
	M	6,206	R. M. 13, 17
Jháná ...	H	469	1, 9, 11, 15, 16
	S	384	16
	M	75	16, 17, 26
Jhánar ...	H	39	9
	M	6	17
Jhandar ...	H	1	9
	S	516	9, 11, 45
	M	2,294	M. 6, 17, 18, 51
Jhándú ...	H	292	6, 8, 9, 10
	S	69	6, 10, 25
	M	527	19, 24, 25, 51
Jhángi ...	H	2,273	1, 6, 8, 9, 10, 15
	S	1,165	6, 9, 10, 45
	M	97	12, 51
Jhángri ...	H	598	1, 3, 9, 10
	S	172	7
Jhangú ...	H	64	49
	S	12	49
	M	1	17
Jhanjar ...	H	535	1, 49
	S	20	49
	M	19	11
Jhanjiál ...	H	45	48
	S	10	48
	M	84	13
Jhankor ...	H	1,491	3, 4
	S	26	10
	M	233	2, 3, 4, 28
Jhánsi ...	H	13	8, 9
	M	2	13
Jhár ...	H	357	1, 2, 9, 10, 13, 32
	S	77	44, 46
	M	648	16, 26, 48
Jhári ...	H	12	5
Jháro ...	H	75	12, 51
	S	8	1
Jhárwál ...	H	817	1, 6
Jhatak ...	M	12	16
Jhati ...	H	247	9, 11, 49
	S	47	6, 49
	M	159	16, 24
Jhatra ...	H	20	44, 49
Jháwali ...	H	255	1, 9
	S	7	12, 17
	M	747	12, 28
Jhawán ...	H	14	15
Jhiwar ...	S	29	15, 19
Jhoda ...	H	5	49
	M	152	23
Jhokar ...	H	162	9, 10
	S	271	9
	M	16	25
Jholi ...	H	252	8, 9, 11, 48, 50
	S	3,017	9, 10, 11, 12, 48, 50
	M	472	11, 16, 48
Jhomar ...	H	3	8, 10
	S	44	12
	M	290	27
Jhonaj ...	M	224	10, 29
Jhonglá ...	M	45	51
Jhotá ...	H	16	8
	M	22	20
Jhoyá ...	S	37	48
Jhugh ...	H	63	12
	M	589	16, 51
Jhún ...	H	543	16
Jiál ...	H	2	5
	M	692	20, 24, 29
Jid ...	H	13	50
	S	221	13, 50
Jidan ...	H	18	27, 48
	S	248	48
	M	2	48
Joba ...	M	352	6, 23
Jobanda ...	H	7	44, 50
	S	669	50
	M	217	27, 50
Jodká ...	M	32	51
Jodru ..	H	16	49
	S	1	49
Jogi ...	H	65	1, 11, 49
	M	21	48
Jogra ...	H	326	15
	S	73	9, 15
	M	1,874	12, 15, 24, 26, 28
Johá ...	M	331	24
Johag ...	S	6	1
	M	73	24
Johal ...	H	964	1, 9, 10, 15, 25
	S	7,578	J. 14, 15, 16, 19, 25, 33, 49
	M	265	12, 15, 25, 29
Johar ...	H	272	1, 2, 3, 5, 6, 9, 12, 30
	S	575	5, 12, 14, 15
	M	145	17, 25, 28
Johbal ...	H	2	48
	S	19	48
	M	7	11, 48
Johta ...	H	5	30
	S	2	19
	M	298	27, 28
Jokar ...	H	16	4, 11
Jokar ...	M	244	27
Jokhi ...	H	41	8, 10, 39
	S	3	12, 46
	M	157	25, 26
Joláh ...	M	18	10, 11
Jolak ...	M	91	9, 26
Jomái ...	M	398	24, 27
Jomar ...	H	10	48
	S	214	48
	M	341	27
Jomná ...	H	22	9
Jon ...	H	1,887	1, 2, 3, 4, 5, 16, 21, 48, 49
	S	22	48, 49, 51
	M	688	27, 29, 51
Jondá ...	H	139	10, 12, 16, 25
	S	1,547	1, 10, 11, 12, 13, 14, 16, 25
	M	588	10, 11, 15, 16, 17, 19, 46
Jondhar ...	M	36	11, 12
Jondi ...	H	108	9, 10, 12, 21, 25
	S	187	1, 9, 10, 12
	M	457	6, 10, 12, 16, 20
Joni ...	H	54	9, 10
	S	22	12
	M	97	26
Jonir ...	M	21	26
Jonkiá ...	H	2	12
	S	122	10
	M	103	17
Jorá ...	H	286	1, 5, 9, 10, 16, 43
	S	884	1, 9, 25
	M	10,166	1, 6, 17, 18, 19, 20, 23, 25, 27
Jorelá ...	H	86	1
	M	221	17, 23, 26
Jos ...	H	2	10
	S	56	51
	M	761	23
Joshánj ...	M	196	16
Jotáb ...	H	66	1, 15
	M	3,644	M. 1, 16, 17, 19, 51
Jotal ...	H	2	46
	S	6	5, 13
	M	157	28, 46
Joth ...	M	14	11
Joti ...	H	12	8, 13
	S	152	9, 10
	M	48	11, 25, 28
Jotin ...	M	28	17
Jotindwá ...	H	125	4
Joyá ...	H	51	8, 11, 25, 50
	S	408	6, 11, 12, 14, 25, 50
	M	15,374	M. 1, 12, 13, 16, 17, 18, 19, 23, 50, 51
Jujalí ...	M	2,615	12, 23
Kábe ...	H	16	50
	S	224	50
	M	8	50
Kabhojar ...	H	8	9
	M	40	9
Kabir ...	H	7	16, 19
	S	1	3
	M	32	11
Kablan ...	H	27	1
	S	2	4
Kabrá ...	S	139	44
	M	356	26, 27, 51
Kábre ...	H	408	5
	S	10	44
	M	3	10
Kachelá ...	H	165	51
	S	27	51
	M	30	44
Kachi ...	H	27	51
	M	30	44
Káchle ...	S	26	9
	M	1	6
Káchoi ...	S	1	24
	M	428	12, 28
Kádán ...	H	117	2, 4, 31
Kádhá ...	H	27	1, 8
	M	60	26

Names of Sub-Castes.		Persons.	Locality.
Kadhár ...	H	18	1
	S	2	9
	M	1,045	26
Kadi ...	M	74	12, 13, 23, 26
Kádián ...	H	10,366	2, 4, 5, 6, 30, 48
	M	153	4, 5, 6
Kadula ...	H	22	30
	S	23	10
Kadwán ...	H	55	48
	M	26	48
Kág ...	H	12	8
Káhal ...	H	413	2, 5, 6, 9, 11
	S	691	11, 49
	M	352	18, 51
Káhan ...	H	171	8, 16, 25
	S	481	6, 10, 14
	M	1,774	14, 27, 44
Kabár ...	H	287	1, 5
	S	27	19, 26
	M	271	18, 26
Káhari ...	H	2	5
	M	545	12, 28
Káhe ...	H	35	1, 8, 9
	S	377	11
	M	172	9
Kahgal ...	M	60	12
Kahlon ...	H	1,021	8, 15, 16
	S	3,180	9, 11, 14, 16, 44
	M	8,133	14, 15, 16, 46
Káhman ...	H	11	8, 9
Kahotra ...	M	158	16
Káhra ...	H	19	9, 16
	M	261	11
Kahror ...	H	16	9
	S	989	5, 25
Káhu ...	H	12	16
	S	63	12
	M	2	18
Kahut ...	M	64	20
Kai ...	S	2	12
	M	15	18
Kaihilá ...	H	56	4
Káil ...	M	115	11, 13
Káili ...	H	13	11, 44
	S	408	11
Káin ...	S	43	10
	M	1	16
Káith ...	H	148	4, 8, 9
	S	71	8, 9
	M	1,414	6, 8, 10, 11
Kájal ...	H	573	1, 5, 34
	S	173	44, 49
	M	22	5, 33
Káji ...	M	40	9
Kájla ...	H	964	1, 2, 4, 5, 10, 30
	S	44	10
	M	229	9, 14, 16, 26
Kájlán ...	H	64	1
Kájlí ...	H	171	2, 6, 9
	S	17	9
	M	70	1
Kákar ...	H	72	3, 8, 9, 30
	S	6	12, 33
	M	14	5, 9
Kakeriá ...	H	3	1
	M	98	28
Kakhá ...	H	29	14
	M	167	28
Kakhal ...	H	35	3, 9
	M	1	11
Kákhat ...	H	17	1
Kaki ...	H	2	12
	M	14	12, 20
Kakli ...	M	16	9, 10, 11
Kaklori ...	H	116	25
	S	130	9
	M	31	13, 20
Kakorá ...	H	40	2, 5, 9, 14
	M	258	9 20, 51
Kakrál ...	H	5	3
	M	1,195	21, 51
Kakri ...	M	248	51
Kaku ...	H	14	39
Kakwáni ...	H	77	1
Kála ...	H	85	9, 11, 16
	S	808	5, 9, 11, 12, 14
	M	615	11, 20, 27
Kaláb ...	H	1	2
	S	26	6
Kalabton ...	M	511	28
Kalál ...	S	36	5, 12, 13, 19, 51
	M	231	12, 18, 27, 51
Kalan ...	H	9	6
	S	65	9
	M	16	10
Kaláná ...	H	406	2, 4, 11, 15
	M	54	13
Kalang ...	M	128	51
Kalár ...	H	720	1, 9, 10, 14, 16, 45
	S	2,832	1, 9, 10, 11, 12, 44, 45, 49
	M	1,636	13, 16, 20, 26, 27, 44, 46, 51
Kalás ...	S	2	45
	M	522	16, 26, 51
Kalásan ...	M	1,364	12, 13, 18, 27
Kalásrá ...	M	2,275	12, 28
Kalátra ...	M	1,006	28
Kaláwat ...	H	1	32
	M	75	51
Kaleb ...	H	522	31
Kaleká ...	M	62	26
Kalel ...	M	38	10, 26
Kaler ...	H	1,774	J. 5, 16, 44
	S	3,709	J. L. 5, 19, 20, 45, 46, 49
	M	1,580	J. L. 18, 20
Kaleron ...	H	190	6
	S	121	51
	M	5	51
Kalerwán ...	H	1,008	5, 33
	S	36	1
Kálham ...	H	26	9
	S	11	9
Kalhar ...	H	45	3, 44
	M	607	10, 23
Kalhora ...	H	7	2
	M	269	16, 51
Kalhum ...	H	80	8
	S	3	19
	M	8	13
Kaliá ...	H	45	2, 8, 9, 12
	S	345	6, 9
	M	1,059	12, 23, 26, 51
Kaliádá ...	H	97	5, 9
Kaliál ...	M	3,035	13, 20
Kaliáná ...	H	58	5, 6, 8, 48
	S	1,568	5, 6, 48
	M	1,409	13, 27, 51
Kaliár ...	H	561	9, 11, 16, 47, 51
	S	17	9
	M	401	6, 9, 18, 26
Káli Bal ...	H	3,852	2, 5, 6, 10, 30, 48
	S	3,533	10, 48, 49
	M	126	26, 48
Kálirání ...	H	4,027	D.
	S	242	12
	M	5	12
Káli Báwal ...	H	371	2
Káli Bawán ...	H	3,278	1, 2, 4, 51
	S	7	6
Kalisá ...	S	1	10
	M	103	14
Kaliwál ...	S	12	2, 45
Kálju ...	S	60	6
	M	12	16
Kal Kali ...	H	47	1, 5, 24
Kál Kandra ...	H	57	2, 5
	S	43	28
Kal Kat ...	H	44	9, 10
	S	526	9, 10, 27
Kaloi ...	H	23	9, 10
	S	100	10, 12, 51
	M	219	9, 14, 16
Kalol ...	H	84	45
	M	84	23, 44
Kálon ...	H	91	5, 9
	S	2,279	9, 10, 33, 49
	M	396	12, 13, 44
Kalorá ...	H	245	1, 8, 12, 49
	M	7	18
Kalos ...	S	25	12
	M	1	5
Kalotá ...	H	172	9, 10
	S	155	9
Kalotrá ...	M	11	13
Kaloya ...	H	12	1, 16
Kálru ...	H	452	1, 9, 17
	S	40	28
	M	155	10, 14
Kalsi ...	H	108	8, 9
	S	16	5, 12, 18
Kalson ...	H	8	5
	M	42	20
Kalú ...	H	74	13, 25
	S	68	10, 13, 27, 44
	M	1,974	9, 10, 13, 14, 16, 23, 26, 28, 44, 51
Kalwa ...	H	94	5, 9
	S	242	9
	M	282	27
Kalwál ...	H	2	3
	S	6	5, 44
	M	20	20
Kalwán ...	H	190	1, 5, 8, 44
	S	117	1
	M	855	26, 27
Kalwárí ...	M	1,114	27
Kamal ...	H	5	12
	M	434	13, 25, 51
Kamáná ...	H	118	1, 3, 35
	S	106	10
	M	211	6, 26
Kamar ...	H	46	1
	S	7	13, 22
	M	1	13
Kamboh ...	H	108	10, 11, 13, 14
	S	738	9, 12, 13, 14, 19, 20
	M	1,667	L. 23, 28, 51
Kamidamni ...	H	27	4
Kamin ...	S	20	10
Kamni ...	H	15	6
	S	7	14
Kamoj ...	M	365	13, 23
Kamoká ...	H	1	26
	M	89	13, 19
Kamra ...	H	2	44
	S	753	14, 19
	M	360	10, 19, 26
Kams ...	S	33	12
	M	84	26
Kanái ...	M	22	20
Kanál ...	H	6	5, 9
	S	8	5
Kanan ...	S	12	6, 14
Kanar ...	H	20	9, 34
	S	6	45
	M	3	26
Kanárí ...	H	12	8
	S	5	8
	M	1,150	28
Kanchal ...	H	22	2, 4
Kanchint ...	H	111	2
Kanda ...	H	373	1, 5, 9
	S	1	5
	M	418	13, 26
Kandal ...	H	936	2, 5, 8, 9, 15, 44, 48, 49
	S	19	24, 48
	M	1,028	27
Kandan ...	H	33	3, 5, 33
	S	1	13
	M	244	19, 23
Kandár ...	H	594	5, 49
	S	67	49
	M	12	26, 49
Kandel ...	H	218	1, 8
Kandera ...	H	41	1, 24
Kanderál ...	H	11	3
Kandhan ...	H	41	9
	S	18	9
Kandharan ...	H	28	3
	S	5	9
Kandhli ...	M	11	9
Kondiwál ...	H	16	9
	M	24	19
Kandli ...	H	24	9
	M	264	5, 51
Kandoki ...	H	996	1, 6, 10, 45, 49
	S	1,459	6, 9, 10, 45, 49
	M	6	10

Names of Sub-Castes.		Persons.	Locality.
Kandoli ...	H	120	5, 9, 11, 44
	S	481	11, 51
Kandor ...	H	11	2, 5, 19
Kanda ...	H	1,338	1, 3, 4, 5
	S	415	9, 11, 33
	M	20	14, 18
Kanera ...	H	16	1, 5
	M	1,114	19, 23, 51
Kang ...	H	2,057	6, 9, 10, 11, 16, 25, 39, 44
	S	9,781	J. 5, 6, 13, 14, 16, 19, 26, 33 44, 46, 51
	M	2,457	J. 6, 13, 14, 16, 18, 19, 44, 46
Kangan ...	H	8	9, 24
	S	182	5, 9
	M	358	9, 11
Kangas ...	H	4	1, 6
	S	11	11, 19
	M	7	5
Kang Dogar ...	M	11	16
Kanghi ...	H	17	1, 6
	S	3	9
	M	73	11
Kangori ...	H	639	6, 9, 11, 16, 48
	S	1,180	6, 11, 12, 16, 44, 46, 48
	M	226	6, 16, 19, 48
Kangotre ...	H	16	16
Kangra ...	H	37	5
	S	595	12, 46
	M	402	6, 11, 16
Kanho ...	H	12	11
Káni ...	H	4	24
	S	56	5, 10
	M	6	12
Kaniál ...	H	3	2,5
	S	2	45
	M	3,872	17, 19, 20
Kanián ...	H	28	2
Kanit ...	M	31	11
Kanita ...	H	28	1
Kánj ...	H	19	9
	S	128	44
	M	118	16, 26
Kánjal ...	S	110	18
	M	1,433	18
Kanjan ...	H	45	1
	M	738	18, 23, 26
Kanjar ...	H	220	1
	S	1	14
	M	76	14, 18, 19
Kanjára ...	M	978	28
Kanju ...	H	28	12, 41
	S	1	14
	M	547	19, 23, 51
Kank ...	H	22	6
	S	252	10, 14, 20
	M	54	12, 14
Kankar ...	H	409	1, 2, 5, 9
	S	3	10
	M	19	5
Kankara ...	H	30	1, 33
	S	104	1
Kankor ...	S	46	9
Kanotra ...	S	108	9
Kanp ...	M	12	11
Káns ...	H	28	2, 3
	M	15	18
Kánsi ...	M	12	45
Kánsouiá ...	H	24	1
Kanun ...	H	9	5, 8
	M	115	51
Kanuri ...	M	99	51
Kánwá ...	M	20	9
Kanwál ...	H	5	9
	S	29	5
	M	1,325	27
Kanwan ...	H	5	21
	M	780	14, 16, 19, 26
Kanwár ...	H	7	2, 14
	S	7	6
Kapál ...	M	191	51
Kapra ...	M	246	29
Kapur ...	H	77	1, 6, 9
	S	5	12, 48
	M	82	51
Kara ...	H	166	1, 2, 15
	S	1,780	14
	M	130	10, 46
Karach ...	H	130	5
	S	8	6
Karag ...	M	36	28
Karál ...	M	126	13
Karaná ...	H	402	4, 49
	S	9	5, 25
	M	9	19
Karangar ...	H	43	3
	S	11	48
Karar ...	H	89	2, 5, 15
	S	484	15, 19
	M	562	12, 16, 19, 20, 26, 46
Karáwat ...	H	5	33
	S	9	9
Karbáni ...	H	47	2, 14
	S	36	6, 9
	M	6	20
Karda ...	H	46	8, 10
	S	1	29
Karel	S	195	14, 24
	M	375	26, 44, 51
Kareri ...	H	11	2, 4
	S	109	48
	M	18	48
Kari ...	H	158	3, 13, 25
	S	361	11, 13, 19
	M	314	9, 16, 23, 28
Kariál ...	H	196	5, 6, 10, 13
	S	4	9
	M	928	9, 13, 20, 27, 28
Karin ...	S	4	13
	M	22	9, 13
Karji ...	M	48	28
Kark ...	H	51	2
Karkará ...	H	1,364	48
	S	49	48
	M	1	48
Karla ...	H	14	1
	M	163	19, 26, 29
Karmán ...	H	139	2, 6, 15, 25
	S	2	12
	M	299	20, 48
Karnáwal ...	H	5	5, 33
	S	11	6, 51
	M	93	27
Karniádágar ...	H	157	4
Karniás ...	H	123	1
Karod ...	H	72	6, 9
Karog ...	M	35	19
Karoiá ...	H	1	1
	S	209	11
	M	45	19
Karor ...	H	15	2, 42
	S	74	2, 11, 17
	M	2	19
Karoti ...	H	17	1, 10, 49
	M	1	11
Karpál ...	M	230	51
Karsani ...	M	17	44
Káru ...	H	26	2, 11
	M	9	15, 19
Kárukath ...	M	43	6, 9, 11
Karursaru ...	H	984	1, 11
	S	101	1
Karwál ...	H	28	3, 8, 25
	S	40	12, 25
	M	398	27
Kárwán ...	H	16	1
Kas ...	H	9	2, 49
	M	330	19
Kásane ...	H	21	1, 48
	M	9	19, 28
Kasar ...	H	2	49
	M	318	19, 20, 23
Káshab ...	H	29	2, 5, 11, 48
	S	10	5
	M	7	12, 18
Kashk ...	M	44	28
Kashmiri ...	S	4	12
	M	538	11, 13, 18, 19, 20, 23, 27, 29, 48
Kási ...	H	65	2, 9, 51
	M	16	12
Kasiá ...	H	867	1
	M	1	6
Kasila ...	H	48	1, 48
Kaskundlá ...	H	263	4
Kásli ...	M	59	28
Kasmiá ...	H	435	2, 6
	S	20	2
	M	95	17
Kasrá ...	M	466	19, 22, 25, 27, 51
Kastur ...	M	54	27
Kasura ...	M	657	26
Kasuran ...	H	5	8, 13
	M	15	10, 11, 21
Kaswal ...	H	498	1, 2, 3, 5
	S	2	12
Kaswán ...	H	1,692	1, 2, 51
	S	60	1, 24
	M	4	13, 25
Kat ...	H	7	4, 23
	S	14	10
	M	462	13, 14, 23, 28, 29
Katara ...	H	1,020	2, 5, 16
	S	48	12, 14, 18
	M	230	11, 14, 18
Katárián ...	H	1,967	1, 3, 4, 9, 16, 48, 49
	S	110	6
	M	80	3, 29, 48
Kathal ...	H	35	33
	S	35	6
	M	303	28, 50
Káthiá ...	S	73	9, 10
	M	459	11, 25
Kathra ...	H	81	1, 11
	S	152	1,
Katiá ...	H	10	10, 19
	S	33	9, 25
	M	399	25, 27
Katiál ...	H	23	2, 8, 24
	M	843	6, 18, 27
Kátián ...	S	1	6
	M	43	9
Katil ...	M	13	46
Katira ...	H	168	1, 5, 9
	S	46	44
	M	195	23, 25, 47
Katoch ...	H	15	1
Katpal ...	M	768	27, 28, 29
Katri ...	H	76	1, 9
	S	239	19, 48
	M	195	9, 14, 28
Kattar ...	M	303	19, 25, 28
Kattu ...	H	92	48
Katwál ...	H	83	2, 12
	S	7	9, 10, 44
	M	305	9, 13, 21, 28
Katwár ...	H	28	5, 51
	M	5	19
Kawál ...	H	13	2, 6
	S	6	19
	M	1	25
Kawálá ...	H	513	3, 4, 12, 48
	S	9	48
	M	1	13
Káwán ...	H	204	1, 5, 21, 31
	M	231	15, 16, 25
Kawár ...	H	11	5
	S	8	25
	M	98	28
Kawárá ...	H	14	2, 11, 24
Keke ...	H	11	51
Kela ...	H	30	16
	S	122	14, 15, 16
	M	792	13, 14, 23, 26
Kelar ...	H	82	9
	S	1	13
	M	7	14
Koli ...	H	278	9, 10
	S	435	8, 9, 10
	M	16	9, 10
Kenjan ...	M	1,555	23
Keora ...	H	8	10
	M	351	18
Keri ...	H	66	9, 11
	S	1	9
	M	1	16
Keruiál ...	M	120	23
Kesar ...	M	46	13, 16
Ket ...	M	280	9, 28

Names of Sub-Castes.		Persons.	Locality.
Kewál ...	H	21	1, 49
	S	2	49
	M	2	49
Khábra ...	H	129	9, 10, 19, 27
	S	571	6, 9, 10
	M	1	19
Khachak ...	M	24	18
Khadái ...	H	19	2
Khadar ...	H	385	4, 18, 39
	S	269	6, 49
	M	48	49
Khagas ...	M	414	6, 19, 28, 51
Khaggan ...	S	529	10
	M	529	9, 19, 26, 27
Khágori ...	H	33	9
	S	7	9
Khaira ...	H	42	9, 11
	M	209	11, 14, 50
Khaka ...	H	298	4, 10
	S	211	9, 10
	M	317	19, 28
Khákan ...	H	107	9
	S	380	9, 10
	M	962	27, 28
Khakhákhel...	M	290	29
Khakhar ...	H	445	1, 10
	S	7	10
	M	505	10, 29, 51
Kháki ...	S	3	12
	M	918	11, 29, 44, 51
Khakori ...	S	347	10
Khákot ...	H	2	11
	M	470	27
Khákre ...	H	18	9
	S	9	10
Khál ...	H	2	11
	S	103	11
	M	351	51
Khalái ...	H	79	1
	M	3	27
Khaláni ...	H	20	2, 9
	S	46	9
	M	731	13, 29
Khalerá ...	H	23	9
	M	625	25, 27, 51
Khaleri ...	H	61	1, 18
Khálí ...	H	155	1
	S	50	12
Khaliár ...	H	171	1, 12, 49
	S	89	49
	M	60	49
Khálig ...	H	30	8, 51
	M	36	19
Khalkar ...	H	117	6
Khallan ...	H	6	9
	S	19	10
Khallo ...	S	720	15
Khálri ...	H	16	33
Khamán ...	H	24	9
	S	53	12, 33
	M	888	12, 44, 51
Khambá ...	H	8	49
	S	18	28, 49
	M	50	25, 49
Khán ...	H	171	9, 49
	S	3	49
	M	338	29, 49
Khana ...	H	291	2
	M	56	17
Khanchak ...	M	199	12, 29
Khand ...	H	577	1, 3, 10, 11, 25
	S	1	10
	M	4,198	23, 26, 27, 28, 51
Khandela ...	H	12	8
	M	321	29
Khander ...	H	109	1, 5, 51
	S	3	13
	M	137	29
Khandwán ...	H	1	25
	S	13	19
Kháne ...	H	1	25
	S	22	19
	M	125	27, 51
Khangar ...	H	391	2, 10
	S	91	11
	M	1,152	9, 11, 20
Khangi ...	H	56	9, 25, 50
	S	168	6, 45, 50
	M	181	16, 50
Khangori ...	H	196	6, 16
	S	1,581	9, 11, 12
	M	97	13, 16
Khangot ..	H	13	10
	S	16	16
	M	30	18
Khanke ...	H	45	9, 10
	S	3	14, 24
	M	130	16, 17
Khanna ...	H	56	4
Khápariá ...	H	822	5
	S	1	4
	M	2	2
Khapra ...	M	28	20
Khárá ...	H	696	5, 6, 10, 25
	S	8,873	3, 6, 8, 9, 10, 11, 13, 14, 18
	M	3,321	13, 14, 17, 19, 28, 51
Kharad ...	H	1,157	2, 5, 6, 49
	S	88	13, 45
	M	290	19, 49
Kharái ...	H	67	5
	S	70	10
	M	715	19
Kharal ...	H	143	1, 34
	S	147	14, 18, 19, 33
	M	13,776	L. 1, 10, 20, 25, 27, 44, 50
Kharalá ...	H	172	49
	S	167	46, 49
	M	1,327	16, 25, 51
Kharáni ...	H	15	19, 25
	M	1,561	16, 20, 28
Kharat ...	H	225	1, 6
	M	672	27
Kharáti ...	H	15	2, 49
	S	46	19, 49
	M	16	5, 15
Kharchar ...	H	28	30
Khardí ...	H	496	1
Kharhar ...	S	424	9, 15
	M	41	17
Khári ...	H	6	31
	S	451	13, 33
	M	579	12, 13, 15, 28
Khariá ...	H	67	4, 5, 21
	S	3	17
	M	100	51
Khark ...	H	4	2, 11
	S	8	17
	M	88	20
Khárkas ...	H	1,736	8, 25
	S	177	17
	M	274	25, 27
Kharkhar ...	H	95	5, 10
	S	1	10
Kharl ...	H	12	2
	M	1,729	11, 26
Kharman ...	H	160	6
	S	16	17
	M	5	25
Kharmár ...	H	75	1, 4
Kharod ...	H	1,202	5, 8, 25, 39
	S	247	10, 45
	M	533	27
Kharog ...	H	15	30
	M	14	23
Kharoki ...	H	466	6
	M	860	51
Kharor ...	H	102	9, 10, 11, 18, 30
	S	90	9, 12, 46
	M	1,960	9, 10, 22, 27, 51
Kharsara ...	M	104	13, 48
Khársi ...	H	3	6
	S	268	48
Kharwá ...	H	28	3, 12
Kharwál ...	H	29	12, 30
	M	79	25
Khasará ...	H	500	48
	S	11	48
	M	28	48
Khási ...	S	2,582	6, 19, 48
	M	34	50
Khata ...	H	8	2
	S	90	11, 46
	M	311	11, 13, 23, 25, 51
Khatal ...	H	46	4
	M	25	13, 51
Khatar ...	H	1,777	2, 16, 17, 25
	S	10	24
Khatarwál ...	H	432	1, 2, 15
	M	2,040	15, 20
Khateri ...	H	416	5, 25
	S	24	1
	M	1,069	4, 15, 18, 25
Khatka ...	H	47	4, 5
	S	359	9, 48
	M	2	48
Khatlál ...	H	12	2, 21
Khatmáriá ...	S	3	18
	M	1,354	18
Khatrái ...	H	776	11, 50
	S	1,484	9, 11, 45, 50
	M	61	11, 50
Khatráwal ...	H	106	49
	S	105	49
Khatri ...	H	4,510	2, 3, 4, 5, 8, 33
	S	108	9, 12
	M	106	2, 3, 13
Khatwál ...	H	824	3, 4
	S	5	10
	M	225	22, 51
Khawárá ...	M	72	26
Kháwrá ...	H	1	9
	M	194	26
Khel ...	H	344	9, 10
	S	57	10, 27
	M	41	16, 17
Khera ...	H	146	8, 9, 10, 16
	S	1,921	10, 11, 12, 14, 16, 19, 33, 46
	M	1,657	10, 13, 16, 17, 20, 46, 50
Kherrá ...	M	12	17
Khes ...	H	180	5
	M	260	26
Khetwál ...	H	86	48
	S	39	48
	M	2	48
Khichá ...	M	1,829	13, 16, 20, 23, 26, 51
Khijianá ...	M	67	20, 26
Khílá ...	H	7	9
	S	355	11
	M	32	25
Khirá ...	S	25	9, 19
Khitráni ...	H	9	14
	S	338	14
Khobál ...	H	17	24, 25
	S	58	25, 27
Khod ...	H	70	2, 6
	S	13	9, 12
	M	400	1, 11, 12
Khog ...	H	5	51
	S	87	1, 6
	M	1,153	8, 17, 25, 28, 29
Khohán ...	M	496	23
Khohri ...	S	22	25
Khoja ...	H	8	12
	M	182	9, 10, 11, 13, 14, 44, 51
Khojan ...	H	87	1
	M	57	9, 12
Khokha ...	H	52	1, 19
	S	141	46
	M	1,655	16, 19, 21, 27
Khokhar ...	H	677	2, 6, 16, 50, 51
	S	5,746	6, 10, 11, 12, 14, 15, 17, 24, 46
	M	25,059	1, 12, 13, 14, 17, 20, 21, 23, 26, 28, 51
Kholá ...	H	386	42, 48
	S	96	6, 14
	M	6	11
Kholrá ...	H	9	9
	M	3,470	39, 44
Khoná ...	H	10	14
	M	458	14, 20, 25
Khondál ...	H	464	3, 48
	S	835	46
	M	28	48
Khopra ...	H	35	4, 9
	S	25	9

Names of Sub-Castes.		Persons.	Locality.
Khorach ...	M	719	18
Khoráná ...	S	140	25
	M	4	13
Khoriá ...	H	1,307	1, 4, 50, 51
	S	1,238	5, 11, 25, 50
	M	1,616	16, 23, 28, 29, 50, 51
Khorwál ...	S	147	14
	M	5,288	19
Khosa ...	H	112	4, 9, 11, 48
	S	1,369	10, 11, 12, 25, 29, 33, 46, 51
	M	1	10
Khosal ...	H	26	4, 49
Khoswál ...	H	770	5, 30
Khot ...	H	255	1, 5
	M	779	12, 18, 26, 28
Khotal ...	H	843	49
	M	1,055	19
Khoti ...	H	2	16
	M	1,268	20, 27
Khotre ...	H	33	30
	S	202	11
	M	204	14, 23
Khudyali ...	M	205	23
Khullar ...	M	13	13
Khunda ...	H	77	4, 14
	M	5	11
Khurásán ...	H	127	48, 50
	S	368	48
	M	62	48
Khúsra ...	S	2	6
	M	58	14
Khyárá ...	M	786	1, 17, 23
Kiara ...	H	277	49
	S	110	1
Kijhon ...	H	3	13
	M	72	5
Kilkali ...	H	934	1
	M	133	19
Kimu ...	H	186	2
	S	20	27
Kine ...	H	137	2, 3
Kingrá ...	H	159	16
	S	19	46
	M	587	12, 17, 18, 20, 51
Kira ...	H	1	12
	S	1	10
...	M	25	14
Kobál ...	M	261	29
Kobár ...	M	258	51
Kochar ...	H	18	19
	M	37	26, 51
Kochi ...	M	627	11, 44
Kodán ...	H	1	32
	M	27	26
Kodi ...	H	166	2, 3
	S	3	6
	M	12	44
Koháji ...	M	231	10, 50
Kohál ...	H	193	1, 10, 16
	S	4	9
	M	249	27
Kohára ...	H	1,535	1, 2, 4, 10, 16, 33
	S	400	10, 16, 22, 44
	M	2,157	6, 16, 46, 51
Koháwár ...	H	149	1
	S	202	6
	M	6	12
Koiá ...	M	21	6
Koila ...	M	265	27
Kojáli ...	H	24	6
	M	7	51
Kojár ...	M	149	9
Kokar ...	H	175	9, 12
	S	50	9
	M	632	27
Kokára ...	S	632	26
	M	39	16, 27, 28, 46
Kokarti ...	H	129	1, 9
	M	440	12, 19, 25
Kokeri ...	M	68	15, 51
Kokram ...	H	3	51
	M	23	12, 14
Kolár ...	H	56	11
	S	277	10, 11, 14
	M	125	17, 23, 44

Names of Sub-Castes.		Persons.	Locality.
Koli ...	H	15	6
	S	5	12
	M	9	8, 20
Koliár ...	M	20	11, 22
Koloti ...	M	32	23
Kolrái ...	M	76	23
Koluwáná ...	H	7	8
	M	32	19
Komár ...	S	8	51
	M	57	20
Konar ...	H	795	9, 10, 11, 12
	S	852	10
	M	3	10, 11
Kondal ...	H	1,025	8, 9, 39
Kondar ...	S	41	12
	M	2	20
Konde ...	H	10	2
	M	11	13, 23
Kondu ...	H	1,159	2, 32
Konjal ...	H	282	4
Kont ...	H	1,687	46, 50
	S	2	50
	M	29	10, 15
Kontar ...	S	100	11
	M	262	9, 20
Kopra ...	H	115	2, 11
Korá ...	H	278	2, 12, 13, 14, 46
	S	110	10, 12, 13, 16
	M	2,256	5, 13, 18, 20, 27, 28, 51
Koral ...	M	289	11, 19
Korija ...	M	181	21, 28, 51
Kornal ...	H	2,097	1
	M	197	20
Korutáná ...	H	17	10, 16
	S	947	5, 12, 33
	M	1,217	11, 14, 16, 18, 19, 51
Kosal ...	H	3	12, 47
	S	9	47
	M	2	2
Kosiá ...	M	40	28
Koswál ...	M	308	21, 27
Kot ...	M	166	17, 20
Kotar ...	H	346	6, 19, 21
	S	2	12, 20
	M	353	9, 11, 19, 26, 27
Kothalá ...	H	31	4, 8
	S	1	8
Kothra ...	M	31	20
Krola ...	H	23	6
Kuchála ...	H	1	12
	M	120	23
Kuchra ...	M	160	10
Kuláná ...	H	33	49
	M	765	27
Kular ...	M	65	16
Kulár ...	H	105	9, 11
	S	252	11
Kunb ...	H	52	2
Kunda ...	H	97	4
Kung ...	M	917	10, 29
Kurmi ...	H	72	11, 13
	M	556	25
Labál ...	S	61	6, 20, 27
Labána ...	H	42	17, 19, 46, 48
	S	260	L. 9, 19, 24, 48
	M	294	9, 10, 19, 28
Lábar ...	M	14	27
Lácha ...	H	738	4, 16, 48
	S	157	48
	M	9	48
Lachar ...	H	45	4
	S	828	9, 10
Lád ...	H	64	4, 8, 38, 39
	S	167	9, 15
Ladá ...	H	6	1
	M	57	5, 17
Ládan ...	H	28	2, 11
Ladhá ...	H	40	16
	S	6	14, 17
Ladháná ...	M	47	27
Ladhar ...	H	764	9, 10, 11, 13, 14, 16, 17, 50
	S	1,771	6, 9, 11, 14, 15, 16, 17, 25, 50
	M	2,774	J. L. 28, 29, 44, 46, 51

Names of Sub-Castes.		Persons.	Locality.
Ládi ...	H	34	9, 11
	S	28	9
	M	8	11
Ladiál ...	M	84	19, 27, 51
Ladiki ...	H	26	8
	M	1	13
Ladkin ...	H	24	39
	M	22	14
Ladwál ...	S	30	9
Laga ...	H	12	16
	M	43	16, 29
Lagándi ...	M	44	17
Lágar ...	H	698	32, 48
	M	10	13, 17, 24
Lághan ...	M	19	28
Láhal ...	M	89	6
Láhan ...	H	21	16
Láhar ...	H	782	1, 2, 9, 13
	S	345	9, 10, 12, 14, 44
	M	129	12, 13, 19, 24, 27
Lahot	H	20	16
Lahotari	S	23	6
Lahná ...	H	144	3
	M	37	17
Lahr ...	H	396	48
	S	70	48
	M	479	16
Lahta ...	H	201	9
	S	235	9, 25
Láhori ...	S	23	6
	M	2	46
Láiá ...	H	40	1, 50
	S	1	50
	M	178	10, 17, 19
Laigári ...	M	476	27
Laigiá ...	H	72	1
Láil ...	H	275	9
	S	131	6
	M	279	12, 24, 26, 27, 28,
Lak ...	H	14	2
	M	9,129	M. 18, 19, 20, 23, 51
Lakariá ...	H	24	49
	M	49	24
Lákhá ...	M	2,199	18, 27, 28, 29, 51
Lakhanpál ...	S	68	1
	M	164	13, 24
Lakhar ...	H	35	4
	M	46	17, 51
Lakherá ...	H	233	2
	M	25	26
Lakhí ...	S	1	49
	M	22	11
Lakhiál ...	M	28	24
Lakhiwál ...	S	389	9
	M	944	51
Lakhoka ...	M	557	51
Lakhlan ...	H	601	1, 6, 49
	S	270	9, 25
	M	850	9, 15, 16, 24, 51
Lakhoti ...	M	235	27
Lakhráná ...	M	14	26
Lakhri ...	H	76	3
Lakhwáli	H	56	3
Lákri ...	H	823	4
	M	42	29
Lál ...	H	48	9, 15
	S	403	9, 11, 14, 25
	M	165	16, 28, 51
Lalak ...	M	428	27
Lalar ...	H	30	16
	S	142	14, 16, 51
	M	80	9, 16, 17, 44
Lali ...	H	307	10, 44
	S	1,954	5, 9, 10, 12, 14, 44
	M	4,852	L. R. 9, 24, 26, 27, 33
Lalhar ...	H	14	49
Lallwál ...	H	13	2
	M	49	19
Lamará ...	H	124	4, 8
	M	387	15, 16
Lanbe ...	H	3,180	4, 6, 12, 20, 48, 49
	S	357	6, 9, 19, 48
	M	65	48
Landá ...	H	1	14
	S	283	8, 14

Names of Sub-Castes.		Persons.	Locality.
Landari ...	H	26	9
	S	21	9
	M	48	25
Láng ...	S	15	4, 19
	M	4,030	M. 12, 19, 51
Langáh ...	H	377	1, 3, 11, 12, 18, 48, 49
	S	323	11, 12, 25, 33, 48, 49
	M	8,170	B. M. 10, 12, 15, 16, 51
Langar ...	M	220	13, 29
Langargál ...	M	3,763	18, 51
Langráh ...	H	358	4
	M	2,195	27, 51
Langriál ...	H	150	16, 18, 19, 51
	S	54	16, 18, 19
	M	1,940	M.16,19,21,23,51
Láni ...	H	30	1, 16
	M	145	11, 13, 19, 44
Láníán ...	H	438	1, 2, 13, 31
Lár ...	H	42	25
	S	26	50
	M	2,238	5, 13, 24, 28, 29, 51
Larson ...	M	868	10, 27
Lasár ...	H	53	9
	M	192	13, 17, 29
Lashari ...	M	242	25
Lat ...	H	59	10, 11
	S	608	4, 7, 11, 49
	M	192	9, 14, 15
Latera ...	H	104	1, 9
	S	62	11
Láthá ...	H	196	1, 4, 30
	S	86	6, 44
	M	87	13, 19, 51
Láthar ...	H	2,172	2, 16, 49
	S	141	11, 49
	M	325	5
Lathwál ...	H	79	49
	M	39	5
Lati ...	M	64	23
Latián ...	H	28	49
Latu ...	M	18	14, 15
Laung ...	M	33	13
Láwá ...	H	175	12, 25
	S	2	9
	M	99	25, 28, 29
Láwár ...	H	39	9
	M	37	49, 51
Lawás ...	H	21	4
Láwat ...	H	279	6, 50
	S	63	6, 50
	M	1,095	25
Ledri ...	M	46	13
Legá ...	M	42	28
Leki ...	H	141	1
Leri ...	M	298	19, 27
Lesi ...	M	71	25
Lespal ...	H	196	10
Lidor ...	H	73	48
	S	18	48
	M	1	48
Lobhi ...	S	3	48
	M	68	48
Loch ...	M	97	6
Lochak ...	S	130	6, 15
	M	65	5
Locham ...	H	80	6, 48
	S	273	48
Lochan ...	H	170	9
	S	116	6, 49
Lochat ...	H	1,081	1, 2, 5, 12, 50
	S	13	12, 50
	M	598	1, 5, 10
Lodha ...	H	130	6, 11, 13, 16
	S	9	9
	M	4,246	L. 9, 18, 19, 26, 27, 28
Lodhar ...	H	6	49
	M	93	9, 24
Lodhará ...	H	76	17, 24
	M	2,571	M. 10, 18, 20, 23
Logáriá ...	H	1	44
	S	47	6
Loh ...	H	89	2, 6, 10
	M	153	26, 28
Loháchi ...	H	900	1, 2, 48, 49
	S	3	48
	M	180	5, 27, 29, 48
Lohán ...	H	1,445	1, 13, 15, 16, 48, 49
	S	18	13, 48
	M	2,085	1, 5, 11, 16, 18, 23, 25
Lohánch ...	M	420	23, 28
Lohár ...	H	790	1, 3, 6, 11, 18, 48
	S	812	9, 11, 13, 48
	M	2,156	1, 5, 27, 28, 48
Lohat ...	H	27	48
	S	46	48
	M	498	12, 48
Lohchan ...	H	48	13, 49
	S	7	49
Lohchit ...	H	371	1
	S	38	25
Lohi ...	M	43	11, 17
Lohrá ...	M	34	24
Loi ...	H	8	4
	M	347	13, 27
Lojat ...	M	148	6
Loká ...	H	35	25
	M	74	27, 29, 46
Lokára ...	H	1,128	3, 4, 6
Lokhar ...	H	33	6, 12
	S	5	6
	M	52	23
Lolariás ...	H	38	2
	M	171	18, 20, 26
Lole ...	H	203	9, 10, 48
	S	182	10
	M	1,076	15, 18, 25, 44, 48
Lomal ...	S	2	49
	M	22	11
Lomarár ...	H	95	1
	S	8	12
	M	37	26
Loudá ...	H	263	6
	S	29	48
	M	44	10, 20, 48
Longi ...	H	32	12
	M	157	26, 27, 51
Lopá ...	H	73	1, 50
	S	21	50
	M	181	5, 50
Lopal ...	M	11	23
Loprál ...	M	1,609	27
Lor ...	H	808	1, 9, 49, 50
	S	189	9, 12, 50
Lore ...	H	208	1
	S	15	16
	M	670	M. 10, 23, 51
Lorna ...	M	27	27
Losar ...	H	13	4
	M	468	27, 29
Lot ...	H	1	44
	S	192	12, 25, 48
	M	575	9, 11, 17, 44, 48
Lotri ...	H	1	14
	S	66	10, 17
	M	14	13, 16
Lund ...	M	29	29
Luráj ...	M	65	17
Lurka ...	M	3,038	17, 25, 27
Machal ...	H	11	4, 6
	S	11	5, 14, 44
Machhána ...	H	100	16, 44, 46
	S	662	9, 10, 13, 14, 44, 45
	M	199	15, 16, 18, 48
Máchhar ...	H	106	1, 2, 4, 12
	S	41	5, 12, 19, 44
	M	311	24, 25, 26
Máchhi ...	S	66	9, 19, 45
	M	911	13, 28, 29, 51
Máchrá ...	H	109	1
	S	9	5, 12
	M	147	15
Madar ...	H	22	3, 9, 13
	S	2	2
	M	35	17, 24
Madári ...	H	28	5, 16
	S	24	6, 10, 13, 33
	M	27	2, 10, 14, 17, 24
Madhán ...	H	974	2, 5, 10, 15, 16
	S	9	14
	M	49	5, 6, 13, 20
Madhar ...	H	199	2, 5, 10, 11, 16, 33
	S	121	19, 27, 44, 46
	M	144	12, 17, 24, 25, 29
Madharán ...	H	1	2
	M	15	1
Madhari ...	H	62	9, 13
	S	224	6, 10
	M	2	10
Mádho ...	H	28	5, 8, 48
	S	13	48
	M	51	19
Madhorá ...	H	106	2, 48
	S	83	27, 48
	M	502	12, 17, 29
Madi ...	H	25	4
	S	1,971	6, 9, 25
	M	10	2, 9
Mado ...	M	49	14, 20
Madráe ...	H	284	1, 6
	S	50	6, 48
Madwál ...	H	212	48
	S	2	48
Magál ...	H	261	2, 5, 12, 14
	S	1	44
	M	303	15, 19, 23, 24, 26
Magan ...	S	66	10, 16, 19
	M	45	10, 15, 25
Mágar ...	H	529	1, 9, 11, 44
	S	8	12
	M	181	6, 13, 19, 25, 44
Maghá ...	H	51	9, 12, 49
	S	37	1, 9
	M	538	1, 28
Magiál ...	H	5	13, 24
	M	72	14, 17, 21
Magwán ...	H	72	48
	S	8	48
Máhal ...	H	2,403	J. 1, 2, 4, 14, 15, 17, 19, 25, 30, 44, 48, 50
	S	5,222	8, 9, 14, 15, 19, 25, 46, 48, 50
	M	3,269	11, 13, 17, 20, 23, 24, 26, 27, 28
Mahán ...	H	274	5, 9, 10, 25, 48
	S	57	14, 25, 48
	M	1,067	12, 13, 16, 25, 26, 29
Mahande ...	H	1	5
	S	88	6, 19
	M	7	20
Mahant ...	H	51	5, 9, 11
	S	33	17
Máhar ...	H	1,292	2, 3, 5, 11, 16, 17, 41, 46, 48
	S	4,296	4, 11, 12, 13, 17, 25, 27, 46, 48
	M	12,945	L. M. except (27), 1, 10, 11, 12, 18, 19, 20, 48, 51
Maharu ...	H	11	9, 12
	S	7	19, 24
	M	93	19, 25, 28
Mahdolrá ...	H	5	33
	M	13	51
Mahelán ...	H	193	1, 2, 6, 45
	S	6	5, 6
	M	41	6
Mahes ...	S	551	13, 34
	M	516	14, 16
Mahgáli ...	M	25	29
Mahi ...	H	484	1, 11, 15, 16, 25, 48
	S	1,897	L. except (17), 12, 25, 44, 48
	M	1,099	15, 16, 17, 18, 25, 26, 29, 46
Mahil ...	H	2,091	1, 6, 8, 9, 10, 42, 49
	S	3,455	5, 8, 9, 10, 12, 14, 16, 33, 45, 49, 51
	M	3,540	1, 3, 6, 9, 10, 15, 16, 17, 18, 23, 24, 26
Mahin ...	S	19	48
Mahjar ...	H	13	4, 50
Mahjo ...	H	26	18

Names of Sub-Castes.		Persons.	Locality.
Mahlá ...	H	1,872	1, 2, 3, 4,10, 12, 32
	S	170	12, 25
	M	755	1, 17, 18, 20, 28, 51
Máhlon ...	H	574	1, 5, 45, 48, 49
	S	418	6, 10, 48, 49
	M	434	10, 13, 17,23,26, 48
Mahmá ...	H	9	46
	S	27	9, 10
Mahniwál ...	H	8	12
	M	4	17
Maho ...	H	5	46
	M	97	13, 24, 25
Máholia ...	H	22	1
	S	2	9
Máhot ...	H	392	48
	S	1,252	48
Máhotrá ...	H	58	15
Mahrán ...	H	211	1, 2, 48
	S	77	25
Mahre ...	H	353	1, 2, 3, 5, 12, 24, 32
	S	107	9, 14, 15, 16
	M	2,726	13, 16, 29, 47, 51
Mahta ...	H	24	2, 9, 11, 24, 48
	S	483	12, 48
	M	1,191	9, 13, 15, 16, 19, 24, 44
Mahtam ...	M	23	17
Mahtun ...	S	367	6, 12, 17, 46
	M	429	10, 12, 13, 24,25
Maihman ...	S	34	48
Maikan ...	M	20	17
Mains ...	H	412	4, 25, 41
	S	212	12, 19, 27
	M	681	14, 17, 19, 24,25
Majahade ...	M	11	14
Májar ...	H	963	1, 4, 5, 9, 25
	S	131	9
	M	117	9, 17, 25, 26
Majhiál ...	H	14	6, 25
	S	7	5, 10
	M	252	18, 19, 20
Májlá ...	H	3	1
	M	163	23
Majlan ...	H	19	1, 5
	M	107	5, 23
Majotre ...	H	641	16
	S	10	16
Majuka ...	M	25	19
Majun ...	H	108	1, 2, 5, 6
	S	276	14, 25, 45
	M	684	19, 23, 25, 29
Make ...	S	61	9, 14
	M	318	14, 51
Makhal ..	S	8	6
	M	612	19, 23, 25, 51
Makhan ...	H	2	2
	S	2	19
	M	470	9, 17, 23, 24, 26, 51
Makhar ...	H	180	4, 10, 25, 48
	S	113	6, 14, 25, 48
	M	631	6, 17, 51
Makhdum ...	M	47	17, 18, 19, 20
Makhnu ...	H	111	1, 6
	S	29	6
Makiár ...	H	6	5, 9
	M	513	23, 24
Makiwál ...	S	8	33
	M	2,309	28, 51
Makore ...	H	46	2, 5, 48, 49
	S	47	6, 10
	M	16	6, 10, 18
Maku ...	H	1	11
	M	37	12, 23
Mal ...	H	126	5, 6, 10, 12, 14, 25, 26, 47, 48
	S	383	6, 9, 14, 25, 26, 44
	M	217	6, 13, 15, 26, 51
Malá ...	H	344	1, 2, 3, 4, 8, 9
	S	172	10, 14
	M	1,065	2, 4, 5, 10, 26, 27, 28,
Maláhar ...	M	54	48
Malák ...	H	891	1, 2, 3, 4, 9, 19, 25. 31, 51
	S	11	12, 46
	M	5,144	2, 4, 11, 12, 13, 14, 17, 20, 26,51
Malalhá ...	H	2	12
	M	44	17
Malán ...	H	312	1, 2, 5, 49
	S	10	5, 49
	M	837	15, 27, 29, 33,51
Malána ...	H	217	10, 11
	S	193	6, 48
	M	7,237	6, 23, 27, 28,29, 25
Malang ...	H	6	
	S	194	9, 10, 44
	M	1	9
Maláwat ...	H	376	3
Malgo ...	M	12	19
Malhan ...	H	1,389	2, 10, 39
	S	9	29
	M	732	9, 13, 19
Malhar ...	M	11	16
Malhi ...	H	1,693	5, 6, 9, 16, 17, 27
	S	2,677	L. 6, 10, 11, 21, 19, 33, 46
	M	1,655	6, 8, 9, 13, 14, 16, 17, 24, 25
Malhot ...	H	22	8
	S	108	44
	M	185	13, 17
Máli ..	H	542	1, 6, 12, 15, 25, 44
	S	3,258	J. except (S), 6, 14, 15, 17, 24,45
	M	892	14, 15, 16, 24, 25, 26, 29, 44
Malián ...	H	197	1, 3, 5, 11
	S	46	1, 5, 9, 10, 37
	M	37	10, 17, 20
Maliár ...	H	113	11, 12, 19
	M	796	19, 20 23, 26,28
Málipotrá ...	M	68	51
Malkhán ...	H	10	11, 48
	S	22	1, 46, 48
	M	467	18, 24, 28, 48
Maloi ...	H	158	11, 12, 46
	S	10	24, 33
	M	603	28, 44
Malorkhi ...	S	2	1
	M	46	23, 26
Malot ...	H	18	8, 9, 10, 39
	S	11	6,9
	M	36	1,9
Malrá ...	H	6	2,12
	M	128	23, 25, 26, 28
Malri ...	H	28	12
	S	49	48
	M	1	14
Mami ...	H	1,064	15, 44
	S	348	15, 34, 51
	M	223	10, 12, 15, 24,25
Mamrá ...	S	45	48
	M	5	48
Mán ...	H	12,587	D. J. except(8), L. 19, 25, 30,33 48, 49, 50
	S	37,482	J. except(8), L. 6, 25, 48, 49, 50
	M	5,261	J. except (8),L. except (13), 6, 25, 49
Mának ...	H	49	10, 19, 44
	S	211	9, 33, 44
	M	2,209	19, 23, 27, 29
Manan ...	H	17	9
	S	610	10, 13, 14, 19, 25
	M	561	5, 10, 12, 14, 44, 51
Manar ...	H	22	5
	M	356	14, 15, 24, 26
Mánat ...	H	52	2, 48
	S	4	39
	M	1	1
Manchari ..	H	74	1, 5
	S	118	9
	M	102	9, 17
Mand ...	H	105	9, 10, 12, 17,25, 34
	S	850	6, 9, 10 12, 13, 17, 25
	M	1,163	6, 9, 10, 16, 17, 18, 25, 28
Mandá ...	H	691	J. except (8), 5, 50
	S	371	5, 15, 50
	M	604	14, 23, 24, 50,51
Mandábar ...	H	495	1, 8, 11, 12, 44, 48
	S	2,588	12, 48, 49
	M	909	11, 17, 18, 25,48
Mandal ...	H	497	2, 4, 5, 6, 9, 10, 12, 48
	S	1,433	6, 9, 14, 48
	M	1,037	5, 16, 17, 19, 23, 24, 48
Mandar ...	H	1,053	5, 9, 16, 42, 48
	S	2,564	1, 6, 9, 11, 25, 48, 49
	M	644	2, 12, 15, 24, 25, 28, 44, 48
Manderná ...	S	242	48
	M	3	48
Mandhán ...	H	1,059	2, 5, 9, 11, 34, 47, 49
	M	365	29, 51
Mandhare ...	H	950	2, 5, 6, 11, 40,45
	S	1,850	1, 5, 6
	M	840	6, 16, 17, 19, 20, 29, 45
Mandi ...	H	1,100	5, 6, 9,11, 16,25, 45, 48
	S	1,580	6, 15, 44, 48
	M	114	10, 25,28, 48,51
Mandiál ...	H	19	1, 12
	S	60	48
	M	152	23,24
Mandiár ...	H	127	1, 25, 30, 39, 42
	S	993	6, 10, 11, 25, 44, 45
	M	241	10, 11, 25
Mandiná ...	H	24	16
Mando ...	H	230	6, 11, 49
	S	3	46
	M	180	17, 29
Mandori ...	H	126	50
	S	315	50
	M	58	50
Mandotre ...	H	33	16
Mandwán ...	H	33	5, 48
	S	30	5
	M	23	17
Mángá ...	H	379	4, 6, 11, 12, 16
	S	44	10, 13
	M	195	16, 26, 51
Mangálá ...	H	94	1, 4, 5, 10, 12,25
	S	340	1, 9, 10, 11, 14
	M	1,771	14, 19, 20,28,29, 51
Mángar ...	H	412	4, 9, 11, 12, 13, 25
	S	767	1, 9, 12, 14, 19, 25, 48
	M	10,53	18, 19, 25,28,51
Mangariál ...	M	22	51
Mangat ...	H	535	J. except (8), 3, 6, 16, 45, 46 48, 50
		6,838	J. except (8), L. except (14),1,6, 20, 25, 48, 50
	M	3,743	L. except(14), 6, 10, 11, 12, 18, 20, 25, 26, 48, 51
Mángi ...	H	250	9, 48
	S	171	9, 44, 48
	M	52	9, 28, 51
Mangloi ...	H	23	24, 25
	M	78	19, 51
Mongori ...	H	18	1, 46
	M	112	13, 19, 51
Mangotrá ...	H	163	16
Mangu ...	H	152	5, 8, 11, 12
	S	42	5, 6, 49
	M	688	24, 29, 51

Names of Sub-Castes.		Persons.	Locality.
Mauháns ...	H	3	50
	S	76	50
Mauhás ...	H	80	7, 8, 9, 11, 16, 49
	S	584	9, 15, 16, 22, 48
	M	2,825	12, 13, 17, 18, 19, 20, 25
Manhi ...	S	63	10, 25
	M	156	17, 20, 51
Manj ...	H	588	11, 12, 16
	S	29	12
	M	14	11, 18
Manjko ...	H	49	1, 9
	S	60	6, 14
	M	4,385	9, 18, 29
Manohar ...	H	1	48
	S	97	48
Mansi ...	H	54	8, 9, 10, 11, 25
	S	193	17, 25
	M	478	10, 12, 14, 24, 27
Manu ...	H	172	10
Manwál ...	H	29	2, 6
	S	4	2, 10
	M	87	5, 11
Maráne ...	H	12	5
	M	1,019	9, 20, 25, 26, 28, 51
Marar ...	H	75	12, 46, 48
	S	210	12, 20, 25, 48
	M	327	17, 25
Márath ...	S	25	18, 24
	M	2,101	6, 18, 19, 20, 25, 28
Marchin ...	H	48	2
	M	135	23, 51
Marhatta ...	H	37	11
	M	156	29, 49
Mariá ...	H	109	1, 2, 6, 16, 48
	S	106	9, 11, 14, 48
	M	101	18, 25, 28, 29, 48
Mariál ...	H	185	11
	S	90	6, 9, 12, 48
	M	847	18, 26, 27
Mark ...	H	1	48
	S	16	48
	M	1	48
Maroe ...	S	27	48
Maroná ...	H	3	27
	S	20	19, 25
	M	92	20, 21, 25
Marral ...	H	11	48
	S	11	27
	M	1,073	17, 26, 29
Marri ...	H	46	5, 21, 24
	S	7	12, 25
	M	203	13, 15, 29
Marth ...	H	62	4, 9, 12
	M	194	3, 18, 20, 25
Maru ...	H	5	1, 12, 44
	S	29	9, 46
	M	241	9, 13, 24, 26, 29
Marwá ...	S	12	10, 12, 19
	M	189	18, 26, 27, 28
Marwáha ...	H	43	16
	S	11	5, 33
	M	1,386	5, 25, 26, 51
Marwáhi ...	H	11	19, 24
Marwat ...	S	16	11
Masandá ...	H	68	44, 48
	S	62	10, 48
Máshki ...	M	96	26
Maslan ...	H	78	4, 44
	S	75	6, 9, 17, 25
	M	1,328	12, 17, 23, 27, 28
Másrai ...	H	34	6, 25
	S	7	25
	M	58	9, 17
Mastur ...	M	535	29
Maswána ...	S	9	9
	M	106	23, 28, 51
Mat ...	H	21	10, 45
	S	2	44
	M	490	24, 25
Matá ...	H	18	1, 18
	M	289	17, 18, 19
Matái ...	H	9	5
	S	95	15
	M	661	18
Matán ...	H	66	5, 9, 15
	S	386	10, 19, 25, 48
	M	48	12, 19
Matar ...	H	163	6, 9, 25, 34
	S	129	14, 25
	M	758	9, 14, 20, 28, 29, 51
Matel ...	H	282	1, 2, 3, 5
	M	1,010	18, 21, 25, 26, 29, 51
Mathárwál ...	H	145	1, 49
	S	2	12
	M	6	16
Mathián ...	H	162	1, 6, 9
	S	6	6, 46
	M	30	19
Mathol ...	H	47	15
	S	15	3, 6, 44, 45
	M	1,922	16, 19, 24, 26
Matodi ...	H	34	6
Mattu ...	H	364	9, 10, 16, 25
	S	912	J. except (8), 14, 17, 25, 44, 48
	M	1,131	13, 16, 17, 18, 19, 20, 25, 28
Matwáli ...	S	30	48
Mawaliá ...	H	53	10
	S	78	15
Mawánch ...	H	1	48
	S	66	48
	M	1	48
Máware ...	H	92	2, 5, 6, 25
	S	21	12, 19
	M	298	5, 12, 24, 27, 28
Mawásan ...	H	25	48
	S	5	48
Máwi ...	H	239	6, 49
	S	82	9
Mazbabi ...	S	15	12
Meáda ...	M	18	17
Medal ...	H	41	48
	S	4	48
	M	1	19
Medo ...	H	5	49
	S	68	9
	M	5	13
Medwál ...	H	37	1, 25
	M	34	15
Megal ...	H	1	17
	M	32	16, 17
Mehrás ...	S	12	10
Mekhí ...	M	12	17
Mekná ...	H	6	11, 25
	M	4,381	12, 18, 19, 20, 27, 28
Melá ...	H	361	1, 25
	S	84	10, 25
	M	168	18, 20
Melar ...	M	45	24
Meo ...	H	4	12, 42
	S	39	12
	M	641	17, 18, 23, 29
Metla ...	H	299	1, 16, 27
	S	119	3, 9, 16, 44, 51
	M	4,497	M. except (25), 11, 15, 19, 20, 51
Mewáni ...	H	61	12, 49
	S	22	9
	M	65	9, 15, 25
Mez ...	M	28	20
Miána ...	H	52	5, 11
	S	10	9
	M	676	12, 14, 17, 19, 20, 23, 26, 29
Michu ...	H	266	27
Mikushari ...	M	1,206	27
Mir ...	H	3	11
	S	91	11, 17, 51
	M	1,605	13, 21, 23
Mivánkhel ...	M	23	23
Mirási ...	S	1	48
	M	285	16, 23, 28, 29
Mirdah ...	M	31	16
Mistari ...	M	173	27
Mochán ...	S	1	20
	M	774	9, 13, 19, 20, 27, 51
Modalá ..	M	35	51
Modi ...	H	271	1, 4, 25
	S	39	10
	M	30	26, 29
Mogali ...	H	5	12
	M	215	25, 27, 29
Mogharu ...	M	29	51
Mohan ...	H	176	1, 2, 9, 16, 49
	S	68	1, 9, 14, 48
	M	2,095	16, 19, 24, 26, 28, 29, 51
Mohár ...	H	122	1, 2
	S	2	1, 51
	M	1,027	1, 23, 25, 27, 51
Mohari ...	H	52	8, 25
	M	216	27, 51
Mohiál ...	H	34	13
Mohta ...	H	9	12
	M	751	1, 9, 27, 28
Mokhar ...	H	6	2, 9
	S	12	1, 12
	M	21	25, 51
Molá ...	H	72	1, 2, 9, 12, 49
	S	10	1
	M	1,123	1, 17, 24, 25, 29, 51
Molhi ...	H	58	9, 11, 19
	S	35	13
Monar ...	H	4	2
	M	186	18, 19, 24, 25
Mondh ...	H	437	1, 12, 19
	S	22	10
	M	305	16, 28
Mondhorá ...	H	12	2, 9, 12
	M	717	28
Mondi ...	H	871	1, 2, 9, 10, 48
	S	365	10, 19, 25, 48
	M	103	13, 16, 19, 33
Moudiál ...	M	30	19
Mondtur ...	H	1,244	2, 4
Mongrá ...	H	38	16
Moni ...	H	50	5, 9, 16, 48
	S	334	25, 44, 48
	M	77	1, 23, 26
Mor ...	H	5,754	1, 2, 4, 5, 25, 49
	S	616	1, 12, 25, 50
	M	505	16, 25, 27, 28
Mori ...	H	1,346	2, 5, 13
	M	198	13, 27, 28
Moriwál ...	H	35	1, 2
	S	3	10
Mosar ...	H	43	1, 12
	S	14	48
Motá ...	H	5	10, 16, 19
	S	11	12, 45
	M	608	12, 16, 17, 26, 27
Mothsare ...	H	902	1, 3, 4, 9, 10, 12, 48, 49
	S	54	5, 10, 48
	M	217	17, 18, 28, 51
Moti ...	H	17	9, 13, 48
	S	2	48
	M	198	1, 9, 16, 27, 48
Motil ...	H	11	12
	S	6	12
	M	22	51
Mughal ...	H	74	2, 5, 46, 48
	S	23	12, 14
	M	990	12, 13, 17, 18, 23, 27, 48
Multani ...	H	28	12, 13, 46, 48
	S	3	12, 48
	M	183	16, 18
Murjána ...	M	77	27
Murli ...	M	56	33
Nabbar ...	S	46	4, 48
	M	7	27, 48
Nach ...	H	219	29
	M	187	27, 28
Nacháranti ...	H	19	48
Nadhar ..	H	14	9, 48
	S	5	10
	M	254	17
Nadboli ...	H	23	25
Nadiál ...	H	3	6, 12
	S	84	48
	M	7	13
Nádir ...	H	2	5
	S	553	48

SUB-CASTES OF CERTAIN SELECTED CASTES—*continued*.

Names of Sub-Castes.		Persons.	Locality.
Nadisar ...	S	18	14
Nadmál ...	S	18	4
Nág ...	S	87	14, 19
	M	62	18, 26
Nágal ...	H	495	1, 2, 30, 31, 44, 49
	S	2	44
	M	17	25
Nágar ...	H	2,511	5, 8, 9, 10, 50
	S	2,254	10, 11, 14, 16, 50
	M	526	L. 10, 11, 19, 20
Nagariál ...	M	550	19, 20, 24
Nagarpál ...	H	8	18, 19
	S	1	19
	M	36	16, 17, 18
Nágauri ...	H	7	47
	S	18	25
Naggáh ...	H	14	2, 20
	S	21	2
	M	55	2, 14, 17
Naggiál ...	H	19	18
	S	59	12, 18
	M	1,933	20, 25, 28
Nághra ...	S	577	4, 9, 27
	M	1,657	16, 18
Nagiáná ...	M	144	19, 23
Nagwán ...	H	35	4, 48
	S	9	10, 24, 48
Náhal ...	H	127	10, 44
	S	1,104	10, 12, 24
	M	35	10, 13, 16
Náhar ...	H	372	5, 29, 44
	S	331	5, 11, 25
	M	1,271	17, 19, 25, 26, 27, 51
Náhra ...	H	1,924	1, 2, 48, 49, 51
	S	120	12, 48, 49
	M	8,484	19, 21, 23, 26, 28, 49, 51
Nahráu ...	H	3	32
	M	65	19
Nahriwál ...	H	149	2, 4, 6, 12
	S	33	1, 17
Naicha ...	H	1	51
	M	575	23, 26, 29, 51
Nail ...	H	2,231	1, 11
	S	99	1, 6, 17
	M	265	17, 24, 28
Nainbaj ...	H	295	6, 48
Najhar ...	S	96	10, 19
	M	18	14, 16
Najotrá ...	M	12	19
Najpar ...	H	570	8, 9, 44
	S	942	9, 14, 44, 49
	M	876	14, 16, 19
Najri ...	H	225	16
	S	2	51
Nak ...	M	95	14, 51
Nakat ...	H	82	1
Nákhar ...	S	3	19
	M	115	9
Nakiál ...	M	135	27
Nakri ...	H	13	48
	S	2	48
Nakwál ...	H	226	3
Nal ...	H	370	5, 8, 48
	S	7	3
	M	123	2, 16, 48
Nalohte ...	H	28	8
Námal ...	S	849	44, 48
Namáni ...	H	42	50
	S	935	10, 25, 44, 50
	M	159	50
Nának ...	H	24	2, 8, 33
	S	47	12
Nándal ...	H	2,303	2, 4, 5, 31, 48
	S	18	48
	M	548	26, 27
Nandan ...	H	39	5, 12, 49
	S	9	45, 49
	M	6	24, 25
Nandolo ...	M	214	27
Nandpál ...	H	25	6
	S	1	20
Nandu ...	H	36	5, 10, 16
	M	5	13
Nang ...	M	116	14, 27
Nángal ...	H	38	2, 8
	S	46	9, 15, 16, 19
	M	61	21
Nangári ...	S	266	6, 12, 19
	M	32	13
Nangi ...	S	5	44
	M	123	16, 17
Nangli ...	S	2	51
	M	44	21
Nangpál ...	H	1	27
	S	14	51
	M	65	17, 19
Nángra ...	H	677	12, 16
	S	150	14, 15, 25
	M	76	16, 17, 19
Nangri ...	H	3	19
	S	288	15, 19, 33
	M	66	25
Nanshábi ...	M	167	17
Nárá ...	H	1,650	1, 2, 5, 6, 21, 49, 53
	S	64	2, 5, 13, 49
	M	220	3, 13, 18, 19, 20, 28
Naráin ...	H	888	5, 6, 11, 12, 48
	S	1,668	6, 12, 45, 48
	M	194	1, 5
Nárang ...	M	356	17, 23, 25, 27
Narhale ...	H	23	8
	S	68	6
Narinjini ...	S	74	10, 12, 14
	M	28	24
Nármat ...	H	649	4
Náru ...	H	1,604	1, 5, 8, 9, 48
	S	26	48
	M	1,562	L. 12, 18, 19, 23, 24, 25, 27, 28
Narwál ...	H	853	3, 4, 5, 31, 46, 49
	S	653	9, 10
	M	227	12, 20, 29
Narwán ...	H	358	5, 48, 49
	S	2,797	1, 4, 5, 6, 48, 49
	M	100	1, 5, 10, 11, 48, 49
Násí ...	M	123	27
Nasir ...	H	1,053	2, 3, 4, 44, 48
	M	537	26
Nat ...	H	653	10, 13, 15, 17, 33, 39, 40, 48
	S	1,917	13, 15, 16, 17, 19, 25, 48, 49
	M	1,731	15, 16, 17, 18, 23, 44, 48
Náth ...	H	57	9, 48
	S	6	5
	M	4,093	51
Nathaiá ...	H	35	8, 14, 16
	S	2	8
Nathal ...	H	10	25
	S	64	14
	M	144	16, 17, 18, 20, 23
Nathar ...	S	230	9
	M	3	14
Nathora ...	M	55	13, 19
Naumuslim ...	M	58	3
Nawáde ...	H	48	10, 49
	S	16	49
	M	28	9
Náwal ...	H	4	4
	S	156	17, 48
	M	139	29
Nawán ...		106	11
	S	58	12, 48
	M	31	29
Nawári ...	S	14	5, 33, 48
	M	739	14, 23, 28, 29
Nehdhe ...	H	186	3, 5
Nekokara ...	M	859	19, 24, 26
Nen ...	H	6,443	2, 4, 5, 6, 10, 13, 44, 48, 49
	S	1,680	11, 13, 48, 49,
	M	1,770	1, 4, 14, 27, 28, 29, 48
Niár ...	M	14	13, 29
Nidrá ...	S	23	10, 17
	M	138	13, 29
Nigah ...	H	33	9, 16
Nihare ...	H	70	3, 9
	M	16	17
Nija ...	S	101	11, 48
Niká ...	H	4	48
	S	32	33, 48
Nikku ...	M	1,094	17, 51
Nil ...	H	29	5
	S	297	10
Nilar ...	S	36	15
Nili ...	H	19	48
	S	545	10
	M	285	16, 17, 18, 29, 48
Nimbar ...	H	27	49
Ningi ...	H	7	10, 39
	M	39	28
Nirhas ...	H	351	1
Nirlán ...	H	6	5
	S	13	33
Niswáná ...	M	505	19
Nol ...	H	514	1, 2, 12
	M	8,372	13, 17, 24, 25, 26, 27
Non ...	H	4	5
	S	16	12
	M	9,884	M. 17, 19, 20, 51
Nonár ...	H	9	12
	M	5,125	12, 24, 25, 26, 29, 51
Nonbansi ...	S	9	20
	M	21	20
Nonun ...	M	975	25, 27
Norá ...	M	411	16
Note ...	H	135	9
	S	12	1
Nungi ...	M	1,247	27
Nur ...	H	287	6
	M	1,239	23, 51
Obáhar ...	H	38	16
	S	1	16
	M	1	19
Obháni ...	M	160	28
Odar ...	H	22	2, 3
Odási ...	H	598	11, 12
Odhá ...	H	51	51
	S	65	51
	M	64	14, 29
Odi ...	H	28	4, 35, 49
	S	3	17, 46
Odole ...	M	52	20
Ogan ...	H	39	6
	S	106	15
Ogh ...	H	46	32, 39
Ohág ...	S	54	15
Ohári ...	H	25	2
Ohí ...	S	27	17
Oj ...	H	11	12
	S	7	12
Ojal ...	H	1,397	5, 6, 44, 45
	S	2,056	10, 45
	M	8,153	16, 45
Okhál ...	S	42	6
	M	83	29
Olá ...	H	652	1, 4, 12, 30, 32
	S	620	10, 11, 33
	M	2	14
Olál ...	H	53	9
Olániá ...	H	96	2
	S	42	1, 10
Onaj ...	S	73	1
	M	92	28
Onas ...	H	107	9
	M	65	19
Onerá ...	M	373	29
Ongá ...	M	337	28
Opal ...	H	1,841	2, 10, 11, 12, 14, 15, 16, 17, 45, 46,
	S	5,554	J. 5, 6, 16, 17, 19, 20, 24, 25, 45, 49, 50, 51
	M	1,037	L. 10, 11, 18, 19, 25, 50,
Oráni ...	M	130	13, 27
Othál ...	H	1	39
	S	262	10
Othe ...	H	325	16, 25
	S	341	10, 14, 16
	M	951	13, 14, 16, 17, 20, 24, 26, 29
Pacháhráb ...	H	78	1
	S	2	10
	M	110	1, 5, 7
Pachaun ...	H	26	1

Names of Sub-Castes.		Persons.	Locality.
Pachkará ...	H	77	1, 3, 4, 12
	S	32	5, 10
	M	115	28
Pádarián ...	S	67	48
	M	66	1, 18, 19
Paddá ...	H	125	15, 16
	S	2,241	1, 6, 10, 14, 15, 16
	M	1,575	14, 15, 16, 19, 25, 26
Padhán ...	H	1	16
	S	13	5
	M	86	17, 18, 24, 25, 29
Pádri ...	H	5	2
	S	1	6
	M	25	25, 26
Padwál ...	H	78	1, 48
	S	48	25, 48
	M	123	18, 19, 25, 51
Págban ...	H	201	2, 3, 16, 30
	S	1	44
	M	127	9, 27, 51
Paghwárá ...	H	79	3, 12
	S	47	10, 13, 17
	M	99	27, 31
Páhar ...	H	5	11, 48
	S	23	5, 19
	M	126	5, 9, 25, 28, 51
Páhlán ...	H	21	2, 3, 9, 10
	S	17	25
Páhpáli ...	H	51	3, 16
	M	1	9
Pájre ...	H	26	48
Pajwár ...	H	92	1, 2
	S	10	25
	M	382	25, 27
Pakale ...	M	726	25, 51
Pákar ...	H	5	48
	S	29	48
Pákián ...	H	16	49
Pakoriá ...	H	387	1, 4, 25, 44
	M	644	16, 27, 28
Pál ...	H	509	1, 2, 6, 11, 12, 13, 33, 48, 49
	S	91	11, 14, 25, 48
	M	69	27
Pálá ...	H	183	1, 12
	M	4	4
Paláhá ...	M	55	13, 16, 26
Palámi ...	H	29	2, 6
	S	1	25
	M	10	18
Palán ...	H	815	2, 6, 48
	S	52	48, 48
	M	1	25
Palang ...	H	67	2, 6, 9, 11
	S	146	5, 11, 45, 48
	M	4	44
Paláníá	H	514	1, 2, 12, 30
	S	14	13, 25
	M	230	19, 23
Palardál	H	219	2
	M	15	51
Pále ...	H	2	48
	S	18	48
Palelá ...	H	39	19, 30
	S	7	6
	M	61	19, 51
Páli ...	H	117	1, 2, 44
	S	2	6
	M	6	25
Palohári ...	H	140	8
	M	59	29
Pálon ...	H	68	1, 4
	S	138	14
	M	43	14, 22, 29
Paloniá ...	H	75	9, 27, 33
	M	13	27
Palrá ...	H	18	8, 39
	M	196	12, 13, 27, 29, 48
Palul ...	H	234	49
Paná ...	H	187	1, 4, 9, 11, 16, 51
	S	163	9, 11
	M	338	5, 10, 11, 13, 16, 24, 25, 27, 28
Panág ...	H	61	50
	S	645	48, 50
Panáich ...	H	47	17, 33, 50
	S	202	50
Panál ...	H	13	49
Panámal ...	H	52	1, 11
	S	50	1, 9
	M	485	6, 13, 21, 25, 27, 51
Panchád ...	H	31	1, 2
	S	2	19
Panchaná ...	M	446	5, 11, 13
Pandál ...	H	20	9, 11, 25, 44 48
	S	246	6, 9, 10, 11
	M	20	13, 15, 44
Pandáre ...	H	672	8, 9, 16, 44, 46, 48
	S	918	6, 9, 10, 15, 16, 33
	M	206	9, 15, 19, 21, 44
Pandhán ...	H	32	1
Pandhár ...	H	7	9, 11, 16, 45
	S	2,306	11, 16, 45
	M	93	16
Pándi ...	H	85	1, 2, 8
	S	12	48
	M	48	5, 18, 29, 48
Pandir	H	114	8, 12, 25, 39, 49
	S	1,814	9, 10, 11, 21, 13, 15, 25, 48
	M	413	9, 15, 27, 28, 48
Pandit ...	S	20	6, 16
	M	8	10, 17
Pandwál	S	47	6, 11, 33
	M	9	13
Panere ...	H	49	8, 49
Pangál ...	H	8,451	1, 2, 3, 6, 9, 15, 44, 48, 49
	S	385	1, 2, 9, 44, 48
	M	1,027	1, 2, 3, 5, 14, 24
Pángri ...	S	11	48
Pangú ...	H	16	8, 16
	S	435	1, 6, 9, 11, 44, 46
	M	28	14
Pani ...	H	38	6
	S	306	6, 11
	M	347	3, 10, 16, 25, 27
Panir ...	H	1,804	3, 11, 31, 49
	M	234	14, 25, 26, 28
Paniwál ...	H	36	1
	M	62	21, 25, 31
Panjá ...	H	247	1, 8, 9, 48
	S	459	33, 48
	M	367	11, 19, 25, 26
Panjábi ...	H	22	4, 19
	S	21	4, 7, 16
	M	29	6, 13
Panjál	S	116	5, 48
	M	1	25
Panjar	H	6	9
	S	13	11
	M	143	5, 28
Panjaso ...	H	58	48
Panje ...	H	10	15, 29
	M	4	19, 29
Panjhatte ...	H	103	2, 5, 6
	S	19	6, 14, 17
	M	651	5, 18, 19, 25, 33
Panjo ...	H	295	12, 50
	S	1	12
	M	28	27
Panjol ...	H	4	8, 45
	M	38	8, 16
Panjota ...	H	66	3, 49
	S	64	5, 12, 14
	M	341	5, 10, 13, 19, 20
Pánkale ...	H	1	48
	S	21	48
Pannún ...	H	728	1, 2, 15, 48, 49
	S	9,363	J. 14, 15, 16, 19, 25, 27, 45, 48
	M	2,136	7, 9, 10, 14, 18, 19, 25, 26, 27
Pans ...	H	4	42
	S	433	9, 11, 13
	M	1,045	9, 25, 26
Panwá ...	S	5	12
	M	893	2, 3
Panwár ...	H	885	1, 2, 3, 6, 9, 25, 29, 46, 48, 50, 51
	S	819	5, 6, 9, 12, 13, 16, 17, 25, 48, 50, 51
	M	9,367	L. M. 48, 49, 51
Panwi ...	H	9	1, 33
	S	288	48
	M	1 699	23, 48, 51
Papál ...	M	849	9, 5, 21, 28
Parádal ...	H	4	6
	M	6	25, 47
Paráe ...	H	331	2
	S	42	14
	M	120	6, 16, 22, 26, 29
Párál ...	H	6	3, 9
	S	31	10, 24, 25
	M	133	1, 16, 25, 28
Pardesi ..	M	67	9, 28
Pargat ...	H	22	1
	M	26	23
Parhár ...	H	25	1, 12, 42, 51
	S	3	51
	M	15,392	M. 12, 13, 14, 17, 16, 19, 20, 47, 51
Pari ...	H	50	4, 8, 10, 49
	S	46	9, 17, 34, 48
	M	45	48, 49
Paridon ...	S	4	10
	M	134	6, 17, 19, 23
Parniá ...	S	84	14
	M	31	14, 24
Parnwál ...	H	26	32, 43, 44, 48
	S	282	10, 44, 45, 46
	M	3	13
Párohá ...	H	1	48
	M	269	18, 19, 23, 27
Parohlá ...	H	1	10
	M	2,187	M. 6
Paroiá ...	S	12	14
	M	339	16, 17, 19, 24, 25, 26, 28
Parewál ...	H	443	2, 13
	S	1	20
	M	589	17, 19
Parti ...	M	72	25
Pas ...	S	21	46
Pasi ...	H	32	1, 13, 16, 19
	S	3	16
	M	295	15, 25, 27, 28, 51
Pasoli ...	H	13	9
	M	1,603	9, 25, 26, 27
Páson ...	H	7	9
	M	12	14, 16
Passa ...	M	18	27
Paswál ...	H	3	30
	S	1	16
	M	22	5, 15, 18, 24
Pat ...	H	9	38
	M	22	13
Patá ...	H	1	9
	S	7	6
	M	357	25, 48
Pátal ...	H	537	10
	S	6	8, 9, 33
	M	71	10, 14, 24
Patáni ...	H	279	49
Pátar ...	H	464	2, 8, 9, 10, 48
	S	95	10, 25
	M	186	1, 5, 10, 15
Pathál ...	H	1	8
	S	5	45
	M	168	20
Pathán ...	H	42	6, 8, 13, 16
	M	192	5, 9, 13, 16, 17, 18, 23, 24, 25, 26, 27
Páthar ...	H	10	8, 19
	S	58	1, 9, 11, 12, 20, 44
	M	98	1, 13, 19, 20,
Patodi ...	H	18	12
Páton ...	H	185	2, 10
	S	22	6, 9, 11
	M	148	9, 11, 14, 16, 19, 24, 25, 29
Pátor ...	H	113	1, 2
	M	121	9, 23, 24, 25
Patori ...	H	152	5, 6, 12
	S	2	44
	M	471	5, 6, 24, 25, 29
Patri ...	H	3	34
	S	292	12, 14, 19, 44,

Names of Sub-Castes.		Persons.	Locality.
Patri ...	M	175	27
Patrol ...	S	29	25, 48
	M	266	1, 5, 24, 26, 48
Patsádal ...	H	9	10
	M	60	18
Patwáná ...	H	6	6, 9
	S	20	6, 14
	M	503	9, 29
Pauri ...	S	41	6, 9
Pauriá ...	H	192	49
Pawád ...	H	1	12
	S	34	9
	M	143	11, 51
Pawál ...	H	7	9, 50
	S	7	11
	M	27	21, 23, 25, 51
Páwan ...	H	76	11, 12
	S	16	12
Pawaniá ...	H	9	9, 13
	M	22	27
Pawár ...	H	357	1, 2, 3, 4, 10, 19, 39
	S	763	2, 10, 14, 15, 25, 33, 44
	M	1,207	2, 13, 16, 17, 19, 20, 23, 24, 25, 28, 29
Petwár ...	H	127	40
	S	129	49
Phagi ...	H	81	3, 30, 48
	S	99	4, 15, 48
	M	6	6
Phabáriá	H	1	30
	M	363	13, 27
Phahera ...	H	24	9, 12, 19
	S	299	6, 11, 12
	M	258	13, 21, 24, 25
Phalon ...	S	3	12
	M	480	12, 13, 17, 23, 25, 26, 27, 29
Phalron ...	H	32	2, 11
	S	6	10
	M	2,057	9, 13, 16, 17, 19, 20, 24, 25, 26, 27, 28
Phalwál ...	H	11	49
Phalwáná ...	H	242	3, 12, 30
	M	240	19, 21, 25, 26
Phalwár ...	H	737	1, 2, 4, 6
	S	11	5
	M	480	13, 17, 19, 20, 26, 51
Phanwár ...	H	3	16
	S	33	13, 33
	M	356	18, 21, 25
Pharái ...	H	7	9, 2
	M	164	25, 27
Phará ...	S	12	5, 13
	M	850	19, 29
Phári ...	M	1,625	5, 16, 19, 23, 25, 26, 28, 48, 51
Phartá ...	H	2	2, 10
	S	8	8
	M	102	19
Pherná ...	M	52	19, 51
Phogát ...	H	3,960	1, 3, 4, 9, 16, 21, 30, 49
	S	46	2, 44, 48
	M	1,656	2, 5, 25, 49, 51
Phokát ...	S	93	1, 2, 11, 16, 48
Phokri ...	S	11	13, 44
	M	29	13
Pholá ...	H	15	9
	S	2	44
	M	39	16, 44
Pholiá ...	M	674	16, 19, 20
Pholwár ...	S	5	18
	M	426	18, 43
Phondal ...	S	10	11
	M	2	18
Phor ...	H	265	9, 49
	S	7	19, 49
	M	787	5, 10, 11, 14, 19, 23, 24, 25
Phosmád ...	M	127	6, 9, 25
Phota ...	H	20	10, 11
	S	2	12
	M	118	1, 11, 28
Phular ...	H	54	6, 9, 17
	M	292	18, 19
Pia ...	H	23	8, 9
	M	17	14, 19
Pinas ...	H	11	48
	S	35	48
Pirwál ...	H	24	2, 8, 42
Podan ...	H	128	9, 10, 11
	M	41	10, 16, 19
Pohan ...	H	15	2, 44
	M	378	10, 11, 19, 23, 44
Pohar ...	H	3	9
	S	87	10, 15
	M	330	16, 17, 19, 23, 25, 27, 28
Pohiá ...	H	12	1, 9, 12
	S	6	19
	M	51	11, 19, 24, 25
Pohni ...	H	1	9
	S	2	25
	M	9	16
Pojab ...	S	86	48
	M	2	48
Pole ...	S	10	48
	M	2	48
Polerái ...	H	1	2
	M	74	16, 23, 29
Pon ...	H	95	8, 9
	S	340	12
	M	86	12, 14, 24, 27
Pondal ...	H	44	11, 48
	S	168	5, 11, 33
Pondi ...	H	77	8
	S	31	20, 33
	M	35	11, 16, 20
Ponghal ...	H	2	16
	S	175	14
	M	24	25
Poni ...	H	555	2, 3, 8, 12, 25, 30, 44
	S	161	5, 25, 44
	M	307	10, 11, 19, 27, 44
Poniá ...	H	13	11, 12, 48
	S	248	11, 15
	M	4	11
Popre ...	H	596	48, 49
	S	33	48, 49
Porán ...	H	35	2, 12, 16
	S	987	12, 15, 25
	M	471	16, 18, 19, 23, 24, 25
Porial ...	H	89	2, 16, 48
	S	260	14, 25
	M	50	16
Posi ...	H	14	2, 12, 19, 51
	M	101	13, 23
Poswál ...	M	13	25
Pota ...	H	239	8, 9, 10, 21, 41
	S	37	20, 25, 44
	M	203	9, 11, 27, 28
Potán ...	H	124	9, 12
	M	4	44
Pothi ...	H	212	6, 9, 12
	S	6	12
	M	1,084	9, 16, 19, 25, 27
Potri ...	H	36	6, 9, 12
	M	10	23, 25
Pottar ...	H	1	10
	S	1,530	9
Pujári ...	H	83	48
	S	1	48
Pujtayo ...	H	24	48
Pumán ...	H	47	6
	S	30	51
	M	12	12
Púni ...	H	51	9, 10, 39
	S	113	9, 11, 19
	M	109	5, 13, 29
Punián ...	H	6,498	2, 4, 5, 6, 9, 10, 11, 12, 25, 38, 48, 49, 50
	S	3,791	1, 6, 9, 12, 25, 46, 48, 49, 50
	M	3,442	1, 5, 6, 11, 27, 45, 48, 49, 50
Punwár ...	H	92	6, 16
	M	846	5, 23, 27
Purbá ...	H	247	6, 8
	S	6	14
	M	133	12, 23
Purbia ...	H	102	1, 11, 14, 15, 45, 48
	S	107	1, 15
	M	21	24, 25
Pure ...	H	1	48
	S	91	48
Puriá ...	H	16	12, 49
	S	25	6, 49
	M	402	9, 16, 17, 27
Puriwál ...	H	289	9, 10, 16
	S	769	10, 12, 16, 19
	M	675	17, 19, 22, 27
Purniá ...	H	48	6
	S	6	11
	M	130	27
Pusiá ...	H	7,885	1
Putná ...	H	214	1
Qádri ...	H	6	10
	M	59	16, 17, 19, 20
Qandhárí ...	M	20	29
Qandhoe ...	S	1	14
	M	145	27
Qanúngo ...	M	50	13, 27
Qasbá ...	S	16	48
Qassái ...	M	15	27, 29
Qázi ...	M	23	27, 48, 51
Qureshi ...	M	128	11, 13, 16, 17, 20, 23, 25, 27, 29, 48, 51
Qutabkhel ...	M	62	13, 19
Qutbi ...	M	12	19
Rában ...	M	322	19, 27
Rábar ...	H	68	1
	S	1	6
	M	6	25
Rabri ...	H	10	5
	S	27	10
	M	246	10, 14, 29, 51
Rád ...	H	3	2
	S	309	12
	M	1,760	18, 27, 28, 29, 51
Radáwál ...	H	5	4
	M	12	5, 12
Radhábái ...	H	5	2
	S	97	44
Radhán ...	H	20	1, 5
Radháwáli ...	H	17	9
	S	140	10 25, 27
	M	151	10, 25, 27
Radnáwe ...	H	55	9, 51
	S	302	51
	M	3	48
Rádhu ...	H	918	1, 2, 30
	S	1	17
Ragh ...	M	360	20, 26, 51
Raghar ...	H	6	45
	M	138	5, 14, 27
Raghni ...	M	31	27
Raghobansi ...	H	267	3
Rahá ...	H	25	1, 2
	S	1	10
	M	188	10, 27, 29
Ráhái ...	H	24	17
	M	4	14
Ráhal ...	H	446	1, 5, 45, 48
	S	1,236	9, 10, 15, 45, 50
	M	218	9, 10, 25, 28
Ráhán ...	H	490	17, 19, 33, 39
	S	21	9, 45
	M	2,947	13, 18, 19, 25, 26, 27
Rábar ...	H	566	1, 2, 16
	S	13	5, 25
	M	391	6, 12, 17, 45
Rahatwál ...	M	37	28
Ráhdári ...	S	49	1, 5
	M	19	19
Rahiál ...	H	21	8, 9, 11, 12
	S	223	10
	M	533	10, 27, 28
Ráhikhel ...	H	144	8
Ráhkar ...	H	44	10
	S	85	10, 44
Rahli ...	H	35	16
	M	7	24

Names of Sub-Castes.		Persons.	Locality.
Rahmán ...	M	162	20, 26, 50
Rahún ...	S	25	13, 27
Ráhwál ...	M	24	9
Rái ...	H	2,806	D. 8, 9, 10, 11, 16, 17, 18, 47, 48, 51
	S	6,652	J. except (8), L. except (17), 6, 19, 25, 44, 45
	M	714	J. except (8,9,10), L. except (15), 6, 25, 44
Ráibdár ...	H	268	3
Raik ...	H	10	1
	M	75	51
Ráil ...	H	27	5, 12, 14, 30
	S	101	15, 19
	M	1	25
Ráin ...	H	298	5, 7, 10, 11
	S	172	6, 9, 10, 25
	M	37	10, 11, 28, 48
Ráipurbá ...	H	15	5
Rájá ...	H	92	4
	S	502	15, 25, 44
	M	86	2, 10, 17, 18, 25, 29
Rajáká ...	M	1,271	12, 17, 18, 24, 25,
Rájan ...	H	322	2, 3, 9
	S	3	9, 25
	M	168	M. 13, 27
Rájar ...	M	1,686	9, 19, 20, 24, 25, 29, 50
Rajhán ...	H	25	3, 4, 5
	S	23	1
	M	142	13, 29
Rajhwáni ...	M	95	26, 29
Rajiá ...	H	11	1
	M	13	26, 48
Rájiál ...	H	1	2
	M	60	13, 19, 20
Rájo ...	H	191	11, 14, 16
	S	221	11, 14, 16
	M	319	5, 14, 15, 16, 19, 25
Rájor ...	H	19	2, 50
	S	1	18
	M	6	16
Rájpál ...	M	826	18, 25, 51
Rájpát ...	H	182	12, 13, 16, 17, 18, 25, 27, 51
	S	19	12, 13, 17, 24
	M	794	12, 13, 14, 17, 18, 19, 20, 21, 22, 27
Rajwál ...	H	53	1, 2, 6, 32
	S	8	31
Rakh ...	H	2	9
	M	345	10, 27
Rákhari ...	H	65	11, 12
	S	31	22, 25
Rakhin ...	H	53	6
	S	4	44
	M	280	14, 26, 27
Rakhiyá ...	M	747	23, 27
Rál ...	H	213	11
	S	15	10, 15
	M	277	15, 20, 24, 25, 29
Rálá ...	M	12	8, 26
Ráli ...	H	13	25
	S	97	11
	M	103	10, 12, 25
Rallá ...	M	32	23
Rálo ...	H	129	10
	M	29	27
Ralui ...	H	25	9
Ramái ...	H	64	44
Ramal ...	H	3	2
	S	12	12
	M	25	18
Ramang ...	H	6	50
	S	130	1, 12
	M	6	26
Ramáná ...	H	53	9, 40
	S	343	40, 49, 51
	M	4	13
Ramár ...	H	16	13
	M	21	25
Rámdási ...	H	14	16
	S	180	12, 16, 25, 45
	M	78	8
Rámdhan ...	H	12	5
	S	256	41
Rámgarhi ...	H	649	48
	S	438	48
	M	269	48
Rambhál ...	H	24	48
	S	12	48
Rámi ...	H	2	5, 48
	S	45	17
Rámjwál ...	H	12	4
Ramle ...	S	133	12, 44, 46
	M	3	12, 44
Ramná ...	H	28	10
Rámoká ..	S	50	1
	M	142	24, 27
Rámrái ...	H	13	18
	S	7	10
Ramsare ...	H	37	48
	M	21	48
Rán ...	H	22	18
	S	84	13, 16, 17, 44
	M	5,755	12, 13, 16, 17, 18, 19, 23, 25, 27, 28, 29, 44, 50
Ráná ...	H	23	2, 5, 51
	S	20	25, 44
	M	267	16, 17, 24, 51
Ranádi ...	H	118	2, 10, 11, 13
Ránar ...	M	16	16
Randev ...	H	242	45
	S	20	9
Randháwá ...	H	1,021	L. 10, 11, 25, 44, 48
	S	28,304	J. except (8), L. except (14), 19, 20, 24, 25, 46, 49
	M	8,764	L. 9, 11, 12, 18, 19, 25, 27, 46
Randwáná ...	H	9	5
	M	101	19
Rang ...	H	6	2, 27
	M	103	18, 19
Rangae ...	M	52	24, 28
Rangán ...	H	4	8
	M	22	20, 22 26
Rángar ...	H	2	9, 13
	S	15	6, 15, 19
	M	27	13, 14, 25
Ranghri ...	H	2	1, 5
	S	132	12, 51
	M	18	1, 18, 19
Rangi ...	H	603	5, 6, 9, 10, 11, 33, 45
	S	939	1, 6, 9, 11, 12, 25, 33, 45, 46, 49
	M	304	9, 11, 27
Rangiá ...	M	689	27
Rangú ...	M	264	27, 29
Ráni ...	H	82	45
	S	30	5, 13, 45
	M	16	14
Raniáh ...	S	13	8
Raniál ...	M	477	19, 20, 21, 24
Ranján ...	M	32	6, 9, 16, 26
Ranjate ...	H	61	16
	M	34	16
Ránjhá ...	H	1	44
	S	153	12, 14, 18
	M	18,411	M. except (28), 16, 17, 18, 19, 20, 22, 44, 50
Ranojá ...	M	638	28, 29
Ránú ...	H	809	1, 5, 9, 10, 40, 44
	S	1,149	5, 9, 10, 19, 25, 49
Ranún ...	H	75	5, 9
	S	498	5, 11, 45
	M	14	51
Ranwál ...	H	116	12
	S	33	9
	M	162	23
Ráo ...	H	715	1, 2, 5, 6, 10, 12, 25, 30, 44, 49
	S	9	33
	M	251	1, 25, 26
Raprá ...	H	1,741	1, 3, 4, 5
	M	8	9, 23
Rará ...	H	15	1, 11, 44
	S	18	11
Rará ...	M	136	27
Rásá ...	H	1	24
	M	59	9, 13
Rasil ...	S	14	12
	M	4	9, 23, 25
Rasodá ...	S	17	17
Rasondhi ...	H	165	6, 9
Raswál ...	H	157	1, 12, 17, 48
	S	2	5
Rát ..	H	1	1
	M	11	13
Ráthá ...	H	413	11, 51
	S	425	51
	M	342	1, 14, 24, 29, 51
Ráthi ...	H	8,454	2, 4, 6, 30, 31, 32
	S	320	2, 4, 5, 6, 33
	M	163	2, 25, 51
Rathol ...	H	9	16, 21
	M	8	19
Ráthor ...	H	636	1, 2, 17, 50
	S	834	1, 2, 14, 16, 17, 18, 24, 25, 50
	M	412	13, 19, 28, 29, 48, 49, 51
Rathwál ...	H	25	6, 18
	S	39	14
Rati ...	H	241	1, 8
	M	194	8, 9, 16, 27, 28
Ratiál ...	M	367	19, 20, 21, 50
Ratiwál ...	H	39	9, 30, 49, 51
	S	102	6, 9, 45
Rátri ...	M	55	27
Rátu ...	H	6	11
	S	52	10, 12, 25
	M	2	22
Ráwá ...	H	119	1, 19
	S	1	9
	M	307	25
Ráwál	H	1,812	2, 5, 9, 10, 12, 42, 51
	S	389	8, 25, 45, 49
	M	177	12, 13, 14, 15, 19, 20, 28, 42, 45
Rawáná ...	H	194	5, 6, 8, 9, 10
	S	44	2, 6, 9
	M	491	19, 23, 24, 25, 26
Rawár ...	H	35	1, 5, 12
	S	1	43
	M	1	25
Ráwat ...	H	1,895	1, 2, 4, 15, 17, 24
	S	8	2
Rayán ...	S	4	13, 15
	M	1,995	20, 27, 46
Redhú ...	H	3,342	49
	S	14	49
Rehál ...	S	10	5, 9
	M	58	29
Rehrú ...	S	149	10, 44
	M	1	19
Rer ...	H	122	1, 2, 19, 48
	S	9	9
	M	19	12, 14, 29
Reru ...	H	21	5
Rewári ...	H	189	1, 2, 5
	M	258	29
Riái ...	M	160	17, 27
Riál ...	H	136	9
Riár ...	H	67	8, 9
	S	1,711	6, 9, 10, 13, 14, 15, 16
	M	134	9, 15
Rind ...	M	299	23, 29
Ringhá ...	M	126	18
Riri ...	H	15	1
	S	11	9
Ris ...	M	80	13, 14, 26, 27
Riwáná ...	H	25	1
	M	22	13, 19
Roobal ...	M	101	48
Rodá ...	H	25	10, 12, 50
	S	9	6, 9, 50
	M	141	23
Rodár ...	H	30	1, 2
Rodhwál ...	H	36	2, 49
Rohach ...	H	16	12
Rohal ...	H	439	1, 2, 8, 9, 10
	S	86	1, 25, 49

Names of Sub-Castes.		Persons.	Locality.
Rohan ...	H	183	6, 49
	M	179	1, 23
Rohej ...	H	11	12
Rohiá ...	S	1	51
	M	18	25
Rohihár ...	M	81	12
Rohilá ...	H	19	9
	M	158	23, 26, 29
Rohra	H	5	11
...	M	56	26
Rojáká ...	M	42	28
Rojha ...	H	354	1, 2, 49
	S	1	13
Rojhariá ...	H	33	2, 30, 49
Rojhda ...	S	26	49
Rojhgawáliá	H	45	51
	S	10	51
Rojke ...	M	28	24
Rojlá ...	H	91	1
	M	72	1
Rokh ...	M	24	29
Rokhan ...	H	6	2, 14
	S	424	11, 29
Rolái ...	H	75	1
	M	4	25
Rolán ...	H	27	31, 49
	M	15	12, 17
Roliá ...	S	7	10
	M	4	10
Ronk ...	S	9	10
	M	2	14
Ropré ...	H	15	31, 42
	M	99	25, 50
Ror ...	H	39	1, 12, 48
	S	1	49
	M	31	28
Rorá ...	H	10	2
	S	12	43, 51
	M	5	14, 29
Rorakh ...	S	33	1
Rori ...	H	5	8
	M	215	18, 25
Rosál ...	H	8	30, 48
	S	13	13
Rosi ...	S	5	46
	M	14	12, 17
Rosori ...	S	165	10
Rot ...	S	113	14, 20
Rotal ...	H	3	12
	M	8	6
Rothi ...	H	88	1, 33
	S	10	19
	M	51	23
Rudi ...	H	26	1
	M	4	25
Ruiwál ...	M	129	19
Runwál ...	H	37	1
Sabál ...	H	1	9
	S	747	9, 11
	M	85	11, 13, 15, 23
Sabáni ...	H	28	2, 11, 18, 46
	S	2	9
	M	56	11, 18, 28
Sabári ...	H	217	6, 9, 44
	S	7	44
	M	20	16
Sábia ...	S	6,496	46, 51
	M	3	6
Sabrán ...	H	20	11, 16
	S	9	45
	M	11	14, 27
Sabwál ...	S	195	6
	M	41	27
Sabzá ...	S	47	5
Sach ...	M	31	19
Sadál ...	H	338	1, 5, 8, 11, 12, 14
	S	2,505	14
	M	896	11, 26, 27
Sadána ...	H	76	9
	S	143	6, 14, 25
	M	175	21
Sadánjha ...	H	88	9
	S	24	9
	M	7	18
Sadaráhá ...	M	158	16, 17
Sádári ...	H	31	6, 14
	S	1	10
Sades ...	H	4	19
	M	974	27
Sadháni ...	S	4,715	25, 45
	M	1,090	26, 27
Sadhár ...	H	4	9
	S	2	9
	M	426	12, 17, 19, 20, 24
Sadhún ...	H	1	46
	S	27	12
	M	153	16, 44
Sadí ...	H	1	9
	S	163	25
	M	94	20
Sádiál ...	H	224	8
	M	10	20, 24
Sadíqí ...	S	1	8
	M	299	12, 27
Sadrá ...	H	18	9, 16
	S	94	16, 19
	M	648	19, 27, 29
Sadrúká ...	M	52	17, 27
Sádú ...	H	676	2, 6, 8
	S	1	9
	M	378	10, 23, 24, 27
Ság ...	S	196	14
	M	109	26, 28
Ságal ...	H	79	5, 25, 30
	S	240	12, 15, 25
	M	1,124	12, 24, 26, 27
Sagan ...	M	24	17, 25, 46
Sagáodi ...	H	133	48
	S	2	48
	M	38	27
Sagará ...	H	40	2, 8, 12
	S	8	10, 49
	M	93	10, 11, 16, 24, 27
Sagarkí ...	S	21	12, 51
Sagarwal ...	H	1	2
	S	22	12
Sagi ...	H	4	9, 10
	S	805	9, 12
	M	35	24, 26, 29
Sagoí ...	H	13	6
Sagpál ...	M	19	24
Sagú ...	H	43	9, 12
	S	230	6, 16, 25
	M	1,215	19, 27, 28, 29
Sagwál ...	M	84	19, 21, 26, 29
Ságwán ...	H	1,514	2, 5, 9, 21, 48
	S	768	14, 48
	M	248	23
Sabáí ...	H	182	11, 19
	M	486	20
Sabáin ...	H	15	2
	M	5	11
Sáhákhel ..	M	21	23
Sahal ...	H	189	2, 9, 14, 19
	S	234	15, 16, 25
	M	263	14, 18, 19, 20, 26, 27, 28
Sahar ...	H	1	16
	S	251	10, 12, 51
	M	906	26, 27
Sahárin ...	H	5,766	1, 2, 5, 9, 12, 13, 30, 48
	S	4	9, 48
	M	933	11, 16, 17, 19, 28, 29, 48
Sáhd ...	M	17	10, 17
Sáhdará ...	H	571	9, 10
	S	197	9, 10
Sáhí ...	H	221	9, 10, 16, 17, 19
	S	1,131	L. 9, 10, 12, 19, 20, 25
	M	4,999	L. 10, 12, 18, 19, 23, 25, 29
Sáhín ...	H	14	4, 14, 19
	S	15	18
	M	287	11, 13, 24
Sahli ...	S	18	12
	M	1	17
Sáhmál ...	S	3	51
	M	74	10, 16, 28
Sáhní ...	H	537	3, 5, 8, 10, 16, 17, 44
	S	2,768	6, 9, 10, 25, 46
	M	728	8, 10, 16, 17, 23, 26
Sáho ...	H	181	1, 3, 8, 51
	S	4	19, 27
	M	2,045	19, 24, 26, 29
Sahojí ...	S	20	25
Saholat ...	H	33	48
	S	250	48
	M	119	48
Sáhon ...	H	21	10, 48
	S	77	48
	M	317	28, 51
Sáhore ...	S	11	48
	M	216	24
Sahota ...	H	2,243	1, 4, 8, 9, 10, 16, 30
	S	3,311	9, 10, 11, 19, 25, 27, 44, 50
	M	717	6, 10, 11, 16, 18, 44
Sahotrí ...	H	439	6, 9, 13, 17, 25
	S	13	9, 13, 15, 18
	M	1,072	10, 11, 16, 17, 26, 29
Sahrál ...	M	32	10
Sahráwat ...	H	6,549	2, 3, 4, 48
	S	378	48
Sahrí ...	H	34	4, 12, 19
	M	254	11, 26
Sahúní ...	H	1	19
	S	12	21, 26, 27
Sahúr ...	M	552	24, 26, 27, 28
Sahwál ...	H	1,007	1, 2, 9, 14, 49
	S	172	9, 12, 49
	M	1,751	19, 26, 28, 49, 51
Sáhwán ...	H	37	1
	S	1	19
	M	205	26, 27, 28
Sahwár ...	H	7	1, 9, 50
	S	9	5
	M	71	28
Sáí ...	H	181	6, 10 12
	S	177	12, 16, 17
	M	22	24
Saián ...	H	5	9
	S	53	46
	M	73	20, 28
Said ...	M	482	17, 18, 51
Saidwál ...	H	217	1, 8, 48
	S	5	48
Saigí ...	M	50	17
Saihgal ...	H	89	2, 3, 12
	S	198	9, 10, 14
	M	439	17, 18, 24, 27
Saihl ...	H	3	10
	M	557	13, 51
Saihúí ...	H	1	23
	S	311	12
Saikar ...	M	110	51
Sáil ...	H	7	12
	S	112	15
	M	174	6, 17, 21, 44
Sain ...	H	211	1, 8
	S	12	10, 14, 25
	M	832	11, 28, 51
Saingí ...	H	14	2
	S	2	19
	M	2	16
Sainí ...	H	228	10, 11, 17, 25, 44
	S	1,010	10, 17, 26, 44
	M	97	10, 17, 26
Sajan ...	S	187	9, 10
	M	27	10, 13
Sajrá ...	H	8	9
	S	32	10
	M	1,972	13, 19, 20, 23, 27, 29, 51
Sajrál ...	S	2	12
	M	30	26, 27
Sajú ...	H	30	9
Sajúd ...	H	464	4, 8
	S	29	5
Sakandá ...	H	67	3, 14
	S	117	25
	M	7	3
Sakhal ...	H	216	2, 6, 9, 44
	S	156	6, 44
	M	38	2, 17
Sakham ...	H	106	10, 11, 14

Names of Sub-Castes.		Persons.	Locality.
Sakhán ...	H	3	31
	S	559	11, 15, 25
Sakháre ...	M	92	24, 26, 51
Sákhi ...	H	3	2, 5
	S	22	14, 48
Sakhrál ...	H	19	1, 25
	M	6	21
Sakhún ...	H	682	3, 10, 11, 45, 46
	S	4,500	11, 14, 25, 45, 46
	M	142	11, 12, 25
Salagiál ...	H	1	8
	M	15	21
Saláhat ...	H	6	9
	S	5	5, 9
	M	1	16
Salan ...	H	55	1, 2, 5, 9
	S	70	9, 13, 49
	M	34	5, 26, 49
Salár ...	H	19	2, 5, 48
	S	16	48
	M	369	6, 23, 27, 48
Saléárán ..	H	134	2, 13, 14, 21, 25
	S	285	6, 14, 16, 48
	M	364	12, 16, 17, 26, 29
Salhál ...	H	87	1
	M	487	19, 20, 21
Saloch ...	S	6	14
	M	15	17
Salodhá ...	S	98	48
Saloí ...	H	37	1, 16
	S	3	14, 51
	M	166	11, 23
Salotriá ...	H	109	1, 16
	S	30	17, 21
	M	322	13, 16, 19, 23, 24
Sálú ...	M	58	21, 24, 28
Sálútiá ...	H	11	48
Samá ...	S	4	47
	M	1,072	51
Samág ...	H	42	1, 12
	S	175	12, 49, 51
Sámágar ...	S	7	17
	M	11	12
Samal ...	H	333	44, 51
	S	733	29, 48
Samán ...	H	148	3, 10, 49
	S	92	49
	M	1,236	12, 27
Samár ...	H	13	9
	S	239	5, 9, 17
	M	52	10, 19, 42
Samás ...	M	41	11, 12, 15
Sámbal ...	H	43	2, 5, 9
	S	20	9, 10
	M	406	17, 25
Sambar ...	H	115	1, 2
	M	15	14
Sámí ...	H	23	1, 30, 42
	S	12	15
	M	78	29
Samnol ...	H	68	1, 2, 12
	S	10	6
	M	4,250	12, 14, 17, 19, 20, 24, 27, 29, 51
Samoká ...	M	28	19
Samol ...	H	198	4, 45
	S	1,029	11
	M	189	24, 51
Sámotá ...	H	88	1, 2, 25
	S	4	5
	M	5	16
Samrá ...	H	2,574	15, 48, 49
	S	4,844	10, 48, 49
Samrol ...	H	371	49
	M	798	19, 28, 49
Samúr ...	M	397	19, 24, 51
San ...	S	204	5, 25
	M	64	19, 23
Sanáhar ...	H	2,555	12, 15, 30, 44
	S	174	44
Sánan ...	H	549	27
Sanániá ...	M	779	23, 24, 28
Sanárán ...	S	1	2
	M	577	19
Sánbal ...	H	4	45
Sánbal ...	S	250	11
	M	1	48
Sánbhar ...	S	225	44
	M	10	18
Sanboí ...	S	13	44, 48
Sand ...	H	11	2, 10
	S	1	10
	M	933	10, 23, 51
Sandá ...	H	473	1, 7, 11, 14, 25, 27
	S	60,923	11, 13, 14, 24, 25
	M	3,977	6, 10, 14, 19, 25, 26, 28
Sandái ...	S	423	12, 44
	M	510	27
Sándal ...	H	96	8, 9
	S	11	9
	M	1,413	12, 14, 26, 27, 28
Sandán ...	H	52	1, 8, 48
	S	15	19, 25, 28
	M	1,059	2, 5, 10, 16, 18, 20, 23, 26, 27, 29
Sandohí ...	H	28	8
	S	364	9, 10
	M	154	24, 26
Sandel ...	H	103	5, 8
	M	41	23
Sandhal ...	H	104	8, 49
Sandhar ...	H	2,406	1, 8, 10, 48
	S	5,400	10, 11, 25, 48
	M	3,172	26, 28, 48, 51
Sandhará ...	H	73	2, 30
	M	23	20
Sandhiá ...	H	102	2, 8
	S	252	12
	M	511	11, 23
Sandhiwárí ...	H	102	2
	M	6	25
Sándí ...	H	458	9, 27, 44
	S	40	10, 25
	M	1,391	19, 23, 28
Sandlí ...	H	27	8
	M	1,576	19, 28, 29
Sandohil ...	H	6	1
	S	2	49
	M	79	51
Sandoí ...	H	7	8
	S	4,811	13
Sandol ...	H	67	1, 8, 11, 47
	S	438	8, 9, 10
	M	1,081	9, 14, 21, 24, 26, 27
Sandrána ...	M	1,553	17, 18, 24, 27
Sandrí ...	H	1,488	1, 21
	M	115	15, 24, 27
Sándú ...	H	59	4, 40, 41
	S	354	22, 23, 44
	M	1,170	11, 12, 15, 21, 23, 27
Sandwána ...	M	18	23
Sanekí ...	M	79	19
Sanerí ...	H	2	13
	S	799	8, 14
Sang ...	H	26	5, 8
	M	1,343	17, 20, 28
Sángá ...	H	172	1, 9
	S	836	11, 46
	M	389	11 16, 22, 25, 26
Sangal ...	H	16,39	1, 2, 4, 17
	S	86	4, 12, 25
	M	386	12, 18, 28, 46
Sangán ...	H	2,564	2, 5, 30
	S	98	12, 32, 44
	M	80	26
Sanghál ...	H	700	4
	S	166	15
	M	10	19
Sangí ...	H	595	1, 5, 10, 14, 48
	S	2,452	10, 12, 25, 44, 46, 48
	M	3,697	6, 10, 12, 15, 16, 27, 28, 29, 44, 48
Sanglá ...	H	6	5, 6
	S	31	6, 44
	M	148	10, 51
Sangohá	S	2,151	9, 10, 12
	M	225	27
Sangotrá ...	H	1,047	1, 48, 49
	S	74	25, 48
	M	68	14, 48
Sangriál ...	M	19	18, 19, 27
Sangrolí ...	H	316	5
	S	142	10, 18
Sangroriá ...	H	10	10
	M	6	44
Sangwál ...	H	10,505	2, 3, 4, 5, 31, 49
	M	4,350	3, 29, 31, 51
Sángwán ...	H	4,184	1, 2, 3, 4, 5, 30
	M	23	21
Sanhás ...	H	76	3, 4
	M	50	27
Sániá ...	H	48	4, 45
	S	2	28
	M	9	10
Saniál ...	H	89	2, 4, 10
	S	32	24, 25
	M	52	19
Sanjoá ...	H	5	45, 48
	S	7	8, 48
	M	33	18, 19, 20
Sanjrá ...	H	10	45
	M	216	19, 51
Sankhal ...	H	205	2, 4, 5
Sanodí ...	M	87	16, 25
Sanog ...	M	267	25, 51
Sanotre ...	H	80	1, 16, 25
	S	8	16, 25
	M	4	20
Sanpál ...	S	461	14, 44
	M	581	25, 26, 27, 29
Sánsi ...	H	1,191	14, 15, 17, 18
	S	266	10, 16 25, 27
	M	1,140	14 15, 16, 25, 27
Sant ...	H	8	30
	S	7	25
	M	476	26, 27, 28
Sanwál ...	H	1,842	1, 3, 4, 5
	S	35	5, 25
	M	792	9, 23, 25, 51
Sanwánkhel	M	240	23
Sapal ...	M	874	18, 19, 23, 25, 28, 29
Sapar ...	S	28	25
	M	1,822	16, 24, 25, 26, 29, 51
Saprái ...	H	110	18, 51
	S	130	10, 18
	M	3,163	18, 20, 25, 28
Saprál ...	M	807	24, 25
Sapul ...	H	5	4
	S	52	14
	M	337	27, 28
Sará ...	H	736	1, 11, 15, 27, 49
	S	161	3, 9, 25
	M	464	20, 24, 29, 45, 51
Sarab ...	H	71	3, 5, 8, 11
	S	205	13, 15
	M	362	12, 15, 29, 46
Sarádat ...	H	1,127	4, 5, 19
	S	20	12
	M	52	2
Sarágí ...	H	153	5, 30, 33, 49
	S	2,359	14, 25, 49
	M	921	5, 16, 18, 27
Saráh ...	S	5	51
	M	22	51
Saráhat ...	H	22	1, 4
	S	1,067	9, 19
Saráí ...	H	2,585	10, 11, 12, 15
	S	10,865	10, 11, 12, 48
	M	1,909	10, 11, 19, 20, 28, 29
Sarákí ...	M	693	26, 28
Sáral ...	M	31	20, 21
Sarálí ...	H	431	5, 9
	S	15	6, 45
	M	17	25
Saráliyá ...	H	76	48, 49
	M	1	48
Sarán ...	H	353	1, 3, 4, 5, 25, 33
	S	783	5, 10, 12, 13, 33, 49
	M	67	25, 27, 49
Sárang ...	H	523	5, 25
	M	42	27

SUB-CASTES OF CERTAIN SELECTED CASTES—*continued.*

Names of Sub-Castes.		Persons.	Locality.
Saráni ...	H	26	25, 30, 44
	S	244	4, 33
	M	36	10
Sarár ...	H	17	38
	S	1,012	6, 10, 14, 33
	M	8	29, 33
Saras ...	H	927	43, 50
	S	8,736	13, 48, 49
	M	17	2, 50
Sárátá ...	H	41	8, 48
	S	11	12
	M	145	12, 29, 48
Saráwá ...	S	31	5
	M	3	24
Sarawál ...	H	64	1, 30
	S	44	5
Saráwán ...	H	346	4, 31
	S	34	12, 19
Sarbal ...	S	122	44, 45
	M	12	10
Sardári ...	H	82	5
Sardí ...	H	195	11
	S	32	11, 25
	M	25	12, 15, 29
Sardú ...	H	5,462	3, 5, 44
Sardúl ...	H	10	1
	M	79	13
Sardwárí ...	H	15	4, 30
	M	6	6
Sarerí ...	S	4	19, 45
	M	586	15
Sargandí ...	M	308	18, 19, 24, 25
Sargoj ...	H	32	30, 49
	S	5	19
Sarbáí ...	H	87	48
	S	21	5, 48
	M	7	48
Sarhán ...	H	29	4
Sarí ...	H	29	5, 8, 25
	S	90	33, 44
	M	142	15, 29
Sarín ...	H	19	8, 10, 13
	S	13	10
Sarír ...	M	151	25
Sarkerá ...	M	101	27, 48
Sarkílá ...	H	5	48
	S	55	48
Sarmár ...	H	262	4, 13, 19
	S	13	44
	M	5	20
Sarní ...	S	315	46
	M	4	44
Sarodá ...	H	253	1, 11
Sarohe ...	H	897	1, 10, 48
	S	7,758	10, 19, 48
	M	714	10, 13, 19, 24
Saroj ...	H	19	8, 10
	S	4	19
	M	195	20, 26, 29, 51
Sarol ...	M	234	10, 21, 28
Sarowá ...	H	155	1, 9, 13, 44
	S	11	6
	M	114	15, 25
Saroíláh ...	M	157	27
Sarú ...	H	35	1
	S	134	6, 25
Sarút ...	H	199	3, 4
Sarwál ...	H	83	5, 12, 13
	S	58	6, 25
	M	238	10, 24, 27
Sarwáná ...	S	8	6
	M	70	6, 15, 25
Sarware ...	S	11	7, 16
	M	145	12, 18
Sarwarí ...	H	827	48
	S	909	48, 49
	M	259	13, 24, 48
Sásí ...	M	496	13, 15
Saswál ...	H	289	1, 4
	M	802	2, 11, 19
Satar ...	H	14	13
	S	2	10
	M	834	19, 26
Sateri ...	M	50	27
Sáthi ...	H	15	1, 25
	S	287	20, 27
	M	202	23, 26, 29, 51
Sathián ...	M	39	12
Satiá ...	H	1	15
	S	8	46
	M	38	18, 21
Satiár ...	H	743	1, 9, 44
	S	5	25
	M	86	12, 19, 23
Saton ...	H	6	48
	S	2	48
	M	13	10, 44
Sawág ...	H	347	2, 31
	M	27	12
Sawáí ...	H	35	4
Sawáich ...	H	1,696	1, 11
	M	60	10, 11
Sawábak ...	H	401	2
Sawál ...	H	172	2, 6, 9
	S	38	8, 16, 25
	M	969	20, 23, 26, 29, 51
Sáwan ...	H	89	1, 2, 13, 31
	S	2	51
	M	675	5, 12, 25, 27, 28, 29
Sáwará ...	H	114	1, 15
	S	193	19, 25
	M	2,080	14, 17, 20, 23, 28,
Sedhá ...	H	268	5, 11, 14
	S	64	5, 6, 10
	M	282	16, 26
Sedrá ...	M	392	11, 16, 50
Sebrá ...	H	305	50
	M	68	19
Sekhún ...	H	69	11, 19
	S	2,583	8, 11, 12
	M	506	11, 23, 25, 28
Sekrí ...	M	28	29
Self ...	M	223	23, 50
Selre ...	H	11	9
	M	8	18
Sen ...	H	3	12
	M	90	11, 46
Senoí ...	S	162	16, 24
	M	8	13, 16
Ser ...	H	74	49
	S	74	25, 49
	M	88	28, 29, 49
Será ...	H	402	2
	M	9	19, 50
Serí ...	H	207	46
	S	11	13
	M	232	10, 25, 45
Serwál ...	M	27	13
Set ...	H	8	1
	M	52	28
Sethí ...	H	10	12
	S	11	12, 26
	M	249	11, 27
Sewá ...	H	182	1, 48
	S	21	14, 48
Sewí ...	M	85	10, 51
Sewkí ...	H	1	10
	M	85	23, 46
Sewrag ...	H	451	49
	M	16	13
Shábá ...	H	8	8, 11
	S	56	9
	M	116	14, 29
Shabání ...	H	2	11
	M	389	11, 18, 19, 28
Shábí ...	M	217	25, 51
Shábpura ...	S	1	20
	M	51	16, 23
Shajrá ...	H	69	51
	M	1,872	25, 27, 28, 29
Shakárí ...	M	1,428	14, 18, 29
Shakorá ...	M	84	27
Shál ..	M	33	18
Shámí ...	H	205	1
Shamrá ...	M	31	10
Shamsí ...	M	447	13, 26, 28, 50
Sharal ...	H	162	2, 14, 31
	S	11	13, 16
Shekh ...	M	304	18, 19, 26, 29
Shekhúká ...	M	122	27
Shergil ...	H	235	10, 12, 46, 48
	S	1,188	10, 11, 12, 19, 48
	M	355	11, 18, 25, 48
Shergir ...	M	24	26
Sherú ...	H	111	2
Shiál ...	H	100	1, 44
	M	113	13, 14
Shiání ...	H	60	38
Shimár ...	S	9	27
	M	12	6, 11
Shodí ..	S	48	13, 27
Shohar ...	H	111	2
	S	12	5, 10
	M	261	23, 25
Shobáz ...	M	723	19, 27
Sholí ...	H	12	15
	M	713	19, 23
Shorá ...	H	79	1, 51
	M	7	25
Shorán ...	H	6,561	1, 2, 3, 49
	S	289	14
	M	174	1, 3, 11
Siág ...	H	1,234	2, 15, 25
	S	15	4
Siahl ...	H	39	1
	M	99	23
Siáí ...	M	30	15, 44
Siál ...	H	43	12, 19
	M	15,271	8, 9, 11, 15, 18, 19, 25, 26, 28, 29, 44, 46, 51
Sián ...	H	519	1, 2
	S	53	10, 42
	M	273	19, 44
Siár ...	H	15	11, 13
	S	28	16, 33
	M	130	2, 11
Sibiá ...	H	2	11
	S	54	49
Sich ...	H	15	49
	S	53	10, 49
	M	175	15, 16, 26, 27
Sidán ...	H	7	1, 8
	M	164	27
Sidhú ...	H	4,266	2, 5, 10 to 13, 15, 19, 45, 46, 48, 49
	S	123,526	5, 9 to 12, 14, 19, 45, 48, 49
	M	62,665	11, 12, 18, 26, 44, 46, 48, 49
Sidí ...	H	20	10, 11
Sigál ...	H	188	1
	M	237	23
Sigárí ...	H	196	1, 2, 5, 6
Sighú ..	H	1,683	1, 5
Sihák ...	S	12	13
Sikh ...	H	52	4, 6, 15, 26
	S	181	3, 9, 19, 20, 24, 49
	M	196	13, 19, 28
Sikhú ...	S	692	5, 13, 25, 33
	M	41	19
Sikhúl ...	H	2	12
	S	46	5, 24
Sikor ...	S	311	16
Sikú ...	H	295	14
	S	20	5, 13
	M	100	16
Sil ...	H	15	9, 12
	S	105	10, 25, 49
	M	535	14, 15, 16
Siláí ...	H	13	2
Silakhán ...	H	982	3, 49
	S	1	49
	M	3	49
Silwál ...	H	30	1
Sim ...	M	20	15, 25
Simár ...	H	284	2
	S	1	49
	M	895	29
Simí ...	H	5	8
	S	31	13
	M	334	10, 29
Símos ...	H	734	4, 13, 46
	S	6	5
	M	136	50
Sin ...	H	32	9
	M	152	18, 25
Sinámár ...	H	56	1
	M	14	28
Sindhu ...	H	8,117	5, 8, 10, 12, 16, 38, 40, 44
	S	96,210	10, 12, 14, 15, 25
	M	54,649	8, 10, 12, 15, 19, 44, 46

Names of Sub-Castes.		Persons.	Locality.
Sindí	S	209	3, 10, 13
	M	186	6, 13, 29
Síngbera	H	1,547	1, 9, 10, 15
	S	4,981	9, 10, 11, 25
	M	525	11, 15, 24, 25
Siotí	H	28	8
Siprá	H	217	10, 19
	S	31	19
	M	4,162	10, 19, 20, 25, 26, 28, 29, 51
Siprál	M	61	18
Sisán	H	15	12
Sitale	H	4	11
	M	109	13
Siur	H	122	6, 10
	S	192	10
	M	20	10
Soba	H	223	15
	M	632	11, 46
Sobhriá	M	1,157	15, 19
Soch	H	550	1, 12, 14, 15
	S	376	1, 11, 28
	M	2	11
Sodal	H	11	14
	S	9	49
Sodan	H	15	2
Sodání	H	300	14
	M	5	10
Sodar	H	33	11, 14, 49
	M	19	19
Sodha	H	355	1, 4, 8, 15
	S	142	9, 16
	M	64	11, 19, 25
Sodí	H	330	2, 10, 48
	S	199	5, 11, 48
	M	15	29, 48
Sodíttú	H	41	11
Sogal	H	223	2, 14
	M	25	19
Sohá	H	1,436	3, 10, 11, 15, 33, 49, 50
	S	2,548	5, 9, 10, 11, 24, 50
	M	705	10, 11, 18, 19, 26, 29, 49, 50
Soság	H	2,809	1, 2, 12, 13, 48, 49
	S	623	48, 49
	M	225	28, 48, 49
Sohal	H	1,639	J. 15, 19, 34, 50
	S	3,256	9, 10, 11, 19, 25, 26, 45, 50
	M	2,005	9, 10, 11, 13 to 16, 18, 19, 28, 29
Sohan	H	554	2, 6, 48
	S	627	10, 25, 48
	M	1,067	10, 12, 18, 21, 26, 29, 48
Soháni	H	260	1, 12
	S	290	44, 45
	M	181	12, 15
Sohantrá	M	350	20, 51
Sohar	M	1,284	10, 14, 28, 50
	S	19	2, 15
Sohattá	S	324	6
Sohdí	S	449	10, 13, 25
	M	1	10
Sohdrí	M	115	18
Sohndí	H	116	2, 10, 11, 14
	S	5	16
	M	247	50
Sohrán	H	39	11, 30
	M	37	28
Sohriá	H	6,538	44, 46
	M	15	20
Soí	H	602	1, 11, 44
	S	685	5, 6, 10, 11; 25
	M	1,198	11, 14, 15
Soján	H	21	10, 44
Sokandá	H	16	4, 31
Sokandlá	H	425	4
Sokhal	H	67	4, 14, 45
	M	166	27, 44
Sokhandá	H	45	4
	M	486	4
Sokhedí	H	1,073	4
	M	34	44
Sokú	S	13	25
	M	1	14
Solá	H	118	1, 14
	M	253	29
Solakhní	H	675	4
	S	9	4
Solan	H	3	47
	S	356	47, 50
	M	90	29
Solgan	M	21	19
Solí	H	103	45
	M	39	29, 44
Solkí	H	591	1, 4, 14; 50, 51
	S	2	24
	M	133	24, 26, 28, 45
Solú	H	150	48
	S	3,003	48
	M	46	28, 48
Solút	H	178	1, 3, 48
	S	12	48
Soman	H	59	30, 50
	S	239	9, 25
	M	814	10, 23, 25, 29
Somará	H	182	14
Somrí	H	740	9, 12, 51
	S	86	51
Sonet	M	100	11, 51
Sopráh	M	308	23
Sorá	H	647	1, 2, 14
	S	31	13
	M	67	13, 14
Soráhan	H	730	1, 5, 13
	S	301	27
Sorái	H	3,395	11, 30
	S	2,314	1, 13
Során	H	18	13
	S	2	6
Sorídíal	H	13	1
	M	370	51
Sorút	H	5	8
	M	139	12, 51
Sosí	S	18	10
	M	31	51
Sotá	S	6	11, 19
	M	753	11, 28
Sotal	H	100	2, 8, 10, 12, 15
	M	17	51
Sotrí	H	423	10, 13, 14, 16
	S	2	12
	M	219	29, 50, 51
Sowálí	H	386	13, 14
	M	11	5
Sowár	S	12	13
Soyá	H	1	10
	S	115	12
	M	968	26, 27, 28, 29
Sozí	M	122	51
Súchan	H	38	12
	M	1	11
Súd	H	132	14
	S	1	5
	M	335	51
Súgar	H	8	3
	S	12	11
Sugárú	H	14	13
Súj	H	38	1
Sújan	M	14	11
Sújol	M	2,423	23, 51
Sultání	H	90	10, 51
Sundará	H	338	12, 14, 41
	S	21	10
	M	391	1, 12, 14, 15, 28
Súntar	H	196	1
Súrág	H	293	9, 15, 31
	M	142	29, 50
Súraj	H	23	13, 48
	S	267	48
	M	59	48
Súrajbansí	H	48	4, 47, 49
Súrí	H	559	2, 6, 8, 11, 12, 30
	S	2	19
	M	674	11, 15, 27
Suswál	H	466	1, 2
	M	3	13
Sút	M	18	13
Suthrá	S	11	5
	M	208	13, 23
Suttan	H	8	12, 48
	S	7	27, 48
	M	469	12, 23, 27, 48
Tadí	H	48	49
Tag	H	34	1, 4
	S	32	10, 25
	M	6	16, 23
Taghar	H	201	10
	S	15	10
	M	36	11, 12
Táhá	M	12	16, 44
Táhal	H	8	1, 9
	S	208	17, 27
	M	35	44
Tahím	S	50	9, 17
	M	11,974	L. 12, 18, 19, 23, 24, 26, 27, 28, 29, 44, 51
Tahír	S	70	6, 18
	M	258	16, 20, 24
Tahríja	H	16	8, 44
	S	17	46
	M	213	13
Táir Khel	S	84	12
	M	126	25, 29
Tajo	M	18	27
Takn Khel	H	4	31
	S	15	50
	M	611	25, 50
Tákhar	H	612	1, 2, 3, 10, 41, 49, 50
	S	1,168	11, 12, 16
	M	113	10, 16, 17, 28
Taklí	H	29	5
	M	48	27
Takrá	H	262	50
Tal	H	4	2, 4
	S	191	13
	M	40	25
Talág	M	30	18
Tulátí	H	22	6, 8, 16
	S	2	44
Talhí	M	59	27
Tálí	H	17	9, 16
	S	1	11
	M	59	11, 25
Talíwál	H	4	50
	S	1	1
	M	6	9
Tálkí	H	18	8
Tállá	H	9	8, 9
	S	53	49
	M	196	18, 24
Talo	H	6	2, 9
	S	8	44
Talod	M	241	24
Talodiá	M	164	28
Talokar	M	2,307	19, 20, 23, 26
Taloní	M	247	20
Talwárá	H	6	2, 9
	S	23	4, 9, 46
	M	3	9
Talyání	H	72	4
	M	1	18
Tama	S	1	5
	M	746	20, 21
Tamal	H	98	2, 5
	S	1	6
	M	27	6
Tamána	S	444	11, 12
Tamar	H	78	5
Tambolí	H	27	6, 9
	S	2	44
Tamhál	S	55	10, 14
	M	30	13, 20
Tamíd	H	2	44
	M	144	21
Tanar	H	15	11, 30, 34
	S	2	49
	M	403	25, 26, 27, 28, 44
Tandá	H	11	1
	S	8	49
	M	7	20, 49
Tandásí	H	4	2, 25
	M	11	2, 6
Tánde	H	107	1, 10, 12
	S	93	11, 12
	M	57	17, 23, 26

Names of Sub-Castes.		Persons.	Locality.
Tandiál ...	H	3	8
	S	26	13, 25
	M	142	10
Taudián ..	H	20	2, 30
	M	100	9, 29
Tanhad ...	S	49	1
Táni ...	H	13	4
	S	12	3
	M	105	20, 26
Taniál ...	H	31	18
	M	4	28
Tanká ...	H	1,846	2, 4, 5, 6, 9, 17
	M	275	15, 29
Tánk Pawár ...	H	346	4, 41
	M	12	25
Tanná ...	H	15	4, 11
	M	216	17, 51
Tanorí ...	H	256	3, 4, 33, 48
	S	382	6, 33, 48
	M	1,068	1, 3, 25, 27
Tanwár ...	H	1,515	2, 3
	S	62	5, 14, 17
	M	66	5, 17, 27
Táparwál ...	H	1	12
	M	1,691	51
Tár ...	H	206	1, 5, 16
	S	391	5, 9, 10, 12, 16, 33, 48
	M	136	1, 10, 12, 15, 16, 27
Tarag ...	M	16	26
Taráh ...	H	112	1, 5, 8, 13
	S	617	9, 25, 50
	M	777	11, 12, 13, 17, 29
Tarál ...	H	3	8, 9
	S	6	33
	M	7	25
Taráo ...	H	35	6
	S	106	6
	M	4	51
Taráomí ...	S	3	33
	M	26	29
Tárár ...	H	567	1, 2, 12, 17, 19
	S	118	16, 17
	M	11,104	9, 14, 15, 16, 17, 18, 19, 21, 23, 24, 26
Tardá ...	M	136	12, 29
Targar ...	S	9	13
	M	5,359	17, 19, 20, 23, 24, 26, 27, 28
Tariál ...	H	5	7, 13
	S	31	13, 25
	M	2	2
Tárícharí ...	M	602	51
Tárin ...	H	3	5
	S	5	25
	M	6	18, 27
Tarjá ...	H	9	2
	M	194	18, 23, 27
Tarka ...	H	1,572	4, 5, 6, 33
	S	1,223	5, 6, 25
	M	621	5, 6, 28, 29
Tarkhel ...	M	255	23
Tarlí ...	H	4	24
	M	243	23, 27, 28, 51
Tarmal ...	H	163	48
	M	2	19
Táro ...	S	8	11
	M	120	17
Tároki ...	H	1,403	4, 30, 49
	S	1	14
	M	287	5, 9, 17, 24, 25
Taror ...	H	421	1
	M	9,734	10, 13, 18, 24, 51
Tasar ...	H	38	16
	M	108	27, 28
Tashiál ...	H	6	49
	M	57	18
Tat ...	H	4	9
	S	245	10, 15, 17, 25
	M	118	16, 18, 19
Tátar ...	H	31	3
	S	42	17
	M	4,448	18, 26, 28
Tathiál ...	S	237	25, 48
	M	1,203	9, 18, 19
Tatle ...	H	47	11
	S	919	11, 12
	M	12	9
Tattí ...	H	34	9, 15
	M	549	26, 28, 29
Táwal ...	H	398	6, 12
	S	15	6, 9
Táwarí ...	H	365	2, 6, 26, 48
	S	868	6, 48
	M	561	1, 13, 17, 18, 19, 24, 26, 48
Tefí ...	M	187	51
Tejá ...	H	12	1, 10, 19
	S	29	4, 12
	M	613	10, 11, 15, 25, 29
Tejor ...	M	30	16
Telí ...	H	393	10, 25, 48
	S	186	12, 25, 48
	M	808	6, 8, 11, 16, 48, 51
Telor ...	H	7	51
	M	274	16, 51
Ter ...	H	4	10
	S	37	48
	M	22	48
Terí ...	H	237	49, 50
	M	6	18, 19
Tetla ...	H	130	16
	S	74	12
	M	2,547	11, 14, 16
Tetrí ...	S	183	11
	M	11	51
Thabal ...	S	12	16
	M	453	16, 18
Thabrál ...	H	71	48
	S	75	48
	M	7	19, 48
Thachar ...	H	3	48
	M	19	27, 48
Thágo ...	H	348	2, 48
	M	58	15
Thagrá ...	H	1	48
	M	123	11, 16
Tháhan ...	H	155	12
	S	1	14
Tháil ...	M	13	6, 44
Thákan ...	H	424	1, 3, 12, 25
	S	90	10, 12
	M	80	3, 4, 13, 18
Thakpál ...	H	6	48
	S	2	9
	M	248	25
Thákrán ...	H	19	9, 12, 16
	S	9	25
Thákrí ...	H	57	4, 27, 29
	S	1	19
	M	20	9, 19, 25
Thala ...	H	270	1, 2, 9, 10, 25, 39
	S	279	17, 19
	M	329	11, 12, 19, 25, 28
Tháliwál ...	H	13	1, 9, 25
	S	122	50
	M	1	9
Thálo ...	H	117	1, 48
	S	45	9, 12, 19, 24
	M	2	15
Thálod ...	H	223	1, 2, 12, 42
	S	1	9, 18
	M	11	25
Thamál ...	H	3	2, 19
	S	87	6, 10
	M	272	16, 17
Thamí ...	H	248	9
	S	1	27
	M	5	13, 17
Thamuá ...	H	109	9
	S	2	5
Thána ...	H	14	9
	S	22	9, 11
Thand ...	H	588	1, 5, 6, 10, 50
	S	2,591	6, 9, 10, 11, 19, 25, 50
	M	1,461	10, 11, 13, 24, 26, 27, 28
Thandar ...	H	269	2, 9, 48
	S	121	9
	M	4	11, 13
Thándí ...	H	720	1, 5, 16
	S	2,787	1, 14, 33
	M	613	14, 25, 27
Thandwál ...	H	13	6
Thankrá ...	H	183	3, 4
	M	97	51
Thápal ...	S	4	6
	M	267	10
Thäprán ...	H	40	3, 48
Tharání ...	H	78	4, 9, 10, 15
	S	77	12, 26, 48
	M	309	26, 27
Tháríwal ...	H	58	1, 10, 12
	S	2	48
	M	31	19, 20
Tharpar ...	H	18	10, 12
	S	6	48
	M	38	13, 29
Thata ...	H	152	9
	S	180	9, 48
	M	508	15, 16, 17, 19
Thatál ...	H	8	17
	M	1,276	19, 20
Thatálí ...	S	38	48
Thataní ...	M	609	6, 11
Thatúgil ...	M	230	10, 25
Thela ...	S	16	48
	M	94	19, 23
Thethí ...	H	6	8, 48
	M	121	18
Thiáu ...	S	24	10, 48
	M	251	27
Thoká ...	H	149	1, 9, 16, 46
	S	18	9, 10
	M	87	2, 10, 28
Thokar ...	H	37	9, 11, 29, 30
Tholar ...	H	4	12
	M	32	48
Tholat ...	S	7	8
	M	52	48
Tholiá ...	H	19	12
	M	2	48
Thorá ...	H	381	1, 16
	S	20	12, 16, 17
	M	1	48
Thoran ...	M	203	14, 24
Thorí ...	H	101	2, 12, 44
	S	902	9, 19, 48
	M	131	28, 29
Thotá ...	M	70	11
Thotan ...	H	9	48
	M	88	28
Thoth ...	H	159	25, 49
	S	127	14, 25, 48
	M	22	19, 28, 29
Thothia ...	H	569	4
	S	2	48
Thothliá ...	S	162	17, 25
	M	7	9
Thothrá ...	H	14	5
	S	69	10, 48, 49
	M	289	9, 19
Tiáj ...	S	77	10, 48
Tihorá ...	H	2	9
	S	22	14, 49
Tíla ...	H	20	8
	S	13	16, 48
	M	398	17, 20
Tílí ...	H	17	9, 10
	M	14	15, 28
Tilodí ...	S	7	48
	M	389	11, 27, 48
Tinde ...	H	559	49
	M	575	16, 27, 48
Tiwáná ...	H	233	10, 12
	S	1	16
	M	81	16, 19
Todha ...	S	120	48
	M	175	27, 29
Todí ...	H	6	9, 51
	S	85	6, 9, 25
	M	207	12, 14, 16, 20, 23, 29
Toh ...	M	189	19
Tohan ...	H	25	12
Tomání ...	S	24	48
	M	2	11
Tongar ...	S	376	12, 48
	M	109	11, 19, 27
Toní ...	H	1	48
	S	31	13
	M	270	13, 27

Names of Sub-Castes.		Persons.	Locality.
Tonk ...	M	14	16
Torí ...	H	45	4
	M	4	19, 48
Tosa ...	H	28	9
	M	8	48
Tota ...	M	11	19, 47
Totáhar ...	M	404	23, 48
Totlaní ...	M	28	11, 21
Trolí ...	H	1	1
	S	157	48
	M	48	27
Túaikmán ...	S	4	24
	M	148	25
Túár ...	S	12	25
	M	164	27
Túíre ...	H	5	9
	S	1	14
	M	1,451	16, 17, 19
Tung ...	H	12	17
	S	797	10, 11, 17
Tunj ...	H	40	27
Túr ...	H	8	48
	S	152	9, 19, 49
	M	2,362	16, 17, 18, 19, 20, 23, 24, 26, 28, 29, 46, 51
Túram ...	S	57	10, 13
Turandí ...	H	2	49
	M	28	21
Tútí ...	H	8	25
	M	72	13, 14, 24
Tútiá ...	H	5,400	3, 9, 29, 49, 50
	S	300	49
	M	160	3, 14, 20, 23, 49
Tutlái ...	H	31	9, 50
	S	58	11, 50
	M	23	20, 25, 50
Ubbhe ...	S	85	9, 11
Udási ...	S	192	9, 10, 44, 46
Udhamá ...	M	687	27
Ulamá ...	M	24	51
Unnar ...	M	358	51
Uppal ...	H	2	11
	S	358	11
	M	36	11, 19, 44
Úran ...	M	48	27
Úrchí ...	M	2,409	27
Ustrá ...	M	112	13, 28
Útál ...	H	5	11
	S	28	9
	M	6	9
Úterá ...	M	58	27
Útrádí ...	M	103	24, 27
Vacha ...	M	18	16, 27
Vachha ...	M	21	17
Vachhal ...	S	117	15
Vad .	M	62	24, 27
Vadá ...	M	210	19, 28
Vadáhá ...	M	14	24
Vaddan ...	M	1,042	13, 16, 18, 20, 27, 28
Vadha ..	M	148	27, 28, 29
Vadhar ..	H	470	16, 19, 27
Vadhará ...	M	409	19, 27
Vadhflech ...	M	101	27
Vádhíwál ...	M	57	27
Vadhor ...	H	221	16
	M	28	28
Vadhrái ...	M	20	19
Vadú ..	M	364	26, 27, 28
Vag ...	M	422	15, 19, 26, 27, 28
Vagar ...	M	348	23, 26, 27
Vaggal ...	M	37	12, 24
Vaggan ...	M	58	24, 27
Vaggí ...	M	207	27
Vághá ...	S	5	51
	M	141	28
Vaghí .	M	159	27, 28
Vágrá ...	M	671	19, 26, 29
Vagrí .	M	41	17, 26
Váhá ..	M	39	18, 24
Vahachá ...	M	188	26, 27, 28, 29
Váhai ...	S	2	16
	M	703	14, 19, 26, 27, 29, 51
Vahar ...	S	159	15, 16
	M	5	14
Vahd ...	S	3	10
	M	364	24, 29
Váhdre ...	M	16	19
Váhga ...	M	1,623	16, 17, 28, 29
Váhia ...	M	37	26, 29
Vahíl ...	S	1,035	15
	M	100	12, 13, 18, 28, 46
Vahín ...	H	9	9
	M	178	19, 29
Váhínd ...	M	104	18, 19
Vahinwál ...	H	13	16
	M	585	19, 27, 28
Váhir ...	M	77	16, 28
Vahla ...	H	18	44
	S	85	13
	M	2,416	13, 16, 17
Váhlár ...	M	29	24
Váhle ...	H	139	13, 15, 16, 17, 51
	S	538	16, 17
	M	45	15, 17
Vahocha ...	M	208	19
Vahoká ...	M	61	19
Vahora ...	H	5	19, 50
	S	126	19, 50
Vahrí ...	M	145	19, 24, 28
Vahú ...	S	4	28
	M	66	26
Vahúcha ...	M	291	27
Váía ...	S	45	10
Váin ..	M	102	13, 20
Vains ...	H	13	12, 16, 17
	S	125	12, 16
	M	3,618	16, 17, 18, 19, 20, 24, 27, 28, 46
Vaish ...	M	569	18, 21, 23
Vajehí ...	M	25	27
Vajhor ...	M	65	24
Vájí ...	M	275	18, 19, 28
Vajjar ...	M	146	19, 24, 29
Vajokha ...	M	97	19
Vajúka ...	M	119	19, 24, 26, 46
Vájwá ...	M	862	27
Vájwáin ...	M	24	23
Vák ...	H	10	9
	S	1	9
	M	479	13, 15, 23, 29
Váká ...	S	32	27
Vákh ...	M	33	29, 51
Vakhar ...	M	119	27
Vál ...	H	1	12
	S	1	13
	M	339	46
Vála ...	H	4	20
	M	457	13, 15, 19, 27
Válak ...	M	1,135	12, 14, 15, 19, 27
Valálí ...	M	24	14, 28
Valána ...	M	60	12, 18
Valaráil ...	M	57	24
Valhar ...	M	92	29
Válí ...	H	16	15
	S	2	6, 10
	M	74	6, 24
Valíra ...	M	71	13, 17
Válíwál ...	S	1	17
	M	161	15, 27
Vallan ...	H	1	16
	M	328	20, 28
Valláns ..	M	399	13, 16, 17, 23, 24, 27
Vallar ...	M	48	15, 24
Vallíe ...	M	202	17, 27, 28
Vallí Sulemán	M	151	26
Vallú ..	S	48	10
Valohá ...	M	13	17
Valtá ...	M	321	15, 16, 19
Valút ...	M	967	27, 28
Valwá ...	M	52	27, 28
Vámín ...	M	20	14
Ván ...	S	812	17
	M	14	17 19
Vandar ...	H	18	12
	S	2,124	1, 12, 13
	M	762	12, 24, 27, 28
Vandua ...	S	1	24
	M	727	28
Váng ...	S	753	12
	M	68	18
Vangí ...	S	1	12
	M	155	17
Vanglá ...	H	10	9
	M	3,612	12, 16, 27, 48
Vángra ...	H	8	17
	M	156	17, 19, 27, 46
Vaníál ...	M	131	26
Vanjhára ...	M	170	27, 28, 46
Vanní ...	M	176	18, 19, 23
Vánoh ...	S	18	6
	M	70	29
Vánúwál ...	H	18	13, 51
	S	1	19
	M	158	12, 26, 28
Vanwáí ...	M	19	19
Vár ...	M	11	16, 19
Varácha ...	H	41	16
	S	3	15
	M	272	26, 27
Varáh ...	H	82	9, 16
	S	30	16
	M	810	17, 20, 21, 26, 28
Varáich ...	H	1,222	L. 18, 19, 24
	S	6,172	5, 11, 14, 15, 16, 17, 18, 19
	M	67,131	L. 9, 10, 18, 19, 20, 21, 25, 27, 28, 29, 51
Varáim ...	M	62	29
Varáj ...	H	11	27
	M	644	27
Varána ...	M	140	17, 27
Varának ...	S	35	19
Varaní ...	M	18	17
Varar ...	S	20	48
	M	128	28
Varga ...	M	703	13, 19, 24, 26, 27
Vargoh ...	M	521	16
Varháí ...	S	15	13
Varbind ...	M	167	10, 16,
Variáh ...	H	313	10, 13, 16
	S	60	10, 16, 17
	M	2,908	13, 14, 15, 16, 19, 20, 26, 27, 29, 51
Varián ...	S	4	12
	M	54	28
Variár ...	M	295	28
Varíhan ...	M	22	46
Varing ...	S	302	24, 46
	M	60	48
Várlú ...	M	122	48
Varmán ...	H	1	10
Varoh ...	M	85	24, 26, 28
Varor ...	M	15	28
Varrú ...	M	15	17
Varsang ...	H	24	5
Varvasa ...	H	47	5
	S	20	12
Vás ...	S	20	12
	M	18	12, 13, 15
Vasákhi ...	H	11	2
	S	1	19
Vasand ...	M	225	24
Vásbin ...	M	24	27
Vásinda ...	M	113	23
Vasli ...	S	4	12
	M	809	12, 27
Vassal ...	M	110	13, 29
Vassan ...	H	2	17
	S	481	12
	M	1,599	10, 14, 15, 17, 26
Vasseír ...	S	1	17
	M	868	12, 13, 24, 27, 29
Vassúhá ...	M	66	29
Vassúr ...	M	127	26
Vastar .	M	92	23
Vasúd ...	M	41	23
Vat ...	M	32	23
Vátal ...	M	18	23
Vathwál ...	M	52	23
Vatikhel ...	M	19	23
Vatrá ...	S	44	15
	M	172	10, 15, 19, 20, 29
Vattí ...	S	2	12
	M	58	46
Vattú ...	H	3	51
	S	18	12, 24
	M	1,376	12, 13, 15, 17, 19, 23, 26, 28, 29, 46, 51

Names of Sub-Castes.	Persons.	Locality.	Names of Sub-Castes.	Persons.	Locality.	Names of Sub-Castes.	Persons.	Locality.
Ves ... H	12	8, 20	Virk ... H	1,488	12, 15, 16, 17, 19, 44	Yúsan-Kháwr S	52	48
S	7	9				Zamindár ... H	40	15, 24, 25, 46, 51
M	1,987	8, 14, 19, 20, 24, 29	S	21,354	10, 12, 13, 15, 16, 17, 18, 20, 24, 51	S	6	12, 24
						M	192	13, 20, 24
Vesar ... M	1,223	17	M	16,290	10, 12, 13, 14, 15, 17, 18, 19, 20, 24, 26, 27	* Minor ... H	1,310	
Vest ... M	21	19, 24				S	537	
Vioh ... M	17	29				M	847	
Vírag ... M	46	24, 28	Yúnse ... H	1	10	Unspecified H	51,213	
Virar ... S	21	20, 24	S	5	48	S	160,614	
M	200	24, 27, 28	M	20	19	M	267,597	
						J	38	

* DETAIL OF MINOR.

Abehar 3, Abradhí 8, Achamba 2, Achharna 1, Achob 1, Adádí 1, Adak 5, Adoh 3, Adrák 3, Adrala 1, Adwána 9, Agrálí 3, Abat 2, Aberdayá 3, Ahígar 4, Ahran 1, Ajhana 10, Ají 8, Akhal 2, Aknárí 5, Akswál 3, Aláchí 2, Alíra 2, Alohán 2, Alorál 2, Alot 1, Alothí 7, Alwán 3, Alyás 2, Ámal 3, Anarwál 6, Anbán 8, Andadí 2, Andal 6, Andhámí 2, Androya 1, Andwáliá 1, Angh 5 Ankál 2, Ankas 9, Anksar 2, Anna 9, Antarí 2, Antarwál 1, Aphas 1, Aploká 3, Árel 1, Árke 7, Arnoh 4, Arooh 1, Aserwál 4, Asjál 1, Askandrál 9, Asoj 10, Asroj 3, Astán 1, Asúkhel 1, Atarya 2, Atfí 1, Athothar 1, Athriya 1, Atmand 1, Atoi 9, Aton 9, Audní 1, Augla 3, Aukhra 6, Aunar 2, Annoh 5, Aunsal 2, Ausra 3, Áwádí 6, Azlí 4, Bachartá 7, Bachhwal 3, Badangrí 5, Badawna 6, Badbar 6, Badhale 2, Badlá 1, Bagherá 3, Bagram 2, Bailwál 6, Baiso 8, Bajáda 3, Bakadmál 2, Bakal 1, Baláhú 10, Báliá 5, Baliárá 1, Baloche 3, Balortá 1, Bandwán 2, Baner 5, Bánjú 4, Banre 1, Bánsíwal 3, Bansrúp 1, Baraniá 8, Bargat 9, Bárhí 8, Barsá 2, Bázdúliá 4, Bhabayán 7, Bhagal 8, Bhagarwá 6, Bhagwái 9, Bharáwín 10, Bhárbon 1, Bharelá 6, Bharniband 3, Bharwe 9, Bhathúnia 8, Bhawájí 5, Bhogí 9, Bhojh 3, Bhojul 3, Bhongarí 8, Bhonjí 2, Bhoras 1, Bíchú 8, Bíd 6, Bikí 2, Bipodá 2, Bisbamrá 3, Bishan 1, Bochan 8, Bochhal 11, Bohán 3, Boral 3, Búndí 6, Chadhí 4, Chadhúke 1, Chakwál 3, Chamání 6, Chamanrái 5, Chamár 4, Chamidá 1, Chanchí 10, Chandel 8, Chandesh 6, Chandharí 4, Chandwál 4, Changrí 1, Chap 1, Charáhá 10, Chároliá 2, Charswál 1, Charwá 7, Chasan 8, Chelí 2, Chief-Khálsa 8, Chiks 6, Chír 3, Chohál 2, Chobí 3, Chond 4, Chorí 10, Chot 3, Chúhá 4, Chúláh 3, Chúnj 2, Chúrásia 5, Dádúpanthí 10, Dáhlúr 8, Dáhwán 7, Dákat 2, Damlot 2, Darjuán 1, Darwáj 6, Derián 3, Dhadaryá 2, Dhadhán 5, Dhánrí 5, Dhárwání 2, Dhatái 4, Dhawan 8, Dhawas 7, Dhedí 4, Dhesal 9, Dhindá 9, Dhohá 8, Diko 1, Diláhan 2, Dobat 6, Dohí 3, Dokal 10, Domandi 1, Doti 7, Dúdbání 7, Fand 1, Gadíl 8, Galol 3, Gandaras 3, Gandholí 6, Ganes 5, Gardhárí 2, Garin 4, Garmáná 1, Garní 4, Ghaltá 10, Ghanil 2, Gharka 6, Ghúsá 8, Gilwál 1, Gobind 4, Goghá 2, Gokar 1, Golab 5, Goláh 7, Gorádar 2, Gorakh 4, Gordwárá 1, Gorewáh 9, Gorsal 3, Gort 1, Gotar 10, Groí 2, Haddí 1, Harchandí 5, Harbas 10, Harjál 1, Hogí 6, Jábak 6, Jadwái 6, Jadwál 5, Jadwán 2, Jagdá 2, Jagwála 1, Jalgotrá 1, Jalokh 8, Jalotí 3, Jalwán 1, Jand 1, Jandú 7, Janesará 5, Janráj 1, Janwí 5, Jarar 1, Jasal 3, Jasrodí 3, Jhakhwáná 4, Jhambhán 1, Jhárkhán 8, Jhesí 4, Jhil 1, Jhráng 2, Jhrír 1, Jigar 3, Jolia 7, Jong 1, Joral 2, Jorwán 1, Joswál 5, Jowán 1, Júgat 10, Káblí 2, Kabúlar 4, Kachhlál 2, Kachotar 3, Kachúrí 4, Kádal 10, Kadáwá 1, Kadorá 5, Kainthal 3, Kalíta 9, Kalíz 1, Kálkí 8, Kamálkhel 8, Kamiál 3, Kaminál 7, Kamírá 1, Kamíwál 1, Kamwál 4, Kanchák 1, Kanet 3, Kángat 5, Kanjiál 1, Kanjiwál 4, Kánsal 6, Kantha 9, Karái 1, Karáng 1, Karátár 3, Karcháná 4, Karg 6, Kargal 2, Karkál 2, Karkárá 1, Karmáli 3, Kárnb 1, Karorwál 3, Kasko 1, Katála 10, Katáni 5, Katarwál 9, Katáyá 3, Katol 4, Katoná 6, Katofá 8, Káwe 2, Kerwán 9, Kesdhári 2, Khajjar 7, Khambál 7, Khánirá 4, Khánwáli 1, Kharb 1, Khátún 7, Khawál 4, Khijoní 4, Khillo-Kháni 6, Khilwá 6, Khíwa 6, Khiyáli 1, Khodális 3, Khurmá 1, Kiálkat 1, Kiáng 3, Kíchar 4, Kíkri 2, Kilo 2, Kisán 1, Kogi 8, Kokhia 1, Koklá 5, Kokuána 2, Koláchí 3, Koran 10, Koriwál 2, Kúká 7, Landán 1, Lasonbate 6, Liah 3, Lodiná 2, Longarkhel 5, Mabri 3, Madígí 3, Maing 2, Maisrí 8, Majparlá 4, Malíwal 8, Mamti 9, Maugan 1, Mangásar 1, Mangbáná 2, Mangwáná 1, Manodí 1, Maráúd 3, Marore 5, Marot 1, Marwádí 3, Matmál 9, Mehá 1, Mehton 1, Merái 1, Mewál 5, Mihi 1, Moechal 7, Mogiáná 7, Mohách 1, Mohal 4, Mohjo 6, Mohlak 3, Mondwál 1, Mongá 2, Muftí 1, Muprái 2, Musle 5, Nában 2, Náhanwál 2, Nábja 2, Nahli 4, Naipál 1, Najlá 5, Nálag 8, Nambal 6, Namír 1, Namrái 2, Nandi 3, Nániá 1, Nanri 6, Nappál 9, Nargáná 4, Narhán 5, Narkí 8, Narsangh 3, Narsí 6, Nátak 2, Nathú 3, Neul 7, Niát 1, Nihand 9, Ním 2, Nímádíá 4, Nimmarhá 8, Nitáj 8, Nitári 7, Noháli 3, Notan 1, Obhál 2, Odan 7, Ogar 1, Ogwáná 1, Ojám 2, Opar 7, Orál 10, Otáni 6, Pacháde 1, Pachí 7, Pachrí 1, Pancham 2, Pandole 1, Pandú 1, Panesar 2, Panwáli 1, Parwán 1, Patwár 2, Patwe 5, Perián 9, Phal 1, Pharar 1, Phat 6, Phátak 1, Phawái 3, Phokwár 1, Phond 5, Photar 1, Phúká 6, Phumman 2, Phungi 5, Pirthí 1, Pogo 1, Popjan 4, Popnún 4, Potalya 1, Potiá 3, Premar 2, Pújman 1, Pulási 4, Punjí 1, Púrk 1, Qabláni 5, Qásmání 4, Qiman 1, Qutab-Sháhí 1, Rachhí 1, Rachhpál 9, Rádar 5, Ráde 6, Radhá 1, Rádhor 1, Radi 8, Rági 3, Rágor 8, Ragwái 2, Raholá 10, Ráhor 8, Rahotlá 3, Ráigal 3, Ráigan 1, Ráikorí 5, Rai-Miwál 1, Ráiti 2, Ráiwál 3, Rajále 2, Rajant 4, Rajhia 1, Rájlol 3, Rajogí 3, Rájra 3, Rájsalori 2, Rájshám 3, Rakbál 2, Rakwál 4, Raltí 4, Rámán 10, Ramáwat 2, Rám-Bansí 1, Rámdes 2, Rám ghan 4, Rámghore 1, Rámkan 1, Rám-San 1, Randá 1, Randhaurí 3, Randhílá 3, Randhor 3, Ranglí 4, Rangro 2, Rániká 1, Ranjobár 4, Ranjrá 6, Rankíd 6, Raolí 2, Ránthí 1, Ránút 1, Rarang 3, Rardhan 2, Rarká 9, Rasanu 3, Rasírá 1, Rason 5, Rasor 1, Rasprá 6, Ratan 4, Ratanmál 5, Ráthán 1, Ratírá 2, Rawáich 3, Ráwli 3, Rebi 2, Regará 1, Rehiá 3, Rehsá 7, Rehtá 3, Reldár 3, Retí 9, Rodádá 4, Rogariá 6, Rogbál 5, Rohádú 1, Roháwal 8, Rohí 6, Rojgal 4, Rokhail 4, Romál 6, Román 6, Rondal 3, Rondí 4, Rongiá 1, Roni 7, Ropyál 2, Roz 5, Rujhi 1, Rupáh 1, Sabeti 2, Sabrái 1, Sáhri 1, Sádá 2, Ságot 1, Sagotí 2, Sáhanpál 1, Sáhbáni 7, Sáhgoná 5, Sahibrang 7, Sahjpálháti 3, Sakání 7, Sakará 10, Sakhúwál 9, Sakiyáná 9, Salban 2, Sallhan 2, Salrí 9, Sanádá 5, Sándáwi 2, Sandaryá 2, Sangrán 10, Sanholi 1, Sanjorá 2, Sanjwál 1, Sankh 6, Sankhí 3, Sankon 6, Sanwár 10, Sardácharn 4, Sarhang 5, Sarjan 8, Sarkali 3, Sarobat 1, Sáron 7, Sarsiá 2, Sasan 1, Seusar 4, Serál 8, Shághla 4, Shahbázi 4, Sháhmadár 1, Shamír 3, Sikhláná 4, Sinkari 1, Sirgul 9, Sitá 4, Sobandá 8, Sodún 3, Sodúr 5, Sogí 1, Sohníbhandár 1, Soilá 8, Sokhariá 4, Sond 5, Soní 3, Soplá 3, Sotrak 7, Sukha 6, Sukham 4, Tadiál 3, Tagáh 2, Tagál 10, Tagrá 6, Tahror 8, Tájak 6, Takrál 1, Talákhel 5, Talásúr 3, Talkhal 1, Tambhan 1, Taudar 2, Tandwál 7, Tanen 4, Tang 10, Tangarí 5, Tarkhán 3, Tarksar 2, Tarmíná 7, Tatrál 2, Tekwál 4, Thákardit 3, Thákí 9, Thakrál 2, Thakreeá 9, Thamráyá 7, Thánesar 10, Tháyá 5, Thod 8, Thog 10, Thostar 5, Tigoliá 9, Tond 5, Tosbak 2, Towár 9, Úde 2, Ukerwand 10, Umokhá 2, Unohá 5, Untwál 2, Utam 4, Uterkhel 7, Utí 1, Vachí 5, Vachrá 2, Vadhal 9, Vadíwál 2, Vágrí 2, Váhndí 10, Vajlá 3, Vál 5, Valiá 10, Vamúká 6, Vandat 6, Vángal 2, Vanjhon 1, Varad 8, Varándá 9, Varb 3, Varhál 2, Varíwál 2, Vástí 1, Vaswál 8, Vatokí 2, Vedí 10, Vehgal 5, Veharú 5, Verfá 4, Viál 1, Zabzál 6, Zahúrí 6, Zání 1, Zargar 5, Zírak 1.

Names of Sub-Castes.	Persons.	Locality.	Names of Sub-Castes.	Persons.	Locality.	Names of Sub-Castes.	Persons.	Locality.
Khatri ...	432,727 { H. 312,024 S. 90,426 M. 232 J. 45		Ahluwáliá ... H	31	9, 12, 14, 15 17, 25	Angrás ... H	333	3, 9, 25, 27, 28, 34, 39, 44
			S	23	17, 21, 25, 27	S	120	9, 10, 14, 44
			Ail ... H	2	24	Aplashdari ... H	13	11, 26, 28, 44
			S	28	24	Arand ... S	20	21, 27
Abarwál ... H	103	8, 10, 12, 15, 19	Ailás ... H	29	9, 39	Arol ... H	25	12
Abhi ... H	21	9, 14, 15, 21	Ajáni ... H	34	20, 25, 28	Arorá ... H	535	1, 3, 4, 5, 7, 9, 10, 11, 15, 18, 21, 25, 29, 34, 40
Ablas ... H	15	9, 10, 11, 14, 44	Akal ... H	15	25			
S	12	11, 14	Akásmohlá ... H	224	17, 23, 26, 27 29			
Abrái ... H	2	12, 25	Amrái ... H	12	8	S	14	4, 27, 29
S	66	4, 14, 19, 20	Amról ... H	30	8, 9	Aryá ... H	17	1, 14, 25
Abrúl ... H	185	1, 16, 21, 25, 44	Anand ... H	631	15, 18, 28, 47	S	5	14
S	12	21, 25	S	150	17, 21	Asal ... H	56	9, 14, 25
Adirái ... H	31	9	M	5	8	Astri ... H	16	37
Agarwál ... H	41	8, 9, 11, 14, 25, 28, 44	Anant ... H	16	28	Atál ... H	10	11
			Anb ... H	22	15	S	1	25
Agriá ... H	64	11	And ... H	581	L. R 16	Atánk ... H	59	8, 9
Ahal ... H	3	24	S	10	9 14, 15	S	3	24
S	8	12	Andogar ... H	20	16	Atrorá ... H	15	17
Ahir ... H	68	11, 17, 18, 19, 21, 25, 27	András ... H	32	5	Atlas ... H	11	6
			Andwál ... H	29	12	Atrá ... H	192	1, 23, 24, 25, 28, 29
S	11	11, 19, 21, 25	Angiásh ... H	57	4, 21			

Names of Sub-Castes.		Persons.	Locality.
Aul	... H	94	15
	S	2	26
Aulakh	... H	26	26
	S	6	27
Aur	... H	28	15
	S	3	27
Awánd	... H	24	15
Aweldal	... H	17	44
Bable	... H	25	9
Báchain	... H	13	9, 39
Bachá	... H	40	18
Badháre	... H	110	6, 9, 11, 14, 19, 22
	S	13	25
Badhwál	... H	116	8, 12, 18, 41
Badhwán	... H	17	6, 12, 14
Badhwár	... H	130	8, 9
Badiái	... H	272	4, 14, 26
Badiár	... H	20	9
	S	2	5
Bagani	... H	32	9, 12, 17
	S	4	19
Báhi	... H	107	15
Báhman	... H	27	15
Báhri	... H	23,197	B. except (2, 3, 4)
	S	2,078	4, 8, 16, 17, 19, 21, 24, 25, 27, 48, 49, 50, 51
Bajje	... H	60	8
	S	16	9
Bajror	... H	16	8
Baláhi	... H	79	9, 11, 14, 47
Bálás	... H	34	6
	S	5	19
Balgeriá	... H	36	15
Balkar	... H	56	9
Balotá	... H	14	2
Bamdá	... H	17	22
Bamluk	... S	15	21
Bándhi	... H	169	8, 14
	S	21	19
Bangar	... H	9	19, 44
	S	2	11
Banjárá	... H	980	11, 17, 19, 20, 23
	S	6	21
Banole	... H	12	19, 20, 23
	S	25	19, 20
Báns	... H	351	5, 6, 9, 10, 11, 14, 15, 18, 19, 21, 39, 44
	S	10	14, 23, 27
Bánsal	... H	34	3, 9
Bansháhi	... H	67	9
Bansi	... H	20	39
Bárá	... H	932	5, 8, 11, 17, 21, 27, 37, 45
	S	36	11, 19, 23
Baráich	... H	230	9, 20
	S	55	8
Barághar	... H	124	10
	S	4	27
Baraj	... H	104	9, 15, 29
Bardwáni	... H	58	8, 18, 25
	S	3	25
Barham	... H	20	8, 51
Barsál	... H	35	9
Barún	... H	34	39
Basáhin	... H	20	10
Basájhú	... H	24	42
Báeal	... H	30	11, 41
Basári	... H	53	15
Báshisht	... H	64	40, 41, 42
Basi	... H	613	J. 1, 4, 13, 14, 41, 44, 45, 50
	S	53	15
Bátansarin	... H	22	9
Báti	... H	145	1, 7, 8, 10, 11, 25, 27, 41, 44, 45
	S	12	1, 14, 20
Batohi	... H	23	3
Battá	... H	38	12, 25
Báwá	... H	57	8, 12, 13, 14, 27, 44
	S	37	15, 19
Bazáz	... H	114	9, 10, 14, 15, 17, 44, 47
	S	9	14, 17
Bedi	... H	938	J. L. M. R. 4, 5, 6, 40, 41, 42, 44, 46, 49, 50
Bedi	S	2,012	L. R. M. 4, 6, 8, 9, 10, 12, 44, 46, 47, 50
Bedwál	... H	15	8, 14
Begi	... H	30	9, 15
	S	1	15
Beko	... H	16	9, 14
Belá	... H	10	9, 14, 44
	S	19	12
Beri	... H	727	4, 8, 9, 12, 14 15, 24, 26, 27 44
	S	36	4, 10, 13, 17, 24, 27,
Bhágal	... H	12	21
Bhágáh	... H	36	14
	S	3	23, 26
Bhagiár	... H	20	9, 10
Bhálgri	... H	24	11, 12
Bhal Bhárdawáj	H	69	39
Bhali	... H	662	5, 8, 9, 12, 14, 20, 27
	S	18	10, 24, 25, 44
Bhallan	... H	1,340	J. L. M. 1, 5, 7, 21, 39, 44, 45, 47
	S	325	9, 12, 14, 15, 19, 24, 25, 28, 33
Bhambri	... H	116	24
Bhandári	... H	5,079	J. L. 1, 6, 21, 22, 25, 41, 44, 47
Bhangáhliá	... H	143	42
Bhangon	... H	315	16, 27
	S	39	25
Bhangási	... H	58	15
Bhárag	... H	26	9, 15
Bharál	... H	17	27
Bhardwar	... H	22	47
Bharihok	... H	21	27
	S	24	12, 42
Bhasin	... H	89	4, 9, 10, 17, 20, 27
Bhat	... H	312	14, 26
	S	84	19
Bhátiá	... H	241	12, 14, 23
Bhalowále	... H	20	12, 25
Bhuriá	... S	16	4, 6
Bhutejá	... H	12	27
Bhuttal	... H	4	45
	S	21	25, 44
Bhuttar	... H	46	1, 44
Bidábará	... H	19	5
Bij	... H	87	9, 11, 15, 44
Bindrá	... H	49	19
	S	98	19, 20, 21, 24, 27
Borá	... H	622	6
	S	3,606	22
Bothal	... H	57	12
Botri	... H	29	42
Bunjáhi	... H	86,388	B. except (4, 5, 28, 29) 33, 34, 39, 40, 44 46, 48, 49, 50
	S	53,976	B. except (2, 4, 7, 18) 33. 44, 46, 48, 49, 50, 51
	M	19	9, 48, 49, 50
	J	1	48
Chábi	... H	82	11
Chadhá	... H	812	7, 8, 11, 14, 15, 17, 18, 19, 20, 21, 24
	S	95	14, 19, 20, 21, 25, 45
Chágar	... H	241	10
Chagoná	... H	11	11
Chagotá	... H	17	9
Chakoi	... H	30	39
Cham	... H	78	1, 5, 11, 25
Chámal	... H	59	9, 11
Chamere	... H	28	8, 11, 26
Chanan	... H	38	14, 44
Chanbed	... H	22	14
Chandá	... H	47	14
	S	5	26
Chánde-Hok	M	2	21
Chándel	H	20	11, 14, 41, 47
Chánde	... H	58	9, 10, 14, 25, 29, 30
	S	13	14, 19, 24
Chándi-phonk	H	114	27, 29
Chandor	... H	4	5, 24, 42
	S	11	24
Chánpare	... H	53	15
Chari	... H	26	14, 25, 42
Chárghare	... H	3,542	10, 13, 14, 17, 24, 48
	S	91	13, 16, 17, 48
Chatálá	... H	74	29
Chathrath	... H	16	17, 42, 44
Chandhri	... H	643	12, 17, 39
Cháwalá	... H	20	14
	S	2	12, 19
Chetu	... H	250	8, 15, 20
Chhalke	... H	11	9
Chhanná	... H	7	27
	S	11	19
Chhapar	... H	31	25
	S	2	19, 45
Chhat	... H	84	12, 19
	S	3	19
Chhattri	... H	72	27
	S	3	21
Chhatwál	... H	3	26
	S	20	12, 19, 21, 25
Chhohre	... H	473	10, 27, 29
	S	16	1
Chhotre	... H	52	10, 20, 45
Chini	... H	27	45
Chirimár	... M	61	3
Chitar	... H	28	12
Chobe	... H	23	9
Choborá	... H	11	11
Choni	... H	13	15, 47
	S	6	15
Choplá	... H	13	9, 40, 47
Choprá	... H	3,197	J. L. R. M. 1, 4, 5, 7, 39, 41, 43 44
	S	377	28, 30, 45, 47
Choriá	... H	48	15, 21, 25
	S	1	17
Chunda	.. H	165	9, 10
Chundhor	... H	38	17
Dabar	... H	22	15, 25, 26
	S	1	19
Dabe	... H	12	14, 25
Dadon	... S	12	21
Daggal	... H	438	7, 15, 25, 28, 34, 44
Daggar	... H	45	25, 28, 29
Dhat	... H	475	9, 20
Dahe	... H	167	28
Dáhr	... H	42	13, 23, 26, 51
Daláwari	... H	11	18
Dalorí	... H	17	11
Dalun	... H	64	19
Dandáná	... H	70	19, 25, 27
Dándharm	... H	82	29
Dándi	... H	30	27
Dánd Dobná	... H	22	19, 27
	S	2	23
Dandwadh	... H	10	17
	S	3	16
Dang	... H	26	21, 23, 25
	S	5	16
Dángwál	... H	214	42
Darare	... H	23	25
Dári	... H	21	11, 14, 15, 27
	S	6	14, 20
Darshan	... H	33	8, 25
	S	5	18
Darwáli	... H	16	28
Dasrá	... H	117	12, 18, 25
Desi	... H	11	27
Deswáli	... H	35	6
Dewáne	... H	82	4, 8
Dewárá	... S	299	7, 19, 26
Dhagwál	... H	11	8
Dháigar	... H	7,372	J. L except (16), 6, 21, 25, 44, 48 51
	S	284	23, 26, 28
Dhákal	... H	21	8
Dhal	... H	137	17, 19, 24, 25
	S	106	23, 26, 28
Dhali	... H	121	45
	S	2	13
Dháliwál	... H	108	11
Dham	... H	75	9, 10
	S	20	20

Names of Sub-Castes.		Persons.	Locality.
Dhan ...	H	168	11, 14, 42, 47
	S	43	13
Dhándhar ...	H	142	11
Dhandi ...	H	90	13, 14, 15
Dhandolá ...	H	11	14
Dhaniwál ...	S	16	12
Dhanni ...	H	120	13
	S	6	21, 27
Dhánsi ...	H	4	9
	S	12	11, 12
Dhar ...	H	200	7, 14, 15, 21, 25, 27, 33
	S	9	13, 19, 25
Dháre ...	H	2	11
	S	13	11, 39
Dharmi ...	H	22	17, 18
	S	2	19
Dháran ...	H	25	27
Dher ...	H	546	1, 5, 11, 12, 27, 29, 44
	S	80	12, 28
Dhingrá ...	H	50	14
Dholi ...	H	54	9, 12, 37
	S	7	23
Dhon ...	H	1,105	L. except (16), 9, 21, 25, 27, 42
	S	74	12, 19, 24
Dhondi ...	H	113	12, 24, 28, 47
	S	4	12
Dhopar ...	H	14	12, 19, 24
Dhorá ...	H	14	8, 14, 17
Dhosi ...	H	26	8, 9, 14, 15
	S	11	9, 13
Dhurál ...	H	12	11
Dodi ...	H	130	9, 11
Dogal ...	H	4,110	11, 12, 14, 15, 22
	S	58	12, 16, 19, 21
Dogar ...	H	241	14, 15, 16, 23
Dobál ...	H	2,815	18, 25
	S	7	13, 19
Dohrá ...	H	102	18
	S	22	19, 25, 27, 33
Dombir ...	H	1,929	18, 29, 47
	S	5	19
Dong ...	H	27	14, 28
Dorá ...	H	19	1, 5, 14, 19
Dosá ...	H	1	6
	S	18	13
Gadu ...	H	48	15, 19, 25
	S	42	19, 21, 27
Gaddi ...	H	70	8, 11
	S	26	21
Gábi ...	H	354	9, 11, 12, 14, 39, 44
Gáhndi ...	H	924	11, 12, 14, 19, 23, 25, 27
	S	33	1, 12, 21, 33, 47
Gakri ...	S	75	21
Galghotu ...	H	38	39, 43
Galon ...	H	20	25, 51
	S	2	25
Galotá ...	S	34	16
Gandotrá ...	H	197	15, 16
Gangáh ...	H	84	9
Gariál ...	H	22	8, 45
	S	11	13, 26
Garhok ...	H	295	1, 20, 25, 39
	S	7	12
Gatti ...	H	39	9, 10, 14, 41
	S	4	13, 25
Gaur ...	H	15	11
Gawál ...	H	42	4, 5, 18, 45
Gawál Mohlá	H	49	29
Ghalri ...	H	13	13, 18
Gharj ...	H	21	15
Gheti ...	H	94	5, 9, 11, 12, 13, 21, 25, 28, 29
Girath ...	H	56	14
	S	1	13
Ghore ...	H	8	45
	S	12	29
Ghota Ghorá	H	17	6
Gidar ...	H	13	14, 17, 27
Gildiá ...	H	34	11
Gilo ...	H	25	9, 13, 16, 19, 24, 25
Giri ...	H	11	42
Gil ...	H	81	42
Ghoman ...	H	11	14
Gobinde ...	H	40	18
Gochar ...	H	65	18
Gond ...	H	37	17, 27
Gondwál ...	H	16	14
Gorath ...	H	69	24
Gori ...	H	85	13, 17
Gorkhá ...	H	46	7, 21
Gosáin ...	H	118	7, 14, 20, 21, 25, 28, 29
Gosálá ...	H	12	11, 12
Gotam ...	H	136	2, 8, 14, 15, 34
Gujrál ...	H	42	19, 25, 27, 44
	S	107	12, 13, 16, 21, 24, 25, 27
Gurupári ...	H	1	25
	S	18	16
Had ..	H	87	11, 42
	S	2	6, 46
Hádún ...	H	102	9, 10, 18
	S	4	19
Haláli ...	H	41	9, 10
	S	4	19
Hamri ...	H	16	17, 41
	S	3	14
Hándá ...	H	701	10, 12, 14, 17, 18, 19, 24, 43, 47,
Hándi ...	H	234	5, 8, 14, 16, 17, 45
Handir ...	H	52	9
Handon ...	H	19	14, 20
Hans ...	H	132	4, 5, 11, 14, 44
Harijá ...	H	15	26
Harjái ...	H	205	19, 25, 26
	S	5	19, 25
Harotrá ...	H	66	26
Has ...	H	15	10
	S	2	14
Hatwáls ...	H	50	42
Homi ...	H	24	14
Jabbal ...	H	44	9, 19, 29
Jádam ...	H	33	12
Jaddi ...	H	49	9, 45
Jadoi ...	H	21	12
Jadrath ...	H	28	42, 43, 46
Jaggáná ...	H	20	45
Jaggi ...	H	58	20, 21, 25
Jagga ...	H	13	14, 42
Jagjiwálál ...	H	11	27
Jagote ...	H	22	8
Jaitli ...	H	15	11
Jájwáh ...	H	59	12
Jakálie ...	H	360	14, 17
Jali ...	H	60	8, 10, 14, 15, 21
	S	13	14, 19, 21, 27
Jalká ...	H	79	14, 15, 16, 44
	S	3	14
Jalote ...	H	71	44
Jame ...	H	11	11
Jamhol ...	H	11	45
Jamon ...	H	14	10, 14, 42
	S	5	14
Jándá ...	H	12	11
Jándak ...	H	30	10, 21
Janji Báz ...	H	69	11
Jare ...	H	14	12
	S	2	11
Jaswál ...	H	59	9, 29
Jaswár ...	H	44	9
Jat ...	H	15	25, 34
Jatáni ...	H	15	11
Jathi ...	H	85	5, 14, 25, 45
	S	15	19, 24
Jatho ...	S	20	12
Jatori ...	H	11	11, 14
	S	12	12
Jeli ...	H	15	10
Jene ...	H	108	12, 41
Jetaki ...	H	51	9
Jhal ...	H	18	15, 19
Jhals ...	H	11	45
Jhámráni ...	H	12	51
Jhandá ...	H	19	11
Jhanji ...	H	33	33
Jhat patie ...	H	15	8
Jhoji ...	H	108	5, 11
Jidki ...	H	117	12
Jirath ...	H	57	11, 12, 25, 36, 44
	S	15	9
Joohuhal ...	H	12	47
Johar ...	H	43	3, 4, 14, 17, 19
	S	33	14, 19, 20, 24, 27
Jomar ...	H	5	11
	S	7	12
Jongi ...	H	36	8
	S	20	25
Kabar ...	H	22	9
Kad ...	H	1,346	14, 15
Káhal ...	H	18	11, 25, 28
	S	4	11
Káhan ...	H	29	9, 14
Káith ...	H	231	14, 17, 42
	S	1	27
Kakkan ...	H	2,743	22
Kakkar ...	H	572	M. 4, 11, 12, 41, 15, 17, 19, 21, 47, 51
	S	31	12, 14, 20
Kákko ...	H	49	1, 15
	S	41	24
Kakrá ...	H	15	15
	S	43	8, 17, 19, 20, 24
Kakrán ...	H	3,413	13, 18, 25, 26
Kalál ...	H	123	1
Katarbansi ...	H	13	27
Kalási ...	H	94	9, 11
	S	15	12
Kalo ...	H	28	1, 26
	S	6	14
Kalib ...	H	54	1
	S	1	10
Kalotre ...	H	45	42
Kambo ...	H	29	14, 15
	S	12	4, 17, 19
Kamhár ...	H	41	42
Kamrá ...	H	54	11, 14, 44
	S	9	14, 44
Kamri ...	H	118	13, 14, 42
	S	4	44
Kán ..	H	12	5, 11
	S	15	5
Kanab ...	H	98	7, 9, 28
Kanári ...	H	119	9, 47
Kanasáe ...	H	43	9
	S	10	9
Kand ...	H	62	41
	S	5	5
Kaneri ...	H	14	19, 26
Kanet ...	H	27	5, 10, 14
Kangár ...	H	12	36
Kángi ...	H	163	27
Kaniá ...	H	31	10
Kániál ...	H	19	4, 18, 24
Kanjan ...	H	11	19
Kannal ...	H	17	14
Kanochiá ...	H	13	27
Kanohre ...	H	20	9, 15
Kansare ...	H	13	8
Kántá ...	H	13	42
Kap ...	H	96	11, 14, 15, 26, 48
Kappal ...	H	67	1, 15, 41
Kapúr ...	H	10,548	J. L. except (16), R. except (22), M. 4, 5, 6, 7, 34, 39, 42, 47
	S	696	J. except (10), L. 1, 4, 5, 6, 18, 19, 21, 34, 25, 27, 44, 48
	M	62	6, 8
Karar ...	H	15	45
Karari ...	H	41	9
	S	13	14, 17
Kari ...	H	52	1, 14, 25
	S	11	14
Karir ...	H	12	44, 45
Kas ...	H	40	5, 9
Kasal ...	H	257	1, 4, 8, 24
Kasar ...	H	37	14
Káshab ...	H	478	1, 4, 6, 14, 17, 25, 34, 39, 40, 41, 47
	S	31	4, 5, 9, 13, 14, 19, 44

Names of Sub-Castes.		Persons.	Locality.
Kataní ...	H	24	8, 15, 44
Katárá ...	H	74	9, 42, 45
	S	1	1
Katári ...	H	35	6, 9, 11, 14
Katármal ..	H	22	19
Kathá ...	H	205	42
Kathiál ...	H	478	9, 13, 19, 25, 26, 27
	S	32	14, 16, 24, 27
Kathrál ...	H	21	42
	S	1	12
Kesar ...	H	14	15
	S	8	24, 25, 44
Keshdhári ...	H	12	7
	S	30	21
Khakhar ...	H	48	14, 17
Khakhráin ...	H	11,923	R. 6, 7, 8, 11, 12 15, 17, 23, 25, 46, 49, 51
	S	4,025	19 to 21, 24, 26, 27
Khakhrinchand	H	9	14, 41
	S	247	16, 23, 25, 44
Khallá ...	H	142	7, 15
Khalli ...	H	72	9
Khálsá ...	H	14	28, 29
	S	67	9
Khandrái ...	H	25	17
	S	2	12, 24
Khanná ...	H	5,617	4, 7, 12 to 14, 17, 18, 21, 23 to 25, 44
	S	277	12, 14, 17, 19, 21, 24, 25, 27, 51
Khanotre ...	S	62	17
Kharpál ...	H	22	9
Khat ...	H	12	14
	S	4	17
Khatan ...	H	1,653	25
Khatiál ...	H	14	47
Khatpál ...	H	19	25, 28
Khatrin ...	H	51	28
Khatti ...	H	182	1, 5, 8, 9, 28, 39
	S	9	10, 25
Khokhar ...	H	11,940	5, 11
	S	427	12, 20
Khokhariál ...	H	51	14
	S	25	13, 19, 21, 24
Khola ...	H	60	14, 15, 51
Kholar ...	H	70	5, 14
Khorá ...	H	14	1, 14
Khosá ...	H	125	9, 14, 23, 28, 42
	S	16	12
Khoshal ...	H	14	1
Khosle ...	H	548	1, 5 to 7, 9, 13, 14, 15, 18, 19, 39, 44, 45
	S	8	11
Khotrá ...	H	116	8, 15
Khollar ...	H	452	11
	S	4	11
Kochar ...	H	264	8, 12, 14, 17, 19
	S	119	14, 21, 25
Kohí ...	H	13	5, 47
	S	4	25
Kohli ...	H	1,272	L. except (13), 12, 20, 21, 27, 33, 40, 48
	S	181	14, 15, 17, 19 to 21, 26, 27
Kohni ...	H	1,631	27, 29
Kohri ...	S	12	14, 15
Koke ...	H	5	29
	S	32	25
Kol ...	H	47	4, 11, 43, 45
Komlí ...	H	46	18
Korchhá ...	H	152	13, 14
	S	7	14, 17
Kori ...	H	99	8, 9, 11, 14
	S	16	14, 15
Koshale ...	H	1,159	2, 5, 7, 11, 14, 21, 25, 26, 28, 41, 44
	S	19	27
Kundal ...	H	88	42
Kushal ...	H	296	11
	S	41	27, 50
Labáná ...	S	26	51
Ladri ...	H	15	14, 41
Lajji ...	H	184	11
Lakhne ...	H	9	17
	S	11	17
Laki ...	H	21	11
Lál ...	H	36	8
Lallotará ...	H	22	14
Lambak ...	S	33	21
Lámkiáru ...	H	79	42
Lámniá ...	H	87	21
Lángri ...	H	14	14, 26, 41
Larni ...	H	111	9, 15
Latter ...	H	12	9
Lawáná ...	H	145	9
Likhará ...	H	48	9
Lodi ...	H	54	12
Loháníá ...	H	24	17
Lohári ...	H	482	10
Lohrá ...	H	28	9, 42
Lotoriá ...	H	35	10
Machhal ...	H	81	9, 14, 24, 42
Madhea ..	H	418	14
Madhok ...	H	22	9
Madhrá ...	H	47	14
Madkan ...	H	24	17
Magon ...	H	18	17, 47
Magri ...	H	41	14, 25, 27
	S	2	14
Magú ...	H	196	9, 14, 19, 27, 29
	S	109	19, 24, 25
Maháján ...	H	64	14, 42
	S	56	21, 25, 27
Mahan ...	H	60	14
Mahandru ...	H	104	24, 33
Mahol ...	H	39	9, 27
Mahote ...	H	101	5, 11
Mahotrá ...	H	12	44
Mahrá ...	H	554	21, 29
Mahtá ...	H	991	12, 14, 17, 20, 24
	S	1,967	9, 12, 23 to 25, 27
Mahtam ...	H	11	12
Maingan ...	H	58	12
Mainrál ...	H	80	8
	S	9	14
Majgotre ...	H	27	19
Makar ...	H	41	2, 8, 9
	S	1	21
Makhne ...	H	14	29
Makhri ...	H	18	24, 42
Maki ...	H	12	12
Málan ...	H	68	11, 12, 44
Malhotra ...	H	5,376	13, 14, 17, 18, 24, 25
	S	207	12, 13, 17
Malli ...	H	61	15, 28
Malok ...	H	20	9
Maman ...	H	61	44
Mand ...	H	36	11, 18
Mandí ...	H	70	9
Mandri ...	H	94	25
Mandú ...	H	2	5
	S	21	19, 24, 27
Mangal ...	H	16	11, 15, 41
Manliá ...	H	83	25
Manohar ...	H	114	14
Márang ...	H	44	28
Marobá ...	H	18	17
	S	22	5, 9
Marothá ...	H	67	15
Marotrá ...	H	2,475	11, 27
	S	6,313	19, 22, 27
Marrá ...	H	136	14
Marwáhi ...	H	338	8, 9, 16, 24, 44
	S	49	14, 15, 21
Marwári ...	H	25	5, 6, 27
Mathre ...	H	138	9, 14, 17, 20, 27
	S	2	27
Matras ...	H	25	5
Matte ...	H	143	9, 11, 20
Matten ...	H	10	1, 25
	S	85	17, 18
Matu ...	H	15	9, 25, 27
Megi ...	H	14	12, 25
Mehr ...	H	768	4, 14, 19, 26
Mehtar ...	H	13	51
Miál ...	H	35	15
Miná ...	H	30	15, 24, 44
Mir ...	H	14	8, 9
Mirkan ...	H	23	11
Misráni ..	H	91	26
Mohne ...	H	43	5, 19, 21
Moli ..	H	1,997	15
Mon ...	H	10	9, 14, 19
	S	12	14
Monde ...	H	79	9, 11, 12, 26
Moti ...	H	31	15
	S	5	12
Multáni ...	H	58	4, 6, 13
Mundrá ...	H	82	15
Múni ...	H	11	9
Múnjngí ...	H	11	5
Múnji ...	H	17	11
Murádhare ...	S	34	9
Murgái ...	H	22	9, 44
	S	5	9, 20
Murri ...	H	19	11
Nágí ...	H	18	11, 19
	S	10	19, 21
Nágon ...	H	65	29
Náglí ...	H	80	21, 28
	S	6	14
Nágpál ...	H	33	14
	S	11	14
Náhan ...	H	20	28
Náhrí ...	H	62	11
Najháwan ...	H	59	23, 24, 25, 27
	S	3	23
Najján ...	H	384	14, 25, 29
Najjár ...	H	189	14, 15, 16, 44
Nakhrá ...	H	20	29
Nandal ...	H	100	9
Nand Chábil	H	123	8, 9, 45
	S	35	9, 19
Nandí ...	H	531	11, 12, 14, 15, 18
	S	47	17, 19, 21
Nará ...	H	27	14, 18
Narli ...	H	14	9
Nárú ...	H	17	8, 47
Negar ...	H	14	9, 29
Nep ...	H	17	14, 15
Niar ...	H	230	8, 9, 11, 15, 27
	S	9	9
Níhál ...	H	12	29
Niháwan ...	H	65	29
	S	4	20
Nílá ...	S	46	25, 27
Obhí Rái ...	H	13	17, 20
Od ...	H	53	23, 27
	S	4	24
Ohr ...	H	32	9, 12, 16
	S	11	9
Omat ...	H	24	9, 12
Opan ...	H	20	15, 24, 39
Orí ...	H	41	44
Pajái ...	H	64	38
Pájí ...	H	11	47
Paknál ...	H	13	15
Palte ...	H	83	12
Pambe ...	H	13	21
Pandárí ...	H	590	1, 11, 15 to 17, 47
	S	89	14, 21, 27
Pándí ...	H	48	5, 9, 11, 15, 27
	S	4	14, 15
Pándrú ...	H	11	6
Pangá ...	H	18	10, 17
Pangás ...	H	19	15
Panjábí ...	H	13	16
	S	12	3, 12, 21
Panjáit ...	H	82	12
Panjiáwal ...	H	29	41
Panjdáss ...	H	197	13
Panj ghar ...	H	28	11, 25
Panj rathá ...	S	70	15
Panj zátí ...	H	40	4, 10
Pappí ...	H	9	9, 41
	S	11	25
Pará ...	H	54	9, 24
Parwál ...	H	5	12, 47
	S	9	19
Pásbí ...	H	146	9, 11, 14, 29, 33
Pát ...	H	3	5
	S	21	25, 33
Pathere ...	H	48	14, 25
Patli ...	H	18	8, 25, 47
Pátní ...	H	248	27
	S	32	21

SUB-CASTES OF CERTAIN SELECTED CASTES—*continued.* KHATRI.

Names of Sub-Castes.		Persons.	Locality.
Patphí ...	H	64	15
Pattí ...	H	108	12
	S	14	16
Petre ...	H	17	8
Phal ...	H	34	8, 14, 27
Phaladh ...	H	20	39
Phalog ...	H	11	6
Phárgú ...	H	11	28
Pharok ...	H	43	24
Phárú ...	H	95	42
Phátiá ...	H	23	12, 26
Phedu ...	H	62	44
Pholí ...	H	13	14
Phular ...	H	21	9, 15
Phuman ...	H	19	14
Pole ...	H	67	4, 14, 42
	S	5	14
Pujyálá ...	H	98	39
Púrbiá ...	H	18	25
Púrí ...	H	2,531	D. J. L. 18, 24, 42, 47
	S	117	L. 24, 48
Qandhárí ...	H	290	9, 11, 13 to 16, 21 44
Rái ...	H	58	8, 16, 20, 21
Ráin Jháin ...	H	193	28
Rajbwán ...	H	42	39
Rájpút ...	H	204	11, 14, 17, 20, 25 to 27, 51
	S	53	12, 13, 14, 20
Rámdás ...	H	33	26
	S	18	16, 20, 26
Rámgirí ...	S	12	14, 21
Ramí ..	H	12	11
Ránd ...	H	87	9, 11, 24
Rang ...	S	18	21
Rangras ...	H	7	8, 9
	S	13	9
Raphál ...	H	18	11
Ráre ...	H	14	11
	S	44	10, 14, 21, 24
Rasáin ...	H	15	12
Rasíle ...	H	18	13
Ratan ...	H	42	39, 47
Ratangot ...	H	16	14
Rathwál ...	H	156	39
Batrá ...	H	41	8, 28
Rattí ...	H	20	14 to 16
Ríhán ...	H	45	9, 10, 44
Rorá ...	H	206	8, 9, 16, 39, 41, 42, 43
Sabárí ...	H	19	5, 17, 47
Sabharwál ...	H	317	9, 14, 17, 19, 23, 24, 25, 44
	S	21	10, 12, 14, 24
Sabhi ...	H	25	2, 17
	S	2	14
Sachdev ...	H	137	5, 15, 21, 25, 27
Sádwál ...	H	18	14
Sagal ...	H	13	5, 8, 9, 11, 19, 26
Sagar ...	H	58	11
Saghari ...	H	21	9, 12, 24
Sagú ...	H	43	9, 10, 12, 14
	S	6	21, 27
Saháran ...	H	11	10
	S	10	14, 15
Sáhdí ...	H	19	9
Sahgal ...	H	2,705	L. M. 4, 10, 11, 12, 20, 21, 41, 47
	S	255	14, 17, 18, 20, 21, 24, 25, 26, 27
Sáhí ...	H	42	12, 14, 25, 27, 33
	S	4	9, 25
Sáhín ...	H	248	12, 18, 19
	S	3	23
Sáhis ...	H	19	5
Sahjari ...	H	68	9
	S	2	28
Sáhni ...	H	7,268	8 to 17, 19 to 21, 45
	S	171	14, 17, 19, 21, 25, 27
	M	5	9
Sahote ...	H	61	6, 45, 47
Sahwále ...	H	15	27
Sainí ...	H	190	14, 18, 21, 26, 44
	S	3	26, 27
Sajjal ...	H	32	3, 12, 44
Sajrá ...	H	12	11, 26
Sákái ...	H	87	19
	S	4	27
Sake ...	H	25	19, 25
Sakhán ...	H	18	8, 27
Sakhrí ...	H	92	9, 14, 15, 44
Sálah ...	H	42	39
Salhok ...	H	35	14, 27
Salhotre ...	H	12	12
Salí ...	H	87	10, 28
Salolí ..	H	16	9, 39
Salone ...	H	16	9
Salorí ...	H	18	11
	S	18	14, 21
Sámán ...	H	30	8, 12, 21
	S	14	14
Same ...	H	221	8, 25 to 28
	S	2	26
Samra ...	H	69	19, 41, 44
Sánan ...	H	35	39
Sánátan ...	H	43	44
Sándal ...	H	37	11, 17, 25, 41
Sandí ...	H	104	8, 11, 15
	S	7	24
Sangal ...	H	13	1, 4, 15
Sangar ...	H	160	9, 12, 15, 17, 18, 28, 44
	S	17	1, 12, 14
Sanjrí ...	H	14	45
Sapálok ...	H	148	19, 28, 29
	S	1	19
Sapní ...	H	35	9, 41
Sappal ...	H	35	14
Sapparwál ...	H	6	24
	S	16	18
Sarhán ...	H	1,148	6, 9, 11, 16, 45
Sarín ...	H	50,514	B. except (7,22), 38, 44, 46, 48, 50
	S	3,513	9, 10, 12, 13, 14, 16, 20, 22, 24, 44, 48, 50
	M	35	9
Sarín Dágí ...	H	194	9
Sarín Khokhar	H	32	9
Sarín Tej ...	H	28	9
Saroí ...	H	1,070	8, 9, 10, 14, 21, 27
	S	249	15, 20, 21
Saromál ...	H	72	6, 11, 18
	S	6	27, 44
Sarotre ...	H	17	10
Sarpál ...	H	154	9, 14, 15, 25
	S	2	14
Sársut ...	H	11	9, 11, 14
Saru ...	H	23	5, 14
Sarwál ...	H	23	5, 15, 20
	S	7	4, 25
Satgajrá ...	H	16	23
Sathá ...	H	165	21, 26
	S	9	14
Satpati ...	S	11	25
Sawái ...	H	8	21
	S	3	25
Sekho ...	H	72	11, 12
Seth ...	H	341	4, 5, 6, 8, 9, 14, 33
Sethi ...	H	851	8, 9, 12, 14, 17, 21, 26
	S	181	14, 17 to 21, 25, 27
Shábi Koshal	H	12	6
Shamas ...	H	50	8
Shám dási	H	96	5
Siái ...	H	11	6
Sial ...	H	544	11, 12, 14, 15, 19, 21, 29
	S	19	14, 20, 21
Sibal ...	H	22	15, 17, 29
	S	14	27
Sikar ...	H	46	9, 26, 39, 46
Simádhi ...	H	27	28
Siná ...	H	49	15, 27, 37
Sindhu ...	H	71	14, 15
	S	10	13, 29
Singar ...	H	34	9
Singh ...	H	459	19, 25, 26, 27
Siri ...	H	11	4, 15
	S	6	25
Sirmál ...	H	28	4
Sitá ...	H	123	14, 15, 45
Sodhbans ...	H	54	19
	S	209	19, 21
Sodhi ...	H	805	1, 6, 8, 10, 12, 20, 21
	S	967	5, 6, 9, 12, 13, 14, 15, 17, 19, 22, 27
Sodri ...	H	14	8
Sofi ...	H	13	25
Sohái ...	H	56	11
Sohal ...	H	118	9, 39
	S	38	9, 15
Sohan ...	H	13	14
Soi ...	H	111	8, 11, 14, 25, 45
	S	5	17, 25
Sojhatá ...	H	22	1
Somin ...	H	28	9
Sona ...	H	1,090	5, 8, 14, 15, 17 19, 25, 27, 29, 34
	S	166	14, 15, 17, 20
Sondhi ...	H	183	10, 14, 21
	S	11	15
Soti ...	H	11	5
Sud ...	H	264	2, 5, 12, 14, 15 25
Sudbansi ...	H	5	19
	S	223	19, 21
Sundrání ...	H	23	1, 9, 15
Suniár ...	H	50	14, 27
Suraj Bansí...	H	35	14, 15, 18, 27
	S	14	14, 17
Súrí ...	H	277	10, 11, 15, 16, 17, 21, 28, 47
	S	50	16, 17
Sutbrá ...	H	16	12
	S	19	21, 27
Tábolá ...	H	22	12
Tágrí ...	H	29	15, 41
Takhiál ...	H	13	44
Takiár ...	H	29	8, 9, 15
Tále ...	H	1	19
	S	55	14, 17, 27
Talwár ...	H	703	2, 7, 14, 15, 17, 18, 19, 21, 23, 26, 27, 44
	S	65	9, 12, 14, 17, 27,
Tan ...	H	68	8, 9, 18
Táube ...	H	80	28
Tauan ...	H	380	9, 11, 14, 15, 17, 19, 24, 25, 27
	S	17	14, 27
Tand ...	H	63	1, 11
Tandal ...	H	27	14, 15
Tandan ...	H	124	9, 24, 26, 28, 29
Tángre ..	H	22	12, 25, 27
Tánk ...	H	108	10, 17, 21, 27
	S	72	10, 27
Tarbiá ...	H	29	14
	S	8	25
Tarbún ...	H	18	16, 18
Tarkhán ...	H	29	9, 11
Taroi ...	H	6	41, 47
	S	7	10
Tárwár ...	H	19	11
Teli ...	H	139	15, 26
Thákre ...	H	80	9, 11, 14, 25, 27
Thaman ...	H	129	8, 9, 11, 25, 47
Thau ...	H	46	8, 11, 15
	S	1	9
Thánk ...	S	48	17
Thápar ..	H	462	1, 10, 11, 12, 14 17, 21, 27
Thappále ...	H	1	11
	S	12	10, 12, 19
Thare ...	H	18	12
Thathiár ...	H	25	14, 26
Torí ...	H	14	9, 11, 39
	S	13	10
Tulí ...	H	143	15, 16, 17, 27
Ubrái ...	H	32	15, 16
	S	44	20

Names of Sub-Castes.	Persons.	Locality.	Names of Sub-Castes.	Persons.	Locality.	Names of Sub-Castes.	Persons.	Locality.
Udásí ... H	9	9, 11, 21, 41	Vag ... H	294	14, 19, 26, 27	Vasht ... H	28	14
S	2	25	S	97	19	Vásin ... H	47	15, 26
Úná ... H	14	28	Vaham ... H	62	26	S	23	14, 17, 24
Uppal ... H	1,884	8, 9, 11, 12,14, 15, 18, 26, 45	S	10	17, 21	Vástí ... H	26	19
S	240	5, 12, 14,24,26, 27	Vábari ... H	629	12, 14 19,25 26, 27, 28	Vedi ... H	66	11, 25, 41
Utrádhí ... H	12	1, 11, 18	S	62	26, 27	S	6	1, 14
S	6	14, 20	Váhí ... H	243	14, 19, 21, 27	Viálak ... H	73	28
Vachhá ... H	14	29, 51	S	8	19, 21	Vij ... H	472	12, 19, 23,24, 26, 27
Vadháwan ... H	96	12, 19, 24, 25, 27	Váhil ... H	20	44	S	79	24, 26
S	47	12, 17, 24	Vahore ... H	72	27	Zargar ... H	72	27, 28, 29
Vadhre ... H	12	17	Vájwah ... H	60	26	S	30	17, 27
S	57	21, 26	S	1	14	*Minor ... H	2,327	
Vadhwa ... H	109	14	Vandholí ... H	66	14	S	567	
S	1	10	Vánsal ... S	23	12, 24	M	1	
			Vasan ... H	103	14, 24	Unspecified... H	4,024	
			Vásdev ... H	55	14, 19	S	734	
						M	42	
						J	44	

*DETAIL OF MINOR.

Abasti 3, Abbrá 4, Abirál 1, Achárji 1, Achint 2, Adal 1, Adham 7, Agrat 4, Ailchha 1, Ajjal 1, Ajo 2, Ajpáni 1, Ajrái 1, Akbari 4, Aki 3, Akshak 1, Álbári 4, Alg 1, Alkh 4, Allu 10, Alons 8, Alri 3, Alúche 2, Alsi 2, Alt 3, Ambarwáni 3, Amláni 1, Amratkapal 9, Amrogh 4, Anangpál 1, Andar 8, Andhapanjghar 2, Andhe 9, Andotre 3, Angri 6, Ankrá 1, Apotre 2, Aprás 3, Apwárthi 6, Aráti 1, Arband 7, Arorbans 2, Asarwál 2, Atárman 2, Audási 1, Augal 6, Awámal 1, Bach 2, Bachher 4, Badhau 9, Badherá 5, Badkáwri 4, Bagar 4, Baggi 1, Bajes 1, Baksará 4, Bale 2, Baliá 1, Balsan 1, Balwábári 1, Bándá 3, Baniá 10, Banre 2, Banwáriá 6, Barahman 1, Barágisart 2, Barándi 8, Barári 4, Barohe 4, Basás 1, Básath 3, Batak 10, Batre 1, Báwe 7, Behi 6, Bekhi 10, Berági 8, Berie 1, Bhábre 1, Bhadar 2, Bhagotre 3, Bhagrá 10, Bhajhái 1, Bhajrá 3, Bhákán 1, Bhalle 4, Bhamarwál 6, Bhanbhar 8, Bhand 4, Bhandaulá 1, Bhandi 10, Bhangal 4, Bhani 6, Bháras 1, Bharbhujá 1, Bhárichopre 1, Bhárti 1, Bharwál 3, Bhas 5, Bhasre 4, Bhátla 2, Bhatti 10, Bhel 4, Bhoj 1, Bhojh 1, Bhojratti 8, Bholar 1, Bhorigot 1, Bhuchar 6, Biás 10, Bobáue 2, Bohre 2, Bore 7, Bukare 5, Chachrá 1, Chajal 1, Chajjar 5, Chák 1, Chakete 10, Chalgi 1, Chalián 3, Chálúi 8, Chamhok 2, Chandarbansi 10, Chandmál 3, Cháng 3, Changádá 2, Change 2, Chanetha 1, Charingi 3, Charke 3, Charkoni 6, Charohá 2, Chátli 1, Chatoi 3, Chatro 4, Chawár 3, Chere 8, Chothe 1, Chhadak 1, Chhakore 7, Chhárchi 3, Chhaniál 2, Chharliá 3, Chharu 6, Chháwre 1, Chhib 2, Chhimba 4, Chhínji 1, Chhochhe 5, Chochar 4, Chojah 6, Chojir 6, Chokhare 3, Choprebansi 8, Chote 8, Chugiánar 6, Chúhán 1, Chúhr 2, Chúki 1, Chúnchrá 9, Dáh 1, Dakhná 8, Dalwáli 4, Dandoriá 1, Danir 2, Daráwne 2, Daríbán 3, Dars 1, Darul 1, Dat 1, Derá 2, Desarrabhá 3, Devi 1, Dhagotiá 2, Dhain 2, Dhaliá 4, Dhalwái 2, Dhaman 5, Dhange 9, Dharkhán 3, Dhundhál 3, Dhel 2, Dho 1, Dibá 1, Dohi 8, Dohre 6, Domrá 6, Dosaj 1, Dosal 2, Duppal 1, Duriál 3, Faqir 8, Gadh 7, Gádzi 2, Gágre 8, Gájri 3, Gandal 1, Gangár 8, Gangotri 1, Gárab 2, Gárian 2, Gawál Bans 1, Gáwari 1, Ghanále 4, Ghangi 1, Gharáin 3, Gháretiá 2, Gharoge 3, Ghas 8, Ghoke 1, Ghoslá 8, Ghurar 1, Ghurcharhe 2, Gila 2, Gobar 7, Gok 1, Gondri 4, Goriá 8, Gujráti 9, Gulgul 1, Gulsan 1, Gulzári 7, Gumtalá 1, Gunjati 4, Gur 2, Guruwaráh 1, Hadar 1, Haggan 2, Hajjá 3, Hangári 3, Harar 2, Hardoi 5, Haroná 2, Határcho 1, Hattá 4, Hawat 6, Hinjrá 2, Hir 6, Hujjá 1, Isht 1, Jádá 3, Jadhá 5, Jádu Bansi 7, Jagriál 4, Jáhre 1, Jajrá 6, Jákar 4, Jal 6, Jand 2, Jandiál 9, Jandre 2, Janewar 10, Jangotre 7, Jángrá 6, Janjuá 8, Jariál 2, Jási 1, Jasorá 1, Jassal 6, Jatah 1, Jatal 1, Jatphal 1, Jaur 1, Jawal 1, Jetha 6, Jhadeok 2, Jhako 1, Jhakrá 1, Jhangi 7, Jhángal 10, Jhangre 6, Jhotre 2, Jog 2, Johal 1, Johi 6, Jon 1, Kachari 5, Káchhí 3, Kahhar 3, Káhí 7, Kajrae 6, Kakaí 1, Kakkrak 2, Kaland 1, Kaleche 6, Kalechi 10, Kalesrí 1, Kalián 4, Kalor 6, Kamiár 1, Kandarí 4, Kandí 1, Kandoiá 1, Kandotar 1, Kandre 2, Kandru 1, Kandwál 6, Kangotre 7, Kaniáni 3, Kanjrá 8, Kankar 10, Kannal 8, Kanotrí 4, Kanojá 4, Kanrá 1, Kanshikhel 1, Kantari 1, Kanungoi 4, Kaplas 1, Karnímal 5, Karj 4, Karkat 2, Karnatho 4, Karorwál 1, Karpál 1, Kasái 3, Kashmiri 2, Kaslá 4, Kasobni 1, Kathuri 1, Katiál 2, Kelad 9, Khag 3, Khandur 4, Khanuat 2, Khar 2, Kharar 3, Khari 2, Khastí 4, Khattar 5, Khinge 3, Khir 5, Khisí 3, Khoi 8, Khurná 2, Kír 1, Kishan 10, Kodí 8, Kontrá 2, Kopási 1, Korahoh 8, Korang 3, Kotrí 1, Kundari 5, Lagge 4, Lagrian 1, Lahar 9, Laboriá 1, Lajjur 2, Lakhanpál 6, Lakh-Dátá 1, Lakhrá 2, Lálí 5, Lalia 3, Lamb 10, Langah 3, Lániá 3 Larove 5, Lathí 1, Láwar 5, Lobhani 1, Lodhar 8, Lohre 1, Loke 6, Loní 3, Lophe 2, Lorí 2, Lote 5, Lowá 4, Lund 2, Lurká 1, Madhohá 1, Madhon 2, Madhrá 1, Madwalie 4, Mahand 3, Máhí 9, Máhil 5, Máhír 1, Mahlog 1, Maigal 2, Majhál 4, Majitha 8, Makan 5, Makhol 8, Makol 2, Makrár 1, Mál 1, Maleku 3, Malin 6, Malpotre 2, Malwálá 6, Manahar 2, Mandar 3, Mandháwan 7, Mandiál 4, Mangárí 1, Mange 6, Mangwál 5, Máni 1, Manir 5, Manjar 1, Mankalí 2, Manwál 4, Marahta 5, Maráti 2, Marawát 1, Marhon 2, Marichá 5, Marjai 4, Marrao 5, Masihán 2, Mathur 5, Matil 3, Matkan 9, Med 6, Mehar 3, Melá 1, Melar 4, Mialok 1, Mini 2, Mithádu 1, Mithádu 1, Mitru 3, Modak 9, Modí 2, Mogal 1, Mohri 5, Mokhi 6, Molit 10, Molrí 3, Moni 9, Mothia 6, Mothre 2, Mujra 7, Mukhe 6, Mulla 4, Murlí 2, Murrí 4, Nabsar 1, Nachiál 5, Nachithar 6, Nádore 4, Nágre 10, Náhí 10, Nain 10, Najas 9, Nákhar 9, Nalhor 1, Nálwár 1, Nánakpál 5, Nánakpanthí 7, Nának-Shábí 1, Nandjar 8, Nandkorá 4, Nando 2, Nandrajog 4, Nangiáre 10, Nan Shahí 1, Napák 7, Naqúl 1, Naráthie 3, Naríte 4, Narjoí 3, Narolí 2, Narosí 3, Narsinghí 9, Norwál 7, Nátak 1, Natal 1, Náwá 1, Nechari 2, Negad 10, Negí 4, Niáhal 9, Nie 1, Nígar 4, Nigráth 4, Nibág 1, Nirmalá 4, Ochar 1, Ochhal 1, Odiál 1, Ogar 8, Ohri 5, Ol 3, Omban 3, Ondái 5, Oprí 5, Orsí 2, Pachiál 1, Padar 1, Pádrí 5, Paháríí 5, Pahiál 5, Pakhar 8, Pakkú 2, Palghí 5, Palahtá 8, Palhorí 3, Pálí 3, Palk 4, Palol 1, Palpak 8, Pámal 7, Panál 6, Pandáoí 1, Pandárí 7, Pandôl 3, Pandwárí 7, Paní 6, Panjárál 1, Panjariá 1, Panjratan 1, Panjú 1, Panjúke 4, Panún 6, Panwár 3, Parail 1, Paral 2, Paras-Rámi 2, Parathí 2, Pariál 3, Parmáre 4, Párti 4, Páse 2, Pasián 5, Pásin 3, Pate 5, Pathán 2, Pátiárí 6, Patoí 3, Patrí 8, Patwál 4, Puwár 7, Páwí 1, Payálí 4, Pekhí 1, Pení 2, Perí 3, Pewálá 2, Phágan 2, Phagiár 1, Phallá 2, Phalná 6, Phalol 8, Phándi 2, Pharárí 3, Phúl 4, Pindí 3, Pochhke 5, Polat 2, Popal 1, Poprí 2, Pottá 2, Punjái 7, Púngo 8, Púranpurí 4, Purhiál 1, Qánúngo 7, Rabbí 1, Rachhbandi 3, Rad 1, Raghbír 5, Raghúbansí 2, Ráhan 1, Ráhi 1, Ráhli 9, Rahor 8, Rájahíl 2, Rajor 1, Rájpbal 7, Rájpút Parhár 1, Rájrú 4, Rájún 3, Rajwál 3, Rakha Singh 2, Rakhrái 1, Rál 6, Rálan 5, Rálash 7, Rámá-Nandí 3. Rám Chandí 2, Rám Dashti 2, Rám garhí 9, Rámpál 1, Rámrá 1, Rááá 5, Ranchal 5, Rangrí 6, Ranpál 6, Rásan 5, Rásiání 4, Ráswár 1, Rátár 4, Ráthí 2, Ráwal 9, Ráwarí 5, Ráwat 1, Rekhí 9, Remán 5, Ret 9, Rind 7, Rode 2, Rohan 2, Ropar 4, Rúhel 2, Rúkí 1, Sabohar 2, Sabhalá 1, Sabhán 3, Sabhúnlá 2, Sachar 3, Sadarít 1, Saddáná 2, Sádí 1, Sadráuch 5, Sagrá 3, Sáhal 6, Sahán 5, Sahárán 9, Sahkal 10, Saholi 8, Sahontrá 6, Sahr 3, Sabrá 1, Sái 9, Sajní 2, Sakandrí 6, Sakrí 3, Sakúí 3, Salarwál 6, Salojá 1, Salohní 10, Salondi 3, Salwán 1, Samal 4, Samáhal 1, Samandrí 7, Samánjí 1, Sámohí 1, Sámpaní 3, Sanbhálá 1, Sandar 6, Sandásan 7, Sandodí 2, Sandok 3, Sang 3, Sangotri 6, Saniási 2, Sánsí 1, Sapálá 9, Saparwál 3, Saprolí 1, Sarb Mukhí 10, Sarit 3, Sárítá 8, Sarjá 2, Sarothá 3, Sarswál 1, Sárwár 6, Satar 5, Sathea 1, Sathíthan 4, Sathwál 1, Satí 4, Satwál 3, Sawátí 1, Seh 1, Selok 5, Serwál 3, Sewgí 1, Shambhú 4, Sharif 1, Shif 1, Shimlá 2, Shinjre 8, Shohar 7, Sholak 4, Siálok 9, Siání 7, Sígár 7, Sikhpál 3, Silái 2, Sillí 4, Sitá Wál 2, Sobti 7, Soghe 9, Sohat 3, Sohígal 3, Sohpale 2, Sohrá 2, Sojí 3, Sokhat 1, Solí 2, Solor 4, Solsí 1, Sondrá 3, Sonthe 1, Sopin 4, Soptí 7, Sosaní 3, Sotat 2, Súmá 2, Súntrá 2, Súrbál 1, Súrian 1, Tabní 3, Tágwál 1, Táhan 3, Táhe 2, Tahím 7, Tajrá 4, Taki 1, Takte 5, Tál 2, Tálbáz 8, Talhotal 2, Talí 9, Talká 8, Tamb 2, Támro 2, Tanchhal 9, Tanojá 1, Tangro 10, Tanwárí 3, Tapre 1, Tarande 2, Tarángrí 7, Targotre 10, Tarkhá 6, Tarlú 6, Tárwál 5, Tate 9 Tatri 2, Tatwálí 1, Thalad 9, Thálká 1, Thals 4, Thandan 5, Thandrí 9, Thárgiál 5, Thiá 6, Tilwán 1, Tír 1, Tirlon 2, Tohar 1, Tolí 5, Údhal 2, Ujále 3, Ulakh 2, Umáotre 5, Umdártán 7, Ummat 2, Umrání 5, Uppásí 1, Upres 5, Utre 3, Vachhir 2, Vágal 5, Valái 2, Vallí 10, Vanesh 1, Varí 3, Vark 3, Varl 1, Varmotre 1, Varoí 3, Vasái 1, Vazírí 1, Vedak Purí 5, Vekhlá 4, Vind 3, Vishan 3, Vishar 8, Zangháre 2, Zirá 1.

Names of Sub-Castes.	Persons.	Locality.	Names of Sub-Castes.	Persons.	Locality.	Names of Sub-Castes.	Persons.	Locality.
Lohar 323,477 { H. 84,441			Adhi ... H	1	48	Agánkhatrí ... H	259	8, 34
S. 35,363			S	21	15, 48	Agarwál ... H	11	10
M. 203,281			M	6	33	M	25	48
B. 392			Adli ... H	6	25	Agnoí ... H	170	39
Achhál ... S.	11	14	M	29	9	Agpál ... S	102	39

SUB-CASTES OF CERTAIN SELECTED CASTES—*continued*.

Names of Sub-Castes.		Persons.	Locality.
Agrá ...	H	38	8
Agrán ...	M	23	1
Agwán ...	M	14	49
Ahangar ...	H	14	42, 47
	M	25	13, 25
Ahir ...	H	24	39
	M	67	17, 25, 27
Ahl ...	H	164	6, 9, 34, 39
	S	2	45
	M	9	9, 15
Ahni ...	H	18	13, 27
Airái ...	M	14	10
Ajirá ...	H	11	17, 19
	M	45	17, 19
Ajmal ...	H	24	8, 9, 10
	S	95	9
	M	18	9, 13
Akosi ...	M	15	14
Akrálиá ...	H	59	4, 47
	M	47	20
Akwál ...	H	30	16
Alráb ...	M	48	9
Alrol ...	H	33	8
Alsar ...	H	69	8, 9, 13, 43
	S	52	8
	M	121	13, 14, 15
Alserá ...	H	2	51
	M	13	22
Alsi ...	H	26	9
	S	4	48
	M	1	48
Amari ...	M	66	22, 51
Amin ...	S	13	15
Ánd ...	M	174	9, 17, 18, 19, 20, 25
Androi ...	S	13	15
Angiá ...	H	85	8
	M	11	44
Angotre ...	H	65	15, 16
Ansári ...	M	41	3, 10, 26, 27
Aphiál- ...	H	9	39
	S	55	11
	M	1	22
Aprá ...	S	5	24
Arab ...	H	2	45
	S	26	44
	M	1020	9, 10, 12, 14, 15, 25, 26
Aráin ...	M	33	16
Arbi ...	M	78	10, 11, 15, 25, 27, 38
Ari ...	H	263	4, 13, 43
	S	104	10, 14, 15, 19, 27, 43
	M	207	3, 13, 14, 15, 16, 17, 25, 27, 48
Arli ...	M	100	13, 15, 25, 44
Arnot ...	H	338	8, 37, 43
Arorá ...	H	5	2
	S	68	14
	M	27	10, 25
Arsán ...	M	13	44
Asir ...	H	1	1
	S	8	9
	M	245	17, 25, 48
Asni ...	S	83	9, 10
Aspál ...	H	10	48
	M	84	16, 19
Ast ...	H	2	48
	M	23	48
Athar ...	H	152	8, 9, 15, 47
	S	3	15
Athwán ...	M	55	14, 25
Atlane ...	M	18	48
Atli ...	H	6	48
	S	19	14
	M	3	48
Áttar ...	H	17	39
Auchhán ...	S	25	15
	M	7	10, 18
Audeshi ...	H	20	42, 47
	M	87	17
Aujah ...	H	24	4
Auli ...	H	2	3
	M	35	9, 10
Aupal ...	H	44	9, 11, 12, 17, 20
	S	25	4, 10, 25
	M	1,882	9, 14, 16, 17, 20, 24
Aushán ...	H	8	16
	S	64	15, 16, 17, 27
	M	85	12, 14, 17, 18
Awán ...	M	2,532	R. 13, 15, 16, 17, 24, 25, 27
Awán Qutab Sháhi	M	63	20, 21
Babrál ...	H	68	1, 9, 10, 15
Babre ...	H	44	9, 10, 15
	S	229	9, 14, 15, 17
	M	316	14, 16, 17, 18 to 20, 26, 44
Babru ...	M	33	13
Bachhu ...	H	4	16
	S	7	13
Badal ...	H	49	15, 42, 48
	S	52	9, 11, 14, 48
	M	65	10, 11, 14 to 17, 21
Badan ...	H	12	48
	S	16	46
Badgujar ...	H	214	2, 3, 4
	M	211	3
Badhwán ...	H	236	8, 15
	M	48	21, 25
Bádiál ...	H	43	2, 8, 9, 47
	M	84	21, 22
Bádla ...	H	29	48
	M	2	12
Badoli ...	M	18	13
Bágai ...	H	22	5, 8, 34
	M	22	14, 18, 20
Bagal Badwál	M	11	15
Bágar ...	H	95	5, 8
	S	15	15
	M	55	5, 16, 44
Bágri ...	H	39	39
	M	10	14
Báhal ...	H	281	8, 9, 15, 48
	S	30	8, 44, 48
	M	81	15, 48, 49
Bahalar ...	H	4	11
	S	12	9
	M	36	13, 15, 25
Báhri ...	H	31	2, 16, 44, 47
	S	21	9, 11, 25, 46
	M	2	13
Báhrlá ...	H	405	11
Bahun ...	M	47	15, 18
Baiá ...	M	49	49
Baid ...	H	10	3
	M	1	3
Bain ...	H	13	5
	S	7	5, 34
Bains ...	S	8	48
	M	97	20, 48
Bais ...	H	10	9, 43
	S	2	10
	M	204	9, 10, 12, 19, 44
Bájrái ...	H	25	5
	M	8	17
Bajre ...	S	7	12
	M	28	13, 27
Bajwá ...	H	8	10
	S	12	15
	M	503	5, 13, 14 to 19, 25
Bákari ...	M	453	1, 12, 16, 25, 45
Baksir ...	M	21	15, 25
Bál ...	H	30	10, 12, 25
	S	7	25
	M	115	9, 13, 14, 16, 25, 33 44
Baláhi ...	H	87	1, 4, 5, 6, 8, 11, 19
	S	62	9, 10
	M	14	21
Balán ...	H	35	5, 49
Baldár ...	M	114	18, 44, 48
Balhodar ...	S	31	9
Balhore ...	H	17	48
Báli ...	H	28	39
Baliá ...	H	23	6
	S	6	8
Balián ...	H	17	48
	S	5	48
Balkhi ...	M	82	2
Balkhokhar ...	H	41	9, 10, 11, 40
	S	4	10, 25
	M	34	14, 44
Balotre ...	H	1	16
	M	15	15, 16
Bálri ...	H	13	6
Balshir ...	M	75	14
Baltar ...	M	424	10, 15 to 18, 25, 28
Bamráh ...	H	53	1, 6, 15
	S	325	9, 12, 15, 16, 19, 25
	M	49	1, 13 to 16, 25
Bamrái ...	H	18	13, 48
	S	352	10 to 15, 19, 25, 44, 46
	M	6	19
Bams ...	M	17	10
Banchun ...	S	29	10
	M	2	25
Band ...	H	8	11
	M	91	3, 10, 13, 16, 17, 44
Bándhal ...	H	6	3
	M	215	L. 12, 25
Bandhyál ...	H	39	39
Bandoi ...	M	538	14
Bandoli ...	H	233	3
	M	590	L. except (14), 9, 12
Bángá ...	H	6	8, 10
	S	1	11
	M	35	48
Bangori ...	H	17	15
	S	44	6, 12, 15
	M	74	13, 16
Báninа́ ...	H	60	10, 45
	S	14	25, 45
	M	48	2, 13, 16, 17, 25
Bánori ...	H	21	5, 9, 39
	M	24	10, 14, 21
Banotre ...	H	12	15
	S	6	15
Bánsal ...	H	539	1, 5, 6, 9, 10, 11, 13, 33, 40, 44, 45, 48
	S	469	6, 9, 10, 11, 25, 44, 45, 48
	M	24	10
Bansi ...	H	192	4, 6, 8, 9, 11, 39
	S	24	10, 15
	M	184	9, 10, 11, 14, 15, 25, 44
Bansráo ...	H	87	48
Banswál ...	H	15	48
Banswáti ...	M	16	3
Banwál ...	H	82	2, 34
Banwáti ...	H	11	6
Bar ...	H	258	D. 11, 15, 25, 49
	M	8	11, 13
Baráich ...	H	20	47
	M	6	13
Barákah ...	H	320	2 to 5, 42
Barar ...	H	19	48
	S	1	48
	M	96	14, 48
Barde ...	H	104	1, 6, 9, 10, 11, 15, 48
	S	272	6, 9, 10, 11, 14, 25, 48
	M	54	6, 13, 25, 48
Bargi ...	H	22	25
	S	4	14, 48
	M	138	5, 9, 33, 48
Bargiál ...	H	313	8
Barhár ...	H	136	1, 2, 9, 42, 47
	S	30	13
	M	1	19
Bariácharaj ...	H	36	9
	S	56	9
Bariáh ...	H	63	1, 8, 9, 48
	S	21	9, 48
	M	619	8, 10, 11, 13, 45, 48, 49
Bariál ...	H	34	42, 19
Bariwál ...	H	16	2

Names of Sub-Castes.		Persons.	Locality.
Barji ...	S	16	14
	M	41	10, 14
Barká ...	H	65	3
	M	3	3
Barkhukhel ...	S	10	15
	M	32	18
Bárkiá ...	H	21	3
Bárlas ...	M	311	6, 18, 21
Bárná ...	H	12	15, 16
	M	1	15
Barmi ...	H	14	15
Barohi ...	H	60	9, 12, 15, 16, 45, 47
	S	261	7, 9 10, 12, 15, 41
	M	139	J. 7, 13, 14, 17, 44
Basan ...	H	192	6, 9, 10, 11, 14
	S	99	9, 10, 44
	M	61	15, 16, 25
Básar ...	H	8	15
	S	1	48
	M	24	16, 19, 25
Basir ...	H	4	10, 15, 47
	S	17	9, 48
	M	243	1, 5 11, 12, 13, 14, 17, 18, 25, 33, 48
Basrái ...	S	57	14
	M	191	14, 16
Basrál ...	H	2	36
	M	122	14, 15, 16
Bát ...	H	30	5, 9
	S	11	9, 44
	M	380	2, 5, 6, 9, 11, 12, 13, 44, 45
Bater ...	H	4	9
	S	4	14
	M	37	6, 14, 24
Báth ...	M	67	12, 26
Batiál ...	H	18	8, 45
	M	102	9, 14, 18
Batil ...	H	9	8
	M	32	15, 16
Batoi ...	H	23	48
	S	2	48
Batoli ...	H	107	4, 5, 6
	M	45	14, 16, 17, 18
Báwári ...	H	402	D. 11, 31, 39, 49
	S	5	11
	M	13	13
Bedi ...	H	11	48
	S	6	48
	M	5	48
Beg ...	M	14	13
Beli ...	H	33	3, 15
	S	1	9
	M	71	10, 14
Beri ...	S	54	48
	M	25	48
Beru ...	H	48	8, 25
Bhad ...	H	13	2
Bhádá ...	H	39	2
Bhadiár ...	H	638	2, 8, 9, 48, 49
	M	4	17
Bhadoi ...	H	108	4, 5
	M	187	9, 10, 12, 13, 14, 17, 18, 25, 33
Bhadráj ...	H	16	47
Bhágal ...	H	50	11, 15, 25, 45
	S	19	6, 41, 44
	M	10	13, 15, 18
Bhági ...	S	6	L. 6
Bhágre ...	M	97	16
Bhagu ...	H	4	15
	S	4	25
	M	36	15, 16, 17, 25
Bháhu ...	H	18	16
Bhái ...	H	31	39
	S	53	11, 44
	M	93	1, 2, 4, 30
Bhain ...	H	20	6
Bháj ...	H	24	9, 25
Bhajju ...	H	25	9
	M	200	10, 11, 12
Bhalánd ...	H	41	2
Bhali ...	H	91	1, 9, 15, 48
	S	48	10, 15
	M	24	10, 11, 19, 25, 48
Bhalim ...	M	433	2, 3, 18, 49
Bhalin ...	M	42	2
Bhambar ...	H	83	2, 4, 8
	S	63	10, 11, 17
	M	136	27, 28
Bhamrái ...	H	691	J. 2, 5, 6, 25, 33, 34, 40
	S	389	1, 5, 9, 11, 14, 15
	M	207	L. 4, 11, 12, 44
Bhandá ...	H	71	3, 5, 6, 34, 47
	M	182	10, 17, 25, 44
Bhandál ...	M	118	25
Bhandrá ...	M	198	10, 14
Bhangori ...	M	12	10
Bhángre ...	M	124	10
Bhangu ...	S	25	50
Bháni ...	H	12	9, 13, 33
	M	172	11, 14, 15, 18, 20, 25, 44
Bhárá ...	H	47	2, 5, 8, 9, 48
	S	6	11
	M	65	9, 10, 13, 14, 24, 25
Bharái ...	H	14	5, 15, 47
	S	28	11, 14, 45
	M	129	12, 14, 15, 16, 17
Bháraj ...	S	22	25
Bharajphaniá	H	71	9, 15, 39, 44
	S	104	9, 10
Bhardwáj ...	H	491	4, 9, 14, 15, 34, 37, 39, 40
	S	11	7
	M	18	7, 9
Bhári ...	H	102	1, 2, 6, 8, 42
	S	18	4, 6
	M	258	4, 5, 13, 15, 16
Bharmi ...	H	78	8, 9, 42
	M	677	5, 14, 26, 51
Bhart ...	M	11	13
Bharwál ...	H	59	8
Bhásan ...	H	12	34
Bhatará ...	H	16	5
	M	23	13, 15, 16
Bhatáru ...	H	8	6, 39
	M	9	15
Bhátiá ...	H	12	9, 16
	S	2	25
	M	103	9, 10, 25
Bhatti ...	H	123	1, 8, 9, 12, 15, 25, 39, 49, 51
	S	240	9, 10 .13, 14, 15, 25, 51
	M	12,239	B. except (4, 7, 23), 34, 39, 42, 44, 45, 49, 50, 51
Bhattlahnda	H	26	4
Bháttu ...	H	8	3, 42
	S	58	9, 11
	M	422	13, 17, 18, 24, 25, 39, 45, 51
Bháwá ...	H	47	49
Bháwal ...	H	91	4, 47
	M	36	18
Bhián ...	S	13	6
Bhitrá ...	H	10	48
	S	7	48
Bhogal ...	H	750	6, 8, 9, 10, 11, 15, 39, 40
	S	803	9, 10 11, 12, 17, 25, 44, 45
	M	45	12, 13, 17, 25, 40
Bhoi ...	H	9	15
	M	892	12, 14, 16, 34
Bhojan ...	H	6	48
	S	19	48
Bholá ...	H	85	9, 10, 11
	S	175	9, 10, 11
	M	137	9, 16, 17, 20, 24
Bholi ...	H	8	1, 8, 10, 42
	S	7	9, 12, 14
	M	12	L. 10, 12, 20
Bhoná ...	H	205	5
Bhoni ...	H	56	2, 9
	S	14	5, 11, 12
	M	254	L. except (13), 24
Bhons ...	M	14	20
Bhore ...	H	45	2, 5, 10, 15
	S	47	10, 11, 15, 25
	M	59	9, 10, 12, 13, 15, 44
Bhori ...	H	44	2
Bhosán ...	M	16	33, 34
Bhosiá ...	H	5	33
	M	22	18
Bhotián ...	H	47	2
	M	44	9, 17, 18
Bhubaliá ...	H	31	3, 4, 31
Bhullar ...	H	84	4, 5, 6, 12, 44
	S	202	9, 14, 15, 16
	M	83	7, 14, 16, 17
Bhund ...	H	854	1, 2, 4, 5, 49
	S	9	5
	M	1	20
Bhundál ...	M	18	12, 20
Bhundi ...	H	13	2, 10, 12
Bhuni ...	M	64	25
Bhupál ...	M	12	16
Bhurá ...	H	18	49
Bhután ...	M	71	51
Bhute ...	H	8	2, 42
	M	955	12, 28, 29, 44, 48
Bhutre ...	H	764	9
Bidoch ...	M	11	51
Birj ...	S	3	9
	M	46	9, 11, 15
Birk ...	M	36	51
Bishan ...	H	3	8
Bishisht ...	H	281	15
	S	74	15
Bisoor ...	M	32	14
Biswákárm ...	H	145	36
Bogal ...	M	255	16
Boh ...	H	6	2
	M	29	3
Bobrá ...	M	30	13
Bohri ...	H	36	6, 8
	S	8	6, 9
	M	37	12, 13
Bolan ...	H	11	15
Bole ...	H	120	49
Bonás ...	H	3	15
	M	110	16
Boráná ...	H	33	1
Boránia ...	H	20	1
Bos ...	M	41	13
Budhál ...	H	36	9, 15
	M	18	18, 33
Chadál ...	M	33	16
Chadde ...	H	206	4, 8, 9, 25, 44
	S	121	4, 9, 16, 17
	M	3,725	L. 9, 21, 25, 44
Chadhar ...	S	18	11
	M	150	17
Chadhe ...	H	58	2, 8, 9, 16
	S	4	15
	M	154	17, 18, 19
Chádír ...	H	18	13
	M	192	18, 25
Chágal ...	H	15	15
	M	20	24
Chághrí ...	H	22	8, 9
	S	10	10
Chábí ...	H	20	6, 10
	S	11	11,
	M	14	13, 22
Cháhil ...	H	39	39
	S	1	48
	M	43	15
Cháhir ...	H	1	2
	M	19	9, 17
Chábní ...	M	154	45
Chain ...	H	10	5, 40
	S	32	10, 11
	M	34	10, 13
Chakrán ...	H	319	36
	M	13	13, 14, 44
Chakwál ...	M	96	18, 21, 22
Chalí ..	H	17	25
	S	18	25, 48
Chalotre ..	H	167	15
	S	38	15, 16, 25
	M	39	15

SUB-CASTES OF CERTAIN SELECTED CASTES—*continued.*

Names of Sub-Castes.	Persons.	Locality.
Chamá ... M	27	25
Chammár ... H	2	11
S	2	18
M	157	18, 25
Chamnár ... M	197	18
Chan ... S	14	46
M	19	14, 18
Cháná ... H	60	11, 45
S	180	10, 11, 12, 19
M	105	18
Chanchab ... H	11	45
S	3	45
Chanchi ... M	24	11
Chand ... H	176	8, 15, 16
S	24	16, 25
M	1,051	6, 9, 10, 15, 16, 17, 18, 19, 25, 44
Chandá ... H	644	8 11, 13, 15, 16, 17, 18, 25, 43
S	20	11, 44
M	692	L. 4, 12, 18, 21, 25, 26, 51
Chandar ... H	14	14, 33, 45
S	1	11
M	209	6, 10, 14, 16, 18, 44
Chandesar ... M	67	13, 17
Chandbrí ... M	75	18
Chandí ... H	25	6, 9
S	17	45, 9
M	292	13, 17, 19, 26
Chandiál ... H	22	38, 40, 47
M	16	16
Chandú ... H	18	10, 44
M	10	33
Chang ... H	7	9
M	91	15, 16, 44
Changar ... H	2	8, 11
S	14	44
M	307	9, 10, 13, 14, 15
Changotrá ... H	46	15, 16
Chángrú ... H	187	8
Chání ... H	51	6, 12, 15, 44
S	317	9, 12, 14, 15, 17, 25, 44, 45
M	240	6, 11, 12, 49
Chánir ... M	28	13, 21, 25
Chapotrá ... H	18	47
Cháprái ... H	28	21, 45
M	11	21
Charái ... M	30	14
Chárak ... H	24	8
M	2	24
Charand ... H	2	2
M	289	L. 9, 10, 11, 12, 25
Charbo ... M	16	10
Chariál ... H	21	3
Chatrál ... H	22	8, 15
Chatwán ... H	276	8, 36
Chauhán ... H	2,758	1, 2, 4, 5, 7, 8, 12, 14, 15, 34, 37, 42, 43, 48, 49, 50
S	86	1, 12, 14, 15, 48, 50
M	2,003	D. 14, 16, 19, 24, 27, 48, 49, 50, 51
Chawál ... H	43	9, 15
M	4	7
Chhadde ... M	193	16, 18
Chhán ... H	10	30
M	68	14, 18, 30
Chhárand ... M	24	16
Chhárí ... H	14	40
M	16	15
Chharkalot ... M	10	3
Chhatrí ... M	17	14, 25
Chhatte ... H	46	10, 42
S	28	10
M	153	13, 16, 18, 20
Chhibbar ... M	220	16, 18, 19, 20
Chhimbá ... M	97	10, 13, 18, 20
Chhokar ... H	24	3
Chhunjí ... M	28	16
Chimá ... M	70	16, 17
Chírí ... H	5	9
M	6	17
Chishtí ... H	8	12
S	25	12
M	76	13, 20, 27, 44
Chodí ... H	74	9
S	24	9
M	20	13, 15, 17
Choghattá ... M	1,024	L. M. 12, 18, 19, 20, 21, 45
Chohal ... M	49	5
Chuhánar ... H	129	9, 45
M	168	18, 45
Chohándí ... H	13	2
M	34	16, 18
Choí ... H	20	1
S	1	25
M	20	14
Chojái ... M	18	18, 19
Chonj Sarai ... M	12	15
Choprá ... H	16	48, 49
M	23	48
Chori ... H	33	8, 47
S	15	9, 14
M	7	12, 17
Chote ... S	1	6
M	29	1
Chotwál ... H	108	8
Chúhá ... H	19	51
Chuhre ... S	31	1, 10
M	105	12, 13, 17, 25
Chúnd ... M	35	20
Dabal ... H	25	6, 9
S	1	6
M	4	15
Dabrá ... H	29	1
S	2	9
Dadiálí ... H	11	16, 18
S	94	14, 15
M	65	15, 16, 17, 25
Daffú ... H	23	10, 45, 48
Dafsul ... S	29	9, 33
Dágar ... H	116	2, 3, 4, 48
Dághán ... H	26	4, 15
Daghotre ... H	121	15, 16
Dágí ... H	7	5, 8
M	34	21
Dáhlí ... H	46	9
M	1	27
Dáhri ... H	301	1, 2, 4
S	2	48
M	48	2, 9, 13
Dalál ... H	56	9, 15
S	6	14
M	2	14
Dalangar ... H	17	3
Dalji ... H	7	34
M	5	15
Dalwál ... H	231	3, 4, 8, 9, 49
Dandhál ... H	17	2, 6, 8
M	49	1, 4, 9, 14
Dandí ... M	22	19
Dáng ... H	21	2, 48
M	1,076	1, 2, 4, 48, 49
Dángal ... H	41	2, 6, 47
Dángan ... H	18	11
S	18	12
Dángar ... H	16	3
M	10	10
Dángi ... H	1,435	D. 38, 48, 49
S	23	5, 6, 48
M	112	48
Daugwál H	48	2, 8
Danjil ... H	12	15, 47
S	3	48
M	6	25
Danmand ... H	232	48
M	54	48
Dár ... H	19	2
M	3	20
Dáraj ... H	12	3, 33
Dardi ... H	5	15
S	18	10, 13
M	4	16
Darhál ... H	9	14
S	1	44
M	4	13
Dárí ... H	1	2
S	20	26
M	9	14
Dariá ... M	11	11, 14
Darwál ... M	86	6, 13, 18
Darzí ... S	7	14, 15
M	29	23, 44
Datorí ... M	42	6, 19
Dawáre ... H	2	16
S	1	44
M	10	15
Degan ... H	68	9, 11, 47
S	77	9, 11, 14, 44
Demán ... H	9	45
S	10	45
M	3	51
Deogan ... H	13	48
S	74	48
Deorá ... H	53	10, 50
S	4	10, 50
M	29	16, 50
Deorí ... H	15	2, 45
M	122	9, 14, 16
Desí ... H	51	4, 5
S	17	25
M	651	2, 4, 12, 18, 49
Deswál ... H	186	2, 4, 5, 6, 49
S	7	5
M	467	4, 6, 33, 48, 49
Deswálí ... H	188	2, 5, 6, 25, 33
S	11	5, 6
M	593	4, 5, 6, 30
Dewáne ... H	12	48
M	9	17
Dewí ... S	29	6
Dewrí ... H	18	9
S	4	17
M	219	13, 17, 19, 25
Dhábrú ... S	25	44, 46
M	17	13, 16
Dhaddí ... H	313	8
M	194	4, 12, 17, 26, 27, 28
Dhadháli ... S	34	8, 14
Dhagatrí ... H	64	15, 17
S	6	26
Dhák ... H	1	2
S	41	15
M	16	5, 6
Dhakú ... S	105	13, 14
M	4	24
Dhálíwál ... H	92	6, 12, 42
M	23	12, 25
Dhallú ... H	60	6, 8, 41
S	15	14
M	35	17, 18, 25
Dhamán ... H	1,177	J. 5, 6, 7, 25, 33, 34, 39, 40, 41, 48, 49, 50
S	1,810	J. 6, 14, 25, 41, 44, 46, 48, 49, 50, 51
M	367	1, 6, 10, 11, 12, 15, 16, 48, 50
Dhámial ... H	2	6
M	128	2, 15, 21
Dhammal ... H	25	9, 41
S	17	11
M	95	12, 14
Dhammar ... H	24	5, 27
M	30	5, 15
Dhamun ... H	210	9, 42
S	16	16
M	49	11, 25
Dhan ... H	49	11, 37
S	6	48
M	8	13, 51
Dhaná ... H	123	1, 33, 34
M	1	5
Dhanaulá ... M	13	25
Dhand ... H	4	49
M	10	10
Dhándal ... H	1	49
S	17	15, 48
M	34	14, 48
Dhandi ... M	44	10, 15, 25, 44
Dhandiál ... H	119	8
S	15	12
M	45	6, 13
Dhandore ... M	13	14
Dhandwál ... H	16	8
Dhang ... M	43	3, 5, 44
Dhangwál ... H	21	3
M	1	13

Names of Sub-Castes.		Persons.	Locality.
Dhání ...	H	13	1, 45, 48
	S	46	9, 15, 48
	M	4	15
Dhanjal ...	H	68	2, 9, 11, 39, 47
	S	172	9, 11, 14, 15
	M	553	13, 14, 15, 25
Dhanjan ...	S	15	10, 14, 25, 44
	M	11	25
Dhanmál ...	H	1	49
	S	10	12
Dhanoi ...	S	36	9, 45
Dhanwál ...	H	6	9
	M	81	16
Dhará ...	H	773	1, 2, 4, 5, 41
	S	14	5
	M	27	13, 17, 19
Dharálí ...	H	11	42
	M	31	5, 12
Dharan ...	H	7	32
	M	35	5, 25
Dhariálá ...	H	12	5
	S	1	48
Dháriwál ...	H	126	1, 2, 8
	S	11	6, 25
	M	55	12, 13, 22
Dharle ...	H	82	48
	S	2	48
Dharú ...	H	188	1, 2, 4, 5, 19, 49
Dhaun ...	S	7	14
	M	8	12
Dhaunsi ...	M	14	16, 18
Dhawál ...	H	35	2, 8, 10
	S	55	5
Dhawán ...	H	2	5
	M	21	13
Dhei ...	H	54	3, 4, 6, 33
	S	1	48
	M	112	1, 12
Dhillo ...	S	17	17, 25
	M	20	16, 25
Dhillon ...	S	86	11, 12, 15
	M	172	11, 12, 15, 24, 46
Dhilwál ...	H	785	1, 2, 4, 5
Dhir ...	H	1	11
	S	16	44
	M	43	13, 17
Dhiru ...	H	83	32, 49
Dhobi ...	H	11	25
	S	4	17
	M	12	26
Dhodi ...	H	2	9
	M	580	1, 13, 16, 17, 18, 19, 24, 25, 27
Dhodiál ...	M	20	18
Dhogri ...	H	91	8, 15, 42, 47
Dhol ...	H	76	9, 12, 49
	S	18	12
	M	29	12, 13, 18
Dholri ...	H	12	16
	M	17	13, 14
Dhondi ...	M	100	12, 13, 21, 44
Dhopar ...	H	4	9
	S	13	10
Dhorán ...	H	1	12
	M	10	33
Dhorí ...	S	13	5
	M	3	17
Dhowál ...	H	23	5
Dhowán ...	H	48	6, 10
	M	5	27
Dhundí ...	M	23	5
Diál ...	H	214	8, 39, 43, 45
	M	1	25
Dibárá ...	H	85	2, 49
	S	6	48
	M	8	48
Dir ...	M	11	27
Díwáli ...	H	9	2
	S	4	5
	M	136	6, 13, 17, 45
Dode ...	H	5	44
	M	83	6, 18, 27, 44
Dogri ...	H	15	8, 9
Dohálá ...	S	46	11, 27
	M	35	11
Dohang ...	M	58	10
Dohelá ...	S	13	10
Dolál ...	H	73	8
Dolang ...	M	40	16
Domár ...	H	59	15, 39, 41, 43
Dori ...	H	20	2
	M	11	49, 51
Dumál ...	H	140	42
	S	62	10, 14
	M	16	13
Dumná ...	M	13	48
Dungi ...	H	36	1, 4, 5
Ferozwál ...	H	19	39
	M	81	21
Gábrái ...	S	50	14
Gábre ...	H	2	45
	S	6	14
	M	269	13, 14
Gadariá ...	H	35	11, 48
	M	44	5, 6, 33, 34
Gáddí ...	H	6	16
	M	18	15, 28
Gadiál ...	H	54	8
Gádri ...	H	24	5, 16, 45, 48
	S	1	10
	M	129	5, 14, 22
Gaggi ...	M	149	14, 48, 51
Gáhi ...	H	74	33, 42, 45
	S	100	11, 13, 14, 48
	M	5	15, 48
Gáhndí ...	H	12	42
	S	60	15, 17
Gahrái ...	S	11	44
	M	6	14, 25
Gáhri ...	S	17	44
	M	23	13, 14, 25
Galár ...	H	12	9, 25, 46
	M	6	14, 15, 18
Galonián ...	H	13	48
Galot ...	H	35	2, 5, 6
	M	51	2, 5
Galotri ...	H	8	15, 44
	M	40	17, 24, 25
Galsar ...	H	6	9, 48
	M	23	5
Galsur ...	H	9	42
	M	12	28
Gambrá ...	S	18	10, 14
	M	4	10
Gandárá ...	H	62	44
Gandeo ...	H	8	3, 44
	S	31	9, 14, 27
	M	15	25
Gandofa ...	H	29	15
	M	23	13, 14
Gangi ...	H	11	33
	M	483	L. 9, 10, 25, 44
Gangotri ...	H	14	2, 15
Gáni ...	H	12	6
	S	83	12, 15
	M	2	14
Garai ...	H	25	41, 42
	S	4	15
	M	1	15
Gáre ...	H	4	4
	M	11	41, 5
Gareri ...	H	19	1, 48
Garg ...	H	24	48
Garirá ...	H	98	2, 8, 48
	M	29	13
Gariwál ...	H	4	15, 39
	M	52	3
Garlú ...	H	24	42
Gatáwári ...	H	4	6
	S	72	10
Gathāriá ...	H	19	8, 43
	S	5	45
	M	4	13
Gawársá ...	M	154	13
Geti ...	H	9	16, 41
	M	4	16, 27
Ghadárá ...	H	10	11, 12
	S	18	11
Ghadún ...	H	3	9
	S	4	14
	M	30	14
Ghágar ...	S	3	13
	M	19	19, 25
Ghaggi ...	M	569	16
Gháhrá ...	M	21	12, 22
Ghaiá ...	H	18	48
Ghakar ...	M	82	16
Ghalot ...	H	118	1, 4, 45, 48, 49
	M	685	1, 2, 4, 5
Ghamár ...	M	54	18, 20
Ghamwádi ...	H	12	47
	S	1	25
Ghanshe ...	H	17	40
Gháre ...	H	5	38
	M	16	12, 21
Ghassi ...	H	72	6, 33, 39
	S	3	12, 48
	M	1	9
Ghattárorá ...	H	108	9, 11, 12, 25
	S	204	10, 11, 12, 14
	M	678	14, 15, 17, 26
Ghatti ...	H	35	8, 9, 12
	M	11	48
Gher ...	H	19	6, 48
	S	13	9, 48
	M	32	48
Ghore wáh ...	H	3	12
	S	13	10, 48
	M	74	13, 17, 25, 48
Ghori ...	H	33	8, 42, 45
	S	1	14
	M	37	5, 12, 49
Ghoriá Pathán	M	14	1
Ghoti ...	M	59	5
Ghumán ...	S	64	48
	M	10	18
Ghummar ...	H	8	9
	M	848	16, 17, 18
Gianiwál ...	H	24	6, 42
Gil ...	H	15	33, 45, 48
	S	60	11, 13, 14, 15
	M	180	L. 25, 27, 29, 46, 48
Godhán ...	H	31	48
Godhi ...	H	52	8
	M	100	22
Gohír ...	H	1	9
	S	19	10
Gohrí ...	M	91	22
Gole ...	H	26	3, 34, 48
	M	89	6, 12, 27, 34
Golrán ...	H	52	4, 6
Gondal ...	H	412	8, 38
	M	233	18, 19, 20, 44
Goniál ...	H	11	15
Gopál ...	H	27	42, 45, 47
Gor ...	H	425	2, 3, 4, 7, 11
	M	907	1, 5, 25, 48
Gorái ...	M	586	14, 15, 16, 17, 22, 25
Gorár ...	M	55	3, 20
Gori ...	H	44	6, 13, 41
	S	8	51
	M	530	D. 12, 13, 17, 18, 25, 45
Goriá ..	H	30	50
	S	21	11
	M	614	1, 2, 3, 10, 11, 16, 18, 25, 46, 49, 50, 51
Gorse ...	H	4	34
	S	1	10
	M	80	18
Gosal ...	H	48	42
Got ...	H	23	6, 16
	M	14	11, 15
Gudárí ...	H	18	1
Gujar ...	H	1	11
	M	14	4, 25
Gulshíná ...	H	68	2, 4
Gurti ...	M	361	48
Hal ...	H	18	42, 48
	S	7	10, 12
	M	13	11
Hamí ...	H	7	47
	S	4	14
	M	3	25
Hamiál ...	H	5	5, 48
	S	10	13, 25
	M	35	44
Hand ...	M	132	16, 18, 19
Handal ...	H	15	39, 48,
	S	5	50
Handole ...	M	32	9
Hándolí ...	M	65	13, 15, 17
Handre ...	M	25	13
Hangori ...	M	15	17, 18

Names of Sub-Castes.		Persons.	Locality.
Hangú ...	M	17	16
Háns ...	H	2	5, 48
	M	59	13, 17
Hánsa ...	M	31	13, 15
Hanseri ...	H	3	40
	M	29	17
Hanspál ...	H	3	6
	S	135	14, 15, 17, 25
Harakali ...	H	56	16, 48
Haral ...	M	102	13, 15, 17
Hardá ...	H	6	15, 41
	S	1	48
	M	43	10, 14, 17, 44
Harí ...	H	1	5
	M	84	13, 14
Hariá ...	H	8	5, 15
	S	3	46
	M	65	13, 17, 44
Hariál ...	H	4	47
	S	13	14
	M	31	18
Haru ...	M	889	L. 25, 44
Hasan ...	H	11	4, 44
	S	14	44
	M	6	15, 26
Hasan Khel	H	20	15
Hasiál ...	H	1	41
	M	97	21
Határu ...	H	7	2
	S	1	4
	M	25	21, 41
Her ...	H	3	9
	S	21	9, 10, 11
	M	33	17
Heri ...	H	14	9, 44
Hijra ...	H	2	12
	S	5	12, 14
	M	47	12, 18, 25
Hind ...	M	93	17, 18, 21
Hinjrá ...	H	2	17
	S	32	17
	M	521	16, 17
Hinjrái ...	S	41	11, 13
	M	45	13, 16
Hira ...	H	13	15
	S	9	6, 10, 41
	M	32	20
Hodla ...	H	346	2, 5, 8
Hoi ...	H	7	25
	S	13	16
	M	29	12, 13, 44
Honjan ...	H	45	9, 12, 44
	S	138	10, 14, 15, 41
Honjle ...	H	16	48
	S	29	25, 44
	M	49	14, 15, 18
Hons ...	H	9	2
	S	2	14
	M	51	18
Hor ...	H	9	2, 48
	S	11	6
	M	53	12, 13
Horí ...	H	11	5, 48
	M	3	13
Hotre ...	H	1	16
	M	15	12
Jabal ...	H	56	5, 39
	S	151	11, 14, 17, 25, 46
	M	124	10, 11, 48
Jadhe ...	M	80	9, 18, 26
Jadu Bansí	H	42	3
Jago ...	H	26	15
	S	4	12
	M	19	17
Jagdev ...	H	182	6, 33, 44, 48
	S	146	5, 6, 9, 11, 13, 45, 46, 48
	M	26	10, 16
Jaghbár ...	H	1	14
	M	12	44
Jaghatre ...	H	14	15
Jaghwál ...	M	544	20, 22, 25, 27, 28
Jain ...	M	26	13
Jaipál ...	H	16	1, 6, 48
	S	5	48
Jaj ...	M	48	19, 24, 25
Jájam ...	S	3	48
Jajuán ...	H	1	25
	M	51	14, 17, 25
Jakar ...	S	43	9, 15, 48
Jalalí ...	M	32	19, 25
Jalhotre ...	H	90	15
	M	9	14
Jálí ...	H	3	33
	S	9	17, 44
	M	8	12
Jáman ...	H	3	45
	S	9	15
	M	6	15
Jamiál ...	H	16	4, 9, 45
	M	22	15
Jamwál ..	H	62	7, 9, 42
Jamor chián	H	30	48
	S	20	48
	M	346	13, 48
Janan ...	H	103	8
	M	15	13, 15
Jinbar ...	H	2	7
	M	11	24
Jand ...	H	34	15
	S	26	11
	M	150	14, 15, 18, 44
Jándá ...	H	13	6
	S	89	12, 25
	M	162	14, 15, 16
Jándal ...	H	39	7, 37, 49
	S	10	11, 14
	M	29	14, 16, 18
Jánde ...	H	28	8, 25
	S	8	10
	M	85	5, 14, 15, 44
Jandesar ...	H	21	7
	M	105	13, 16, 19, 20, 25
Jandráj ...	M	15	13, 49
Jandrán ...	M	149	48
Jandu ...	H	62	6, 15
	S	130	10, 11, 18
	M	8	10, 13
Jángi ...	H	7	5, 6
	M	29	8, 15
Jangilial ...	H	10	15, 47
	S	2	15
Jangotre ...	H	41	15, 16
Jangro ...	H	125	3, 8
Jáni ...	H	20	44, 45
	S	11	11
	M	106	16, 25
Janjáhí ...	M	293	12, 13, 14, 44
Janjuha ...	H	242	8, 9, 15, 16
	S	32	16
	M	5,006	13, 14, 16, 19, 21, 25, 51
Janjuhán ...	S	1	9
	M	2,345	9, 17, 18, 20, 22, 24, 25, 27
Janjuhe ...	H	91	8
	S	49	10
	M	558	19, 25, 26
Janoi ...	H	19	15, 47
	S	13	25
	M	127	12, 15, 25
Janshi ...	H	14	1
Jar ...	H	136	8, 9
	S	1	25
Jarál ...	H	1	15
	S	12	15, 51
	M	56	13, 20
Jarand ...	M	93	10, 15, 48
Jariál ...	H	117	2, 16, 47, 48
	M	10	5, 8, 48
Jariálí ...	H	45	47
Jarl ...	H	4	47
	M	28	25, 27, 48
Jarri ...	H	5	13
	S	2	4
	M	9	15, 18
Jasan ...	H	19	5, 34
	S	2	11
	M	72	14, 25
Jasiál ...	H	113	3, 6, 34
	S	12	16
	M	67	20, 22
Jaskalián ...	H	79	5, 6, 33
Jaspáli ...	H	271	5, 6, 49
	S	1	1
Jaspán ...	H	220	2, 5
Jasrál ...	H	27	8, 39
	M	127	16, 18
Jastar ...	M	40	15, 16
Ját ...	H	69	4
	M	184	2, 13, 14, 15, 17, 29
Jatoi ...	H	78	2, 3
	M	21	12, 48
Jatolía ...	H	20	3
Jatte ...	H	12	25, 44
	S	49	10
	M	39	11, 19, 44
Játun ...	M	15	2
Jáwár ...	H	76	4
...	M	35	17, 18, 27
Jeunt ...	H	54	48
	S	6	48
	M	24	1, 26
Jhaggar ...	H	4	44
	S	12	25
	M	56	9, 14
Jhagro ...	H	89	9, 39
Jhajjh ...	M	23	16
Jhálas ...	H	69	9, 12
	S	4	10
Jhandu ...	H	83	5, 9, 15, 48
	S	66	9, 48, 49
	M	30	5, 17, 18, 48
Jhang ...	M	32	25, 51
Jhangar ...	H	18	9
	M	131	12, 13, 17, 25
Jháns ...	H	8	16
	S	3	14
	M	108	16, 17
Jharú ...	H	5	11
	S	305	13
	M	15	13
Jhatti ...	H	1	48
	S	1	25
	M	28	10, 16, 25
Jhot ...	H	13	25
Jhoth ...	H	8	6, 47
	M	5	14
Jhunj ...	M	374	10, 13, 14, 16, 24, 44
Jinbar ...	H	2	7
	M	11	24
Jindar ...	H	11	7
	M	237	1, 48
Jirán ...	H	13	4
Jodá ...	M	44	17, 25
Jodí ...	H	1	9
	S	3	9
	M	31	8, 9, 17
Jogí ...	H	18	8
Jogiál ...	H	9	6
	M	39	21, 22
Jogowál ...	M	16	21
Joi ...	M	19	1, 5
Joiá ...	M	1,018	1, 12, 17, 19, 24, 25, 27, 29, 46, 48, 50, 51
Jojal ...	M	388	13, 14, 15, 16, 25, 44
Jojar ...	M	58	14
Jolí ...	H	1	25
	M	54	14, 19, 26
Jondá ...	S	12	17
	M	11	18
Jondí ...	H	4	2
	M	54	14, 18
Jorá ...	H	71	8
	M	7	12, 14
Jorí ...	S	1	17
	M	138	14, 18, 21, 25
Joshi ...	H	1	12
	M	22	14, 25
Jotal ...	H	9	47
	M	19	18
Jothi ...	H	10	40
	S	18	25
	M	63	11
Jotle ...	H	10	9
	S	26	9, 11, 12
Jotrá ...	M	39	13, 15
Jún ...	M	18	5, 49
Junj ...	M	163	14
Junjh ...	S	9	25
	M	8	25

APPENDIX TO IMPERIAL TABLE XIII.—

Names of Sub-Castes.		Persons.	Locality.
Kabir Bansi ...	H	16	7
Kabir Khel ...	H	8	48
	M	4	13
Kachúr ...	H	27	4
	M	1	29
Kachwáí ...	H	39	3, 4
Kadi ...	M	52	13
Kadiál ...	H	37	2, 47
	M	7	27
Kahár ...	H	3	15
	M	14	14
Káhlon ...	M	41	14
Káká ...	M	65	10, 15, 25
Kákaliá ...	H	29	10
	M	3	10
Kakar ...	H	8	2, 5
	M	986	1, 2, 4, 5, 6, 13, 45, 48
Kakore ...	S	16	15
	M	66	14, 49
Kakri ...	M	53	13, 16, 19, 25, 33
Kalankah ...	H	20	16
Kalar ...	H	122	2, 8, 48
	S	43	14, 16
	M	207	1, 2, 5, 12, 14, 17
Kalás ...	H	20	6, 9
	S	4	27
	M	150	9, 13, 14, 15, 16, 17, 18, 25, 48
Kaláei ...	H	56	5, 25, 39, 45, 48
	S	10	25, 45
	M	291	9, 10, 14, 15, 18, 25, 44
Kaláyú ...	H	19	9, 24
Kálí ...	H	4	8, 12, 33
	S	49	9, 11, 12, 14
	M	27	10, 13, 14, 17
Kalián ...	H	39	5, 8, 9, 47
	S	75	6, 9, 10
	M	7	13
Kals ...	H	11	15, 40
	S	14	14
	M	9	9
Kalse ...	H	347	5, 8, 12, 15, 16, 19, 24, 25
	S	658	10, 14, 15, 16, 21, 25
	M	54	11, 14
Kalte ...	H	31	48
Kalu ...	H	1	48
	M	34	11, 16, 25
Kálúwál ...	H	1	16
	S	1	15
	M	48	20, 25, 48
Kamboh ...	H	3	1, 27
	M	9	13, 15
Kanádí ...	H	16	1, 16, 48
	S	1	49
Kanárí ...	M	11	17
Kanchí ...	S	9	9
	M	14	1
Kandál ...	H	13	8, 37, 41, 48
	M	10	15, 18
Kandiá ...	H	31	9, 39
	S	111	9, 10, 12
	M	15	10
Kandrí ...	H	79	6, 9, 44, 48
	S	9	10
	M	10	25
Kangah ...	M	126	48
Kangí ...	H	5	5, 15
	S	1	45
	M	214	13, 16, 17, 48
Kangotr ...	H	24	15, 16
Kangrá ...	H	14	3
Kangrí ...	H	14	3
	M	37	17, 30, 25
Kanjlí ...	H	5	49
	S	3	45, 49
	M	87	13, 20, 49
Kanju ...	H	26	3, 4
	M	16	1
Kankan ...	H	14	5
Kankará ...	H	8	1, 5, 48
	M	86	6
Kane ...	H	68	9, 15, 34, 36, 45
	S	5	9, 10, 45
Kársal ...	H	26	48
Kapuriá ...	M	347	1, 6, 12, 18, 25, 48
Kapurí ...	M	299	1, 2, 30, 49
Karáre ...	H	61	45, 48
	S	5	48
	M	50	15, 18
Karchí ...	M	48	17, 25
Kardgar ...	M	21	44
Karel ...	M	53	14, 15, 29
Kari ...	H	18	5, 41
	M	7	16, 44
Kariál ...	H	22	6, 25, 27, 39
	S	5	12, 14
	M	6	10, 14, 22
Karír ...	H	91	2, 5
	M	173	10, 15, 16, 18, 45
Karirá ...	H	446	1, 2, 4, 5, 33, 49
Karordí ...	H	36	2, 5
	M	6	12
Kasar ...	H	3	2, 9
	M	14	13
Kásbí ...	H	121	15, 36, 37, 47
	S	3	25
	M	3	13, 18
Káshab ...	H	1,011	7, 8, 9, 10, 35, 36, 39 42, 43, 44, 47, 48
	S	14	41, 45, 48
Kashmírí ...	M	41	11, 14, 17, 18, 19, 48
Katárí ...	H	87	2, 15, 18, 39, 45, 48
	S	9	48
	M	57	3, 15, 25, 48
Katardade ...	H	4	48
	S	11	48
Katliáná ...	M	11	3, 27, 28
Katoch	H	76	8, 6
Katorí ...	H	7	10
	S	13	44
	M	4	11
Katte ...	H	31	48
Katwárí ...	H	35	39, 40
	M	33	9, 14, 15, 17, 18, 25
Kaunsái ...	H	2	39
	M	11	3
Kaushal ...	H	131	9
Kawálí ...	H	10	39, 48
	M	86	13, 15
Keere ...	H	16	4
Kesar ...	M	45	15, 17, 18, 24
Kesarí ...	H	12	14, 16
	M	148	14, 16
Khachra ...	M	18	13, 28
Khaggí ...	M	98	5, 21, 26, 48
Khágí ...	S	15	12, 44
	M	106	14, 19, 25
Khakar ...	H	6	5, 47
	M	27	15
Khakhara ...	H	132	2, 5, 6
	M	28	18, 27
Khákí ...	H	4	15
	M	11	16
Khálí ...	H	1	11
	S	23	11
	M	25	13, 48
Khalwá ...	H	11	15, 48
	M	1	13
Khámí ...	M	41	9, 15
Khánbí ...	H	4	5
	M	24	16, 18
Khandrá ...	H	58	2, 4, 5, 48
	M	2	10
Khángrí ...	H	91	1, 2, 6, 15
Khání ...	H	20	8
	S	5	48
	M	6	16, 25
Khánjí ...	S	8	10
	M	44	16
Khankár ...	H	130	1, 2, 5, 6
Khar ...	H	8	3, 6
	M	49	13, 14, 25
Khara ...	H	1	2
	S	44	11, 44, 45
	M	254	4, 12, 13, 14, 17, 46
Kharáj Khatri	M	17	3
Khárás ...	S	1	49
	M	16	13, 18, 19
Kharí ...	H	38	2, 5, 15, 48
	S	14	11
	M	206	12, 15, 17, 25
Khariál ...	H	9	15
	M	80	18, 19
Kharral ...	H	34	5
	M	424	12, 13, 17, 24, 27, 28
Katáwárá ...	H	7	6, 44
	M	25	16
Khati ...	H	1,022	6, 9, 10, 11, 14, 25, 41, 46, 48, 49, 50
	S	478	6, 9, 10, 11, 12, 46, 48, 50
	M	137	9, 12, 48, 50
Khatrí ...	H	110	2, 8, 12, 13
	S	8	10
Khattárorá ...	H	2	13
	S	21	13
	M	32	10, 16
Kheli ...	H	13	4, 42
	M	42	17
Khorá ...	M	200	10, 13, 16, 17
Kherbi ...	H	1	17
	S	3	51
	M	96	12, 17, 25
Khichi ...	H	49	1, 12, 24, 51
	M	72	13, 24, 26, 46
Khilji ...	H	19	12
	M	1,099	1, 3, 6, 10, 11, 12, 25, 48, 49
Khilowálí ...	M	87	16
Khogal ...	H	10	39, 47
	M	1	17
Khohári ...	H	5	8
	M	178	25
Khoja ...	M	63	3, 13, 16
Khoka ...	S	17	25
	M	29	12, 14, 48
Khokhar ...	H	76	2, 8, 9, 15, 16, 18, 19, 25
	S	153	6, 14, 15, 17, 51
	M	11,535	J. L. R. M. 1, 6, 33, 44, 46, 48, 50, 51
Khori ...	H	10	9
	M	11	12, 13, 15, 27
Khotrí ...	H	4	25
	M	64	5, 12, 17, 25
Khrori ...	H	40	1, 2, 8
	M	51	16
Khurikand ...	H	12	12
Kira ...	H	9	8
	M	2	14
Koftgar ...	M	12	17
Kohli ...	H	370	7, 15, 43
	M	7	26
Kokás ...	S	12	14
Kokni ...	M	143	18, 20
Kolas ...	H	5	15, 39
	M	21	14, 15
Kolási ...	H	1	47
	M	144	9, 12, 44
Koli ...	H	13	8, 41, 42, 47
	M	36	5, 6, 10
Komal ...	H	30	14, 48
	M	8	6
Kondal ...	H	86	3, 7, 8, 9, 34, 35, 37, 39, 42, 48
	S	14	7, 9, 37, 44
	M	5	5, 24
Kora ...	H	6	5
	S	6	4, 5
	M	78	4, 13, 15, 16, 47, 51
Korál ...	M	50	12, 21
Korás ...	H	2	15
	M	46	10, 25
Kori ...	H	55	1, 5, 9, 27
	S	2	11, 44
	M	22	5, 6, 15
Korutáná ...	M	39	1, 12
Koti ...	H	1	12
	M	26	9
Kulebri ...	H	2	2, 31
	M	14	1, 50

Names of Sub-Castes.		Persons.	Locality.
Laddubans ...	H	95	9, 39
	S	2	4
Laddubhárat	H	73	9
	S	75	9, 15
Laddumián ...	H	28	9
	M	10	15
Láde ...	*H*	6	47
	S	12	9, 15
	M	21	13, 18
Ladhar ...	M	75	10, 12, 13, 16, 27
Ladhari ...	M	14	8
Lagwál ...	H	36	8, 42
Láhel ...	S	14	11
	M	7	18
Láhir ...	S	32	11
	M	17	14, 25
Láhoriá ...	S	20	44
	M	17	9, 12
Lakhan ...	H	10	2, 10
	M	1	15
Lakhanpál ...	H	2	2
	S	16	14, *15*
	M	7	12
Lakher ...	M	409	1, 12, 13, 17, 18, 20, 23, 24, 26, 29
Lakhirá ...	M	62	17, 18, 27, 51
Lákir ...	M	53	25
Lakisar ...	H	2	2
	M	706	5, 19, 24
Lál ...	H	134	9, 10, 11, 12, 40, 47
	S	218	10, 25
	M	3	10, 25
Lálli ...	H	44	9, 14, 15, 47
	S	6	9
	M	79	14, 15, 48
Lamrái ...	*H*	2	45, *48*
	M	99	17
Lamsári ...	H	12	6, 48
	M	6	48
Landáwál ...	M	17	3
Langáh ...	H	8	16
	S	26	11
	M	1,048	1, 3, 16, 17, 23, 28, 29, 44
Langar ...	M	32	22, 23
Langariá ...	M	18	18
Lange ...	H	9	45
	M	3	16
Lasthar ...	H	83	27, 36
	S	1	9
	M	5	6
Lawár ...	H	1	14
	S	20	48
	M	2	12
Lel ...	S	5	11
	M	8	19, 26
Lelli ...	H	5	11
	M	183	9, 13, 15, 16, 17, 25
Ler ...	M	69	48
Lodi ...	H	79	8
	S	7	12
	M	29	1, 9, 20, 25
Lodri ...	H	1	49
	S	2	48
	M	*13*	*1, 18,* 51
Logal ...	M	55	13, 15, 16, 48
Lobárawán ...	M	72	25, 51
Lohári ...	S	2	2
	M	256	25
Lohi ...	S	40	5, 25
	M	2	18, 25
Lohiá ...	H	117	3, 5, 12
Lohl ...	M	11	25, 46
Lokir ...	M	4	25
Lolá ...	M	83	9, 24, 26
Loláná ...	M	12	48
Loli ...	H	1	1
	S	8	14
	M	19	44, 14
Lon ...	*H*	*10*	*48*
	S	7	11, 48
	M	5	21
Longar ...	H	63	9
	M	21	2
Lor ...	H	15	15
	S	29	11, 15
	M	1	28
Losan ...	M	222	18, 21
Loti ...	H	1,347	3, 5, 6, 11, 25, 41, 45, 47, 49, 50
	S	372	5, 9, 11, 14, 25, 45, 48, 49, 50
Lotiáwár ...	S	15	12
	M	20	27
Lune ...	S	30	14
Mabábalá ...	H	23	13
Madáhar ...	H	84	6, 48
	S	30	10, 48
	M	32	5, 48
Mádi ...	H	20	2, 11, 47, 48
	S	12	48
	M	9	11
Mádli ...	S	11	11
Maghari ...	H	5	6, 42
	M	29	13, 15
Máhal ...	M	15	13, 23
Mahán ...	M	20	25, 26
Mahand ...	M	29	13
Máhandu ...	*H*	*37*	*6*
Máhar ...	H	37	4, 5
	M	264	1, 20, 27, 28, 29, 51
Mahdwál ...	M	16	15
Máhi ...	M	132	16, 28, 25
Máhlon ...	M	94	13, 16, 17, 18
Máhorá ...	H	18	2, 18
Máhori ...	H	3	25, 45
	M	21	16
Máhrà ...	H	9	49
	S	4	14
	M	7	1, 5
Máhru ...	H	3	5, 48
	S	47	48
	M	*104*	*6, 12,* 15, *16,* 17, 48
Máhu ...	H	1	48
	M	252	5, 13, 16, 18 22, 48
Mahul ...	M	54	13
Máhun ...	H	12	15, 16
	M	407	16
Main ...	H	12	6, 25
	S	3	9
	M	83	12, 13, 17, 16
Mair ...	H	7	48
	M	14	15
Makhan ...	S	1	25
	M	15	14
Makhanpál ...	*H*	5	*25*
	S	17	14
	M	7	14
Makhtum ...	H	8	9
	M	15	17
Makjál ...	H	2	9
	M	129	21
Makkar ...	M	12	28, 29
Makrál ...	H	4	39
	M	8	21
Maksar ...	M	57	6, 15, 16
Mál ...	H	20	11, 16, 25
	S	29	14
	M	15	14
Maláhe ...	M	25	15
Malai ...	M	32	*14*
Malak ...	H	27	49
	M	102	5, 48, 49
Malál ...	M	92	2, 25
Maláná ...	H	9	5
	M	274	2, 3, 4, 5, 28, 29, 48
Malan Haus ..	H	12	5
	M	10	19
Malhotra ...	H	62	15
	S	18	16
	M	15	15
Mal Kake ...	H	5	10
	S	6	10
	M	2	12, 17
Mal Kotre ...	*H*	1	15
	S	11	15
Málorí ...	H	12	44
	S	8	12, 14
	M	21	48
Malotre ...	H	53	15
	S	2	16
	M	63	12, 15
Malpotra ...	H	211	8, 15, 16
	S	10	15
Málsi ...	M	67	9, 10, 44
Malwáli ...	H	8	2, 16
	M	156	1, 14
Mamarzi ...	H	5	15
	M	13	27
Mamnun ...	S	20	44
	M	1	2
Mamráh ...	S	21	10
	M	16	15
Manak ...	H	5	48
	M	10	14
Manáru ...	H	4	15
	M	66	14, 15
Mánd ...	H	36	11, 16, 45
	S	1	12
	M	130	16, 21
Mandak ...	*M*	*21*	*48*
Mandál ...	H	18	15, 34, 47
	S	9	14
	M	64	15, 20, 25, 27
Mandial ...	H	39	8, 41
	M	5	10
Mandiár ..	H	49	3, 6, 31, 39
	S	20	10, 15
	M	12	12, 17, 18
Mandri ...	H	18	9, 11
	S	30	10, 44
	M	69	13, 44
Mandru ...	M	82	13, 14
Mang ...	H	33	42
	S	30	11
	M	1	17
Mangá ...	S	23	10, 44
	M	93	13, 17, 18
Mangal ...	H	30	5, 6
Mangar ...	M	28	21, 22 25
Mángat ...	M	129	17, 25
Mangoi ...	H	22	6
	S	28	11
	M	69	15, 19, 21, 25
Mangotre ...	H	41	15, 16
Mangotri ...	H	11	5, 9
	M	36	15
Mangrál ...	M	95	21
Mangwál ...	M	36	22
Manhári ...	H	13	9, 14, 41
Manhás ...	*H*	*171*	*8, 15*
	S	33	9, 15
	M	808	L. R. 8, 9, 10, 12, 25
Manhotre ...	H	21	16
Maniál ...	S	32	9
	M	9	20
Mankothí	H	34	8, 15
Manku ...	H	23	4, 33, 34, 45
	S	214	9, 10, 11, 12, 45
	M	26	9, 12, 14
Manotrí ...	H	43	15
Mánu ...	H	1	10
	M	47	14
Marái ...	H	6	18
	S	6	44
	M	35	13, 19, 26
Marás ...	H	1	7
	M	44	16, 17, 18, 19, 25
Màrdí ...	H	43	6
	S	2	25
Marhattá ...	M	10	12
Mari ...	H	28	9
	S	70	10, 25
	M	18	13, 17, 24
Marmál ...	M	20	1, 15
Maroi ...	S	89	9, 15, 44
Marote ...	H	1	48
	S	83	9, 10, 48
Máru ...	S	2	*6*
	M	58	13, 14, 19
Márukhel ...	M	10	23
Marwahe ...	H	17	6
	S	2	11
Márwi ...	H	4	15
	S	27	9, 44

APPENDIX TO IMPERIAL TABLE XIII.—

Names of Sub-Castes.		Persons.	Locality.
Masán ...	H	7	2
	S	3	14
	M	70	4, 51
Masar ...	H	5	15
	S	32	14, 25
	M	19	5, 15
Masi ...	M	24	15, 25
Maskar ...	M	60	48
Matai ...	M	13	26
Matáru ...	H	13	5, 9, 48
	S	46	9, 19
	M	123	15, 25, 44, 48
Matha ...	H	79	42
	S	17	9, 25
Matharu ...	H	214	6, 9, 10, 11, 12, 15, 25, 41, 44
	S	1,316	6, 9, 10, 11, 12, 13, 14, 15, 21, 25, 44, 49
	M	947	L. 6, 10, 25
Mathru ...	H	11	33
	M	12	25
Mathuriá ...	H	10	4
	M	5	13
Matiál ...	H	79	1, 9, 15, 33
	S	3	45
	M	25	13
Matike ...	S	3	25
	M	7	12
Matirá ...	H	31	1, 3, 39
Mattu ...	H	3	2, 6
	M	170	17, 19
Matuhará ...	H	15	45
	S	111	14, 45
	M	12	14
Máun ...	H	1	15
	M	78	14, 15, 28
Mehiá ...	M	37	22
Mehni ...	H	1	15
	M	123	5, 16
Mehru ...	H	1	6
	M	29	15
Meo ...	M	232	5, 13, 15, 17, 18
Met ...	M	12	16
Mián ...	H	156	6
Mirá ...	H	10	8
	M	21	17
Mirak ...	H	1	9
	M	52	49
Mogu ...	H	41	47
Mohal ...	H	49	1, 2, 4, 9, 12, 48
	S	70	19, 48
	M	256	5, 12, 13, 15, 51
Mohal Gujar	M	34	13
Momi ...	S	15	15
	M	252	16, 18, 22
Mondá ...	H	32	2, 13, 15, 25, 48
	S	115	6, 11, 25, 45
	M	12	14, 16
Moni ...	H	4	16
	S	1	11
	M	6	18
Mori ...	S	53	10
	M	3	10
Mosári ...	H	9	48
	S	7	48
	M	49	48
Moti ...	H	12	16, 48
	S	16	15
Motiár ...	H	104	8, 46
	S	11	46
Mughal ...	M	8,525	D. except (7), L. except (14), R. 8, 9, 10, 12
Mule ...	H	21	5, 51
Multáni ...	H	65	1, 5, 6, 48, 49
	M	1,886	1, 10, 11, 12, 14, 19, 31, 33, 34, 40, 48, 49, 50
Mund ...	H	1	3
	M	11	19
Mundi ...	H	50	5, 40
	S	2	40
Nág ...	H	9	8, 9
	S	203	9, 15
	M	273	8, 9, 13, 14, 15
Naginá ...	S	51	14
	M	234	14, 15, 44
Naglá ...	H	17	6, 34
	S	2	16
Náhal ...	H	7	2
	M	17	4
Najári ...	H	9	42
	M	8	3, 18
Najir ...	H	5	1
	M	49	25
Nakwál ...	H	9	15
	M	6	12
Nálband ...	H	2	3
	M	109	5, 11, 13, 14, 16, 45, 48
Náli ...	H	9	9
	S	24	12, 25
	M	88	11, 14, 15, 16, 21, 44
Nandál ...	H	4	36
	S	1	1
	M	7	12
Nandhari ...	H	10	4
	S	6	45
Nangi ...	H	6	16
	S	23	12, 16, 17
	M	80	11, 18, 20, 25
Nariál ...	H	251	8, 15, 47
	M	4	15
Narmál ...	M	47	13
Narori ...	H	53	8
Narotre ...	M	185	8, 9
Náru ...	H	17	8, 18, 34
	M	72	13, 14, 24, 28, 48
Natál ...	H	27	8
Nathre ...	M	24	14, 18,
Natri ...	H	307	8, 47
	S	5	11
Náwri ...	H	49	6, 10
	S	120	10, 12, 45
Neli ...	H	196	3, 4
	S	10	6, 13, 14
	M	263	8, 10, 16, 24, 25
Niar ...	H	6	11
	S	5	6
Nid ...	S	5	12
	M	46	16, 25
Nilká ...	M	33	12, 27
Nirlean ...	H	14	49
Noche ...	M	22	13, 48
Nol ...	M	47	10, 11, 12, 18
Nonári ...	H	2	48
	M	10	29
Note ...	H	571	9, 10, 34, 39, 44
Ojari ...	H	10	48
	S	8	48
Padan ...	H	12	48
	S	44	13, 14
Paddi ...	S	6	25, 44
	M	69	15
Padhal ...	H	62	8, 47
	M	1	12
Padholá ...	H	2	6
	S	2	25
	M	8	25
Páhan ...	H	14	9, 47
	M	30	13
Páhde ...	H	287	8
	S	6	6, 10, 14
	M	100	8, 10, 16, 17, 24
Páhie ...	S	2	12
	M	20	14
Paik ...	S	1	11
	M	33	10, 12
Pákar ...	H	3	6
	M	52	1, 12, 51
Pálak ...	H	13	1, 5
	S	5	14
	M	29	24, 25, 49
Palaniá ...	H	89	6
Palar ...	H	104	9, 11
Pále ...	H	14	1, 2
	M	16	48
Pálori ...	S	59	9
Palotre ...	H	50	8, 9, 15, 16
Pálsi ...	H	13	9
	S	22	15
	M	23	25
Palti ...	H	214	9
	M	27	12, 25
Paltor ...	H	165	2
	S	2	6
	M	7	9
Pandat ...	M	11	20
Pande ...	H	10	48
	M	275	13, 14, 15, 16, 19, 25, 26, 44
Panden ...	S	4	14
	M	282	16
Pander ...	H	137	34, 40, 48
	S	38	11, 48
	M	29	9, 24
Pándhi ...	M	29	12, 21
Pandoli ...	H	38	2, 41
	M	144	9, 12, 13, 15, 16, 19, 20
Pandori ...	H	5	5
	S	34	10
	M	124	13, 14, 16
Paniár ...	H	75	1, 3, 5, 11
Panir ...	H	235	2, 6, 8, 11, 44, 47
	S	355	9, 10, 11, 13, 14, 15, 17, 25
	M	142	13, 45
Panjábi ...	M	57	13, 17
Panju ...	H	2	11
	S	8	13
	M	74	44, 51
Panlohar ...	M	22	16
Panon ...	M	83	13, 16, 17
Pansir ...	H	17	6, 8, 18
	S	382	9, 11, 14, 44
Panwár ...	H	348	1, 2, 4, 5, 7, 12, 34, 41, 49, 50
	S	38	25
	M	587	2, 3, 4, 12, 13, 17, 24, 27, 28, 45, 49, 50, 51
Parahin ..	H	23	47
	M	3	6
Parbat ...	H	21	15, 18
Parhár ...	H	2	12
	M	10	12, 24, 27
Pári ...	H	20	9, 16
	M	7	25
Pariál ...	H	93	1, 8
Pási ...	H	14	6, 15
	S	17	11
	M	1,144	L. 10, 11, 24, 33, 44
Patal ...	M	9	10, 27
Pátan ...	H	16	5
	M	1	5
Patar ...	H	11	1, 5
Pathe ...	H	999	8
	M	11	3, 30
Pathán ...	H	16	5, 12, 47
	M	582	1, 2, 3, 4, 12, 13, 15, 16, 17, 19, 20, 21, 24, 25, 27, 48
Pathaniá ...	H	509	3, 8, 9
	M	48	8, 30
Páti ...	H	5	8
	M	30	13, 14, 17
Patole ...	H	84	9, 48
Patorá ...	H	54	6, 49
Patpará ...	H	250	4, 5
Pátri ...	H	12	1, 42
Pawár ...	H	140	2, 10, 48
	S	17	13, 16, 48
	M	734	1, 12, 13, 14, 17, 48
Peg ...	M	13	48
Phadal ...	H	16	47
	S	8	9
	M	2	25
Phagwál ...	H	48	47
	M	1	16
Phakrá ...	H	1	5
	M	45	17, 18
Phal ...	H	25	10, 44
	S	76	9, 10, 44
	M	82	10, 13, 14, 23, 25, 44
Phaládi ...	H	47	8
Phalli ...	S	22	11, 12, 24
Phalrai ...	H	53	2
	S	1	33
	M	1	24

Names of Sub-Castes.	Persons.	Locality.
Phamráh ... M	24	19, 20, 44
Phangure ... M	51	18
Phárji ... M	175	5, 9, 15
Pharre ... M	12	13, 18
Phárná ... H	57	5
M	16	3
Phohi ... S	26	16
M	270	13, 16
Phori ... H	2	5
Phosi ... S	24	11, 14
Photi ... M	131	16, 18, 25
Phul ... H	8	18
S	96	10
M	25	14, 18
Phussán ... M	11	16
Pik ... M	17	19, 45
Poi ... S	18	10, 15
Punián ... H	18	5, 16
M	1	16
Puri ... H	18	5, 16
M	6	17, 18
Qanauji H	5	48
S	1	48
M	32	48
Qanib ... M	179	16
Qázi ... M	12	15, 17, 24
Qureshi ... M	260	1, 3, 9, 10, 12, 13, 16, 16, 18, 19, 22, 24, 44
Qutab Shahi M	80	6, 16, 18, 20, 25
Rachhrá ... H	65	4, 10
M	3	25
Raghubansi H	171	6, 7, 8, 9, 15, 39, 41, 48
S	21	6, 15, 48
M	39	14
Ráhab H	16	48
S	31	48, 49
Raháin H	2	33
S	431	9, 45
M	19	14, 15, 18, 25, 29
Rahel H	429	8, 11
S	113	11, 25
M	58	15
Rahsan H	124	15, 17
S	41	9, 10
Ráibhái S	17	10
M	37	17
Ráihin M	62	14
Rail H	65	8, 25
S	187	24
M	14	11
Rait H	369	9
S	239	11, 25
Ráiteli M	46	14
Rájbansi S	5	10
M	18	16
Rájgariá H	5	42
S	3	15
M	5	14, 15
Rájiál H	19	8
Rájmál H	115	6, 9, 47
S	3	9
Rájmardán M	13	20
Rájpál ... H	32	48
S	1	48
Rájput ... H	86	1, 2, 4, 12, 15, 45, 48, 49
S	50	11, 13, 15
M	396	2, 3, 9, 11, 12, 13, 14, 16, 17, 18, 19, 22, 25, 48
Rájoi ... M	26	15, 16, 17
Rájrup ... M	26	14
Ráju ... H	4	6
S	3	6, 9
M	116	9, 14, 15, 25, 45
Rakhanpál ... S	14	15
Rakhi ... M	136	15, 16, 17, 18, 19, 20,
Ral ... H	15	8
M	37	14
Ralhan ... H	13	6
Rámgarhiá ... H	99	7, 8, 9, 15, 21, 23
S	162	9, 14, 15, 18, 23, 24, 44
M	2	13

Names of Sub-Castes.	Persons.	Locality.
Rán Lál ... H	36	6
Rámri ... M	26	44
Ráná ... H	171	8, 47
S	27	12
Ranb ... H	58	16, 39
Randháwá ... H	45	14, 42
Rangránia ... M	36	13
Rangre ... H	9	7, 25
M	6	5, 18
Ránjha H	1	9
M	303	18
Ranot ... H	212	8
Ranpál ... H	136	39, 47
S	173	48
M	6	17
Rásal ... H	32	2, 9,
M	65	13, 21, 44
Rasiál ... H	4	6, 15, 45
S	12	25
M	12	15
Ratanpál ... S	10	48
M	6	48
Rather ... H	425	1, 2, 3, 8, 11, 12, 42, 46, 48, 49
S	3	12
M	7	18
Ratial ... H	53	8
S	17	9, 44
M	35	15
Ratn ... H	184	7, 9, 15, 34, 39
S	57	9, 13, 15
M	1	19
Ráwáit ... H	1,227	3, 4
Rawat ... H	144	7, 8, 32, 39
M	10	3, 13, 45
Regi ... M	33	18
Rekhi ... H	1	25
M	332	8, 16, 25
Renu ... S	68	14, 18
M	18	16, 28
Reri ... H	80	8, 13
Reti ... H	28	8, 9
M	19	18
Rewalia ... H	28	3
Rial ... H	114	9, 33
Riah ... H	20	15
Riait ... H	101	5, 6, 8, 9, 10, 11, 25
S	142	9, 10, 11
M	21	25
Rohela ... H	18	6, 8, 9, 48
S	8	9, 11
M	101	9, 13, 25
Rojbri ... H	2	6
S	24	48
Romani ... H	59	9, 48
Roni ... H	12	1, 10, 11, 25
S	33	11
M	80	10
Rori ... H	3	10
S	7	12, 17
M	23	9, 14, 16, 44
Rupál ... H	20	1
S	9	1, 6, 19
M	52	9, 25
Ruprái ... H	167	9, 11, 33
S	150	9, 10, 33, 44
M	425	9, 10, 11, 12, 13, 14, 15, 17, 25, 44
Sabharwál ... H	197	9, 15
S	151	15, 17
M	6	15
Sábir ... S	55	50
M	3	50
Sabjál ... M	25	18
Sabrán ... S	55	15
M	16	16, 48
Sabzá ... H	13	25
S	8	11
M	31	15, 22
Sachrá ... M	44	17
Sachrál ... H	9	47
M	29	13
Sadal ... M	1,071	L. except (17), 10, 12, 19, 25, 44

Names of Sub-Castes.	Persons.	Locality.
Sadan ... H	38	1, 2, 5, 12
S	52	5, 14
M	2	13
Sadelozi ... M	33	13
Sadhorá ... S	1	12
M	37	19, 25
Sadiqi ... M	11	5, 15, 49
Saglotre ... H	10	15
Saghar ... H	3	15
M	82	1, 11
Sagi ... H	41	9
S	6	12
M	1	12
Sagotre ... H	39	15, 48
S	7	15
Sagu ... H	150	8, 12, 14, 15, 25
S	384	J. except (8), 13, 15, 25, 44, 50
M	146	11, 15, 16, 50
Sagwál ... H	12	44
M	34	22
Saháí ... H	48	16, 31, 42, 47
S	114	5, 43, 50
M	125	12, 18, 25
Sáham ... M	404	21, 25
Sáhan ... H	26	17, 18, 25
M	67	14, 17, 18, 25
Sahárán ... H	91	6, 9, 10
S	8	9, 48
M	251	13, 17, 18, 25, 48
Sahgal ... M	107	14, 28
Sáhi ... H	49	6, 9
S	7	17
M	93	13, 15, 17
Sáhiwál ... H	36	34
M	1	12
Sahman ... M	19	15, 24
Sahnan ... S	4	11
M	9	24
Sahoni ... M	12	10, 17
Sahori ... H	66	6, 9
S	19	9, 44
M	182	13
Sahote ... H	43	1, 9, 10, 44, 46
S	159	5, 9, 10, 44
M	104	4, 5, 6, 19, 25, 44, 48
Sahotre ... H	133	9, 15, 16
M	392	16, 17, 24, 25,
Sabrá ... S	219	9
M	40	13, 15
Sahtariá ... H	13	8
M	53	13
Saidore ... M	16	14
Saihiál ... M	1,777	21, 44
Saine ... H	10	48, 49
S	29	14, 48
M	8	48
Sajhár ... M	41	13
Sákhál ... H	6	6
S	8	1
Sakhun ... S	2	9, 10
M	167	16, 17, 21
Sákiel ... H	68	9
M	7	5, 16
Saki ... H	6	9
M	4	5, 14
Sakrá ... H	8	15
S	1	9
M	12	18, 19
Sál ... H	4	25, 45
S	88	11, 25
M	6	11, 13
Salábat ... M	15	13, 20, 44
Salágh ... M	53	11, 48
Saláich ... H	8	8
M	832	9, 12, 13, 16, 17, 25
Saláit ... M	16	9, 16
Saláije ... S	3	3
M	77	17, 19, 48
Saláukhi ... H	145	3, 4, 26, 49
M	68	17, 18
Salariá ... H	112	5, 8, 15, 16
M	19	15, 16, 25
Salegam ... H	16	9, 17
Salgotre ... H	77	15, 16
M	45	15

Names of Sub-Castes.		Persons.	Locality.
Salhan ...	H	69	9
Salim ...	S	46	9
	M	11	13, 24
Salláh ...	M	37	14
Saloche ...	H	4	47
	M	88	47
Sálorá ...	M	17	15, 28
Salotri ...	H	75	9, 15, 16
	S	45	9, 15
	M	185	15, 17, 24, 25
Samád ...	H	5	5
	M	138	12, 28, 47
Sámal ...	H	237	8
	M	26	15, 25
Samanda ...	M	47	48
Sami ...	H	15	17, 25, 44
	S	122	13, 14, 15, 46
	M	18	20, 25
Samkari ...	H	144	8
	M	14	27
Samlál ...	M	31	15, 28
Samrao ...	H	1	48
	S	81	14, 48, 50
	M	118	13, 14, 15, 25, 50
Sán ...	S	44	11, 15, 25
	M	13	20, 25, 27
Sanbal ...	H	4	4
	M	17	20
Sánd ...	H	3	14
	S	16	14, 25
	M	37	15, 20, 25
Sandá ...	S	22	11
	M	100	11, 16, 17, 18
Sandal ...	H	246	8, 9, 37, 48
	S	55	5, 9, 11, 14
	M	2,050	10, 17, 18, 25
Sandán ...	H	70	4, 5
	M	20	18, 25
Sandar ...	H	1	6
	S	31	47
	M	31	15, 16, 25
Sandhi ...	S	11	50
	M	18	14
Sandin ...	M	17	15, 18, 27
Sandoi ...	M	12	5, 12
Sandu ...	H	29	8, 13, 15, 25
	S	124	11, 14, 15
	M	280	14, 15, 25
Sangál ...	H	22	1, 30, 41, 47
Sangári ...	H	6	5, 8
	S	1	11
	M	6	17, 25
Sangarwál ...	H	30	3
Sange ...	H	7	9
	S	102	10, 11
	M	52	14, 15, 16, 17
Sanghabi ...	S	2	15
	M	29	2, 25
Sánghan Chan	M	18	3
Sanghari ...	M	33	12, 30
Sanghla ...	H	17	51
Sangot ...	M	147	13
Sangotre ...	H	68	15, 16
	M	23	15
Sángra ...	H	5	15, 16
	S	10	15
	M	1	17
Sangrial ...	S	31	49
	M	13	19
Sangu ...	H	89	2, 10, 48
	S	141	11, 14, 15, 48
	M	64	5, 17, 48
Saniál ...	H	17	48
	M	3	48
Sanjal ...	S	29	45, 51
	M	23	13, 15
Sanjali ...	H	35	4
	S	2	9
Sanjor ...	H	1	8
	M	19	19
Sanjotre ...	H	9	16
	S	3	16
Sánk ...	H	223	1, 8, 47
	M	15	13, 17, 18
Sánklá ...	M	692	1, 2, 12, 48
Saukli ...	H	51	1, 10, 25
Sanosi ...	H	52	8, 34
	M	9	9
Sanwária ...	H	43	2, 3, 25
	M	18	4
Sapáril ...	H	1	21
	M	11	22
Saphar ...	H	16	12, 17, 44
	M	34	19, 20
Sappal ...	H	2	45
	M	103	1, 16, 18, 22, 25
Sapur ...	M	47	18
Sarái ...	H	123	8, 12, 15, 34
	S	35	11, 12, 44, 47
	M	332	12, 13, 14, 20
Saráich ...	H	1	15
	S	6	12
	M	56	17
Saral ...	H	26	1, 2, 7, 8, 39
	S	23	13, 18, 20, 25
	M	88	20, 25
Saraste ...	M	16	48
Saráyá ...	M	26	6
Sard ...	H	16	1, 5
	S	1	9
Sárdi ...	H	9	6, 42
	S	63	14, 25, 44
	M	39	14, 15, 25, 33
Sárgotre ...	H	87	16
Sári ...	H	17	2
Sariál ...	H	3	2, 44
	M	11	18, 46
Sarka ...	H	14	2, 48
	M	84	33, 34, 48, 49
Sariwál ...	H	27	2, 3, 32
Sarkande ...	M	57	5
Sarohá ...	H	18	7, 47
	M	56	49
Saroi ...	H	49	5, 17, 48
	S	102	16, 44, 48
	M	700	6, 15, 48, 51
Saroti ...	H	4	5, 9
	M	186	2, 6, 48
Sarswál ...	H	11	6
	M	3	6
Sarwal ...	M	52	15, 29
Sarwari ...	S	26	15, 41
Sarwie ...	H	4	34
	M	284	1
Sási ...	H	1	45
	S	36	9
Sathal ...	H	7	2
	M	5	9, 12
Sathi ...	S	20	25
	M	114	5, 27
Sáwand ...	H	1	42
	M	55	18, 27, 28
Sáwari ...	H	52	2
Sawná ...	H	26	25, 47
	S	9	12
Sehgal ...	M	10	15
Sehi ...	S	77	10, 11, 15
	M	5	44
Sehra ...	H	197	8
	S	14	11
	M	34	15, 18, 24
Sehri ...	H	62	10
	S	5	44
Sehti ...	S	23	10
Sej ...	M	33	15
Sekhar ...	M	27	47
Sekhu ...	S	1	17
	M	159	1, 13, 15, 44
Seli ...	H	42	9, 15
Sengora ...	H	2	8
	S	5	5
	M	219	13, 15, 22
Seti ...	H	39	9
	S	12	9, 11, 15
Shádi ...	M	55	13
Shabad ...	S	12	44
	M	1	51
Shábut ...	M	11	10
Shámáni ...	H	66	48
Shekh ...	M	806	13, 16, 20, 23, 48
Shekhu ...	M	767	1, 2, 5, 13, 22, 23, 27, 44
Shekhuzádá...	M	14	5
Shine ...	H	1	24
	S	7	17
	M	12	5, 15
Shorán ...	M	29	1
Shotre ...	H	14	4
Siál ...	H	27	2, 8, 48
	S	30	9, 14, 48
	M	1,386	M. 9, 17 to 20, 48
Siálkoti ...	H	14	8
Siám ...	H	221	9, 10, 33, 47
	S	35	9, 10
	M	101	17, 20, 22
Sidhán ...	H	54	2
	M	39	1, 45
Sidkar ...	H	88	2, 46
Sikhu ...	H	13	5, 10
	S	84	12, 14, 44, 45
	M	159	1, 5, 17, 25
Sil ...	M	15	9, 17
Sila ...	H	5	48
	M	11	48
Silahat ...	M	17	9
Simál ...	S	10	50
Siná ...	M	46	17, 24
Sindha ...	H	69	1, 12, 48
	S	88	11, 13, 16, 50
	M	520	13, 17, 18
Sindhu ...	H	42	12, 16
	S	69	9, 12
	M	146	11, 12 15, 26
Singhanche ...	M	93	49
Sippa .	H	50	8
Siprá ...	H	26	10
	S	16	15
	M	178	17, 25
Siqligar ...	H	16	5, 12, 47
	S	45	8
	M	152	11, 14, 27, 29, 51
Sirál ..	H	92	2, 5, 9
	S	10	9
Sobhá ...	S	34	15
	M	4	11
Sodáioh .	M	11	5, 13, 16
Sodhans ...	S	17	14
Sohal ...	H	265	9, 14, 15, 41, 48
	S	187	10, 14, 15, 44, 48
	M	535	10, 12, 15, 48
Sohan ...	H	61	1, 6, 9, 48
	S	84	10, 15
	M	188	3, 5, 6, 15, 44
Sohanki ...	H	35	1
Sohanpál ...	H	41	9
Sohdi ...	H	2	2
	S	38	14
	M	73	15, 17, 25
Sohi ...	H	12	5, 6
	S	8	50
	M	28	5, 18
Sohri ..	H	15	15
	S	18	15, 44
	M	29	44
Soi ...	H	27	6, 9, 10, 42
	S	11	11, 14
	M	5	11, 49
Sokhi ...	H	6	14
	S	344	10, 14, 15, 19
Sokhlá ...	H	10	8, 51
	M	11	17
Solakhan ...	H	480	1, 3, 4, 12
	M	63	3
Solar ...	H	4	9, 10
	S	2	11
	M	14	17
Sond ...	S	218	9, 11, 12, 14
Songrup ...	H	98	8
Sonj ...	H	4	3
	S	40	11
	M	1	51
Sonkarwál ...	H	38	15, 41
	M	14	25, 44
Sonkhi ...	H	31	1, 3
Sonta ...	H	15	1, 33
	M	6	10
Sonwál ...	H	56	8
Sorekhi ...	H	52	48
Sorhál ..	H	32	36
Soseri ...	H	10	5
	M	27	12, 13, 28
Sotri ...	H	14	6, 10, 47
	M	327	13, 18, 24, 25

Names of Sub-Castes.		Persons.	Locality.
Srohi ...	H	14	48
Sud ...	H	44	8, 9, 15
	S	16	10
	M	1	11
Sufi ...	H	2	15
	S	5	15
	M	10	15, 48
Suleki ...	H	18	9
Sultáni ...	H	7	12, 45
	M	22	5
Sultánpuriá ...	H	29	50
Sumrá ...	H	4	44
	S	52	11, 12
	M	91	17, 26, 28
Suod ...	H	49	9, 10
	S	20	9
Sur ...	H	288	9, 10, 12, 15
	S	298	9, 14, 15, 25
	M	25	10, 15
Suraj Bansi ...	H	18	7, 15, 41
	S	1	47
Surajmukhi ...	H	20	7, 48
Suri ..	H	12	2, 16
Surjan ...	H	31	9, 25
	S	1	14
	M	3	11
Tadari ...	H	13	31
Tahim ...	S	22	13
	M	394	14, 17, 19
Takáie ...	H	3	6
	M	38	15, 18
Takalti ...	H	580	8, 9, 47
	S	9	47
Taksaliá ...	M	28	44
Talar ...	H	224	9, 17, 18, 20
Tállán ...	H	3	2
	S	5	25
	M	142	11, 25
Talobri ...	H	4	13
	M	27	18
Tanbár ...	S	15	11
Taundi ...	M	13	13
Tandlá ...	H	115	3, 6, 45
	S	3	25
Tángar ...	S	2	9
	M	37	4
Tángri ...	H	22	1, 5
	S	3	25
Tanjal ...	S	1	11
	M	42	14, 15
Tánk ...	H	160	4, 5, 41, 48
	S	5	17
	M	27	12, 16
Tanor ...	H	68	2, 4, 7, 49
	M	80	1, 5, 33
Tansri ...	S	14	14
Tapalwasir ...	M	15	9, 29
Tárá ...	M	18	20, 25
Tarái ...	H	17	5, 15
	S	1	5
	M	2	5
Tarar ...	M	86	14, 19
Táreri ...	H	3	2
	M	124	17, 23
Tárhal ...	H	2	15
	M	31	13
Tariá ...	S	6	15
	M	6	26
Tariánd ...	M	17	13
Tarkhán ...	H	60	7, 42, 47
	S	16	14
	M	232	3, 13, 14, 25
Tarki ...	H	19	1, 4, 15
	M	1	6
Tarpál ...	H	16	6, 47
Tárthe ...	H	11	15
Tatial ...	H	54	6, 9, 15
	M	92	18, 20, 25
Tatri ...	H	164	6, 8, 15, 40, 42
	M	10	18
Táwari ...	H	343	3, 5
	S	19	15
Teli ...	H	126	4, 5, 7, 37
	S	3	10
	M	980	L. except (16), 18, 19, 25, 33, 45
Teriá ...	H	61	2, 12
Thade ...	H	32	8
	S	4	14
Thakke ...	H	80	8
Thakru ...	H	50	8, 42
	M	51	18, 28, 44
Thál ...	S	4	11
	M	83	13, 15, 20, 21
Thálli ...	S	2	9
	M	17	17
Thalrá ...	H	31	42
	M	17	25
Thamiál ...	H	6	10
	M	43	16, 27
Thandiál ...	M	11	9, 13, 51
Thári ...	H	21	5, 16
	M	4	25
Tháru ...	H	19	44, 50
	S	16	10
	M	38	13, 24
Thati ...	H	12	6, 10
	S	221	12, 13, 14, 15
Theli ...	M	15	10, 48
Thodi ...	M	27	12, 48
Thorá ...	H	41	2,
Til ...	H	22	47
	S	1	10
	M	34	13, 18, 47
Titariá ...	H	20	48
	M	5	48
Tite ...	S	25	12, 15
Titru ...	H	3	5
	S	8	11
Tokli ...	H	5	15, 42
	M	8	48
Tol ...	M	73	10, 11, 16, 18
Tolí ...	H	442	2, 14, 36, 39, 41
	M	11	18, 49
Toráit ..	H	16	42
Ton ...	H	1	48
	S	5	11
	M	49	1, 48
Tur ...	H	104	2, 3, 17
	S	8	1, 5, 10
	M	278	8, 11, 13, 18, 24, 25, 45
Ture ...	H	84	1, 2, 5
	S	4	5
	M	42	15, 18
Turk ...	M	27	5
Vadhal ...	S	4	17
	M	10	20
Vadhále ..	M	31	15, 17
Vadhán ...	M	79	12, 16
Vaghomál ...	M	121	27
Váhdi ...	H	4	14
	M	29	15
Váhle	H	14	15, 16
	S	7	15
Vains ...	H	9	25
	M	89	10, 13, 14, 21
Valde ...	S	14	15
Valsir ...	M	55	15
Vanjál ...	M	77	13, 16
Variáh ...	H	62	4, 5
	M	215	12, 14, 24
Varáich ...	M	206	17, 20
Varayá ...	M	215	12, 13, 19, 25
Vardi ...	H	2	9, 15
	S	565	L. except (16), 11, 27
	M	378	L. except (17), 11, 12, 25
Varhál ...	S	16	25, 44
	M	20	13, 14, 28
Vari ...	H	16	5
	S	8	16
	M	2	14
Variáh ...	S	23	44
	M	530	L. except (16), 1, 24, 25, 27, 28, 46
Variál ...	M	92	13, 14, 16, 17, 25, 45
Varji .	M	202	12, 14, 15, 16, 44
Varju ...	S	39	12
Varne ...	S	14	15
	M	3	16
Vásali ...	H	9	9
	S	4	17
	M	25	20
Vasan ...	H	1	10
	M	202	L, 25
Vasir ...	M	604	13, 14, 17, 24, 28, 29
Vattu ...	M	84	12, 17, 24
Vazir ...	M	12	13
Vesar ...	H	4	17
	M	36	18, 19, 25
Vesrá ...	M	24	16, 19
Virk ...	S	12	14, 16
	M	207	1, 13, 17, 25, 48
Yusafzai ...	M	61	18, 48
Yunas ...	S	45	15
	M	24	17, 25
*Minor ...	H	642	
	S	305	
	M	887	
Unspecified ...	H	15,447	
	S	7,543	
	M	42,851	
	B	392	

*** DETAIL OF MINOR.**

Abaránt 10, Abdán 5, Abhi 3, Abir 2, Abto 4, Admal 7, Afghán 1, Agetáne 2, Aghan 5, Agwábl 1, Ajli 2, Akosar 1, Alwán 8, Alyás 2, Amrá 4, Andán 5, Andli 7, Ando 9, Andrl 1, Anoli 10, Arag 2, Arhán 8, Arhár 3, Ashiál 3, Aslámkhel 1, Aujál 4, Aujári 8, Aukhiá 2, Aurhái 10, Bahádará 4, Bahial 5, Bahman 4, Bákan 1, Bála 5, Baliraná 3, Balko 7, Balsaná 2, Banerá 8, Bangol 4, Banuri 4, Bankorá 1, Bánkri 10, Barás 2, Barlko 1, Barwan 8, Baságwál 10, Baskhan 9, Batsar 5, Bawániá 2, Bawársi 2, Behan 9, Bhágal 5, Bhanattel, Bharorá 6, Bhediá 7, Botate 1, Chajjar 8, Chándal 7, Chandoli 1, Chandsur 7, Changal 2, Changhi 5, Chantak 1, Charindi 6, Chattu 9, Chhaman 3, Chhanbal 8, Chhandi 3, Chhariál 2, Chhágwri 7, Chhib 4, Chite 9, Choghtte Kabli 1, Chohdád 1, Chokhá 2, Chondi 8, Choni 8, Chundá 1, Chunj 9, Dabgar 5, Dadh 4, Dadhi Khalo 8, Dadiáná 10, Dagái 10, Dagaryál 1, Dai 8, Dáji 3, Dalore 2, Dálú 3, Dalwái 1, Daniál 2, Danu 8, Danwáná 7, Dariáná 2, Darliáh 3, Darmán 6, Daroi 3, Darotre 4, Darwesh 6, Dasál 1, Dewal 10, Dhal 5, Dhamli 2, Dhandar 2, Dhanmán 6, Dhantár 7, Dharki 1, Dhatoyá 9, Dher 1, Dhillara 2, Dhilwán 4, Dhindsá 5, Dholaniá 7, Dhomi 2, Dhosar 3, Dhotar 8, Dim 5, Din 1, Dipu 2, Diwari 3, Dod 5, Dodáhadiá 1, Dobai 3, Dohgli 6, Dolái 8, Dosál 6, Falás 2, Faqir Gadaria 4, Gad 2, Gadai 3, Gáe 6, Gágal 1, Gahotri 7, Gajjan 10, Galbis 1, Galdeo 4, Galebri 9, Galreri 9, Ganariá 1, Gandháni 7, Gandik 1, Ganesh 8, Ganie 4, Ganshá 8, Gansital 2, Gatarurkhi 1, Gáwár 7, Gedu 7, Genti 7, Ghag 2, Ghái 2, Ghalun 9, Ghamli 1, Ghatpál 9, Gholári 1, Ghuráná 1, Gobie 8, Gogi 1, Guler 6, Hab 2, Hákan 6, Hallu 6 Hamale 1, Hamdal 3, Hamrás 3, Han 1, Hánsi 1, Hantar 2, Harmál 1, Hartál 2, Harwi 1, Hasti 3, Hem 5, Hindal 6, Hirá 4, Hosan 9, Ilbán 6, Jadi 7, Jadik 1, Jál 7, Jám 1, Jandorie 3, Janki 1, Jariá 2, Jarmali 4, Jasrá 9, Jatani 5, Jatoná 3, Jeswál 7, Jeti 2, Jewari 1, Jhajwál 8, Jhami 2, Jharid 1, Jharsiá 5, Jhuji 7, Jobá 4, Johari 4, Johdal 5, Johdi 3, Jojli 3, Jor 1, Jotta 5, Juláhi 1, Kahi 9, Káhri 5, Káhut 4, Kajoi 2, Kákhe 2, Kandoli 1, Kanwál 1, Karnut 9, Katádi 1, Katwádá 5, Khabal 8, Khábi 5, Khádi 6, Khámleiá 3, Khánste 5, Khásá 10, Khatak 4, Khatar 7, Khodare 4, Khoi 4, Khokhar patte 6, Kodan 2, Kokne 6, Korokotri 7, Kotán 1, Ladri 4, Lakhsál 4, Lambe 1, Lambsaras 3, Lamtán 9, Langori 10, Langriálá 5, Lassi 6, Len 10, Lobal 5, Lochgi 1, Lodhar 2, Logan 6,

*DETAIL OF MINOR—*concluded.*

Lohan 6, Lohani 5, Lohargari 3, Lohri 1, Lokhani 7, Lokli 1, Lonas 10, Loni 8, Lotas 10, Lotli 1, Machhál 2, Maddan Machan 4, Madári 1, Madgotre 7, Madhwal 9, Maggi 3, Maghar 1, Mahráli 5, Mahtam 5, Maihne 1, Mailor 5, Majnun 3, Makri 8, Malmotre 8, Malohar 8, Malsari 4, Malswái 2, Mandola 9, Manháru 6, Maniár 3, Manhulá 2, Mansur 7, Mante 3, Marabi 1, Mariá 1, Marji 1, Máse 7, Masur 3, Mathrai 3, Matier 8, Matri 1, Mehun 2, Mel 8, Mewar 6, Modan 1, Mohi 6, Mohka 6, Mojni 1, Mokhar 1, Mor 5, Mulla 1, Mussali 1, Nabku 3, Nabnar 4, Nachar 1, Nahang 1, Náidá 1, Náis 8, Namri 3, Nanakpanthi 8, Nandi 1, Nárá 2, Nárátar 2, Narzá 9, Neru 2, Nirmáhni 5, Odat 5, Osrá 9, Othi 4, Padal 1, Padholi 4, Páji 3, Palku 9, Pangrá 3, Pangure 9, Pankhá 1, Pashnoní 3, Pàsil 7, Pati Potre 3, Pherle 1, Phokra 4, Phologul 1 Pinjrá 3, Pobián 1, Pohal 1, Pohi 6, Qarái 3, Qulbi 1, Ragan 5, Rahai 3, Rájaur 3, Rakeb 1, Rakhiári 1, Rakhni 3, Rakman 5, Ramán 3, Ramián 6, Rámáni 3, Rámdáse 10, Ranbu 1, Ránudi 1, Rao 3, Rasái 5, Rasotre 1, Ratol 1, Ráttu 4, Ráwan 2, Rezbále 4, Rind 4, Rohan 8, Rorat 10, Rup Lál 9, Rup Rám 7, Sabgal 4 Sabbiá 5, Sabwár 9, Sád, 3, Sadách 2, Sadeári 2, Sadu 1, Sáju 5, Sakiá 3, Sáláhan 8, Saláik 2, Salwáu 1, Salwáni 1, Samiá 1, Samián 7, Samotre 4, Sanár 7, Sánbar 3, Sangar Kháni 4, Sangwál 8, Sanju 6, Sanjaru 8, Sánti 4, Sápki 1, Saranob 3, Sárandal 3, Saras 4, Sarfi 8, Sarghál 8, Sewaj 2, Sindal 5, Sital 3, Sohie 2, Sojá 7, Sokan 9, Sokar 6, Sokhan 8, Sonat 4, Sopti 7, Sorangi 6, Sosial 3, Sundar 8, Sundhr 3, Sunhari 1, Suraj 1, Tagiál 4, Takhiar 9, Tamhan 2, Tanri 7, Tapurá 3, Tarad 3, Tarhar 3, Táshe 9, Thajjal 2, This 5, Timber 9, Torangi 1, Torni 1, Vadiáli 6, Vahang 1, Váhgal 2, Vakli 6, Válásál 2, Válásáti 2, Vásal 6.

Names of Sub-Castes.		Persons.	Locality.
Machhi 279,666	H		14
	M		279,652
Abrá ...	M	20	51
Adham ...	M	20	18
Ahal ...	M	43	25, 27
Ahalmaluk ...	M	27	27, 29
Ajri ...	M	36	15, 25
Ambri ...	M	17	25
Auándu ...	M	15	16
Ansári ...	M	27	19, 27
Athal ...	M	57	14, 25
Aulakh ...	M	17	13, 17
Aur ...	M	26	18, 19
Awan ...	M	927	10, 12, 13, 17 to 21, 23 to 28, 44, 51
Badhar ...	M	117	17, 24, 44
Badhelá ...	M	17	19, 24
Badin ...	M	30	18, 25
Baggá ...	M	74	13, 18, 19, 44
Baggan ...	M	89	44
Bájwá ...	M	972	13, 16, 17, 19, 25, 44
Balgan ...	M	19	17
Balhim ...	M	327	12,15, 16, 17,25
Balká ...	M	15	19
Ballar ...	M	14	28
Balri ...	M	34	1, 25
Bambola ...	M	163	27
Bamrá ...	M	61	16
Bangi ...	M	38	25
Banjárá ...	M	33	16, 19
Banmolá ...	M	41	28, 51
Banowár ...	M	20	28
Bansiál ...	M	19	17, 18, 27
Bará ...	M	61	1
Baráre ...	M	11	17, 25
Baráz ...	M	18	17
Bargoti ...	M	55	25
Barhám ...	M	14	13, 17
Bariál ...	M	26	1, 13, 25
Bariár ...	M	111	16, 17, 25
Basráie ...	M	64	17, 18
Bassá ...	M	15	16
Bassin ...	M	40	15
Batál ...	M	44	16, 25
Bathiará ...	M	92	19, 27, 28
Battar ...	M	24	13, 27, 44
Batwál ...	M	11	1
Bhábal ...	M	444	25, 28
Bhádar ...	M	150	12
Bhadiál ...	M	164	13
Bhagar ...	M	13	19, 28
Bhagat ...	M	47	16, 19,
Bhágni ...	M	57	26
Bhákar ...	M	264	25, 27, 51
Bhalan ...	M	48	25, 28, 44
Bhamráj ...	M	11	23
Bhangar ...	M	56	17, 44
Bhangi ...	M	56	12
Bhangri ...	M	66	12, 13
Bhanoi ...	M	44	16, 51
Bhánún ...	M	281	12, 44
Bharál ...	M	59	1, 17, 25
Bharbhunjá ...	M	33	12
Bhari ...	M	112	12, 14, 25
Bhart ...	M	93	13, 17, 18, 24, 25, 26
Bhart-khokar	M	24	16

Names of Sub-Castes.		Persons.	Locality.
Bhat ...	M	30	26
Bhatal ...	M	116	12, 23, 25, 51
Bhatará ...	M	274	12, 24, 26, 29
Bhatpotrá ...	M	59	51
Bhattá ...	M	2,137	12, 16, 17, 19, 24, 25, 26, 51
Bhatti ...	M	17,794	J. L. R. 1, 6,10, 11, 12, 40,44,48
Bhatti Dhorí...	M	80	18
Bhatu ...	M	79	12, 17
Bhokar ...	M	68	26, 44
Bholá ...	M	126	13, 18, 27
Bhore ...	M	27	51
Bhota ...	M	742	12, 13, 16, 17, 24, 25, 27, 28, 44, 51
Bhoti ...	M	839	12, 13, 17, 44
Bhuná ...	M	439	13, 17, 18, 27
Bhutte ...	M	611	13
Biloch ...	M	91	25, 26, 27, 28
Chábar ...	M	171	48
Chadhar ...	M	172	17, 18, 26
Cháhe ...	M	112	15, 16
Chákarni ...	M	12	16
Chakráli ...	M	35	19, 25
Chamár ...	M	12	13, 27
Chamia ...	M	65	18, 25
Chándá ...	M	113	16, 17
Chandor ...	M	17	13
Chandrái ...	M	16	17
Cháng ...	M	64	19, 25, 44
Changre ...	M	114	25
Chantiá ...	M	239	16
Chaugattá ...	M	1,440	12, 23, 24, 26,48
Chauhán ...	M	701	13, 20
Cháwalá ...	M	64	12, 17, 26, 27
Chhab ...	M	27	17
Chhanan ...	M	77	13, 25, 51
Chimá ...	M	39	L. 19
China ...	M	83	17
Chishti ...	M	39	13, 20
Chite ...	M	27	12, 13, 25
Dabhar ...	M	39	27, 51
Dádpotrá ...	M	24	28
Dagan ...	M	26	13, 44
Dáhar ...	M	104	16, 27
Dahomi ...	M	19	44
Dáiá ...	M	530	28, 51
Dakhne ...	M	76	13, 16, 51
Dál ...	M	204	1, 12, 13, 29
Dale ...	M	14	13, 27
Damkan ...	M	21	12
Dang ...	M	34	17, 28
Dangar ...	M	11	11, 17
Dangnalá ...	M	16	27
Darági ...	M	133	15, 17
Dhaddi ...	M	2,418	12, 24, 26
Dhákar ...	M	46	13, 24, 51
Dhaku ...	M	44	24
Dhán ...	M	52	16
Dhándál ...	M	17	14
Dhande ...	M	91	12, 18, 44
Dhándi ...	M	570	15, 17, 26, 27
Dhanori ..	M	12	12
Dhariwál ...	M	12	15, 17
Dharmáne ...	M	71	51
Dharri ...	M	28	12, 15, 17
Dhilwán ...	M	26	11
Dhim ...	M	576	12, 13, 15, 17, 25, 26, 44

Names of Sub-Castes.		Persons.	Locality.
Dhodi ...	M	6,467	12, 13, 14, 16,17, 18, 24, 27, 51
Dhokri ...	M	67	26
Dholi ...	M	117	17, 18
Dholri ...	M	47	14, 17
Dhun ...	M	58	12, 17, 18
Dhosar ...	M	108	23
Diál ...	M	76	18
Diwar ...	M	377	19, 27
Dochak ...	M	22	1
Dode ...	M	96	27
Dogar ...	M	11	12, 19
Doglá ...	M	56	27
Drúdgar ...	M	57	51
Gadár ...	M	11	18
Gadi ...	M	76	12, 13, 15, 26
Gajjan ...	M	17	51
Galar ...	M	242	44, 51
Galoi ...	M	78	44
Gandal ...	M	14	12, 27
Gangar ...	M	133	1, 51
Ghagará ...	M	154	12, 17, 28
Ghakar ...	M	220	13, 16,20, 27,51
Ghallú ...	M	22	27
Ghaman ...	M	405	17, 18
Ghámi ...	M	27	16, 51
Ghindár ...	M	71	27
Ghor ...	M	87	20
Ghorá ...	M	21	12, 27, 28
Ghorewál ...	M	18	12, 13
Gil ...	M	478	12, 13, 16, 17,20
Goháli ...	M	11	17
Golrá ...	M	69	18
Gondal ...	M	274	17, 18, 19, 20
Goria ...	M	146	12, 13, 15, 17, 44, 51
Got ...	M	24	12
Gujráti ...	M	124	51
Hajráh ...	M	23	16, 20
Hamshirá ...	M	51	28
Háns ...	M	571	12, 13, 17, 24, 25, 26, 51
Hánsi ...	M	93	44
Hár ...	M	20	18, 23
Hari ...	M	18	24
Harl ...	M	410	13, 19, 26
Hindi ...	M	14	51
Hinjrá ...	M	403	15, 17, 18, 19,26
Hot ...	M	113	19, 23
Jádle ...	M	33	1, 23
Jagwáne ...	M	147	25
Jái ...	M	137	13, 28
Jalowálá ...	M	1,608	13, 24, 25, 27
Jamáo ...	M	25	27
Jamat ...	M	446	17, 18
Jamwál ...	M	115	29, 51
Janal ...	M	180	13, 26
Jand ...	M	152	12, 18, 19, 28
Jangálu ...	M	16	25
Janjohán ...	M	519	13, 20, 24, 27, 51
Janjuá ...	M	1,416	L. 25, 26
Jásal ...	M	30	13, 18
Jassi ...	M	35	17
Jat ...	M	10,330	13, 29, 51
Jatiál ...	M	158	24, 25
Jáwán ...	M	12	1
Jhagar ...	M	12	12, 23
Jhinwar ...	M	174	25
Jhujá ...	M	47	19

SUB-CASTES OF CERTAIN SELECTED CASTES—*continued.*

Names of Sub-Castes.		Persons.	Locality.
Johi	... M	47	1, 19
Joiá	... M	409	12, 24, 25, 27, 51
Jokhe	... M	36	51
Kadhar	... M	49	19
Káhar	... M	12	19, 25
Káhlon	... M	32	16
Káith	... M	33	13
Kálej	... M	35	12
Kaler	... M	18	26
Kaloi	... M	15	17, 25
Kaloti	... M	52	13, 44
Kamboh	... M	22	13, 20
Kanán	... M	23	24, 25
Kandelá	... M	253	27
Kanglá	... M	27	51
Kangrá	... M	11	16
Kanerá	... M	122	51
Kaniál	... M	14	25
Kanne	... M	56	13, 25
Karelá	... M	99	24, 27
Karichá	... M	97	28, 51
Karri	... M	138	25, 27, 44
Katiál	... M	33	18, 27
Katpál	... M	124	12, 13, 16, 25, 28
Káwán	... M	57	16
Kelá	... M	60	24, 45, 51
Khagá	... M	30	16, 27
Khagar	... M	14	25
Kháikhod	... M	41	19
Khákhe	... M	25	17, 27, 51
Khanna	... M	248	15, 24, 27
Khárá	... M	32	24, 25, 33
Khárak	... M	16	25, 51
Kharal	... M	672	12, 17, 19, 26, 27, 51
Kháre	... M	174	13
Kharkash	... M	358	19, 25
Khathe	... M	61	51
Khichi	... M	18	24, 27
Khohi	... M	34	51
Khohárá	... M	519	15 to 17
Khokhar	... M	60,236	L. R. M. 1, 10, 12, 44, 51
Khomi	... M	48	16, 44
Khosar	... M	116	25
Khot	... M	44	17, 19, 21, 25
Kokári	... M	136	7, 24
Kondar	... M	27	25
Kori	... M	79	18, 25
Lak	... M	52	19
Lakhanpál	. M	14	12, 44
Lakherá	. M	191	10, 51
Lallar	... M	18	16
Lanbáh	.. M	17	19
Lang	... M	30	20, 27, 44
Langáh	... M	976	12, 13, 16 to 19, 24, 25, 27, 28, 51
Láwámar	... M	14	13
Lodháni	... M	213	13, 24, 51
Lodi	.. M	43	13, 18, 20, 26
Lohre	... M	20	13
Machherá	... M	13	18, 19
Madár	... M	53	12, 24, 27
Madráj	... M	23	13, 15
Máhar	... M	72	12, 16, 27
Máhi	... M	100	16, 17, 26, 27, 44
Máhigír	... M	1,073	1, 10, 13, 15, 24, 25
Máhis	... M	16	16, 44
Máhle	... M	33	13, 15, 17
Mahni	... M	235	15 to 17, 27, 44
Máhrá	... M	73	12, 13, 24, 27
Mákan	.. M	75	17, to 19, 27, 28
Malan	... M	39	12, 17, 51
Malan-háns	... M	317	12, 13, 25 to 27, 51
Malás	... M	20	19, 24
Malhi	.. M	11	12, 25
Málk	... M	479	14, 17, 19, 51
Mamráe	... M	76	13, 17, 24
Mánan	... M	99	13
Mand	... M	18	16, 19
Mangáh	... M	288	13, 16, 27
Mangi	... M	279	17, 24, 27
Manhás	... M	794	12, 16, 25
Manir	... M	38	16, 25, 44
Manjotáh	... M	35	16, 29

Names of Sub-Castes.		Persons.	Locality.
Manjyál	... M	102	20
Manale	... M	26	15, 25
Mará	... M	45	27, 51
Maráján	... M	30	17
Márath	... M	12	19
Marhás	... M	203	13, 16, 19, 25, 44
Máshki	... M	17,238	J. L. R. M.
Mássu	... M	22	13, 26
Mathri	... M	23	13
Matoriá	... M	170	17, 18, 25
Matti	... M	11	16, 25
Men	... M	93	12, 17, 24
Minhás	... M	1,772	13 to 15, 17 to 19, 23, 26, 28, 44
Mirdáh	... M	87	20
Mirháns	... M	156	17, 18
Mohi	... M	34	25, 29
Mokhá	... M	17	14, 27, 51
Monglá	... M	17	51
Mothá	... M	101	51
Mughal	... M	626	12, 13, 16 to 20, 24, 25, 27, 44
Mukhrámar	... M	13	23
Multáni	... M	87	13
Nánghi	... M	28	13, 19, 23, 24, 25
Náru	... M	177	12, 13, 25, 27, 29
Nonári	... M	61	27
Nori	... M	111	25
Otár	... M	18	51
Pandál	... M	149	13, 17
Paniál	... M	28	12, 13, 25 to 27
Paniár	... M	108	25, 26, 27
Panwár	... M	1,133	11 to 13, 23 to 25, 27, 48, 51
Parbál	... M	27	17, 25
Parhár	... M	119	19, 27, 51
Pathán	... M	466	M. 13, 16 to 19, 51
Pathárá	... M	40	12, 17
Patoke	... M	51	12
Patrái	... M	43	12
Patri	... M	11	12, 13, 44
Pawár	... M	99	16, 17, 24, 25, 27, 28
Phul	... M	103	12, 13, 24
Phulron	... M	148	17, 18
Piál	... M	71	12
Pori	... M	45	12, 29, 44
Qureshi	... M	55	12, 16, 17, 18, 51
Rahán	... M	1,044	12, 13, 16, 17, 18, 19, 24 to 26
Rái	... M	60	13, 16 to 18, 25
Rájá	... M	27	17, 19, 25
Rájput	... M	274	R. 11 to 13, 25, 51
Ráju	... M	183	16, 19, 25, 27
Rán	... M	192	13, 16, 18, 25, 27
Randháwá	... M	108	12, 13, 16, 25
Rangrá	... M	12	1, 13, 17
Ráni	... M	16	17
Ranjá	... M	548	12, 17 to 19, 25
Ratan	... M	47	13, 16, 44, 51,
Rathal	... M	324	27, 51
Ráthor	... M	14	12, 13, 27
Ratti-Khokhar	M	20	16
Reni	... M	23	12, 13, 44
Rind	... M	44	13, 26, 51
Rondan	... M	12	11
Sadhi	... M	44	1, 19
Sadhráich	... M	2,992	12, 13, 17, 25, 26, 48
Sadhráj	... M	533	20, 23 to 25, 27, 51
Sadrá	... M	97	12, 13, 16
Sadráhat	... M	57	25
Sadreche	... M	207	12, 17
Sagál	... M	236	26
Sagbári	... M	84	44
Saghotre	... M	29	17, 24
Sábi	... M	40	12, 13, 16, 25
Sábil	... M	116	12, 16, 44, 51
Sáhni	... M	23	17, 25
Sahotri	... M	217	13, 16 to 18, 23, 25
Sajrá	... M	20	16, 23
Sajráit	.. M	86	13, 16, 17, 25, 27
Sakhráná	... M	15	23
Sakhri	... M	19	12, 17, 27

Names of Sub-Castes.		Persons.	Locality.
Sálárat	... M	23	26
Saligá	... M	62	27
Sámand	... M	36	26
Sámina	... M	96	51
Samor	... M	325	17, 26
Samrá	... M	49	12, 16, 18
Sánal	... M	31	17
Sandhi	... M	13	25, 44
Sandrá	... M	111	15, 18
Sandráich	... M	83	16, 17
Sandráit	... M	26	24
Sandráj	... M	56	17, 26
Sange	... M	112	13, 17, 25, 26, 28
Sangoliá	... M	175	26
Sangráich	... M	19	12, 17
Sangri	... M	113	12, 14, 17, 25, 44
Sanjrát	... M	13	48
Saprá	... M	1,200	17, 18, 24 to 26
Saqqá	... M	34,838	1, 2, 4, 6, 12 to 14, 25, 49, 50
Sará	... M	14	25
Sáráh	... M	54	13, 26
Saráhat	... M	18	17, 44
Saráe	... M	164	12, 13, 15 to 17, 24, 25
Saraich	... M	567	13, 17, 44
Saráj	... M	68	29
Sárang	... M	19	20, 51
Sarát	... M	20	14
Sardár	... M	22	13
Saroiá	... M	79	17, 51
Sarri	... M	11	15
Sarwáh	... M	96	29, 51
Sáthan	... M	41	27
Satráit	... M	100	27
Sáwind	... M	139	23, 27
Sehria	... M	22	13, 17
Sengre	... M	48	44
Será	... M	22	17
Sethi	... M	16	16
Shajrá	... M	60	27
Sheikh	.. M	156	13, 14, 16, 18, 20, 21, 44
Sial	... M	4,267	1, 12, 13 15 to 18, 23, 25, 27, 28, 41, 51
Sian	... M	11	16, 37
Sidhu	... M	100	1, 12, 17
Siláich	... M	143	16, 20
Simá	... M	39	13
Sindhá	... M	46	13, 27
Sindhú	... M	473	12, 16 to 18, 25
Sochil	... M	317	13, 51
Sokhi	... M	52	17
Solgi	... M	14,767	12, 13, 17, 27, 29, 51
Somere	.. M	160	25, 27, 51
Sond	... M	65	16, 44
Sont	... M	24	44
Tahim	... M	2,056	1, 12, 16 to 19, 23 to 25, 27, 28, 44, 51
Tallá	... M	32	19
Tandi	... M	48	12, 15, 17, 28
Tánk	... M	127	6, 13, 14, 17
Tánori	... M	78	1, 13, 51
Tarar	... M	29	15, 17
Tarkhán	... M	30	12, 13, 28
Tártari	... M	13	13
Tatle	... M	160	1, 13, 16, 18
Tátráin	... M	12	13
Thamná	... M	54	16
Thathiár	... M	11	16
Thind	.. M	11	48
Tolábe	... M	15	1, 12
Tore	... M	41	15, 16, 27
Tot	... M	127	16, 44
Tur	... M	305	11, 13, 14, 16 to 19, 24 27, 44
Vadhan	... M	901	16, 17, 18, 19
Vadhar	.. M	114	16, 27
Vágan	... M	401	12, 13, 16 to 19, 23, 24, 26, 28
Vains	... M	16	18, 19
Vájin	... M	263	14, 24, 44
Valim	... M	33	16, 24
Ván	... M	25	17

Names of Sub-Castes.	Persons.	Locality.	Names of Sub-Castes.	Persons.	Locality.	Names of Sub-Castes.	Persons.	Locality.
Vándal ... M	16	12, 16, 17	Variáh ... M	905	12, 13, 17, 27	Ves ... M	31	13, 14, 17 to 19
Varáich ... M	870	16 to 19, 26, 51	Varji ... M	39	16	Virk ... M	795	13, 17
			Vasir ... M	24	16, 27, 51	*Minor ... M	1,518	
Varhi ... M	34	17	Vattu ... M	13	12, 13, 17	Unspecified ... H	14	
						M	43,172	

*DETAIL OF MINOR.

Abán 3, Achhrál 1, Ahmri 4, Alodia 8, Alri 2, Amín Bhatti 2, Amrá 9, Ande 1, Anghárí 2, Aráin 4, Aro 2, Arora 4, Asrání 2, Aumira 1, Aunt 9, Aur 2, Bábarlágí 8, Bábe 1, Babrái 2, Bábrí 1, Bábúnd 3, Badráj 3, Bágal 5, Báhmán 3, Bakhír 8, Balái 5, Baland 4, Bálra 5, Bamní 4, Bánríkhel 7, Bandán 2, Bangri 10, Bari 6, Bariáh 10, Barná 3, Basrár 1, Basroi 3, Batan 8, Batmak 2, Bhaláí 4, Bhándí 3, Bhandiár 4, Bharwálá 1, Bhata 6, Bhatiára 5, Bháwán 1, Bhír 7, Bhopál 2, Bhúlar 2, Bín 9, Bohar 2, Cháchar 6, Chadha 2, Chadráj 3, Chagrálá 3, Cháhal 7, Chakráti 3, Chamrang 1, Chanchal 7, Chandesar 10, Chanímuní 6, Chantú 1, Charg 4, Chatil 2, Cháyá 8, Chhágan 2, Chhati 3, Chhávle 2, Chíde 5, Chirímár 5, Chotan 1, Chuhrá 1, Dabte 2, Dadhú 1, Dahgan 8, Dajan 6, Dal 4, Damkan 10, Damúre 9, Dane 1, Davat 7, Desí 2, Devarkhel 1, Dháliwál 5, Dhalú 7, Dhamyál 9, Dhásad 2, Dhodo 4, Dhori 2, Díndár 8, Dot 8, Faqír 10, Gadá 7, Gádrí 9, Gadríchal 1, Gagal 8, Gaglot 2, Gáhang 1, Gan 10, Gandári 9, Gándhi 1, Gári 4, Gariál 3, Garjke 5, Ghalot 3, Ghauri 1, Ghíbá 1, Godam 7, Golia 3, Goríwál 8, Gorsiáne 3, Hándah 9, Hánjí 10, Harchand 2, Harjoi 6, Háshmi 1, Hatím 3, Hogar 8, Hola 7, Hoti 3, Isrán 2, Jabráe 3, Jagáli 4, Jaggú 2, Jagráná 5, Jajwál 6, Jáik 2, Jaj 1, Jakhar 1, Jal 3, Jalotre 8, Jandájal 4, Jander 5, Jhálri 4, Jhanjri 7, Jhatmak 3, Jhoichá 6, Jhomri 4, Jodám 7, Jomíne 10, Josh 1, Jotra 1, Káhni 1, Kahwára 1, Kainálkhel 2, Káit 10, Kakah 1, Kákri 6, Kalásan 1, Kálí 8, Kaliána 5, Kallú 3, Kalokí 3, Kálrá 4, Kamálkhel 2, Kandári 6, Kandpár 4, Kangar 2, Kángri 8, Káujan 1, Kankar 2, Kánsbi 2, Kantan 1, Karmáni 5, Kawár 5, Keni 5, Kentú 10, Kesar 2, Khachchí 1, Khangar 2, Kharotal 8, Kharwál 4, Khatáná 6, Khawán 7, Khemi 10, Khokhar 4, Koelakhel 9, Kokári 10, Koli 4, Kotána 5, Ladhar 7, Lagárá 6, Larká 1, Lele 9, Lohri 4, Lolna 2, Londe 10, Loni 3, Lot 5, Lulíra 5, Máchhal 2, Madári 5, Madh 5, Madwán 8, Mahín 5, Máhire 9, Majháná 4, Majíra 2, Mákhas 3, Mal 6, Malain 8, Malhána 1, Malláh 3, Malotre 4, Malshor 9, Mandiáls 2, Mángar 1, Mánge 3, Mángrál 1, Mánír 6, Mankhí 5, Marár 5, Mardankhel 9, Marhwál 6, Mastáni 7, Mástrí 1, Matílá 1, Mehra 7, Meo 7, Mírekhel 4, Moghi 6, Mokhi 10, Morín 4, Multáni 3, Munj 2, Nadre 5, Nagiána 1, Nagpál 10, Nágri 3, Name 1, Nangriál 2, Narmál 5, Naron 1, Nárú 7, Náwal 1, Niárí 1, Niggá 3, Nok 7, Nol 8, Nún 6. Obli 9, Ochh 5, Oháná 3, Padhál 9, Pagáh 6, Pakhíwár 6, Pandít 1, Pandolí 9, Panerá 8, Paniár 5, Panjutha 9, Párach 1, Pasáí 1, Patál 9, Páwali 1, Phakrái 2, Phaman 3, Phiphre 2, Pirtir 5, Podrí 3, Posla 3, Qábla 6, Qáimkháni 1, Qalandar 1, Ráhrání 3, Rájdái 1, Rál 1, Rangrez 3, Ratti 1, Ráwant 1, Rehál 3, Rimán 9, Ronge 3, Ropare 10, Ros 6, Rukne 8, Sadal 5, Sadási 2, Sadhre 5, Sadi 1, Sadíqí 9, Sadmál 1, Sadráni 8, Sagdoi 1, Sagú 8, Sahoch 1, Sajwál 3, Sakhi 4, Sakhíj 1, Salgan 9, Salíja 1, Salím 8, Salop 3, Salotre 2, Sammi 8, Samráne 3, Sandal 8, Sandiá 5, Sandyár 3, Sanjal 6, Sanjotre 6, Sanotre 7, Sanwale 4, Saploch 9, Sappal 6, Sarchat 6, Sardhái 6, Sarhál 3, Sari 9, Sarín 8, Sarkote 2, Sarvesh 1, Sáun 10, Sáwand 4, Sáwe 7, Shanána 2, Shínmár 2, Shomra 6, Sinoh 6, Sirwáre 3, Sísí 8, Sochi 1, Sodhái 5, Sogan 2, Sohan 2, Somal 7, Somar 6, Soni 3, Sontar 1, Ták 1, Talái 3, Talain 1, Talodha 5, Tángre 3, Tarkar 2, Tatáriá 3, Thodi 6, Utrádi 8, Vagar 5, Vákarí 2, Valána 2, Vangar 5, Vard 6, Varáich 1, Varshán 1.

Mussalli including (Kutana) M 309,568

Names of Sub-Castes.	Persons.	Locality.
Ahir ... M	176	17 to 20
Arorá ... M	26	22, 23, 27
Athwál ... M	806	13, 17, 18, 24
Audal ... M	24	18, 51
Aukhat ... M	135	27
Awán ... M	745	R. 17, 28
Bábá ... M	176	19, 20, 28
Báchlair ... M	14	17
Badábí ... M	24	29
Badál ... M	36	21
Badhál ... M	101	21
Badhán ... M	43	24
Bágí ... M	220	17, 23, 26, 27
Baholiá ... M	17	18
Bái ... M	87	27
Bájwáh ... M	19	13, 17, 18
Bál ... M	65	20, 25
Balan ... M	61	27
Balhim ... M	223	20, 24, 25
Báli ... M	76	28
Bandál ... M	14	21
Bangiál ... M	537	21
Bánwá ... M	22	18
Barár ... M	212	12, 17, 18, 25
Barhár ... M	23	20, 25
Bariál ... M	175	13, 20, 23
Bart ... M	94	51
Batál ... M	13	25
Bateja ... M	55	51
Bhábhi ... M	327	21, 27, 28
Bhadál ... M	104	17, 19
Bhádár ... M	127	17, 26
Bhadiár ... M	21	26
Bhadmár ... M	55	13, 25, 51
Bhainswál ... M	47	20
Bhakrul ... M	75	20
Bhalan ... M	98	17
Bhalar ... M	32	18
Bhalarwán ... M	388	17
Bháo ... M	176	18
Bhári ... M	91	12, 13
Bhart ... M	23	28
Bhat ... M	47	16, 17
Bhatti ... M	34,078	L. R. M. 51
Bhim ... M	548	17, 18
Bhoi ... M	13	17
Bhonji ... M	19	51
Bhotrá ... M	11	51
Bhuttá ... M	835	12, 18, 20, 25, 26
Biloch ... M	696	17 to 20

Names of Sub-Castes.	Persons.	Locality.
Bodat ... M	39	20
Boli ... M	24	28
Boná ... M	26	10
Borath ... M	183	17 to 19, 25
Bot ... M	57	27
Bota ... M	11	22
Chaddá ... M	22	19
Chadhar ... M	471	17, 18, 27, 51
Chadu ... M	26	19
Chahá ... M	653	26, 28
Chak ... M	15	51
Chamiá ... M	26	27
Chanál ... M	271	19, 22, 26
Chanár ... M	154	26
Chandál ... M	48	17
Chandhar ... M	156	29
Chandri ... M	126	14, 28
Changrá ... M	176	27, 28
Chánor ... M	65	26 to 28
Chauhán ... M	4,554	R. M. 12, 51
Chhaf ... M	137	28, 29
Chhapriba n ... M	225	17, 18, 24
Chhori ... M	10	21
Chhotri ... M	49	17, 19, 27, 51
Chogan ... M	36	27
Chogatta ... M	1,798	L. R. M. 12, 13, 51
Chohriá ... M	136	22, 26, 28
Chorál ... M	40	17
Chotrá ... M	35	23
Chuhrá ... M	216	12
Daddá ... M	17	29
Dágar ... M	448	17, 19
Dáhrá ... M	164	20, 27, 51
Daiá ... M	94	22
Dálhat ... M	15	13
Danejá ... M	25	28
Desar ... M	10	18
Dhageke ... M	55	25
Dhaji ... M	83	17
Dháli ... M	13	19
Dhán ... M	52	20
Dhának ... M	11	12
Dháni ... M	141	18, 19
Dhanj ... M	175	17, 18, 24
Dhari ... M	115	19, 27, 51
Dharjá ... M	16	16
Dharijá ... M	80	27
Dháru ... M	29	17, 29
Dhodi ... M	804	12, 19, 24, 25, 27, 51
Dhori ... M	94	17, 28

Names of Sub-Castes.	Persons.	Locality.
Díndár ... M	5,785	12, 21, 24, 26, 51
Dodhári ... M	11	16
Dagará ... M	21	19, 22
Dumná ... M	13	25
Faqir ... M	18	17, 19
Galeriá ... M	37	20
Gandára ... M	19	51
Gandere ... M	28	21, 24
Garari ... M	97	28
Ghagat ... M	23	18
Ghángri ... M	59	51
Ghar ... M	13	19
Ghárá ... M	73	19, 22
Ghársu ... M	138	17
Gháru ... M	1,949	M. 12, 17 to 19, 51
Gháseri ... M	29	26
Ghirat ... M	18	17
Ghosar ... M	27	17, 27
Gil ... M	2,714	1, 16 to 19
Gohar ... M	18	17
Golandáz ... M	10	51
Golar ... M	14	18
Gondal ... M	92	18, 28, 51
Gondi ... M	132	27, 28
Gorái ... M	231	17, 18, 20
Gori ... M	910	13, 17 to 20, 51
Goriá ... M	811	12, 17 to 20
Gujar ... M	14	27
Hadire ... M	11	19
Hamman ... M	27	51
Háns ... M	591	12, 24, 25, 27, 51
Harhár ... M	11	26
Hari ... M	30	24, 27
Hariál ... M	25	18, 25
Haror ... M	13	16
Haru ... M	11	17
Her ... M	107	19, 20, 21, 27
Hinjrái ... M	621	15, 18 to 20
Jaba ... M	1,206	27, 51
Jadri ... M	16	18
Jagiál ... M	40	20
Jámi ... M	18	23
Jandál ... M	12	17
Jandotra ... M	14	51
Jángri ... M	11	29
Janjohri ... M	21	51
Janjotrá ... M	121	28, 51
Janjuá ... M	618	17 to 21
Jánori ... M	187	23, 51
Jans ... M	90	18

Names of Sub-Castes.	Persons.	Locality.
Jarái ... M	21	18
Jat ... M	519	27, 39
Jatále ... M	66	19, 27
Jatiá ... M	128	20
Jawán ... M	27	19
Jhakiál ... M	110	17
Jhali ... M	17	51
Jhalwára ... M	207	29
Jhár ... M	33	28
Jhoj ... M	578	18, 29
Jhonch ... M	111	18, 28
Jital . M	120	27
Joi ... M	188	25, 27
Jotrá ... M	53	17, 27
Joyá ... M	9,305	M. 12, 13, 17, 18, 51
Kábi ... M	126	18, 21
Kakar ... M	11	29
Kaláchi ... M	66	28, 51
Kaler ... M	195	14, 23
Kaliáli ... M	26	24
Kalián .. M	35	22, 48
Kaliáná ... M	2,574	17, 19, 23, 26, 27
Kalotre ... M	50	25
Kamboh ... M	11	19, 51
Káná ... M	188	28
Kandári ... M	1,472	19, 20
Kandária ... M	84	25, 51
Kandhári ... M	129	15
Kandiál .. M	365	12, 17
Kandiari ... M	956	17 to 19, 22, 23, 28
Kangar ... M	116	18
Kaniál ... M	11	21
Kaptál ... M	24	51
Kariána ... M	26	50
Kashmiri ... M	12	19
Katári ... M	101	12
Khachi ... M	31	24, 28
Khái ... M	29	51
Kharal ... M	12	28
Kháro ... M	145	17, 19, 23, 29
Khoja ... M	1,327	12, 24, 25, 27, 51
Khokhar ... M	34,659	R. M. 12, 13, 16, 51
Kutáná ... M	10,741	17, 19, 23, 27, 51
Labána ... M	14	20
Ladhar .. M	84	13, 17, 20
Láhar ... M	562	18 to 19
Láhauri ... M	193	18, 19, 24, 27
Láhn ... M	73	25
Lak ... M	11	19, 29
Lakhan ... M	631	27, 51
Lálbegi ... M	37	12, 51
Lanbá ... M	762	10 to 21
Langáh ... M	426	18, 28
Lár ... M	30	27
Lodi ... M	62	19
Lohár ... M	28	17
Lonie ... M	166	21, 25, 26
Lorat ... M	11	28
Lot ... M	3,530	17, 18, 25 to 27
Machhi ... M	25	28
Madhar ... M	686	15, 17 to 19, 24, 27
Mahdanar ... M	12	28
Máhdar ... M	481	17, 25, 26
Mahota ... M	29	18, 19
Máhr ... M	62	20
Makhána ... M	260	26 to 28
Malak ... M	37	13, 17, 20
Malan ... M	80	27, 28
Malanhás ... M	611	27, 51
Maliár ... M	14	29
Malotra .. M	14	27
Mamdáni ... M	37	20, 23, 27
Mampál ... M	37	51
Mán ... M	15	18
Mándal ... M	23	20
Mándhar ... M	286	17, 26, 25
Manhás ... M	958	16 to 21
Manjí ... M	11	29
Marái ... M	205	18 to 20
Maráni ... M	12	28
Marar ... M	81	20
Maráeí ... M	13	25, 26
Marth ... M	12	26
Masur ... M	14	25
Mattu ... M	1,555	13, 16 to 20
Mekan . M	23	28
Modiane ... M	12	51
Mohána ... M	12	28
Mokal ... M	25	12
Mokhar ... M	19	25
Molí ... M	33	20
Moman ... M	22	24, 26
Molá ... M	51	18, 26
Motímadál ... M	21	19
Mughal ... M	353	R. 16, 17, 24
Nagiál ... M	246	20 to 22
Náhar ... M	147	17
Nau Muslam... M	2,053	12, 24 to 27, 51
Pábá ... M	390	17, 19
Padhárí ... M	807	12, 17, 25
Pakhíwárá ... M	29	22, 27
Palhár ... M	61	28
Páli ... M	78	17, 18, 25
Pandás ... M	353	19, 23
Pandit ... M	633	16, 19, 23, 26, 27
Panián ... M	90	20
Pánveu ... M	53	20
Panwár ... M	3,114	12, 18, 23, 24, 27, 28
Parere ... M	67	19
Parhál .. M	769	17 to 20, 25
Parhár ... M	6,452	12, 19, 23, 24, 26 to 28, 51
Parmál ... M	70	18, 19, 51
Pási .. M	96	26
Pathán ... M	603	17 to 19, 24, 27, 51
Páwali ... M	37	19
Phor ... M	123	18, 19, 23
Ponat .. M	32	18
Qalandar ... M	11	13
Qutabsháhí ... M	30	21
Rahásan ... M	363	17, 18
Ráhilá ... M	91	27
Ráhi ... M	102	28, 29, 51
Rahtti ... M	44	18
Rajoká ... M	11	21, 25
Rájpút ... M	130	19, 20, 22, 26
Ramiál ... M	21	21
Rán ... M	87	51
Randháwá ... M	80	18
Ránjhá ... M	383	17 to 19, 26
Ranwál ... M	13	27
Raswál ... M	,13	27
Rattí ... M	1,222	R.M. 13, 17, 20, 22, 26, 51
Ráwal ... M	37	23
Sadhare ... M	83	18, 24, 26
Sagí ... M	42	27
Sáhan ... M	20	21
Sahárú ... M	20	27
Sáhtú ... M	14	28
Saholí ... M	32	27
Sahotá ... M	9,185	R. 17, 24 to 28
Sahr ... M	116	24, 25
Saláich ... M	14	18
Saliáná ... M	57	25
Salothí ... M	28	25
Sálrí ... M	52	17, 18, 25
Samejá ... M	18	26
Samnotrí ... M	48	12, 51
Samrád ... M	45	51
Sándal ... M	196	19, 23, 26, 27, 29
Sándar ... M	439	17, 19, 23, 27, 28
Sandhú ... M	2,414	14, 17, 18, 24, 27
Sándariá ... M	18	26
Sangotri ... M	25	20
Sanotrá ... M	3,775	19
Saprá ... M	209	17 to 19, 26
Sarái ... M	84	19, 20
Sáras ... M	251	17 to 19
Saroh ... M	230	19, 20
Sarohd ... M	54	17
Saroí ... M	799	17 to 19, 25
Saroiá ... M	47	12, 17
Sársar ... M	16	25
Sawárí ... M	11	24
Seoní ... M	19	25
Shabána ... M	12	22
Sháhúkhel ... M	54	21, 22
Sháhzáda ... M	15	20
Shekh ... M	1,217	20 to 22, 27, 29, 51
Siál ... M	386	17, 19, 27, 28, 51
Siálaní ... M	13	18
Siáriá ... M	16	18
Sidhú ... M	484	12, 17, 19, 51
Sohi ... M	36	17 to 19
Solí ... M	29	51
Somrá ... M	226	27, 29, 51
Sonibhandiál... M	136	20
Sontri ... M	31	18, 19, 21
Sotá ... M	13	18
Sotni ... M	17	18
Sotrá ... M	601	12, 21, 23, 51
Tárar .. M	35	17, 20
Tari ... M	22	20
Tawáná ... M	11	19, 28
Tejí ... M	1,716	17 to 19, 24 to 28
Teli ... M	113	27, 28
Thím ... M	213	13, 19, 24, 26, 51
Tor ... M	58	17
Vágri ... M	184	17, 19, 25 to 27
Váhan ... M	51	17, 18
Vahím ... M	44	25
Varáich ... M	141	18, 25
Variáh ... M	2,467	16 to 20
Vasir ... M	671	12, 24, 26, 27, 51
Vattú ... M	283	18, 20, 28
Ves ... M	11	19, 27
Virk ... M	44	18, 20, 25
*Minor ... M	988	
Unspecified ... M	113,852	

*** DETAIL OF MINOR.**

Adíwál 6, Adrá 1, Afghán 4, Altar 2, Andá 1, Arí 5, Asíwál 3, Audarwál 2, Audeswál 4, Awal 2, Badálá 1, Badhara 4, Bagan 1, Balgohar 3, Bálmíkí 5, Bandrá 2, Báns 5, Banú 4, Banwál 7, Barí 7, Barlás 2, Bartál 7, Barwálí 9, Baryár 7, Basir 7, Batoí 6, Beldár 1, Bhandár 4, Bhangí 4, Bhar 3, Bharwál 8, Bharyál 3, Bhatái 3, Bháwlí 2, Bhonge 1, Bhorá 1, Bhorí 1, Bír 1, Bothá 8, Chad 8, Chakwátí 1, Chamár 1, Chanan 5, Chandotri 4, Chandú 8, Cháwlí 3, Chhatábá 4, Chhatí 2, Chohrí 1, Chonch 7, Dabrí 5, Dákas 1, Dakhní 2, Dálat 6, Darkháu 3, Dhálú 1, Dhanwál 3, Dharáli 2, Dháriwál 8, Dhát 8, Dheri 8, Dhotar 8, Diddán 7, Díndiál 1, Doglí 1, Dogrí 4, Dol 2, Gadará 5, Gadhar 2, Gagrá 7, Gajrání 6, Gajrí 1, Galan 8, Galot 2, Galotra 8, Gharí 8, Ghoríwáh 4, Godhí 6, Gophar 4, Goriwál 4, Gurjmár 8, Hajám 2, Hálú 4, Hán 1, Handal 9, Hánjí 4, Háns 5, Harián 9, Háro 2, Hassar 1, Hoi 1, Jabola 4, Jádre 3, Jaindráin 6, Jaj 7, Jamotrá 8, Janái 3, Janálí 5, Jandáliá 1, Jangalá 1, Jánwarí 3, Jarán 9, Jarmán 3, Jawái 4, Jese 3, Jháliá 7, Jhamá 1, Jhandá 4, Jídá 9, Jír 6, Joba 9, Jogí 1, Kajlisí 1, Káli 7, Kaljí 2, Kalní 1, Kalrráhn 9, Kals 8, Kalsrá 2, Kalúniá 8, Kandárá 9, Kanj 2, Karoliá 1, Katál 6, Káti 6, Khagar 4, Khánzáda 6, Khará ri 5, Khiljí 3, Khonjí 3, Khori Nagál 7, Kokára 3, Kori 1, Kort 4, Kot 2, Ladan 1, Ladhra 7, Lakhra 9, Lalriá 5, Lángar 1, Lasí 3, Lochí 2, Lorat 7, Madárí 2, Máhlí 4, Mahtam 4, Makar 1, Makhotrí 6, Malái 8, Málarí 1, Malk Jat 1, Mamrá 1, Mand 6, Mandar 1, Mariáli 5, Mawál 5, Mazhabí 8, Mehra 10, Meo 10, Met 8, Mír 1, Morá 5, Muglí 2, Munj 2, Nádar 3, Nág 4, Náglú 1, Náhal 4, Nakiáná 1, Nal 2, Nárú 1, Natrá 4, Nún 1, Opal 3, Pagúl 7, Páhil 4, Pambi 9, Pandas 2, Panhár 7, Panwál 2, Parochá 3, Parmir 9, Páwat 9, Phalron 1, Phalwál 2, Phiblí 1, Port Láhú 1, Púná 1, Rái 7, Ratiál 6, Ratwál 6, Sachdev 4, Sadhí 3, Saghar 4, Sahwál 9, Sahoná 4, Sái 4, Sainpál 2, Sanálí 8, Sanáthar 8, Sándá 6, Sandhú 2, Sandi 1, Sandílá 4, Sangar 1, Sanglá 1, Sangwáliá 5, Sapádh 10, Sapal 1, Saplí 5, Sarájí 1, Sardí 1, Sarí 5, Sarwái 1, Selí 8, Shahází 1, Shori 1, Síkhon 3, Silán 6, Sodá 5, Sodharí 9, Soi 3, Sondi 1, Sonibarmála 1, Sonibhatiár 1, Sont 2, Sonta 1, Sotri 8, Tabjí 6, Táíká 9, Tandli 5, Teja 6, Thathál 6, Thora 1, Thothá 5, Tittrí 8, Vádhan 3, Vádhar 2, Váhrí 4,

Names of Sub-Castes.		Persons.	Locality.
Rajput 1,685,432	H.	388,544	
	S.	24,810	
	M.	1,222,064	
	J.	14	
Abáin ...	H	16	27
Abdál ...	H	4	8, 23
	M	19	14, 21, 23
Abbe Lagan	H	15	48
Abbi ...	H	85	8
Abbrol ...	H	50	8
Abiál ...	H	103	8
Abkal ...	H	50	4
Abtá ...	M	13	25
Achhar ...	H	68	8
	M	35	19
Achirt ...	H	11	9
Adah ...	H	101	18, 42
Adhári ...	M	219	21, 41
Adhobansi ..	H	27	47
Adin ...	H	12	21
Adráh ...	H	7	1
	M	57	21
Aemán ...	M	35	2
Agál ...	H	2	13
	S	4	17
	M	6	25
Agán ...	H	35	8, 44
	M	569	15
Agastmuni ...	H	15	48
Agbansi ...	H	59	41, 44
	M	5	7
Agiál ...	H	22	8
Agnásh ...	M	28	13
Agni ...	H	96	6
Agnote ...	H	28	9
Agráh ...	H	8	26
	M	17	15, 44
Agráwnt ...	H	15	1, 2
Agwai ...	H	85	4
Ahir ...	H	92	4, 13, 24
	S	57	4
	M	206	1, 13, 19
Ahluwáliá ...	H	82	8, 9, 12, 21, 44
	S	152	8, 14, 18, 27, 44
	M	2	44
Ahlwá ...	H	11	8
Ahouriá ...	H	24	50
Ajer ...	H	13	8
Ajesi ...	H	18	2
Ajnobi ...	H	254	50
Ajowál ...	H	22	44, 47
Ajpál ...	M	73	27
Akerá ...	M	24	26
Akbái ...	M	14	1
Akhrá ...	M	120	15, 20
Akri ...	H	27	4
Akwál ...	H	862	8, 9, 15, 16, 27, 39
	M	16	11
Aliánáh ...	H	7	8
	M	246	1, 26
Alot ...	H	13	9, 10, 15
	S	1	10
Alpiál ...	M	9,303	20 to 22, 25
Alwál ...	H	276	9, 12
Alwari ...	H	17	15
	S	1	15
	M	16	13
Ambale ...	H	48	9
Anadwál ...	H	22	9
Anári ...	H	15	9
Anáwál ...	H	70	1, 9
Anbitere ...	H	61	9
Anbrál ...	M	119	18
Anbre ...	H	84	9
Anda ...	H	45	1, 28
	S	19	20, 28
	M	17	8, 13, 15
Andariál ...	H	73	8
Andarotiá ...	H	19	15
Andotri ...	H	202	15, 24
Angotha ...	H	65	8
Angwálá ...	M	11	44
Anot ...	H	82	9
Anotri ...	H	293	8, 9, 15
Ansári ...	M	119	21
Antál ...	H	178	4, 16
Apal ...	M	11	11, 19, 44
Ár ...	H	11	7, 25
	M	28	25, 44
Aráín ...	M	63	13, 27
Arar ...	M	133	12
Arko ...	H	4	9, 25
	M	11	2
Arnáit ...	H	13	9, 13
	M	4	25
Arorá ...	H	3	6
	M	764	21
Asat ...	H	177	4, 5, 9, 28, 33
Asi ...	H	6	9
	M	190	26
Atar ...	H	1,058	8, 9, 15, 16, 34, 36 to 38, 41, 47,
	M	823	19, 20, 34
Atarbatti ...	M	14	25
Athar ...	H	39	25, 44
	M	5	18
Athwál ...	M	27	14, 25
Ati ...	H	28	9
Atiál ...	H	220	8
Atlas ...	H	35	6, 44, 48
	S	1	48
	M	40	6, 33, 48
Atri ...	H	921	9, 12, 15, 34, 37, 39, 42
	S	18	6, 8, 48
	M	13	8, 25
Audh ...	H	854	24, 51
Augiál ...	H	230	8
Aulháná ...	H	158	4, 8
Aungh ..	H	32	8
Aunkri ...	H	14	8
Awán ...	H	53	8, 13
	S	2	15
	M	4,366	L. 6, 21, 25, 46, 48
Babar ...	S	9	14
	M	29	13, 22
Bábla ...	H	51	27
Báchar ...	H	15	48
Bachár ...	H	61	1, 9, 48
	M	7	1
Bachas ...	H	598	4, 32
Báchbal ...	H	52	4, 34
	M	201	3, 5
Bachhan ...	M	12	21
Bachharwál ..	H	12	39
Bachhiá ...	H	30	50
Bachná ...	H	57	48
Badáhar ...	H	273	1, 8, 49
Badáná ...	H	13	9
Badáu ...	H	39	10, 48
	S	6	14
	M	113	21
Bádawar ...	H	58	1, 8
Bádbani ...	H	14	8
Badbál ...	H	271	8, 9
	M	956	2, 8, 12, to 14, 16, 17, 21
Badháu ...	H	11	9, 21, 47, 48
	S	30	12
	M	2	5
Badhánia ...	H	140	8
Bádhian ...	H	25	4
Badhmániá ...	H	67	9
Badho ...	M	34	13
Badhwán ...	H	42	9
	M	5	3
Badiál ...	H	103	9
	M	9	9
Badmár ...	M	22	48
Bado ...	H	33	39
	M	2	27
Badobá ...	H	150	8
Badoli ...	H	2	12
	M	43	8, 19, 24
Badrál ...	H	13	8
	M	3	8
Badri ...	H	5	14
	M	35	1
Badwál ...	H	28	1
Bagaliá ...	H	11	51
Bagam ...	H	12	48
Bagarwál ...	H	413	8
Bagáwat ...	H	36	1
Bage ...	H	62	9, 11
	S	3	49
	M	7	1, 12
Baghiál ...	H	278	6, 8, 15, 44
	S	16	15
	M	1,015	16, 21, 25
Baghla ...	M	926	24, 25
Bagota ...	H	15	9
Bagotre ...	H	84	8, 9
Bágri ...	H	355	2, 3, 8, 25, 27, 49
	S	1	15
	M	15	5
Baháli ...	H	982	2, 4, 9, 12, 14, 21
	M	74	3, 21
Báhán ...	H	1	9
	M	12	19
Báhdar ...	M	47	13
Bahir ...	H	8	12
	M	11	13
Bahlim ...	M	262	8, 15, 20, 45, 48
Bains ...	H	65	2, 4, 5
	S	1	50
	M	590	5, 21
Bairági ...	H	160	1, 39
Bajalwán ...	H	60	47
Bajori ...	M	25	16
Bajrotiá ...	H	70	8
Báju ...	H	945	16
	M	137	16
Bájwe ...	H	26	50
	M	13	13
Bakhár ...	H	4	48
	M	173	14, 48
Bakhiál ...	M	238	21
Bákhri ...	H	105	15, 51
Bal ...	H	15	25
	S	7	18
	M	2	44
Balásar ...	H	26	7
	M	28	9
Baláwáh ...	H	81	8
Balgán ...	H	2	42
	M	16	8
Bali ...	H	20	13
	M	29	22
Baliál ...	H	32	8
Balkeshan ...	H	18	17
Baloriá ...	H	44	8, 15
Balotha ...	M	14	1
Baluri ...	H	83	47
Balwáná ...	H	13	12, 15, 43
Bámanbán ...	H	25	4
Bamnoriá ...	H	811	9
Banápar ...	H	72	48
Banbhas ...	H	59	8
	M	89	12
Bandár ...	H	105	8, 9
	M	8	9
Bandarhál ...	H	192	8
Bandhár ...	H	22	2
	M	5	13, 48
Bandhela ..	H	166	8, 48
	S	368	10
	M	3	48
Bandhir ...	H	115	8, 39
	S	4	19
Bando ...	H	31	9
...	M	7	1, 48
Bandure ...	M	62	14
Báng ...	H	61	8, 16
	M	2	48
Bángal ...	H	146	8, 9, 20, 42
Baugiál ...	H	48	9
	M	1302	18, 21
Bangore ...	H	46	9
Bangwái ...	H	26	9
Baniál ...	H	661	8, 9, 43
	M	61	16
Banj ...	M	503	6, 10, 14
Banjiál ...	H	108	9
Banjla ...	H	18	8
Banjori ...	H	105	9, 36
	S	1	48
Banore ...	H	72	2
Banoriá ...	H	131	4, 9, 25
Banot ...	H	109	8
Bansi ...	H	122	D. 12, 15, 19, 27
...	M	242	1, 20, 21, 27

Names of Sub-Castes.		Persons.	Locality.
Bansiál ...	H	43	6, 9, 41, 49
	M	5	6
Banwál ...	H	128	2, 15
Banwárá ...	H	64	13, 28
Barái ...	M	589	1
Barána ..	M	99	26
Barangwál ...	H	17	9
Barára ...	H	39	48
	M	45	48
Bargála ...	H	223	4
	M	136	4
Bargi ...	H	22	25, 44
Bargolá ...	H	14	9
Bargujar ...	H	4,307	D. 12, 31, 32, 48 to 50
	M	1,640	D. 13, 31, 48
Barhál ...	H	24	9, 27
	S	1	48
	M	16	22, 39, 48
Barhán ...	H	17	8
	M	9	25
Barhár ...	H	29	1, 12, 51
	S	450	10
Barhiál ...	H	299	8
Bariáh ...	H	673	5, 6, 8, 9, 44, 48, 50
	S	135	25, 48
	M	29,566	5, 6, 9 to 11, 15, 21, 25, 40, 42, 48
Bariál ...	H	592	8, 9, 27, 47
	M	716	8, 9, 11, 44
Bariár ...	H	13	9
Barjáná ...	H	31	8
Barjiá ...	H	5	4, 9
	M	15	48
Barnar ...	M	10	48
Barodiá ...	H	12	50
Baror ...	H	15	4, 9
	S	4	44
	M	56	27, 46
Bárota ...	H	16	44
	S	3	25
	M	27	20
Barsare ...	H	16	8
Barwál ...	H	88	1, 4, 8, 12, 15, 47
	S	80	15
	M	1	28
Barwála ...	M	22	9
Barwáná ...	M	39	26
Barwária ...	H	34	8
Barzah ...	M	212	6
Baserá ...	H	73	39
Bashisht ...	H	54	6, 34, 47
Basí ...	M	799	16
Basrá ...	M	31	14
Baswál ...	H	240	8
Batáriá ...	H	46	8, 25, 44
Batoz ...	S	67	14
	M	4	6
Bath ...	H	264	8, 27
	S	9	16
	M	7	9, 46
Báti ...	H	9	15, 44
	M	661	21
Batiál ...	H	196	9, 15, 44
Batis ...	H	33	48
	M	33	48
Batla ...	H	7	6
	M	200	21
Bátu ...	H	47	48
Batwál ...	H	89	8, 9, 15, 47
	M	67	15
Bawá ...	M	84	2, 21
Bawáli ...	H	11	9
	S	2	7
Bawárá ...	H	88	8, 9, 17
Bawáriá ...	H	1,226	2, 9, 25, 44
	M	141	9, 20, 42
Bedáwat ...	H	82	1
Bedpár ...	H	19	9
Beká ...	H	63	1, 25
	S	1	24
Bekan ...	H	29	12
Bekanirab ...	M	12	2
Beldár ...	H	14	21
Berá ...	S	1	48
	M	16	6
Besh ...	H	33	6, 47
Bháhará ...	H	175	8
Bhabhuri ...	H	313	8
Bhadáni ...	M	50	20, 51
Bhadariá ...	M	152	1, 6
Bhadiár ..	H	882	8, 9
Bhádrán ...	H	17	4
Bhadwáli ...	H	282	8, 9, 15, 47, 48
Bhádwár ...	H	337	8
Bhaga ...	H	67	1, 2, 44
Bhágar ...	H	86	49
Bhagiál ...	M	950	21
Bhágirath ...	H	75	20, 25, 27
	M	28	3
Bhagoriá ...	H	53	8, 44
	S	1	9
	M	26	10
Bhagotrí ...	H	56	8
Bhagrál ...	M	63	18
Bhágri ...	H	7	48
	S	5	48
	M	9	48
Bhágsar ...	H	19	7
Bhagwáli ...	H	190	15
Bhagwe ...	H	28	8
Bhái ...	H	49	12, 27, 49
	S	4	48
Bhains ...	H	29	11, 49
	M	112	20
Bhajiáná ...	M	238	24, 27
Bhajwán ...	H	16	47
Bhakrál ...	H	2	15, 41
	S	1	23
	M	6,626	20 to 23, 51
Bhalán ...	H	25	21
Bhaláníáh ...	H	29	8
Bhalo ...	H	526	2, 4, 44
	S	1	25
	M	3	48
Bhalwál ...	H	43	8, 9, 47
Bhalwán ...	H	461	8, 47, 48
Bhalwat ...	H	196	16
Bhamal ...	H	23	47
Bhamnotre ...	H	60	15
Bhandál ...	H	6	9, 10
	S	122	9, 12
Bhandáwal ...	H	12	27, 42
Bhandiái ...	H	13	8
Bhaneki ...	H	9	1
	M	38	1
Bhangi ...	H	32	7
Bhango ...	H	15	8, 9
	M	163	15, 18
Bhangore ...	H	25	9
Bháni ...	H	19	9
Bhaniál ...	M	54	16
Bhanmoiá ...	H	130	9
Bhanori ...	H	100	8
Bhanot ...	H	1,015	8, 9
	S	24	7
	M	58	24
Bháo ...	H	4	20
	M	706	15
Bhar ...	H	25	25, 27, 44
	S	1	19
Bhará ...	M	341	5, 15, 20
Bhárag ...	H	20	8, 9
Bhárat-sharmá	H	13	48
Bharáwat ...	H	5	2
	M	23	27
Bhardhor ...	H	47	47
Bhárdwáj ...	H	1,373	D. except (3), 9, 13 to 15, 19 25, 27, 34 to 39, 41, 42, 44, 47 to 50
	S	22	7, 14, 15
	M	97	24, 25
Bhare ...	H	96	8
Bharol ...	H	122	2, 7, 9, 39
Bharorath ...	H	59	8
Bharath ...	H	87	21
	M	80	18
Bharwál ...	H	10	8, 27, 44
	M	18	24
Bhatániá ...	H	109	9, 10, 47
Bhater ...	H	93	8, 47
Bháti ...	H	1	44
	M	20	1
Bhátiá ...	H	1,593	L. 12, 18, 19, 24 to 28, 51
	S	71	15, 17, 18, 20, 25
	M	1,913	1, 25, 27, 51
Bhatiárá ...	H	31	1, 10, 15, 44, 46, 47
	S	5	25
Bhatnagar ...	H	8	48
	S	15	4
Bhatnotre ...	H	41	8
Bhátre ...	H	18	8
Bhatti ...	H	2,413	D. J. L. M. except (24), 30, 31, 48 to 51
	S	598	4, 5, 10, 12 to 16, 25, 44, 48, 50
	M	319,860	B. 33, 34, 39 to 42, 44, 45, 47 to 51
Bhatti-Bariál	M	488	12, 44
Bhatti-Bharoli	M	50	24
Bhatti-Faqir	M	13	22
Bhatti-Jat ...	M	851	24
Bhattiwál ...	H	104	1, 2, 4
	M	3	1
Bhawán ...	H	10	11
	M	38	2
Bhawárá ...	H	1	48
	M	21	48
Bhes ...	M	44	4
Bhil ...	H	52	51
Bhindar ...	H	52	9, 12, 15
Bhobariá ...	H	76	8
Bhoi ...	H	29	8, 21
Bholá ...	H	16	8, 15
Bholar ...	H	28	8
	M	2	29
Bhon ..	M	133	26
Bhoriá ...	H	181	2, 9, 37, 39, 42, 44
Bhosan ...	M	108	24
Bhot ...	H	27	10, 29, 51
Bhota ...	M	232	16, 19, 27
Bhotán ...	M	89	24
Bhotia ...	H	12	14
	M	13	6, 26
Bhuri ...	S	306	10
Bhuttan ...	M	311	27
Biál ...	H	63	9, 10, 44
	M	2	24
Biás ...	H	25	2
	M	136	18
Biloch ...	H	132	8, 39, 42
	M	16	1, 2, 44
Bimbi ...	H	39	48
Birgohar ...	M	24	9
Bishan ...	S	14	7, 25
Bobriá ...	H	15	11
Bohán ...	H	33	6
	M	26	10, 51
Bolá ...	M	12	49
Bomi ...	H	4	8, 9
	M	397	1, 19
Bopár ...	H	5	9
	M	11	9
Borá ...	H	78	10, 12, 13
	M	204	1, 2, 19, 48
Buch ...	H	14	9
Chabrá ...	H	13	8, 9
Chachar ...	M	481	19
Chachkáná ...	M	50	26, 27
Chadde .	M	15	16
Chaddbar ...	H	13	12
	M	8,628	19, 20, 25, 26, 51
Chábal ...	H	76	1, 11, 50, 51
	M	141	1, 48
Cháhan ...	H	339	1, 38, 41
	S	5	9
Chaji ...	M	16	12, 44
Chakar ...	H	5	1
	M	10	18, 48
Chakoká ...	M	44	12
Chamáde ...	H	59	8

Names of Sub-Castes.		Persons.	Locality.
Chambiál ...	H	35	34, 47
Chamiál ...	H	309	10, 15, 27, 47
	S	6	10
Chanau ...	H	8	48
	M	59	25, 48
Chánar ...	M	28	27, 51
Chand ...	H	1,311	8, 42
	S	1	4
	M	1	9
Chandá ...	M	112	1
Chandar ...	H	62	7, 37, 42
	M	113	6
Chandarbansi	H	479	1, 2, 4, 6, 7, 10 to 12, 15, 17, 34 to 37, 40 to 42, 44, 47, 48
	S	8	6
	M	24	4, 48
Chánde ..	H	33	5, 14, 17, 25, 42, 50
	S	5	15
	M	425	9, 13, 19, 24, 50
Chandel ...	H	806	6, 9, 10, 25, 37, 42, 43, 48, 50
	S	10	6, 50
	M	175	27, 43, 48
Chander ...	H	31	8, 11, 42
	S	1	25
	M	21	12
Chandbál ...	H	15	15
Chándi ...	H	12	10, 25
Chándiá ...	H	12	13
Chándil ...	H	321	15, 34, 40, 44
	S	29	5, 40
	M	521	1, 5, 6, 10, 47
Chándlá ...	H	1,093	8, 9, 29, 38 to 40, 42
	S	54	9
	M	74	9, 12, 15, 39
Chandmál ...	M	237	15
Chandpuriá ...	H	191	9
Chandrán ...	H	27	44, 47
	M	9	27
Cháng ...	H	17	9, 13, 15, 26
	S	2	26
Changar ...	H	7	8
	M	139	11, 12, 27
Chángare ...	H	390	1, 6, 8, 9
Chángle ...	H	22	8
Chaniál ...	H	28	15
Chaniár ...	M	44	25
Chanjotha ...	H	32	9
Chánle ...	H	24	48
	M	1	48
Chanoria ...	H	1,019	8, 9, 20
	M	53	12
Chanota ...	H	12	8
Chanotare ...	H	37	8
Chap ...	H	5	25
	S	3	14
	M	3	14
Chárak ...	H	475	8, 9, 15, 16, 47
	S	8	18
	M	232	9, 16
Cháran ...	H	407	1, 51
Chastánf ...	M	230	27
Chatiál ...	H	36	9, 27
Chatoria ...	H	11	47
	M	6	9, 11
Chátre ...	H	439	4, 8
	S	21	14, 18
	M	2	26
Chatroniá ...	H	35	47
Chattha ...	M	582	1, 21
Chawái ...	H	94	15, 25, 44
	S	1	25
	M	2	11
Cháwalá ...	H	8	40, 48
	S	2	48
	M	45	13
Chela ...	M	58	26, 45
Chhabale ...	M	12	25
Chhagrayál ...	H	11	8
Chharitio ...	H	84	8
Chhatri ...	H	95	8, 10, 44
	S	64	8, 20
	M	21	20, 21
Chháwant ...	M	13	3
Chhená ...	H	2	8
	M	289	19
Chhokar ...	H	101	2, 5, 11
	M	14	5, 9
Chhotre ...	S	14	9
Chib ...	H	893	8, 9, 15 to 18, 20, 27
	S	3	14, 27
	M	10,805	18 to 22, 25 to 27
Chíma ...	M	107	20
Chinán ..	M	84	1, 25
Chishti ...	M	40	12, 49
Chogattá ...	M	796	1, 12, 15, 18, 19, 20, 23, 24, 26, 27, 29, 51
Chohán ...	H	49,768	P
	S	2,046	P
	M	71,192	P
Cholar ...	H	98	9
Choukar ...	H	548	3, 13, 48
	M	74	3
Chotiá ...	H	4	9
	M	69	1, 26
Chotwál ...	H	81	15
Dabáh ...	H	49	14
	S	1	14
	M	151	12, 26
Dabgí ...	M	38	11
Dádi ...	H	64	9, 11
	M	8	20, 25
Dadwál ...	H	5,774	6, 8, 9, 12, 15, 17, 27, 33
	S	21	9, 15, 25
	M	343	1, 9, 15, 27
Dadwáná ...	H	33	42
	M	78	26, 27
Dáhá ...	M	992	12, 27
Dábar ...	H	3	25
	M	81	1, 12, 18, 48
Dahariás ...	H	8	2
	M	81	17
Dáhi ...	M	379	6, 9
Dáhko ...	M	93	13
Dahwál ...	H	17	10
	M	10	16
Dakhar ..	H	9	15
	M	174	24
Dalá ...	M	55	9, 12, 14, 16, 46
Dalál ...	H	204	4
	M	210	13, 20, 21
Dalalre ...	H	56	9
Daliál ...	H	53	15, 25
	M	7	12
Dálotri ..	H	17	9
Dalpiá ...	M	57	25
Daln ..	S	1	48
	M	30	28
Dalwál ...	H	254	8
	M	3	16
Dalwári ...	H	46	15
Damans ...	H	15	48
Dáná ...	H	672	1, 9, 25
	S	5	27
	M	15	16
Dandan ...	M	42	10, 14
Dandi ...	M	16	17
Dandwál ..	H	85	4, 9, 12, 14, 47
	S	1	9
	M	3	13, 46
Daneri ...	M	193	4
Dangoi ...	H	81	9, 21
	S	2	14
	M	25	1, 9
Dangoliá ...	H	82	8, 9
	M	8	12
Dár ...	H	11	9
	S	2	14
	M	9	13
Darbar ...	H	249	9
Dargáhi ...	M	34	18
Dariál ..	H	14	8, 12
	M	5	15, 21
Darián ...	H	47	43
Dariá-Siál ...	M	159	18, 24
Dariyáh ...	H	133	9, 12
	S	1	14
	M	203	9, 10, 18, 24
Darnage ...	M	432	10
Darob ...	H	8	1
	M	19	1
Daroch ...	M	38	8
Dárogá ...	H	28	1, 25
Darwál ...	H	129	8, 19, 51
Darzi ...	M	34	14, 15, 25
Dasar ...	H	8	25, 42, 44
	S	6	10
	M	11	13
Daswat ...	H	166	1, 2, 4
Datáná ...	H	28	1
	M	15	3
Datiál ...	H	91	8
	M	7	25
Datowál ...	H	35	39
Daulat ...	H	16	1
Dawáná ...	H	119	16
	M	431	16, 27
Debi ...	H	3	10, 42
	S	1	15
	M	40	1, 5, 25
Deorá ...	M	109	9, 13, 16
Deota ...	M	191	15
Dermán ...	H	19	50
Derwál ...	H	141	9, 21
Desi ...	H	14	4, 5
	M	43	15, 22
Detá ...	M	115	10, 25
Dewal ...	H	23	4, 7, 39
	S	1	26
	M	26	4, 20, 25
Dewar ...	H	105	1, 8, 41, 44
	S	4	12
	M	24	46
Dewas	H	29	6, 9, 41
Dewat ...	H	1	10
	M	14	1, 12, 19
Dhád ..	M	108	12
Dhádi ...	M	191	13, 14
Dhadiál ...	H	1,495	8, 14, 16, 25, 42
	S	16	18
	M	2	14, 22
Dhagi ..	H	23	15
	M	2	11
Dhaiwal ...	S	21	12
Dháli ...	H	70	8, 9, 12, 19, 24
	S	48	4, 11
	M	27	15, 44
Dhalwál ...	H	798	8
Dhamán ...	M	21	48
Dhamiál ...	H	1,936	3, 8, 47
	M	8,084	18, 20, 21, 22
Dhamriál ...	H	79	15, 47
	M	2	15
Dhamtiál ...	H	214	8
Dhamyáwál ...	M	42	25
Dhandá ...	M	87	12
Dhándi ...	H	54	8
	M	867	12, 24
Dhándiál ...	H	38	1, 51
Dhandwál ...	H	110	8, 15, 42
	S	1	9
Dhanetta ...	H	20	27, 50
	M	17	50
Dhani ...	H	112	10, 16, 48
	S	71	13, 14, 44
	M	65	9, 14
Dhaniál ...	H	131	6, 8, 9, 12
	S	1	14
	M	6,659	4, 20, 21, 24
Dhanpál ..	H	24	8
Dhans ...	H	24	5, 42
	M	89	15, 18
Dhanwár ...	H	14	50
Dhar ...	H	19	48
	M	1	11
Dharáná ...	H	8	4
	S	2	25
	M	48	25
Dhariál ...	H	83	8
	M	11	24
Dháriwál ...	H	747	8, 17
	S	40	12
	M	14	13, 24
Dharmán ...	H	110	4, 9, 14
	M	127	24
Dharsi ...	M	453	21

SUB-CASTES OF CERTAIN SELECTED CASTES—*continued.*

Names of Sub-Castes.		Persons.	Locality.
Dhart	H	26	6, 8
Dharwál	H	701	8, 10, 19, 27
Dharyáne	H	109	42
Dhatwál	H	28	8, 15
Dhawál	H	42	8, 24, 43
Dhawan	M	439	20
Dher	H	1	13
	S	10	16
	M	5	27
Dhiá	H	1,335	5, 6, 33
	S	114	6, 25
	M	3,259	6, 9, 1 , 25, 33, 44
Dhillon	S	9	12
	M	391	12, 24, 48, 51
Dhímrái	M	105	13
Dhodála	M	55	1
Dholan	M	15	27
Dhond	M	454	9, 12, 19, 20, 21, 22, 25
Dhonikal	H	44	8, 12
Dhori	H	31	8, 18
	M	289	17, 19
Dhudhi	H	7	13
	M	5,802	12
Dhul	H	62	9
	M	458	12, 19
Diá	H	51	1, 8, 10, 24
	M	19	1, 12, 25
Diál	H	120	9, 39
	M	252	8, 14, 16, 20
Dingar	S	34	14
	M	6	9
Diriá	H	7	48
	M	16	48
Dod	H	916	2 to 6, 8 to 10, 15, 25, 29, 39, 44, 48
	S	11	11, 48
	M	53	9, 11, 27
Dodál	H	658	8, 9, 25, 39
	M	4	13, 48
Dodwál	H	501	8, 11, 14
	M	11	6
Dogalí	H	10	42
	M	23	13
Dogar	H	212	3, 4, 13, 14, 17, 19, 21, 22, 26, 27, 41, 46
	S	76	14, 17, 24, 25
	M	1,511	1, 12, 17, 21, 24, 25
Dogra	H	231	6, 8, 16, 18, 20, 21, 24, 27, 39
	S	14	13, 18, 23, 27
	M	346	13, 16, 21, 27, 47
Dogri	H	176	8, 13, 42, 46
	S	21	14
	M	11	17
Dohán	H	25	16, 18, 27
	M	56	13, 25
Doiá	H	42	48
	S	8	48
	M	357	48
Dokat	M	250	13
Dolí	H	56	39
	S	1	9
	M	2	10
Dond	H	567	9
	M	120	24
Dondal	M	8,843	21
Donsiál	M	82	26
Dor	H	23	8
	S	10	24
Dotal	H	8	1
	M	16	1
Dukhore	M	80	8
Duriál	H	28	8
Fairon	M	34	17
Faqír	H	4	10
	S	1	25
	M	47	11, 14, 17, 25, 45
Firozi	M	15	1
Fonsi	H	28	48
Gaddi-Rajput	H	18	8
Gadewak	M	24	20
Gádi	H	3	42
	M	95	51
Gadwáre	H	15	28
Gágaliá	H	50	10
Gagar	M	52	1, 17, 20
Gagi	H	18	11
	S	3	25
	M	8	8, 12, 18, 20
Gagotre	H	103	15
Gágre	H	25	44
	M	6	8, 15
Gahlot	H	607	4 to 6, 21, 48 to 50
	S	7	4, 48
	M	501	1, 3, 5, 48
Gahlotú	H	10	32
	M	10	13, 32
Gajrál	M	66	21
Gakhar	H	96	15, 16, 25
	S	7	13, 14, 19
	M	1,812	L. 4, 6, 8, 10 to 12, 20, 22, 27, 47, 51
Galere	H	468	8, 10, 14 to 16, 26, 44
Galgal	M	15	48
Galgat	H	50	4
	M	35	11, 12
Gali	H	67	9, 11
Galoiá	H	24	6, 10
Galori	H	16	47
	M	1	8
Galotra	H	1	13
	M	64	17, 26
Galsái	H	14	12
Gamrure	M	13	18
Ganáth	H	33	14
Gandál	H	21	14, 42, 48
	S	3	14
	M	337	13, 17, 21
Gandar	H	71	15, 19, 21
	S	2	15
	M	10	14
Gandáriá	H	11	16
	M	1	15
Ganesh	M	36	34
Gangi	H	3	13, 25
	M	42	13
Gangotrá	H	67	9, 16
Ganjiál	M	278	21
Garáin	H	71	14, 47
Gardál	H	190	8
	S	2	12
Gáre	H	165	14, 15, 25, 41
	M	89	10, 21, 49, 50
Garemá	H	12	6
Garg	H	153	9, 12, 15, 21, 34, 51
Garhál	H	164	8, 21, 37
	S	8	12, 18
	M	166	21
Gariál	H	489	4, 8, 14, 41
	S	5	15, 48
	M	849	20, 21, 48
Gárli	H	25	34
	M	1	45
Gaur	H	2,177	1 to 5, 11, 20, 31, 32, 48, 49
	S	44	48
	M	270	46, 48, 49
Gauria	H	54	1, 15, 47, 48
	M	31	48
Gaurwá	H	3,346	3, 12
	M	1,740	3, 18, 26
Gawálbans	H	45	2, 4, 5, 12, 16
Gawáli	H	48	14, 44, 51
Gawár	H	1	3
	M	61	10, 12
Ghagar	H	2	6
	M	10	24
Ghaloriá	H	72	2, 8
Ghalot	H	399	2, 3, 5, 8, 51
	S	1	33
	M	274	2, 6, 25
Ghaman	M	15	16, 28
Ghamiá	H	117	42
Ghamrál	H	24	15
Ghangar	M	1,022	21
Ghantiá	M	12	16, 24
Ghanwán	M	210	10, 24
Ghare	H	192	9, 27
	S	6	11
	M	182	11
Ghariál	H	162	5, 8, 39
	M	11	12
Ghartwál	H	98	14, 42
	M	33	12
Gharwál	H	241	8, 21, 41, 48
	S	116	48
	M	1,778	7, 12, 15, 21, 34, 48
Ghatiál	H	10	8, 15
	S	3	12
Ghemarpuriá	H	119	8
Ghilána	H	25	8
	M	14	22, 26
Ghol	H	52	5, 9
	M	48	5
Ghonan	H	22	8
	M	100	17, 51
Ghor	H	15	13, 20, 27
	M	21	18
Ghorcharhe	M	11	14, 48
Ghorewáh	H	2,583	5, 6, 8 to 11, 15, 19, 41, 50
	S	52	9, 10, 12, 13, 40
	M	12,343	J. 1, 3, 6, 13, 14, 19, 20, 24, 25, 29, 33, 37, 40, 42, 44 to 46, 49, 50
Ghori	H	52	24, 39, 42
	M	147	1, 6, 25, 42, 44
Ghorpurá	H	152	6
Ghorwál	H	10	14, 17
	S	2	13
	M	4	26
Ghot	H	68	12, 15
	M	9	25
Ghotar	H	347	14, 15
	M	41	6
Ghowál	H	3	25
	M	23	22
Giárú	H	127	8, 44
	M	311	27
Gil	H	37	12, 14
	S	13	14
	M	145	12, 14, 21, 27
Gobrá	S	1	48
	M	86	48
Godárá	H	2	25
	M	128	1
Godatyá	H	134	8, 27
Godhá	H	238	8, 15, 29
	S	1	10
	M	37	11, 13, 22
Godháre	H	2	4
	M	68	9
Godlá	H	84	8, 47
	M	3	14
Gogáu	H	10	8
	S	4	25
	M	26	23, 26
Gogar	H	187	8, 11, 41, 48
	M	17	8, 9, 34
Gohal	H	34	7, 14
	M	1	10
Gohána	H	81	8, 44
	M	47	13, 24
Gohrá	H	169	8, 16
	S	4	19, 21
	M	178	16, 20, 25
Goi	H	55	8, 14
Gojarwál	M	79	20, 21
Gol	H	34	8, 15, 19
	M	173	7, 17, 21, 24
Golairi	H	190	6, 19, 42
Goleriá	H	2,904	8, 9, 12, 15, 42, 43, 45, 47
	S	1	21
	M	85	16, 19, 48
Gomráhiá	S	9	12
	M	26	14
Gondal	H	232	13, 14, 39, 48
	S	2	10
	M	484	1, 6, 12, 17, 19, 24, 25, 26

Names of Sub-Castes.		Persons.	Locality.
Gondárá ...	H	5	5, 14
	M	26	12
Gondi ...	H	32	5, 9, 19, 24, 48
	S	22	13, 21, 48
	M	19	1, 15, 16
Gorái ...	M	26	12, 13, 42, 47
Goráié ...	H	57	1, 8
	M	269	3, 4, 8
Goráng ...	H	66	8, 34, 47
Gorchal ...	H	196	8, 25
Gori ...	H	14	2, 12, 17, 25, 44
	S	4	21
	M	375	1, 8, 10, 18, 25, 46
Gorie ...	H	13	8, 14
	M	16	9, 10, 14
Gosáin ...	H	20	13, 14
Gosar ...	H	86	4
	M	1	12
Got ...	H	9	1
	M	128	1, 5, 23, 37
Gotam ...	H	121	7, 8, 50
	S	11	50
Gowáre ...	M	962	21
Gugráné ...	M	79	25, 27
Gujar ...	H	23	4, 12, 14
	S	1	14
	M	96	1, 10 to 13, 20, 27
Gurábá ...	H	5	8, 47
	M	23	8, 11, 17
Gurkhá ...	H	221	7, 8, 13, 21, 39, 41, 42
	S	1	48
	M	18	21, 28, 40
Hábun ...	H	151	8
	S	4	16
Hádi ...	H	2	8, 48
	M	15	5
Hadiál ...	H	169	5, 9, 27
Hadwál ...	H	237	8
Hajaúhá ...	M	125	26
Hajauli ...	H	15	8
Hajráe ...	M	208	1, 12, 19, 24
Halárie ...	M	715	16
Hálú ...	H	1	25
	M	14	12
Hamidkháni	M	12	2
Handál ...	H	31	8, 15, 25
	M	12	21
Handiár ...	H	169	4, 8, 19
Handoli ...	H	30	10, 51
	M	3	25
Hanjoiá ...	M	134	1, 17, 21
Háns ...	H	34	4, 8, 10
	M	799	1, 12, 14, 15, 24, 27, 46, 48
Hansi ...	H	13	13, 27
	M	8	11, 28
Hansráj ...	H	49	4, 8, 48
	M	52	19, 25
Haráj ...	S	20	10
	M	71	14, 24, 26, 27
Haráni ...	M	18	46
Harar ...	M	79	13, 16
Harchand ...	H	1593	8, 15, 25, 47
	M	200	9, 14, 15
Hargan ...	H	23	8, 48
	M	291	17, 19
Hari ...	H	311	4, 8, 9, 15
	S	1	48
	M	447	24, 25, 26
Hariál ...	H	7	8, 48
	M	23	13, 21
Harmi ...	H	13	48
	M	67	13, 25
Harsarié ...	H	160	8
	M	18	14
Hasiná ...	H	50	8
	M	6	8, 13, 20
Hastiál ...	H	50	8
	M	101	21, 27
Hotárié ...	H	41	8, 14, 42
	M	276	19
Hatgala ...	M	38	1
Hati ...	H	84	8
	M	9	11, 45
Hatiál ...	H	7	43
	M	38	10, 21
Hawál ...	H	8	7, 8, 25
	M	3	27
Hazári ...	H	15	8, 13
	M	12	9, 29
Haziál ...	H	2	13
	M	9	10, 13, 22
Hejar ...	H	7	48
	M	71	25, 48
Herwál ...	H	18	4, 17
	M	1	25
Hidan ...	M	55	19
Hinjrá ...	M	16	12, 25
Hir ...	H	3	14
	S	23	12, 46
	M	14	13, 14, 51
Hon ...	M	958	21, 22, 27
Hot ...	H	4	5
	M	126	19
Indorié ...	H	1,822	6, 8, 9, 12, 15
	M	87	51
Jabdál ...	H	1	18
	S	13	46
	M	50	13, 20
Jabhána ...	M	73	9, 18, 26
Jabotre ...	H	114	8
Jabrá ...	M	727	11, 15, 16
Jabwál ...	H	6	30
	S	1	26
	M	4	22
Jadái ...	H	32	11
Jadam ...	H	20	4
	S	10	48
	M	3	48
Jadár ...	S	31	11
	M	12	9, 15
Jaddi ...	H	86	4
Jadhra ...	H	12	1
	M	4	14
Jádu ...	H	14,023	1 to 3, 8, 12, 13, 31, 34, 49
	S	47	5
	M	431	1, 3, 16
Jáe ...	M	18	9, 13
Jagal ...	H	15	47
Jagaryá ...	S	14	44
	M	175	21
Jagatre ...	H	204	8
Jagawat ...	H	8	27
	S	2	48
	M	35	23
Jaggi ...	H	665	15, 42
	M	2	15
Jaghara ...	M	16	26
Jagrál ...	H	16	11, 19
	M	83	9, 12, 21
Jágram ...	H	268	9
Jagta ...	H	11	48
Jáhank ...	H	119	18
Jaidharma ...	M	100	13
Jaijatra ...	M	86	45
Jaikarié ...	H	20	13
Jain ...	H	4	46
	M	875	10, 13
Jaipál ...	H	24	2, 47
	M	7	19
Jajié ..	H	7	14
	M	514	19
Jajohán ...	H	2	9, 25
	M	346	9, 25, 27, 29
Jajori ...	H	19	9
	M	1	28
Jajotar ...	H	541	8, 9, 15
	M	8	9
Jajoti ...	M	12	14
Jajuká ...	H	9	27, 44
	S	2	44
Jajuwán ...	H	7	27
	M	20	9
Jákarié ...	H	22	50
Jakrán ...	M	16	1, 25
Jalál ...	H	16	12, 24
	M	68	25, 48
Jálap ..	H	4	10
	M	10	18, 25
Jalárié ...	H	42	9, 15, 42
	M	39	13, 24
Jale ...	M	18	48
Jaloke ...	M	78	5, 24, 25
Jalphuchar ...	H	13	27
Jam ...	M	11	15, 27
Jamarwál ...	H	168	8, 25
Jamiál ...	H	92	8, 15
	M	9	10
Jamlolié ...	H	113	8
	S	4	11
Jammún ...	M	56	1, 12, 51
Jamrál ...	H	7	9
	M	248	18, 48
Jamunwál ...	H	23	12, 41, 42, 44
	M	5	13
Jamwái ...	H	24	7, 8
Jamwál ...	H	1,122	8, 9, 15 to 17, 39, 42, 47
	S	85	13, 15, 17, 23
	M	46	8, 16, 25
Jáná ...	H	2	12
	M	12	25
Janál ...	H	30	1, 21
	M	51	13, 25, 27
Janáli ...	M	84	51
Jandal ...	H	34	2
	S	4	48
	M	63	12, 48
Jándansi ...	M	30	12
Jander ...	H	8	10
	S	2	10
	M	3	12
Jandhe ...	H	5	10
	M	25	11
Jándi ...	H	29	5, 10
	S	23	18
	M	97	15, 16, 48
Jandiál ...	H	16	9, 48
Jandiáli ...	H	2	9
	M	31	25
Jandil ...	H	1	9
	S	1	9
	M	59	20, 24
Jandiwálé ...	H	12	1
	M	551	24
Jandu ...	H	92	4
	M	834	11, 51
Jangié ...	H	384	3, 42
Jangliál ...	H	103	8
	M	1	15
Jángrá ...	H	148	3, 8, 9, 42
	M	3	25
Jángri ...	H	126	8
Janié ...	H	113	8
	S	1	5
	M	68	10
Janira ...	M	399	26, 27, 29
Janjali ...	H	46	9
	M	871	19
Janjoti ...	H	38	9, 14, 29
	S	2	14
	M	88	9, 11, 12
Janjuá ...	H	2,518	9, 11, 12, 20, 24, 44
	S	30	18, 19
	M	21,284	R. 1, 6, 12, 13, 16, 17, 24, 25, 27, 48, 51
Janjwál ...	H	1	15
	M	35	10
Janohán ...	M	79	11, 25
Janobe ...	M	58	15
Janoi ...	M	258	14, 15
Janooh ...	M	285	11, 25, 44
Janothi ...	H	9	14
	M	82	48
Janwár ...	H	13	4
	S	1	11
Japángi ...	M	131	16
Járáh ...	H	2	15
	S	3	14
	M	51	19
Jarál ...	H	291	8, 9, 15, 42
	S	8	12, 16, 51
	M	218	15, 18, 21, 25
Jarálá ...	H	992	9, 14

Names of Sub-Castes.		Persons.	Locality.
Jaráwat ...	H	181	8, 19
Jarhál ...	H	25	16
	M	31	15
Jari ...	H	19	8, 11, 15
	M	8	13, 15, 25
Jariál ...	H	1,840	9, 14, 17, 47
	M	80	8, 16
Jarián ...	H	179	27, 47
	M	1	15
Jaroti ...	H	752	8, 11, 47
	M	13	15
Jasal ...	H	42	9, 30
	S	1	25
	M	4	49
Jasanwál ...	H	445	9, 13
Jasgám ...	M	200	18, 20
Jasiál ...	H	16	8
	M	5	12, 15
Jasoti ...	H	16	8, 44
Jaspál ...	H	26	8, 9, 42, 48
	S	5	9, 10, 15
	M	126	6, 18
Jasrál ...	H	9	13
	M	28	13, 18, 20
Jasráti ...	H	279	8, 13, 20
	S	2	15
	M	1	19
Jasre ...	H	10	8, 44
	M	16	15
Jasrotiá ...	H	235	8, 9, 15, 16, 19, 42, 47
Jaswál ...	H	6,240	1, 5, 8, 13, 15, 18 to 20, 24, 25, 27, 39, 42, 44, 47, 48
	S	337	10, 15, 16, 19, 25, 43
	M	1,890	4, 9, 10, 13 to 15, 18, 20, 25
Jaswálie ...	H	65	8, 9
	M	33	13, 29
Jat ...	H	118	8, 12, 17, 20, 21, 51
	S	5	14
	M	277	7, 13, 14, 19, 21, 27, 29
Jatál ...	H	8	5
	M	2,498	11, 17, 21, 41
Jatáná ...	H	27	5, 24
	S	1	51
	M	60	1, 26
Jatárá ...	S	1	10
	M	148	9, 20, 29
Játie ...	H	4	9
	M	98	8, 12
Játu ...	H	7,237	1, 2, 4, 5, 12, 30 to 32, 47 to 50
	S	9	12, 48
	M	14,442	1, 2, 4 to 6, 20, 25, 31, 32, 48 to 50
Jaurá ...	H	31	1
Jawán ...	H	31	15, 25, 44
	M	579	12, 14, 20
Jewáti ...	M	105	12
Jhaggar ...	M	133	1, 10, 12, 17, 21
Jhagrán ...	M	12	14
Jhakhál ...	H	628	3
Jhakhar ...	H	11	2, 44
	M	350	24, 25, 51
Jhalobi ...	H	138	8
Jhammat ...	H	34	43
	M	3,483	16, 19, 20, 24
Jháná ...	H	7	9, 24
	M	28	20
Jhandu ...	H	9	12, 24, 39
	M	279	1, 12, 13
Jháng ...	H	9	5, 11, 24, 25
	S	3	14
	M	9	13
Jhangar ...	H	18	1, 4, 9, 15, 39
	M	84	13, 25, 26, 28
Jhangi ...	H	9	10, 18
	M	17	13, 31
Jhawál ...	H	35	8
Jhawán ...	H	14	5
	M	37	12
Jhinwar ...	H	27	8
Jhol ...	H	27	8, 9
Jhonna ...	M	36	12, 13
Jhote ...	H	33	9
	M	4	45
Jiná ...	M	824	13, 20, 24
Jiwál ...	H	9	4
	M	8	12, 13, 15
Jiwár ...	S	1	13
	M	128	13, 16, 17
Jiwári ...	H	30	8
Jodhará ...	H	39	1, 5, 15, 17
	S	14	14, 17
	M	8,821	1, 20, 22, 27
Jogi ...	H	10	2, 15, 51
	M	16	8, 13
Johán ...	H	2	9
	M	148	13, 15, 22
Johar ...	H	128	31
	M	1,011	20
Johi ...	H	6	6
	M	66	15, 25
Joiá ...	H	50	1, 8, 27, 28, 51
	M	87,194	1, 5, 9, 11, 12, 14 to 17, 25 to 27, 29, 46, 51
Jokhá ...	M	24	27
Jonál ...	S	2	16
	M	77	16, 27
Joniá ...	H	6	9, 15
	M	307	12, 13, 21
Jotá ...	H	10	10, 24
	M	667	9, 12, 26, 27, 29
Jotiá ...	H	11	9, 47
	M	70	5, 8, 9
Kabál ...	H	3	5, 24, 41
	M	14	12, 21
Kacháni ...	M	180	19
Kachaurí ...	H	107	1, 14, 48
	M	36	11, 48
Kachauri Kaiála	H	1	15
	M	20	3
Kachchí ...	H	116	1, 20
	M	29	18
Kachhwái ...	H	718	1, 4, 5, 12, 30 to 32, 49
	S	1	12
	M	314	1, 2, 5, 13
Kachwál ...	H	9	12
	M	2	22
Kachwárá ...	H	35	4, 10, 12
	S	1	12
Kadhál ...	H	7	9
	M	13	9
Kahál ...	H	9	10, 15, 19, 27
	M	67	15, 16
Káhalre ...	H	187	8
Kaharwáns ...	H	4	13, 25
	M	64	12
Káhgar ...	M	15	16, 17
Kahí ...	M	47	13, 16
Kahsab ...	H	189	9, 15
Kahút ...	H	2	44
	M	527	15, 19, 20, 23
Káisth ...	H	110	13, 21
	S	10	13
	M	26	6, 10
Kajáwá ...	H	24	1, 3
Kájú ...	M	14	9
Kákar ...	H	18	9, 27
	S	8	19
	M	63	7, 12, 15, 21, 45
Kákariá ...	H	146	9, 15
	M	162	1, 12, 16
Kakohrí ...	H	99	9
Kákre ...	H	8	8
	M	151	12, 22, 51
Kálá ...	H	130	8, 21
	M	747	26
Kaláb ...	H	40	1, 34
	S	1	26
Kalál ...	H	28	9, 11, 12, 25
	S	4	27
	M	138	1, 12, 24, 25, 27
Kalálí ...	H	23	11, 24
Kalándrú ...	H	30	8
	M	1	28
Kálas ...	H	37	4, 9, 13, 27
	S	35	9, 17
	M	376	9, 12, 16, 19
Kaleriá ...	H	15	6
	M	13	1
Kaliál ...	M	5,084	19 to 22
Kálián ...	H	47	8, 12, 14
	M	408	13, 19
Kalísián ...	M	61	16, 22
Kalná ...	H	9	39
	M	6	25
Káloká ...	H	5	1
	M	399	1, 12, 25
Kaloriá ...	H	94	47
	M	22	12
Kalota ...	H	76	8, 9
Kalotrá ...	H	100	8, 15
	M	39	18, 25
Kálrú ...	M	17	19, 25
Kals ...	H	9	15
	M	12	12, 18
Kalsan ...	M	33	13
Kalsí ...	H	1	44
	S	3	14
	M	11	15
Kalsú ...	H	38	41
	S	6	15
Kálú ...	H	41	8
	M	918	19
Kalú Khokar	M	809	10
Kalwal ...	H	33	15
	M	14	10, 25
Kamál ...	M	80	19
Kamáwat ...	H	16	1, 8, 48
Kambo ...	H	6	5, 13, 17, 24
	M	83	13, 27
Kambori ...	H	31	5, 27
	M	1	51
Kamiál ...	H	13	13
	M	28	10, 25
Kamil ...	H	9	2, 9
	M	6	14
Kamlábiá ...	H	28	16
Kamli ...	H	42	8
Kanauj ...	M	22	9, 24
Kanchiá ...	H	20	39, 48
	S	1	12
Kandál ...	H	420	7, 12, 14, 27, 44
	S	4	44
	M	46	10, 15, 27
Kándar ...	H	5	11, 44
	M	7	12, 13
Kandel ...	H	283	1, 8, 9, 13, 40, 41
Kandi ...	H	23	9, 10, 25
	S	9	11, 13, 44
	M	5	13
Kandiál ...	H	19	50
Kandmalya ...	H	41	41
Kandodal ...	H	37	9
Kándwál ...	H	43	8, 10, 15
	M	1	19
Kanet ...	H	27	6, 8, 24
	S	5	33, 45
	M	13	10, 27
Kangar ...	H	48	8
	M	803	21, 25, 27
Kangi ...	H	4	4
	S	8	45
	M	6	13
Kangrá ...	H	39	1, 6, 8, 9, 30
	S	1	19
	M	360	10, 19, 22, 46
Kangwál ...	H	1	7
	M	72	25
Kaniál ...	H	27	8
	M	2,720	18, 19, 21, 22
Kaniáni ...	H	11	4
	M	1	13
Kánjú ...	M	274	1, 12, 19
Kankot ...	H	20	48
Kanojá ...	H	27	7, 13
	M	298	25
Kánoliá ...	H	17	50
	M	4	20, 21
Kánsi ...	H	6	7, 14
	S	2	12
	M	1	13
Kanthwál ...	H	24	4
	M	3	25
Kanwál ...	H	14	8, 13
	M	53	25

Names of Sub-Castes.		Persons.	Locality.
Kanwar ...	H	19	4
	M	128	17, 27
Kanwerá ...	H	147	7, 8
Kapiál ...	H	117	8, 9, 12
Kapúr ...	H	4	7, 9, 36
	M	16	12, 13, 20, 25
Karái ...	H	4	9
	M	21	10, 18
Karáliyá ...	H	11	48
Karáshi ...	M	46	13
Karáwál ...	H	9	9, 11, 15
	M	422	21
Karbalo ...	H	5	11
	M	12	48
Karban ...	H	18	48
Karohhi ...	M	256	15
Kardo ...	S	13	19
Káriá ...	H	6	9, 21
	M	5	16, 45, 51
Kariál ...	H	425	3, 9, 11, 40
	S	3	44
	M	178	10, 12, 20
Karl ...	S	4	15
	M	48	18
Karmor ...	M	384	11, 26
Karniá ...	H	35	42
Karol ...	H	16	11, 13, 25
	S	2	12
	M	438	3, 22
Karore ...	H	39	2, 9, 42
	M	65	1, 9, 10
Karpál ..	M	143	19, 20, 22
Kartiál ...	H	35	5, 11
Kartwála ...	H	13	42
Karwál ...	H	87	1, 5, 25
	S	1	48
	M	231	18, 20
Kas ...	H	106	9, 34
Kasar ...	M	15	12, 18, 19
Kásarke ...	M	80	19, 20, 21
Káshab ...	H	1,297	1, 2, 5, 6, 7, 8, 9, 10, 14, 19, 21, 44
	S	12	27, 39, 41, 42
	M	5	14, 16, 25
Káshabgotri...	H	42	12, 42
Kashatrí ...	H	83	2, 6, 8, 16
	S	4	16
Káshle ...	H	3	6
	S	1	9
	M	919	12, 24
Kashmírí ...	H	12	5, 10, 12
	M	293	14, 25, 27
Kashoriá ...	H	11	19, 21, 44
	M	33	21
Kasoár ...	H	171	8
Kaste ...	H	31	9, 16
Kastwál ...	H	52	9, 14, 16
Kaswál ...	S	81	9, 13
Kaswáre ...	H	22	8
	S	1	8
Katali ...	H	4	10
	S	1	25
	M	10	23
Katán ..	H	12	48
	S	1	45
	M	1	18
Katáni ...	H	29	8, 48
	M	19	10, 14
Katáriá ...	H	215	3, 9, 13
	S	7	44
Káthiá ...	H	27	5, 22, 43
	S	1	25
Káthor ..	H	115	2
	S	1	25
Kátil ...	H	1,194	9, 15, 16, 21
	S	35	15, 48
	M	2 726	16, 17, 20, 21, 22, 25, 51
Kátoch ...	H	2,049	8, 10, 11, 13, 15, 17, 19, 20
	S	9	27, 42, 44, 47, 48
	M	9	9, 18, 21
Katwál ...	H	386	4, 5, 7, 8, 9, 15, 42, 51
	M	3,648	13, 14, 15, 19, 21, 25
Kausi ...	H	17	12
Kawári ...	H	2	44
	M	31	1, 10, 44
Ker ...	M	15	13, 15
Keu ...	M	39	1
Khachori ...	H	55	34
Khagar ...	H	7	48
	S	7	48
	M	495	24, 25, 48
Khajuriá ...	H	302	3, 4, 21
	S	38	50
	M	67	3
Khakhá ...	H	2	27
	M	11,260	5, 9, 11, 13 to 16, 19, 25, 29
Khakhan ...	M	150	11, 20
Khalál ...	H	7	2, 9, 21
	M	19	1
Khalot ...	H	15	3
	S	9	4
	M	83	4
Khalu ...	H	19	8
Khandwál ...	H	148	39
	M	6	6
Khaneu ...	H	16	9, 11
Khanewa ...	M	102	18
Khaniál ...	H	39	15, 20
Khanor ...	H	64	9, 27
	M	3	20
Khánzádá ...	M	13	13, 17
Khar ...	H	13	7, 9, 11, 15, 20, 24, 26
	S	1	14
	M	2	13
Khárá ...	H	6	44
	M	30	24, 27
Kharal ...	H	105	16, 24, 25, 27, 44
	S	1	14
	M	16,010	M. 1, 8, 12, 13, 17, 18, 19
Kharar ...	M	18	13
Kharas ...	M	14	13, 15, 29
Khárí ...	H	7	44
	M	24	10, 24
Kharoch ...	H	67	15
Kharoliá ...	H	14	9
Kharwál ...	H	1,262	8, 14, 27, 51
	M	45	20, 21
Khátál ...	H	170	9, 27
	S	3	10
Khatan ...	H	13	1, 15
Khatar ...	H	64	4, 8, 9, 24
	S	6	51
	M	8	8, 9
Khatogúni ...	H	282	41, 42
Khatral ...	M	117	21
Khatri ...	H	119	5, 8, 14, 16, 21, 27
	S	40	14, 25, 27
	M	12	1, 8
Khawáriá ...	H	14	47
Kherí ...	H	17	8, 10
	M	126	12, 51
Kheriwál ...	H	787	8
	M	2	1
Khichí ...	H	71	1, 2, 16, 44
	S	1	9
	M	4,963	1, 12, 16, 17, 19, 20, 24, 26, 51
Khiljí ...	H	14	9
	M	262	1, 16, 48, 49
Khingar ...	M	174	20
Khod ...	M	29	12, 20
Khohárá ...	H	67	9
	M	29	12
Khoj ...	H	33	42
	M	13	8, 13
Khojá ...	M	24	11, 13, 51
Khokhar ...	H	341	L. 8, 24, 44, 47, 50
	S	227	13, 14, 17, 25
	M	34,043	B. 33, 40, 44, 45, 46, 47, 49, 50, 51
Khokhar Siál	M	162	6, 9, 24, 46
Khore ...	H	2	2, 15
	M	81	5, 11, 20, 22
Khoriál ...	M	249	17
Khosal ...	H	16	9
	M	95	19, 21, 46
Khose ...	H	84	7, 12
	S	19	25
	M	6	19
Khotna ...	H	52	9
Khotrá ...	H	2	8
	M	139	15, 22, 25, 39
Kishan Chandí	S	51	9
Kiyál ...	M	113	18, 20
Kodál ...	H	51	9, 24, 47
	M	13	9, 12
Kohál ...	H	736	8, 11, 15, 42
	M	31	9, 15
Koháleriá ...	H	157	8
Koí ...	H	103	11
	S	5	10
Kokariá ...	H	3	47
	M	80	12, 46
Kolábat ...	H	82	9, 15
Kolar ...	H	20	9, 25
Koláráj ...	H	88	15
Kolí ...	H	11	5, 8, 12
	M	7	11
Kolkaritá ...	H	32	9
Kondá ...	H	57	37, 44
	S	1	9
Kondal ...	H	945	6, 8, 9, 34, 36, 37, 39, 41, 42, 48
	S	11	9, 37, 48
	M	8	9, 39
Kondle ...	H	158	9
Kons ...	H	49	5, 13, 17, 25
	S	2	17, 45
	M	3	13, 25
Kontáwál ...	H	97	8, 24
Korhen ...	M	72	25
Koriá ...	H	40	9, 10, 13, 15, 18, 19, 44, 48
	S	2	44, 49
	M	93	11, 12, 25, 48
Korigar ...	H	11	48
Koriwál ...	M	16	25, 26
Korthi ...	H	12	8
Koshak ...	H	116	4, 14, 34
Koshal ...	H	1,065	D. 9, 12, 25, 34, 35, 36, 41, 47, 48, 49
	M	586	9, 10, 16, 25
Koshash	H	6	1, 8, 25
	M	890	11
Kotál ...	H	15	9
Koth ...	H	29	8, 18
	M	446	15, 19, 27, 51
Kothri ...	H	61	8
	M	5	12
Kotiál ...	H	205	8, 9
	M	2	46
Kotlariá ...	H	24	8, 9
Kowál ...	H	2	7, 14
	M	64	10, 21, 27
Kundal ...	H	498	9
Kurmi ...	H	6	48
	M	16	48
Labáná ...	H	4	25
	S	48	25, 28, 51
	M	27	13, 27, 51
Ladáhrá ...	H	4	9
	M	134	19, 21
Laddu ...	H	1,167	8, 9, 15
	S	135	9, 10, 46
	M	450	9, 10, 25
Ladhál ...	S	2	44
	M	18	19
Ladháná ...	H	5	34
	M	38	26
Ladhar ...	H	32	9, 24
	S	29	9, 17
	M	159	2, 10, 13, 16
Ladhárach ...	H	85	8, 9, 47
	M	11	12
Labáraj ...	H	38	15
Láhauriá ...	H	9	8, 10, 12, 15
	S	5	14
	M	70	9, 13, 15
Láhotri ...	H	5	5, 14
	M	16	10, 13
Lái ...	H	41	24
	M	2	9
Lait ...	H	7	48
	M	25	19, 48
Lak ...	M	78	19, 20
Laker ...	H	3	12, 15
	M	413	1, 12, 24

Names of Sub-Castes.		Persons.	Locality.
Lakhair ...	H	193	11, 43
Lakhana ...	M	30	17, 49, 51
Lakhanpál ...	M	865	12, 13, 15, 16, 44
Lakhanpuri ...	H	41	15
	M	57	12, 13
Lakhi ...	H	14	9, 12, 25
	S	1	49
	M	8	15, 25
Lakhwerá ...	M	73	24, 26
Lakriá ...	II	12	8
Laleri ...	M	25	12, 17, 26
Lalbár ...	H	10	8
	M	19	16
Laliar ...	H	429	15
	M	47	25, 26, 47
Lalotrá ...	H	3	27
	S	23	14, 15
	M	57	15, 26
Laltre ...	H	15	16
Lalyán ...	M	11	26
Lambi ...	H	55	8, 42, 48
	S	146	48
	M	4	8, 13
Lamini ...	H	100	15
Lanbariá ...	H	26	13, 15
	S	10	12
	M	2	27
Lande ...	H	14	9
Langah ...	II	5	8, 11
	M	528	1, 9, 12, 13, 15, 16, 19, 20, 21, 22, 51
Langrál ...	S	1	16
	M	4,959	19, 21, 27
Lár ...	H	144	12, 13, 21, 27
	M	8	1, 27
Lariál ...	H	3	1
	M	10	12
Larjh ...	H	1	48
	M	19	25
Larkojá ...	H	21	4
Lasan ...	H	8	1, 13, 27, 41
	M	29	13, 15
Latu ...	H	16	4, 30
	M	2	13
Lawár ...	H	20	2, 4, 6, 45
	M	8	11
Lel ...	H	6	8
	M	76	24, 45
Lire ...	H	73	8
Lobh ...	H	192	4
Lodan ...	H	21	8, 27
	M	6	13
Lode ...	H	10	48, 50
	M	22	48
Lodhal ...	H	158	8
Lodhar ...	H	18	16, 17
	S	7	51
	M	5	1
Lodhrá ...	H	1	19
	M	81	12, 13, 17
Lodi ...	H	443	8, 27
	M	12	13, 15, 24, 25
Logáhi ...	H	80	8
Lohan ...	H	14	9
Lohár ...	H	16	14, 51
	M	12	12
Lohiách ...	H	13	8
Lohie ...	H	200	4, 9
	M	3	25
Lon ...	H	158	9, 16
	S	2	12, 13
	M	229	5, 12, 16, 25
Londak ...	H	13	4
Lonrá ...	H	14	5
Lor ...	H	18	6, 9, 12, 14, 15
	M	170	9, 12, 13
Loshiáni ...	H	39	8
Lotá ...	H	52	4, 5, 11, 12, 19
	M	11	2
Machán ...	H	71	34
	M	1	12
Máchhi ...	M	29	1, 13
Madan ...	H	18	13, 27, 48
	S	8	13
	M	11	13, 16, 25
Madári ...	H	35	1, 7, 9
	S	7	14
	M	15	10, 15
Madhaná ...	H	2	7
	S	2	14
	M	15	19
Madhwál ...	S	1	9
	M	108	16, 24
Madori ...	H	9	19, 48
	M	22	13
Magar ...	H	22	15, 34
	S	2	14
	M	102	9, 21
Maghal ...	H	1	9
	M	27	26
Maghiáná ...	H	2	7, 9
	M	59	20, 26, 51
Maghral ...	II	1	41
	M	58	21
Maghwál ...	H	11	8
	M	5	10, 41
Magoke ...	M	36	26
Mahál ...	H	27	16, 24, 47
	M	321	9, 13, 21, 48
Mahál Sakhar	H	431	8
Mahán ...	H	4	9, 21
	M	39	1, 6, 19, 22, 23
Mahandu ...	H	10	11, 13
	S	1	47
	M	3	6
Mahár ...	H	74	8, 14, 15, 17
	S	77	14, 25, 40
	M	1,527	1, 12, 13, 16, 48, 51
Mahárájá ...	H	4	21
	S	12	25
	M	2	45
Máhá Rájput	H	15	26, 47
Máhas ...	H	33	8
Mahawál ...	H	129	9
Mahdpuri ...	H	13	26
Mahesh ...	H	9	6, 9
	M	21	12, 18, 43
Máhi ...	H	7	9, 25, 42, 51
	S	1	8
	M	79	17, 27, 51
Mahiál ...	H	56	12, 19
	M	205	21, 22
Máhigir ...	M	38	12
Mahlan ...	H	180	2, 42, 43
	M	43	16
Máhnas ...	H	150	9
Mahotrá ...	H	48	15
Mahráh ...	H	4	19, 24, 27
	S	5	22
	M	72	26
Mahri ...	H	183	2, 8
	S	28	14
Mahtá ...	H	161	9, 24, 47
	S	15	51
	M	21	13, 15, 19
Mahtam ...	H	403	51
	S	1	24
	M	49	11, 12, 13
Mahton ...	H	1,735	9, 10, 11
	M	1	13
Mahur ...	H	153	12, 39
Máián ...	H	27	11, 24
Maijlas ...	H	31	2
Main ...	H	3	5
	S	3	13
	M	2,288	11, 48
Mainpál ...	M	61	13
Máir ...	H	172	11, 18, 20, 44
	S	82	11, 17
	M	15,094	20, 21, 22
Majariál ...	H	30	15
Majbál ...	H	18	15
	S	1	9
Majothá ...	M	11	10, 12, 41
Majwál ...	H	11	16
Makbápariá ...	H	19	18, 44, 48
	M	1	12
Makerá ...	H	9	13
	S	2	19, 20
	M	10	9, 31
Mákhalá ...	H	4	2, 15
	M	23	3, 12
Makhí ...	H	31	9, 25
	M	5	9
Makhiál ...	H	2	8
	M	27	15, 20
Makhotre ...	H	82	15
Makrál ...	M	124	8, 12, 21
Makrí ...	H	24	15, 51
	M	20	20
Makrolar ...	H	315	8
Makwál ...	M	104	25, 27
Mál ...	H	9	9, 14
	M	69	10, 16
Malá ...	H	20	14
	M	5	1
Maláhre ...	H	23	9, 15, 24, 39
Malakzáda ...	M	24	12
Malálí ...	H	21	9
Malamtá ...	M	116	12, 27
Malán ...	H	80	9, 17
Maláná ...	H	19	27
	M	244	25, 27, 51
Malatar ...	H	18	8
Malbírtalí ...	II	95	8
Malhí ...	H	31	8, 19, 27
	M	62	20, 48
Malhotar ...	H	143	8, 39, 47
Málí ...	H	120	4, 20, 37, 48
	S	2	15
	M	6	10
Maliál ...	H	1,046	39, 42
	M	29	27
Malián ...	H	22	4
	M	133	21
Malì-kand ...	H	8	50
	M	98	10, 18, 26, 27
Malírá ...	H	105	5, 9
	M	3	12, 17
Malk ...	H	13	1, 7, 9, 44
	S	1	20
	M	157	13, 17, 21, 29, 51
Málkas ...	H	14	48
	M	6	3, 26
Malkhádá ...	M	18	1
Malkoiá ...	H	101	8, 9
Malkoti ...	H	367	8, 9
	M	63	1
Maloch ...	H	27	8
Malotrá ...	H	201	8, 15
	M	18	16
Malpotá ...	H	70	8, 9
Malwál ...	H	278	1, 5, 39
Mamán ...	H	205	15, 39
	M	7	12, 51
Mamidál ...	H	19	13, 20, 21
Mán ...	H	21	9, 19, 25, 50
	S	49	10, 48
	M	220	2, 6, 9, 10, 12, 13, 15, 17, 45
Manásar ...	M	108	7, 19
Manbah ...	H	1	9
	M	10	1, 18
Manchatá ...	M	61	12, 20
Mand ...	H	68	9, 15, 17, 25, 42
	M	1	14
Mandáhar ...	H	6,901	1, 4, 5, 6, 9, 48, 49, 50, 51
	S	14	5, 6, 48
	M	25,724	3, 6, 11, 21, 48, 49
Mandal ...	H	20	5, 48
	M	96	12, 13, 25
Mándálá ...	H	2	15
	M	22	16, 27, 45
Mander ...	II	28	8
Mandhál ...	S	4	14
	M	173	2, 5
Mandhán ...	H	68	1, 4
	M	2	1
Mándí ...	H	94	8, 48
	M	19	2, 10, 13
Mandiál ...	H	359	8, 9, 17, 42
	M	165	1, 19, 21, 27
Mandíwál ...	H	17	17, 47
	M	22	2, 5, 12
Mandlí ...	H	27	15, 18
	S	11	14
	M	4	14
Mandwáriá ...	H	55	8, 47

Names of Sub-Castes.		Persons.	Locality.
Mangal ...	H	16	1, 8, 15
	M	73	12, 27, 48
Mangládí ...	H	20	8
Manglwál ...	H	86	8
Mangotrí ...	M	36	15
Mangrál ...	M	2,424	13, 19, 20, 25, 27
Manbarse ...	H	157	8
Manbáe ...	H	11,187	L. R. 8, 9, 10, 25, 27, 39, 43, 44, 47
	S	1,592	9, 10, 17, 18, 19, 25, 44
	M	4,569	J. L. R. 1, 25, 27, 28, 44, 45, 49, 51
Máni ...	H	1	9
	M	94	6, 46
Maniál ...	M	18	25
Maniár ...	H	1	12
	M	21	12, 27, 48
Manj ...	H	221	9, 10, 11, 44, 49, 50
	S	36	9, 10, 11, 12, 44
	M	17,903	9, 10, 12, 13, 14, 15, 25, 44, 45, 49
Manjás ...	H	29	39, 43
	S	1	17
	M	163	10, 11, 46
Mankotiá ...	H	1,350	8, 9, 10, 20, 43, 47
Manotrá ...	H	167	15
	M	18	51
Mánsar ...	H	9	10, 13
	S	2	9
	M	160	12, 26
Már ...	H	58	3, 6, 9, 21
	M	484	9, 11, 12, 14, 21
Maráhí ...	H	41	9
	M	44	12, 13, 26
Máráin ...	H	298	8, 28
	M	1	39
Maráj ...	H	12	9, 27
	M	8	24
Maral ...	H	2	19, 44
	M	335	13, 16, 25, 27, 51
Marálie ...	M	253	27
Maráná ...	H	9	2, 16
	M	11	12, 26
Marar ...	H	1	12
	M	187	10, 18, 19, 27
Marásí ...	H	66	14, 15, 27, 39, 41
	M	205	13, 14, 15, 46, 48
Márath ...	H	11	1, 3
	M	84	20
Marbán ...	M	86	2, 11
Marbáljá ...	H	18	9
	M	31	19
Marhattá ...	H	48	13, 14, 24, 50
	M	88	12, 21
Mariá ...	H	10	2, 9, 25
	S	128	10
	M	1	6
Mariál ...	H	219	8, 9, 47
	M	162	21, 22, 27
Markan ...	S	14	11
	M	37	26
Márkandá ...	H	19	25, 34, 42
Maroiá ...	H	10	1, 8
	S	5	12
	M	1	26
Márthán ...	H	23	1, 8, 11
Máru ...	H	7	14, 15, 44
	M	70	15, 25, 49, 51
Marwál ...	H	407	1, 14
Márwár ...	H	33	1, 12, 13, 48
	S	4	11
	M	37	13, 24, 44
Marwárán ...	H	76	1, 8, 48
Marze ...	H	11	28
Masádí ...	M	23	15
Masál ...	H	25	9, 48
	S	30	13
	M	8	15, 44
Masan ...	H	13	1, 14
	S	5	14
	M	15	9, 15, 25
Masáwan ...	H	20	10, 13, 15, 25
	S	7	11
	M	8	9
Mashkíní ...	M	507	13, 21
Masiánd ...	H	5	13
	M	28	26

Names of Sub-Castes.		Persons.	Locality.
Masinor ...	M	22	25
Masurí ...	H	14	9
	S	3	25
	M	5	14
Mátá ...	H	9	22, 25, 26
	S	1	13
	M	62	22
Mátáir ...	H	206	5, 13, 27
	S	3	14
Matal ...	H	21	9
	M	1,326	11, 15, 21
Matárjanjube	H	26	4, 7
	S	5	9
	M	1	11
Maten ...	M	28	1, 10
Mathán ...	H	1	44
	S	28	25
	M	19	12
Mathár ...	H	47	3, 5, 18, 44
	S	38	13
	M	2	25
Mathrás ...	H	21	6, 25, 44
	M	192	6, 10, 11, 14, 44
Mátí ...	H	1	11
	M	548	6, 48
Mátuk ...	H	84	13, 26
Mátwál ...	M	12	48
Mátwáldáh ...	H	74	8
Matwálí ...	H	94	8
Mawál ...	H	292	8, 9, 10, 15, 42
	M	1	24
Mawánat ...	H	81	8
Mawátí ...	H	26	4, 8, 15, 42
	S	3	27
	M	265	1, 5, 13
Mede ...	H	4	44
	S	13	9
	M	4	17
Mehiál ...	H	2	40
	M	13	10, 24
Mehlá ...	H	17	9
	M	53	48
Mehná ...	H	33	7, 9, 42
	M	23	46
Mehrál ...	H	77	8
Mehrás ...	H	143	4, 13, 15, 17, 48
	S	8	15
	M	92	9, 13, 44, 48
Mehrchand ...	H	301	9, 15
	M	4	15
Meí ...	H	133	18, 51
Mekan ...	M	1,709	1, 19, 26, 28
Mer ...	H	77	4, 25, 48
	S	39	44, 48
Merákí ...	H	64	12
Merdah ...	M	42	16
Meriá ...	H	28	8, 9, 48
	M	66	9, 12, 48
Mewál ...	H	17	2, 4, 44
	M	7	3, 12
Miál ...	H	12	9
Mián ...	H	545	13, 24, 47
	S	20	13
	M	1	15
Miáná ...	M	20	20, 24, 27
Miáwat ...	H	168	8
Mír ...	H	116	2, 4, 9, 13, 19
	S	34	12, 16, 21
	M	136	13, 21, 22
Mírwál ...	H	68	50
	M	67	20, 50
Mirzápuriá ...	H	31	8
Mitor ...	H	891	9, 10, 12, 14, 17, 23, 25, 26, 27, 51
	S	190	10, 17, 20, 25, 27
	M	9	15, 25
Mitroká ...	M	108	26
Mochí ...	H	34	12
	M	18	13, 48
Mogá ...	H	21	4
Mohal ...	H	120	1, 25, 42, 49
	M	682	1, 10, 12, 15, 46
Mohkí ...	M	23	16
Mohlá ...	H	153	8, 13, 19, 42
	S	5	12
Mojoká ...	M	31	1
Mukhíharpár	H	23	10
Molak ...	H	66	2, 18

Names of Sub-Castes.		Persons.	Locality.
Mone ...	H	50	9, 12, 13, 15
	M	117	10, 12, 25
Mongrí ...	H	24	50
	M	1	50
Mor ...	H	10	1, 11, 42
	S	7	25
	M	1	12
Mordhaj ...	H	21	48
	S	13	15
Motábal ...	H	25	42, 47
Mothal ...	H	115	42
	M	8	48
Motrí ...	H	13	48
Mughal ...	H	8	12, 48
	M	897	12, 13, 16, 17, 18, 20, 21, 2
Mukhnádal ...	M	852	18
Multání ...	H	18	8
	S	2	5, 27
	M	471	5, 6, 48, 50
Mundlás ...	M	18	10, 27
Munshí ...	M	132	26
Mutal ...	H	19	4
	M	1	9
Muthá ...	S	28	25
	M	3	13
Mutráh ...	H	23	8
Nadábar ...	H	2	8
	S	2	48
	M	7	12, 15
Nádí ...	H	46	9
	M	12	16
Nádní ...	S	18	9
	M	12	25
Nadrál ...	H	55	4
	S	15	9
	M	1	20
Nadwál ...	H	81	9, 16
Nagálí ...	H	49	8
Nagárián ...	H	164	8, 39, 50
	S	26	4, 48
Nágarkí ...	H	158	39, 42
	M	14	9, 24
Nagiál ...	H	9	21
	M	2,165	19, 21, 26
Nágoria ...	H	57	8
Nágpál ...	H	5	27
	M	83	18, 20, 25
Nagrál ...	S	8	8
	M	1,198	1, 20, 21, 24
Nágrí ...	H	1	17
	M	99	13, 51
Nagrokí ...	H	14	42, 47
Nágwál ...	H	25	8
Nagwán ...	H	13	1, 9, 42
	M	8	15
Náhar ...	H	41	9, 13, 15, 48
	S	11	14
	M	35	16, 25, 26
Nahondah ...	H	50	8
Náhrí ...	M	17	25
Náich ...	H	205	24
Náik ...	H	52	5, 13, 19, 46
Náin ...	M	35	13
Náit ...	H	1	9
	M	18	8
Naiwál ...	S	1	27
	M	15	12
Najár ...	H	1	48
	S	9	27, 48
	M	70	13, 18, 22, 2
Najáwat ...	H	12	27
Nakám ...	H	89	13, 19, 36,
	M	2	25
Nakiál ...	H	11	9, 12
	M	44	27
Naktániáh ...	H	58	8
Nálagarh ...	H	155	25, 39
	M	93	26
Nalodrúpatha	H	78	8
Náloní ...	H	16	15
Nalpála ...	H	53	8
Nalwárach ...	H	20	8
Namakkhoi ...	H	148	8, 9
	M	5	13, 48
Namole ...	H	127	8
Nanáre ...	M	150	13
Nand ...	M	56	9, 11, 12

Names of Sub-Castes.		Persons.	Locality.
Nandrál ...	H	678	8, 9, 15
Nánga ...	M	14	18
Nangal ...	H	1	15
	M	32	9, 10, 11, 19, 25
Nángar ...	M	14	4, 11
Nánglachha ...	H	23	4
Nángle ...	H	369	8, 15, 39, 47
	M	5	17
Nánglegaloia	H	19	8
Nánglú ...	H	281	8, 39
Nánsha ...	H	29	25, 39
Nanwál ...	H	200	8, 25
	S	1	25
	M	6	9
Náolí ...	H	3	9
	M	290	12
Náp ...	H	53	8
	M	2	48
Naran ...	M	420	9, 13, 26
Nárang ...	H	31	51
	M	1	12
Narbán ...	H	223	2, 3, 12, 32, 49
	S	1	10
	M	102	2, 32, 49
Nardí ...	M	14	13
Narháraj ...	H	13	15
Nariá ...	H	69	2, 9
	M	6	10, 11, 42
Nariál ...	H	815	8, 9, 42, 43, 47
Narián ...	H	2	16
	M	209	16
Nármá ...	H	35	5, 31
	M	14	18
Narmál ...	H	55	8, 14
Nármián ...	H	19	3
Naroí ...	H	18	7, 9, 12
	M	8	45
Naroká ...	H	38	2, 3, 12, 49
Nároní ...	M	24	12
Narotre ...	H	21	8
Nárú ...	H	125	8, 9, 10, 11, 44, 48
	S	6	9, 10, 15
	M	24,936	J. L. 18, 20, 24, 25, 27, 44, 48, 50
Narwáe ...	M	266	10, 21, 25
Narwál ...	S	7	48
	M	19	21, 48
Narwán ...	H	37	46, 47
	M	481	21
Náse ...	H	18	8
Nat ...	M	14	27, 48
Nau-Muslam	M	52	4, 9, 10, 13, 27, 47
Náwání ...	H	4	10
	M	59	1, 25, 26
Neg ...	H	18	25, 48, 49
	M	16	9, 11, 13, 25
Nekokárá ...	M	58	16
Nepál ...	H	7	41, 44
	S	4	44
	M	644	11, 12, 13, 44
Niál ...	H	12	8
	S	2	9
	M	6	13
Nij ...	M	68	13
Níiá ...	H	3	11, 41, 48
	S	6	9, 49
	M	35	9, 12
Níráj ...	H	69	11, 48
	M	20	10, 11, 13
Nirmál ...	H	201	48
	S	1	9
	M	1	13
Nol ...	H	16	47
	S	1	25
	M	622	13, 16, 17
Nonári ...	M	162	12, 13
Nun ...	M	885	1, 11, 13, 19, 27, 51
Nur ...	H	52	9, 11, 12
	M	37	11, 12, 13, 29
Okhárie ...	H	14	8
Os ...	H	17	4
	M	1	21
Pachádá ...	M	5,632	15, 48
Pachas ...	H	78	4, 31
	M	3	11, 24
Pacherá ...	S	15	15
	M	12	14, 26
Pachrál ...	H	27	8
Padhár ...	H	186	8, 9, 26, 43
	S	1	46
	M	13	14, 15
Padho ...	H	21	8
Pahári ...	H	15	4, 9, 44
	S	2	9
	M	11	8, 12
Pahgoch ...	H	132	8
Pahlwál ...	H	24	9, 44
	M	6	13
Pahor ...	H	20	1, 15, 18
	M	11	26
Pahotrá ...	M	26	1
Pajáhe ...	H	13	9
Pajal ...	H	26	6
	M	4	14
Pakaryál ...	M	11	25
Pakhrár ...	M	685	21
Páli ...	H	3	10, 14
	S	14	11
	M	10	14, 15
Palokan ...	H	242	8
Paloriá ...	H	15	8
Pandál ...	H	4	5
	M	163	13, 16, 17, 21, 48
Pandat ...	H	11	9
Pander ...	H	1,065	5, 6, 8, 48, 49
	S	1	48
	M	111	6, 10, 12, 48, 49
Pandhán ...	H	21	1
Pandhár ...	H	141	1, 8, 12, 23, 33, 42
	M	18	10, 12
Pandhír ...	H	658	1, 3, 5, 6, 8, 34, 39
	S	5	5
	M	322	5, 44
Pándí ...	H	25	12, 14, 21, 25
	M	10	13, 14, 17, 47
Pándo ...	H	312	1, 5, 8, 9
	M	3	12
Pándwán ...	H	33	8, 9, 15, 22, 48
Pango ...	H	25	8
Pangrí ...	H	19	8, 9, 42
Panhe ...	M	15	24, 25
Paniál ...	H	308	1, 9, 14, 15, 19, 48
	S	11	8, 15
	M	58	1, 13, 14, 15, 16
Paníbár ...	H	19	1, 3, 12
Panjhatte ...	M	16	19
Panjíe ...	S	3	25
	M	62	15
Panjnáh ...	H	23	5
Panjor ...	H	58	9, 16
	M	236	16
Panjotre ...	H	13	9
	S	7	48
Panjutá ...	H	15	9
Panor ...	H	91	1, 7, 32
	M	18	1, 14
Panwáí ...	M	69	18
Panwár ...	H	6,404	D. 8, 10, 13, 16, 24, 25, 27, 28, 41, 46, 49, 50, 51
	S	1,861	5, 6, 10, 16, 19, 26, 28, 51
	M	47,318	1, 2, 3, 5, 6, 10, 13, 16, 19, 20, 24, 27, 28, 49, 50, 51
Panwáriá ...	H	340	9
	M	30	16
Páoti ...	M	39	27
Pará ...	S	123	18, 21
	M	44	11, 14
Paráj ...	M	34	11
Parambansí ...	H	21	4, 7
Parásar ...	H	63	42, 48
Parbiá ...	H	13	13, 44
Parhár ...	H	39	1, 27, 47, 51
	S	13	25
	M	280	1, 12, 19, 24, 27, 48, 51
Parí ...	H	14	14, 27
	M	10	38
Pariá ...	H	46	9
Pariál ...	H	27	9, 10, 12, 15, 51
	M	2	12
Parmár ...	H	796	9, 25, 43, 44
	S	249	44
	M	23	13
Paro ...	H	9	8
	M	158	13
Parsrámí ...	H	25	5
Parwál ...	H	16	16, 37, 48
	M	1	47
Pásí ...	H	61	9, 14, 17, 48
	S	7	9
	M	13	13, 22, 24
Patháí ...	H	122	9
Pathán ...	H	629	8, 16, 25, 42
	S	3	16
	M	188	1, 12, 13, 27, 39, 48
Pathániá ...	H	5,143	8, 9, 15, 40, 41, 42, 47
	S	35	9, 15, 20, 22
	M	146	8, 15, 16, 42, 47
Pathánián ...	H	184	9, 16, 39, 42
	M	7	15, 49
Pathanria ...	H	1,120	2, 8
	S	3	22
	M	8	8, 9
Pathará ...	H	8	42
	M	140	12
Pathaurá ...	H	445	8
Pathohar ...	M	12	27
Pathulá ...	H	59	39
Patiál ...	H	6,228	8, 9, 15, 39, 42, 47
	S	16	8, 29
	M	96	16, 17
Patiániáh ...	H	126	9
Patiáraj ...	H	541	8
Patriáh ...	H	25	8, 9
	M	17	1, 11
Pattí ...	H	2	9
	M	445	9
Patwe ...	H	40	8
Pawál ...	H	29	8
Pawániáh ...	H	4	48
	M	31	6
Penes ...	H	14	48
	S	1	48
Permál ...	H	125	8
Phadwál ...	H	222	8
Phál ...	M	93	13, 51
Phalákar ...	H	22	8
Phaliád ...	H	173	8
Phalron ...	M	957	L. 12, 18, 19, 20
Phandáre ...	H	12	8
Pharan ...	H	1	25
	S	9	14
	M	31	25
Pharwáre ...	H	17	47
Phato ...	H	506	8
Phatosáí ...	H	20	8
Phattí ...	M	161	18
Pháw ...	M	110	11, 18
Phalátar ...	H	24	8
Pholar ...	H	18	8
	M	30	17, 27, 44, 46
Phulchhare ...	M	59	27
Phullarwál ...	M	935	24
Phulyáne ...	H	55	20
Pingláne ...	H	35	42
Pohár ...	H	6	13
	M	43	21
Polas ...	H	23	6
	M	3	6
Poná ...	H	66	4, 9, 30, 49
	M	12	49
Panháná ...	M	74	24
Purbiá ...	H	115	6, 15, 16, 19, 47
	S	1	14
	M	52	25, 27
Purí ...	H	43	13, 15, 25, 42
	S	21	9, 25
	M	161	9, 25
Qáim-khání ...	M	4,225	1, 2, 3, 12, 31, 49

APPENDIX TO IMPERIAL TABLE XIII.—

Names of Sub-Castes.		Persons.	Locality.
Qanauj ...	M	129	15
Qásam-khání	M	62	24
Qureshí ...	M	42	1, 15, 16, 20, 25
Qutbí ...	M	30	13, 15, 19
Qutbsháhí ...	M	166	13, 18, 21
Rabaní ...	M	110	51
Ráchar ...	H	18	8
Rachpál ...	M	121	51
Rádat ...	H	86	9, 13
	M	2	25
Rádhor ...	H	46	10
Ráe-kanwár ...	M	44	12
Ráení ...	H	19	25, 47, 48
Raghiál ...	H	24	8, 15, 47
Raghu-bansí ...	H	2,470	L. 3, 5, 6, 7, 8, 9, 10, 21, 22, 25, 27, 34, 36, 39, 41, 48, 49
	S	55	6, 33, 48
	M	4,590	D. 11, 14, 25, 33, 34, 48, 49
Ráh ...	H	122	51
	M	4	15
Rabájan ...	H	89	9
Rahán ...	M	447	12, 19, 24, 26
Ráhar ...	H	35	16, 27
	S	5	14
	M	20	51
Rahmání ...	S	5	25
	M	12	27
Ráí ...	H	359	1, 4, 25
	S	49	25
Rájá ...	H	13	4, 44
	M	11	13, 45
Rajáwat ...	H	85	2, 8, 12, 24, 27
Rajáwle ...	H	13	8
Rájbáuá ...	M	14	27
Rájbansí ...	H	16	4, 13, 14, 51
	S	3	12
	M	16	10
Rájí ...	M	13	20, 23, 26
Rájíá ...	M	25	25
Rajiál ...	H	34	8, 9
Rajokhá ...	H	1	25
	M	476	24, 26
Rájpál ...	H	16	14, 17, 51
	M	30	6, 10, 11, 18
Rájput-nípál	M	528	44
Ráju ...	M	89	1, 51
Rajwán ...	M	30	18, 51
Rajwár ...	H	20	4
	M	38	13, 24, 51
Rakesh ...	H	150	15
Rakhru ...	H	15	4, 14
	M	14	13
Rakhwál ...	H	91	5, 8, 15, 16
	S	5	9, 19
	M	81	5, 15
Rákí ...	M	14	11
Rakiál ...	H	42	8, 9
Rakwál ...	H	126	9, 27
	M	4	16
Ralosí ...	H	24	8
Ramán ...	S	17	51
	M	17	4, 26
Rámdás ...	M	293	19
Rámgare ...	H	48	8, 14
	S	7	27
Ramler ...	M	31	13
Rán ...	S	4	12
	M	67	16
Ráná ...	H	607	8, 15, 16, 42, 47
	S	11	13
	M	62	1, 3, 8, 13
Ráná-tur ...	H	87	8
Ranáwat ...	H	1,483	8, 12, 39
Randháwá ...	H	1	46
	M	45	12
Randhí ...	M	14	1, 10
Randot ...	H	38	47
Raneat ...	H	35	39
Ranghar ...	H	363	12, 13, 14, 21, 36, 42, 48
	S	549	11, 12, 19, 20
	M	1,033	L. 12, 13, 20, 21, 25, 27, 42, 46, 48, 51
Rangor ...	M	14	46
Rangre ...	H	64	2, 4, 7, 8, 17
	S	2	15
	M	103	3, 16, 19, 24, 25, 51
Rangrez ...	M	12	13, 15, 26
Rangwál ...	H	44	4
Raniál ...	H	36	8, 47
Ránjhá ...	H	1	15
	M	18	12, 19, 26, 51
Ránot ...	H	527	8, 9, 10, 20, 27, 39, 42, 49
	S	19	9, 33
	M	7	10, 11
Ransíl ...	M	87	18
Rár ...	H	32	8
Rasáídan ...	M	24	3, 47
Raswál ...	H	73	12, 15, 27
Raswáliá ...	H	107	8
Rátá ...	H	69	9
	M	2	13
Ratan ...	H	16	39
Ratan-bhárdwáj	H	27	39
Ratanpál ...	H	5	17
	S	35	21
Ráth ...	H	3	24, 44
	M	708	14, 24
Rathí ...	H	523	2, 4, 12, 15, 30
	M	16	2, 12
Ráthor ...	H	3,339	B. 34, 35, 44, 46, 48, 49, 50, 51
	S	4,207	L. M. 12, 18, 19, 48, 50, 51
	M	1,516	1, 2, 5, 6, 11, 12, 13, 14, 19, 24, 25, 48, 51
Ráthor-panwár	S	56	13
Rathotrá ...	H	162	8
Rathwál ...	H	5	17
	M	47	12
Ratiál ...	M	551	21
Ratnáwat ...	H	14	1, 48
Rato ...	H	126	9, 16
	M	149	5, 9, 16, 23, 25
Ratre ...	H	11	15
	M	10	10
Ráután ...	H	1	48
	M	23	11
Ráwal ...	H	265	7, 9, 11
	M	24	9, 12, 15, 39
Ráwat ...	H	754	4, 6, 8, 9, 39, 41, 42, 47
	S	5	11
	M	47	9, 10, 11, 25, 44, 46
Ráwí ...	H	76	8, 21
	S	131	51
Razádá ...	H	33	10
Rer-chandr ...	M	13	8
Rewán ...	M	41	1, 11, 14
Reyá ...	H	74	2, 4, 22
	M	3	13
Riál ...	H	6	8
	S	10	10
Ringláná ...	H	35	42
Roch ...	H	20	4
	M	13	25
Rogiál ...	H	11	8, 9
Rohelá ...	H	11	6
	M	1	25
Rokals ...	M	64	13
Rore ...	H	35	1, 9, 12, 25, 48
	S	2	14, 25
	M	4	1, 10
Rot ...	H	14	9, 25
	M	24	13
Rupál ...	H	133	8, 10
	M	204	20, 21
Ruprám ...	M	12	9
Sabádbú ...	H	1	27
	M	133	21
Sabahrá ...	H	17	8
Sabáná ...	M	120	24, 25, 26
Sabetí ...	H	11	7, 47
Sabhariá ...	H	90	20
Sabí ...	H	121	8, 9
Sabráí ...	H	20	12, 13, 16, 25
	M	22	1
Sád ...	H	23	8, 11, 39
	M	9	16
Saddhan ...	H	24	9, 12, 42
	M	3,345	12, 22, 25, 27
Sade	H	9	25
	M	13	13
Sádeti ...	H	22	9
Sadewre ...	H	17	11, 15, 43, 51
	S	9	12, 14
	M	1	24
Sadhar ...	H	4	9, 10, 19
	M	8	25
Sadhárú ...	H	15	9, 25
	S	6	9, 16
Sadhú ...	H	20	1, 11, 12, 44
	S	7	25
	M	77	1, 10, 11, 25
Sadíá ...	H	87	42
	M	216	21
Sadiál ...	H	17	8, 14, 27
Sádkhali ...	H	71	9, 42
Sadná ...	H	65	14, 27
	M	10	25
Sadriá ...	H	57	9, 11, 26
	M	142	16, 51
Sádú ...	H	43	1, 14
	S	1	14
Sadwále ...	H	17	24
Safainá ...	M	19[illegible]	51
Sagal ...	H	12	31
	M	279	12, 19, 21
Sagú ...	S	4	10
	M	109	10, 12, 19
Sáhájar ...	S	1	25
	M	357	21, 26
Sahál ...	H	31	1, 15, 49
	S	3	48, 50
	M	35	11, 12, 22, 28, 46
Sahám ...	M	274	22, 26
Saháns ...	M	693	6, 48
Sahár ...	H	1	9
	M	192	9, 16, 18
Sahárú ...	H	133	8
	M	60	18, 19, 23
Sábí ...	H	18	24, 35
	M	4	20, 27
Sahote ...	H	5	48
	S	13	16
	M	69	25, 44, 48
Sahotrá ...	H	272	8, 9, 41, 43
	M	25	8, 15, 24
Sáhúká ...	S	2	14
	M	14	12, 24
Sahwál ...	H	2	8, 15
	M	388	22
Sai ...	M	12	5, 26
Sain ..	H	649	8, 9, 15, 41, 42
	S	1	14
	M	206	6, 25, 41
Sajan ...	H	43	10, 48
	M	6	10
Sajoka ...	M	334	26
Sakal ...	H	23	39
Sakand ...	H	147	8, 9
Sakaria ...	H	8	12, 18
	M	30	25
Sakarwál ...	H	80	1, 4, 13, 39, 42
Sákel ...	H	14	1, 9, 15, 25, 42
	M	570	12
Sakbán ...	H	346	8, 9, 41
Sakhání ...	M	17	12, 24
Sakharwár ...	H	4	18
	M	61	12
Sakhiál ...	H	131	12, 39
	M	8	19, 22
Sakhláwat ...	H	45	2, 8, 10, 14
Sakhrá ...	H	3	39
	M	563	12, 13, 51
Sakhrí ...	H	2	25
	M	744	1, 10
Sakláníá ...	H	18	8, 14, 42
	M	4	42
Sakrál ...	H	11	25
	S	10	10
	M	134	9, 21
Salábrí ...	H	36	9, 13, 27, 42
	M	37	8, 12, 20, 25
Sálakhia ...	H	32	50
Saláuí ...	H	7	19
	M	7	9, 10

Names of Sub-Castes.		Persons.	Locality.
Salárá ...	H	1,099	9, 15
	M	12	8, 28
Saláran ...	H	1,050	15
	M	18	12, 27
Saláre ...	H	4	14
	S	2	14
	M	32	1, 14, 15, 36, 49
Salátiá ...	H	65	8
Saláwat ...	H	24	1, 5
Salehrí ...	M	30	22
Salehriá ...	H	1,330	8, 15, 20, 21, 27
	S	84	13, 17
	M	25,089	9, 11, 13, 14, 16, 17, 20, 24, 47,
Salerí ...	H	26	47
	M	217	13, 14, 26, 48
Sáleske ...	H	22	21
Salhál ...	M	63	21
Saliách ...	H	26	8
Saliál ...	H	23	8, 15
Salohar ...	H	103	9
	M	19	24
Salorná ...	H	27	4
Salotri ...	M	29	15, 16
Salsjan ...	H	2	4
	M	16	27
Salwání ...	H	4	42
	M	11	13, 25
Samán ...	H	8	4, 10
	M	91	12, 13
Samániah ...	H	46	4
Samariál ...	H	120	8, 47
	M	10	12
Samartí ...	H	13	12
Sambiál ...	H	38	5, 6, 8, 9
	M	101	2, 17
Samdiál ...	H	114	8
Samgorí ...	H	12	9, 12
	M	12	12
Samhál ...	M	58	15, 24
Samiál ...	H	950	8, 9, 15, 16, 47
	M	34	12, 15, 42
Samjah ...	M	101	27
Samkariá ...	H	219	8, 9, 10, 15
	M	3	8
Samlán ...	H	40	8
Samol ...	H	17	8, 25
Sámorá ...	H	10	9
	M	51	12
Sampál ...	H	2	24
	M	53	13, 24
Sánán ...	H	5	5, 19
	M	9	9, 19
Sanár ...	H	61	10, 13, 14, 18, 27
	M	11	1, 11, 15, 24
Sanárú ...	H	76	4, 8, 14
	M	2	9
Sanás ...	H	9	8, 9, 11
	M	2	10, 26
Sánd ...	H	41	11, 12, 42
	S	6	15
	M	1	12
Sandáe ...	H	2	7, 26
	M	10	27
Sándal ...	H	811	1, 4, 34, 38, 43, 48
	S	34	9, 27
	M	49	10, 13, 16, 27
Sándar ...	H	66	11, 35
	S	20	44
Sandárí ...	H	17	14, 25
	S	5	17
	M	11	12
Sandela ...	H	1	27
	M	24	1, 12, 13
Sandhá ...	H	5	15
	S	3	1, 51
	M	88	12, 51
Sandher ...	H	8	5, 9
	M	5	10
Sandhí ...	H	8	9
	M	31	10, 17, 39
Sandbiál ...	H	43	1, 6, 41, 42, 47
	S	3	14
Sandhú ...	H	602	10, 14, 19, 34, 48
	S	22	12, 14, 26, 28
	M	318	12, 14, 15, 16, 21, 48
Sandiál ...	H	72	9
Sandol ...	H	5	7, 9, 34
	M	6	25
Sandore ...	H	1	8
	S	11	51
	M	5	25
Sandránn ...	M	49	9
Sangá khokbar	M	776	10
Sángar ...	H	32	14, 15, 27
	S	2	14
	M	605	8, 9, 13, 16, 25
Sángar-Bansí	H	12	6, 9
Sangariál ...	H	24	14
Sangat ...	M	172	9, 42
Sange ...	H	14	1
	M	1	13
Sanghá ...	M	83	1, 14, 27
Sanghál ...	H	111	8, 12, 25, 39, 48, 51
	M	85	9, 10, 17, 21, 24
Sanghar ...	H	3	27
	S	2	47
	M	31	51
Sangháriá ...	M	22	13
Sangbráe ...	H	32	43, 47
	M	20	17
Sángí ...	H	21	12, 14, 48
	M	26	16
Sangiál ...	H	11	1, 9
	M	28	11, 23
Sánglá ...	H	30	9, 16, 32
	M	34	12
Sangopata ...	H	12	1, 5
	M	26	12, 46
Sangoria ...	H	14	1, 8, 9, 14
Sangotrí ...	H	13	1, 8
	M	1	25
Sángrá ...	H	25	9, 15
	M	160	12, 15, 16, 25, 46
Sangrál ...	H	39	10, 47
	S	12	15
	M	1	10
Sangú ...	M	38	15, 25, 48
Sangwál ...	H	85	5, 13, 15, 47
Saniál ...	H	333	8, 9
	M	4	19
Saníwál ...	H	103	4
Sánjar ...	M	462	26
Sanjdes ...	M	60	13
Sanjotri ...	H	2	25
	M	27	13, 14, 25
Sánkhiá ...	H	1,272	1, 2, 3, 8, 9, 12, 48
	S	9	11, 48
	M	28	1, 8, 9, 48, 49
Sanoriá ...	H	402	8, 15, 42
	M	19	10
Sansál ...	M	43	9
Sánsí ...	H	25	8, 11, 42
	S	2	14
Santrí ...	M	16	14
Sanúpál ...	H	23	8
Sanwál ...	H	33	8
	M	154	5, 16
Sapái ...	H	78	8
Sapal ...	H	7	20, 39, 47
	S	2	50
	M	2,950	10, 11, 20, 21, 25, 26, 27, 49
Sapiál ...	H	11	8
Sapré ...	H	4	9, 19, 25
	M	93	1, 17, 19, 20, 25
Sár ...	H	9	4, 9, 25
	S	2	14
	M	62	9, 11, 24
Sarád ...	H	4	1, 17
	S	12	14
	M	8	9
Sarái ...	H	38	13, 24, 25, 49
	M	45	12, 14, 16
Sarál ...	H	20	8, 21, 39, 49
	M	125	20, 21, 22
Saran ...	H	12	1
Sarár ...	H	23	12, 19, 51
	M	5	6
Sarbahás ...	H	49	4, 35
Sardbá ...	H	9	2, 10
	M	120	2
Sardiá ...	H	3	1, 43
	M	176	1, 6
Sarghaní ...	M	13	25
Sargoí ...	M	41	27
Sarhál ...	H	278	8, 14, 39
Sarí ...	H	10	25, 34
	M	2	1, 15
Sariadiál ...	S	12	10
Sariál ...	H	553	8, 9, 15
	M	138	8, 12, 21, 22
Sarián ...	H	90	2, 9
	M	96	27, 45
Sarmál ...	H	49	7, 8, 9, 15, 27
	S	1	15
Sarodh ...	H	11	11
	S	2	25
	M	129	11, 48
Saroí ...	H	126	1, 5, 6, 8, 9, 15, 16, 25
	S	50	9, 12, 44
	M	407	1, 4, 5, 11, 15, 16
Sarolá ...	H	36	3, 9, 44
Saronch ...	H	583	8, 9, 15, 16
	M	160	16
Sarsawál ...	H	29	1, 48
	M	5	4
Sarsodhe ...	H	25	5
Sarú ...	M	13	9, 25
Sarwá ...	M	64	9, 15
Sarwálí ...	H	36	8, 29, 44
	M	8	1, 24
Sarwánkí ...	H	11	18, 43
	M	30	42
Sarwaria ...	S	165	10, 25
Sashrola ...	M	58	2
Sathwál ...	H	33	4
Satí ...	H	9	8, 11, 24
	M	718	11, 12, 21
Satohia ...	H	93	8
Satráolá ...	M	572	1, 4
Satráwe ...	M	114	5
Satrola ...	M	36	48
Sawál ...	H	28	5, 43
	M	23	22, 49
Sawán ...	H	1	9
	M	11	13, 14, 45
Sawánch ...	H	9	1
	M	25	2
Sáwne ...	H	6	48
	M	15	6, 12, 48
Sáwre ...	H	6	8, 9
	M	15	12
Sawárn ...	H	103	48
Sawátrá ...	H	43	8
Sawiár ...	H	18	2
Sech ...	H	4	4
	M	39	48
Sedal ...	H	16	11
Sehjar ...	M	25	13
Sehre ...	M	19	9
Sekha ...	H	10	9
	M	18	13, 23, 24
Sel ...	H	16	8, 42
	M	2	29
Senpál ...	M	18	12, 14
Será ...	H	11	1, 9
	M	6	1
Sespon ...	H	19	47
Sethí ...	M	11	14, 26
Sewál ...	H	3	2
	M	135	21
Shahídká ...	M	14	1
Sháh-Sarwarí	M	132	10
Shái ...	H	9	42
	M	14	17
Shakar dár ...	H	367	34
Shalílí ...	M	159	19
Shar ...	M	92	51
Sharfí ...	M	34	25, 48
Shátí ...	H	21	24
Shekh ...	M	678	8, 11, 12, 13, 14, 15, 21, 25, 27
Shekháwat ...	H	2,032	1, 2, 3, 12, 17, 21, 32, 48, 49, 50, 51
	S	96	48, 51
	M	82	13, 16, 50
Sheo ...	H	4	14, 23
	M	10	12

Names of Sub-Castes.		Persons.	Locality.
Shiám ...	H	379	7, 9, 39, 41
Shína ...	H	11	42
Shogáwál ...	H	32	12
Shoriá ...	H	3	13
	M	158	16
Siál ...	H	230	8, 10, 13, 18, 51
	S	6	16, 51
	M	83,829	R. M. 1, 10, 12, 16, 42, 51
Siám-Dev ...	H	162	7
Siána ...	H	52	8, 13, 17
	S	97	10
Sikh ...	S	28	12, 25
Sikhon ...	S	92	51
Singh ...	H	12	12
	S	7	14
	M	75	13, 14
Sípí ...	H	79	8
Síratwál ...	H	28	50
Sobhá ...	H	4	8, 24
	S	14	14
	M	29	15, 45
Sodágar ...	H	61	12
Sodan ...	H	13	1, 8, 12
	S	41	14
	M	110	13, 14, 51
Sodána ...	H	9	51
	M	125	13, 51
Sodhá ...	H	56	2, 3, 4, 43
Sodhar ...	H	14	14
Sodhiá ...	H	36	13
	M	4	14
Sodhín ...	M	46	13
Sodí ...	H	16	2, 14
	S	5	17
	M	1	11
Soháll ...	H	241	8
Sohán ...	H	7	8, 27
	M	648	11, 14, 18, 20
Sohána ...	M	13	11, 12, 14, 48
Sohria ...	H	30	8, 15
	M	2	8
Sof ...	H	46	10, 14
Sokhal ...	H	84	9, 12, 42, 48
	M	4	12, 16
Solakh ...	H	31	12, 42
Solakhní ...	H	142	1, 3, 4, 12
	S	19	4
	M	20	2
Solangí ...	H	73	2, 14, 50
	M	3	19
Solgí ...	H	7	51
	M	247	10, 17
Solkia ...	M	11	48
Sombansí ...	H	49	15
Sondí ...	H	2	24
	M	13	15
Sonekí ...	H	83	1, 12, 24
Sonbach ...	H	27	4
Sonk ...	H	45	12, 14
	M	9	14
Sonkhle ...	H	658	8, 9, 12, 39
	M	1	9
Sonthe ...	H	7	43, 47
	M	11	2
Soraj ...	H	13	51
	S	4	12
Soran ...	H	9	4
	M	2	8
Soratwál ...	H	11	3
Sore ...	M	39	13, 21
Sorián ...	H	73	4, 8
Sorjan ...	H	75	9
Soskali ...	H	11	11
Sotí ...	H	4	8, 9
	S	13	5
	M	8	13, 15, 25
Sotra ...	M	36	15, 25, 27
Súd ...	H	82	13, 15, 47
	S	10	13, 14
Súdán ...	H	21	8, 51
	S	48	27
	M	86	20
Súdiál ...	H	29	48
Súherá ...	H	33	8
Sulemána ...	M	92	27
Sultán ...	M	32	25
Súmrá ...	H	3	15
	M	17	27
Supiah ...	H	1,018	8, 42
Surajbansí ...	H	3,687	J. L. 3, 5, 6, 7, 21, 34, 35, 36, 37, 41, 47, 48, 49
	S	190	6, 25, 33, 48, 50, 51
	M	202	7, 10, 13, 18, 25, 48
Súrál ...	H	136	8
Súrath ...	H	14	8
Súrí ...	H	34	14, 37
	M	15	9, 12, 14, 15
Susa ...	H	47	8
Tadí ...	H	1	26
	M	118	13, 15, 25
Tádrí ...	H	8	6, 9
	S	25	9
	M	1	11
Tag ...	H	6	48
	M	9	6
Tagále ...	H	2	48
	M	17	48
Tagar ...	M	12	12
Tagiál ...	M	26	1, 6
Tahgarán ...	S	22	9
Tahím ...	M	200	11, 12, 13, 24, 45
Takariál ...	H	20	39
Takhí ...	H	89	9
	M	2	8
Takhípadhár	M	23	9
Taklí ...	H	158	8
Taknál ...	H	22	8
	S	2	9
Taliál ...	H	17	8, 47
	M	18	22
Talor ...	H	17	8, 9, 15
	M	1,378	2, 15
Tamiál ...	H	1	16
	M	485	21
Tammar ...	H	126	25, 50
	M	103	12, 50
Táná ...	H	49	4, 9
	M	57	21
Tandal ...	H	73	4, 9, 15
	S	6	12, 25
Tandiár ...	H	14	9
Tángá ...	H	12	9
	M	6	11
Tangar ...	H	25	12, 19, 25, 27, 42
	M	22	24
Tangrál ...	H	373	8, 15
	S	13	15
	M	112	21
Tángrí ...	H	14	8
Táuí ...	H	4	5
	M	101	1, 10, 11, 50
Tanjar ...	M	15	14
Táuk ...	H	301	1, 5, 13, 14, 17, 18, 20, 21, 22, 27, 48
	S	77	17, 18, 27
	M	17	14, 17, 26, 45
Tanurbansí ...	H	68	7
Tánwartí ..	H	21	51
	M	547	19
Táon ...	H	2,377	5, 6, 8, 9, 11, 33, 48
	S	48	9, 48
	M	26,116	2, 8, 9, 11, 46, 48
Tapiál ...	H	883	8
Tárach ...	H	6	47
	S	5	25
	M	10	1, 13
Tárak ...	M	12	22, 46
Taráná ...	M	20	1
Tarar ...	M	20	17, 48
Targar ...	H	5	51
	M	868	14, 26, 27, 28
Tarbár ...	M	102	18
Tarhili ...	M	225	51
Táriá ...	H	31	8
	M	18	25, 48
Tarial ...	H	223	8, 9, 19, 20, 25, 47
	M	2	21
Tarián ...	M	48	31
Tarkál ...	H	10	9
	M	16	9, 18
Tarkhán ...	H	3	8
	M	61	10, 13, 16, 28, 29
Tarní ...	M	36	11
Tarond ...	M	94	21
Tarondalá ...	H	218	9, 41, 42
Tarrí ...	M	472	17, 25
Táru ...	H	13	13
	M	901	1, 6, 17, 19, 24, 25
Taswál ...	H	273	9
	S	51	9
Tatálá ...	H	60	15
	S	2	16
Tathiál ...	H	2	25
	S	2	9
	M	1,676	9, 14, 20, 21, 25
Tátre ...	H	7	8, 13, 17
	M	126	19, 22, 45
Tatwál ...	H	101	8, 9
Táwar ...	H	820	3, 12, 24
	S	10	12, 27
	M	12	13, 22
Tekat ...	H	12	1
Telí ...	H	5	8
	M	18	8, 13, 15
Temur ...	M	67	4, 48
Thadár ...	M	13	13
Thadiál ...	H	17	8
Thadri ...	S	28	9
Thákkar ...	H	18,509	L. 4, 6, 7, 8, 12, 18, 19, 23, 25, 48, 50, 51
	S	6	14, 16, 25, 27
	M	258	11, 14, 15, 21, 25
Thákkar-panj-goí.	H	20	48
Thákrí ...	H	21	8, 17
	M	302	8, 12, 16, 18, 25
Thalgí ...	H	33	8, 20
Thaliál ...	H	15	47
Thaliáng ...	H	13	8
Thaloriá .	H	2	27
	M	14	13, 16
Thalwál ...	H	158	8
Thandál ...	M	22	9, 10, 13, 15
Thápá ...	H	47	8, 15, 21, 34, 44, 47
Tharband ...	M	13	9
Thetá ...	S	2	19
	M	342	13, 19
Thorí ...	S	1	9
	M	28	1
Thunthal ...	H	19	8, 9
	M	49	22
Tiách ...	H	5	39
	S	30	10
	M	7	11
Tibí ...	M	18	22
Tihárí ...	H	114	8
Tímár ...	M	19	48
Tingarí ...	H	33	5
Tíre ...	H	46	8
Tíván ...	M	29	12
Tiwáná ...	H	35	24
	M	2,285	16, 19, 20, 25, 27
Todal ...	H	1	9
	M	1,056	12
Tohar ...	H	10	8, 19, 44
	M	455	1, 6, 12
Tokar ...	H	165	8
Tol ...	H	22	6, 15
	S	3	19
	M	70	9, 10, 12, 17, '4
Tomar ...	H	120	25, 34, 41
	S	4	14, 42
	M	81	5
Tongar ...	M	167	12, 20
Topal ...	H	19	8
Torálí ...	H	15	6
Torewál ...	M	45	10, 14
Torgar ...	M	105	27
Tori ...	H	23	9, 17, 19
	S	3	14
Totar ...	H	8	15, 44
	M	1,372	2
Tunwár ...	H	5,520	1, 4, 5, 6, 34, 46
	S	11	3, 12
	M	8,189	1, 3, 4, 6, 19, 33

Names of Sub-Castes.	Persons.	Locality.	Names of Sub-Castes.	Persons.	Locality.	Names of Sub-Castes.	Persons.	Locality.
Tur ... H	2,046	D. J. 21, 24, 31, 48, 49, 50, 51	Vaish ... H	2	27	Vasti-bhattu M	17	24
			S	2	16,	Vásu ... M	19	13
S	87	11, 12, 17, 18 20, 21, 48, 49	M	170	12, 18, 20	Vattu ... H	59	1, 13, 14, 16, 17
			Vajhálká ... M	42	26	S	2	12, 15
M	18,093	D. J. L. R. 25, 44, 45, 46, 48, 49, 50, 51	Vajíáná ... H	9	16	M	24,286	1, 12, 13, 24, 25 46
			M	8	27			
			Valáná ... M	323	20, 26	Vedí ... H	6	17
Tutyál ... H	24	9	Valásar ... M	11	25	S	3	28
Umnál ... H	14	9	Valh ... M	62	14	M	27	13, 14
Unále ... H	25	9	Valiár ... M	299	25	Vehiá ... M	84	25
Uthwál ... M	74	25, 51	Ván ... M	12	17, 18	Veráná ... M	165	25
Uttam ... H	51	7, 9, 47, 48	Vanáká ... M	53	26	Verka ... M	148	1, 26, 27, 46
Vadhán ... H	19	16, 27	Váns ... M	62	12, 14, 21	Virk ... H	1	16
M	11	16	Varáich ... M	149	19, 21, 25	M	110	1, 21, 26
Vaghá ... M	77	51	Varangal ... H	123	15	Zamindár ... H	2	13
Vagor ... M	15	12	Varbhu ... M	124	26	M	11	17
Váhal ... M	476	24	Varí ... H	1	12	Zargar ... H	173	19, 25, 41
Váhanswál ... M	15	25	M	49	13	S	6	14
Váhí ... H	48	13	Variál ... M	872	2, 13, 15, 18, 20	M	13	13, 14, 25
S	9	13	Varoj ... M	18	14	* Minor ... H	3,318	
M	160	25	Varsiál ... M	49	15, 51	S	425	
Vahídi ... M	12	13	Vasáldárí ... M	27	12, 51	M	2,423	
Vahorí ... M	19	25	Vasand ... M	42	24	Unspecified ... H	36,159	
Váhrí ... H	82	12	Vaser ... H	2	9	S	4,106	
Vajns ... H	7	16, 48	M	1,257	12, 17, 24, 25	M	122,632	
S	2	16	Vasht ... M	355	24	J	14	
M	110	M. 13, 16, 19	Vasti ... M	29	24, 25			

* DETAIL OF MINOR.

Abanse 1, Abdodiá 3, Abdoh 3, Abejas 4, Abí 1, Ablohe 4, Abrás 2, Abráwat 1, Abrí 4, Abrole 1, Abú 1, Achjariál 10, Achú 2, Adaryál 3, Adese 1, Adhkhásiá 1, Adiál 1, Adjariál 1, Adráná 2, Adwál 2, Agarbansí 1, Agárná 1, Agarwál 7, Aghar 1, Aghián 4, Agiárí 2, Agot 1, Agpál 3, Agrániá 1, Agrás 1, Agrí 6, Agtáh 2, Agwál 5. Ahal 2, Áhangar 2, Ahí 7, Aholi 1, Ai 9, Aindar 2, Airi 3, Ajbar 2, Ajmeriá 8, Ajoráh 9, Ajpat 1, Ajrá 1, Ajrál 1, Ajroe 6, Ajrot 4, Akár 1, Akhárí 3, Akhroliá 1, Akhtaryál 1, Akotaliá 2, Alone 9, Amdo 6, Amhál 2, Amír 10, Amkoriá 1, Amlá 2, Amrá 6, Anand 2, Anarwál 2, Anas 7, Anat 4, Anbrái 6, Anbotah 5, Andat 1, Andhan 2, Andíl 1, Andlá 8, Andoí 5, Andro 3, Angrer 5, Angrás 1, Anmol 1, Anot 4, Antre 6, Anwán 8, Anwar 1, Arakwál 1, Arbali 6, Arbola 6, Ard 1, Ariál 4, Aro 1, Arond 2, Asáin 3, Asar 9, Ashkandrál 4, Ashláníár 8, Aspot 3, Asráb 1, Aster 2, Astwál 1, Atal 2, Ath 1, Athál 3, Athán 6, Atras 3, Aujhá 10, Aukáwat 3, Aulakh 1, Aule 5, Aur 1, Aurál 8, Aurwál 8, Ayál 6, Bábá 2, Babián 2, Babnotí 5, Bábot 5, Babyál 1, Báchhol 3, Badáiál 10, Badália 2, Badar 10, Baden 3, Badgal 2, Badh 6, Badhegí 1, Badhí 3, Badhro 1, Badhuri 3, Bádí 10, Badkí 1, Badmániá 3, Badorat 5, Badyánti 4, Bagána 1, Bágbán 4, Baghlána 3, Bagoí 1, Bagrath 9, Bagriál 2, Bahaur 2, Báhí 7, Bahmoriá 9, Báhrí 9, Báhú 8, Bair 10, Bajat 10, Bajgotí 1, Bajha 3, Bajhar 10, Bajkar 5, Bajlána 1, Bajoí 2, Bajwál 2, Bajwáthá 10, Bakáwal 3, Bakerá 2, Bakbáriá 10, Bakhslána 1, Baláhar 9, Balánia 2, Balarya 2, Balháua 10, Balkhan 2, Balpál 3, Balwál 5, Bamhatí 8, Bámjáh 10, Bamrál 1, Bána 5, Banáua 10, Banaut 10, Banar 5, Banársí 7, Banartha 8, Bandal 1, Banderaghau 1, Bándhiál 5, Bandhián 3, Bandiár 8, Bandwál 3, Banetí 1, Bangáne 1, Bángar 5, Bangátie 3, Bangriál 1, Bangú 4, Bangwál 4, Baní 4, Banírot 4, Banjáhí 9, Bánke 1, Bankoh 1, Bankoí 7, Bankotiá 1, Banoí 2, Bansarí 1, Bantáne 4, Bantorí 5, Banún 2, Bánwái 3, Bar 4, Barága 4, Baráj 1, Baráj-Mal 2, Barál 1, Baránjí 4, Baras 8, Baráthí 2, Baráwat 2, Bardí 4, Bargháin 1, Barghwál 5, Bargojí 1, Bargola 1, Bargota 6, Barhat 3, Barhwála 3, Bári 3, Barín 2, Barkando 1, Barkí 4, Barliál 4, Barmá 3, Barmálá 5, Barmár 5, Barnáhrí 1, Barnála 2, Barnoliá 1, Barogal 2, Baroghá 3, Baroí 4, Barondhiá 6, Barpál 2, Barser 3, Barsil 2, Barthí 1, Barwáia 1, Básau 9, Básdev 1, Bashír 1, Bashúkarma 9, Báso 1, Bastán 3, Batak 9, Bátal 3, Batehrí 2, Bathlániá 1, Batka 7, Bátrán 9, Batrárí 9, Batrasí 3, Bed 2, Beg 1, Ben 4, Beraghwá 6, Berjana 8, Berwál 3, Bet 2, Betam 1, Bethere 6, Bhabhal 4, Bhabúle 1, Bhadíga 1, Bhador 7, Bhadrí 10, Bhágalwál 1, Bhagáotí 2, Bhagriál 10, Bhagat 1, Bhagiánián 1, Bhagwán 8, Bhágwas 2, Bhagwatí 2, Bháj 10, Bhajwál 1, Bhakolá 5, Bhalbansí 5, Bhalgot 3, Bhaloriá 8, Bhalotrí 7, Bhande 2, Bhandián 3, Bhanewál 6, Bhangar 9, Bhankána 1, Bhansar 10, Bharái 2, Bharáich 10, Bháraj 4, Bharákh 6, Bharbhúnja 3, Bharí 3, Bharwána 10, Bhadin 2, Bhatiál 2, Bhatián 1, Bhati-Tánk 2, Bhator 9, Bhatúl 7, Bháwal 8, Bháwja 2, Bheji 1, Bherí 1, Bhet 4, Bhilmar 1, Bhindál 5, Bhitah 2, Bhodal 1, Bhodet 7, Bhogla 1, Bhojal 5, Bhokal 8, Bhoke 1, Bhonán 2, Bhonsar 1, Bhonse 4, Bhont 1, Bhorjia 4, Bhorle 9, Bhorna 10, Bhosá 1, Bhotú 1, Bhowálí 1, Bhudam bans 2, Bhúndant 10, Bhúp 10, Bhúpál 2, Bhúrna 4, Bhút 1, Biámí 2, Bij 2, Bijro 2, Biláspawálie 8, Bodh 3, Bodí 9, Bodla 3, Bohar 5, Bojwál 2, Bokar 1, Bolachh 5, Boldal 1, Bolián 9, Bone 3, Bong 3, Bonián 2, Bopárái 1, Borána 1, Bordián 2, Bosara 1, Búdí 2, Chábá 9, Cháchh 1, Chadarwed 1, Chagartárí 3, Chágarú 8, Chagriál 2, Chakbansí 1, Chakrále 1, Chakwál 3, Chal 1, Chalorthá 1, Chamál 1, Chambah 4, Chamiárat 1, Chanáiá 4, Chanál 2, Chanára 7, Chandan 7, Chándáwat 4, Chandharí 1, Chandhoria 1, Chandú 2, Chandí-Púj 2, Chandre 1, Changiál 4, Chankárá 2, Chánon 3, Chánwalí 1, Chanwán 1, Chánwara 8, Chappal 3, Charál 1, Charantia 2, Charban 8, Charmán 1, Charne 3, Charnotiá 7, Charoj 2, Charore 4, Chars 1, Charwágar 4, Charwál 10, Charwán 1, Cháryárí 1, Chaskí 1, Chatána 2, Chatror 1, Chatroí 6, Chechlá 1, Chechrí 1, Cherá 2, Chhachhor 7, Chhachhrí 7, Chhad 1, Chhaj 10, Chhal 10, Chhaní 10, Chhania 10, Chhanot 1, Chhawán 3, Chháwariá 1, Chhe 3, Chhore 10, Chhoria 1, Chiáne 1, Chíbá 1, Chír 2, Chirí-Már 2, Chisar 2, Chitro 6, Chobdár 1, Chodhan 1, Chohá 6, Chobánbhattí 3, Chohán-Khokhar 6, Chohán-Konsal 1, Chohar-Kháni 4, Chohatta 4, Chobra 8, Chokhar 10, Chong 1, Chonj 4, Chopar 5, Chora 3, Chorat 1, Chore 3, Chotrí 1, Chanble 1, Chúníe 2, Churia 1, Dabána 3, Dabarwál 1, Dablia 5, Dabrár 2, Dádúpotra 1, Dádre 1, Dáffú 6, Dágú 3, Dágwál 5, Dahal 2, Dahití 6, Dáhliá 7, Dáhra 1, Dáimí 8, Dáin 9, Dakhna 5, Dakol 6, Daksara 5, Dalán 10, Daláwar-Kháni 8, Daloga 6, Daloporia 2, Dalotrí 1, Dalwan 5, Dambal 1, Daurú 4, Damtiál 2, Dandár 2, Dandosia 10, Dánkí 2, Dáns 3, Dánsara 2, Darambál 5, Darchand 2, Dardkháni 10, Darege 6, Dares 1, Dariáíbáf 2, Darnáth 8, Daror 3, Darsang 5, Darúsat 3, Dasáín 4, Daska 6, Daslim 10, Dastí 6, Datí-Poriá 1, Datar 3, Dáúdke 9, Daugalia 1, Daul-Rathor 4, Dawái 6, Dayál 9, Dayás 2, Dehona-Malál 4, Dela 8, Dengoí 2, Deoke 1, Deoní 4, Der 9, Derkalbái 8, Desar 1, Desí-Lán 2, Dhabba 3, Dhadarwál 1, Dhadpál 5, Dhágar 8, Dhagwán 1, Dhakú 1, Dhalárí 10, Dhalwána 3, Dhamáí 9, Dhamsbái 1, Dhan 10, Dhángal 2, Dhange 4, Dhank 4, Dhanoí 3, Dhanzí 1, Dháral 3, Dharás 1, Dhargwál 2, Dhatríjoh 2, Dhárka 3, Dharkháne 2, Dharní 2, Dhatse 7, Dhaunchak 2, Dhawí 7, Dhawra 2, Dhesí 5, Dhilána 2, Dhím 8, Dhíndsa 3, Dhirpat 3, Dhobí 2, Dhode 6, Dhokar 1, Dholea 4, Dholú 6, Dhongat 7, Dhor 8, Dhoriál 9, Dhotí 5, Dhotri 1, Dhúmrat 3, Dhúndlor 10, Didár 1, Díndár 1, Deorá 4, Diptí 1, Dípú 4, Dírwál 1, Dobaj 4, Dobalá 1, Dohata 2, Dober 1, Dod-Khandar 5, Doeja 6, Dogálon 2, Dogarwál 5, Dohdí 10, Dopar 3, Doraj 4, Doráne 8, Dosála 1, Dosánjah 6, Dostán 2, Doyálá 9, Dún 5, Far 3, Fargáh 2, Faríd 1, Farsí 1, Fárú 9, Fatehtawárí 6, Fatejí 3, Fatú 1, Fegwál 5, Gabára 1, Gachwáhe 2, Gadotí 1, Gadri 7, Gagwál 5, Gagyán 4, Gahír 6, Gaí 4, Gaisí 1, Gákhal 2, Galans 2, Galesar 6, Galgorí 1, Galoranwál 5, Galori 1, Galrí 2, Gamarpur 1, Gamroiá 4, Gamyár 8, Ganbariá 3, Gánda 5, Gandhan 2, Gandlí 6, Gandpuria 1, Gandsar 1, Gandú 2, Gandwália 3, Gang 9, Gangot 2, Ganj 10, Ganaur 2, Garal 3, Garánbal 1, Garanjí 3, Garewál 3, Gargágarí 2, Gark 1, Garojandí 1, Gashtí 5, Gasrátia 4, Gathe 1, Gatiál 3, Gatriál 3, Gandí 2, Gauhra 2, Gází-Khán 6, Gehla 9, Gehlon 4, Gelor 2, Gerat 2, Ghagú 6, Ghagyál 2, Ghakhí 1, Ghallan 1, Ghamar 5, Ghandwál 2, Ghang 1, Ghant 10, Ghantiál 5, Gharále 1, Ghart 1, Ghárú 4, Ghenas 1, Gherparia 1, Ghí 1, Ghiál 5, Ghís 6, Ghons 3, Ghorakh 1, Ghorsita 3, Ghosí 4, Gidarpiyára 2, Gikhoka 3, Girwál 6, Gítí 9, Giwál-Pore 1, Giyán 2, Giyat 1, Gobar 2, Godbhákar 7, Godharí 6, Godí 2, Gog 9, Gogáli 1, Goges 1, Goghna 5, Gogtí 1, Gohat 1, Gojhale 3, Gokhápir 8, Gole 7, Golmár 2, Gomalí 1, Goman 5, Gona 2, Gondhi-Lára 3, Gopál 8, Gopí-Rái 1, Gopra 6, Gorál 1, Gork 6, Gorle 1, Gorti 3, Gosal 5, Gotangí 1, Gotar 6, Gowálsí 3, Gowána 6, Gujrátí 2, Guláb-Dásí 6, Gulhát 1, Gul-Sharhí 3, Gurúbans 1, Gurwára 1, Gusábí 2, Guwárda 1, Hadín 3, Hájíke 1, Hajwán 1, Hakím 5, Hakorí 2, Hakút 2, Halál 3, Halápa 9, Halíp 1, Halkar 10, Halwál 5, Ham 7, Hamal 3, Hamas 3, Hamír-Puria 5, Hamra 7, Hamwál 1, Handrika 4, Hanera 6, Hankárí 2, Hanún 1, Harápál-Chattí 2, Harát 1, Harga 1, Hargra 9, Harl 8, Harlát 7, Harnál 9, Haro 2, Harpál 1, Haryás 2, Hatámí 3, Hathárí 10, Hazrat-Pir-Madan 2, Hech 6, Hem 2, Hemráh 1, Híkh 2, Hindú 10, Hingria 10,

* DETAIL OF MINOR—*concluded.*

Hinsar 1, Hír-bans 2, Hitar 2, Hitwár 2, Hodí 7, Hokrí 1, Holar 4, Hole 1, Homar 1, Honiál 6, Húngarh 8, It 8, Jabal 1, Jaddev 1, Jadhaut 1, Jadol 1, Jadosl 2, Jadwál 1, Jagdi Pur 6, Jagpál 1, Jagrí 5, Jagríth 7, Jagzai 4, Jáhí 7, Jaikam 4, Jaiswár 2, Jájam 1, Jalál-Kháni 10, Jálo 7, Jalot 4, Jálwá 8, Jamání 1, Jámar 1, Jamble 1, Jamna 10, Jamorá 1, Jamwáli 4, Jandara 4, Jandole 8, Jándrán 2, Janglí 5, Janglohtí 3, Janiál 1, Janj 8, Jankálí 5, Jankí 2, Janwán 9, Jar 6, Jarán 1, Jaráwalia 3, Jarbár 1, Jarpálí 1, Jasta 1, Jastroba 9, Jatak 2, Jatia 4, Jatwál 1, Jáwara 2, Jedbár 1, Jehdo 3, Jehlú 1, Jethí 7, Jhájor 9, Jhatwál 6, Jhokar 4, Jhokari 5, Jhongri 1, Jhonkar 4, Jhotra 1, Jipál 1, Jiriálah 6, Jirmál 4, Jiwán 1, Jodhan 8, Jogiánor 10, Johal 6, Joslí 7, Kabír-Bansí 7, Kabona 10, Kachávar 1, Kachhár 5, Kadore 4, Kahant 1, Kahiál 4, Kabli 8, Káhr 1, Kahtar 2, Kajar 8, Kak 7, Kal 1, Kalánot 4, Káliá 6, Kalián-Chand 2, Kaliás 3, Káli-Kat 4, Kalodhan 1, Kalohia 5, Kaleiá 6, Kamálap 2, Kamera 2, Kanan 3, Kánár 6, Kanbti 1, Kand 1, Kandka 1, Kangar 4, Kangas 10, Kanjhán 4, Kanoch 2, Kánpalia 1, Kánpúr 10, Kanth 1, Kanwáwán 5, Kapáhtia 6, Kapái 10, Kaprí 6, Karáni 2, Karánia 9, Karáthí 6, Kardwál 2, Kargandle 10, Karháua 1, Karhoi 3, Karjan 1, Karián 2, Karuási 3, Karnáwat 2, Karnpál 9, Karodh 5, Kart 2, Kartha 1, Kásab Dawál 9, Kasán 8, Kasdai 1, Kasorí 2, Kasotar 3, Kastúl 1, Kású 9, Kátah 3, Kataur 8, Katbáwat 9, Kátbia 3, Káth-pália 2, Káwália 4, Kawátáh 4, Kegar 4, Kellí 4, Kelo 2, Kental 10, Keza 3, Khabra 4, Khadára 6, Khadyál 1, Khagre 1, Kháil 6, Khairátí 3, Khakhrail 2, Khakri 8, Khalária 10, Khálik 1, Khaloria 9, Khámar 1, Khán 6, Khande 3, Khapí 1, Kharak 6, Kharkhodia 4, Khartoí 1, Khatak 2, Khataryálí 2, Khatloria 7, Khatran 10, Khatwál 7, Khatwára 2, Kheti 10, Khí 3, Kholáia 1, Khona 4, Khonar 1, Kilole 1, Kior 7, Kírath 1, Kirk 1, Kirwál 6, Kochan 6, Kochgar 10, Kodán 2, Kogas 4, Kohr 10, Kokas 8, Kokolrí 3, Koldher 9, Kolere 6, Konar 6, Konetra 3, Koriál 9, Korra 6, Koskí 4, Kotlás 1, Kottárí 9, Kotwálí 2, Labár 1, Labhúma 5, Ladan 8, Ladharial 6, Ladí 7, Lagan 1, Lágar 8, Lagwái 2, Lagwál 8, Laharwá 2, Lábní 1, Lakesar 4, Lakhatrá 4, Lakháwat 2, Lákhwán 2, Lakriál 2, Lálí 5, Lángas 8, Langto 6, Lanká 2, Lánkar 4, Laret 3, Largaralgán 2, Lashárí 1, Latarí 4, Látghál 4, Láthra 9, Latka 5, Láwní 1, Lodú 1, Lohaskarn 3, Lolárie 6, Lonbán 9, Losáí 1, Lotar 3, Lotní 3, Lotrá 3, Mách 1, Machhána 3, Madáwat 3, Madíra 10, Magerú 7, Magharám 4, Magí 3, Magodiá 1, Magri 7, Mahájan 3, Mahammad 1, Mahammal 1, Mahándras 4, Mahangán 8, Mahansi 6, Mahant 7, Maháthi 7, Maháwan 2, Mahgo 5, Máhíwál 9, Mahriál 4, Máhtari 6, Maindar 4, Majroí 1, Majrotia 1, Majtál 2, Makandhá 3, Makandwál 1, Makhoria 1, Malagrál 7, Maláhtar 1, Malanhás 3, Malárine 2, Malas 2, Malghora 2, Malhati 2, Mállidharo 2, Malohriá 2, Málri 7, Málsi 6, Mán 1, Manálo 1, Manchhi 1, Mandaro 6, Mandáwar 2, Mandiáni 4, Mangar 2, Mángat 4, Mangiál 4, Manwai 4, Mangwali 2, Maniái 9, Manjál 9, Manjarial 5, Manjtor 6, Mankal 1, Mankoi 6, Manpál 1, Manwál 1, Marádwál 1, Marás 3, Mare 9, Marhwán 1, Márjan 9, Markha 3, Márni 5, Marot 3, Mársot 1, Marwái 9, Masand 5, Masandiál 2, Mashgori 5, Maska 8, Masú 8, Matar 9, Matás 8, Mathiás 9, Matíla 7, Matíre 9, Matirhána 1, Matkábí 7, Matolia 2, Matra 8, Mattú 2, Megrámot 5, Mehra 5, Mehráwat 3, Mehtor 1, Melí 9, Mendhí 6, Menhosí 8, Mental 2, Merath 1, Merdhar 1, Merhú 5, Mesúr 8, Mewá 4, Mewán 1, Mewár 1, Míka 4, Míkan 6, Milka 8, Minbár 1, Miráki 9, Miral 6, Mirhán 5, Modes 1, Mohiál 5, Mosla 4, Moth 6, Muftí 5, Mungí 4, Nadhandi 5, Nadmál 1, Nág 1, Nágái 1, Nágaro 1, Náglí 5, Nagoshi 1, Náhal 7, Nabol 3, Naboti 1, Nahrál 1, Nákas 8, Nakhán 4, Nakhiár 1, Nalúra 3, Náná 6, Nandbár 6, Nandorí 1, Nandúka 6, Nanhá 6, Nanotri 9, Nanwár 6, Napar 4, Nargan 1, Narhál 10, Narkí 2, Narnihal 2, Nární 10, Narol 10, Nast 1, Naswál 1, Náth 3, Náthak 10, Naul 2, Nauráh 10, Nausherwání 3, Nawáb-zádí 2, Nob 5, Niáman 1, Niás 2, Nigáh 2, Nigiál 3, Nijáwar 1, Ním 1, Nímar 3, Nistrá 9, Nclara 2, Noloí 1, Nondíwat 3, Nongar 1, Nonúwán 3, Odemán 4, Odín 1, Oniábnia 8, Onshábí 3, Ontwál 2, Pabrœ 1, Pachhal 2, Pachísi 2, Padal 1, Padwál 1, Paghan 1, Pagwáli 1, Páhgot 3, Páhra 9, Pakhíwárá 7, Pakhrál 6, Palálá 1, Palastar 2, Paliál 9, Palkálí 2, Palotá 6, Palwál 9, Panch 8, Pandá 1, Pandpur 10, Pangál 2, Pángalá 9, Pangián 8, Panglan 5, Panhárá 8, Paniáwá 8, Pánír 2, Panjábí 8, Panjal 10, Panjália 5, Panjwál 3, Pantal 3, Paráke 8, Paran 3, Parhár-Lakhni 3, Parhwál 1, Párkárá 2, Parmál 6, Parochal 2, Parohtí 3, Pasháwrí 3, Pasiál 1, Pasnot 5, Pát 5, Patálí 5, Patang 2, Pathiára 5, Patiána 3, Patíj 7, Phadiár 2, Phagwárá 4, Phakar 8, Phali 5, Phalor 10, Phalra 1, Phangí 1, Phatána 5, Phedrú 8, Phol 6, Phon 4, Phorí 10, Phote 1, Píál 9, Pilkan 1, Piple 2, Pitách 1, Podar 3, Pode 2, Pondar 6, Popal 5, Pople 4, Posír 7, Potí 2, Pujan 1, Pwálah 2, Qádar 2, Qanúngo 8, Qassáb 2, Rabí 4, Radhonka 1, Radwái 6, Ragan 2, Ragetí 1, Raghnáth 2, Raghoriá 1, Raghúsan 4, Rágian 1, Raglál 2, Ragpál 1, Rahál 7, Ráibans 2, Railwáí 1, Ráín 1, Ráisal 5, Rajádá 3, Rájbandar 1, Rájbar 4, Rájíná 1, Rájkaur 7, Rájkos 2, Rájoá 7, Rájoí 4, Rájon 3, Rájpút-Náikí 1, Rájtúr 3, Rakhán 10, Rakhbansí 6, Rákho 6, Rakhráj 4, Rákot 1, Raláich 2, Rallá 9, Ramáwat 2, Rámbansí 6, Rámiál 6, Rámorká 5, Rámportiá 1,Ráná gaddí 1, Randán 4, Rang 1, Rangas 3, Rání 8, Ranián 3, Ráo 5, Ráon 1, Rásí 9, Rasotre 5, Ratan hardawár 4, Ratan-jot 2, Ratrám 2, Ratti 1, Ratúria 5, Rawáiá 1, Rawánch 2, Rechhí 2, Reta 6, Rodá 3, Roghat 5, Rogi 2, Rohlí 2, Rol 10, Roleti 2, Roshan 3, Rudiál 7, Rukmáná 10, Rúp-Rái 9, Sabhá 3, Sabiál 7, Sabkhál 8, Sabráin 6, Sabráne 6, Sachdev 1, Sadáná 5, Sadesar 4, Sadhánch 1, Sadiqi 6, Sadmárá 3, Saghar 10, Sagi 7, Sagiál 1, Sagliri 1, Ságol 3, Sagonte 2, Sagotre 1, Sagrál 6, Saháwá 10, Saháwan 4, Sahdev 5, Sáholiá 6, Sahorá 8, Sáhu 3, Saiád 1, Saidhorá 4, Saiyadpurá 8, Sajád 2, Sájgor 1, Sájí 8, Sajre 2, Sajumán 1, Sakam 4, Sakarwár 5, Sakhiá 1, Sákhli 7, Sakhot 9, Sakhotrá 5, Sakhpán 1, Sákhti 5, Saki 4, Sakohliá 3, Sakotiá 2, Sakpál 1, Saktál 4, Sál 3, Salabati 2, Salás 7, Sálbáhan 1, Salege 1, Saliáná 5, Salkaná 9, Sálochá 5, Salohke 5, Salohri 4, Saloi 2, Salonki 7, Saloriá 6, Sálot 2, Sálu 10, Samágan 3, Samáji 1, Sámet 7, Samián 3, Samotri 7, Samri 6, Samrichohadá 10, Sanál 10, Sanámi 5, Sanbal 4, Sanbu 6, Sandan 6, Sandáná 6, Sandarke 1, Sandeorá 4, Sandhan 4, Sandháwe 1, Sandhil 2, Sandhwál 2, Sandirás 1, Sandok 1, Sandrál 9, Sángá 4, Sangálí 9, Sanghu 4, Sánglo 2, Sangni 6, Sangniál 3, Sangot 1, Sangrat 1, Sangwáná 5, Saniás 9, Sanibhale 8, Sanihori 5, Sanikand 3, Sánj 1, Sánkh 2, Sankri 2, Sanloká 10, Sanod 1, Sanoi 3, Sanon-Kalár 3, Sanorwál 8, Sanpati 4, Sanre 4, Sapáne 5, Saped 3, Saphal 1, Saptál 2, Saqá 1, Sarájá 5, Sárbán 1, Sarbat 5, Saretwal 1, Sargot 5, Sárhoi 3, Sariá 6, Sarmá 10, Sarmande 5, Sarmor 1, Sarniál 1, Saropál 3, Sarsáná 1, Sarsoi 1, Sársut 3, Sartiál 2, Sásan 7, Sasre 2, Satáliá 7, Satás 1, Satgorá 1, Sáthá 4, Sathot 1, Satori 1, Satriá 6, Saundwál 1, Saung 5, Sawá 2, Sawár 10, Sawár-bansí 2, Sawáriá 2, Sawáriál 1, Sayone 1, Sedan 1, Sehwál 2, Selrá 10, Selurthá 1, Sená 7, Sendu 4, Sengu 3, Seswár 3, Shabáh 2, Shabáná 1, Shábrí 3, Sháh-sarwán 8, Shabad 7, Sháj 8, Shaloí 2, Sháuá 3, Shánkaliá 1, Shariál 6, Shawál 3, Shehnál 5, Shahwál 2, Shekh 6, Shekh-qureshi 8, Shekhu 5, Shergil 7, Sherwáli 2, Shewáni 5, Sialag 4, Sídor 5, Sídu 1, Sílo 5, Silodiá 5, Siná-wár 4, Síndar 9, Siráj-wál 1, Sirí-darsam 7, Sital 2, Sobágh 2, Sobhángí 7, Sochal 7, Sodar 4, Sodharká 2, Sogal 8, Sogan 7, Sogar 3, Soháí 1, Sohong 2, Sokhdá 9, Solá 5, Solar 1, Soliá 4, Somí 7, Son 4, Songi 5, Soní 4, Sonkar 5, Sonkelá 3, Sonsi 2, Sontrá 2, Sorthiá 3, Soterí 8, Sotwál 2, Sukhpál 1, Suthre 5, Tabálí 2, Tábar 1, Tadniál 1, Tagání 10, Tagarwál 1, Táil 6, Tajorí 1, Taknet 5, Takáhí 1, Takrí 9, Taksái 2, Taláí 1, Talká 2, Talmán 1, Talok Chande 3, Tánaní 4, Taniá 8, Tankmál 2, Tanwál 1, Taqi 8, Tarat 2, Tarewál 5, Tarwál 1, Tarmán 2, Tarogá 1, Taroí 1, Tarore 1, Tarwál 8, Tatá 7, Tatá-wáliá 6, Tatkhal 7, Tawánar 1, Tawle 8, Tevár 1, Thegiá 6, Thakiál 2, Thakrá 6, Thal 7, Thalá 1, Thalwárá 1, Thamán 2, Thand 1, Thápal 2, Thar 1, Thrál 9, Thárí 6, Thathí 1, Thunj 4, Tílo 1, Tilwár 8, Tipal 1, Títari 5, Todar 2, Togariá 2, Toháná 4, Tobawre 1, Tokhal 8, Toláí 1, Tonban 3, Topan 3, Toriál 1, Tul-bághán 3, Tulsí 1, Turk 7, Tut 2, Ulmán 3, Undhar 1, Utrádhí 2, Utre 8, Váchhá 3, Vachhíwár 1, Vachhole 1, Vadá 7, Vadh 9, Vadhál 9, Vadpálíá 6, Vadwál 1, Vákh 4, Vakoriá 1, Valím 5, Vándar 2, Vangar 3, Vanjárá 3, Varang 3, Varmái 1, Varvegá 3, Vasiál 3, Yusaf-zái 2, Zandán 7, Zangu 9.

Names of Sub-Castes.	Persons.	Locality.	Names of Sub-Castes.	Persons.	Locality.	Names of Sub-Castes.	Persons.	Locality.
Sheikh ... M.	338,873		Anand ... M	444	17, 18, 19, 21	Babbar ... M	176	13, 17, 27
			Andí ... M	541	9, 14, 15	Badár ... M	90	44, 51
Abbásí ... M	966	1, 5, 6, 9, 10, 48, 51	Ansárí ... M	8,047	B. 37, 44, 45, 48, 51	Badgujar ... M	60	3, 30
						Badhál ... M	22	21
Abú halím ... M	56	6	Apalkarí ... M	14	9	Badhan ... M	88	9, 11
Adhalie ... M	24	9, 20	Aráin ... M	37	13, 17, 48	Badiá ... M	15	44
Afghán ... M	17	13, 14, 27	Arbí ... M	209	10, 11, 28, 47	Bádrí ... M	13	10, 12
Afulá ... M	16	1	Arorá ... M	108	L. except (16), 21, 22, 24	Badu ... M	18	10, 15, 36
Agarwál ... M	23	1, 3, 12				Baghiál ... M	32	15, 17
Agg ... M	36	21	Asmání ... M	19	15, 17	Báglí ... M	553	3
Ahí ... M	20	12	Aspál ... M	18	12, 46	Bágri ... M	15	3, 25
Ahir ... M	61	13, 17, 47	Atáre ... M	28	9, 11, 13, 14	Báhal ... M	89	9, 10, 24, 44
Ahmadí Khel M	26	13, 15	Athwál ... M	45	13	Bain ... M	17	11, 17, 36
Akhtiári ... M	56	14	Atrá ... M	227	11, 15, 17, 51	Bajwál ... M	22	12, 44
Alághi ... M	26	51	Aulakh ... M	67	12, 13	Bájwe ... M	66	11, 15, 16
Aláuí ... M	25	51	Awán ... M	506	9, 12, 16, 17, 19	Bákhar ... M	11	13
Amarwál ... M	12	15	Azwál ... M	23	11	Bálá ... M	58	9, 10, 11, 44

SUB-CASTES OF CERTAIN SELECTED CASTES—*continued.*

Names of Sub-Castes.		Persons.	Locality.
Balai	... M	22	15
Balán	... M	77	4, 11, 45
Bálbi	.. M	47	15
Báli	... M	92	11, 17
Bálím	... M	839	1, 2, 3, 5, 6, 8, 9, 32, 48
Baloe	... M	148	5
Bám	... M	24	10
Bambhal	... M	156	13, 14
Bandar	... M	20	15, 19, 21
Bándi	... M	37	10, 16
Bangar	... M	45	8, 13. 44
Bángí	... M	35	11, 19
Bániá	... M	57	14, 15, 18, 20, 47
Bani Isráil	... M	105	D. except (7) 9, 11, 46
Banjárá	M	58	8, 12, 13, 46
Bansi	... M	80	12, 14, 17
Bánwá	... M	69	3, 48
Baránia	... M	11	11
Barár	... M	125	7, 14, 41
Báráwál	... M	52	3, 12
Barbon	... M	24	11
Bárí	... M	51	9, 13, 46
Bariáh	... M	81	15, 47
Bariáná	... M	23	17
Bariár	... M	86	15, 17, 18, 25
Barjí	... M	11	10
Barlás	... M	121	11, 16, 21, 44
Barol	... M	55	13, 19
Barwálá	... M	28	14, 44
Básiá	... M	23	11, 18
Basie	... M	53	10, 11, 12
Basrá	... M	11	11
Basroí	... M	21	17
Bat	... M	366	13, 14, 21, 22
Báth	... M	164	10, 12, 16, 46
Báti	... M	32	22
Batotre	... M	21	15
Bazáz	... M	283	5, 9, 13
Bedí	... M	51	13, 17
Begí	... M	13	10, 11
Bekal	... M	11	24
Beri	... M	15	9, 10
Bhággú	... M	86	7, 29, 36
Bhákri	... M	12	9, 10, 36
Bhallá	... M	85	9, 17, 25, 45
Bhammau	... M	17	11
Bháud	... M	39	3, 20
Bhandál	... M	13	13, 20
Bhandárí	... M	214	14, 15, 17, 44
Bhangu	... M	264	11, 13, 36, 41
Bharáí	... M	2,191	J. except (8) L. except(17), 1, 5, 18, 25, 51
Bharás	... M	16	15
Bhárdwáj	... M	107	10, 15, 47
Bhartgolar	... M	87	17
Bhás	... M	34	1, 3
Bhasle	... M	20	47
Bhat	... M	239	9, 13, 25, 47
Bhattá	... M	195	13, 24, 27, 51
Bhátiá	... M	83	15, 17, 44
Bhatiará	... M	123	3, 9, 13
Bhatnágar	... M	58	4
Bhattí	... M	2,539	J.L.R. except(22, 23), M. except (26), 1, 2, 51
Bhír	... M	38	14, 29
Bhochár	... M	21	10, 11
Bholí	... M	44	10, 17, 19, 20
Bhondu	... M	16	11, 18
Bhopálí	... M	36	3
Biloch	... M	67	13, 17, 20
Bisátí	... M	20	11, 20, 33
Bismal	... M	16	12
Bodlá	... M	162	12, 17, 27
Bohre	... M	166	J. 1, 17, 24
Boiá	... M	35	6, 17, 25, 51
Boriwál	... M	53	13
Botar	... M	102	5, 11, 17
Brahman	... M	54	13, 20, 21, 24
Brálí	... M	21	16
Bubak	... M	40	17
Bukhárí	... M	359	J. 6, 13, 14, 19, 21, 44, 48
Búnjáhi	... M	23	17, 25
Chadar	... M	23	17, 19, 25
Chadarwál	... M	37	9
Chadde	... M	120	9, 10, 14, 17
Cháhil	... M	35	13, 17
Cháki	... M	48	51
Chamár	... M	152	16
Chamine	... M	21	9, 13
Chand	... M	43	16, 20, 28
Chándiá	... M	13	9, 27
Changar	... M	328	13, 25
Char	... M	18	11
Charághi	... M	149	12
Charand	... M	13	10
Chatrath	... M	28	17
Chatri	... M	46	15
Chauhdrí	... M	190	9, 12, 17
Chauhán	... M	2,513	D. J. except (9) L. except (16), 41, 48
Cháwalá	... M	623	9, 12, 13, 17, 51
Chechre	... M	27	27
Chhattá	... M	34	9, 17
Chher	... M	12	11
Chhimbá	... M	74	12, 13, 17
Chhina	... M	111	13, 14, 21
Chhittar	... M	238	9, 17, 20
Chhokar	... M	12	15
Chhor	... M	24	11, 15
Chima	... M	99	15, 16, 17
Chishti	... M	1,641	J, except (8), M. except (26), 1, 5, 23, 51
Choghattá	... M	62	11, 12, 13, 15, 27
Chougar	... M	24	11
Chopre	... M	42	11, 17, 44
Chuhra	... M	43	16, 18, 24
Churigar	... M	30	11, 14, 24
Dad	... M	43	20
Dadbán	... M	19	1
Dadhirá	... M	196	16, 18
Dadhoí	... M	69	10, 13
Dádí	... M	12	11, 13, 15, 16
Daggal	... M	40	14, 15, 19
Dahálí	... M	53	2, 13, 28
Dáhar	... M	297	12, 28, 41
Dakhná	... M	18	10, 13, 16, 17
Dakháwaná	... M	80	13
Dakotrá	... M	31	19
Dál	... M	38	11, 15, 21
Daláwí	... M	51	18
Dán	... M	19	16
Dáná	... M	25	13, 17
Dámá	... M	19	1, 13, 18
Darí	... M	112	13, 17
Dark	... M	110	10, 13, 17
Darwesh	... M	18	10, 13, 31
Darzi	... M	51	13, 14, 17, 18
Dat	... M	89	17, 18, 20
Daure	... M	95	13, 17, 23
Degar	... M	40	1, 10, 15
Desí	... M	15	14, 19, 24, 45
Deslán	... M	98	4
Deswál	... M	50	4
Dewat	... M	15	12
Dhálí	... M	20	3, 11, 13
Dhammál	... M	18	9, 22
Dhangrí	... M	405	12, 13, 16, 17, 21
Dhari	... M	47	10, 13, 15, 25
Dháríwál	... M	71	11, 12, 17, 25, 44
Dháun	... M	26	12, 17, 25, 45
Dhillon	... M	48	11, 14, 24, 46
Dhim	... M	144	13, 17, 18, 21
Dhobi	... M	56	11, 12, 13, 14
Dhodi	... M	167	12, 13, 14, 20
Dhojá	... M	42	28
Dhondí	... M	171	13
Dhorá	... M	22	17
Dhusar	... M	21	15, 46
Dindár	... M	3,192	1, 8, 10, 13, 14, 19, 25, 29, 51
Díngrí	... M	71	16
Diwán	... M	16	13
Dobrí	... M	41	18, 20, 21
Dode	... M	119	14, 17, 19
Dogar	... M	37	1, 21
Dográ	... M	55	12, 13, 19, 20, 21
Dokhar	... M	42	13, 51
Donchí	... M	84	5
Dontí	... M	14	33
Dorán	... M	14	9
Doráth	... M	19	14
Faqír	... M	35	13, 15, 20
Farangí	... M	604	48
Farídí	... M	14	10, 17, 25
Fársí	... M	14	13
Faruqi	... M	8,481	D. except (7), J. except (8), L. except (17), 20, 25, 44
Gádí	... M	13	10, 11, 44
Gadyok	... M	300	17, 18, 20, 27
Gagre	... M	13	12, 17
Galijá	... M	31	45, 51
Gandwál	... M	116	2, 21
Garanjá	... M	55	44
Garchá	... M	23	10, 44
Gashtí	... M	21	3
Gasorá	... M	21	2
Gaur	... M	259	3, 7, 13, 36
Gawálbansi	... M	21	2
Ghalorá	... M	20	51
Ghaurí	... M	1,289	3, 4, 5, 13, 17, 28, 31, 47, 49, 51
Ghakhar	... M	44	2, 17, 25, 47
Ghef	... M	95	13, 21
Gholá	... M	68	2
Ghorewáh	... M	26	12, 13
Ghosí	M	29	1, 12, 13, 33
Gil	... M	21	1, 16
Gilání	... M	25	9, 14, 15, 23
Gilot	... M	92	4, 10
Gobindi	... M	300	10, 17, 18, 19
Godgad	... M	69	2
Gol	... M	67	2, 5, 13
Golimár	... M	131	6, 46
Gondal	... M	217	2, 14, 17, 18, 19
Gondi	... M	122	14, 15, 20, 44
Gopáng	... M	56	29
Gorai	... M	95	13, 14, 16
Goranj	... M	23	44
Gorwárá	... M	302	12, 13, 19, 27
Gujar	... M	37	12, 16, 20, 51
Gujarwál	... M	62	20
Gul	... M	583	L. 12, 19, 25, 45
Guryáni	... M	27	10, 13, 46
Haidri	... M	15	10
Halim	... M	16	3
Hánde	... M	82	10, 13, 16
Hanfi	... M	97	1, 2, 22, 45
Hang	... M	456	13, 16, 17, 19
Hans	... M	105	14, 24
Hansári	... M	52	10, 13, 17
Hansiál	... M	11	12, 13
Haráni	... M	22	19
Harar	... M	15	14, 16, 17
Háshmi	... M	508	D. 9, 13, 17, 27, 44, 48, 51
Hazúri	... M	20	15, 47
Hirá	... M	47	10, 11, 47
Hoji	... M	182	L. 25
Horiá	... M	27	50
Hosbáz	... M	18	9
Husani	... M	380	3, 9, 15, 17, 27, 34, 44
Jabání	... M	121	28, 29
Jádá	... M	45	13, 14
Jáfiri	... M	62	1, 6
Jagi	... M	108	11, 21
Jagrál	... M	71	6, 9
Jáhdi	... M	25	1, 12, 15
Jalál	... M	65	4, 15, 49
Jálí	... M	202	L. 9, 12, 25
Jand	... M	52	13, 17, 51
Jandrán	... M	178	1, 10, 16, 25, 41, 51
Jango	... M	50	8, 9, 47
Janjuá	... M	326	R. except (28), 5, 17, 25, 51
Jaskání	... M	18	29
Jaswál	... M	67	9, 18, 29, 51
Jat	... M	115	5, 13, 14, 25, 27, 29
Jawán	... M	33	18
Jawarde	... M	21	9, 11, 17

APPENDIX TO IMPERIAL TABLE XIII.—

Names of Sub-Castes.	Persons.	Locality.
Jhabar ... M	95	13, 17, 27
Jhálí ... M	58	11, 15
Jhángotar ... M	81	9
Jhár ... M	42	12, 15, 17
Jhinwar ... M	70	12, 45
Jhonjárá ... M	61	13, 17
Jílání ... M	142	6, 29, 51
Johál ... M	18	13, 27
Joí ... M	22	10, 13
Joíá ... M	389	12, 25, 29
Jonfe ... M	39	50
Jorí ... M	32	50
Jugiá ... M	16	3, 24
Juláhá ... M	24	11, 13, 14, 27, 44
Kadáre ... M	24	5, 12, 13
Kaith ... M	40	10, 12, 39, 43
Kajwáne ... M	47	12, 51
Kákákhel ... M	31	14, 27
Kakezaí ... M	2,627	J. except (8), L. except (16), M. 6, 21, 25, 44
Kakre ... M	105	8, 11, 14, 15, 25
Kakríobá ... M	35	14, 15
Kalál ... M	281	5, 6, 12, 21
Kalánaurfá ... M	17	13, 22
Kalet ... M	35	11, 17
Kaliál ... M	12	47
Kaliáná ... M	11	24, 25
Kalíjá ... M	144	12, 13
Kálíposh ... M	77	6
Kálre ... M	163	12, 16, 28, 50
Kaleiá ... M	49	44
Kálúká ... M	59	24
Kamángar ... M	13	3
Kamboh .. M	123	5, 17, 18, 20
Kandrá ... M	183	9, 11, 15, 16
Kanjará ... M	44	3, 13, 14, 15, 21
Kapur ... M	574	J. except (10), L. R. except (23), 25
Karane ... M	52	12, 13, 16
Karár ... M	27	17
Karmán ... M	18	5, 17
Kashmiri ... M	1,148	J. L. R. M. except (29) 1, 6, 7, 46, 47
Káshtkár ... M	152	13
Katáre ... M	103	10, 13, 17
Katármal ... M	13	11, 22
Katiál ... M	40	16, 17, 27
Khaish ... M	20	11, 15, 47
Khaldár ... M	46	6
Khahual ... M	56	16, 49
Khárá ... M	11	17
Kharál ... M	486	L. except (15), 19, 20, 21, 25, 47
Kharar ... M	103	13, 17
Kharbande ... M	13	17
Khatik ... M	43	9, 13, 16, 51
Khatrí ... M	332	J. except (9) L. 3, 25, 27
Khattí ... M	36	10
Khawájá ... M	3,355	5, 8, 13, 16, 27
Khiohi ... M	11	24
Khiljí ... M	233	5, 9, 16, 17, 49
Khojá ... M	13,557	J. L. R. M. except (26) 1, 44, 48, 51
Khokhar ... M	535	L. 1, 11, 12, 18, 24, 25, 36, 49, 51
Khor ... M	46	3, 17, 24
Khoráná ... M	75	12, 15, 17, 25
Khori ... M	11	11, 13, 21
Khúmre ... M	16	13, 24
Khurásání ... M	31	1, 4, 12, 13, 19, 49
Kokáre ... M	602	11, 13, 15, 18, 25, 27, 51
Koldhár ... M	78	11
Kolí ... M	213	L. 10, 22, 25, 27, 44, 49
Korá ... M	99	8, 13, 17
Kuttaná ... M	221	29, 50
Labáná ... M	23	9
Lábsi ... M	40	14
Lád ... M	1,579	1, 11, 29, 51
Láhorí ... M	60	4, 44
Lákhar ... M	40	12, 17, 25
Lálí ... M	39	15
Langáh ... M	819	12, 13, 17, 18, 19
Lár ... M	7,689	51
Lawár ... M	16	17
Lodhá ... M	36	2, 12, 13, 29
Lodhí ... M	40	6, 11, 17
Lodhrá ... M	84	10, 17, 27
Logiohá ... M	39	14
Lohár ... M	51	11, 13, 25, 28, 51
Lohrá ... M	83	11, 17, 51
Loní ... M	11	13, 21, 47
Máchhi ... M	15	10, 16
Madáhar ... M	14	10, 49
Madárí ... M	314	5, 6, 11, 12, 49
Magár ... M	112	14, 15, 25
Mago ... M	48	12, 16, 17, 24
Mahájarín ... M	174	4, 13, 21, 25, 27
Mahet ... M	70	9, 10, 16
Máhí ... M	47	11
Mahir ... M	36	11, 12, 14, 51
Mahrá ... M	33	12, 13, 15, 25
Mahtá ... M	193	12, 13, 17, 24, 46
Mahwál ... M	18	2, 24
Mairí ... M	27	11
Majáwar ... M	196	3, 5, 28, 29
Majázi ... M	17	14
Makri ... M	27	17, 24
-malak ... M	44	3, 5, 13, 20, 47
Malán ... M	157	9, 15, 25, 27
Malawání ... M	34	6, 13
Málí ... M	27	9, 12, 16, 18, 44
Malmans ... M	42	5
Malotre ... M	87	16, 21, 24, 44
Mán ... M	25	12, 16, 21
Mándah ... M	16	11, 24
Mandrá ... M	267	9, 11, 12, 15, 16
Mángat ... M	27	9
Manhás ... M	118	11, 13
Maniár ... M	15	11, 12
Manj ... M	46	11, 13
Mansúrí ... M	139	13, 21, 49
Marwáhá ... M	362	16, 12, 22, 24
Marwání ... M	58	9, 24, 33, 51
Masní ... M	196	9, 25, 27, 51
Mathrá Dásí ... M	12	9
Matiála ... M	437	27, 51
Mawájí ... M	15	27
Mazárí ... M	566	13
Medán ... M	25	14
Mekhar ... M	53	25
Miáná ... M	72	13, 20, 23, 28
Mír ... M	91	8, 9, 11, 21, 22
Miráliwádhan M	355	51
Mirdhá ... M	11	3
Mohammadí M	120	9, 11, 22, 51
Moháná ... M	44	14, 24, 25, 27
Mohiál ... M	33	9, 12, 14, 25
Mohotre ... M	49	17, 25
Moman ... M	157	L. except (15), 11, 12
Mote ... M	62	13, 24
Mufti ... M	11	15, 27
Mughal ... M	134	J. except (10), 1, 17, 21, 25
Multání ... M	294	1, 3, 7, 10, 13, 34
Mundní ... M	43	51
Musákhel ... M	24	23, 24
Muslmán ... M	438	13, 20
Mussalli ... M	65	28
Nágí ... M	89	5, 11, 12, 14
Nágre ... M	30	6, 10, 11
Nái ... M	17	13, 20, 21
Nakokárá ... M	242	27, 51
Nand ... M	14	11, 15
Nandar Jág ... M	49	28
Nárag ... M	463	12, 13, 26
Nardaie ... M	56	14
Narolá .. M	48	12, 13, 24
Náru ... M	14	11, 20
Nasain ... M	16	3
Nat ... M	12	12, 21, 25
Naumuslim ... M	28,955	D. except (5), J. L. M. 19, 21, 22, 23, 46, 48, 51
Núrbáf ... M	33	13, 14
Núr Sháh ... M	62	2, 12
Ogáhí ... M	109	24
Okárí ... M	21	9
Osáin ... M	15	16, 17
Páhal ... M	78	9
Pál ... M	892	13, 14, 16, 27
Pálá ... M	14	16, 51
Palledár ... M	545	48
Pándhá ... M	66	10, 13, 15, 28, 47
Pandit ... M	120	13, 18, 20, 25
Panjáe ... M	16	17, 24
Paunun ... M	17	13, 14, 19
Panwár ... M	237	2, 3, 5, 20, 27
Páoli ... M	29	18, 27, 29
Paráchá ... M	243	1, 2, 13, 21, 22, 24
Parhár ... M	21	19, 21
Pasái ... M	15	14
Páef ... M	34	2, 10, 17
Patále ... M	24	9, 11
Pathán ... M	316	J. 1, 13, 14, 25, 29, 47
Pátní ... M	28	12
Patwár ... M	46	21
Peraín ... M	33	19
Pharáe ... M	38	10, 17, 21
Phondwál ... M	31	4
Phupal ... M	12	10
Pírí ... M	581	13, 18
Pople ... M	19	10, 28
Purí ... M	574	L. 6, 8, 9, 11, 18, 24, 25, 28
Qadariá ... M	14	1, 8, 51
Qádiáni ... M	50	5, 24
Qádirí ... M	113	5, 12, 18, 27, 29
Qalandar ... M	42	4, 5, 10
Qánángo ... M	2,371	J. L. R. M. 1, 44, 51
Qárumi ... M	53	9, 16, 18, 27
Qassáb ... M	52	4, 10, 14, 15, 27
Qází ... M	90	13, 15, 20, 27
Qureshí ... M	95,267	P. except (35, 38)
Qureshí Háshmí. M	30	15
Qureshí Sadíqí M	1,463	9, 12, 15, 27
Rad ... M	24	11
Ráhan ... M	30	9
Ráhar ... M	80	3, 22
Ráhlá ... M	33	8, 9, 14, 25
Rahmání ... M	61	51
Ráí ... M	117	6, 13, 21, 46
Rájá ... M	286	9, 10, 18, 21, 49
Rajal ... M	29	51
Rájput ... M	165	R. except (23) 1, 8, 12, 13, 47
Rakhrah ... M	15	9, 13, 46
Randháwá ... M	191	12, 13, 20, 25
Rangrez ... M	11	9, 24, 44
Ranial ... M	51	21
Ratrá ... M	179	8, 9, 18, 25, 51
Ráwal ... M	112	12, 13, 25
Ráwat ... M	15	51
Rawrá ... M	51	13, 31
Rind ... M	51	8, 17
Robáná ... M	13	25
Rongá ... M	92	28
Royat ... M	24	9
Runí ... M	47	10, 15
Ruprái ... M	13	9
Sabíl ... M	19	12, 13
Sachdev ... M	112	12, 16, 17, 24
Sadái ... M	62	16, 23
Sadal ... M	113	9, 10, 45
Sadáná ... M	15	12
Sadiqáni ... M	4,231	6
Sadíqí ... M	67,252	B. 31, 32, 34, 45, 48, 49
Sado ... M	12	10, 25
Sadrá ... M	27	25
Sago ... M	61	12, 25
Sáhdu ... M	106	9, 17
Sahgal ... M	832	L. except (16), R. except (19) 3, 10, 27, 36. 44, 51
Sáhí ... M	56	19, 21, 27
Sáhní ... M	113	17, 21
Sáhotre ... M	180	8, 9, 17, 20, 25
Saíad ... M	64	12, 28, 51
Saídan ... M	20	25
Saídí ... M	86	12, 24, 27, 51
Saini ... M	28	12, 13, 25

Names of Sub-Castes.		Persons.	Locality.
Sajdi ...	M	21	14, 18
Sakri ...	M	26	15
Sal ...	M	21	11
Saláh ...	M	23	14, 19
Salái ...	M	291	9, 14, 15
Salámat ...	M	19	10
Salhári ...	M	15	2
Salímkhel ...	M	23	4
Saloni ...	M	27	9, 13, 21
Sámal ...	M	78	11, 22, 50
Samrái ...	M	40	12, 13
Sandal ...	M	113	15, 16, 18, 25
Sandan ...	M	62	15, 17, 45
Sánde ...	M	84	10, 15
Sandhu ...	M	374	11, 12, 17, 25
Sangar ...	M	143	1, 13, 14, 44, 45
Sání ...	M	480	10, 13, 16, 21
Saniasi ...	M	14	12
Sánjhí ...	M	22	16
Sanotre ...	M	13	12, 13
Sará ...	M	286	1, 5, 15, 17, 44
Saráf ...	M	51	16, 25
Saráj ...	M	27	15, 42
Sareqi ...	M	22	14, 22, 28
Sarí ...	M	125	11, 17, 21
Sarpal ...	M	14	14
Sarwári ...	M	22	10, 14
Satar ...	M	44	12, 28
Sathí ...	M	284	12, 13, 15, 16, 21
Saweki ...	M	14	25
Sekun ...	M	174	11, 12
Semar ...	M	76	11
Sepal ...	M	53	11, 12, 25
Shadán ...	M	18	14
Shahzádi ...	M	34	10, 27
Shamsí ...	M	53	9, 13
Shekho ...	M	169	11, 19, 20
Shinh Már ...	M	121	10, 11
Shirázi ...	M	37	20, 51
Siál ...	M	94	15, 16, 17, 28
Siharwál ...	M	93	8, 15, 16, 21
Sindhu ...	M	366	11, 14, 16, 44
Sobin ...	M	12	21, 51
Suigar ...	M	17	45
Sunár ...	M	93	6, 22, 26
Suraj Bansi ...	M	13	13, 47
Surkhni ...	M	19	3
Tabákh ...	M	20	5
Tablá ...	M	30	7
Tagiár ...	M	214	16
Tahím ...	M	19	12, 13, 18, 24
Takhíál ...	M	135	9, 15
Talwár ...	M	85	9, 22, 25, 36
Tandé ...	M	22	13, 15, 25
Tangarí ...	M	15	14
Tánk ...	M	67	5, 11, 25, 44
Tapián ...	M	28	9
Taprídár ...	M	11	16
Tarák ...	M	71	1, 11, 13
Tarálí ...	M	14	15, 25
Tarár ...	M	14	16 18
Tarásí ...	M	72	13, 17
Táru ...	M	72	5, 16, 17, 21
Telí ...	M	44	13, 17
Thadíál ...	M	14	9
Thákrí ...	M	34	51
Thápar ...	M	98	15, 16, 20
Toná ...	M	28	13
Tonáhar ...	M	27	1, 5
Tonjah ...	M	42	27
Totar ...	M	17	5
Tukiár ...	M	17	15
Tur ...	M	121	1, 2, 5, 14
Ulwi ...	M	79	3, 4, 9, 17, 51
Uppal ...	M	412	8, 9, 11, 12, 13, 16, 17, 44
Usmání ...	M	1,053	D. Except(2), 8, 11, 13, 24, 48, 49
Vadhan ...	M	15	13, 15, 24
Vadhánwan ...	M	64	12, 16
Vadhrá ...	M	342	14, 15, 16, 25
Vahá ...	M	33	51
Vahde ...	M	25	19
Vahorá ...	M	20	24
Váhwá ...	M	26	17
Vain ...	M	23	15
Valáná ...	M	23	16
Valím ...	M	24	11, 14
Varaich ...	M	14	16, 18
Variah ...	M	36	17
Vasegí ...	M	58	14
Vaslí ...	M	37	16
Vedí ...	M	61	16
Vena ...	M	17	13, 25
Virk ...	M	32	15, 21, 46
Yaqub Rái ...	M	11	13
Yusafzai ...	M	41	4, 6, 13, 47
Zahurí ...	M	66	6
Zamán ...	M	12	12
Zamíndarí ...	M	33	8, 13, 26
Zargan ...	M	76	18, 20, 27
Zulkarni ...	M	28	9
Minor* ...	M	1,867	
Unspecified ...	M	25,424	

* DETAIL OF MINOR.

Abábí 8, Abdál 1, Abí 6, Achand 7, Adham 2, Afrídí 10, Ahangar 1, Ahmdál 6, Aibzái 5, Ain 4, Airaf 1, Áliáná 7, Alimán 5, Aloij 3, Alsadiqi 3, Alsará 3, Aman 6, Amamiá 4, Amír 3, Amráná 2, And 4, Andar 5, Andi 4, Antri 2, Ashábí 3, Ashpáni 6, Atári 10, Atiálj 3, Awir 1, Azmi 1, Bábá 8, Bápalsai 1, Baohak 9, Badáni 1, Badeji 2, Badhe 2, Badhíroí 5, Baßudá 3, Bágá 8, Bagal 1, Baghadádí 8, Bagon 1, Bahau 1, Bahishti 7, Bahmini 2, Bajwan 2, Balekhel 2, Báliá 9, Balír 2, Balkh 4, Balotre 1, Baman 5, Bamat 5, Banal 7, Bandhá 1, Bangalí 4, Banjola 4, Bausgo 1, Banan 1, Bauwár 1, Barag 1, Barwál 6, Bás 2, Bázígar 6, Beldár 8, Beopárí 6, Bhadi 6, Bhái 7, Bhaksí 8, Bhalun 1, Bhan 1, Bhanjáná 3, Bharochi 2, Bharta 2, Bhatoi 5, Bhaun 2, Bhíní 5, Bhotí 5, Bhullar 8, Bhuttar 3, Bolak 9, Bote 8, Botrí 1, Chálor 1, Chambal 7, Chándan 2, Chandasar 1, Charamfrosh 9, Charmí 2, Chastoí 6, Chatrad 8, Cheti 3, Chhey 3, Chhodi 4, Chhor 4, Chirimár 6, Chohlí 4, Chokrá 1, Chuharwand 2, Dabgar 5, Dabwál 1, Dadiá 8, Dakrá 2, Dandu 6, Danejá 3, Dangrá 5, Daria 3, Dariálá 4, *Dándzái* 10, *Dawalgrain* 1, *Dawaliá* 9, *Dazír* 10, *Delá* 9, Deob 2, Detí 3, Dháigar 7, Dhalkows 4, Dhamraya 1, Dhana 8, Dhaniál 7, Dhanjái 5, Dharojal 5, Dhawar 1, Dhol 4, Dhorán 6, Dhotar 6, Dobán 9, Dobani 9, Dográl 8, Durráni 4, Dyal 1, Gadágar 1, Galotre 2, Gándí 3, Gandra 4, Gáni 8, Gánjal 1, Garíwál 9, Gelan 4, Ghamman 6, Gharwál 8, Gilgo 2, Golre 5, Goricha 5, Gorowál 3, Gorsí 1, Gosáin 3, Gumbar 7, Guruzi 7, Hajjám 7, Hajji Ahmadi 1, Haklo 9, Hamdáni 5, Hamza 2, Handraf 4, Hansí 3, Haqání 7, Hart 3, Hastí 1, Hathi 10, Hatiál 2, Hatrás 4, Hedí 1, Hem 5, Hindrí 7, Hindroí 10, Hindustání 2, Hoti 9, Isháqi 5, Jádu Bansí 6, Jagádhri 6, Jahází 4, Jaímal 3, Jálaf 1, Jamanke Bábe 1, Janjuhán 6, Jasor 8, Jatgil 5, Jatiál 9, Játú 10, Jawálá 1, Jawlái 6, Jehar 1, Jhábe 2, Jhaggar 10, Jhamat 5, Jhandrí 10, Jhás 1, Jhatá 4, Jhatoí 2, Johá 1, Jolí 2, Jopáin 1, Jotá 2, Jothre 1, Jutá 8, Kabáhue 6, Kabáti 4, Kabutrí 2, Kahut 1, Kakan 1, Kakbandí 7, Kakí 1, Kálas 5, Kalu 4, Kamhár 10, Kamlá 6, Kanchan 6, Kanethí 7, Kangu 2, Kaní 2, Kanshí 10, Karasi 5, Kardantí 2, Karkhwál 10, Kárliá 5, Kerí 1, Khákí 3, Khal 9, Khánzádá 3, Khar 1, Khargore 3, Khatpan 1, Khatri Siál 8, Khawárí 5, Kherí 3, Khokhráin 9, Khole 1, Khoráq 1, Khurshíd 2, Kiár 1, Kochar 3, Kotál 6, Kot Dolá 1, Kot Hindu 2, Kotwál 4, Kundal 2, Lak 6, Lakhárá 10, Lakhí 5, Lakhowal 3, Lal Isákhel 1, Lalrí 1, Lániá 1, Laran 1, Lohikhel 1, Loje 2, Longe 3, Loráná 1, Lund 5, Mahdí Ratta 4, Mahdiwál 1, Mahiás 10, Mahtám 1, Mahún 9, Makhdumí 10, Mal 5, Malang 1, Malanhans 4, Malásí 2, Maliá 2, Malokhá 9, Malwání 10, Mamyána 7, Maná 10, Manau 7, Mandau 3, Manghe 9, Mangrol 3, Manjohí 1, Mankot 3, Márá 3, Marake 7, Marán 2, Marechá 3, Marí 8, Marod 9, Marok 4, Marolí 5, Maryal 3, Masjedin 5, Máski 6, Maslaji 1, Mastadi 3, Math Banrí 1, Malotí 1, Med 7, Mekhi 3, Mel 3, Melo 3, Mewáti 4, Milke 2, Mín 7, Momí 8, Mullán 10, Munsi 1, Murgha 1, Nadáf 3, Nadáki 1, Nágpál 3, Nahar 4, Náich 10, Nakiál 1, Nal 1, Nali Band 3, Nanak Panthi 4, Nanhár 3, Naráin 4, Nayyar 2, Niárná 9, Niází 4, Nigamí 1, Nikobárí 2, Nilárí 3, Nurí 2, Nursí 10, Padhár 1, Panjábí 8, Panjáhal 10, Panjariá 9, Paráji 1, Páslí 10, Paswál 9, Patáfi 2, Pawár 3, Phágau 5, Phalarwál 9, Phálí 2, Pharthi 1, Phoi 1, Phor 4, Phuliyara 6, Pírzádá 3, Porsí 1, Pung 6, Purbiá 2, Puzí 6, Qabaz 2, Qaimkhání 1, Qariání 1, Qásmí 2, Qaul 7, Qazái 4, Qesri 3, Qutab Sháhí 3, Rágú 6, Rahel 5, Rabgar 1, Ráhní 6, Rábd 10, Rahtar 5, Ráin 7, Rajíd 1, Rajpál 5, Rajuhí 1, Rakni 7, Rámá 1, Rangar 6, Ránjá 1, Rasdí 1, Rasílí 4, Ratanpál 10, Ráthne 2, Ráthor 5, Ratnágar 3, Ritá 6, Rorá 4, Rupí 1, Sahkal 1, *Sadásí* 3, *Sadkal* 3, *Sadráj* 5, *Sakjá* 2, *Salat* 2, *Samlána* 3, *Sandal* 9, *Saugi* 10, *Sangri* 5, *Sanisári* 3, *Sárun* 10, *Sáras* 5, *Sardál* 10, Sat-Nágar 5, Shaidí 3, Shámchurási 5, Shámí Nái 5, Shariát Wai 6, Shekhwál 2, Shiá 1, Shirgil 7, Sirwál 4, Sital 3, Sodágar 1, Sud 3, Suji 9, Sulaimání 9, Sultání 1, Surí 3, Sumrá 3, Sunní 10, Tadiálá 3, Tagála 3, Tallan 2, Tallí 2, Talyál 1, Talwál 4, Tamboli 2, Tanwár 9, Tanwári 10, Tap 4, Tará 1, Targar 1, Tarí 4, Tartárí 2, Tasádar 1, Tatál 3, Tawaif 1, Tawáná 10, Thatar 1, Thodí 4, Tirmázi 6, Turkman 8, Ulmá 4, Umri 4, Utrádhí 2, Uttamdayal 3, Vagrá 9, Vahán 7, Vahgal 2, Vahmi 2, Vájdiá 1, Vají 3, Vajwá 1, Vák 9, Valkan 1, Ván 4, Vandarah 1, Vasan 3, Vástí 1, Viráich 9, Zai 1.

Names of Sub-Castes.		Persons.	Locality.
Sunar 158,318	H.	102,997	
	S.	27,567	
	M.	27,745	
	J.	8	
	B.	1	
Adhar ...	H	48	8, 19, 25
	S	16	25
	M	10	24
Agarwál ...	H	77	1
Agásilohe ...	H	84	23
Ahi ...	H	510	19, 20, 21, 22, 23
	S	470	20, 21, 22
	M	96	20, 22, 25
Ajal ...	H	18	3, 4
Ajimali ...	H	85	7, 11, 38
Ajote ...	H	235	D. J. M. except (29), 19, 20, 23
	S	1	25
Akásmohlá ...	H	375	13, 17, 26, 28
	S	6	17, 28
Alf ...	H	113	15, 27, 38
	M	55	9, 18

Names of Sub-Castes.		Persons.	Locality.
Amír ...	H	39	43
Anati ...	H	48	2, 13, 15
	S	1	10
Anchahá ...	H	11	1, 3
Anchal ...	H	177	1, 2, 3
And ...	H	20	11, 16, 19
	S	5	25
Arorá ...	H	136	1, 8, 19, 31
	M	21	18, 20, 21, 23
Ashat ...	H	261	4, 6, 8, 11, 12, 13, 14, 15, 25, 33, 34, 41, 48
	S	275	1, 5, 12, 13, 14, 24, 25, 48
	M	17	48
Ashtal ...	H	103	1, 11
	M	3	24
Atan ...	H	10	21
	S	8	14
Atar ...	H	56	8, 11, 14, 15, 25, 45
	M	2	9
Atatrá ...	H	27	16, 21, 45
Ath ...	H	32	16
	S	12	21
	M	23	13
Awán ...	M	36	12, 13, 19, 44
Bable ...	H	16	13
Babrá ...	H	276	1, 2, 11, 14, 15, 19, 20
	S	14	14, 20, 25
	M	53	17, 24, 27
Badária ...	H	5	18
	S	10	48
	M	44	25
Badiwárí ...	H	14	15
Badri ...	H	177	1
	S	9	16, 21, 44
	M	3	25
Badyál ...	H	15	1, 2
	S	1	16
Bagarál ...	H	52	4, 20
	M	66	16
Bágarí ...	H	91	2, 4, 12, 16, 40, 50
Baggi ...	H	399	4, 6, 10, 11, 14, 15, 16, 18, 25, 34, 40, 44, 45
	S	218	9, 10, 13, 14, 16, 25, 43
	M	16	9, 44
Báhal ...	H	44	2
	S	6	4, 12, 14
	M	12	9, 19, 23
Báham ...	H	11	22
	S	12	9, 11, 12
Báhrí ...	H	152	10, 14, 16, 20, 21
	M	2	26
Báí ...	H	37	11, 14
Bajániá ...	H	48	10, 11
	S	5	11
Bají ...	H	29	2, 8
Bajlash ...	H	23	3
Bájwah ...	H	13	1
Bakhal ...	H	20	2, 8, 15
Bakre ...	H	89	15, 16, 28
Bandará ...	H	29	3, 51
	M	12	15, 18, 25
Bangáli ...	H	7	2, 12
	S	4	12
Bangar ...	S	12	9, 11, 12
Bangi ...	H	32	6, 8, 19
	S	8	16, 44
	M	16	17, 22
Báníá ...	H	13	29
Baníwál ...	H	16	3
Bannán ...	H	15	17
Bans ...	H	79	2, 3, 4, 11, 12
Barári ...	H	260	1, 2, 4, 21
	S	14	13, 25
	M	2	9, 18
Barbar ...	H	31	2, 8, 45
	M	4	15, 45
Bark ...	H	47	4, 25, 51
Baráli ...	H	34	15
Barwáh ...	H	42	1, 2, 45
	S	16	17
Basáwan ...	H	32	2, 15
	S	7	9, 11
	M	29	1
Basauí	H	12	15, 19
Basí ...	H	55	15, 21
	M	15	16
Bátal ...	H	19	2, 14
Batjiá ...	M	24	20
Bator ...	H	12	15, 18
	S	95	5, 14, 18, 25
	M	3	9
Batrá ...	S	42	14
Báwaliá ...	H	108	2, 3, 4
Bed ...	M	22	9, 10, 25
Begí ...	H	18	12
	M	10	10
Bel ...	H	31	6, 15, 16
	M	1	9
Ber ...	H	357	4, 8, 12, 13, 15, 16, 24, 25, 37
	S	31	14
	M	10	13, 44
Bewál ...	H	49	2, 4, 11
Bhabar ...	S	86	20
Bhadwáli ...	S	18	17
Bhagolí ...	H	20	11
	M	1	8
Bhakrá ...	H	14	25
Bhál ...	H	25	1, 8, 21, 27
	S	7	24
Bhalle ...	H	193	22, 23, 26
	S	29	18
	M	10	17
Bhalí ...	H	20	18
Bhalan ...	H	345	8, 19, 23, 26
	S	14	17, 25
	M	195	15, 19, 24, 27
Bhaman ...	H	165	1, 2, 15
Bhamb ...	H	10	1, 5, 11
	S	17	21
Bhámi ...	H	25	4, 12, 20, 25
	S	4	46
Bhand ...	H	29	8
	S	1	25
Bhair ...	S	35	14
Bhardwás ...	H	68	1, 4, 7, 8, 14, 25, 26, 40, 45, 47
Bharlí ...	H	12	25, 45
Bharmi ...	H	25	42, 45
Bhatal ...	H	21	4, 51
Bhattá ...	H	204	1, 12, 14, 24, 25, 40
	S	20	13, 17
	M	647	12, 17, 18, 19, 23, 24, 25, 51
Bhattar ...	H	24	25, 51
	M	11	51
Bhattí ...	H	76	1, 13, 15
	S	163	12, 14, 16, 17, 24
	M	1,136	7, 12, 13, 14, 15, 16, 27, 28, 44
Bherá ...	S	19	18, 25
	M	4	28
Bhím ...	H	59	2, 4, 25
	S	28	12
Bho ...	H	35	2, 4, 6, 14, 16, 18
	S	17	17, 22
Bholan ...	H	310	15, 17, 18, 22, 23, 28
	S	54	17, 18, 24
	M	4	13
Bholar ...	H	34	2, 28
	S	6	28
	M	30	17, 24
Bholí ...	H	1,715	R. 13, 15, 25, 27, 51
	S	741	R. 14, 16, 17, 51
	M	108	14, 15, 17, 20 25
Bhon ...	H	7	49
	M	7	18, 19
Bhond ...	H	186	1, 2, 12, 20 51
	S	1	23
Bhonsí ...	H	48	4, 12, 21
Bhotí ...	H	104	18, 24, 41
	M	390	9, 10, 12, 13, 27, 28
Bir ...	H	71	17, 18
	S	14	17, 18.
Birwal ...	H	168	2, 3, 4, 17
Bobal ...	H	32	28
	S	1	25
Bobar ...	H	124	18, 19
Bohal ...	H	251	17, 18, 20, 21, 22, 23, 27
	S	59	20, 22
Bole ...	H	9	8
	M	13	17
Bora ...	H	16	11, 12
	M	10	49
Bota ...	H	17	2, 27, 28
Botan ...	H	55	1, 24
	S	16	11
	M	8	1
Bunjái ...	H	103	11, 12, 17, 19, 24, 25, 26, 46
	S	37	13, 18, 19, 25
Cháchal ...	H	11	1
Chadi ...	H	26	10, 11, 14
Cháli ...	H	70	1, 11, 28
	M	1	12
Chándal ...	H	77	1, 2, 8, 20, 39, 43
Chandole ...	H	44	7, 8, 38, 39, 51
Chaughattá ...	M	68	15, 27, 28
Chauhán ...	H	658	1, 2, 3, 4, 6, 7, 8, 10, 11, 12, 14, 15, 25, 34, 37, 41, 43, 48
	S	75	9, 12, 13, 14, 16
	M	1,542	D. except (3) L. 19, 25, 48, 49, 51
Cháwlá ...	H	13	13, 51
	S	1	20
Chhabrá ...	H	9	4, 5
	S	3	14
Chhaji ...	H	12	8
Chhanan ...	H	12	8, 44
	S	1	14
Chhángá ...	H	19	3
Chhángal ...	H	17	21
Chhatri ...	H	329	2, 4, 13, 14, 15, 22, 25, 45
	S	6	17, 21
Chhimbá ...	H	57	6, 10, 11, 25, 44
	S	32	11, 12, 13, 44
	M	4	17
Chhiná ...	H	54	11
	S	4	44
Chikná ...	H	70	2, 4, 11
Choprá ...	H	141	1, 12, 13, 14, 19, 26, 29, 45
	S	81	12, 17, 20, 27
	M	11	13
Chor ...	H	17	2, 14, 44, 45
	S	4	25
Chura ...	H	18	2, 10
	M	124	23, 25, 27
Dágar ...	H	36	2, 25
Dági ...	H	39	21, 25
	M	1	9
Dáhar ...	H	72	1, 11, 15, 16, 25
	S	31	10, 11, 20, 25
Dahla ...	H	32	15, 25
	S	3	16
Dahri ...	H	17	15, 25
	S	25	10, 12, 20
Dahsan ...	S	24	21,
Dalál ...	H	108	11, 25, 28, 34
	S	10	12, 45
	M	4	12
Daloná ...	H	16	1
Dámar ...	H	52	3, 12
	M	1	13
Damí ...	H	15	45, 46
Damirá ...	H	15	4, 45
Dandi ...	H	281	25, 26, 29
	S	80	13, 14, 18
	M	3	8
Dandiwál ...	H	65	3
	M	1	1
Dar ...	H	59	11
Darad ...	H	340	10
Dáriá ...	H	52	17, 19, 45
Dasar ...	H	18	2, 21, 49
Dasáwar ...	H	111	4, 6, 12, 25
	S	7	9, 41, 44
Dasor ...	H	71	1, 6, 8, 10, 12, 21
	S	2	9, 10

SUB-CASTES OF CERTAIN SELECTED CASTES—*continued.*

Names of Sub-Castes.		Persons.	Locality.
Dasti ...	H	23	1
Dehli ...	H	7	10, 15
	S	17	17
	M	47	9, 12
Desi ...	H	4	4
	S	19	12
	M	10	27
Devi ...	H	12	4, 11
Deswáli ...	H	67	1, 4, 12, 49
	S	6	12
Dewári ...	H	68	1, 25, 45
	M	2	5
Dhadi ...	H	39	12, 25, 27, 51
	S	12	51
	M	59	17, 19, 24, 51
Dhaí ...	H	168	16, 50
	S	1	9
	M	9	25
Dhal ...	H	23	1, 25
	S	4	1, 11
	M	4	24
Dhala ...	H	370	1, 2, 12, 14 to 16, 25, 40, 46
	S	94	13, 19, 24, 25
	M	134	15, 24, 25, 27
Dháriwál ...	S	19	12, 14
Dhalú ...	H	114	12, 25
	S	140	12, 13, 17, 24
	M	117	10, 16, 24, 25
Dhamán ...	H	33	1, 2, 12
	S	1	49
	M	2	10
Dhamwál ...	H	45	11, 12, 14
	S	156	12 to 14, 25
	M	144	L. 1, 9, 10, 12, 22, 25
Dhán ...	H	13	11, 44
	S	25	25
	M	1	25
Dhaná ...	H	766	J. L. 11, 12, 14, 17, 25, 44, 51
	S	34	9, 10, 11, 14, 19, 25, 44
	M	76	9, 10, 12, 14, 19, 24, 26, 51
Dhandí ...	H	51	18, 19
	S	13	17, 26
	M	1	16
Dhariá ...	H	38	1, 12, 21, 25, 27
	S	39	17, 21, 25
	M	121	12, 14, 20, 23, 25, 27, 51
Dharmí ...	H	2	3, 25
	M	141	13, 27
Dharná ...	H	197	8, 16, 17, 25
	S	5	16, 28
	M	418	12, 13, 14, 17, 22, 24, 25, 27
Dháter ...	H	52	4, 11, 15
Dhele ...	H	17	1, 14
Dhil ...	H	302	11, 16, 44
	S	48	12, 25
	M	76	15, 24, 25, 44, 51
Dhillon ...	H	73	6, 15, 16, 25
	S	272	11 to 14, 17, 19, 21, 25
	M	10	15
Dhim ...	H	188	17, 23, 25, 26
	S	54	12, 17, 18
Dhingar ...	H	44	15, 28
Dhir ...	H	96	16, 19, 26
	S	53	14, 16, 17, 26, 28
Dhobí ...	S	3	9, 10
	M	52	10, 51
Dhokar ...	H	17	28
Dhon ...	H	251	10, 12, 17, 20, 26, 34
	S	47	12, 25
	M	9	13
Dhoná ...	H	169	12 to 14, 25
Dholar ...	H	269	17, 21, 24
Dhongi ...	H	191	12, 14, 22
	S	16	12, 14
	M	91	17 to 19, 25
Dhopar ...	H	104	1, 33, 34, 40
Dhor ...	H	464	8, 14, 17, 18, 21, 25, 44
Dhotí ...	H	47	2, 27
	S	12	9
	M	17	40, 44
Dodar ...	H	15	11, 13
Dogar ...	M	15	18
Dogne ...	H	17	1, 16
	S	44	21, 22
	M	11	13
Dohí ...	S	33	14
Dolá ...	H	41	1, 2
	S	36	21
Dontre ...	H	26	1
Dora ...	H	113	6, 8, 12, 19, 25, 26, 51
	S	2	21
Dotar ...	H	54	24, 25, 27
Gadar ...	H	127	13, 19, 25, 26
Gadoná ...	H	20	2, 20
Gádrí ...	H	150	5, 11, 25
Gand ...	H	322	16, 18 to 21, 25
	S	74	20, 21, 25
	M	44	16
Gande ...	H	22	17
	S	87	1, 17, 25
	M	1	5
Gandwara ...	H	3	45
	M	9	51
Gangánía ...	H	25	5
	S	3	24
Gangáras ...	H	164	1, 2, 5, 11, 27
Gar ...	H	12	7, 11, 14
	S	7	12, 14
	M	7	17
Gargor ...	H	1	4
	S	32	15
Gatárí ...	H	36	6
Gáwrí ...	H	27	1, 5
	S	4	51
Ghakar ...	H	45	17
	M	1	16
Ghal ...	H	79	1, 5
Ghiásmola ...	H	127	28, 29
Ghon ...	H	105	1, 5, 6, 33
Giárí ...	H	91	19, 26
	M	1	27
Gil ...	H	268	14, 17
	S	65	1, 12 to 14, 17, 25
	M	65	1, 15, 16, 25
Gobra ...	H	196	8, 20
	S	71	20
Gogá ...	H	15	25
Gogal ...	H	47	25, 26
	M	36	15
Gogan ...	H	198	44
	S	3	44
Goghí ...	H	52	25
Gogane ...	H	501	1, 2, 5, 6, 10, 11, 15, 25, 45
	S	35	9, 12
	M	8	15
Gogash ...	H	21	4, 40
Gográ ...	H	405	3, 4, 14, 15, 17, 25, 31
	S	4	17
	M	4	40, 51
Goharikhait ...	H	20	15
Gokal ...	H	45	10, 22
	S	27	44
Goíá ...	H	29	3, 4
Golariá ...	H	3	5
	S	13	11
Goliá ...	H	3	11
	S	8	14
Gomal ...	M	25	1, 42
Gond ...	H	253	R. except (23)
	S	518	R. except (23)
Gandal ...	H	6	13, 15
	S	11	18
	M	205	13, 16 to 19
Gonga ...	H	13	25
	S	71	13
Gonghar ...	H	13	1, 3
	S	13	12, 17
Gore ...	H	91	12, 15, 21, 22
	S	127	13, 21, 22
	M	9	5, 15, 17
Goriá ...	S	12	21
Gorwál ...	H	3	13
	S	8	13
Gujjar ...	H	35	45
Gulábu ...	H	26	7
Hakhári ...	H	28	15, 16, 23
Hándi ...	H	87	2, 15, 44
	S	12	1, 14, 25
Háns ...	M	14	1, 28
Har ...	H	7	12, 17, 25
Hasi ...	H	4	3
	S	2	12, 25
	M	7	51
Hech ...	H	28	5
Heri ...	H	21	21
	S	27	21
Isat ...	H	85	2
Jágal ...	H	75	23, 41
	S	34	17, 23
Jaghar ...	H	31	4
	S	6	17
Jagi ...	H	9	2, 15, 33
	S	3	22
Jagoiá ...	H	15	8, 51
Jáho ...	H	7	6
	S	30	1, 11, 12
	M	4	25
Jahrá ...	H	23	28
Jálo ...	H	47	1, 2, 5, 12
	S	31	14
	M	23	18, 25
Jámlo ...	H	31	5, 8
Jándal ...	H	4	2, 19
	S	49	18
Jángal ...	H	131	1, 6, 19, 29, 30
	S	2	17
	M	34	20, 29
Jangi ...	H	305	1, 4, 5, 34
	M	96	20, 22, 27
Jangogi ...	H	40	1, 27, 28
Janjuhán ...	H	11	25
	M	4	28
Janjuá ...	S	1	21
	M	86	17, 19, 20
Jankal ...	H	52	24, 27
Jarái ...	H	95	5, 14, 27, 51
	S	28	17
	M	13	15
Jariá ...	H	959	1, 12, 15, 28, 51
	S	509	16, 44
	M	691	19, 23, 27
Jaspál ...	H	33	1, 2, 8
	M	11	19
Jasrátiá ...	H	38	10, 25, 40
	M	2	18
Jat ...	H	12	13, 14
	S	11	11, 13, 25
	M	3	19, 29
Jatálá ...	H	21	31, 34
	S	5	12, 13
	M	4	22
Jatiá ...	H	16	5
Játu ...	H	49	1, 4, 5
Jhaggal ...	H	55	11, 40
Jhalo ...	H	34	1, 6, 44
	M	30	16
Jhangi ...	H	285	1, 2, 5, 18, 34
	S	78	16, 19, 20, 26
	M	61	18
Jhori ...	H	11	8, 11, 28
	S	88	1, 13
	M	71	16
Johrá ...	H	47	24, 51
Joiá ...	H	8	25, 27
	M	493	12, 19, 23, 24
Joji ...	H	9	10
	S	5	12
Jolá ...	H	9	4
	M	3	14, 15
Kachhare ...	H	90	1, 5, 8, 44
	S	5	44
	M	143	13, 27
Káhlon ...	H	25	9
Kaikán ...	H	22	5
Kájli ...	H	5	11
	S	20	12
Kakar ...	H	54	16, 18
	S	7	18, 19
	M	9	18, 19

Names of Sub-Castes.		Persons.	Locality.
Kaki ...	H	323	13, 15, 18, 20
	S	56	17, 18, 25
	M	112	16, 19, 26
Kalandar ...	M	20	28
Kalo ...	M	15	27
Kalodiá ..	H	2	10, 12
	M	12	28, 29
Kalwará ...	H	12	3
Kamboh ...	M	66	20, 51
Kámri ...	H	50	9, 19, 28
Kán ...	H	46	19, 26
	M	28	25, 28
Kandhere ...	H	15	27
Kandi ...	H	959	J. 9, 11, 25
	S	730	13, 14
	M	643	L. 9, 10
Kang ...	H	24	11, 16
	M	10	18
Kangal ...	H	25	2
	M	9	16
Kangar ...	H	112	1, 2, 5
	M	33	13, 19
Kangoriá ...	H	35	4
Kánjal ...	H	1	2
	M	13	16
Kanjar ...	H	14	14
Kankál ...	H	67	2, 26
	S	54	14, 22
	M	4	14
Kankhán ...	H	66	2, 29, 31
	S	71	22
Kans ...	H	22	4
Kansal ...	H	28	8, 34
Kántiwál ...	H	64	3, 4
Kapal ...	H	28	1, 49
Kaphle ...	H	81	1, 5
Kaplas ...	H	13	41, 48
Kapur ...	H	534	R. M. 8
	S	25	26, 27
	M	20	15, 16, 18
Karbar ...	H	37	9, 15
Karil ...	H	153	4, 9, 10, 14
	S	72	9, 11
	M	63	5, 24
Karor ...	H	331	L. 1, 25
	S	164	13 to 15
	M	68	12, 13, 24
Karwál ...	H	957	D. 9, 11, 12, 15
	S	130	11 to 13
	M	111	1, 24, 49
Karwári ...	H	35	25
Kásab ...	H	188	3 to 5, 36
	S	12	11, 21
	M	3	25
Kashal ...	H	46	15, 42
Kashmíri ...	H	14	4, 8, 44
	S	3	46
Katámal ...	H	196	R. 27, 28
	S	29	20, 28
	M	65	18, 22
Katar ...	H	286	D. 18, 20
	S	32	12, 18, 20
	M	23	18
Katára ...	H	82	13, 18
	S	2	12
Kattan ...	H	12	9, 10, 34
Kedi ...	H	48	12
	S	1	14
Keji ...	H	13	44
Kekhan ...	H	59	2
Khábre ...	H	14	15
Khaggar ...	H	29	1, 18
	S	22	10, 13
	M	52	15, 18
Khankar ...	H	19	14
Khanná ...	H	65	12, 14, 18
	S	27	10, 21, 25
Khari ...	H	121	J. 4
	S	12	11, 12, 25
	M	8	12, 25
Kharil ...	H	50	12, 17
	S	12	10 to 12
	M	303	24, 25, 27
Khárji ...	H	11	9, 44
	S	17	1, 10
Kharkhoda	H	14	2
Kharman ...	H	39	1, 5, 42
	S	4	12, 17
Kharoli ...	H	9	2, 41, 51
	S	1	12
	M	25	13, 16
Khátodia ...	H	55	2, 8, 11
Khatri ...	H	730	J. R. M.
	S	159	12, 23, 25
	M	6	12, 15, 25
Khel ...	H	419	D. except (6, 7)
	S	97	1, 11, 12
Khichi ...	H	11	24, 51
	M	68	12, 44, 51
Khoiá ...	H	28	5
	M	1	44
Khokar ...	H	54	4, 15
	S	6	11, 16
	M	667	12, 13, 15, 26 to 28
Khol ...	H	36	5, 8
	S	29	1, 5, 12
Khor ...	H	49	5
	S	8	12
	M	139	15, 24
Khurmi ...	H	287	J. except (8)
	S	112	11, 12, 25
	M	47	12
Kohli ...	H	15	16, 21, 44
Kokal ...	H	186	18 to 20, 23
	S	160	R. except (22)
	M	123	14, 15, 22, 23
Kokar ...	H	100	1, 2, 12, 20
	S	21	17
	M	17	15, 18, 23
Kokas ...	H	50	1, 2, 4
	M	1	14
Kolariá ...	H	28	1, 51
Kondal ...	H	17	9
Kori ...	H	16	9, 15
Koshal ...	H	163	9, 10, 36, 42
Lacho ...	H	13	25
	S	61	25
Ládhar ...	H	371	2, 9, 14, 25
	S	267	12, 13, 16, 24, 46
	M	78	25, 29
Lágan ...	H	17	2
Lágore ...	H	42	9
Láhar ...	H	359	L. 9 to 11, 19, 25
	S	158	14, 17, 19, 24, 25
	M	120	14 to 17, 19
Láhi ...	H	30	1, 2
	M	1	1
Láhori ...	H	138	18 to 20
	S	8	9, 11
	M	2	10
Lál ...	H	34	9, 16, 18
	S	4	14
Lálori ...	S	14	9
Lámbe ...	H	56	4, 49
Lán ...	H	71	25
	S	4	14
Lánbi ...	H	24	3, 19
Landi ...	M	41	12
Landori ...	M	18	12
Lang ...	H	56	12, 14, 19, 25
	S	4	25
	M	7	25
Lár ...	H	1	11
	S	1	12
	M	12	18, 17
Lásá ...	H	31	2, 9
Lodhar ...	H	508	9, 13, 14, 16, 23, 26
	M	53	15, 16, 27
Machchal ...	H	31	18, 28
Máchh ...	H	45	2, 4
Maderi ...	H	14	12
	M	20	12, 15
Máhaj ...	H	383	1, 2, 4, 5
Máhal ...	H	27	12
	S	5	19
Máhan ...	H	22	16
	S	32	13, 25
Mahandri ...	H	16	9
	S	5	10, 15
Máhar ...	H	105	1 to 3, 9, 12, 13, 14, 21, 25, 26, 47
	S	10	14
	M	121	1, 5, 6, 10, 44, 51
Mahát ...	H	21	1, 5
Mahon ...	H	1	1
	S	39	14, 21
	M	5	17
Mahta ...	H	42	12, 25, 26, 45
	M	57	11, 15, 16, 24, 26
Máipotre ...	H	31	51
Mair ...	H	18,459	J. L. 2 to 4, 6, 7, 25, 34, 40, 44, 46, 48, 49
	S	4,482	13 to 16, 18 to 20, 48, 49
	M	941	16, 48
Makkar ...	H	31	29
	S	1	51
	M	10	15
Mál ...	H	882	9, 50, 51
	S	191	12, 50, 51
Málak ...	H	21	15, 20
	S	4	46
Malan ...	H	45	11
Malhotre ...	H	27	17, 25
Mán ...	H	195	9, 15, 20, 22, 44, 49, 51
	S	3	11, 12
	M	8	11
Mánaj ...	H	26	1, 45
Mánan ...	H	52	9, 10, 13, 15
	S	15	13, 15
	M	23	13, 17, 19
Mandal ...	H	32	2, 24, 25, 41, 51
Mándan ...	H	292	1 to 5, 12, 21
	S	5	13
	M	33	17, 25
Manderi ...	H	26	1, 45
	S	2	15
Mándi ..	H	23	2, 8, 12, 25, 44
	M	3	9
Mándoriá ...	H	50	50
Mangan ...	H	159	26
Manghá ...	H	233	13, 19, 20, 21, 26, 28
	S	136	22, 24
	M	64	18, 24, 26
Mangpál ...	H	14	22
Máni ...	H	11	15, 25, 42
Manotra ...	H	92	26
Már ...	H	29	31
Márkandi ...	H	29	1, 9, 13
Maro ...	H	141	5, 8, 10
	S	14	25
	M	36	13, 15, 24
Maror ...	H	3	11
	M	24	15
Marotra ...	H	27	9, 19
Marwáhi ...	H	51	9, 13
	S	4	13
	M	2	9
Marwári ...	H	33	4, 18, 42
	S	16	13
	M	1	51
Masáwan ...	H	342	1, 5, 6, 9 to 13, 16, 17, 20, 24, 25, 44
	S	281	10, 12, 13, 16, 17, 24, 44, 46
	M	110	1, 3, 10, 12, 15, 16, 24, 27, 44, 51
Mashon ...	H	1,177	1, 6, 9, 10, 12, 14, 17 to 19, 24 to 26, 33
	S	129	14, 16, 18, 24, to 26, 45
	M	217	1, 9, 16, 17, 25, 44
Masur ...	H	96	9, 11, 45
Matan ...	H	44	1, 9, 12, 44, 45
	S	14	25, 46
	M	19	25
Matardewál ...	H	15	4, 14
Mathe ...	H	4	16
	S	24	21
	M	11	23
Matrija ...	H	19	51
Matto ...	H	78	9, 13, 25, 44, 45
	S	2	15
	M	41	5, 13, 27

SUB-CASTES OF CERTAIN SELECTED CASTES—*continued.*

Names of Sub-Castes.		Persons.	Locality.
Mod ...	H	32	12, 15, 42
Medal ...	H	17	16
Mege ...	H	9	26
	S	15	13
Meich ...	H	25	33
Meon ...	H	63	1, 14, 25
	S	9	5, 12, 46
	M	26	10, 14, 15
Merki ...	H	27	26
Mes ...	S	182	5, 9, 11, 12, 17
	M	141	9, 17, 18, 24
Mesiá ...	H	14	5
Minhás ...	H	362	9, 25
	M	50	9, 19, 27, 51
Mirajput ...	H	45	32
Miran ...	M	13	14
Mitar ...	H	1,995	1, 4, 5, 9, 15, 19, 20, 51
	S	11	15
	M	102	15, 24
Mohal ...	H	45	1, 2, 5
	S	11	15
	M	4	51
Mohan ...	H	12	19, 47
	S	4	17
	M	62	12 to 14
Mohni ..	H	76	18
Mol ...	H	29	1, 27
	M	21	10, 13, 19
Mon ...	H	346	1, 6, 12, 16, 19, 25, 26, 40, 41
	S	17	14
	M	214	1, 12, 17, 18, 24, 25
Moriwál ...	H	24	12
Mughal ...	H	71	16, 21, 25
	M	71	15, 16, 20, 25, 28, 51
Munchal ...	H	13	1
Nachal ...	H	171	15, 16, 23, 28
	S	1	25
Nágauri ...	H	19	4, 9, 14
Nági ...	H	141	8, 21, 25
	S	167	5, 14, 16, 21, 25
Nágle ...	H	17	1, 12
Náhal ...	H	60	14, 16, 18, 25
	S	48	14, 24
	M	120	24, 25
Náhangar ...	H	24	3
Náhar ...	H	13	19
Nái ...	H	8	28
	M	4	3
Náich ...	H	21	2
Najhon ...	H	33	1, 29
Nákoru ...	H	14	47
Náli ...	H	41	20, 27
	S	3	20
Namchári ...	B	14	12
Nának ...	H	34	11
Nánaksháhi ...	H	26	9
Nándal ...	H	52	2
Nang ...	H	50	8
	S	2	13
	M	4	23, 25
Nárandiá ...	H	13	3
Nárnoli ...	H	73	5, 12
Náru ...	H	54	9, 10, 14, 18
	M	28	13
Nasáwas ...	H	61	1, 2, 5
Naspán ...	H	16	9
Nathal ...	H	13	16
Naumuslim ...	M	34	19, 24, 27
Nir ...	H	24	9, 11
	M	1	11
Nis ...	M	42	23
Noli ...	H	27	18
Noná ...	H	11	23
Nosáwar ...	H	12	1
Obbi ...	M	18	18
Ochhe ...	H	27	4
Odh ...	H	32	51
	M	7	5, 13
Odhare ...	M	32	16
Ohi ...	H	22	22
Oholiá ...	H	22	3
Okas ...	H	11	4
Okhar ...	H	30	27

Names of Sub-Castes.		Persons.	Locality.
Otam ...	H	12	1
Pachi ...	H	226	8, 16, 25, 34, 41
	S	3	34
Padi ...	H	18	8, 6
	M	14	8, 16
Páji ...	H	144	34
Panje ...	H	20	8, 11, 45
Pann ...	H	12	12
	S	2	12
Panwár ...	H	7	1, 33
	S	6	17
	M	392	1, 2, 5, 6, 12, 24, 27, 51
Parán ...	H	12	8
Parasrámi ...	H	22	18, 20
Parwáhi ...	H	34	1, 5, 9
Pasán ...	H	21	2, 9, 18, 25
	S	11	2, 25
Patas ...	H	89	4
Pathán ...	M	22	13, 27, 28
Patrohi ...	H	10	5
Pawár ...	H	131	2, 10 to 12, 40
	S	3	48
	M	29	2, 16, 28, 29
Phálan ...	H	26	17, 30
Phári ...	H	5	9
	S	8	25
Phil ...	H	27	25
	S	5	9
Pholá ...	M	11	19, 20
Phulan ...	H	2	51
	M	23	23
Phular ...	M	292	23, 44
Pirnálas ...	H	14	25
Punjabi ...	S	13	13, 21
Puri ...	H	13	6, 8
	S	1	14
	M	6	15, 25
Puriwál ...	H	40	31
Qureshi ...	M	55	5, 11, 20, 22
Raghobansi ...	H	88	17, 44
	S	5	17
Rahta ...	H	10	2, 5
	S	1	14
Rajále ...	H	21	13, 14
Rájniati ...	H	40	14
Rajorá ...	H	95	4, 8, 14
Rajpál ...	H	69	6, 11, 45, 48, 49
	M	1	48
Rájput ...	H	4,772	B. except (7, 28)
	S	2,072	L. R. 6, 10, 25, 46
	M	729	J. L. 6, 18, 24, 25
Rájput Kande	S	36	14
Rali ...	H	84	12, 18
Rámgarhiá ...	H	12	15
	S	1	12
Ramrá ..	H	19	5
Randwál ...	H	13	1
Rangar ...	H	111	12, 20 to 22
	S	290	12, 19 to 22, 25
	M	8	13, 16, 22
Rásul ...	H	11	1
Ratanpál ...	H	35	21, 39
	S	242	20, 21
Ratgar ...	H	43	19
Rati ...	H	126	1, 3, 15, 17, 26
	S	51	14, 18, 19, 26
	M	195	9, 14, 16, 18, 19
Ratre ...	H	344	1, 8, 9, 11, 45
Rián ...	H	20	15
	S	9	20
Rodá ...	H	433	1, 5, 12, 15, 17, 19, 48
	S	53	17, 24 to 26
	M	39	12, 13, 26 to 28
Rodhá ...	H	159	23, 25, 26, 29
	M	77	19, 24, 25
Rodhi ...	H	18	2
Rodki ...	S	22	14
Rojá ...	H	15	4
Ropar ...	H	14	12, 29
Rorá ...	H	221	1 to 4, 17, 18, 28
	S	14	13, 14
	M	3	15, 51
Rori ...	M	18	8, 17, 25
Roti ...	H	34	26
	M	8	16

Names of Sub-Castes.		Persons.	Locality.
Sabi ...	H	28	18
	S	23	11, 25
Sachawáre ...	S	1	13
	M	116	12
Sachde ...	H	92	16, 24
	S	95	24
	M	4	24
Sadá ...	H	20	1, 5, 8, 12
	S	3	14
Sadhar ...	H	199	1, 17, 18
Sadhare ...	H	1,447	L. 1, 9, 18, 24, 25
	S	746	L. 1, 11, 12, 24, 46
	M	1,187	15, 24 to 27
Sadho ...	H	137	12
Sadhwán ...	H	11	16
Sadporá ...	H	105	17, 18, 44, 46
	S	6	11, 25
	M	1	15
Sahgal ...	H	34	1, 11
	M	21	25, 44
Sahotre ...	H	5	8
	M	8	27
Saini ...	H	173	1, 14, 15, 18
	S	55	1, 18, 28
	M	52	10, 28
Sajhorá ...	M	19	17, 18
Sakhi ...	H	5	2, 4
	M	10	16
Sálan ...	H	35	8, 9, 11
	M	1	9
Salwariá ...	M	19	44
Sami ...	H	976	13, 16, 19, 22, 26 to 29, 47
	S	114	13, 23, 25, 28
	M	53	12, 15, 23, 44
Sán ...	H	34	1, 5, 45
	S	6	18, 45
	M	6	10
Sanáriá ...	H	7	2, 27
	M	239	17, 18, 24, 26
Sanas ...	H	15	44
	S	14	4, 16
	M	6	25
Sanchal ...	M	16	16
Sándas ...	H	36	2
	M	2	25
Sandhan ...	H	66	1, 3, 5, 8, 15
	S	5	17
	M	43	10
Sandhari ...	H	278	1, 11, 21
	S	136	15, 18, 21
Sandhawál ...	H	61	1
Sandhil ...	H	118	1, 2, 5
	M	65	11, 12
Sandolá ...	H	19	1, 18
	M	5	18, 20
Sandwari ...	H	266	51
	S	13	11
	M	152	2, 9, 24
Sang ...	H	10	14, 16, 51
	S	12	13, 44
	M	72	16, 17, 27
Sangal ...	H	46	2, 4
	S	7	12, 21
Sangat ...	H	135	1, 3 to 5
Sangwárá ...	H	12	31, 44
Sank ...	H	374	16, 26, 39
	S	16	9, 13, 14, 46
	M	284	13, 15, 16, 20 25
Sapal ...	S	8	10, 14, 18
	M	28	16, 18, 21, 25, 27
Sara ...	H	232	8, 13 to 15, 46
Sarán ...	M	18	13
Sarás ...	H	33	2, 25, 28
	M	1	17
Sardái ...	H	2	5
	S	5	17
	M	12	12
Saroet ...	H	2	51
	M	9	8
Sarwál ...	H	66	1, to 3, 8, 12, 14, 25
	S	34	14
	M	5	1, 8, 27

APPENDIX TO IMPERIAL TABLE XIII.—

Names of Sub-Castes.		Persons.	Locality.
Sárwán ...	H	48	1, 5, 12, 15
	S	17	17, 25
	M	392	10, 15, 16, 25, 40, 44
Sarware ...	H	6	9, 13
	S	17	11, 17, 25
	M	42	14, 15, 27
Satráni ...	H	12	2
Sáwan ...	H	471	4, 6, 9, 12, 14, 16, 17, 18, 25
	S	174	6, 9, 10, 11, 13, 14, 17, 25, 44
	M	62	13, 15, 17, 19, 20, 25
Sedhi ...	H	379	1, 2, 5, 10, 11, 25
	S	9	11, 25
	M	29	25
Segiá ...	H	29	2
Sela ...	H	21	10
Seti ...	H	30	5, 14, 15
Sewári ...	H	19	2, 9
	S	14	25
	M	2	25
Sháh ...	H	18	11
Sháhná ...	H	94	11, 12, 17, 25
	S	40	13
Shakarpuri ...	M	11	9, 10
Shakriá ...	H	23	2
Shamshi ...	H	22	12, 27
	S	9	10
Shashan ...	H	150	12
Sheikh ...	S	7	12
	M	76	1, 5, 16, 19, 20, 22, 28
Shelan ...	H	18	16
Shina ...	H	255	5, 10, 11, 12, 15, 16, 17, 25, 46
	S	30	14, 19, 46
Shudar ...	H	105	13, 28
Siáh ...	H	4	25, 30
	S	35	22
Siál ...	M	11	27
Sib ...	H	35	45
Sidha ...	H	13	2, 11
Sidhu ...	H	76	12, 45
	S	88	24, 46
Sindhu ...	H	81	1, 5, 9, 17, 18
	S	249	12, 15, 17, 29
	M	196	13, 15, 16, 19, 25
Sir ...	S	36	15
Soda ...	H	6	14
	S	4	9
	M	26	10, 51
Sodrá ...	S	34	9, 17
	M	26	51
Sohal ...	S	27	14
	M	3	11, 22
Sohán ...	H	19	2, 9, 14, 15
	S	43	14, 25
	M	4	21
Sokh ...	S	12	14
Sol ...	H	7	15
	M	21	22
Son ...	H	296	2, 9, 13, 15, 16, 24, 25
	S	105	13, 14
	M	31	1, 9, 15, 19
Song ...	S	12	11
Sopal ...	H	63	9, 18, 25
	M	2	51
Sor ...	H	282	8, 11, 12, 13, 16, 18, 24, 25
	S	312	L. 9, 11, 12
	M	6	1, 12
Soti ...	M	20	15
Sotre ...	H	8	12
	S	16	12, 17, 25
Sud ...	H	201	12, 13, 15, 29
	S	258	12, 14, 15, 17
Sudar ...	H	36	29
Surajbansi ...	H	32	4
Suri ...	H	20	17, 44
	S	34	46
Tahim ...	M	100	20, 24, 27, 28
Taneli ...	H	12	13
Tánk ...	H	8,185	D. J. L. R. except (3, 7, 23), 25, 26 S. except . (30, 31, 32, 33, 34, 39, 43)
	S	1,190	J. L. R. except (8, 12, 22, 23)
	M	69	9, 13, 14, 17
Tanur ...	H	62	3, 4, 34
	M	36	2, 5
Tarámi ...	H	1	29
	S	14	25
Targar ...	H	20	12
Tasáwar ...	H	22	1, 3
	M	14	24
Tatwál ...	H	80	2
Tawán ...	H	11	12
Táwegar ...	H	38	3
Tekán ...	H	40	2
Tezi ...	H	83	7, 8, 34
Thákar ...	H	172	3, 4, 24, 47, 50
Thathwál ...	H	23	2
Tindle ...	H	11	19
Tohla ...	H	23	19
Tor ...	H	74	8, 21
	S	21	12
	M	610	5, 6, 12, 26
Toriwál ...	H	28	10, 31
	M	83	5, 7, 15, 25, 29
Tosbánar ...	H	37	2
Total ...	M	73	12, 14
Upal ...	H	26	13
Utradhi ...	H	13	28
Vabiá ...	H	17	18
Variáh ...	M	74	17, 24, 25
Váshdev ...	H	22	20
Vasra ...	H	64	20
Ved ...	H	236	9, 13, 16, 12
	S	38	
	M	1.	
Vedo ...	H	39	[illegible]
	M	24	10, 18
Vela ...	H	11	15
Vens ...	M	12	9, 17, 27
Zargar ...	H	239	25, 26, 27, 29
	S	17	12, 25, 29
	M	36	18, 25, 26,
Zargarmarichá	H	21	51
*Minor ...	H	2,189	
	S	496	
	M	647	
Unspecified	H	14,238	
	S	5,327	
	M	6,078	
	J	8	
	B	1	

* DETAIL OF MINOR.

Abbi 1, Ablas 2, Abri 1, Achání 9, Achhal 7, Adhi 1, Adil-khán 3, Agand 1, Agál 2, Agangotre 4, Agoriá 4, Agroi 1, Ahángar 5, Abat 2, Abdo 4, Aheri 7, Ahír 1, Ahmadi 1, Abwál 8, Ailráwáh 3, Ait 4, Alat 8, Andháná 4, Angres 2, Ankras 9, Anotri 6, Anpál 4, Appátti 3, Aráin 9, Arath 1, Arjan 3, Aroki 5, Arsi 9, Ashgal 6, Asi 4, Asiri 3, At 2, Atale 1, Bagaliári 3, Bagle 9, Babláudi 4, Balál 8, Baláwat 1, Báli 3, Balim 6, Banchal 2, Bandal 1, Bandhad 6, Bangotre 7, Banhár 2, Báni 6, Barahmn 2, Barás 4, Bárgar 3, Bargil 2, Barotre 1, Básas 4, Basije 3, Basin 10, Batoi 4, Bayábi 1, Bedrale 3, Bedwán 3, Bekál 8, Beli 4, Bhábra 4, Bhad 10, Bhagna 3, Bhagotre 10, Bháigo 6, Bhair 2, Bhájji 2, Bhákan 2, Bhandlá 1, Bhang 1, Bhangá 1, Bhárath 1, Bhárdwáj 1, Bhárwáj 6, Bhasá 10, Bhat 7, Bhatan 6, Bhatiári 1, Bhatwáli 4, Bháwal 1, Bhok 6, Bholra 4, Bhopál 7, Bhor 5, Bhori 5, Bichar 8, Bikhani 1, Biloch 1, Bode 1, Bodil 7, Bodry 6, Bujogo 1, Bulái 1, Bungar 1, Chábil 3, Chamre 3, Chander-Bansi 8, Cháudiá 1, Chandrániá 8, Chandwánd 5, Chángal 7, Chángar 4, Chánk 1, Chansarái 1, Charlá 5, Chatoriá 10, Chátiá 4, Cháure 6, Chhal 3, Chhalwál 4, Chidi 7, Chisti 4, Choohi 1, Chodhar 5, Chodi 1, Chokar 6, Choreti 2, Chorke 5, Chotre 10, Dabkar 1, Dadbá 3, Dakhni 6, Dakondal 1, Dalogá 1, Dálor 7, Danri 6, Dárá 3, Darghiri 2, Daswán 3, Dasoldi 1, Dasoriá 6, Dátor 6, Dáwar 7, Dáwas 9, Dhagi 1, Dhakri 10, Dhalni 3, Dham 6, Dhánajait 6, Dhandiál 9, Dhandbir 1, Dhanoj 5, Dharal 1, Dhásiá 4, Dháwan 6, Dhilwán 1, Dhobri 10, Dhokalá 5, Dhokar 1, Dimbaláh 2, Diná 4, Dindár 10, Ditá 5, Dodhi 6, Doge 1, Doháli 1, Dohárá 8, Dohmi 1, Dokal 7, Dolar 2, Doli 1, Dooji 10, Elahi 1, Faggi, 9 Fálo 3, Fare 2, Ferozi 4, Gadgane 7, Gadhágiá 9, Gadoja 1, Gáhan 5, Gáhi 3, Galáti 1, Ganbar 1, Gandori 2, Garer 6, Gargas 10, Garkhal 4, Garni 4, Garta 4, Gashágiá 9, Gehung 1, Geri 5, Ghar 6, Gharal 3, Gharan 4, Gharwálá 3, Ghate 2, Ghol 8, Gholán 3, Ghori 6, Ghosan 5, Ghote 1, Ghumman 4, Ghuna 10, Gichar 2, Gobind 1, Gochi 1, Godal 1, Godhájiá 6, Godiál 7, Gogli 7, Gohi 5, Gomáh 10, Gomri 1, Gon 3, Gopál 7, Gophri 7, Gorási 5, Gorbhá 5, Gordan 1, Goriá 7, Goriál 1, Gorni 1, Gorowárá 8, Gosal 1, Gotal 5, Gugái 6, Gujjar-Khel 3, Gundh 2, Gurgái 1, Gurge 5, Gyár 8, Hachu 8, Háili 1, Hajure 4, Hakal 2, Hálar 1, Handar 7, Hande 8, Hanji 1, Hanjrád 1, Hanskawár 1, Harbái 1, Hármeá 4, Hash 1, Hathar 3, Háwan 1, Heggi 2, Hinjrá 4, Hirsi 7, Hodeá 2, Hojal 1, Holi 10, Hoc 1. Hotipál 3, Jábar 2, Jáchongá 1, Jádalá 3, Jagdev 5, Jagru 1, Jáhlan 10, Jáiswárá 1, Jájal 1, Jájan 9, Jájátri 1, Jajdái 3, Jámal 7, Jámalá 4, Jamwál 5, Jangáras 3, Janjukhel 4, Janjwár 9, Jansun 7, Jaral 5, Járáli 2, Jari 9, Jarwe 9, Játán 5, Jáwan 9, Jáwará 8, Jepál 3, Jewáni 3, Jhádal 2, Jhagar 5, Jhagi 6, Jhairwál 5, Jhajaká 2, Jhán 3, Jhime 10, Jhoj 1, Jhokar 1, Jhorlo 2, Jiwári 6, Joil 1, Jojan 3, Jondián 1, Jopal 2, Jore 9, Jotáh 1, Jotal 1, Juláhi 4, Kabir-Bansi 1, Kabiri 2, Kachhal 2, Kachhi 6, Kachri 2, Kadke 1, Kadri 5, Kafáh 4, Kagle 5, Kahlan 3, Kahrámi 2, Káist 1, Káith 2, Káiwál 8, Kajái 10, Kajlán 5, Kákas 4, Kakerá 9, Kakezai 5, Kakrán 5, Kakriá 5, Kalál 5, Kalasrá 4, Kálejo 1, Kálgal 2, Kalinni 9, Kalkhásiá 10, Kalle 2, Kálo 1, Kamani 1, Kambore 1, Káuá 2, Kanchari 7, Kandare 1, Kandela 1, Kandlor 4, Kandli 5, Kanet 1, Kanj 6, Kanjro 9, Kanjuran 1, Kanki 7, Kanol 5, Kanri 1, Kánthá 2, Kantia 3, Kantre 2, Kanwál 10, Kanwár 1, Kapalas 4, Kappi 4, Kariband 1, Karkhal 1, Karmar 9, Karmi 8, Karni 8, Karnil 6, Karorá 2, Kasati 6, Kasiare 1, Kásrá 2, Katán 8, Katáwára 1, Kate 4, Kathal 1, Kathoriá 3, Katiwál 7, Katoriá 1, Katri 1, Katwál 2, Keni 3, Kenthal 7, Kewál 2, Khábrá 1, Kháí 6, Khákan 9, Khakariá 2, Khákas 1, Khakhe 4, Kháli 7, Khamil 1, Khándá 3, Kháni 10, Khanná 2, Khánpurá 5, Khante 1, Kharar 7, Kháras 2, Khárjal 5, Kharkhori 10, Kharwálá 9, Khárwas 6, Khásia 1, Kheari 10, Khekan 9, Kher 5, Khojá 1, Kholu 1, Khorsi 5, Khorsni 2, Khukarián 1, Khusháni 6, Khushhál 9, Kián 6, Kitbit 1, Kochá 2, Koghli 5, Kohi 6 Kohigál 4, Koknár 5, Kondras 2, Kongi 1, Konjgar 3, Konjiwál 2, Konni 1, Kontná 2, Kor 8, Korái 2, Koral 9, Koriwál 3, Kotan 4, Kothá 4, Kotharmal 9, Kotri 10, Kotu 1, Kotwálá 1, Kumárá 1, Kundan 3, Kurbal 4, Kuriál 6, Labojiá 6, Lachí 2, Ladhirwál 7, Lágas 3, Lagí 1, Lahin 9, Laiq 1, Lakhwárá 3, Lakria 1, Lala 1, Lamari 2, Lamasirá 1, Lánbá 7, Landhir 4, Langah 2, Langaria 1, Lánkdhi 6, Lawán 1, Láwát 4, Ledhi 4, Lek 1, Lekas 3, Lodhi 2, Lohán 3, Lon 3, Lonas 1, Lond 2, Lop 6, Lor 6, Lotan 5, Ludhari 7, Machar 4, Machin 2, Mad 8, Madál 1, Magian 4, Magli 2, Mahant 5, Maharet 3, Maharkaror 6, Máhi 10, Máho 2, Mahtáni 1,

SUB-CASTES OF CERTAIN SELECTED CASTES—*concluded.*

DETAIL OF MINOR—*concluded.*

Máin 2, Mairlo 1, Májal 5, Máji 2, Majoke 4, Malah 1, Male 2 Mámau 2, Manchal Mir 2, Mándas 4, Mandú 7, Mandwál 9, Mangal 2, Mangaldiá 2, Manhote 4, Manj 2, Manjorá 1, Manráh 1, Manre 4, Mansum 1, Mantráná 9, Mánurá 2, Máon 10, Maráich 7, Marbotrá 8, Mariá 3, Mariná 5, Marol 2, Marou 1, Marwáli Kashab 3, Márwár 5, Másie 10, Mathádu 1, Mathora 2, Matra 1, Matwáli 10, Mazári 6, Medane 5, Medke 7, Meharwál 3, Mekar 1, Melar 1, Mensi 1, Menu 6, Merdbání 4, Merkhattri 1, Metak 1, Metes 6, Mittarpál 1, Mochi 8, Mohala 1, Mohangar 2, Mohli 7, Mobte 8, Mokh 1, Molání 3, Mondá 1, Mondal 2, Mondhrí 2, Mosál 1, Mudkán 2, Mugi 3, Multáni 2, Nachalmer 1, Nachar 2, Nagrál 1, Náhar 5, Naik 3, Naimoo 1, Náin Bagrí 8, Nainpál 3, Nál 4, Nandli 1, Nandorá 2, Nandwár 9, Nangá 4, Nangiáná 1, Nánuksab 1, Naráin 9, Narankárí 1, Nargis 3, Nathál 5, Narní 1, Nárnobiá 2, Nársoni 4, Narwál 7, Nasbin 6, Náwal 1, Nechar 9, Neori 3, Nigas 3, Nihál 4, Nijáwan 1, Nikori 2, Nimráni 3, Nimrázi 3, Nohda 8, Nongar 10, Nongarma 5, Nonián 1, Nothwán 8, Nujarnojáti 4, Nunári 1, Oda 3, Odák 3, Odhare 2, Odkhansí 4, Olakh 7, Opál 3, Patkarwal 1, Pachhora 4, Padan 1, Padattair 4, Padhar 1, Páhar 2, Paitas 5, Pakbori 7, Palhat 3, Paloh 1, Paloria 2, Palotre 3, Pambá 7, Pane 7, Panaáin 2, Pantas 5, Panti 3, Part 5, Parwal 4, Pathanján 5, Pathán Puri 5, Pathwál 8, Patodia 4, Páwal 1, Páwan 1, Petar 5, Pháh 2, Phal 10, Phal Bhái 1, Pholi 5, Pindri 6, Pirahámahí 10, Pith 1, Pithar 5, Pocham 6, Podan 5, Podi 6, Popal 1, Purbia 2, Qázi 3, Radan 1, Ragiál 4, Rahal 2, Rahani 7, Rabna 10, Rabni 7, Raib 1, Rája 1, Rájan 10, Rajhans 1, Rákhal 1, Ralyath 9, Ramant 4, Rimgáriá 3, Rammal 3, Randat 9, Rang 2, Ranghar 1, Ráníwál 6, Rasht 2, Rasne 4, Rasore 2, Rást 2, Ratan 1, Ratanpál 8, Ráthor 10, Ratiá 8, Ratri 5, Rattí 3, Rekiwár 2, Remare 7, Rewái 6, Rewári 2, Robbe 6, Rochi 2, Rodháran 1, Rodki 4, Rohanki 1, Rojan 1, Rojha 2, Rolí 4, Romimal 1, Rons 1, Ropál 3, Rotá 7, Rotre 5, Rup 1, Ruppar 1, Sabde 2, Sablon 1, Sacho 6, Sadan 5, Sadela 2, Sadhráj 2, Sadra 3, Sadráni 8, Sadwál 2, Saga 1, Ságand 7, Ságro 5, Sagwál 7, Sában 10, Sahate 3, Sahgotre 1, Sahlore 10, Sahro 5, Sahto 7, Saidi 7, Sailare 8, Sain 1, Sainpuro 2, Sair 4, Saith 4, Sajwár 3, Sakera 1, Saket 9, Sakhar 2, Sakhpál 1, Sakráni 1, Saka 1, Sala 3, Salet 1, Salhar 9, Salmániá 4, Saloni 1, Saloniá 5, Salotre 5, Salwál 3, Salwáli 2, Samble 3, Samrani 2, Sanbá 3, Sanda 7, Sandi 4, Sane 3, Sangar 8, Sangba 1, Sankáriá 7, Sánkpuri 1, Sant 1, Sanwál 3, Sanwar 4, Sap 3, Sapún 7, Sara 1, Saraj 1, Saral 5, Sarána 3, Sarás 4, Sargal 3, Sariacha 1, Sarie 1, Sarire 1, Sarmore 3, Sarni 5, Sarohi 7, Sarorni 2, Satakmel 1, Satal 1, Sathrolá 2, Satwán 5, Sawa 3, Sawal 2, Sedhá 1, Sejore 1, Selak 1, Selánkand 5, Sewari 1, Shabar 9, Shabir 4, Sháhrá 1, Sháli 1, Shangariá 5, Shator 1, Shekharjan 6, Sharjil 4, Shian 3, Shoshap 1, Shollá 4, Sialon 3, Sidiqi 1, Sidur 4, Silot 3, Sim 2, Sinah 8, Sing 3, Siprá 1, Sirbare 2, Sita 1, Sital 1, Sithian 2, Sohdtáni 9, Sohni 7, Soi 4, Solich 7, Som 3, Somri 3, Sonáni 2, Songar 5, Soppan 1, Soppar 1, Során 2, Sored 8, Sot 6, Sudha 6, Sudhi 7, Sukdá 1, Soltani 1, Sumal 2, Supja 9, Suter 5, Swani 7, Tabli 3, Talána 3, Talwár 10, Tandan 1, Tandi 1, Tandli 1, Tang 8, Tangar 1, Tani 1, Tarai 5, Tarain 8, Taria 5, Tarni 1, Tarodi 9, Taror 1, Tarot 1, Tarwan 8, Tasádar 7, Tashám 4, Taspur 1, Tegi 6, Telan 2, Thal 5, Thali 3, Thang 1, Tharal 1, Thatha 1, Thongar 2, Thopar 5, Thori 1, Tij 2, Tohan 1, Tohar 3, Toki 1, Torhaj 7, Torni 1, Tosáwálá 3, Tosiwal 4, Tumar 1, Tunija 3, Tutrái 1, Tyore 7, Udasi 2, Udbaki 1, Ude 2, Udere 7, Udiji 1, Ujani 3, Vad 1, Vadhawan 10, Vagi 2, Vahar 1, Vahara 1, Vahim 1, Vak 1, Val 2, Valaicha 1, Vali 2, Vandal 3, Vani 4, Var 1, Vardi 1, Vari 3, Variwal 7, Varwar 1, Vasbishat 1, Vatgar 8, Vedan 3, Versal 1, Vindhi 2, Vist 8, Zangal 1.

APPENDIX TO IMPERIAL TABLE XIV.

CIVIL CONDITION BY AGE AND CASTE OF CERTAIN SECTS IN SELECTED DISTRICTS.

1. This table has been prepared according to Census Commissioner's instructions contained in his Nos. 1227 and 1255, dated the 25th August 1911, and 29th August 1911, respectively, and shows for certain districts, the Civil Condition by Age, of the castes of Aryas, Brahmos and the followers of Dev Dharm (*vide* para. 4, Title page of Imperial Table XIV).

2. The Districts selected are those where the followers of these sects are found in considerable strength.

3. Only 40 Sikhs have returned themselves as Aryas and 22 as Brahmos in these Districts. They have not, therefore, been included in the figures shown in this table.

4. Castes returning less than 10 persons have been grouped under 'Others.'

APPENDIX TO IMPERIAL TABLE XIV.—CIVIL CONDITION

1. ARYA.

Serial No.	Caste.	Locality.	Sex.	Population.	Unmarried. Total.	0—5.	5—12.	12—15.	15—20.	20—40.	40 and over.
	1	2	3	4	5	6	7	8	9	10	11
1	TOTAL		Male ...	47,125	24,098	9,225	6,226	3,575	3,257	1,447	368
2			Female ...	35,363	15,686	6,823	4,564	2,481	1,634	132	52
3	AHÍR ...	TOTAL ...	Male ...	57	18	5	5	2	2	4	...
4			Female ...	39	12	3	8	...	1	...	...
5		Hissar ...	Male ...	14	6	1	1	...	2	2	...
6			Female ...	3	...	...	...	...	...	..	...
7		Delhi ...	Male ...	34	8	2	2	2	...	2	...
8			Female ...	30	8	2	6	...	...	...	...
9		Hoshiarpur ...	Male ...	1	...	...	...	...	...	...	...
10			Female ...	...	...	...	...	...	...	...	...
11		Jullundur ...	Male ...	8	4	2	2	...	...	...	...
12			Female ...	6	4	1	2	...	1	...	...
13	ARORÁ	TOTAL ...	Male ...	6,211	3,295	1,290	916	528	348	152	61
14			Female ...	4,336	2,128	873	780	300	151	18	6
15		Hissar ...	Male ...	39	23	6	12	...	3	2	...
16			Female ...	27	11	5	2	1	3	...	...
17		Kangra ...	Male ...	8	5	1	1	2	...	1	...
18			Female ...	5	3	1	2	...	...	...	...
19		Hoshiarpur ...	Male ...	5	1	1	...	...	...	...	...
20			Female ...	10	6	...	...	1	3	2	...
21		Jullundur ...	Male ...	20	13	3	5	3	2	...	...
22			Female ...	16	10	3	2	2	1	...	2
23		Lahore ...	Male ...	1,242	632	276	243	74	34	5	...
24			Female ...	634	280	168	71	29	12	...	...
25		Amritsar ...	Male ...	260	124	64	32	17	6	3	2
26			Female ...	185	60	35	16	6	3	...	...
27		Gurdaspur ...	Male ...	85	37	18	8	3	5	2	1
28			Female ...	67	22	13	6	2	1	...	...
29		Sialkot ...	Male ...	602	297	135	62	60	18	14	8
30			Female ...	479	236	112	83	36	3	...	...
31		Gujranwala ...	Male ...	560	288	139	87	39	18	4	1
32			Female ...	349	117	60	32	16	8	1	...
33		Gujrat ...	Male ...	74	30	8	6	5	5	3	8
34			Female ...	99	23	6	5	6	6	...	...
35		Shahpur ...	Male ...	523	303	96	68	73	48	15	3
36			Female ...	351	179	78	44	32	21	4	...
37		Lyallpur ...	Male ...	933	533	245	99	98	57	24	10
38			Female ...	628	376	123	153	50	47	3	...
39		Multan ...	Male ...	1,424	797	271	239	119	96	55	17
40			Female ...	1,177	662	234	308	82	34	4	...
41		Muzaffargarh ...	Male ...	436	212	27	54	35	56	24	16
42			Female ...	279	143	35	56	35	9	4	4
43	BAIRÁGI ...	TOTAL ...	Male ...	14	4	3	...	1	...	...	...
44			Female ...	5	4	2	2	...	...	...	...
45		Delhi ...	Male ...	12	4	3	...	1	...	...	...
46			Female ...	5	4	2	2	...	...	...	...
47		Hoshiarpur ...	Male ...	2	...	...	...	...	...	...	...
48			Female ...	...	...	...	...	...	...	...	...
49	BÁNIA. Aggarwál ...	TOTAL ...	Male ...	1,164	561	183	186	89	44	46	13
50			Female ...	819	332	158	115	36	18	3	2
51		Hissar ...	Male ...	184	96	19	33	18	9	8	9
52			Female ...	125	50	16	22	7	3	2	...
53		Delhi ...	Male ...	300	112	48	41	8	8	7	...
54			Female ...	209	67	39	21	3	4	...	...
55		Karnal ...	Male ...	322	152	38	50	24	14	23	3
56			Female ...	252	101	43	38	14	6	...	...
57		Hoshiarpur ...	Male ...	35	21	3	8	7	1	2	...
58			Female ...	12	3	...	3	...	...	...	...
59		Jullundur ...	Male ...	42	24	7	8	6	1	1	1
60			Female ...	34	22	4	8	5	2	1	2
61		Lahore ...	Male ...	133	77	34	22	15	3	3	...
62			Female ...	75	40	27	9	3	1	...	...
63		Amritsar ...	Male ...	5	3	2	1	...	...	...	...
64			Female ...	2	...	...	...	...	...	...	...
65		Gurdaspur ...	Male ...	50	24	11	6	4	3	...	...
66			Female ...	41	15	10	4	1	...	...	...
67		Sialkot ...	Male ...	68	40	15	14	6	4	1	...
68			Female ...	50	26	13	9	3	1	...	...
69		Gujranwala ...	Male ...	20	9	5	2	1	1	...	...
70			Female ...	14	5	4	1	...	...	...	...
71		Gujrat ...	Male ...	5	3	1	1	...	...	1	...
72			Female ...	5	3	2	...	...	1	...	...
73	BÁNIA. Unspecified ...	TOTAL ...	Male ...	23	9	2	4	...	1	2	...
74			Female ...	22	10	...	2	2	5	1	...
75		Kangra ...	Male ...	1	...	...	...	...	...	...	...
76			Female ...	...	...	...	...	...	...	...	...
77		Hoshiarpur ...	Male ...	3	1	...	1	...	...	...	...
78			Female ...	5	2	...	1	1	...	...	...

BY AGE AND CASTE OF CERTAIN SECTS IN SELECTED DISTRICTS.

1. ARYA.

Married. Total.	Married. 0—5.	Married. 5—12.	Married. 12—15.	Married. 15—20.	Married. 20—40.	Married. 40 and over.	Widowed. Total.	Widowed. 0—5.	Widowed. 5—12.	Widowed. 12—15.	Widowed. 15—20.	Widowed. 20—40.	Widowed. 40 and over.	Serial No.
12	13	14	15	16	17	18	19	20	21	22	23	24	25	
19,506	...	178	661	2,901	9,291	6,475	3,521	6	19	68	210	1,175	2,048	1
16,682	1	155	967	3,140	7,211	5,208	2,995	...	15	61	200	935	1,784	2
31	...	...	...	6	14	11	8	...	...	...	1	4	3	3
20	...	...	1	3	10	6	7	...	...	...	...	3	4	4
7	...	...	...	...	4	3	1	...	...	...	1	...	...	5
3	...	...	1	...	1	1	...	...	...	...	...	...	...	6
20	...	...	...	5	7	8	6	...	...	...	...	4	2	7
15	...	...	...	2	8	5	7	...	...	...	...	3	4	8
1	...	...	...	...	1	...	...	...	...	...	...	...	...	9
...	...	...	...	...	...	...	...	...	...	...	...	...	...	10
3	...	...	...	1	2	...	1	...	...	...	...	...	1	11
2	...	...	...	1	1	...	...	...	...	...	...	...	...	12
2,504	...	8	71	393	1,154	878	412	2	14	33	22	134	207	13
1,868	...	23	168	505	553	619	340	...	...	6	26	112	196	14
14	...	...	4	...	7	3	2	...	...	...	1	...	1	15
10	...	...	...	...	10	...	6	...	...	...	...	2	4	16
3	...	...	...	...	2	1	...	...	...	...	...	...	...	17
2	...	...	...	...	2	...	...	...	...	...	...	...	...	18
4	...	...	...	...	4	...	...	...	...	...	...	...	...	19
4	...	...	...	3	1	...	...	...	...	...	...	...	...	20
5	...	...	...	2	2	1	2	...	...	...	...	1	1	21
5	...	...	1	...	2	2	1	...	...	...	...	1	...	22
524	...	...	3	58	239	224	86	...	...	...	...	28	58	23
331	...	...	3	50	140	138	23	...	...	...	1	7	15	24
111	...	...	12	21	34	44	25	...	...	...	2	8	15	25
108	...	4	14	21	31	38	17	...	...	...	2	4	11	26
40	...	...	1	5	16	18	8	...	...	...	...	...	8	27
34	...	...	...	4	9	21	11	...	...	...	...	3	8	28
261	...	...	4	27	112	118	44	2	14	28	...	...	...	29
208	...	...	12	20	89	87	35	...	...	...	...	14	21	30
198	...	...	5	27	62	104	74	...	...	1	3	27	43	31
193	...	...	5	25	53	110	39	...	...	1	3	9	26	32
38	...	...	1	13	14	10	6	...	...	...	...	2	4	33
65	...	2	9	15	17	22	11	...	...	...	4	3	4	34
188	...	1	4	55	65	58	37	...	...	...	2	15	20	35
160	...	2	10	26	68	54	42	...	...	...	3	15	24	36
368	...	3	8	72	195	90	32	...	...	3	1	15	13	37
233	...	5	92	129	4	3	19	...	...	3	2	6	8	38
554	...	4	20	65	316	149	73	...	...	1	6	27	39	39
402	...	10	13	179	96	104	113	...	...	2	6	39	66	40
201	...	...	9	48	86	58	23	...	...	...	7	11	5	41
113	...	...	9	33	31	40	23	...	...	...	5	9	9	42
8	...	...	1	1	4	2	2	...	...	...	...	...	2	43
1	...	...	...	...	1	...	...	...	...	...	...	...	...	44
6	...	...	...	...	4	2	2	...	...	...	...	...	2	45
1	...	...	...	...	1	...	...	...	...	...	...	...	...	46
2	...	...	1	1	...	...	...	...	...	...	...	...	...	47
...	...	...	...	...	...	...	...	...	...	...	...	...	...	48
511	...	8	26	87	255	135	92	...	...	...	4	39	49	49
388	...	3	22	66	187	110	99	...	...	...	3	27	69	50
78	...	6	6	6	44	16	10	...	...	...	...	6	4	51
61	...	...	2	7	39	13	14	...	...	...	...	3	11	52
155	...	2	11	29	75	38	33	...	...	...	3	15	15	53
107	...	2	10	16	47	32	35	...	...	...	1	9	25	54
150	...	...	5	31	80	34	20	...	...	...	1	10	9	55
116	...	1	6	25	62	22	35	...	...	...	1	10	24	56
12	...	...	...	4	5	3	2	...	...	...	...	...	2	57
9	...	...	1	3	4	1	...	...	...	...	...	...	...	58
16	...	...	3	6	6	1	2	...	...	...	...	1	1	59
9	...	...	2	3	3	1	3	...	...	...	1	2	...	60
49	...	...	...	6	24	19	7	...	...	...	...	3	4	61
33	...	...	...	2	17	14	2	...	...	...	...	1	1	62
1	...	...	...	...	...	1	1	...	...	...	...	1	...	63
1	...	...	...	...	1	...	1	...	...	...	...	...	1	64
17	...	...	1	3	4	9	9	...	...	...	...	2	7	65
21	...	...	1	4	6	10	5	...	...	...	...	1	4	66
24	...	...	...	1	12	11	4	...	...	...	...	...	4	67
20	...	...	...	3	5	12	4	...	...	...	...	1	3	68
7	...	...	...	1	3	3	4	...	...	...	...	1	3	69
9	...	...	...	2	3	4	...	...	...	...	...	...	...	70
2	...	...	...	...	2	...	...	...	...	...	...	...	...	71
2	...	...	...	1	...	1	...	...	...	...	...	...	...	72
13	...	...	1	4	8	...	1	...	...	...	...	...	1	73
11	...	...	2	...	6	3	1	...	...	...	...	...	1	74
1	...	...	...	...	1	...	...	...	...	...	...	...	...	75
...	...	...	...	...	...	...	...	...	...	...	...	...	...	76
2	...	...	...	...	2	...	...	...	...	...	...	...	...	77
3	...	...	...	...	3	...	...	...	...	...	...	...	...	78

APPENDIX TO IMPERIAL TABLE XIV.—CIVIL CONDITION

1. ARYA—*continued.*

Serial No.	Caste.	Locality.	Sex.	Population.	Unmarried. Total.	0—5.	5—12.	12—15.	15—20.	20—40.	40 and over.
	1	2	3	4	5	6	7	8	9	10	11
1	BÁNIÁ (UNSPECIFIED)—*concld.*	Jullundur	Male	5	3	1	1	...	...	1	...
2			Female	5	4	...	...	1	3	...	...
3		Lahore	Male	2	1	1	...	...	...	...	...
4			Female	1	...	...	...	...	...	...	...
5		Gurdaspur	Male	12	4	...	2	...	1	1	...
6			Female	10	3	...	...	...	2	1	...
7		Gujranwala	Male	...	...	...	...	...	...	...	...
8			Female	1	1	...	1	...	...	...	...
9	BHÁT	TOTAL	Male	8	5	3	1	1	...	...	...
10			Female	3	1	...	1	...	...	...	...
11		Amritsar	Male	8	5	3	1	1	...	...	...
12			Female	...	...	...	...	...	...	...	...
13		Gurdaspur	Male	...	...	...	...	...	...	...	...
14			Female	3	1	...	1	...	...	...	...
15	BHÁTIÁ	TOTAL	Male	31	17	9	4	1	1	1	1
16			Female	33	12	8	3	1	...	...	...
17		Jullundur	Male	3	1	...	1	...	...	...	...
18			Female	3	1	1	...	...	...	...	...
19		Lahore	Male	7	4	3	1	...	...	...	...
20			Female	5	3	2	1	...	...	...	...
21		Amritsar	Male	...	...	...	...	...	...	...	...
22			Female	9	4	2	1	1	...	...	...
23		Gujranwala	Male	13	6	4	...	...	1	...	1
24			Female	7	3	2	1	...	...	...	...
25		Gujrat	Male	8	6	2	2	1	...	1	...
26			Female	9	1	1	...	...	...	...	...
27	BRAHMAN	TOTAL	Male	4,139	2,131	752	538	344	246	205	46
28			Female	3,101	1,314	545	376	232	186	17	8
29		Hissar	Male	97	46	7	14	10	6	7	2
30			Female	71	38	16	14	4	2	...	...
31		Delhi	Male	196	67	26	12	14	6	8	1
32			Female	118	40	19	14	4	2	...	1
33		Karnal	Male	72	31	14	8	5	1	3	...
34			Female	46	23	10	6	2	5	...	...
35		Kangra	Male	315	150	40	27	51	23	6	3
36			Female	284	129	48	21	42	18	...	...
37		Hoshiarpur	Male	300	156	27	39	28	38	23	1
38			Female	206	114	28	40	26	18	2	...
39		Jullundur	Male	152	71	22	26	18	3	2	...
40			Female	110	44	10	16	11	3	3	1
41		Lahore	Male	805	411	179	121	48	45	18	...
42			Female	466	225	113	72	35	5	...	...
43		Amritsar	Male	191	95	47	22	15	8	3	...
44			Female	142	56	26	15	10	3	2	...
45		Gurdaspur	Male	609	293	104	72	62	29	15	11
46			Female	462	192	53	45	30	54	7	3
47		Sialkot	Male	597	398	108	73	39	46	108	24
48			Female	511	214	109	58	48	4	...	...
49		Gujranwala	Male	483	238	125	76	24	11	2	...
50			Female	327	96	56	29	10	1	...	...
51		Gujrat	Male	93	48	18	15	6	4	3	2
52			Female	144	38	14	8	4	8	1	3
53		Shahpur	Male	90	59	21	15	11	8	3	1
54			Female	74	42	19	14	6	3	...	...
55		Lyallpur	Male	84	39	11	17	5	4	1	1
56			Female	120	60	22	22	5	9	2	...
57		Multan	Male	30	20	8	1	8	5	8	...
58			Female	10	4	2	2	...	...	...	...
59		Muzaffargarh	Male	25	9	...	...	...	9	...	...
60			Female	10	1	...	...	...	1	...	...
61	CHAMÁR	TOTAL	Male	154	69	18	30	9	4	7	1
62			Female	157	69	23	31	10	5	...	...
63		Hissar	Male	16	7	4	3	...	...	...	...
64			Female	16	7	4	3	...	...	...	...
65		Kangra	Male	113	51	11	21	7	4	7	1
66			Female	118	55	16	26	8	5	...	...
67		Hoshiarpur	Male	9	1	...	1	...	...	...	...
68			Female	12	1	...	1	...	...	...	...
69		Lahore	Male	4	2	1	1	...	...	...	...
70			Female	2	...	...	...	...	...	...	...
71		Amritsar	Male	4	3	1	1	1	...	...	...
72			Female	3	2	1	...	1	...	...	...
73		Sialkot	Male	5	3	1	2	...	...	...	...
74			Female	6	4	2	1	1	...	...	...
75		Gujrat	Male	3	2	...	1	1	...	...	...
76			Female	...	...	...	...	...	...	...	...

BY AGE AND CASTE OF CERTAIN SECTS IN SELECTED DISTRICTS.

1. ARYA—*continued.*

Married.							Widowed.							Serial No.
Total.	0—5.	5—12.	12—15.	15—20.	20—40.	40 and over.	Total.	0—5.	5—12.	12—15.	15—20.	20—40.	40 and over.	
12	13	14	15	16	17	18	19	20	21	22	23	24	25	
2	...	...	...	1	1	...	...	...	...	...	...	...	...	1
1	...	...	...	...	1	...	...	...	...	...	...	...	...	2
1	...	...	...	...	1	...	...	...	...	...	...	...	...	3
1	...	...	...	...	1	...	...	...	...	...	...	...	...	4
7	...	...	1	3	3	...	1	...	...	...	...	..	1	5
6	...	...	2	...	1	3	1	...	...	...	...	...	1	6
...	...	...	...	...	...	...	...	...	...	...	...	...	...	7
...	...	...	...	...	...	...	...	...	...	...	...	...	...	8
2	...	...	...	..	1	1	1	...	...	...	...	...	1	9
2	...	...	...	1	...	1	...	...	...	...	...	...	...	10
2	...	...	...	...	1	1	1	...	...	...	...	...	1	11
...	...	...	...	...	...	...	...	...	...	...	...	...	...	12
...	...	...	...	...	...	...	...	...	...	...	...	...	...	13
2	...	...	...	1	...	1	...	...	...	...	...	...	...	14
9	...	...	...	1	5	3	5	...	...	...	1	...	4	15
17	...	...	...	3	8	6	4	...	...	...	1	1	2	16
1	...	...	...	...	1	...	1	...	...	...	...	...	1	17
1	...	...	...	...	1	...	1	...	...	...	...	1	...	18
3	...	...	...	...	1	2	...	...	...	...	...	...	...	19
2	...	...	...	...	2	...	...	...	...	...	...	...	...	20
...	...	...	...	...	...	...	...	...	...	...	...	...	...	21
4	...	...	...	...	2	2	1	...	...	...	...	...	1	22
4	...	...	...	1	2	1	3	...	...	...	...	...	3	23
4	...	...	...	...	2	2	...	...	...	...	...	...	...	24
1	...	...	...	...	1	...	1	...	...	...	1	...	...	25
6	...	...	...	3	1	2	2	...	...	...	1	...	1	26
1,621	...	6	91	241	686	597	387	...	1	7	35	146	198	27
1,519	...	35	129	276	557	522	268	...	1	8	31	89	139	28
43	...	...	2	4	21	16	8	...	...	...	...	4	4	29
28	...	...	1	8	16	3	7	...	...	...	3	2	2	30
104	...	...	9	18	42	35	25	...	...	...	4	10	11	31
58	...	...	5	16	20	17	20	...	...	...	2	11	7	32
36	...	...	3	4	18	11	5	...	...	...	...	3	2	33
18	...	...	...	1	14	3	5	...	...	...	1	1	3	34
126	...	...	...	22	80	24	39	...	...	...	...	22	17	35
127	...	6	9	27	69	16	28	...	1	2	5	14	6	36
122	...	...	5	26	64	27	22	...	...	...	2	10	10	37
74	...	1	8	22	35	8	18	...	...	...	...	8	10	38
70	...	...	7	16	32	15	11	...	...	...	...	2	9	39
55	...	1	5	11	23	15	11	...	...	1	1	5	4	40
336	...	...	4	20	170	142	58	..	...	...	5	19	34	41
211	...	...	...	17	105	89	30	...	...	...	2	10	18	42
72	...	1	5	12	25	29	24	...	...	1	2	6	15	43
69	...	2	6	10	26	25	17	...	...	...	2	6	9	44
237	...	3	37	49	49	99	79	...	...	5	14	31	29	45
236	...	10	34	54	55	83	34	...	...	3	9	10	12	46
167	...	...	3	18	68	78	32	...	...	...	1	11	20	47
250	...	...	7	34	88	121	47	...	...	...	...	9	38	48
178	...	1	9	26	47	90	72	...	1	1	6	24	40	49
193	...	3	8	25	57	100	38	...	...	...	4	10	24	50
37	...	...	...	13	18	6	8	...	...	...	1	1	6	51
102	...	8	19	23	23	29	4	...	...	...	1	1	2	52
28	...	...	5	5	11	7	3	...	...	...	...	2	1	53
29	...	...	3	7	11	8	3	...	...	...	...	1	2	54
44	...	1	2	5	18	18	1	...	...	...	...	1	...	55
56	...	4	24	21	7	...	4	...	...	2	1	1	...	56
10	...	...	...	...	10	...	...	...	...	...	...	...	...	57
4	...	...	...	...	4	...	2	...	...	...	...	...	2	58
16	...	...	...	3	13	...	...	...	...	...	...	...	...	59
9	...	...	...	...	4	5	...	...	...	...	...	...	...	60
79	...	2	3	5	34	35	6	...	...	...	...	1	5	61
80	...	3	1	4	43	29	8	...	...	...	...	3	5	62
8	...	...	...	1	6	1	1	...	...	...	...	...	1	63
8	...	...	...	1	6	1	1	...	...	...	...	...	1	64
59	...	2	3	4	20	30	3	...	...	...	...	1	2	65
56	...	3	1	2	22	28	7	...	...	...	...	3	4	66
7	...	...	...	...	4	3	1	...	...	...	...	...	1	67
11	...	...	...	...	11	...	...	...	...	...	...	...	...	68
2	...	...	...	...	2	...	...	...	...	...	...	...	...	69
2	...	...	...	1	1	...	...	...	...	...	...	...	...	70
1	...	...	...	...	...	1	...	...	...	...	...	...	...	71
1	...	...	...	...	1	...	...	...	...	...	...	...	...	72
1	...	...	...	...	1	...	1	...	...	...	...	...	1	73
2	...	...	...	...	2	...	...	...	...	...	...	...	...	74
1	...	...	...	...	1	...	...	...	...	...	...	...	..	75
...	...	...	...	...	...	...	...	...	...	...	...	...	...	76

APPENDIX TO IMPERIAL TABLE XIV.—CIVIL CONDITION

1. ARYA—*continued.*

Serial No.	Caste.	Locality.	Sex.	Population.	Unmarried. Total.	0—5.	5—12.	12—15.	15—20.	20—40.	40 and over
	1	2	3	4	5	6	7	8	9	10	11
1	CHHIMBÁ ...	TOTAL ...	Male ...	42	17	3	6	3	2	3	...
2			Female ...	26	10	2	6	2	...	...	...
3		Hissar ...	Male ...	1	...	...	...	...	...	...	...
4			Female ...	...	...	...	...	...	...	...	...
5		Kangra ...	Male ...	10	3	...	2	...	...	1	...
6			Female ...	11	4	1	2	1	...	...	...
7		Hoshiarpur ...	Male ...	9	4	...	1	...	1	2	...
8			Female ...	3	1	...	1	...	...	...	...
9		Jullundur ...	Male ...	9	4	1	1	1	1	...	...
10			Female ...	7	3	...	2	1	...	...	...
11		Lahore ...	Male ...	5	3	2	1	...	...	...	...
12			Female ...	3	1	1	...	...	...	...	...
13		Amritsar ...	Male ...	3	2	...	1	1	...	...	...
14			Female ...	2	1	...	1	...	...	...	...
15		Gurdaspur ...	Male ...	5	1	...	...	1	...	...	...
16			Female ...	...	...	...	...	...	...	...	...
17	DÁGI AND KOLI ...	TOTAL ...	Male ...	32	14	6	1	5	2	...	...
18			Female ...	35	17	4	6	4	2	1	...
19		Delhi ...	Male ...	6	2	2	...	...	...	...	...
20			Female ...	3	1	1	...	...	...	...	...
21		Kangra ...	Male ...	26	12	4	1	5	2	...	...
22			Female ...	32	16	3	6	4	2	1	...
23	DHOBI ...	TOTAL ...	Male ...	28	11	7	3	...	1	...	...
24			Female ...	5	1	...	...	1	...	...	...
25		Delhi ...	Male ...	14	6	5	...	...	1	...	...
26			Female ...	1	...	...	...	...	...	...	...
27		Karnal ...	Male ...	1	...	...	...	...	...	...	...
28			Female ...	...	...	...	...	...	...	...	...
29		Jullundur ...	Male ...	13	5	2	3	...	...	...	...
30			Female ...	4	1	...	...	1	...	...	...
31	DUMNÁ ...	Kangra ...	Male ...	50	30	10	12	3	3	...	2
32			Female ...	44	26	7	14	4	1	...	...
33	GADARIÁ ...	Delhi ...	Male ...	19	5	3	1	...	...	...	1
34			Female ...	11	2	1	1	...	...	...	...
35	GHIRATH ...	TOTAL ...	Male ...	30	14	4	7	1	2	...	...
36			Female ...	11	5	1	3	1	...	...	...
37		Kangra ...	Male ...	15	7	3	3	...	1	...	...
38			Female ...	8	4	1	2	1	...	...	...
39		Hoshiarpur ...	Male ...	15	7	1	4	1	1	...	...
40			Female ...	3	1	...	1	...	...	...	...
41	GUJJAR ...	TOTAL ...	Male ...	39	10	...	7	2	...	...	1
42			Female ...	30	18	6	8	2	2	...	...
43		Hissar ...	Male ...	2	...	...	...	...	...	...	...
44			Female ...	...	...	...	...	...	...	...	...
45		Delhi ...	Male ...	25	5	...	5	...	...	...	...
46			Female ...	17	10	5	8	...	2	...	...
47		Karnal ...	Male ...	9	3	...	2	1	...	...	...
48			Female ...	9	5	1	3	1	...	...	...
49		Kangra ...	Male ...	2	1	...	...	1	...	...	...
50			Female ...	4	3	...	2	1	...	...	...
51		Gujrat ...	Male ...	1	1	...	...	...	...	...	1
52			Female ...	...	...	...	...	...	...	...	...
53	JAT ...	TOTAL ...	Male ...	5,057	2,170	678	684	197	158	352	101
54			Female ...	4,146	1,519	637	659	133	79	7	4
55		Hissar ...	Male ...	1,345	544	170	165	51	43	90	25
56			Female ...	1,057	337	153	145	19	17	...	3
57		Delhi ...	Male ...	1,209	435	165	205	38	12	13	2
58			Female ...	1,065	396	144	225	27	...	...	...
59		Karnal ...	Male ...	1,147	389	125	174	39	26	23	2
60			Female ...	963	289	128	139	12	7	3	...
61		Kangra ...	Male ...	3	1	...	...	...	...	1	...
62			Female ...	1	...	...	...	...	...	...	...
63		Hoshiarpur ...	Male ...	49	41	14	3	13	5	6	...
64			Female ...	29	22	7	7	8	...	...	...
65		Jullundur ...	Male ...	6	4	...	2	1	1	...	...
66			Female ...	3	2	1	...	...	...	1	...
67		Lahore ...	Male ...	150	81	46	28	4	3	...	...
68			Female ...	57	31	17	8	6	...	...	...
69		Amritsar ...	Male ...	9	5	5	...	...	...	...	...
70			Female ...	6	1	1	...	...	...	...	...
71		Gurdaspur ...	Male ...	190	87	34	22	16	10	3	2
72			Female ...	123	38	10	11	9	5	2	1
73		Sialkot ...	Male ...	823	512	80	71	27	54	213	67
74			Female ...	765	375	160	118	48	49	...	...
75		Gujranwala ...	Male ...	113	53	35	14	6	3	2	3
76			Female ...	74	27	16	5	4	1	1	...
77		Gujrat ...	Male ...	13	8	4	...	2	1	1	...
78			Female ...	3	1	...	1	...	...	...	...

BY AGE AND CASTE OF CERTAIN SECTS IN SELECTED DISTRICTS.

1. ARYA—*continued*.

Married.							Widowed.							
Total.	0—5.	5—12.	12—15.	15—20.	20—40.	40 and over.	Total.	0—5.	5—12.	12—15.	15—20.	20—40.	40 and over.	Serial No.
12	13	14	15	16	17	18	19	20	21	22	23	24	25	
23	...	...	...	3	13	7	2	...	...	...	...	1	1	1
14	...	...	...	1	11	2	2	...	...	...	...	1	1	2
1	...	...	...	...	...	1	...	...	...	...	...	...	...	3
...	...	...	...	...	...	...	...	...	...	...	...	...	...	4
5	...	...	...	...	3	2	2	...	...	...	...	1	1	5
5	...	...	...	...	3	2	2	...	...	...	...	1	1	6
5	...	...	...	1	3	1	...	...	...	...	...	...	...	7
2	...	...	...	...	2	...	...	...	...	...	...	...	...	8
5	...	...	...	2	2	1	...	...	...	...	...	...	...	9
4	...	...	...	1	3	...	...	...	...	...	...	...	...	10
2	...	...	...	...	2	...	...	...	...	...	...	...	...	11
2	...	...	...	...	2	...	...	...	...	...	...	...	...	12
1	...	...	...	...	1	...	...	...	...	...	...	...	...	13
1	...	...	...	...	1	...	...	...	...	...	...	...	...	14
4	...	...	...	...	2	2	...	...	...	...	...	...	..	15
...	...	...	..	...	...	..	...	...	...	...	...	...	...	16
15	...	...	...	3	4	8	3	...	...	...	...	1	2	17
16	...	1	...	1	3	11	2	...	...	...	1	1	...	18
3	...	...	...	...	...	3	1	...	...	...	...	...	1	19
2	...	...	...	...	...	2	...	...	...	...	...	...	...	20
12	...	...	...	3	4	5	2	...	...	...	...	1	1	21
14	...	1	...	1	3	9	2	...	...	...	1	1	...	22
10	...	...	...	2	5	3	7	...	...	...	2	...	5	23
3	...	...	...	1	1	1	1	...	...	...	...	...	1	24
5	...	...	...	2	1	2	3	...	...	..	...	...	3	25
1	...	...	...	...	...	1	...	...	...	...	...	...	...	26
1	...	...	...	...	1	...	...	...	...	...	...	...	...	27
...	...	...	...	...	...	...	...	..	...	...	...	...	...	28
4	...	...	...	...	3	1	4	...	...	...	2	1	1	29
2	...	...	...	1	1	...	1	...	...	...	...	1	...	30
18	...	...	...	...	13	5	2	...	...	...	...	1	1	31
16	...	...	...	2	11	3	2	...	...	...	...	1	1	32
10	...	...	1	3	1	5	4	...	...	...	...	1	3	33
8	...	1	2	1	2	2	1	...	...	...	...	...	1	34
14	...	...	1	...	10	3	2	...	...	...	1	...	1	35
6	...	...	...	1	4	1	...	...	...	...	...	...	...	36
8	...	...	...	...	6	2	...	...	..	...	...	...	...	37
4	...	...	...	...	3	1	...	...	...	...	...	...	...	38
6	...	...	1	...	4	1	2	...	...	...	1	...	1	39
2	...	...	...	1	1	...	...	...	...	...	...	...	...	40
26	...	1	...	4	4	17	3	...	...	...	...	...	3	41
8	...	...	...	2	4	2	4	...	...	...	...	1	3	42
2	...	...	...	...	2	...	...	...	...	...	...	...	...	43
...	...	...	...	...	...	...	...	...	...	...	...	...	...	44
18	...	...	...	4	1	13	2	...	...	...	...	...	2	45
4	...	...	...	2	1	1	3	...	...	...	...	...	3	46
6	...	1	...	...	1	4	...	...	...	...	...	...	...	47
4	...	...	...	...	3	1	...	...	...	...	...	...	...	48
...	...	...	...	...	...	...	1	...	...	...	...	...	1	49
...	...	...	...	...	...	...	1	...	...	...	...	1	...	50
...	...	...	...	...	...	...	...	...	...	...	...	...	...	51
...	...	...	...	...	...	...	...	...	...	...	...	...	...	52
2,272	...	114	117	338	1.175	528	615	...	4	11	58	291	256	53
1,886	...	40	178	273	906	489	741	...	11	22	55	277	376	54
663	...	53	26	82	357	145	138	...	2	1	20	43	72	55
441	...	14	25	48	274	80	279	...	11	18	45	141	64	56
658	...	33	55	97	357	116	118	...	...	5	2	75	34	57
518	...	5	34	91	289	99	151	...	...	4	...	53	94	58
547	...	26	27	106	276	112	211	...	1	5	26	119	60	59
501	...	16	90	57	223	115	173	...	...	...	5	51	117	60
1	...	...	...	...	1	...	1	...	...	...	...	...	1	61
1	...	...	...	...	1	...	...	...	...	...	...	...	...	62
8	...	...	...	4	2	2	...	...	...	...	...	...	...	63
6	...	...	...	1	5	...	1	...	...	...	...	...	1	64
1	...	...	...	...	1	...	1	...	...	...	...	1	...	65
1	...	...	...	...	1	...	...	...	...	...	...	...	...	66
63	...	...	...	5	39	19	6	...	...	...	...	1	5	67
23	...	...	...	3	18	7	3	...	...	...	...	...	3	68
8	...	...	...	...	...	8	1	...	...	...	...	...	1	69
4	...	...	1	1	...	2	1	...	...	...	...	...	1	70
71	...	2	6	14	19	30	32	...	1	...	3	11	17	71
65	...	1	9	13	19	23	20	...	...	...	1	8	11	72
213	...	...	2	27	106	78	98	...	...	...	2	40	56	73
291	...	3	18	55	71	144	99	...	...	...	4	20	75	74
40	...	...	1	3	15	21	10	...	...	...	...	1	9	75
38	...	1	1	3	9	19	14	...	...	...	...	4	10	76
4	...	...	...	...	2	2	1	...	...	...	...	...	1	77
2	...	...	...	1	1	...	...	...	...	...	...	...	...	78

APPENDIX TO IMPERIAL TABLE XIV.—CIVIL CONDITION

1. ARYA—*continued.*

Serial No.	Caste.	Locality.	Sex.	Population.	Unmarried. Total.	0—5.	5—12.	12—15.	15—20.	20—40.	40 and over.
	1	2	3	4	5	6	7	8	9	10	11
1	JHINWAR ...	TOTAL ...	Male ...	282	127	52	30	20	9	10	6
2			Female ...	189	73	35	16	12	10	...	...
3		Delhi ...	Male ...	18	4	3	...	...	...	1	...
4			Female ...	6	1	1	...	...	...	...	...
5		Hoshiarpur ...	Male ...	11	6	...	...	1	2	2	1
6			Female ...	17	11	4	4	2	1	...	...
7		Jullundur ...	Male ...	8	1	1	...	...	...	...	...
8			Female ...	14	5	1	...	3	1	...	...
9		Lahore ...	Male ...	16	7	5	1	1	...	...	...
10			Female ...	12	3	2	1	...	...	...	...
11		Amritsar ...	Male ...	23	12	8	8	1	...	...	...
12			Female ...	12	5	3	1	1	...	...	...
13		Gurdaspur ...	Male ...	82	42	17	11	8	4	2	...
14			Female ...	48	16	8	4	2	2	...	...
15		Sialkot ...	Male ...	67	27	9	8	3	1	2	4
16			Female ...	51	25	13	4	3	5	...	...
17		Gujranwala ...	Male ...	34	18	7	5	3	1	1	1
18			Female ...	16	3	1	1	1	...	...	...
19		Gujrat ...	Male ...	23	10	2	2	3	1	2	...
20			Female ...	13	4	2	1	...	1	...	...
21	JOGI ...	TOTAL ...	Male ...	21	9	7	1	...	...	...	1
22			Female ...	...	...	...	...	...	...	...	...
23		Hissar ...	Male ...	2	1	...	...	...	...	...	1
24			Female ...	...	...	...	...	...	...	...	...
25		Gurdaspur ...	Male ...	11	5	4	1	...	...	...	...
26			Female ...	...	...	...	...	...	...	...	...
27		Gujranwala ...	Male ...	8	3	3	...	...	...	...	...
28			Female ...	...	...	...	...	...	...	...	...
29	JULÁHÁ ...	TOTAL ...	Male ...	354	180	38	60	32	33	12	5
30			Female ...	271	134	35	51	25	21	2	...
31		Delhi ...	Male ...	3	...	...	...	...	...	...	...
32			Female ...	...	...	...	...	...	...	...	...
33		Kangra ...	Male ...	84	48	10	17	3	15	3	...
34			Female ...	92	56	15	22	4	15	...	...
35		Hoshiarpur ...	Male ...	145	76	13	31	20	10	2	...
36			Female ...	81	43	8	18	13	3	1	...
37		Gujrat ...	Male ...	122	56	15	12	9	8	7	5
38			Female ...	98	35	12	11	8	3	1	...
39	KALÁL ...	TOTAL ...	Male ...	167	102	24	34	11	17	15	1
40			Female ...	152	71	28	16	11	7	9	...
41		Hissar ...	Male ...	7	5	...	2	...	2	1	...
42			Female ...	5	1	1	...	...	...	...	...
43		Delhi ...	Male ...	4	1	...	1	...	...	...	...
44			Female ...	3	...	...	...	...	...	...	...
45		Karnal ...	Male ...	27	15	4	3	...	5	3	...
46			Female ...	28	10	5	3	2	...	...	...
47		Kangra ...	Male ...	5	4	1	1	...	1	1	...
48			Female ...	2	1	...	...	1	...	...	...
49		Hoshiarpur ...	Male ...	87	52	12	15	6	8	10	1
50			Female ...	81	40	16	9	5	2	8	...
51		Jullundur ...	Male ...	16	11	2	6	3	...	...	...
52			Female ...	16	11	4	2	2	3	...	...
53		Lahore ...	Male ...	9	6	3	2	1	...	...	...
54			Female ...	7	4	2	1	1	...	...	...
55		Amritsar ...	Male ...	6	6	2	4	...	...	...	...
56			Female ...	4	2	...	1	...	1	...	...
57		Gurdaspur ...	Male ...	6	2	...	...	1	1	...	...
58			Female ...	6	2	...	...	...	1	1	...
59	KAMBOH ...	TOTAL ...	Male ...	65	28	10	7	1	4	6	...
60			Female ...	57	12	4	2	4	1	1	...
61		Karnal ...	Male ...	63	27	9	7	1	4	6	...
62			Female ...	54	10	4	1	4	1	...	...
63		Jullundur ...	Male ...	2	1	1	...	...	...	...	...
64			Female ...	3	2	...	1	...	...	1	...
65											
66	KÁYASTH ...	TOTAL ...	Male ...	205	86	32	20	10	17	3	4
			Female ...	182	43	24	11	5	1	2	...
67		Hissar ...	Male ...	24	13	2	1	...	7	1	2
68			Female ...	11	5	1	3	...	...	1	...
69		Delhi ...	Male ...	138	45	20	9	6	7	1	2
70			Female ...	89	21	15	4	2	...	...	...
71		Karnal ...	Male ...	8	4	2	...	1	...	1	...
72			Female ...	...	...	...	...	...	...	...	...
73		Hoshiarpur ...	Male ...	7	5	...	3	2	...	...	...
74			Female ...	9	5	1	1	2	1	...	...
75		Jullundur ...	Male ...	5	4	1	2	...	1	...	...
76			Female ...	5	4	2	1	...	...	1	...

BY AGE AND CASTE OF CERTAIN SECTS IN SELECTED DISTRICTS.

1. ARYA—*continued.*

Married.							Widowed.							
Total.	0—5.	5—12.	12—15.	15—20.	20—40.	40 and over.	Total.	0—5.	5—12.	12—15.	15—20.	20—40.	40 and over.	Serial No.
12	13	14	15	16	17	18	19	20	21	22	23	24	25	
119	...	...	2	20	44	53	36	...	...	...	...	11	25	1
92	...	1	6	15	28	42	24	...	...	...	...	8	16	2
11	...	...	...	1	3	7	3	...	...	...	...	1	2	3
3	...	...	...	...	...	3	2	...	...	...	...	...	2	4
4	...	...	...	1	3	...	1	...	...	...	...	1	...	5
6	...	...	1	2	2	1	...	...	...	...	...	...	...	6
4	...	...	...	1	2	1	3	...	...	...	...	1	2	7
8	...	...	...	1	6	1	1	...	...	...	...	1	...	8
6	...	...	...	1	2	3	3	...	...	...	...	2	1	9
8	...	...	...	1	1	6	1	...	...	...	...	1	...	10
9	...	...	...	...	3	6	2	...	...	...	...	1	1	11
6	...	...	1	1	1	3	1	...	...	...	...	1	...	12
34	...	...	1	8	10	15	6	...	...	...	...	...	6	13
22	...	1	2	3	6	10	10	...	...	...	...	3	7	14
30	...	...	...	2	15	13	10	...	...	...	...	2	8	15
20	...	...	1	3	6	10	6	...	...	...	...	1	5	16
11	...	...	...	2	3	6	5	...	...	...	...	2	3	17
11	...	...	...	1	4	6	2	...	...	...	...	1	1	18
10	...	...	1	4	3	2	3	...	...	...	...	1	2	19
8	...	...	1	3	2	2	1	...	...	...	...	...	1	20
8	...	...	...	...	2	6	4	...	...	...	1	1	2	21
...	...	...	...	...	...	...	...	...	...	...	...	...	...	22
1	...	...	...	...	1	...	...	...	...	...	...	...	...	23
...	...	...	...	...	...	...	...	...	...	...	...	...	...	24
3	...	...	...	...	...	3	3	...	...	...	1	1	1	25
...	...	...	...	...	...	...	...	...	...	...	...	...	...	26
4	...	...	...	...	1	3	1	...	...	...	...	...	1	27
...	...	...	...	...	...	...	...	...	...	...	...	...	...	28
143	...	...	5	16	73	49	31	...	...	1	3	11	16	29
111	...	1	10	15	46	39	26	...	...	...	3	9	14	30
2	...	...	...	...	...	2	1	...	...	...	...	...	1	31
...	...	...	...	...	...	...	...	...	...	...	...	...	...	32
32	...	...	...	2	16	14	4	...	...	...	...	...	4	33
29	...	...	...	2	14	13	7	...	...	...	...	4	3	34
62	...	...	...	3	36	23	7	...	...	...	1	2	4	35
32	...	...	1	8	20	8	6	...	...	...	...	2	4	36
47	...	...	5	11	21	10	19	...	...	1	2	9	7	37
50	...	1	9	10	12	18	13	...	...	...	3	3	7	38
57	...	...	1	3	29	24	8	...	...	...	...	3	5	39
64	...	1	2	12	36	18	17	...	...	...	...	4	18	40
2	...	...	...	...	2	...	...	...	...	...	...	...	...	41
2	...	...	...	...	1	1	2	...	...	...	...	...	2	42
2	...	...	...	...	...	2	1	...	...	...	...	1	...	43
2	...	...	...	...	1	1	1	...	...	...	...	...	1	44
11	...	...	...	...	2	9	1	...	...	...	...	...	1	45
13	...	...	...	...	11	2	5	...	...	...	...	...	5	46
1	...	...	...	...	1	...	...	...	...	...	...	...	...	47
1	...	...	...	...	1	...	...	...	...	...	...	...	...	48
80	...	...	...	2	19	9	5	...	...	...	...	2	3	49
38	...	...	2	9	15	7	8	...	...	...	...	3	5	50
4	...	...	1	...	1	2	1	...	...	...	...	...	1	51
4	...	...	...	2	2	...	1	...	...	...	...	1	...	52
3	...	...	...	1	2	...	...	...	...	...	...	...	...	53
3	...	...	...	...	1	2	...	...	...	...	...	...	...	54
...	...	...	...	...	...	...	...	...	...	...	...	...	...	55
2	...	...	...	...	2	...	...	...	...	...	...	...	...	56
4	...	...	...	...	2	2	...	...	...	...	...	...	...	57
4	...	1	...	1	2	...	...	...	...	...	...	...	...	58
29	...	...	...	3	13	13	8	...	...	...	...	7	1	59
35	...	...	1	7	20	7	10	...	...	...	...	2	8	60
28	...	...	...	3	12	13	8	...	...	...	...	7	1	61
34	...	...	1	7	19	7	10	...	...	...	...	2	8	62
1	...	...	...	...	1	...	...	...	...	...	...	...	...	63
1	...	...	...	...	1	...	...	...	...	...	...	...	...	64
94	...	...	1	15	47	31	25	...	...	...	1	6	18	65
75	1	...	2	14	32	26	14	...	...	1	1	4	8	66
8	...	...	...	...	6	2	3	...	...	...	1	...	2	67
5	...	...	...	1	4	...	1	...	...	...	...	...	1	68
71	...	...	1	15	30	25	22	...	...	...	...	8	16	69
55	...	...	2	10	22	21	13	...	...	1	1	4	7	70
4	...	...	...	...	3	1	...	...	...	...	...	...	...	71
...	...	...	...	...	...	...	...	...	...	...	...	...	...	72
2	...	...	...	...	1	1	...	...	...	...	...	...	...	73
4	...	...	...	1	1	2	...	...	...	...	...	...	...	74
1	...	...	...	...	1	...	...	...	...	...	...	...	...	75
1	...	...	...	...	1	...	...	...	...	...	...	...	...	76

APPENDIX TO IMPERIAL TABLE XIV.—CIVIL CONDITION

1. ARYA—*continued.*

Serial No.	Caste.	Locality.	Sex.	Population.	Unmarried.						
					Total.	0—5.	5—12.	12—15.	15—20.	20—40.	40 and over.
	1	2	3	4	5	6	7	8	9	10	11
1	KÁYASTH—*concld.*	Lahore	Male	*20*	13	6	4	1	2	...	...
2			Female	*17*	8	5	2	1	...	...	...
3		Gurdaspur	Male	*3*	2	1	1	...	...	...	...
4			Female	*1*	...	...	...	...	...	...	...
5	KHATRI	TOTAL	Male	**10,389**	**5,194**	**2,083**	**1,474**	**891**	**530**	**204**	**62**
6			Female	**6,848**	**2,958**	**1,222**	**954**	**499**	**226**	**31**	**26**
7		Hissar	Male	*69*	30	6	12	3	6	3	1
8			Female	*41*	20	11	7	1	...	...	1
9		Delhi	Male	*191*	67	34	17	5	6	3	2
10			Female	*134*	48	23	15	3	...	1	1
11		Karnal	Male	*36*	22	10	5	5	1	1	...
12			Female	*35*	18	5	11	2	...	...	...
13		Kangra	Male	*85*	51	12	14	11	8	6	...
14			Female	*52*	20	2	7	6	5	...	...
15		Hoshiarpur	Male	*546*	298	52	82	67	55	33	9
16			Female	*357*	195	49	86	44	15	1	...
17		Jullundur	Male	*1,027*	526	162	197	109	40	15	3
18			Female	*719*	389	102	157	63	34	16	18
19		Lahore	Male	*3,124*	1,516	705	382	274	127	28	...
20			Female	*1,447*	594	303	178	97	16	...	...
21		Amritsar	Male	*914*	468	208	104	78	43	25	10
22			Female	*690*	318	174	63	49	28	4	...
23		Gurdaspur	Male	*533*	243	105	70	41	16	8	3
24			Female	*451*	171	75	48	25	18	3	2
25		Sialkot	Male	*1,389*	689	317	219	80	29	30	14
26			Female	*1,116*	494	232	134	91	37	...	...
27		Gujranwala	Male	*663*	325	165	93	40	21	4	2
28			Female	*473*	147	91	41	10	5	...	...
29		Gujrat	Male	*487*	211	60	43	33	39	24	12
30			Female	*350*	139	32	73	13	16	1	4
31		Shahpur	Male	*560*	318	95	100	51	70	1	1
32			Female	*403*	161	62	47	40	12	...	...
33		Lyallpur	Male	*397*	198	52	65	51	24	4	2
34			Female	*204*	108	28	20	27	31	2	...
35		Multan	Male	*297*	194	45	62	37	34	15	1
36			Female	*320*	120	27	58	26	7	2	...
37		Muzaffargarh	Male	*71*	38	6	9	6	11	4	2
38			Female	*56*	21	6	9	3	2	1	..
39	KUMHÁR	TOTAL	Male	**197**	**93**	**30**	**18**	**18**	**15**	**10**	**2**
40			Female	**116**	**44**	**17**	**10**	**8**	**6**	**2**	**1**
41		Hissar	Male	*44*	22	2	8	3	5	4	...
42			Female	*22*	9	2	7	...	...	...	...
43		Delhi	Male	*17*	3	3	...	...	...	...	...
44			Female	*2*	...	...	...	...	...	...	...
45		Hoshiarpur	Male	*19*	11	4	3	2	2	...	...
46			Female	...	...	...	...	...	...	...	...
47		Jullundur	Male	*13*	8	2	1	3	2	...	...
48			Female	*2*	...	...	...	...	...	...	...
49		Lahore	Male	*1*	...	...	...	...	...	...	...
50			Female	*2*	1	1	...	...	...	...	...
51		Amritsar	Male	*4*	3	2	1	...	...	...	...
52			Female	*3*	1	1	...	...	...	...	...
53		Gurdaspur	Male	*48*	23	8	3	6	4	2	...
54			Female	*47*	18	7	1	5	2	2	1
55		Sialkot	Male	*29*	10	1	...	2	1	4	2
56			Female	*27*	13	4	2	3	4	...	...
57		Gujranwala	Male	*19*	13	8	2	2	1	...	...
58			Female	*11*	2	2	...	...	...	...	...
59		Gujrat	Male	*3*	...	...	...	...	...	...	...
60			Female	...	...	...	...	...	...	...	...
61	LOHÁR	TOTAL	Male	**24**	**10**	**2**	...	**5**	**3**	...	...
62			Female	**18**	**7**	**2**	1	**3**	**1**	...	...
63		Hissar	Male	...	...	...	...	...	...	...	...
64			Female	*1*	...	...	...	...	...	...	...
65		Kangra	Male	*18*	7	...	...	4	3	...	...
66			Female	*13*	6	1	1	3	1	...	...
67		Hoshiarpur	Male	*5*	2	1	...	1	...	...	...
68			Female	*3*	1	1	...	...	...	...	...
69		Jullundur	Male	*1*	1	1	...	...	...	...	...
70			Female	*1*	...	...	...	...	...	...	...
71	MAHÁJAN	TOTAL	Male	**74**	**43**	**9**	**9**	**12**	**8**	**4**	**1**
72			Female	**34**	**11**	**5**	...	**4**	**2**	...	...
73		Kangra	Male	*47*	29	4	3	12	6	3	1
74			Female	*21*	9	3	...	4	2	...	...
75		Lahore	Male	*3*	2	1	1	...	...	...	...
76			Female	*1*	...	...	...	...	...	...	...
77		Sialkot	Male	*23*	12	4	5	...	2	1	...
78			Female	*12*	2	2	...	...	...	...	...

BY AGE AND CASTE OF CERTAIN SECTS IN SELECTED DISTRICTS.

1. ARYA—*continued.*

Married.							Widowed.							
Total.	0—5.	5—12.	12—15.	15—20.	20—40.	40 and over.	Total.	0—5.	5—12.	12—15.	15—20.	20—40.	40 and over.	Serial No.
12	13	14	15	16	17	18	19	20	21	22	23	24	25	
7	...	...	...	...	5	2	...	...	...	...	...	...	...	1
9	...	...	...	2	4	3	...	...	...	...	...	...	...	2
1	...	...	...	...	1	...	...	...	...	...	...	...	...	3
1	1	...	...	...	...	...	...	...	...	...	...	...	...	4
4,308	...	7	140	607	2,115	1,439	887	...	...	5	33	262	587	5
3,326	...	27	208	646	1,367	1,078	564	...	2	12	34	163	353	6
37	...	...	1	3	21	12	2	...	...	...	...	2	...	7
17	...	...	...	3	14	...	4	...	...	...	...	1	3	8
87	...	...	1	10	41	35	87	...	...	...	1	13	23	9
71	...	..	7	11	29	24	20	...	...	...	1	6	13	10
12	...	...	...	...	7	5	2	...	...	1	...	1	...	11
16	...	...	...	3	11	2	1	...	...	...	...	1	...	12
29	...	...	...	2	16	11	5	...	...	...	...	2	3	13
28	...	..	...	6	13	9	4	...	...	...	...	3	1	14
208	...	...	4	27	122	55	40	...	...	...	1	15	24	15
138	...	...	4	25	77	32	24	...	...	...	...	9	15	16
432	..	...	18	60	277	77	69	...	...	...	5	31	33	17
297	...	1	26	73	164	33	33	...	...	2	6	8	17	18
1,329	...	...	20	188	764	862	279	...	...	...	5	33	241	19
735	...	...	12	187	327	258	118	...	...	...	...	19	99	20
382	...	...	24	64	94	200	64	...	...	1	5	19	39	21
341	...	3	27	63	133	115	31	...	...	...	...	13	18	22
232	...	5	15	40	90	82	58	...	...	2	4	20	32	23
235	...	4	18	58	66	89	45	...	1	...	5	17	22	24
543	...	...	9	56	244	234	157	...	...	...	4	47	106	25
519	...	1	16	78	208	216	103	...	...	...	7	23	73	26
275	...	1	11	38	85	140	63	...	...	..	...	26	37	27
269	...	...	8	28	92	141	57	...	...	1	6	19	31	28
249	...	1	15	48	95	90	27	...	...	...	2	10	13	29
192	...	8	44	58	55	27	19	...	...	3	4	6	6	30
202	...	...	10	42	80	70	40	...	...	...	2	22	16	31
190	...	...	10	35	103	42	52	...	...	...	3	19	30	32
177	...	...	7	15	123	32	22	...	...	1	4	10	7	33
84	...	6	30	23	11	14	12	...	...	6	...	5	1	34
89	...	...	5	16	42	26	14	...	...	...	...	8	6	35
164	...	4	5	24	56	75	36	...	1	...	2	13	20	36
25	...	...	...	3	14	8	8	...	...	...	...	3	5	37
30	...	...	...	21	8	1	5	...	...	...	...	1	4	38
85	...	1	5	16	33	30	19	...	...	...	...	6	13	39
59	...	3	6	6	19	25	13	...	...	...	...	3	10	40
21	...	1	3	1	11	5	1	...	...	...	...	...	1	41
10	...	...	1	1	5	3	3	...	...	...	...	...	3	42
13	...	...	2	4	2	5	1	...	...	...	...	...	1	43
1	..	...	...	...	...	1	1	...	..	...	...	...	1	44
6	...	...	...	1	4	1	2	...	...	...	...	...	2	45
...	...	...	...	...	...	...	...	...	...	...	...	...	...	46
4	...	...	...	1	2	1	1	...	...	...	...	1	...	47
2	...	...	...	...	2	...	...	...	...	...	...	...	...	48
1	...	...	...	...	1	..	...	...	...	...	..	...	...	49
1	...	...	...	...	1	...	...	...	...	...	...	...	...	50
1	...	...	...	...	...	1	...	...	...	...	...	...	...	51
2	...	...	...	...	...	2	...	...	...	...	...	...	...	52
20	...	...	...	8	5	7	5	...	...	...	...	2	3	53
25	...	3	4	3	6	9	4	...	...	...	...	1	3	54
18	...	...	...	...	4	9	6	...	...	...	...	2	4	55
11	...	...	1	2	4	4	3	...	...	...	...	1	2	56
4	...	...	...	1	2	1	2	...	...	...	...	1	1	57
7	...	...	...	...	1	6	2	...	...	...	...	1	1	58
2	...	...	...	...	2	...	1	...	...	...	...	...	1	59
...	...	...	...	...	...	...	...	...	...	...	...	...	...	60
13	...	...	...	2	8	3	1	...	...	...	...	...	1	61
7	...	...	...	1	4	2	4	...	...	...	...	3	1	62
...	...	...	...	...	...	...	...	...	...	...	...	...	...	63
...	...	...	...	...	...	...	1	...	...	...	...	1	...	64
11	...	...	...	2	8	1	...	...	...	...	...	...	...	65
6	...	...	...	1	4	1	1	...	...	...	...	...	1	66
2	...	...	...	...	...	2	1	...	...	...	...	...	1	67
1	...	...	...	...	...	1	1	...	...	...	...	1	...	68
...	...	...	...	...	...	...	...	...	...	...	...	...	...	69
...	...	...	...	...	...	...	1	...	...	...	...	1	...	70
25	...	...	1	2	12	10	5	...	...	...	1	4	1	71
21	...	...	...	2	10	9	2	...	...	...	...	...	2	72
15	...	...	...	1	8	6	3	...	...	...	...	3	...	73
11	...	...	...	1	6	4	1	...	...	...	...	...	1	74
1	...	...	...	...	1	...	...	...	...	...	...	...	...	75
1	...	...	...	...	1	...	...	...	...	...	...	...	...	76
8	...	...	...	1	3	4	8	...	...	...	1	1	1	77
9	...	...	...	1	3	6	1	...	...	...	...	...	1	78

APPENDIX TO IMPERIAL TABLE XIV.—CIVIL CONDITION

1. ARYA—*continued.*

Serial No.	Caste.	Locality.	Sex.	Population.	Unmarried. Total.	0—5.	5—12.	12—15.	15—20.	20—40.	40 and over.
	1	2	3	4	5	6	7	8	9	10	11
1	MAHÁJAN—*concld.*	Gujrat	Male	*1*	...	...	...	...	...	...	...
2			Female	...	...	...	...	...	...	...	...
3	MAHTON	Hoshiarpur	Male	16	13	7	3	3	...	...	...
4			Female	13	9	1	7	1	...	...	...
5	MÁLI	TOTAL	Male	72	19	7	4	5	1	2	...
6			Female	44	11	8	3	...	...	..	...
7		Hissar	Male	*9*	5	...	...	2	1	2	...
8			Female	...	...	...	...	...	...	...	...
9		Delhi	Male	*53*	9	7	1	1	...	...	...
10			Female	*40*	10	8	2	...	...	...	...
11		Karnal	Male	*10*	5	...	3	2	...	...	...
12			Female	*4*	1	...	1	...	...	...	...
13	MEGH	TOTAL	Male	12,120	6,513	2,863	1,190	902	1,362	187	9
14			Female	9,995	4,690	2,344	667	858	806	14	1
15		Lahore	Male	*2*	1	...	...	1	...	...	...
16			Female	*1*	...	...	...	...	...	...	...
17		Gurdaspur	Male	*1*	...	...	...	...	...	...	...
18			Female	...	...	...	...	...	...	...	...
19		Sialkot	Male	*11,565*	6,240	2,774	1,116	842	1,321	179	8
20			Female	*9,542*	4,515	2,232	626	843	802	12	...
21		Gujrat	Male	*552*	272	89	74	59	41	8	1
22			Female	*452*	175	112	41	15	4	2	1
23	MINÁ	Delhi	Male	12	2	2	...	...	...	...	...
24			Female	7	1	1	...	...	...	...	...
25	NÁI	TOTAL	Male	58	32	9	14	5	3	1	...
26			Female	40	15	7	4	3	1	...	...
27		Hissar	Male	*4*	3	2	1	...	...	...	...
28			Female	*5*	2	1	1	...	...	...	...
29		Delhi	Male	*6*	2	...	2	...	...	...	...
30			Female	*7*	...	...	...	...	...	...	...
31		Karnal	Male	*2*	1	...	...	...	...	1	...
32			Female	...	...	...	...	...	...	...	...
33		Kangra	Male	*8*	4	1	2	1	...	...	...
34			Female	*6*	2	...	1	1	...	...	...
35		Hoshiarpur	Male	*21*	13	3	5	2	3	...	...
36			Female	*7*	4	3	1	...	...	...	...
37		Jullundur	Male	*9*	6	1	3	2	...	...	...
38			Female	*7*	3	1	...	1	1	...	...
39		Gurdaspur	Male	*8*	3	2	1	...	...	...	...
40			Female	*8*	4	2	1	1	...	...	...
41	OD	TOTAL	Male	2,778	1,749	647	547	200	224	106	25
42			Female	2,324	1,199	458	485	164	83	9	...
43		Shahpur	Male	*90*	51	7	17	5	22	...	...
44			Female	*84*	36	7	15	10	4	...	...
45		Lyallpur	Male	*238*	133	14	46	25	42	6	...
46			Female	*171*	115	88	28	37	11	1	...
47		Multan	Male	*1,838*	1,161	477	341	108	123	88	24
48			Female	*1,451*	659	242	317	66	27	7	...
49		Muzaffargarh	Male	*612*	404	149	143	62	37	12	1
50			Female	*618*	389	171	125	51	41	1	...
51	RÁJ	TOTAL	Male	9	5	1	2	1	1	...	...
52			Female	4	2	...	...	1	1	...	...
53		Jullundur	Male	*8*	5	1	2	1	1	...	...
54			Female	*4*	2	...	...	1	1	...	...
55		Karnal	Male	*1*	...	...	...	...	...	...	...
56			Female	...	...	...	...	...	...	...	...
57	RÁJPUT	TOTAL	Male	1,458	674	220	170	126	111	40	7
58			Female	945	373	134	137	57	32	11	2
59		Hissar	Male	*105*	48	9	22	8	4	3	2
60			Female	*132*	48	16	27	2	2	1	...
61		Delhi	Male	*349*	145	61	81	18	28	6	1
62			Female	*208*	57	22	31	4	...	...	...
63		Karnal	Male	*66*	26	11	4	6	4	1	...
64			Female	*48*	18	10	6	2	...	...	...
65		Kangra	Male	*79*	46	11	10	13	9	3	...
66			Female	*55*	24	8	12	4	...	...	...
67		Hoshiarpur	Male	*120*	65	12	12	14	19	8	...
68			Female	*81*	51	18	17	11	3	1	1
69		Jullundur	Male	*154*	78	19	24	20	14	1	...
70			Female	*133*	65	15	16	19	9	5	1
71		Lahore	Male	*168*	87	39	24	11	11	2	...
72			Female	*69*	31	19	9	3	...	...	...
73		Amritsar	Male	*68*	32	17	12	2	1	...	...
74			Female	*48*	14	6	4	2	2	...	...
75		Gurdaspur	Male	*294*	116	27	24	29	17	15	4
76			Female	*154*	55	12	13	10	16	4	...

BY AGE AND CASTE OF CERTAIN SECTS IN SELECTED DISTRICTS.

1. ARYA—*continued.*

Married.							Widowed.							
Total.	0—5.	5—12.	12—15.	15—20.	20—40.	40 and over.	Total.	0—5.	5—12.	12—15.	15—20.	20—40.	40 and over.	Serial No.
12	13	14	15	16	17	18	19	20	21	22	23	24	25	
1	...	...	1	...	...	...	...	...	...	...	...	...	...	1
...	...	...	...	...	...	...	...	...	...	...	...	...	...	2
2	...	...	1	1	...	...	1	...	...	...	...	1	...	3
1	...	...	...	...	1	...	3	...	...	...	...	...	3	4
43	...	2	1	11	10	19	10	...	...	...	...	3	7	5
26	...	1	2	5	10	8	7	...	...	...	...	2	5	6
3	...	...	...	...	1	2	1	...	...	...	...	1	...	7
...	...	...	...	...	...	...	...	...	...	...	...	...	...	8
36	...	2	1	11	9	13	8	...	...	...	...	2	6	9
23	...	1	2	5	7	8	7	...	...	...	...	2	5	10
4	...	...	...	...	...	4	1	...	...	...	...	...	1	11
3	...	...	...	...	3	...	...	...	...	...	...	...	...	12
5,117	...	3	102	724	2,512	1,776	490	...	...	1	31	96	362	13
4,911	...	3	133	740	2,507	1,528	394	...	...	3	16	75	300	14
1	...	...	...	...	...	1	...	...	...	...	...	...	...	15
1	...	...	...	...	...	1	...	...	...	...	...	...	...	16
1	...	...	...	...	1	...	...	...	...	...	...	...	...	17
...	...	...	...	...	...	...	...	...	...	...	...	...	...	18
4,852	...	...	77	667	2,427	1,681	473	..	...	...	28	89	356	19
4,658	...	...	98	695	2,449	1,416	369	...	...	2	12	67	288	20
263	...	3	25	57	84	94	17	...	...	1	3	7	6	21
252	...	3	35	45	58	111	25	...	...	1	4	8	12	22
7	...	...	...	...	3	4	3	...	...	...	...	1	2	23
6	...	...	...	3	2	1	...	...	...	...	...	...	...	24
24	...	...	1	5	13	5	2	...	...	...	...	...	2	25
20	...	...	1	3	12	4	5	...	...	...	...	1	4	26
1	...	...	...	...	1	...	...	...	...	...	...	...	...	27
2	...	...	...	...	...	2	1	...	...	...	...	...	1	28
4	...	...	...	...	2	2	...	...	...	..	...	...	...	29
6	...	...	...	...	5	1	1	...	...	...	...	...	1	30
1	...	...	...	...	...	1	...	...	...	...	...	...	...	31
...	...	...	...	...	...	...	...	...	...	...	...	...	...	32
4	...	...	...	...	3	1	...	...	...	...	...	...	...	33
4	...	...	...	1	3	...	...	...	..	...	...	...	...	34
7	...	...	1	2	4	...	1	...	...	...	...	...	1	35
2	...	...	...	1	1	...	1	...	...	...	...	...	1	36
3	...	...	...	1	1	1	...	...	...	...	...	...	...	37
4	...	...	1	1	2	...	...	...	...	...	...	...	...	38
4	...	...	...	2	2	...	1	...	...	...	...	...	1	39
2	...	...	...	...	1	1	2	...	...	...	...	1	1	40
916	...	2	16	124	410	364	113	...	...	6	5	32	70	41
945	...	5	22	314	321	283	180	...	1	4	11	41	123	42
32	...	...	...	...	16	16	7	...	...	...	1	4	2	43
38	...	...	3	16	7	12	10	...	...	...	2	1	7	44
100	...	...	...	31	38	31	5	...	...	3	...	1	1	45
53	...	...	1	9	27	16	3	...	...	2	1	...	...	46
587	...	2	16	50	285	234	90	...	...	3	4	27	56	47
640	...	1	10	243	177	209	152	...	1	2	8	40	101	48
197	...	...	...	43	71	88	11	...	...	...	...	...	11	49
214	...	4	8	46	110	46	15	...	...	...	...	...	15	50
3	...	...	...	...	1	2	1	...	...	...	...	...	1	51
2	...	...	...	...	1	1	...	...	...	...	...	...	...	52
2	...	...	...	...	1	1	1	...	...	...	...	...	1	53
2	...	...	...	...	1	1	...	...	...	...	...	...	...	54
1	...	...	...	...	...	1	...	...	...	...	...	...	...	55
...	...	...	...	...	...	...	...	...	...	...	...	...	..	56
642	...	15	37	144	283	163	142	...	...	2	11	48	81	57
470	...	4	39	99	199	129	102	...	...	2	11	36	53	58
46	...	1	4	3	26	12	11	...	...	1	...	2	8	59
62	...	...	8	6	32	16	22	...	...	...	...	6	16	60
179	...	2	15	48	72	42	25	...	...	...	...	7	18	61
121	...	...	9	26	57	29	25	...	...	2	3	8	12	62
38	...	...	...	6	21	11	2	...	...	...	2	...	...	63
26	...	...	...	5	18	3	4	...	...	...	...	3	1	64
28	...	...	...	2	21	5	5	...	...	...	...	3	2	65
28	...	...	...	6	18	4	3	...	...	...	1	2	...	66
42	...	...	...	12	18	12	13	...	...	...	1	6	6	67
26	...	...	1	6	16	3	4	...	...	...	1	3	...	68
53	...	...	2	20	26	5	23	...	..	...	1	8	14	69
55	...	...	7	20	20	8	13	..	...	...	1	5	7	70
75	...	...	...	9	53	13	6	...	...	...	1	4	1	71
25	...	...	...	3	11	11	3	...	...	...	...	...	3	72
23	...	...	...	5	7	11	3	...	...	...	...	...	3	73
23	...	...	2	4	7	10	6	...	...	...	1	2	3	74
137	...	12	16	34	31	44	41	...	...	1	5	14	21	75
81	...	3	12	18	14	34	18	...	...	...	4	5	9	76

APPENDIX TO IMPERIAL TABLE XIV.—CIVIL CONDITION

1. ARYA—*continued.*

Serial No.	Caste.	Locality.	Sex.	Population.	Unmarried. Total.	0—5.	5—12.	12—15.	15—20.	20—40.	40 and over.
	1	2	3	4	5	6	7	8	9	10	11
1	RÁJPUT—*concluded.*	Gujranwala	Male	57	27	13	7	4	2	1	...
2			Female	33	9	7	2	...	...	...	...
3		Gujrat	Male	8	4	1	...	1	2	...	...
4			Female	4	1	1	...	...	...	...	...
5	RÁTHI	Kangra	Male	278	130	28	34	30	16	19	3
6			Female	311	152	58	42	45	7	...	...
7	ROR	Karnal	Male	144	84	17	36	15	12	4	...
8			Female	102	53	26	24	1	2	...	...
9	SAINI	TOTAL	Male	185	94	26	23	13	20	8	4
10			Female	116	54	15	21	10	8	...	...
11		Delhi	Male	42	19	10	...	3	5	1	...
12			Female	44	15	5	10	...	...	...	...
13		Kangra	Male	4	2	...	...	1	1	...	...
14			Female	2	1	...	1	...	...	...	...
15		Hoshiarpur	Male	138	72	16	23	9	14	7	3
16			Female	70	38	10	10	10	8	...	...
17		Jullundur	Male	1	1	...	...	...	...	...	1
18			Female	...	...	...	...	...	...	...	...
19	SUD	TOTAL	Male	189	91	25	23	20	15	6	2
20			Female	117	38	7	12	8	7	3	1
21		Delhi	Male	3	...	...	...	...	...	...	...
22			Female	...	...	...	...	...	...	...	...
23		Kangra	Male	18	8	...	1	1	5	1	...
24			Female	8	3	...	1	1	1	...	...
25		Hoshiarpur	Male	21	12	4	...	2	4	2	...
26			Female	9	3	...	2	...	1	...	...
27		Jullundur	Male	109	49	11	16	14	5	2	1
28			Female	88	29	5	8	7	5	3	1
29		Amritsar	Male	38	22	10	6	3	1	1	1
30			Female	12	3	2	1	...	...	...	...
31	SUNÁR	TOTAL	Male	575	277	100	76	44	28	27	4
32			Female	434	171	86	60	16	7	1	1
33		Hissar	Male	12	4	...	2	...	...	2	...
34			Female	12	6	2	3	...	1	...	...
35		Delhi	Male	30	10	3	2	2	...	3	...
36			Female	24	8	3	3	2	...	...	...
37		Karnal	Male	8	6	4	2	...	...	...	...
38			Female	7	2	...	2	...	...	...	...
39		Hoshiarpur	Male	129	72	19	22	10	12	8	1
40			Female	77	43	16	23	3	1	...	...
41		Jullundur	Male	16	6	1	1	2	1	1	...
42			Female	12	4	2	...	1	...	1	...
43		Lahore	Male	31	17	10	4	3	...	...	...
44			Female	29	7	5	2	...	...	...	...
45		Amritsar	Male	77	37	16	12	6	3	...	...
46			Female	64	25	9	10	3	2	...	1
47		Gurdaspur	Male	78	28	7	7	5	2	6	1
48			Female	72	24	18	4	...	2	...	...
49		Sialkot	Male	50	17	4	2	2	3	6	1
50			Female	42	29	14	4	4	...	...	...
51		Gujranwala	Male	131	70	34	20	11	4	1	...
52			Female	77	23	14	7	2	...	...	...
53		Gujrat	Male	18	10	2	2	3	1	1	1
54			Female	18	7	3	2	1	1	...	...
55	TARKHÁN	TOTAL	Male	311	144	55	40	22	14	8	5
56			Female	242	76	35	22	16	3	...	...
57		Hissar	Male	2	1	...	...	...	...	1	...
58			Female	...	...	...	...	...	...	...	...
59		Delhi	Male	17	4	1	...	1	...	...	2
60			Female	11	2	1	1	...	...	...	...
61		Karnal	Male	5	1	...	...	...	...	1	...
62			Female	1	...	...	...	...	...	...	...
63		Kangra	Male	11	6	2	1	1	2	...	...
64			Female	9	5	1	2	2	...	...	...
65		Hoshiarpur	Male	16	8	1	3	...	1	2	1
66			Female	6	2	...	1	1	...	...	...
67		Jullundur	Male	34	20	7	5	5	3	...	...
68			Female	16	8	1	2	4	1	...	...
69		Lahore	Male	7	4	1	2	1	...	...	...
70			Female	8	2	1	1	...	...	...	...
71		Amritsar	Male	1	1	...	...	1	...	...	...
72			Female	2	1	...	...	1	...	...	...
73		Gurdaspur	Male	153	65	28	17	8	8	4	2
74			Female	118	30	13	9	6	2	...	...
75		Sialkot	Male	42	25	18	8	4	...	...	...
76			Female	46	16	11	4	1	...	...	...

BY AGE AND CASTE OF CERTAIN SECTS IN SELECTED DISTRICTS.

1. ARYA—*continued.*

Married.							Widowed.							
Total.	0—5.	5—12.	12—15.	15—20.	20—40.	40 and over.	Total.	0—5.	5—12.	12—15.	15—20.	20—40.	40 and over.	Serial No.
12	13	14	15	16	17	18	19	20	21	22	23	24	25	
18	...	...	...	4	7	7	12	...	...	...	1	3	8	1
20	...	...	...	4	6	10	4	...	...	...	...	2	2	2
3	...	...	...	1	1	1	1	...	...	...	...	1	...	3
3	...	1	...	1	...	1	...	...	...	...	...	...	...	4
121	...	1	12	19	46	43	27	...	...	...	1	15	11	5
128	...	...	15	27	58	28	31	...	...	...	3	20	8	6
49	...	...	...	5	24	20	11	...	...	...	...	5	6	7
37	...	...	1	7	22	7	12	...	...	...	...	3	9	8
73	...	...	2	17	37	17	18	...	...	...	...	4	14	9
52	...	1	1	10	29	11	10	...	...	...	1	7	2	10
19	...	...	...	4	8	7	4	...	...	...	...	...	4	11
20	...	...	...	6	6	6	9	...	...	...	...	7	2	12
2	...	...	...	...	2	...	...	...	...	...	...	...	...	13
1	...	...	...	...	1	...	...	...	...	...	...	...	...	14
52	...	...	2	13	27	10	14	...	...	...	...	4	10	15
31	...	1	1	4	20	5	1	...	...	...	1	...	...	16
...	...	...	...	...	...	...	...	...	...	...	...	...	...	17
...	...	...	...	...	...	...	...	...	...	...	...	...	...	18
85	...	2	12	17	29	25	18	...	...	...	...	6	7	19
64	...	...	8	12	35	14	15	...	...	...	1	5	9	20
3	...	...	...	...	1	2	...	...	...	...	...	...	...	21
...	...	...	...	...	...	...	...	...	...	...	...	...	...	22
8	...	...	...	...	7	1	2	...	...	...	...	1	1	23
5	...	...	...	1	4	...	...	...	...	...	...	...	...	24
6	...	...	...	1	5	...	3	...	...	...	...	3	...	25
4	...	...	...	...	4	...	2	...	...	...	...	1	1	26
54	...	2	12	14	14	12	6	...	...	...	...	2	4	27
47	...	...	2	10	24	11	12	...	...	...	1	3	8	28
14	...	...	...	2	2	10	2	...	...	...	...	...	2	29
8	...	...	1	1	3	3	1	...	...	...	...	1	...	30
227	...	1	6	33	101	86	71	...	...	1	1	21	48	31
218	...	1	5	38	94	80	45	...	...	1	1	15	28	32
8	...	...	...	...	2	6	...	...	...	...	...	...	...	33
4	...	...	...	1	1	2	2	...	...	...	...	1	1	34
14	...	1	3	3	4	3	6	...	...	1	...	2	3	35
10	...	...	...	4	3	3	6	...	...	...	...	...	6	36
2	...	...	...	...	...	2	...	...	...	...	...	...	...	37
4	...	...	...	...	3	1	1	...	...	...	...	...	1	38
44	...	...	...	5	31	8	13	...	...	...	...	3	10	39
26	...	...	1	3	18	4	8	...	...	...	...	4	4	40
10	...	...	...	5	5	...	...	...	...	...	...	...	...	41
8	...	...	...	3	4	1	...	...	...	...	...	...	...	42
9	...	...	...	1	3	5	5	...	...	...	...	3	2	43
19	...	...	...	1	7	11	3	...	...	1	...	...	2	44
33	...	...	...	6	18	9	7	...	...	...	...	2	5	45
36	...	...	...	6	19	11	3	...	...	...	...	1	2	46
36	...	...	2	5	15	14	9	...	...	...	...	4	5	47
43	...	1	1	8	15	18	5	...	...	...	...	3	2	48
27	...	...	1	3	7	16	6	...	...	...	1	1	4	49
15	...	...	...	1	6	8	5	...	...	...	...	1	4	50
39	...	...	...	6	14	20	22	...	...	...	...	6	16	51
43	...	...	1	7	15	20	11	...	...	...	1	4	6	52
5	...	...	...	...	2	3	3	...	...	...	...	...	3	53
10	...	...	2	4	3	1	1	...	...	...	...	1	...	54
132	...	5	4	24	51	48	35	...	...	...	2	12	21	55
132	...	1	6	22	45	58	34	...	...	2	1	17	14	56
1	...	...	...	...	...	1	...	...	...	...	...	...	...	57
...	...	...	...	...	...	...	...	...	...	...	...	...	...	58
12	...	...	2	1	3	6	1	...	...	...	...	1	...	59
9	...	...	...	2	4	3	...	...	...	...	...	...	...	60
4	...	...	...	2	2	...	...	...	...	...	...	...	...	61
1	...	...	...	1	...	...	...	...	...	...	...	...	...	62
4	...	...	...	...	4	...	1	...	...	...	...	...	1	63
4	...	...	...	...	4	...	...	...	...	...	...	...	...	64
7	...	...	...	1	5	1	1	...	...	...	...	...	1	65
3	...	...	...	1	2	...	...	...	...	...	...	...	...	66
10	...	...	...	4	4	2	4	...	...	...	...	1	3	67
6	...	...	1	1	4	...	2	...	...	...	...	...	2	68
2	...	...	...	...	1	1	1	...	...	...	...	...	1	69
5	...	...	...	...	2	3	1	...	...	1	...	...	...	70
...	...	...	...	...	...	...	...	...	...	...	...	...	...	71
...	...	...	...	...	...	...	1	...	...	...	...	1	...	72
67	...	5	2	16	20	24	21	...	...	...	2	8	11	73
64	...	1	5	14	13	31	24	...	...	1	1	13	9	74
15	...	...	...	...	7	8	2	...	...	...	...	1	1	75
27	...	...	...	2	10	15	3	...	...	...	...	2	1	76

APPENDIX TO IMPERIAL TABLE XIV.—CIVIL CONDITION

1. ARYA—*concluded.*

Serial No.	Caste.	Locality.	Sex.	Population.	Unmarried. Total.	0—5.	5—12.	12—15.	15—20.	20—40.	40 and over.
	1	2	3	4	5	6	7	8	9	10	11
1	TARKHÁN—*concld.*	Gujranwala ...	Male ...	18	9	4	4	1	...	...	...
2			Female ...	23	7	4	2	1	...	...	...
3		Gujrat ...	Male ...	6	...	...	...	...	...	...	...
4			Female ...	3	3	3	...	...	...	...	...
5	OTHERS* ...	TOTAL ...	Male ...	44	19	5	6	3	2	3	...
6			Female ...	29	9	1	4	2	2	...	...
7		Hissar ...	Male ...	2	2	...	...	2	...	...	...
8			Female ...	...	...	...	...	...	...	...	...
9		Delhi ...	Male ...	23	8	4	2	...	...	2	...
10			Female ...	15	1	1	...	...	...	...	...
11		Kangra ...	Male ...	8	3	...	...	...	2	1	...
12			Female ...	6	3	...	1	1	1	...	...
13		Hoshiarpur ...	Male ...	1	...	...	...	...	...	...	...
14			Female ...	...	...	...	...	...	...	...	...
15		Jullundur ...	Male ...	1	...	...	...	...	...	...	...
16			Female ...	4	3	...	2	1	...	...	...
17		Amritsar ...	Male ...	4	3	...	2	1	...	...	...
18			Female ...	2	2	...	1	...	1	...	...
19		Sialkot ...	Male ...	3	2	1	1	...	...	...	...
20			Female ...	...	...	...	...	...	...	...	...
21		Gujrat ...	Male ...	2	1	...	1	...	...	...	...
22			Female ...	2	...	...	...	...	...	...	...

**Detail of others.*—Agári Males 3; Bharbhunja Males 4, Females 3; Dhának Females 2; Báwariá Males 2; Bhábrá Males 2; Kanet Males 3, Females 4; Mochi Males 2, Females 2; Sangtrásh

2. BRAHMO.

Serial No.	Caste.	Locality.	Sex.	Population.	Unmarried. Total.	0—5.	5—12.	12—15.	15—20.	20—40.	40 and over.
1	TOTAL	...	Male ...	353	153	84	43	15	5	3	8
2			Female ...	274	97	54	28	9	3	2	1
3	ARORÁ ...	TOTAL ...	Male ...	70	25	14	8	3	...	...	...
4			Female ...	56	23	13	7	3	...	...	...
5		Ferozepore ...	Male ...	3	1	...	1	...	...	...	...
6			Female ...	3	1	1	...	...	...	...	...
7		Lahore ...	Male ...	26	14	9	3	2	...	...	...
8			Female ...	25	15	7	6	2	...	...	...
9		Gurdaspur ...	Male ...	1	...	...	...	...	...	...	...
10			Female ...	4	1	1	...	...	...	...	...
11		Shahpur ...	Male ...	35	8	3	4	1	...	...	...
12			Female ...	18	4	3	1	...	...	...	...
13		Montgomery ...	Male ...	3	1	1	...	...	...	...	...
14			Female ...	6	2	1	...	1	...	...	...
15		Lyallpur ...	Male ...	4	1	1	...	...	...	...	...
16			Female ...	...	...	...	...	...	...	...	...
17	BÁNIA (AGGARWÁL)..	TOTAL ...	Male ...	10	5	3	1	1	...	...	...
18			Female ...	10	3	...	1	1	...	1	...
19		Hoshiarpur ...	Male ...	6	4	3	1	...	...	...	...
20			Female ...	5	2	...	1	1	...	...	...
21		Ferozepore ...	Male ...	4	1	...	...	1	...	...	...
22			Female ...	3	...	...	...	...	...	...	...
23		Gurdaspur ...	Male ...	...	...	...	...	...	...	...	...
24			Female ..	2	1	...	...	...	...	1	...
25	BRÁHMAN ...	TOTAL ...	Male ...	135	65	33	18	9	2	2	1
26			Female ...	101	35	20	10	4	1	...	...
27		Delhi ...	Male ...	16	6	3	1	1	...	1	...
28			Female ...	13	5	3	1	1	...	...	...
29		Simla ...	Male ...	7	4	1	2	1	...	...	...
30			Female ..	7	3	2	1	...	...	...	...
31		Lahore ...	Male ...	53	30	19	9	2	...	...	...
32			Female ...	26	10	7	3	...	...	...	...
33		Amritsar ...	Male ...	18	8	3	2	1	1	...	1
34			Female ...	18	5	3	1	1	...	...	...
35		Gurdaspur ...	Male ...	19	7	2	1	2	1	1	...
36			Female ...	15	3	2	1	...	...	...	...
37		Rawalpindi ...	Male ...	21	10	5	3	2	...	...	...
38			Female ...	21	8	3	2	2	1	...	...
39		Montgomery ...	Male ...	1	...	...	...	...	...	...	...
40			Female ...	1	1	...	1	...	...	...	...
41	KALÁL ...	TOTAL ...	Male ...	12	9	4	2	...	2	...	1
42			Female ...	10	4	1	1	...	1	1	...
43		Hoshiarpur ...	Male ...	8	6	2	1	...	2	...	1
44			Female ...	7	3	...	1	...	1	1	...
45		Lahore ...	Male ...	4	3	2	1	...	...	...	...
46			Female ...	3	1	1	...	...	...	...	...

BY AGE AND CASTE OF CERTAIN SECTS IN SELECTED DISTRICTS.

1. ARYA—*concluded.*

Married.							*Widowed.*							Serial No.
Total.	0—5	5—12	12—15	15—20	20—40	40 and over.	Total.	0—5	5—12	12—15	15—20	20—40	40 and over.	
12	13	14	15	16	17	18	19	20	21	22	23	24	25	
5	...	...	...	...	1	4	4	...	...	...	...	1	3	1
13	...	...	...	1	6	6	3	...	...	...	...	1	2	2
5	...	...	...	...	4	1	...	...	...	...	...	...	...	3
...	...	...	...	...	...	...	...	...	...	...	...	...	...	4
18	...	...	...	2	9	7	7	4	...	1	1	1	...	5
17	...	...	1	2	6	8	3	...	...	...	...	1	2	6
...	...	...	...	...	...	...	...	...	...	...	...	...	...	7
...	...	...	...	...	...	...	...	...	...	...	...	...	...	8
11	...	...	...	1	5	5	4	4	...	...	...	...	...	9
11	...	...	...	1	3	7	3	...	...	...	...	1	2	10
3	...	...	...	1	1	1	2	...	...	1	1	...	...	11
3	...	...	1	...	2	...	...	...	...	...	...	...	...	12
...	...	...	...	...	...	...	1	...	...	...	...	1	...	13
...	...	...	...	...	...	...	...	...	...	...	...	...	...	14
1	...	...	...	...	1	...	...	...	...	...	...	...	...	15
1	...	...	...	1	...	...	...	...	...	...	...	...	...	16
1	...	...	...	...	1	...	...	...	...	...	...	...	...	17
...	...	...	...	...	...	...	...	...	...	...	...	...	...	18
1	...	...	...	...	1	...	...	...	...	...	...	...	...	19
...	...	...	...	...	...	...	...	...	...	...	...	...	...	20
1	...	...	...	...	...	1	...	...	...	...	...	...	...	21
2	...	...	...	...	1	1	...	...	...	...	...	...	...	22

Bhanjrá Female 1 ; Faqir Males 3, Females 2 ; Báhti Male 1, Females 3 ; Gurkha Male 1 ; Gosáin Males 3, Females 2 ; Jogi-Ráwal Males 3 ; Male 1 ; Minor Castes Males 16, Females 10.

2. BRAHMO.

Total.	0—5	5—12	12—15	15—20	20—40	40 and over.	Total.	0—5	5—12	12—15	15—20	20—40	40 and over.	Serial No.
163	...	1	7	31	61	63	37	...	...	...	...	7	30	1
152	...	...	4	28	70	50	25	...	...	...	...	6	19	2
38	...	...	3	9	14	12	7	...	...	...	...	2	5	3
29	...	...	1	9	13	6	4	...	...	...	...	1	3	4
2	...	...	...	...	2	...	...	...	...	...	...	...	...	5
2	...	...	...	1	1	...	...	...	...	...	...	...	...	6
8	...	...	...	1	3	4	4	...	...	...	...	1	3	7
9	...	...	...	...	5	4	1	...	...	...	...	...	1	8
1	...	...	...	...	1	...	...	...	...	...	...	...	...	9
2	...	...	...	...	1	1	1	...	...	...	...	...	1	10
22	...	...	3	6	7	6	3	...	...	...	...	1	2	11
12	...	.	1	6	4	1	2	...	...	...	...	1	1	12
2	...	...	...	1	...	1	...	...	...	...	...	...	...	13
4	...	...	...	2	2	...	...	...	...	...	...	...	...	14
3	...	...	...	1	1	1	...	...	...	...	...	...	...	15
...	...	...	...	...	...	...	...	...	...	...	...	...	...	16
4	...	...	...	1	2	1	1	...	...	...	...	...	1	17
5	...	...	...	1	4	...	2	...	...	...	...	...	2	18
2	...	...	...	...	2	...	...	...	...	...	...	...	...	19
3	...	...	...	1	2	...	...	...	...	...	...	...	...	20
2	...	...	...	1	..	1	1	...	...	...	...	...	1	21
2	...	...	...	...	2	...	1	...	...	...	...	...	1	22
...	...	...	...	...	...	...	...	...	...	...	...	...	...	23
...	...	...	...	...	...	...	1	...	...	...	...	...	1	24
54	...	...	1	8	20	25	16	...	...	...	...	4	12	25
57	...	...	1	7	25	24	9	...	...	...	...	3	6	26
9	...	...	...	...	3	6	1	...	...	...	...	...	1	27
8	...	...	...	...	3	5	...	...	...	...	...	...	...	28
3	...	...	...	1	1	1	...	...	...	...	...	...	...	29
3	...	...	...	1	2	...	1	...	...	...	...	1	...	30
19	...	...	...	2	8	9	4	...	...	...	...	1	3	31
13	...	...	...	...	8	5	3	...	...	...	...	...	3	32
7	...	...	...	2	1	4	3	...	...	...	...	1	2	33
11	...	...	...	2	4	5	2	...	...	...	...	1	1	34
7	...	...	...	1	4	2	5	...	...	...	...	2	3	35
10	...	...	...	1	4	5	2	...	...	...	...	1	1	36
9	...	...	1	2	3	3	2	...	...	...	...	...	2	37
12	...	...	1	3	4	4	1	...	...	...	...	...	1	38
...	...	...	...	...	...	...	1	...	...	...	...	...	1	39
...	...	...	...	...	...	...	...	...	...	...	...	...	...	40
3	...	...	...	...	2	1	...	...	...	...	...	...	...	41
6	...	...	...	1	4	1	...	...	...	...	...	...	...	42
2	...	...	...	...	2	...	...	...	...	...	...	...	...	43
4	...	...	...	1	3	...	...	...	...	...	...	...	...	44
1	...	...	...	...	...	1	...	...	...	...	...	...	...	45
2	...	...	...	...	1	1	...	...	...	...	...	...	...	46

APPENDIX TO IMPERIAL TABLE XIV.—CIVIL CONDITION

2. BRAHMO—*concluded.*

Serial No.	Caste.	Locality.	Sex.	Population.	Unmarried. Total.	0—5	5—12	12—15	15—20	20—40	40 and over.
	1	2	3	4	5	6	7	8	9	10	11
1	KHATRÍ ...	TOTAL ...	Male ...	94	36	20	11	2	1	1	1
2			Female ...	77	23	14	7	1	...	...	1
3		Lahore ...	Male ...	*30*	15	10	5	...	...	...	...
4			Female ...	*31*	12	7	5	...	...	...	...
5		Amritsar ...	Male ...	*12*	6	4	1	1	...	...	...
6			Female ...	*6*	2	1	1	...	...	...	...
7		Gurdaspur ...	Male ...	*31*	10	4	2	1	1	1	1
8			Female ...	*22*	5	3	1	1	...	...	...
9		Gujrat ...	Male ...	*2*	...	...	...	...	...	...	...
10			Female ...	*4*	1	1	...	...	...	...	...
11		Shahpur ...	Male ...	*11*	2	1	1	...	...	...	...
12			Female ...	*11*	2	1	...	...	...	...	1
13		Montgomery ...	Male ...	*2*	1	...	1	...	...	...	...
14			Female ...	*3*	1	1	...	...	...	...	...
15		Lyallpur ...	Male ...	*6*	2	1	1	...	...	...	...
16			Female ...	...	...	...	...	...	...	...	...
17	RÁJPUT ...	TOTAL ...	Male ...	8	3	2	1	...	...	...	...
18			Female ...	3	2	1	1	...	...	...	...
19		Ferozepore ...	Male ...	*3*	1	1	...	...	...	...	...
20			Female ...	*1*	1	...	1	...	...	...	...
21		Lahore ...	Male ...	*4*	2	1	1	...	...	...	...
22			Female ...	*2*	1	1	...	...	...	...	...
23		Gurdaspur ...	Male ...	*1*	...	...	...	...	...	...	...
24			Female ...	...	...	...	...	...	...	...	...
25	SUÑÁR ...	TOTAL ...	Male ...	17	7	5	2	...	...	...	...
26			Female ...	6	3	2	...	...	1	...	...
27		Lahore ...	Male ...	*3*	2	2	...	...	...	...	...
28			Female ...	*2*	1	1	...	...	...	...	...
29		Gurdaspur ...	Male ...	*10*	5	3	2	...	...	...	...
30			Female ...	*2*	1	1	...	...	...	...	...
31		Gujrat ...	Male ...	*4*	...	...	...	...	...	...	...
32			Female ...	*2*	1	...	...	...	1	...	...
33	OTHERS * ...	TOTAL ...	Male ...	7	3	3	...	...	...	...	...
34			Female ...	11	4	3	1	...	...	...	...
35		Lahore ...	Male ...	*2*	1	1	...	...	...	...	...
36			Female ...	*1*	...	...	...	...	...	...	...
37		Gurdaspur ...	Male ...	*5*	2	2	...	...	...	...	...
38			Female ...	*6*	2	2	...	...	...	...	...
39		Lyallpur ...	Male ...	...	...	...	...	...	...	...	...
40			Female ...	*4*	2	1	1	...	...	...	...

* *Detail of others.*—Jat Males 2, Females 4; Jhinwar

3. DEV DHARM.

Serial No.	Caste.	Locality.	Sex.	Population.	Unmarried. Total.	0—5	5—12	12—15	15—20	20—40	40 and over.
1		TOTAL ...	Male ...	1,321	465	115	154	69	62	41	24
2			Female ...	996	372	134	145	75	17	1	...
3	ARORÁ ...	TOTAL ...	Male ...	186	35	16	10	3	6	...	...
4			Female ...	151	32	11	7	8	6	...	...
5		Ferozepore ...	Male ...	*128*	25	13	8	1	3	...	...
6			Female ...	*109*	25	9	4	6	6	...	...
7		Lyallpur ...	Male ...	*58*	10	3	2	2	3	...	...
8			Female ...	*42*	7	2	3	2	...	...	...
9	BÁNIÁ (AGGARWÁL)	TOTAL ...	Male ...	17	6	1	...	5	...	...	...
10			Female ...	36	6	2	2	2	...	...	...
11		Delhi ...	Male ...	...	...	...	...	...	...	...	...
12			Female ...	*2*	...	...	...	...	...	...	...
13		Hoshiarpur ...	Male ...	...	...	...	...	...	...	...	...
14			Female ...	*2*	1	...	1	...	...	...	...
15		Ferozepore	Male ...	*17*	6	1	...	5	...	...	...
16			Female ...	*32*	5	2	1	2	...	...	...
17	BRAHMAN ...	TOTAL ...	Male ...	80	24	7	7	4	5	1	...
18			Female ...	62	15	4	5	5	1	...	...
19		Simla ...	Male ...	*13*	2	...	...	—	2	...	...
20			Female ...	...	...	...	...	—	...	...	...
21		Hoshiarpur ...	Male ...	*23*	13	3	6	1	2	1	...
22			Female ...	*11*	8	...	1	2	...	...	...
23		Ferozepore ...	Male ...	*25*	5	3	1	1	...	...	...
24			Female ...	*30*	9	4	3	2	1	...	...
25		Lyallpur ...	Male ...	*19*	4	1	...	2	1	...	...
26			Female ...	*21*	3	...	2	1	...	...	...
27	CHAMÁR ...	TOTAL ...	Male ...	401	181	42	68	26	11	15	19
28			Female ...	269	173	61	68	39	5	...	...
29		Simla ...	Male ...	...	...	...	...	...	...	...	...
30			Female ...	*2*	...	...	...	...	...	...	...
31		Hoshiarpur ...	Male ...	*344*	169	40	65	19	11	15	19
32			Female ...	*234*	159	54	64	36	5	...	...
33		Kapurthala ...	Male ...	*57*	12	2	3	7	...	...	...
34			Female ...	*33*	14	7	4	3	...	...	...

BY AGE AND CASTE OF CERTAIN SECTS IN SELECTED DISTRICTS.

2. BRAHMO—*concluded.*

Married. Total.	0—5	5—12	12—15	15—20	20—40	40 and over.	Widowed. Total.	0—5	5—12	12—15	15—20	20—40	40 and over.	Serial No.
12	13	14	15	16	17	18	19	20	21	22	23	24	25	
50	...	1	3	13	18	15	8	...	...	...	...	...	8	1
45	...	...	2	9	18	16	9	...	...	...	...	2	7	2
11	...	...	...	...	6	5	4	...	...	...	...	...	4	3
18	...	...	...	3	9	6	1	...	...	...	...	...	1	4
5	...	...	...	...	2	3	1	...	...	...	...	...	1	5
3	...	...	...	1	1	1	1	...	...	...	...	...	1	6
19	...	1	1	11	8	3	2	...	...	...	...	...	2	7
13	...	...	1	2	4	6	4	...	...	...	...	1	3	8
2	...	...	...	1	1	...	...	...	...	...	...	...	...	9
2	...	...	...	...	1	1	1	...	...	...	...	...	1	10
8	...	...	2	1	3	2	1	...	...	...	...	...	1	11
7	...	...	1	2	2	2	2	...	...	...	...	1	1	12
1	...	...	...	...	1	...	...	...	...	...	...	...	...	13
2	...	...	...	1	1	...	...	...	...	...	...	...	...	14
4	...	...	...	...	2	2	...	...	...	...	...	...	...	15
...	...	...	...	...	...	...	...	...	...	...	...	...	...	16
3	...	...	...	...	1	2	2	...	...	...	...	...	2	17
1	...	...	...	...	1	...	...	...	...	...	...	...	...	18
1	...	...	...	...	...	1	1	...	...	...	...	...	1	19
...	...	...	...	...	...	...	...	...	...	...	...	...	...	20
1	...	...	...	...	...	1	1	...	...	...	...	...	1	21
1	...	...	...	...	1	...	...	...	...	...	...	...	...	22
1	...	...	...	...	1	...	...	...	...	...	...	...	...	23
...	...	...	...	...	...	...	...	...	...	...	...	...	...	24
8	...	...	...	...	3	5	2	...	...	...	...	1	1	25
3	...	...	...	1	1	1	...	...	...	...	...	...	...	26
1	...	...	...	...	...	1	...	...	...	...	...	...	...	27
1	...	...	...	...	...	1	...	...	...	...	...	...	...	28
3	...	...	...	...	...	3	2	...	...	...	...	1	1	29
1	...	...	...	...	1	...	...	...	...	...	...	...	...	30
4	...	...	...	...	3	1	...	...	...	...	...	...	...	31
1	...	...	...	1	...	...	...	...	...	...	...	...	...	32
3	...	...	...	...	1	2	1	...	...	...	...	...	1	33
6	...	...	...	...	4	2	1	...	...	...	...	...	1	34
1	...	...	...	...	...	1	...	...	...	...	...	...	...	35
1	...	...	...	...	1	...	...	...	...	...	...	...	...	36
2	...	...	...	...	1	1	1	...	...	...	...	...	1	37
3	...	...	...	...	1	2	1	...	...	...	...	...	1	38
...	...	...	...	...	...	...	...	...	...	...	...	...	...	39
2	...	...	...	...	2	...	...	...	...	...	...	...	...	40

Males 2, Female 1; Tarkhán Males 3, Females 6.

3. DEV DHARM.

Married. Total.	0—5	5—12	12—15	15—20	20—40	40 and over.	Widowed. Total.	0—5	5—12	12—15	15—20	20—40	40 and over.	Serial No.
757	4	24	66	109	329	225	99	...	...	1	6	31	61	1
525	3	8	51	120	251	92	99	...	...	1	5	31	62	2
128	...	1	16	42	42	27	23	...	...	...	3	11	9	3
104	...	...	10	26	50	18	15	...	...	1	1	6	7	4
86	...	1	11	34	31	9	17	...	...	...	2	8	7	5
74	...	...	4	21	36	13	10	...	...	1	1	3	5	6
42	...	...	5	8	11	18	6	...	...	...	1	3	2	7
30	...	...	6	5	14	5	5	...	...	...	...	3	2	8
10	...	...	...	1	5	4	1	...	...	...	...	1	...	9
28	...	...	1	4	12	11	2	...	...	...	1	1	...	10
...	...	...	...	...	...	...	...	...	...	...	...	...	...	11
2	...	...	...	...	2	...	...	...	...	...	...	...	...	12
...	...	...	...	...	...	...	...	...	...	...	...	...	...	13
1	...	...	...	1	...	...	...	...	...	...	...	...	...	14
10	...	...	...	1	5	4	1	...	...	...	...	1	...	15
25	...	...	1	3	10	11	2	...	...	...	1	1	...	16
48	...	...	4	9	23	12	8	...	...	...	1	2	5	17
42	...	...	1	12	12	17	5	...	...	...	...	2	3	18
9	...	...	...	...	9	...	2	...	...	...	...	1	1	19
...	...	...	...	...	...	...	...	...	...	...	...	...	...	20
10	...	...	...	2	4	4	...	...	...	...	...	...	...	21
6	...	...	1	4	1	...	2	...	...	...	...	1	1	22
16	...	...	4	4	6	2	4	...	...	...	1	1	2	23
19	...	...	...	2	7	10	2	...	...	...	...	...	2	24
13	...	...	...	3	4	6	2	...	...	...	...	...	2	25
17	...	...	...	6	4	7	1	...	...	...	...	1	...	26
200	...	11	15	22	94	58	20	...	...	...	...	3	17	27
84	...	3	14	14	49	4	12	...	...	...	3	4	5	28
...	...	...	...	...	...	...	...	...	...	...	...	...	...	29
1	...	...	...	...	1	...	1	...	...	...	...	1	...	30
157	...	10	8	16	76	47	18	...	...	...	...	2	16	31
68	...	3	6	11	46	2	7	...	...	...	2	2	3	32
43	...	1	7	6	18	11	2	...	...	...	...	1	1	33
15	...	...	8	3	2	2	4	...	...	...	1	1	2	34

APPENDIX TO IMPERIAL TABLE XIV.—CIVIL CONDITION

3. DEV DHARM—*concluded.*

Serial No.	Caste.	Locality.	Sex.	Population.	Unmarried. Total.	0—5	5—12	12—15	15—20	20—40	40 and over.
	1	2	3	4	5	6	7	8	9	10	11
1	DÁGI AND KOLI ...	Simla ...	Male ...	19	9	...	2	3	2	2	...
2			Female ...	18	2	...	2	...	...	...	...
3	DHOBI ...	Simla ...	Male ...	12	9	3	...	3	3	...	...
4			Female ...	3	1	...	1	...	...	...	...
5	JAT ...	TOTAL ...	Male ...	150	60	17	26	7	6	3	1
6			Female ...	119	51	23	16	9	3	...	...
7		Hoshiarpur ...	Male ...	68	42	11	20	2	5	3	1
8			Female ...	51	34	13	10	8	3	...	...
9		Ferozepore ...	Male ...	5	...	...	...	...	...	...	...
10			Female ...	1	...	...	...	...	...	...	...
11		Lyallpur ...	Male ...	28	4	...	1	2	1	...	...
12			Female ...	22	4	2	1	1	...	...	...
13		Kapurthala ...	Male ...	51	14	6	5	3	...	...	...
14			Female ...	45	13	8	5	...	...	...	...
15	KANET ...	Simla ...	Male ...	18	3	...	...	...	...	3	...
16			Female ...	18	2	...	1	1	...	...	...
17	KHATRÍ ...	TOTAL ...	Male ...	117	24	5	8	4	6	1	...
18			Female ...	92	13	5	6	2	...	...	...
19		Delhi ...	Male ...	2	1	...	...	...	...	1	...
20			Female ...	8	1	1	...	...	...	...	...
21		Ferozepore ...	Male ...	78	17	3	6	4	4	...	...
22			Female ...	63	8	2	4	2	...	...	...
23		Lyallpur ...	Male ...	37	6	2	2	...	2	...	...
24			Female ...	21	4	2	2	...	...	...	...
25	KUMHÁR ...	TOTAL ...	Male ...	19	9	3	1	4	...	1	...
26			Female ...	15	8	1	5	2	...	...	...
27		Simla ...	Male ...	5	3	1	1	...	...	1	...
28			Female ...	4	2	...	2	...	...	...	...
29		Hoshiarpur ...	Male ...	14	6	2	...	4	...	...	...
30			Female ...	11	6	1	3	2	...	...	...
31	LOHÁR ...	TOTAL ...	Male ...	14	8	...	2	...	4	2	...
32			Female ...	6	5	1	2	2	...	...	...
33		Simla ...	Male ...	6	3	...	...	...	3	...	...
34			Female ...	...	...	...	...	...	...	...	...
35		Hoshiarpur ...	Male ...	8	5	...	2	...	1	2	...
36			Female ...	6	5	1	2	2	...	...	...
37	MIRÁSI ...	TOTAL ...	Male ...	10	6	...	...	2	1	3	...
38			Female ...	7	1	...	1	...	...	...	...
39		Simla ...	Male ...	...	...	...	...	...	...	...	...
40			Female ...	4	...	...	...	...	...	...	...
41		Hoshiarpur ...	Male ...	10	6	...	...	2	1	3	...
42			Female ...	3	1	...	1	...	...	...	...
43	NÁI ...	Hoshiarpur ...	Male ...	7	2	...	1	1	...	...	...
44			Female ...	7	3	...	2	...	1	...	...
45	NÁIK ...	Delhi ...	Male ...	191	70	17	24	6	15	6	2
46			Female ...	162	46	23	21	1	...	1	...
47	RÁJPUT ...	TOTAL ...	Male ...	20	8	...	2	...	3	3	...
48			Female ...	3	2	1	1	...	...	...	...
49		Delhi ...	Male ...	...	...	...	...	...	...	...	...
50			Female ...	1	1	1	...	...	...	...	...
51		Simla ...	Male ...	17	6	...	...	...	3	3	...
52			Female ...	...	...	...	...	...	...	...	...
53		Hoshiarpur ...	Male ...	3	2	...	2	...	...	...	...
54			Female ...	2	1	...	1	...	...	...	...
55	SUNÁR ...	TOTAL ...	Male ...	13	5	1	2	...	...	...	2
56			Female ...	9	4	2	2	...	...	...	...
57		Hoshiarpur ...	Male ...	2	2	...	...	...	...	...	2
58			Female ...	3	1	1	...	...	...	...	...
59		Kapurthala ...	Male ...	11	3	1	2	...	...	...	...
60			Female ...	6	3	1	2	...	...	...	...
61	TARKHÁN ...	TOTAL ...	Male ...	25	2	2	...	...	...	...	...
62			Female ...	12	6	...	3	2	1	...	...
63		Hoshiarpur ...	Male ...	2	...	...	...	...	...	...	...
64			Female ...	...	...	...	...	...	...	...	...
65		Ferozepore ...	Male ...	23	2	2	...	...	...	...	...
66			Female ...	12	6	...	3	2	1	...	...
67	OTHERS* ...	TOTAL ...	Male ...	22	4	1	1	1	...	1	...
68			Female ...	7	2	...	...	2	...	...	...
69		Delhi ...	Male ...	4	...	...	...	...	...	...	...
70			Female ...	...	...	...	...	...	...	...	...
71		Simla ...	Male ...	12	2	...	1	...	...	1	...
72			Female ...	6	2	...	...	2	...	...	...
73		Hoshiarpur ...	Male ...	6	2	1	...	1	...	...	...
74			Female ...	1	...	...	...	...	...	...	...

* *Detail of others.*—Báhti Male 1; Bairági Male 1; Bhát Males 3; Chanal Females 2; Ghirath Males 2; Jaiswára Males 6

BY AGE AND CASTE OF CERTAIN SECTS IN SELECTED DISTRICTS.

3. DEV DHARM—*concluded.*

Married.							Widowed.							Serial No.
Total.	0—5	5—12	12—15	15—20	20—40	40 and over.	Total.	0—5	5—12	12—15	15—20	20—40	40 and over.	
12	13	14	15	16	17	18	19	20	21	22	23	24	25	
10	...	...	...	...	8	2	...	...	...	...	...	...	...	1
10	...	...	...	2	6	2	6	...	...	...	...	4	2	2
3	...	...	...	...	3	...	...	...	...	...	...	...	...	3
2	...	...	...	..	2	...	...	...	...	...	...	...	...	4
84	4	5	11	14	34	16	6	...	...	...	...	4	2	5
58	3	4	11	5	22	13	10	...	...	...	...	6	4	6
26	1	...	...	3	15	7	...	...	...	...	...	...	...	7
15	...	...	2	1	12	...	2	...	...	...	...	2	...	8
3	...	...	...	1	2	...	...	...	...	...	...	...	...	9
1	...	...	...	1	...	...	...	...	..	..	...	...	...	10
21	..	...	3	7	5	6	8	...	...	...	...	1	2	11
16	...	...	1	1	5	9	2	...	...	...	...	...	2	12
34	8	5	8	3	12	3	3	...	...	...	...	3	...	13
26	3	4	8	2	5	4	6	...	...	...	...	4	2	14
12	...	...	1	...	6	5	3	...	...	...	...	...	3	15
8	...	...	...	..	6	2	8	...	...	...	...	2	6	16
78	...	5	13	8	30	22	15	...	...	1	1	6	7	17
71	...	...	7	23	32	9	8	...	...	...	...	2	6	18
1	...	...	...	...	1	...	...	...	...	...	...	...	...	19
6	...	...	...	1	4	1	1	.	...	...	...	...	1	20
50	...	5	7	3	21	14	11	...	...	...	1	4	6	21
50	...	...	3	20	22	5	5	...	...	...	...	1	4	22
27	...	...	6	5	8	8	4	...	...	1	...	2	1	23
15	...	...	4	2	6	3	2	...	...	...	..	1	1	24
10	...	..	...	...	6	4	...	...	...	...	...	...	...	25
7	...	...	...	2	4	1	...	...	...	...	...	...	...	26
2	...	...	...	...	...	2	...	...	...	...	...	...	...	27
2	...	...	...	2	...	...	...	...	...	...	...	...	...	28
8	...	...	...	...	6	2	...	...	...	...	...	...	...	29
5	...	..	...	...	4	1	...	...	...	...	...	...		30
4	...	...	...	1	2	1	2	...	...	...	...	...	2	31
1	...	...	...	1	...	...	...	...	...	...	...	...	...	32
2	...	...	...	...	2	...	1	...	...	...	...	...	1	33
...	...	...	..	...	...	...	...	...	...	...	...	...	...	34
2	...	...	...	1	...	1	1	...	...	...	...	...	1	35
1	...	...	...	1	...	...	...	...	...	...	...	...	...	36
4	...	..	...	..	3	1	...	...	...	...	...	...	...	37
3	...	...	...	3	...	...	3	...	...	...	...	...	3	38
...	...	...	...	...	...	...	...	...	...	...	...	...	...	39
2	...	...	...	2	...	...	2	...	...	...	...	...	2	40
4	...	...	...	...	3	1	...	...	...	...	...	...	...	41
1	...	...	...	1	...	...	1	...	...	...	...	...	1	42
5	...	...	...	...	4	1	...	...	...	...	...	..	...	43
4	...	...	...	1	3	...	...	...	...	...	...	...	...	44
107	...	2	1	...	41	63	14	...	...	...	1	3	10	45
90	...	1	5	24	48	12	26	...	...	...	...	2	24	46
12	...	...	...	...	12	...	...	...	..	...	...	...	...	47
1	...	...	...	...	1	...	...	...	...	...	...	...	...	48
...	...	...	...	...	...	...	...	...	...	...	...	...	...	49
...	...	...	...	...	...	...	...	...	...	...	...	...	...	50
11	...	...	...	...	11	...	...	...	...	...	...	...	...	51
...	...	...	...	...	...	...	...	...	...	...	...	...	...	52
1	...	...	...	...	1	...	...	...	..	...	...	...	...	53
1	...	...	...	...	1	...	...	...	...	...	...	...	...	54
8	...	...	...	5	3	...	...	...	..	...	...	...	...	55
5	..	...	1	1	2	1	...	...	...	...	...	...	...	56
...	...	...	...	...	...	...	...	...	...	...	..	...	..	57
2	...	...	..	...	1	1	...	...	...	...	...	...	...	58
8	...	...	...	5	3	...	...	...	...	...	...	...	...	59
3	...	...	1	1	1	..	...	...	...	...	...	...	...	60
16	...	...	4	6	3	3	7	...	...	...	...	1	6	61
6	...	...	1	2	1	2	...	...	...	...	...	...	...	62
1	...	...	...	...	1	...	1	...	...	..	...	1	...	63
...	...	...	...	...	..	...	...	...	...	...	..	...	...	64
15	...	...	4	6	2	3	6	...	...	...	...	...	6	65
6	...	...	1	2	1	2	...	...	...	...	...	...	...	66
18	...	...	1	1	10	6	...	...	...	...	...	...	...	67
1	..	...	..	...	1	...	4	...	...	...	...	2	2	68
4	...	...	...	...	3	1	...	...	...	...	...	...	...	69
...	...	...	...	...	...	...	...	...	...	...	...	...	...	70
10	...	...	...	...	6	4	...	...	...	...	...	..	...	71
...	...	...	...	...	...	...	4	...	...	...	...	2	2	72
4	...	...	1	1	1	1	...	...	...	...	...	...	...	73
1	...	...	...	...	1	...	...	...	...	...	...	...	...	74

Jhinwar Male 1, Female 1; Juláhá Male 1, Females 4; Kurmi Males 2; Mochi Males 8; Sarera Males 2.